Big Data Analytics with Hadoop and Spark

A hands-on guide to big data engineering and scalable analytics

Shikha Mehta

www.bpbonline.com

First Edition 2026

ISBN: 978-93-65894-745

Distributors:

BPB PUBLICATIONS
20, Ansari Road, Darya Ganj
New Delhi-110002
Ph: 23254990/23254991

DECCAN AGENCIES
4-3-329, Bank Street,
Hyderabad-500195
Ph: 24756967/24756400

MICRO MEDIA
Shop No. 5, Mahendra Chambers,
150 DN Rd. Next to Capital Cinema,
V.T. (C.S.T.) Station, MUMBAI-400 001
Ph: 22078296/22078297

To View Complete BPB Publications Catalogue Scan the QR Code:

Published by Manish Jain for BPB Publications, 20 Ansari Road, Darya Ganj, New Delhi-110002 and Printed by him at Repro India Ltd., Rewari.

www.bpbonline.com

Dedicated to

My loving daughter, Teana, my dear son, Aayush, and my beloved husband, Rajesh, whose love, patience, and unwavering support have been my greatest strength and inspiration throughout this journey.

About the Author

Dr. Shikha Mehta is an academician, researcher, and technology professional with extensive experience in computer science education, data analytics, and big data technologies. She is the HOD, Department of Computer Science and Engineering and Information Technology, at Jaypee Institute of Information Technology, Noida. She has been actively involved in teaching, curriculum design, and faculty development, with a strong focus on bridging theoretical foundations with real-world industry practices.

With deep expertise in big data analytics, distributed computing, and machine learning, Dr. Mehta has designed and delivered advanced training programs on Hadoop, Apache Spark, Python, and data-driven decision-making frameworks for students, faculty members, and working professionals. Her academic contributions include the development of structured, application-oriented learning modules and executive-level instructional content tailored to emerging industry demands.

Dr. Mehta has played a key role in mentoring faculty and learners in adopting modern data analytics tools and scalable data processing frameworks. Her work emphasizes hands-on learning, real-world case studies, and ethical considerations in data usage, enabling learners to build industry-ready skills. Through her teaching, research, and academic leadership, she continues to contribute to the advancement of big data education and analytics-driven innovation.

About the Reviewers

- **Gaurav Khare** is a seasoned senior data engineer with 16 years of experience in the finance domain. He is an expert in Python, Hadoop, Spark, NLP, and big data technologies, specializing in data analysis and data science. Throughout his career, he has built scalable data infrastructure and implemented advanced analytics solutions to improve banking operations and decision-making.

  An avid reader and technical reviewer, he stays at the forefront of emerging technologies. He actively contributes to technical communities, sharing insights and mentoring peers, earning a strong reputation as a skilled professional and thoughtful leader.

- **Nandhakumar Raju** is a visionary technology leader with over 25 years of experience in digital transformation, AI/ML innovation, and large-scale enterprise modernization. As director of technology at a leading healthcare organization, he has played a critical role in revolutionizing health systems that impact millions of lives across the United States. His work focuses on building scalable, intelligent, and people-centric solutions that improve access, efficiency, and equity in healthcare.

  He is also the co-founder of My Ayur Health and Mazo Solutions, ventures that reflect his passion for blending technology with purpose. Through these platforms, he empowers individuals and businesses with tools for wellness, automation, and operational excellence.

  An award-winning innovator, published researcher, and mentor, Nandhakumar is committed to nurturing the next generation of global leaders and driving meaningful change through responsible technology.

- **Praneeth Reddy Amudala Puchakayala** is an accomplished data scientist and AI researcher with experience designing and deploying scalable, data-driven solutions across financial services and healthcare domains. His work focuses on machine learning, artificial intelligence, advanced analytics, and modern data architectures that enable organizations to make accurate, explainable, and impactful decisions. Praneeth has a strong foundation in applied research and real-world problem solving, combining deep technical expertise with practical implementation. He has contributed to enterprise-scale AI systems, open-source initiatives, and research publications, with a particular interest in explainable and responsible AI. In addition to his industry work, Praneeth is an active member of the global AI community, serving as a speaker at international conferences, a technical reviewer for journals and books, and a mentor to early-career professionals.

Acknowledgement

I would like to express my deepest gratitude to my family and friends for their constant support, patience, and encouragement throughout the writing of this book. Their constant motivation and understanding made this demanding journey both possible and meaningful.

I sincerely thank the BPB Publications for their guidance, support, and professional expertise in bringing this book to completion. The process of revising and refining this manuscript was a long and enriching journey. This was made possible through the valuable participation and collaboration of reviewers, technical experts, and editors, whose insights significantly improved the quality and clarity of this work.

I am also grateful to my colleagues and co-workers from my years in academia and the technology industry, who have shared their knowledge generously, challenged my thinking, and provided constructive feedback that shaped many of the ideas presented in this book.

I extend my appreciation to my institution for providing the academic environment, infrastructure, and resources necessary to support this work. I am thankful to my mentors and academic leaders who gave me opportunities to teach and explore emerging subjects in big data analytics, which deeply influenced the direction and depth of this book.

Finally, I offer my sincere thanks to my parents, to the divine for guidance and strength, and to all the readers who have taken an interest in this book. Your encouragement and support have been invaluable and truly rewarding.

Preface

Big data has emerged as a transformative force in the digital era, enabling organizations to extract meaningful insights from massive, complex, and diverse datasets. With the rapid growth of data generated from social media, IoT devices, enterprise systems, and online transactions, there is a growing demand for scalable data storage, efficient processing frameworks, and advanced analytics platforms. This book is designed to provide a comprehensive and hands-on understanding of big data analytics, covering both foundational concepts and practical implementations using Hadoop, Spark, and associated ecosystem tools within the Cloudera platform.

The book adopts a structured, step-by-step approach, beginning with the fundamentals of big data and gradually progressing toward advanced data processing, data warehousing, NoSQL databases, and large-scale machine learning applications. Through real-world case studies, hands-on exercises, and practical demonstrations, readers will gain the skills required to design, implement, and analyze big data solutions effectively.

Chapter 1: Exploring Big Data - This chapter introduces the fundamental concepts of big data, including its characteristics, evolution, and significance across industries. It explores big data architectures, platforms, and technology components while highlighting key drivers for adoption. The chapter also addresses critical concerns such as security, compliance, auditing, privacy, and ethics in big data systems.

Chapter 2: Introduction to Hadoop - This chapter discusses the storage and computation challenges posed by big data and introduces Hadoop as a solution. It explains the origins, architecture, and advantages of Hadoop, compares it with traditional RDBMS and distributed databases. It explains the Hadoop ecosystem through a practical stock data analysis case study.

Chapter 3: Hadoop Distributed File System and MapReduce - This chapter explains traditional and distributed file systems, emphasizing the need for HDFS. It details the architecture and properties of HDFS and introduces MapReduce as Hadoop's processing model. Concepts such as key-value pairs, map and reduce phases, shuffling, and logical data flow are explained through a weather data analysis case study.

Chapter 4: Big Data Analysis with Cloudera - This chapter provides hands-on exposure to commercial Hadoop distributions, focusing on the Cloudera framework. It guides readers through installing and configuring the Cloudera QuickStart VM and introduces basic HDFS commands for working in a Hadoop environment.

Chapter 5: Stock Data Analysis using Cloudera - This chapter demonstrates end-to-end stock market data analysis using Hadoop and Cloudera. It covers data ingestion into HDFS, execution of Hadoop jobs, and development of MapReduce programs in Java to analyze stock market data.

Chapter 6: Understanding Pig for Big Data Processing - This chapter introduces Apache Pig as a high-level data processing platform for Hadoop. It explains Pig architecture, execution modes, Pig Latin syntax, data models, operators, and user-defined functions, along with practical execution in the Cloudera environment.

Chapter 7: Operators in Pig Latin- This chapter focuses on practical application development using Pig Latin operators. Readers learn to load, filter, group, join, sort, split, and combine data using Pig, enabling efficient processing of large datasets.

Chapter 8: Functions in Apache Pig - This chapter explores built-in and user-defined functions in Pig. It demonstrates string functions, UDF development, and real-world stock market data analysis using Pig, emphasizing reusable and extensible data transformation logic.

Chapter 9: Hive-data Warehousing and SQL-like Queries - This chapter introduces Apache Hive as a data warehousing solution on Hadoop. It explains Hive's data model, architecture, HiveQL, DDL, and DML operations, SerDes, and compares Hive with Pig and traditional SQL-based systems.

Chapter 10: Data Analysis Using Hive - This chapter provides hands-on experience with Hive, covering table creation, data loading, querying, partitioning, clustering, aggregation, grouping, and joins. It focuses on practical data analysis tasks using HiveQL in Cloudera.

Chapter 11: Data Storage and Processing Using HBase - This chapter introduces HBase as a column-oriented NoSQL database for big data analytics. It explains HBase architecture, data storage model, and shell commands, and demonstrates the design and development of a stock market application using HBase.

Chapter 12: MongoDB - This chapter introduces NoSQL databases and the CAP theorem, followed by an in-depth exploration of MongoDB. It covers the MongoDB data model, CRUD operations, aggregation operators, and application development using real-world examples.

Chapter 13: Introduction to Spark for Big Data Processing - This chapter introduces Apache Spark as a fast, in-memory distributed computing framework. It covers Spark architecture, Spark vs. Hadoop comparison, Spark application concepts, RDDs, DataFrames, transformations, actions, and lazy evaluation through practical examples.

Chapter 14: Getting Started with Scala Programming - This chapter introduces Scala programming fundamentals required for Spark development. It covers data types, operators, control structures, functions, classes, inheritance, and running Scala applications in the Cloudera environment.

Chapter 15: Data Analysis with Spark SQL - This chapter explains Spark SQL and structured data processing using DataFrames and datasets. It covers Spark SQL architecture, data ingestion from multiple formats, DataFrame operations, and end-to-end application development using Spark SQL.

Chapter 16: Machine Learning Application Using PySpark - This chapter introduces machine learning concepts and explains why Spark is suitable for large-scale ML applications. It demonstrates classification and clustering using Spark ML pipelines, covering data preparation, model training, evaluation, and prediction using PySpark.

Code Bundle and Coloured Images

Please follow the link to download the
Code Bundle and the ***Coloured Images*** of the book:

https://rebrand.ly/eww2omz

The code bundle for the book is also hosted on GitHub at
https://github.com/bpbpublications/Big-Data-Analytics-with-Hadoop-and-Spark.
In case there's an update to the code, it will be updated on the existing GitHub repository.

We have code bundles from our rich catalogue of books and videos available at **https://github.com/bpbpublications**. Check them out!

Errata

We take immense pride in our work at BPB Publications and follow best practices to ensure the accuracy of our content to provide an indulging reading experience to our subscribers. Our readers are our mirrors, and we use their inputs to reflect and improve upon human errors, if any, that may have occurred during the publishing processes involved. To let us maintain the quality and help us reach out to any readers who might be having difficulties due to any unforeseen errors, please write to us at: **errata@bpbonline.com**

Your support, suggestions and feedback are highly appreciated by the BPB Publications' Family.

Piracy

If you come across any illegal copies of our works in any form on the internet, we would be grateful if you would provide us with the location address or website name. Please contact us at **business@bpbonline.com** with a link to the material.

If you are interested in becoming an author

If there is a topic that you have expertise in, and you are interested in either writing or contributing to a book, please visit **www.bpbonline.com**. We have worked with thousands of developers and tech professionals, just like you, to help them share their insights with the global tech community. You can make a general application, apply for a specific hot topic that we are recruiting an author for, or submit your own idea.

Reviews

Please leave a review. Once you have read and used this book, why not leave a review on the site that you purchased it from? Potential readers can then see and use your unbiased opinion to make purchase decisions. We at BPB can understand what you think about our products, and our authors can see your feedback on their book. Thank you!

For more information about BPB, please visit **www.bpbonline.com**.

Join our Discord space

Join our Discord workspace for latest updates, offers, tech happenings around the world, new releases, and sessions with the authors:

https://discord.bpbonline.com

Table of Contents

CHAPTER 1
Exploring Big Data

In God we trust; all others must bring data.

-W. Edwards Deming

Introduction

Digital advancement in the last few years has led to the explosion of data like never before. This abundance of data, known as **big data**, has emerged as a driving force behind innovation, decision-making, and transformation across industries. Big data refers to vast volumes of structured and unstructured data that are too large, complex, and dynamic to be effectively managed and processed using traditional data processing techniques. Big data technologies and techniques enable organizations to harness the power of this data for valuable insights, predictive analytics, and informed decision-making. The ability to process and analyze large-scale data sets in real-time or near real-time has opened up new possibilities in various fields, including healthcare, finance, marketing, logistics, and more.

This chapter will explore the rise of data to big data and the types and characteristics of big data. It also introduces the readers to big data analytics and the types of analytics done in the industry for getting insights and better decision-making. The objective is to familiarize the readers with the capabilities and trade-offs of various tools and technologies to store, process, and analyze big data. This will facilitate making well-informed decisions when selecting the most appropriate database for the development of the application.

Structure

In this chapter, we will cover the following topics:

- Introduction to big data
- History of big data innovation
- Big data architecture
- Significance of big data
- Big data applications
- Big data governance

Objectives

By the end of this chapter, the readers will be able to understand the need and importance of big data, and will be able to define the types, characteristics, architecture, and applications of big data. They will build a thorough understanding of the various processes, policies, and controls that are put together by the organizations to ensure the proper management, quality, security, and compliance of big data.

Introduction to big data

Big data refers to extensive and complex data sets that are difficult to process and analyze using traditional data processing methods. The term gained popularity around the early 2010s when organizations started grappling with the challenges of managing and making sense of vast data. The rapid growth and adoption of big data are attributed to multiple factors known as drivers of big data. These drivers are instrumental in shaping and driving the big data landscape's ongoing development. As organizations have recognized the transformative potential to harness and analyze large and diverse data sets effectively, these drivers collectively contribute to the growth and adoption of big data. The prime drivers for big data are:

- **Data explosion**: The exponential growth of data is one of the primary drivers for big data. The proliferation of digital technologies like social media, **Internet of Things** (**IoT**) devices, mobile applications, and online transactions has generated enormous volumes of data every second. This data explosion drives the need to harness and analyze vast amounts of data for valuable insights.
- **Technological advancements**: Advancements in technologies have played a significant role in enabling big data. The development of more powerful and affordable computing infrastructure, cloud computing, distributed storage systems, and parallel processing frameworks such as *Hadoop* and *Spark* has made it feasible to store, process, and analyze massive data sets.
- **Cost reduction**: The declining costs of storage and computing resources have made big data more accessible. Organizations can now utilize scalable cloud-based solutions that provide cost-effective storage and processing capabilities. The cost reduction has enabled businesses of all sizes to leverage the benefits of big data technologies.
- **Connectivity and IoT**: The increasing connectivity and growth of IoT devices have generated vast amounts of data. IoT sensors embedded in various devices and environments, such as smart homes, wearables, industrial machinery, and transportation systems, are continuously capturing and transmitting data. This interconnectedness has contributed to the growth of big data by generating real-time data streams from various sources.
- **Social media and user-generated content**: The rise of social media platforms and user-generated content has created enormous data sources. Social media platforms generate vast amounts of textual, image, and video data, user interactions, and behavior patterns. This social media data has become a source for organizations to gain valuable insights into consumer sentiment, brand perception, market trends, etc.
- **Business intelligence and competitive advantage**: Organizations identify the potential value of big data in gaining a competitive edge. Analysis of large and diverse data sets helps businesses to discover hidden patterns, trends, and correlations that can drive strategic decision-making, optimize operations, and improve customer experiences. The pursuit of business intelligence and the desire to stay ahead in a data-driven world have further fueled the adoption of big data.
- **Personalization and customer insights**: Big data analytics helps organizations to gain deeper insights into their customers. Businesses can personalize products, services, and marketing campaigns by analyzing customer behavior, preferences, and feedback, improving customer satisfaction and loyalty. Therefore, personalization and customer-centric approaches have become key drivers for leveraging big data.
- **Scientific research and innovation**: Big data has substantially impacted scientific research and innovation. In fields like genomics, astronomy, climate science, and particle physics, huge data sets are generated and analyzed to make groundbreaking discoveries and advance knowledge. Big data analytics provides scientists with the tools to process, model, and simulate complex phenomena, which lead to new insights and innovations.
- **Decision-making and predictive analytics**: Big data analytics has the potential to enable data-driven decisions and predictions based on historical and real-time data. Organizations leverage advanced analytics techniques, such as **machine learning** (**ML**) and predictive modeling, which require huge amounts of data, to identify patterns, forecast outcomes, and optimize decision-making processes. The desire to make informed decisions and anticipate future trends drives the adoption of big data analytics.

Characteristics of big data

Big data is a term used to describe extremely large and complex datasets that exceed the processing capabilities of traditional data management and analysis tools. The characteristics of big data highlight the key features that differentiate it from traditional data sources. These are commonly summarized using the 3 Vs framework, which consists of volume, velocity, variety, and sometimes with the addition of veracity. The following list provides a detailed understanding of the frameworks:

- **Volume**: It refers to the sheer size of the data. It involves managing and analyzing massive amounts of data that exceed the capabilities of traditional data processing systems. The size of data may be estimated from the data generated from IoT devices, satellites, large-scale scientific experiments, or from the number of monthly active users available on various social media portals such as *Facebook* (958 billion), *Instagram* (2 billion), *WhatsApp* (2 billion), *TikTok* (1.051 billion), etc. The volume of data is expanding in two dimensions—horizontally, with the increase in rows, and vertically, with the increase in columns or dimensions/attributes. The increase in the number of dimensions has given rise to the *curse of dimensionality* problem. These challenges require new tools and technologies to store and analyze large datasets.
- **Velocity**: It reflects the speed at which data is generated, processed, and analyzed. It involves dealing with high-velocity data streams that require real-time or near-real-time processing and decision-making. For example, in one minute, *Netflix* streams 452K hours of videos, approximately 5.7M searches are performed on *Google*, *Amazon* customers spend $283K, and 65K photos are shared on Instagram. Besides, there are financial transactions, stock market data, or geospatial data where data is constantly being created and updated.
- **Variety**: It represents the diversity in types and formats of data that are generated. The unprecedented growth of digital information led to the birth of the concept of the digital universe, which encompasses all the data generated, collected, and stored in the digital realm. Digital data can be categorized into various types based on its format, structure, or content.

  It includes structured data (e.g., traditional databases), semi-structured data (e.g., XML or JSON files), and unstructured data (e.g., text documents, videos, images) as shown in *Figure 1.1*. Big data analytics systems must handle this variety of data sources and extract meaningful insights from them.

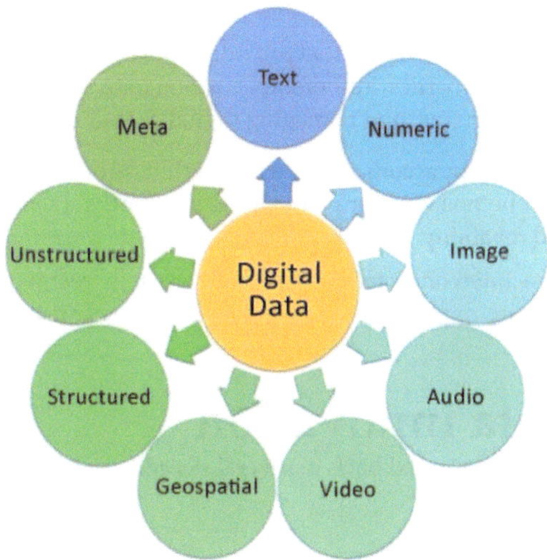

***Figure 1.1**: Types of digital data*

  - The following list outlines the different types of digital data:
    - **Text data**: Text data refers to alphanumeric characters, including letters, numbers, symbols, and punctuation marks. It can include documents, emails, instant messages, web pages, and any other textual information.

  - **Numeric data**: Numeric data represents numerical values, such as integers, decimals, or floating-point numbers. It is commonly used in scientific, financial, or statistical applications for calculations, analysis, and modeling.
  - **Image data**: Image data consists of visual representations, such as photographs, graphics, or digital images. It can be in various formats, including JPEG, PNG, GIF, or TIFF, and is used in fields like photography, design, computer vision, and medical imaging.
  - **Audio data**: Audio data includes sound and auditory information. It can include music files, spoken recordings, podcasts, or any other type of audio content. Common audio formats include MP3, WAV, AAC, or Ogg.
  - **Video data**: Video data comprises moving visual content. It includes recordings, movies, television shows, video clips, or any other visual sequences. Video data is often stored in formats like MP4, AVI, MKV, or MOV.
  - **Geospatial data**: Geospatial data refers to information related to geographic locations and spatial features. It includes maps, satellite imagery, GPS data, **geographic information system (GIS)** datasets, and geo-referenced data used in fields like cartography, urban planning, or environmental science.
  - **Structured data**: Structured data is organized and stored in a predefined format, typically using database systems. It is characterized by a fixed schema or data model, and examples include tables in relational databases, spreadsheets, or data represented in XML or JSON formats.
  - **Unstructured data**: Unstructured data has no predefined format or organization. It includes free-form text, social media posts, emails, multimedia content, or any data that does not fit neatly into a structured format.
  - **Metadata**: Metadata refers to data that provides information about other data. It describes various aspects such as file properties, authorship, creation date, file size, or data source. Metadata helps in organizing, categorizing, and managing digital data effectively.
- **Veracity**: It specifies the reliability, accuracy, and trustworthiness of the data. As big data is generated from a variety of sources, it can be noisy, incomplete, or inconsistent. Veracity encompasses the challenges of ensuring data quality and reliability, as well as dealing with data uncertainty and errors.

The characteristics of big data are interconnected and often coexist in real-world scenarios. The appropriate technologies, tools, and approaches are required to address these unique characteristics for effective management and analysis of big data.

History of big data innovation

The history of big data innovation can be traced back to several decades. *Figure 1.2* depicts some of the significant events in the evolution of big data:

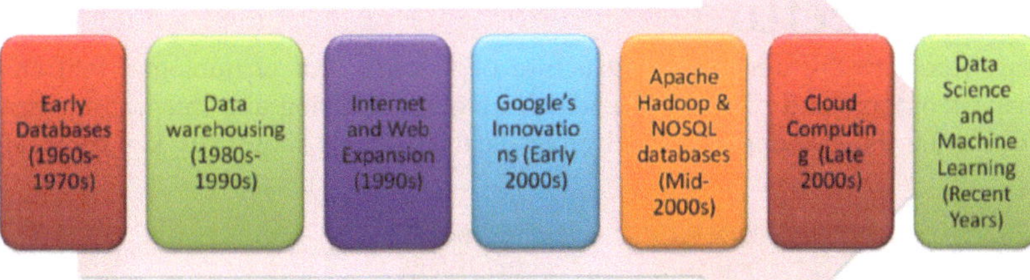

***Figure 1.2**: Evolution of big data*

The various stages in the evolution of big data are as follows:

- **Early databases (1960s-1970s)**: The development of **database management systems** (**DBMS**) in the 1960s and 1970s created the foundation for structured data storage and management. These systems were designed and developed for efficient storage and retrieval of structured data in a controlled manner.
- **Data warehousing (1980s-1990s)**: Relational DBMS like *Oracle* and *Microsoft* SQL *Server* became prominent during this period. The concept of data warehousing and **online analytical processing** (**OLAP**) also emerged in the 1980s and 1990s. It involves the consolidation of data from multiple sources into a centralized repository for analysis and decision-making. It led to advancements in data integration, data modeling, and query optimization techniques.
- **Internet and web expansion (1990s)**: The swift growth of the Internet and the proliferation of websites in the 1990s generated huge amounts of data. The rapid surge in volume and variety of online data sources is the prime catalyst behind escalating challenges and opportunities presented by big data.
- **Google's innovations (early 2000s)**: In this era, Google introduced technologies like the **Google File System** (**GFS**) for distributed storage and the MapReduce framework for parallel processing and distributed computing. These innovations for managing and analyzing large-scale data sets played a significant role in the evolution of big data. The term big data gained prominence during this decade. These technologies also formed the basis of the Apache Hadoop ecosystem.
- **Apache Hadoop (mid-2000s)**: It is an open-source framework for big data storage and processing. **Hadoop Distributed File System** (**HDFS**) and MapReduce programming model enabled scalable storage and parallel data processing at reduced cost with clusters of commodity hardware.
- **NoSQL databases (mid-2000s)**: The rise in the variety of digital data sources beyond structured data led to the emergence of **Not only SQL** (**NoSQL**) databases. NoSQL databases offered a flexible, schema-less approach for the storage of data, facilitating efficient handling of unstructured and semi-structured data.
- **Cloud computing (late 2000s)**: The introduction of cloud computing provided scalable and cost-effective infrastructure for storing, processing, and analyzing big data. Cloud-based platforms, such as **Amazon Web Services** (**AWS**), Microsoft Azure, and **Google Cloud Platform** (**GCP**), offer on-demand resources and managed services for big data processing.
- **Data science and ML (Recent years)**: The advent of data science and ML techniques has further propelled big data innovation. Advanced analytics, predictive modeling, and **artificial intelligence** (**AI**) driven algorithms have been applied to big data to extract insights, patterns, and predictive capabilities from large and complex data sets.

These milestones reflect the progression of significant data innovations driven by the increasing volume, variety, and velocity of data and advancements in computing power, storage, and analytical techniques.

Big data architecture

Big data architecture refers to the design and structure of systems and technologies that enable the storage, processing, and analysis of large and diverse data sets. It involves selecting and integrating various components and technologies to handle the challenges posed by big data. *Figure 1.3* shows the key components in big data architecture:

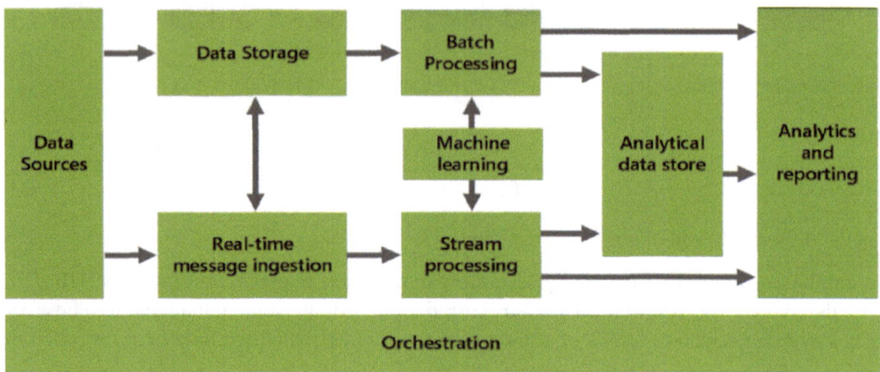

***Figure 1.3:** Big data architecture*

The following list provides a detailed understanding of the key components of big data architecture:

- **Data sources**: Data sources are the starting point of every big data system. Depending on the type of application or problem to be solved, data sources may vary, e.g., application data stores (relational databases or NoSQL databases), static files (log files, CSV files), or real-time data sources (IoT devices, sensors, social media feeds). These sources provide the raw data that needs to be processed and analyzed.
- **Data ingestion and storage**: The next step is to ingest the data into a big data architecture for storage and processing. Latest technologies like Apache Kafka, Apache NiFi, or cloud-based services are often used for data ingestion. The ingested data is stored using robust and scalable solutions such as traditional relational databases (like MySQL, PostgreSQL), NoSQL databases (like MongoDB, Cassandra), distributed file systems (like Hadoop HDFS), and cloud-based storage (like Amazon S3, Google Cloud Storage), etc. In the applications involving real-time data, big data architectures include a component for message ingestion. Real-time data streaming from sources like IoT devices or event-driven systems needs to be captured and stored for further processing. Technologies like Azure Event Hubs, Azure IoT Hub, or Kafka are used to handle the real-time message ingestion and provide reliable, scalable, and durable message queues.
- **Data processing**: Once data is ingested and stored, the next step is to process the data. Based on the type of application, this may involve batch processing or stream processing. In batch processing, large volumes of data are processed in batches. The data is read from the storage layer and processed using frameworks like Apache Hadoop (including Hadoop MapReduce), Apache Spark, or other distributed computing frameworks. Batch processing is usually preferred for tasks like data cleaning, filtering, aggregation, or running complex algorithms on the entire dataset.

  Stream processing is responsible for real-time data processing, allowing for immediate analysis and action on incoming data streams. It involves processing and analyzing the data as it flows rather than in batches. Stream processing frameworks like Azure Stream Analytics, Apache Spark Streaming, Apache Flink, or Apache Storm perform operations like filtering, aggregation, windowing, and joining on real-time data streams.

- **Machine learning (ML)**: ML algorithms play a key role in big data analytics. These algorithms are used to analyze large datasets to discover useful insights and patterns from data. They are trained on large datasets to perform various tasks like building predictive models, performing classification or clustering tasks, anomaly detection, **natural language processing** (**NLP**), recommendation systems, optimization, and decision making. ML models can be continuously trained and updated with the availability of new data, which enables the big data architectures to adapt to changing patterns and trends. Platforms like Google Cloud AI, Amazon SageMaker, and Microsoft Azure provide tools and frameworks to develop, train, and deploy ML models on big data.
- **Analytical data store**: An analytical data store or an analytical repository is a type of database specifically designed to store data for data analysis, reporting, and business intelligence. These databases are optimized to perform complex queries, aggregations, and data exploration tasks, unlike conventional transactional databases, which are optimized to handle numerous read and write operations concurrently.

  These storage systems are characterized by high performance, scalability, parallel processing, and data integration. The various analytical stores include columnar databases (Amazon Redshift, Google BigQuery, and Snowflake), in-memory databases (SAP HANA and MemSQL), and data warehouses (Teradata, Oracle Exadata, and Microsoft Azure Synapse Analytics).
- **Analysis and reporting**: It refers to the processes that derive meaningful insights and generate valuable information from large and diverse datasets, which are ingested and processed in the previous steps. Analysis and reporting are performed with the specialized tools and technologies for data exploration, visualization, and business intelligence. For example, Azure Analysis Services performs multidimensional analysis and modeling, Power BI supports interactive data visualization and reporting, and Jupyter Notebooks or Microsoft R Server perform data exploration and advanced analytics. Visualization tools also play an important role in data analysis and reporting meaningfully and clearly. They help analysts, business users, and decision makers to explore, analyze, and interpret data visually, create interactive dashboards, and generate reports. Tools like *Power BI*, *Tableau*, *QlikView*, *Qlik Sense*, *D3.js* (a JavaScript library), *ggplot2* (an R package), *Matplotlib* (a Python library), and *Google Data Studio* are used by organizations to perform data analysis and reporting for generating impactful insights.
- **Orchestration**: Orchestration refers to the coordination and management of the various tasks involved in the processing and analysis of data across the various components and stages of the data pipeline of big data architecture. It ensures the smooth and efficient execution of dataflows between the components, coordination of processes, and tasks in the data pipeline. Technologies like Azure Data Factory, Apache Oozie, Apache Airflow, Apache NiFi, etc., are widely used platforms for orchestrating data pipelines, managing dependencies, and handling data movement.

Significance of big data

In this digital era, big data is important across various industries and sectors as it has transformed how organizations operate, make decisions, and innovate. Enterprises are harnessing the potential of big data from multiple perspectives. The details are as follows:

- **Insights and informed decision-making**: Big data enables organizations to make informed decisions based on the wealth of information available from various sources and formats. Big data analytics allow organizations to uncover patterns, trends, and correlations that would be challenging to discover using smaller datasets. Enterprises can utilize this information to identify new opportunities and optimize business strategies.
- **Enhanced customer understanding**: Big data helps organizations to understand their customers better. Customer data analytics enables organizations to understand customer behavior, their product, service, or feature preferences, and feedback. Organizations use this information to drive business growth by personalizing products and services, planning marketing campaigns, and improving customer experiences.

- **Increased operational efficiency**: The companies analyze the Organization's operational data to identify the bottlenecks, inefficiencies, or areas for improvement. This helps in better management of resources, streamlining the workflows, reducing costs, and improving productivity.
- **Risk management and fraud detection**: Big data analytics plays an important role in risk management and fraud detection. Due to increased online transactions, organizations are compelled to analyze data to detect anomalies, patterns of fraudulent activities, and potential risks. This helps in taking preventive measures to avoid financial losses, protect against security threats, and ensure regulatory compliance.
- **Competitive advantage**: Big data analytics has become a new tool to provide a competitive edge. Organizations leverage data analytics to understand market trends, customer behaviors, and competitors' strategies to design and implement innovative business strategies and stay ahead of the competition in today's data-driven world.

Big data applications

The vast amount of data generated in the recent past has empowered various industries across all major domains to gain insights, make informed decisions, and drive innovation. Some prominent use cases, along with applications, are discussed in this section.

Retail and e-commerce

Millions of transactions are performed every few minutes across various online platforms. Web and mobile applications monitor all activities of the users, for example, purchase history, browsing behavior, click-through rate, time spent on pages, etc. The companies analyze these details to design personalized marketing campaigns, recommend products, and improve customer engagement. For example, recommendations for products, movies, videos, music, etc., generated by *Amazon, Netflix, Spotify, YouTube, Pandora, Reddit*, etc., are based on customer data analysis.

Companies leverage their historical data related to sales of products or services to predict demand for products, optimize inventory management, and reduce stockouts. For example, companies like *Procter & Gamble, Walmart, Amazon, Coca-Cola, Airbus, Starbucks, FedEx, Zara, Nestle*, etc, use sophisticated algorithms for demand forecasting to maintain optimal stock levels, meet customer demands and preferences, plan production schedules, optimize delivery routes, and manage inventory. Analyzing competitor pricing is another prime focus of the companies to develop optimal pricing strategies for maximizing revenue. For example, airlines adjust ticket prices based on real-time demand and market conditions.

Healthcare

Hospitals and healthcare systems across the globe have incorporated healthcare data analytics into their operations for improved patient care, optimization of resources, and enhanced decision-making. Analysis of patient data, medical records, and research data helps to gain real-time insights, detect disease outbreaks, predict epidemics, develop personalized treatment plans, and facilitate early intervention for improved diagnosis and treatment outcomes. For example, *IBM Watson for Oncology* is employed to assist physicians in cancer treatment decisions, *Google Flu Trends* predicts flu activity based on search queries, *The Cancer Genome Atlas* (*TCGA*) project is using big data to advance cancer research and personalized medicine, *Mayo Clinic* employs analytics to personalize treatments, predict patient outcomes, and optimize clinical workflows.

Financial services

Financial data analytic tools like *SAP, Qlik, Anaplan, Backline, SAS, and TIBCO* are gaining immense popularity over the years. Companies employ financial data analysis to optimize financial performance, budgeting, and forecasting, identify fraudulent activities, risk assessment and management, and enhance security. Credit card companies like *Visa, Mastercard, American Express, Chase*, etc., employ advanced data analytics and ML algorithms to detect and prevent fraudulent transactions in real-time, analyze spending patterns, etc. Companies like *Goldman Sachs*, *JPMorgan Chase & Co.*, *Morgan Stanley*, *Two Sigma*, etc., use big data analytics to enhance trading strategies and manage market risk more effectively.

Manufacturing and supply chain

Data from the machine sensors, equipment performance, historical maintenance records, supply chain data, and quality metrics are analyzed by companies to predict and prevent equipment failures, optimize maintenance schedules, minimize downtime, improve delivery efficiency, identify quality issues, and enhance product quality and consistency. For example, *General Electric* (*GE*) uses *Predix*, *Siemens* offers *MindSphere*, and *ABB* utilizes its *ABB ability* platform to perform big data analytics for predictive maintenance in industrial equipment. *Walmart* performs data analytics to optimize inventory management and improve supply chain operations. *Tesla*, *Ford*, *General Motors*, *Toyota*, and others use big data to monitor vehicle performance and analyze telematics data to identify quality concerns.

Transportation and logistics

Companies involved in transportation and logistics business leverage their big data repositories to analyze real-time traffic data, historical patterns, and weather conditions for optimizing transportation routes, minimizing delivery time, and reduce fuel consumption, for example, *UPS*, *FedEx*, *DHL*, *Uber freight*, *Amazon logistics* utilize big data analytics to optimize delivery operations, streamline logistics operations, and improve driver scheduling and route optimization. *Ryder* and *Uber* leverage big data analytics to effectively manage a global fleet of vehicles. *Delta Airlines* uses big data analytics to forecast demand and dynamically adjust fares. *CN Rail* analyzes data to optimize rail operations, track cargo movements, and enhance its freight transportation services.

Big data governance

Big data governance refers to the set of processes, policies, and controls that an organization puts together to ensure the proper management, quality, security, and compliance of big data. For organizations dealing with large volumes of sensitive and valuable data, it is vital to establish a data governance framework to maintain data integrity, ensure regulatory compliance, and enable responsible and efficient use of data assets. The following section highlights some of the key aspects of big data governance that are critical for managing and safeguarding large and complex data sets.

Privacy

It refers to the issues and challenges associated with safeguarding the privacy of individuals while collecting personal or sensitive data for big data analysis. The following list outlines the key considerations for organizations to ensure the privacy of individuals:

- Organizations must obtain informed consent from individuals before collecting and using their data. The purpose and scope of data collection should be precisely stated in accordance with relevant privacy laws and regulations.
- Organizations may employ techniques like anonymization and pseudonymization to hide or alter **personally identifying information** (**PII**) from the collected data sets. This helps in minimizing the risk of linking any data with an individual's identification.
- Organizations may collect only the specific or necessary data required to solve the problem. This principle of data minimization would help organizations to reduce privacy risks and improve data protection.
- Big data platforms should implement robust security measures to protect data during storage and transmission. This includes encryption, access controls, secure network protocols, and regular security audits to safeguard against unauthorized access, breaches, and data leakage.

Security

Big data security refers to the protection of data from unauthorized access, breaches, and malicious activities. A variety of measures are adopted by the organizations to address these concerns and to ensure the confidentiality, integrity, and availability of data, e.g., encryption technologies, access control methods, authentication mechanisms, and secure network protocols.

Compliance

Big data compliance means ensuring the legal, industry-specific, and regulatory requirements while handling and managing data. Compliance frameworks like **General Data Protection Regulation** (**GDPR**), **Health Insurance Portability and Accountability Act** (**HIPAA**), or **Payment Card Industry Data Security Standard** (**PCI DSS**) outline the guidelines to be followed for privacy, security, retention, and disclosure of data. Organizations follow big data compliance to avoid legal consequences, reputational damage, and financial penalties.

Auditing

It is a process to track and monitor the access, usage, and modifications of data. Organizations implementing auditing mechanisms are able to track the activities of users who accessed the data, when it was accessed, and what actions were performed on it. Auditing helps to identify and investigate potential security breaches, policy violations, or anomalies in data access patterns in an organization.

Protection

Big data protection encompasses measures to safeguard data from loss, corruption, or unauthorized modifications. This includes implementing data backup and disaster recovery strategies, ensuring data quality and consistency, and implementing data governance frameworks. Data protection also involves identifying and mitigating risks associated with data storage, data transmission, and data processing.

Big data ethics

Organizations with massive amounts of data should have ethical guidelines in place to ensure the responsible and ethical use of data. They should perform big data analytics with ethical considerations and avoid using methods or processes that may harm individuals or violate their rights. Ethical considerations for the collection and analysis of data are as follows:

- Fairness and unbiased big data analysis must be the key priority of the organizations. To ensure the same, appropriate methods must be used for data collection, processing, and algorithms such that decisions are not based on any sensitive attributes like race, gender, or religion.
- Transparency and justification with respect to data collection and analysis practices are the responsibility of the organizations. They should provide clear explanations on the usage of data, insights that are derived, and the likely impact on individuals. Transparency helps in fostering trust and helps individuals make informed decisions.
- Stringent data governance practices help in establishing accountability of the organizations to handle data ethically.
- Organizations should behave responsibly when sharing or selling individuals' data to third parties. They must obtain prior consent and ensure that shared data is used for legitimate purposes only.
- Data retention and disposal policies should align properly with the privacy regulations. Data should be retained only for the desired duration and disposed of securely thereafter.

Conclusion

This chapter focused on big data, which refers to the large and complex data sets that have evolved over the years due to the rapid growth of the **World Wide Web (WWW)**, technological advancements, connectivity, IoT, and so on. Big data is mainly characterized by high volume, velocity, and variety of data (structured, semi-structured, and unstructured). Organizations have designed big data architecture for seamless processing and analysis of big data. It is used in various applications like finance, healthcare, and manufacturing. The chapter finally discussed big data's privacy, ethics, security, compliance, auditing, and protection aspects.

In the next chapter, we will discuss the challenges that arise while handling the storage and computation of vast volumes of data and how Hadoop is used as a solution to deal with the prevailing issues. The chapter will also explain the types of data analytics done by organizations for various applications.

Points to remember

The following list outlines the key takeaways from this chapter:

- Big data refers to extremely large and complex data sets that are difficult to process and analyze using traditional data processing methods.
- The primary drivers of big data are technological advancements, cost reduction, connectivity, IoT, social media, and user-generated content.
- The characteristics of big data are volume, velocity, variety, and veracity.
- The digital data exists in multiple forms, for example, text, numeric, image, audio, video, geospatial, structured, unstructured, and metadata.
- The evolution of big data is traced back to relational database management systems, evolving over time to data warehouses, Hadoop, NoSQL databases, and cloud for storage and processing. The big data architecture represents the data pipeline used by enterprises to ingest, store, process, and analyze the huge amount of data.
- Big data is seen as an important asset by organizations for getting useful insights, informed decision-making, enhanced customer understanding, increased operational efficiency, risk management, fraud detection, and a competitive advantage.
- The worth of big data has already been established in varied applications in different domains, such as retail, e-commerce, healthcare, financial services, manufacturing and supply chain, transportation, and logistics.
- Organizations with a huge amount of data need to follow the security compliances and be responsible for the privacy of users and ethical considerations.

Multiple choice questions

1. **What type of data is collected when a user writes a tweet on Twitter?**
    a. Structured
    b. Unstructured
    c. Semi-structured
    d. Relational

2. **The given figure shows______ a type of data?**

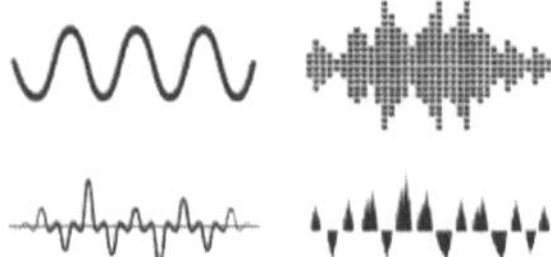

Figure 1.4: Audio data

   a. Structured
   b. Signal
   c. Unstructured
   d. Semi-structured

3. **Which format represents the semi-structured data?**
   a. Excel
   b. HTML
   c. Relational
   d. JSON

4. **What is the primary characteristic of big data that refers to the vast amount of data generated and collected?**
   a. Variety
   b. Velocity
   c. Volume
   d. Veracity

5. **Which of the following is not a driver of big data adoption?**
   a. Cost reduction
   b. Social media and user generated content
   c. Technological advancements
   d. Data simplicity

6. **Which historical development in the timeline of big data innovation is associated with the introduction of Apache Hadoop?**
   a. Google's innovations
   b. Cloud computing
   c. NoSQL databases
   d. Early databases

7. **Which type of data includes information like location coordinates and map data?**
   a. Structured data
   b. Geospatial data
   c. Numeric data
   d. Unstructured data

8. **Which component of big data architecture involves preparing data for analysis and modeling?**
   a. Data processing
   b. ML
   c. Data ingestion and storage
   d. Analytical data store

9. **Which of the following is not a significance of big data?**
   a. Increased operational efficiency
   b. Enhanced customer understanding
   c. Entertainment
   d. Insights and informed decision making

10. **Which sector can benefit from big data applications in detecting fraudulent activities?**
    a. Entertainment
    b. Healthcare
    c. Financial Services
    d. Transportation and logistics

Answers

1. b.	2. c.	3. d.	4. c.	5. d.
6. a.	7. b.	8. a.	9. c.	10. c.

Questions

1. Explain the concept of big data and discuss why traditional data processing methods areinadequate for handling it. Provide examples to illustrate your points.
2. What are the drivers of big data adoption? How do technological advancements, social media, and business intelligence contribute to the growth of big data? Provide real-worldexamples for each driver.
3. Describe the four key characteristics of big data: volume, velocity, variety, and veracity. For each characteristic, provide an example of how it manifests in real-world scenarios.
4. Trace the history of big data innovation from the 1960s to the present day. Highlight key developments such as the introduction of early databases, the role of Apache Hadoop, and the emergence of data science and ML.
5. Explain the components of big data architecture in detail. How do data ingestion, storage, processing, ML, and analysis collectively contribute to extracting value from big data?
6. Discuss the significance of big data in modern business and technology landscapes. How does it enable insights, enhance customer understanding, and provide a competitive advantage? Provide examples from different industries.
7. Explore the applications of big data in the healthcare sector. How can it be used to improve patient care, medical research, and operational efficiency in healthcare organizations?
8. Describe the concept of big data governance. What are the key aspects of governance, including privacy, ethics, security, compliance, auditing, and protection? Why is effective governance crucial in the era of big data?
9. Analyze the role of big data in risk management and fraud detection within the financial services sector. Provide examples of how financial institutions can leverage big data to mitigate risks and prevent fraudulent activities.
10. Choose a specific industry (e.g., manufacturing, transportation, retail) and explain how bigdata can be applied to optimize processes and improve overall efficiency within that industry.

CHAPTER 2
Introduction to Hadoop

The goal is to turn data into information, and information into insight.

-Carly Fiorina

Introduction

The chapter begins by addressing the key challenges of big data, focusing on storage and computation complexities that arise with the vast volumes of data. It then explains the concept of data analysis, exploring the various analytic processes and modern tools used to gain valuable insights from the data. It then follows the introduction to Hadoop, tracing its origin and the reasons behind its widespread adoption in the industry. A comparative analysis of Hadoop with distributed databases sheds light on the advantages offered by its data and computing models. The chapter further compares Hadoop to traditional **relational database management systems** (**RDBMS**), clearly distinguishing between the two paradigms. Finally, the Hadoop ecosystem and its various components are explored, providing readers with a comprehensive understanding of this robust big data processing framework.

Structure

In this chapter, we will cover the following topics:

- Big data analytics
- Big data challenges
- Case study: Stock data analysis
- Introduction to Hadoop
- Hadoop ecosystem
- Hadoop versus relational database management system
- Hadoop versus distributed databases

Objectives

By the end of this chapter, the readers will be able to understand the fundamental concepts of big data analytics and its types. They will be able to identify the storage and computation challenges posed by conventional systems in processing big data and performing big data analysis, and will understand how organizations use Hadoop to solve the problems posed by traditional systems. Furthermore, they will build an understanding of the origin of Hadoop, the various components of Hadoop ecosystems, and its comparison with distributed databases and RDBMS.

Big data analytics

Big data analytics is collecting, examining, and analyzing large amounts of data to discover hidden patterns or correlations, understand market trends, and gain insights for making better business decisions. It began with the introduction of the first computer system by *IBM* in 1960, capable of processing large amounts of data. This was followed by the development of databases and data-processing software in the 1970s and 1980s. Subsequently, the emergence of the cloud led to the industries' significant adoption of big data. When used in business, data analytics is often called **business analytics**.

Currently, **artificial intelligence** (**AI**) and **machine learning** (**ML**) techniques are applied prominently to make big data analytics actionable and transform big data into insights. It is popularly called **intelligent data analysis** and provides engagement capabilities for data scientists, enterprise analytics strategists, data intelligence warehouse architects, implementation and development experts, etc. Enterprise data intelligence is used for business intelligence operations, analyzing sales, evaluating inventories, and building customer data intelligence. Organizations implementing big data analytics are driving a huge value impact to support their decision-making process and maintain their competitive advantage along various dimensions, such as:

- **Data-driven decision making**: The analysis of huge volumes of data from a variety of sources helps companies to gain valuable insights and make informed strategic choices, optimize operations, and improve overall decision-making processes.
- **Improved customer understanding**: Organizations perform data analysis to improve their understanding of customer behaviors, along with their preferences and sentiments. This helps enterprises to perform more personalized marketing and product recommendations and provide improved customer experiences. For example, companies perform trend analysis to gain insights into purchase history and future buying intentions of customers for product development decisions. Customer data is generated faster than ever before. New technologies, like *Google Analytics* and mobile apps, can track customer behavior on your website or when they interact with your services.
- **Enhanced product and service development**: In this digital era, organizations analyze ratings, reviews, etc., to gain insights into customer needs and preferences. This helps organizations develop new products and services that are better aligned with market demands.
- **Cost reduction**: Big data analysis helps reduce costs by identifying opportunities to optimize processes, reduce inefficiencies, and minimize waste. Data is also analyzed to predict maintenance needs and reduce downtime and maintenance costs for equipment and assets.
- **Risk management**: Businesses perform data analytics to identify potential risks and fraud by analyzing patterns and anomalies in data and develop solutions for managing those risks.

According to the studies, the global data analytics market size was USD 30 billion in 2022 and is projected to surpass around USD 393.35 billion by 2032, as shown in *Figure 2.1*. This clearly indicates that big data analytics empowers organizations to harness the power of data to gain insights, make informed decisions, improve operations, and stay competitive in today's data-driven world. Nowadays, many companies, including *Netflix*, *Amazon*, and *Spotify*, use big data analytics to uncover valuable insights for their business. Its applications span across various industries and functions, making it a transformative technology with far-reaching benefits.

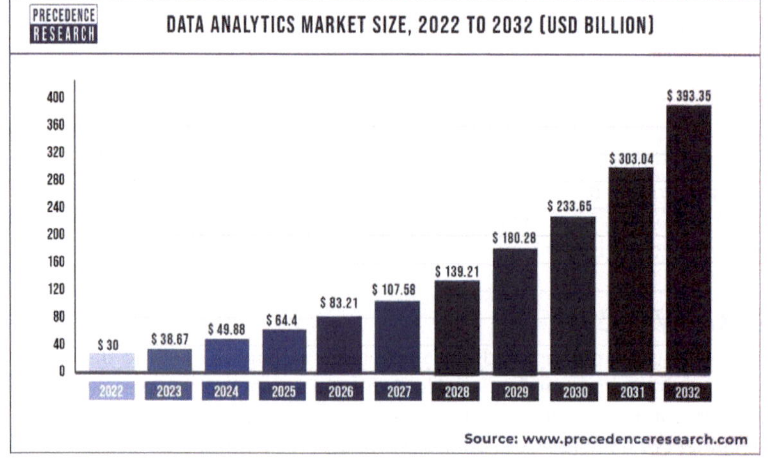

Figure 2.1: *Global big data analytics size*

*(**Source**: https://www.precedencestatistics.com/)*

Types of big data analytics

There are mainly four types of analytics being performed by companies with different objectives, such as descriptive, diagnostic, prescriptive, and predictive analytics. They use a variety of tools and techniques for data mining, cleaning, integration, visualization, etc., in order to improve the process of data analysis for maximizing profits and informed decision-making.

Descriptive analytics

Descriptive analytics is performed to discover patterns and gain insights into historical data. It helps to answer the question: *what happened in the past?* or *what is happening?*. For example, a company may check the sales data of their products to identify the trends in sales of products by season, region, change in the number of users, total revenue per subscriber, etc. Descriptive analytics may reveal to a toy company that a trend of an increase in sales of *PlayStations* and video games is observed during a particular period in the year in India.

Diagnostics analytics

Companies do diagnostics analytics to understand the reasons behind a particular trend or behavior observed via descriptive analytics. These types of analytics are performed to answer questions like *why did it happen?* For example, through diagnosis, a toy company observed a spike in sales during May, June, October, and November. A deeper analysis of the historical data revealed that sales were high in northern India as summer vacations fall in May and June, so people may have been purchasing games to keep their children busy during vacations. Sales were high during October and November, due to the festive season, and toys were purchased for gifting purposes. In another study, it was observed that sales were decreasing despite customers adding items to the shopping cart. Diagnostics analytics helped identify that the online payment system was not working correctly for a few weeks. Thus, big data technologies and tools aid companies in recognizing the problems and opportunities for better planning and implementation.

Predictive analytics

In predictive analytics, the past and present data are analyzed to make predictions about the future. It answers the question, *what may happen in the future?* Various **artificial intelligence** (**AI**), **machine learning** (**ML**), and data mining techniques are applied to the data to predict market trends. For example, after diagnostic analytics, the toy company applies various techniques to predict the sales of PlayStation/toys in the coming year. This type of analytics was also performed to predict the spread of COVID-19 in various countries at different levels. It helps in better planning of resources in the future.

Prescriptive analytics

Prescriptive analytics helps businesses to make better and more informed decisions. Its goal is to answer the question, *what should be done next?* It may be performed post-diagnostics or predictive analytics. It relies on AI and ML techniques to analyze the data and generate recommendations. It is a valuable tool for data-driven decision-making. For example, the toy company may recommend offering discounts or some offers to increase its profits further. The doctors recommend medicines after diagnosing the diseases. The government recommended a lockdown to control the spread of COVID-19.

Big data challenges

Data's rapidly increasing size and complexity have presented companies with enormous challenges in storing and processing large amounts of data in recent years. Traditional tools and technologies that were good at addressing the storage and computing challenges of previous paradigms have become inefficient due to the sheer volume, speed, variety, and intricate data structures inherent in today's data landscape. Let us understand the challenges enterprises face due to the mushrooming size of data. Imagine a large retail company, *A2Z*, selling its goods online via an e-commerce portal. A2Z wants to harness the power of big data collected over a period of time to enhance its customer experience and optimize inventory management. Significant data challenges faced by companies are as follows:

- **Scalability**: Conventional tools and databases are designed to handle relatively small to medium-sized data sets. They find it difficult to cope with the massive amounts of data generated in big data environments. Scaling often requires significant hardware and software upgrades, resulting in higher costs.
- **Performance**: As data size escalates, traditional tools experience performance bottlenecks. Queries and operations that used to work well on smaller data sets can become slow and inefficient when applied to large data sets. This may lead to delays in data processing and analysis.
- **Data processing speed**: The retail company wants to analyze data in real-time or near real-time to make instant decisions about inventory management and personalized marketing. However, traditional batch-oriented **extract, transform, load** (**ETL**) processes may not be optimal solutions for real-time data ingestion and processing. Handling data streams with low latency requirements can be challenging for these systems.
- **Data variety**: The retail company has data from various sources, such as customer browsing and shopping data, **point of sale** (**POS**) systems, supply chain, social media, customer support, etc. All sources provide data in different formats and structures. For instance, the e-commerce website data might be in JSON format, while the POS data is stored in relational databases. Traditional ETL tools may struggle to handle these diverse data formats seamlessly.
- **Complex data models**: Big data mainly involves complex data models, such as graph data, time-series data, and geospatial data. Conventional relational databases may not be well-suited to handle these data models efficiently.
- **Storage costs**: Traditional storage solutions can be expensive to use, as they require additional costs to purchase, maintain, and upgrade the hardware components. Big data storage systems are designed to store massive datasets cost-effectively by distributing data across commodity hardware.
- **Data integration challenges**: Integrating data from various sources can be complex with traditional tools. Big data often involves seamless ingestion and integration of data from various sources and formats, which may not be achievable with legacy systems.
- **Data processing paradigm**: Traditional tools typically follow batch processing, while big data often requires real-time or stream processing. Traditional batch processing systems are not well-suited for analyzing data as it arrives. Therefore, delays in data processing and integration can lead to missed opportunities and decreased operational efficiency.
- **Limited analytics capabilities**: Traditional data analytical tools like Excel or essential relational databases have limited built-in analytics and ML capabilities. As data size increases to terabytes or petabytes, traditional tools may not scale easily, leading to slower analysis and decision-making processes. Big data analytics often requires specialized tools and frameworks designed for distributed processing and advanced analytics.

Case study: Stock data analysis

Let us understand the challenges with a case study of stock data analysis. Analyzing stock market data is essential for making informed investment decisions in the modern financial world. Assume that a small financial company has stored 1 TB of stock data of various companies on the server. Now, the company wishes to explore the data and wants to know how much time will be required to answer queries like **`the maximum closing price of each stock`** or **`the minimum opening price of each stock`**. Let us understand how the data analyst computes the execution time of the given query :

- **Total execution time of query**: Data access rate + Program computation time + Network bandwidth and where:
  - o Assume HDD, data access rate is 122 MB/sec.
  - o Time required to access 1TB of data is 10^6MB/122=8196.72 seconds, which is 2.278 hours.
  - o Assume that the program execution time for the query is 60 seconds or 1 hrs.

Hence, the total execution time of the query is approximately. 3.28 hrs+ Network bandwidth.

The total execution time of 3.28 hours to process a single query is too high using conventional tools and techniques. One solution may be replacing the HDD with a **Solid State Drive** (**SSD**) to improve the data access rate. However, this solution is not cost-effective as SSDs are very expensive. Personal machines face limitations in storage capacity, slower data fetch times, and restricted processing power, affecting both data retrieval and execution time. Conversely, servers offer more storage options, better hardware configurations, and improved data center management. However, they come with higher costs, maintenance responsibilities, and potential latency issues depending on their location and bandwidth availability. The choice between personal machines and servers depends on factors like budget, data volume, performance requirements, and accessibility. Besides, computation time and network bandwidth still remain a challenge.

This shows that the amount of data generated in this digital era is too much to be processed efficiently by traditional tools. Therefore, the following key challenges need to be addressed:

- To reliably store a large amount of data at a reasonable cost.
- To reduce the time required for analyzing the stored data.

To address these limitations, organizations often turn to big data technologies and platforms like Hadoop, Spark, NoSQL databases, data lakes, and cloud-based solutions. The landscape [1] of technologies and platforms used by the industries for big data analytics, as shown in *Figure* 2.2, is provided every year. These technologies are designed to handle the challenges posed by big data and provide the scalability, performance, and flexibility needed for modern data analytics and processing requirements. A few of the modern data analytics tools and techniques used by enterprises to gain valuable insights from data are as follows:

- **Data visualization tools**: Tools like Tableau, Power BI, and Matplotlib/Seaborn in Python are used by organizations to create interactive and visually appealing charts, graphs, and dashboards to explore and communicate insights from data.
- **ML platforms**: Platforms like TensorFlow, PyTorch, and scikit-learn provide libraries and frameworks to build, train, and deploy machine learning models to uncover patterns and relationships in data.
- **Big data processing tools**: Technologies like Apache Hadoop, Apache Spark, and Apache Flink enable distributed processing of large datasets, which helps organizations to analyze and derive insights from massive amounts of data efficiently.
- **Natural language processing (NLP) tools**: NLP tools like spaCy, NLTK, and Hugging Face's Transformers facilitate the analysis of unstructured text data to perform sentiment analysis, named entity recognition, and document classification.
- **Data wrangling and preparation tools**: Tools like Pandas, dplyr, and Apache NiFi help in cleaning, transforming, and preparing data for analysis, ensuring that it is in the right format and structure for further processing.
- **Data mining and pattern recognition tools**: Software like RapidMiner, KNIME, and IBM SPSS Modeler offer drag-and-drop interfaces to perform data mining, pattern recognition, and predictive analytics tasks without the need for extensive programming knowledge.
- **Data storytelling platforms**: Platforms like Narrative Science and DataRobot's Paxata enable users to create compelling narratives and stories from data, which help effectively communicate insights and findings to the stakeholders.
- **Cloud-based analytics platforms**: Cloud-based platforms like **Google Cloud Platform** (**GCP**), **Amazon Web Services** (**AWS**), and Microsoft Azure provide scalable infrastructure and services to store, process, and analyze data, along with built-in tools for ML, data visualization, and business intelligence.

- **Collaborative analytics platforms**: Tools like Databricks, Dataiku, and Alteryx enable collaboration among data scientists, analysts, and business users by providing centralized environments for sharing, exploring, and collaborating on data and analytics projects.
- **Automated analytics and AI tools**: Automated analytics platforms like DataRobot, H2O.ai, and AutoML provide automated machine learning capabilities, allowing users to build and deploy predictive models quickly without extensive manual intervention.

All these tools and technologies empower organizations to extract valuable insights from data, drive data-driven decision-making, and gain a competitive edge in today's data-driven world.

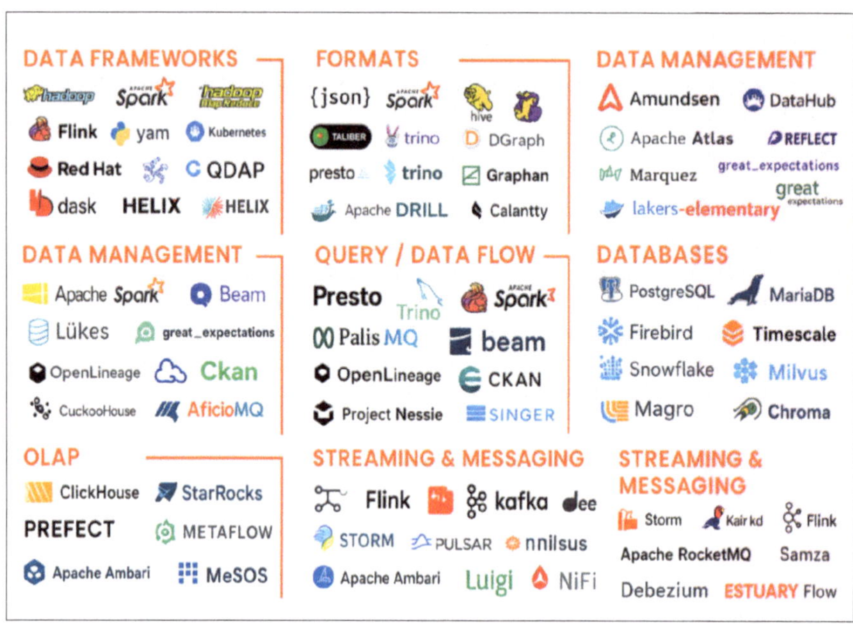

Figure 2.2: Big data landscape

Introduction to Hadoop

Apache Hadoop is an open-source framework for distributed processing of large datasets across clusters of commodity computers. It can easily store and process large-size datasets ranging from gigabytes to petabytes. Hadoop performs this task in parallel by distributing the task among multiple computers in the cluster, which enables fast processing of massive datasets. The framework is managed by the Apache Software Foundation and is licensed under the Apache License 2.0. It is written in Java.

With the rapid rise of applications generating huge amounts of data, Hadoop has become an important part of the database world. Although the computational power of application servers has increased dramatically in recent years, databases have been performing poorly due to their limited speed and capacity. This software gave the data analysts a new ray of hope for handling big data. Due to its enhanced features, its market size is continuously growing. According to the studies, the world will generate 181 zettabytes of data by 2025. Therefore, the global market revenue of Hadoop is projected to reach USD 851.4 billion by 2030 with a **Compound Annual Growth Rate** (**CAGR**) of 37.3% from 2022 to 2030, as shown in *Figure 2.3*:

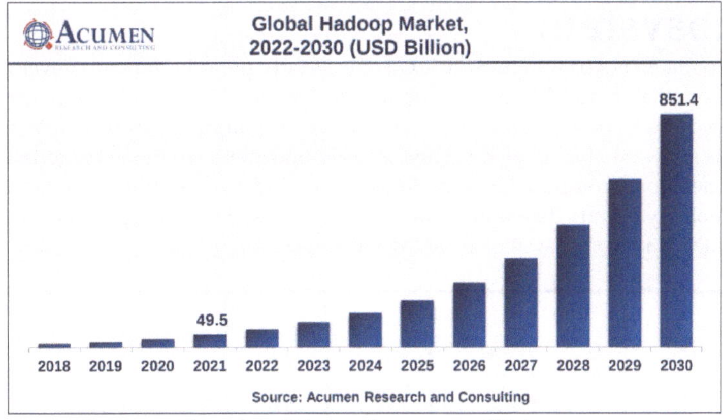

***Figure 2.3**: Global market revenue of Hadoop*

*(**Source**: https://www.acumenresearchandconsulting.com/hadoop-market)*

Evolution of Hadoop

The evolution of Hadoop began in 2002 when *Doug Cutting* and *Mike Cafarella* started working on the Apache Nutch project to build a search engine that could index billions of pages. They were searching for a feasible, low-cost solution to store and process large datasets. In 2003, Google published a paper that explained the architecture of Google's distributed file system, called **Google File System** (**GFS**), for storing large data sets. In 2004, Google published another paper with a solution to process large datasets, MapReduce. Doug Cutting and Mike Cafarella implemented GFS and MapReduce as open-source in the Apache Nutch project.

In 2006, *Doug Cutting* joined *Yahoo*, along with the Nutch project, with the goal of providing people with an open-source, reliable, scalable computing framework with the help of Yahoo. At Yahoo, he separated the distributed computing parts from Nutch and created a new project named Hadoop. In 2007, Yahoo successfully tested Hadoop on a 1000-node cluster, and in 2008, Yahoo released Hadoop as an open-source project to the **Apache Software Foundation** (**ASF**). In 2009, Hadoop was successfully tested to sort a **petabyte** (**PB**) of data in less than 17 hours to handle billions of searches and index millions of web pages. In 2011, ASF released Apache Hadoop version 1.0. In 2013, version 2.0.6 was released, and the latest Apache Hadoop version 3.0 was released in December 2017. The complete timeline for the evolution of Hadoop is shown in *Figure 2.4:*

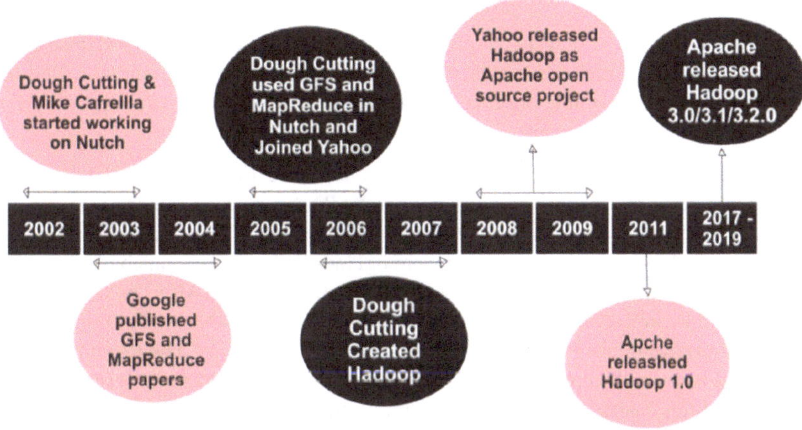

***Figure 2.4**: Evolution of Hadoop*

Hadoop ecosystem

The Apache Hadoop ecosystem is a comprehensive set of open-source projects and tools developed by the ASF. It is a collection of softwares for reliable, scalable, and distributed computing. The various components of this framework enable the distributed processing of large data sets across clusters of computers using simple programming models. The components of this software library are designed to scale up from a single server to thousands of machines, where each machine offers local computation and storage. It provides an inbuilt capability to detect and handle failures at the application layer, thus delivering a highly-available service on top of a cluster of computers. The various components of the Hadoop ecosystem are shown in *Figure 2.5*:

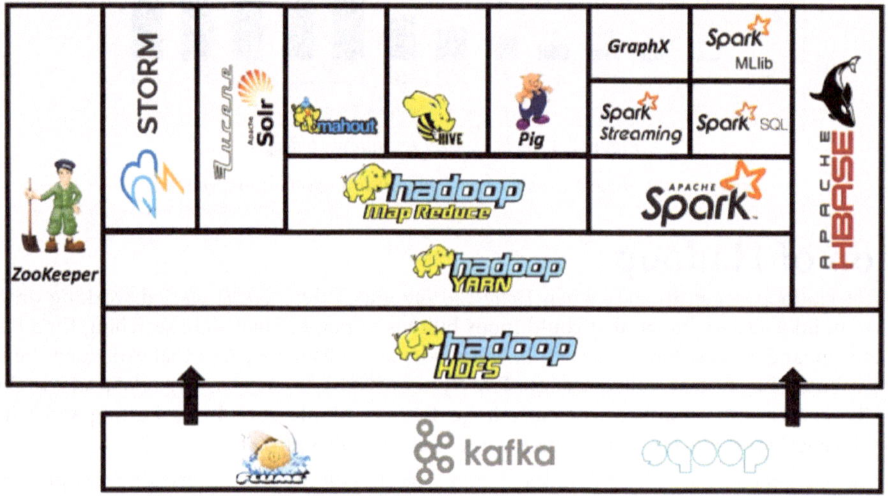

***Figure 2.5**: Hadoop ecosystem*

The role of various components of Apache Hadoop ecosystem are:

- **Hadoop Distributed File System (HDFS)**: It is one of the primary components of the Hadoop ecosystem. It is a distributed storage system that can store and distribute data across multiple nodes in a Hadoop cluster. It is highly fault-tolerant and is designed to handle large files and streaming data.
- **MapReduce**: It is the data processing component of Hadoop. MapReduce is basically a programming model and processing engine that helps in the distributed processing of large datasets. It consists of two phases, the Map phase, which processes data in parallel across nodes, and the Reduce phase, which aggregates the results. It is capable of processing large structured as well as unstructured data for big data analytics.
- **Yet Another Resource Negotiator (YARN)**: It is a resource management tool that enables multiple applications to share resources in a Hadoop cluster. YARN became part of the Hadoop ecosystem YARN became part of hadoop ecosystem in Hadoop2.x to allow different workloads. Hadoop 2.x to allow different workloads. It is like the operating system of Hadoop and is responsible for managing workloads, monitoring, and the implementation of security controls. The YARN has two main components, NodeManager and ResourceManager. The fundamental idea of YARN is to split up resource management and job scheduling/monitoring functionalities into separate daemons. The ResourceManager is the main authority that allocates resources among all the applications in the system. It tracks the resources in the cluster and schedules tasks, for example, the map-reduce jobs. The NodeManager is responsible for maintaining containers, monitoring their resource usage (CPU, memory, disk, network), and reporting the same to the ResourceManager. NodeManager is usually one per cluster.

- **Apache Hive**: It is an ETL and data warehousing tool in the Hadoop ecosystem. It provides an SQL-like interface and query language, **Hive Query Language** (**HQL**), which creates a layer of abstraction over the map-reduce jobs. It is primarily used in industries for data summarization, querying, and analysis of unstructured and semi-structured data in Hadoop. It is highly scalable and suitable for real-time processing and batch-processing applications.
- **Apache Pig**: This platform is specially designed to simplify Hadoop's complex data processing tasks. It has two components, Pig Latin and Pig engine. Pig Latin is a high-level scripting language that allows operators to perform big data analytics. Pig engine transforms the scripts written by programmers into MapReduce jobs to be executed in Hadoop. As Pig helps to achieve ease of programming and optimization, it is widely used by companies like *Informatica, Salesforce, JPMorgan Chase, Netflix*, etc., for processing web log data, ad-hoc queries, complex data transformations, etc.
- **Mahout**: This component of Hadoop is primarily developed to create scalable ML algorithms. It provides a ready-to-use framework for tasks such as recommendation systems, classification, clustering, etc, on large volumes of data. It has in-built libraries for several MapReduce-enabled clustering implementations such as k-means, fuzzy k-means, Canopy, Dirichlet, and Mean-Shift. It provides classification implementations for distributed and complementary naive Bayes. It also supports distributed fitness function capabilities for evolutionary programming.
- **Apache Spark**: Spark is an open-source general-purpose cluster computing framework that supports in-memory processing. It is a distributed processing system optimized for fast analytic queries against big data workloads. It is suitable for developing diverse applications requiring batch processing, interactive queries, real-time analytics, ML, graph processing, etc. Spark supports deployment using several **application programming interfaces** (**APIs**), such as Java, Python, Scala, and R programming. Spark is best suited for real-time or nearly real-time data processing, whereas Hadoop is best suited for batch processing; hence, both are used in most companies interchangeably.
- **Apache HBase**: HBase is a type of NoSQL database. It is an open-source, distributed, scalable, and consistent database that provides real-time read/write access to large datasets. It is a non-relational database modeled after Google's Bigtable, thus able to work on big data sets effectively. It is designed to support all kinds of data and is thus capable of handling anything in the Hadoop Database. It provides an easy-to-use Java API for programmatic access and Thrift and REST API for non-Java front-ends. HBase is suitable for both write-heavy applications, as well as applications that need to provide fast, random access to vast amounts of available data, e.g., storing clickstream data for downstream analysis, storing application logs for diagnostic and trend analysis, storing document fingerprints used to identify potential plagiarism, and so on.
- **Apache Oozie**: It is a workflow scheduler system designed to manage Apache Hadoop jobs. It provides a Java Web application that allows users to define and run workflows as single logical units of work. It is integrated within the Hadoop stack and supports Hadoop jobs for Apache MapReduce, Apache Pig, Apache Hive, and Apache Sqoop. Oozie is highly scalable and can easily manage the timely execution of thousands of workflows in a Hadoop cluster. It consists of two parts, namely the **Workflow Engine** (**WE**) and the **Coordinator Engine** (**CE**). The WE is responsible for storing and running workflows composed of Hadoop jobs, whereas the CE runs workflow jobs based on predefined schedules and data availability.
- **Sqoop**: Sqoop is a data ingestion tool that efficiently transfers bulk data between Hadoop and structured data stores such as relational databases. It uses the YARN framework to import and export data. It provides connectors for the majority of the structured data stores so that data can be moved into HDFS/Hive/HBase from MySQL/ PostgreSQL/Oracle/SQL Server/DB2 and vice versa. It supports incremental loads of a single table or a free-form SQL query and saves jobs that can be run multiple times.
- **Apache Storm**: Apache Storm is an open-source, real-time data streaming tool to process large volumes of high-velocity data. It can reliably process unbounded streams of data from sensors, weblogs, and other applications. It is designed to process streaming data with high ingestion rates in a fault-tolerant manner. It is horizontally scalable, easy to use, and can be deployed using any programming language on real data in parallel. It has the ability to process over a million records per second per node on a modest-sized cluster.

It is widely used for real-time analytics, online ML, continuous computation, distributed RPC, ETL, etc., in financial services, telecom, retail, manufacturing, and so on. It is used by popular real-time data streaming platforms like *X* (formerly known as *Twitter*), *Yahoo*, *Spotify*, *WebMD*, etc.

- **Kafka**: Apache Kafka is an open-source distributed streaming system that was initially created at *LinkedIn* in 2011 to handle real-time data feeds. It is primarily designed to handle real-time streaming data requiring continuous analysis of large volumes of data as it is generated. It uses a publish-subscribe messaging system to process the real-time data. It is also a data ingestion tool that can ingest data from various sources like databases, applications, and **Internet of Things** (**IoT**) devices. It is a horizontally scalable, high-performance tool designed for high availability. It is reliable and ensures data durability and fault tolerance via a distributed architecture that replicates data across multiple nodes. Kafka is well known for its capability to ingest and process trillions of records per day while maintaining impeccable performance even as data volumes continue to scale. *Fortune 500* companies, such as *Target*, *Microsoft*, *Airbnb*, and *Netflix*, rely on Kafka to deliver real-time, data-driven experiences to their vast customer base.
- **ZooKeeper**: ZooKeeper is an open-source coordination service for a cluster in distributed applications. It is a centralized service to maintain configuration information and naming, along with distributed synchronization and group services. ZooKeeper provides a simple interface and maintains a standard hierarchical namespace, similar to files and directories. It records all transactions, which may be used for higher-level abstractions like synchronization primitives. ZooKeeper is fast with workloads where data reads are more common than writes. It is suitable for applications with an ideal read/write ratio of about 10:1. It is reliable as it is replicated over a set of hosts, and the servers are aware of each other, so there is no single point of failure. As long as the servers are up and running, the ZooKeeper service remains available. It runs in Java and has bindings for both Java and C.
- **Apache Solr**: It is a full-text search engine that is built on Apache Lucene, which is a Java library that provides indexing and search technology along with spellchecking, hit highlighting, and other advanced analysis/tokenization capabilities. Solr provides an easy mechanism for programmers to develop sophisticated, high-performance search applications with advanced features, such as faceting (arranging search results in columns with numerical counts of key terms). Solr supports batch, real-time, and on-demand data indexing of any type. It is highly reliable, scalable, and faults liberal with automated failover and restoration. Due to its fast exploration capabilities, it is used by *Apple* as the search engine for its support site, *Netflix* uses it for searching its content catalog, *eBay* for its search functionality, etc.

Hadoop versus relational database management system

Hadoop is optimized for storing and processing large volumes of unstructured data across distributed clusters, while RDBMS are better suited for structured data and transactional workloads. *Table 2.1* presents a comparison of both on various criteria:

Criteria	RDBMs	Hadoop
Database	It is a database.	It is a distributed file system that can store and process large volumes of data.
Data volume	Works better for constant and predict-able low load, e.g., gigabytes of data.	Good for fluctuating data demands, e.g., terabytes or petabytes of data.
Data structure	Structured	Structured and unstructured
Access	Interactive and batch processing	Suitable for batch processing applications.
Updates	Read and write many times	**Write once and read many** (**WORM**) times.
Schema	Static schema	Dynamic schema

Criteria	RDBMs	Hadoop
Integrity	High	Low
Throughput	Low	High
Speed	Reads are fast.	Both reads and writes are fast.
Scalability	Vertical	Horizontal
Hardware requirements	Commodity / Utility hardware	High-end servers
Transactions	**Atomicity, consistency, isolation, and durability** (**ACID**)	None
Data objects	Relational tables	Works with key-value pairs
Cost	Licensed	Free
Examples	Oracle, MySQL, SQL Server, etc	Hadoop implementations by Cloudera, Hortonworks
Applications	Time-sensitive data analysis, real or near-real-time analysis of small data sets.	Ideal for tasks such as running end-of-day reports to review daily transactions, scanning historical data, and performing analytics where a slower time-to-insight is acceptable.

***Table 2.1**: Comparison of Hadoop with RDBMS*

Hadoop versus distributed databases

Hadoop and distributed databases both provide solutions to handle large volumes of data across distributed systems. However, they utilize different data and computing models. The details are as follows:

- **Data model**: Hadoop uses HDFS as its primary storage. HDFS is a distributed file system designed to store big data in large files across multiple machines in a fault-tolerant manner. It stores data in a distributed manner across a cluster of commodity hardware. Distributed databases like *Cassandra*, *MongoDB*, or *Amazon DynamoDB* use various data models, including key-value, document, or columnar. They distribute data across multiple nodes in a cluster.
- **Data structure**: Hadoop primarily stores data in the form of files, often in a semi-structured or unstructured format like text, JSON, or XML. It is optimized for batch processing. In distributed databases, data is generally organized into tables (for relational databases), collections (for document databases), or key-value pairs (for key-value stores). They support structured, semi-structured, and sometimes unstructured data.
- **Computing model**: Hadoop uses a batch processing model, where data is processed in large chunks, typically using MapReduce, Spark, or other distributed computing frameworks. The access pattern in Hadoop is usually read-heavy, focusing on scanning large datasets. On the other hand, distributed databases offer real-time or near-real-time access to data. They support both **online transaction processing** (**OLTP**) and **online analytical processing** (**OLAP**) workloads. These systems have varied access patterns, including reads, writes, updates, and deletes.
- **Scalability**: Both Hadoop and distributed databases are designed to scale horizontally, but distributed databases often provide more granular control over scalability and performance tuning.
- **Transaction support**: Distributed databases offer ACID transaction properties, making them suitable for transactional workloads. Nevertheless, Hadoop lacks built-in transaction support.

- **Latency**: Hadoop is optimized for high throughput but generally has higher latency due to batch processing. It is not suitable for real-time or interactive applications. Distributed databases are designed for low-latency access to data. They provide quicker responses to queries and updates compared to Hadoop's batch processing.
- **Use cases:** Hadoop is commonly used for processing and analyzing large volumes of data where latency is not critical, such as log processing, data warehousing, and batch analytics. Distributed databases are suitable for a wide range of use cases, including OLTP, real-time analytics, fraud detection, and recommendation systems, where low latency and high concurrency are essential.
- **Complexity:** Hadoop requires more complex programming with MapReduce or other distributed processing frameworks, whereas distributed databases often provide simpler query languages (e.g., SQL) and APIs.

On the whole, Hadoop is suited for batch processing of large datasets with higher latency. In comparison, distributed databases offer real-time processing with lower latency, making them suitable for interactive and transactional workloads.

Conclusion

This chapter focused on understanding the various types of big data analytics in organizations that enable improved data-driven decisions. The two main challenges conventional systems face in analyzing big data are storage and processing. Apache Hadoop is a distributed file system that provides two main components, HDFS and MapReduce, for storage and processing, respectively. These components originated from the MapReduce framework and the GFS published by *Google* in 2004. The chapter further provided brief discussions about various components of the Hadoop Ecosystem such as HDFS, MapReduce, YARN, Hive, Pig, HBase, Spark, etc. Finally, the chapter compared Hadoop with RDBMS and distributed databases.

In the next chapter, we will understand the fundamental concepts and architecture of HDFS and MapReduce. The chapter will also provide a case study to build an understanding of the concept of MapReduce in detail.

Points to remember

The following list outlines the key takeaways from this chapter:

- Big data analytics is done by organizations from various perspectives, such as descriptive analytics, diagnostic analytics, predictive analytics, and prescriptive analytics.
- Big data poses two main challenges to the conventional systems, which include storage and processing.
- Hadoop is a distributed file system to store and process large volumes of data. It has two main components, HDFS and MapReduce, for the storage and processing of big data.
- Hadoop originated from a paper published by Google in 2004 on the MapReduce framework and the GFS. Doug Cutting and Mike Cafarella then developed an open-source implementation at Yahoo! in 2005, which later became Apache Hadoop.
- The Hadoop Ecosystem is a collection of open-source components for the distributed storage and processing of big data. It includes tools like HDFS, MapReduce, YARN, Hive, Pig, HBase, Spark, and many others, providing a comprehensive platform for various big data tasks.
- Hadoop is designed to store and process large volumes of unstructured data across distributed clusters, while RDBMSs are better suited for structured data and transactional workloads.
- Hadoop is designed for batch processing of large volumes of unstructured data, while distributed databases are optimized for real-time or near-real-time access to structured or semi-structured data.

Multiple choice questions

1. **What is Hadoop primarily designed for?**
    a. Small-scale data processing
    b. Real-time analytics
    c. Big data processing
    d. Web development
2. **Which of the following is a key characteristic of big data analytics?**
    a. Processing small datasets
    b. Analyzing data in real-time only
    c. Handling large and diverse datasets
    d. Using only structured data
3. **What challenges do conventional systems face when dealing with big data?**
    a. Limited storage capacity
    b. Difficulty in processing real-time data
    c. Inability to handle large volumes of data
    d. All of the above
4. **What is one of the main challenges associated with big data?**
    a. Lack of data variety
    b. Limited data volume
    c. Inadequate data velocity
    d. Unstructured data
5. **How does Hadoop differ from an RDBMS?**
    a. Hadoop is better suited for transactional data
    b. RDBMS is more scalable for large datasets
    c. Hadoop is designed for structured data only
    d. RDBMS lacks fault tolerance
6. **Which component in the Hadoop ecosystem is used for workflow automation and coordination?**
    a. HDFS
    b. Apache Hive
    c. Apache Oozie
    d. Apache HBase

7. **In what scenario would an RDMS be more suitable than Hadoop?**
   a. Handling large-scale unstructured data
   b. Real-time data processing
   c. Complex and structured data relationships
   d. Batch processing of data
8. **What is the primary function of Hadoop YARN in the Hadoop ecosystem?**
   a. Data storage
   b. Data processing
   c. Resource management and job scheduling
   d. Data querying
9. **Which Hadoop component provides a high-level, SQL-like interface for querying the data stored in Hadoop?**
   a. Hadoop MapReduce
   b. Hadoop Pig
   c. Hadoop Hive
   d. Hadoop Spark
10. **Which type of data analytics involves analyzing historical data to identify patterns and trends?**
    a. Descriptive analytics
    b. Predictive analytics
    c. Prescriptive analytics
    d. Diagnostic analytics

Answers

1. c.	2. c.	3. d.	4. c.	5. d.
6. c.	7. c.	8. c.	9. c.	10. a.

Questions

1. Explain the concept of big data analytics. Provide examples of industries or applications where big data analytics has demonstrated significant value. What are the key challenges associated with implementing big data analytics?
2. Discuss the limitations of traditional data processing systems in handling large volumes of data. How do these challenges contribute to the need for alternative solutions like Hadoop?
3. Provide a detailed overview of Hadoop, its architecture, and the key components that make up the Hadoop ecosystem. How does Hadoop address the challenges posed by big data?
4. Trace the origins of Hadoop, highlighting the key events and contributors. How has the evolution of Hadoop influenced the field of big data processing?
5. Explore the components of the Hadoop ecosystem and their respective roles. Describe a use case where multiple Hadoop ecosystem components work together to solve a complex data processing problem.

6. Compare and contrast Hadoop and RDBMS in terms of their architecture, data processing capabilities, and suitability for different types of data. When would you choose one over the other for a specific task?

7. Explain the four main types of big data analytics—descriptive, diagnostic, predictive, and prescriptive analytics. Provide real-world examples of how each type is applied in different industries. Discuss the challenges and considerations organizations may face when implementing these analytics approaches.

8. Analyze a scenario where a healthcare organization faces challenges managing and analyzing a massive volume of patient data. Propose a Hadoop-based solution, outlining the specific components of the Hadoop ecosystem that would be most beneficial.

9. Examine how a retail company could leverage Hadoop to process and analyze customer data for personalized marketing strategies. Discuss the potential benefits and challenges of implementing such a solution.

10. Let us imagine a case study of enhancing customer experience through various types of big data analytics. The following are the details:

    - **Background**: A multinational e-commerce company aims to improve its customer experience by leveraging different types of big data analytics. The company collects vast amounts of customer data, including purchase history, website interactions, and customer feedback.

    - **Objective**: The goal is to implement a comprehensive big data analytics strategy to gain actionable insights into customer behavior, preferences, and potential issues. The company wants to enhance its marketing strategies, optimize the website for better user experience, and proactively address customer concerns.

    - **Implementation**:

        - **Descriptive analytics**: The company starts with descriptive analytics to gain a holistic view of customer behavior. It analyzes historical data to understand common purchasing patterns, peak activity times, and frequently visited website pages. Describe how descriptive analytics helps the company establish a baseline understanding of customer interactions.

        - **Diagnostic analytics**: Upon identifying certain trends through descriptive analytics, the company utilizes diagnostic analytics to investigate the root causes of specific customer behaviors. For example, it examines the reasons behind an increase in customer complaints during certain periods and correlates it with website changes or marketing campaigns. Discuss how diagnostic analytics aids in identifying and addressing underlying issues.

        - **Predictive analytics**: Using insights from descriptive and diagnostic analytics, the company implements predictive analytics to forecast future customer behavior. It builds models to predict purchasing trends, potential product preferences, and customer churn. This illustrates how predictive analytics helps the company proactively tailor marketing strategies and offerings.

        - **Prescriptive analytics**: Finally, the company employs prescriptive analytics to recommend specific actions to enhance customer experience. For instance, if predictive analytics indicates a potential increase in demand for a specific product, prescriptive analytics might suggest adjusting inventory levels or launching a targeted promotion. Explain how prescriptive analytics guides the company in making data-driven decisions.

    - **Challenges and considerations**: Discuss the challenges the company may face during the implementation of each type of analytics, such as data quality issues, resource requirements, and the need for skilled personnel. Additionally, it explores how the company addresses privacy concerns and ensures compliance with data protection regulations throughout the analytics process.

- **Outcomes**: Conclude the case study by highlighting the positive outcomes achieved by the company through integrating various types of big data analytics. Emphasize improvements in customer satisfaction, increased sales, and the overall enhancement of the customer experience.

CHAPTER 3
Hadoop Distributed File System and MapReduce

Data is a precious thing and will last longer than the systems themselves.

–Tim Berners-Lee

Introduction

The chapter begins by introducing the concept of file systems, providing an overview of traditional file systems and their limitations in handling large-scale data. It then outlines the need for distributed file systems, explaining how they offer improved scalability and fault tolerance. The focus then shifts to the **Hadoop Distributed File System** (**HDFS**), a cornerstone of the Hadoop framework, where readers gain insights into its architecture, including a detailed explanation of the roles of the NameNode and DataNodes. The chapter explores the properties that make HDFS suitable for storing and processing big data effectively. Moving forward, the chapter discusses the fundamental concepts of MapReduce, the key processing framework in Hadoop, illustrated through an example of log data analysis. Next, job scheduling and monitoring processes are examined in detail. Finally, this chapter outlines the various file formats supported by Hadoop, along with their merits, demerits, and applications.

Structure

In this chapter, we will cover the following topics:

- Traditional file system
- Distributed file system
- Hadoop Distributed File System
- Architecture of Hadoop Distributed File System
- Properties of Hadoop Distributed File System
- Processing data using MapReduce
- Working of MapReduce
- Job scheduling and monitoring in MapReduce
- File formats

Objectives

By the end of this chapter, the readers will understand the limitations of traditional file systems in managing big data challenges. They will be able to explain the necessity and various types of distributed file systems, and will gain a detailed understanding of the architecture, properties, and functioning of the HDFS. They will also learn to write MapReduce programs to analyze data stored in HDFS and will gain insights into how job scheduling and monitoring are performed in MapReduce. Finally, they will learn about the various types of file formats, such as text-based, binary, and columnar, which are supported by Hadoop for data processing. These formats are discussed along with their pros, cons, and applications.

Traditional file system

File system (**fs**), as shown in *Figure 3.1*, is a method used by operating systems to store and organize data on physical storage devices such as hard drives, **Solid State Drives** (**SSDs**), or other storage media. In traditional file systems, all data is stored on a single machine. A file system mainly consists of files and directories as perceived by users. However, it maintains a lot of additional information that is required for storage, retrieval, and organization of data on a storage medium, for example, file metadata (file name, size, creation date, modification date, and permissions), file paths, access controls, file system operations, etc. For storage and management of data on physical devices, they need to be partitioned and formatted before their first use. Partitioning is splitting a storage device into several logical regions, for instance, creating multiple drives in the Windows OS. Next, partitions are formatted. For example, while formatting a partition on Windows OS, users can choose among FAT32, NTFS, and exFAT file systems. Through formatting, storage devices are divided into blocks, and each block is composed of fixed-sized sectors. A block is the basic unit of storage in formatted partitions. It is the largest contiguous amount of disk space that can be allocated to a file and also the maximum amount of data that can be accessed in a single I/O operation. Therefore, each file the user creates is segmented into blocks to be stored on the storage device. As the file systems vary according to the operating system, the block size also varies accordingly. For example, most of the file systems in popular **operating systems** (**OS**) such as Windows (FAT32, NTFS, and exFAT), macOS (HFS+, APFS), and Linux (Ext3, Ext4, XFS) are optimized for a block size of 4KB and are tunable up to a 64KB block size. Due to the small size of blocks, the efficiency and performance of these systems are reduced with the increase in file size. The increase in size of files escalates the I/O operations, hence leading to performance degradation. Besides, traditional systems are not cost-effective for handling big data as they are vertically scalable and involve significant investments for hardware upgrades. These systems also lack the resilience for reliable big data processing, particularly at scale. Therefore, these systems are more suitable for small applications or personal use.

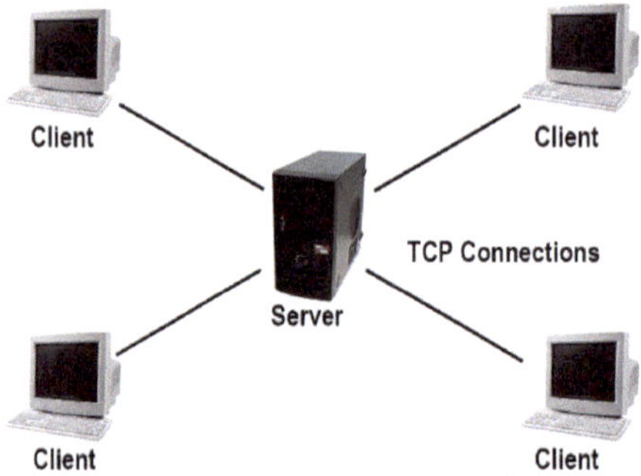

***Figure 3.1**: Traditional file system*

Distributed file system

The amount of data generated in this digital era is too large to be processed by the traditional file systems on a single server, regardless of the massive storage capacity or computing power that the server possesses. After a certain point, scaling up is no longer economically and technically possible. Therefore, organizations tend to distribute the data across multiple nodes in a cluster by scaling out. A **distributed file system** (**DFS**) is a file system that spans across multiple file servers or multiple locations, as shown in *Figure 3.2*. In DFS, data/files can be accessed as if they were stored locally, from any device, and anywhere on the network. It enables organizations to read big data quickly, perform multiple reads, and write in parallel from multiple nodes.

The various benefits provided by distributed file systems for big data processing are as follows:

- **Location independence**: Users need not be aware of the exact physical location of the file, and still can have seamless access to it.

- **Transparency**: Data appears to the users as if located on the local system.
- **Scalability**: DFS has the ability to scale out massively by adding more machines. These systems can scale to large clusters with thousands of servers.

Other features, such as fault tolerance, replication, and concurrency, are specific to the DFS implementation.

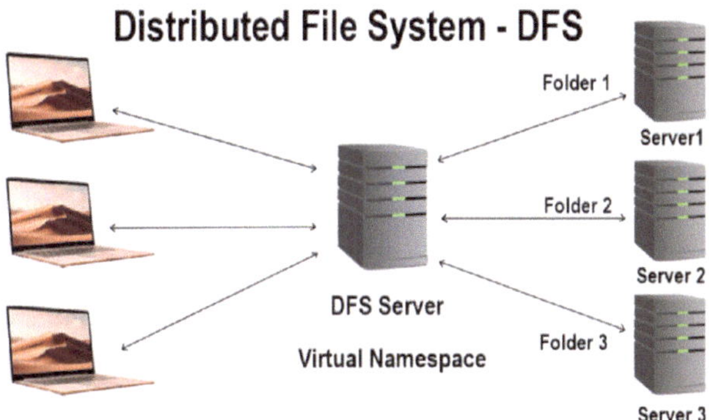

***Figure 3.2**: Distributed file system*

The most common DFS implementations are:

- Windows DFS
- **Network file system** (**NFS**)
- **Server message block** (**SMB**)
- **Google File System** (**GFS**)
- Lustre
- HDFS
- GlusterFS
- Ceph
- MapR file system

Hadoop Distributed File System

The two main challenges in big data analysis are storage and computation. The two main components of Hadoop that handle these challenges are HDFS and MapReduce, as illustrated in *Figure 3.3*:

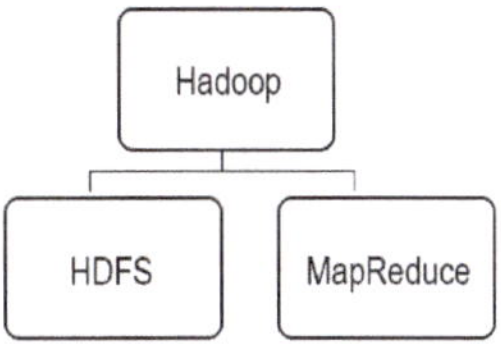

***Figure 3.3**: Components of Hadoop*

HDFS is a DFS designed to run on commodity hardware. It is one of the primary components of Hadoop, used for storing large amounts of data in big data applications for big data analytics. It is suitable for scaling a single Apache Hadoop cluster to hundreds or thousands of nodes. HDFS offers efficient access to application data with high throughput, which makes it appropriate for handling extensive datasets. It is highly fault-tolerant and is designed to be deployed on low-cost hardware. The various assumptions and goals underlying HDFS are:

- **Hardware failure**: HDFS is designed with the assumption that hardware failure is the norm rather than the exception. Since an HDFS instance may consist of hundreds or thousands of server machines, each storing part of the file system's data, there is a high probability that some components of HDFS may always be non-functional. Therefore, detection of faults and quick, automatic recovery from them is a core architectural goal of HDFS.
- **Streaming data access**: Applications running on HDFS require streaming access to their data sets. As HDFS is designed mainly for batch processing applications, it emphasizes high-throughput data access rather than low-latency access to data.
- **Large data sets**: HDFS is designed to run applications with data sets with a typical file size varying from gigabytes to terabytes. Therefore, it provides high aggregate data bandwidth, which is scalable to hundreds of nodes in a single cluster, and support tens of millions of files in a single instance.
- **Simple coherency model**: HDFS is suitable for applications that need a write-once-read-many access model for files. It assumes that a file must not be changed once created, written, and closed. This simplification will streamline data coherency challenges and facilitate high-throughput data access. This model aligns well with applications such as MapReduce or web crawlers, where the data is predominantly read and processed batch-like.
- **Moving computation is cheaper than moving data**: For applications dealing with large datasets, efficient computation is greatly enhanced when computation is performed near the data it operates on. This approach minimizes network congestion and significantly boosts the overall system throughput.
- **Portability across heterogeneous hardware and software platforms**: HDFS is designed to be easily portable from one platform to another. This has become the prime reason for its widespread adoption for big data analytics.

Architecture of Hadoop Distributed File System

HDFS is based on a master/slave architecture. An HDFS cluster consists of a single master node known as the **NameNode** and multiple slave nodes called **DataNodes**. The same is illustrated in *Figure 3.4*. A NameNode is a server that is responsible for managing the metadata and file system namespace for regulating access to the data files by the clients. A DataNode is usually one per node in the cluster; it stores and manages data on the nodes that it runs on. NameNode and DataNode are the software built to run on commodity machines. These machines mainly run a GNU/Linux OS. HDFS is written using the Java programming language, so NameNode or the DataNode software can be run on any machine that supports Java. The inherent portability feature of Java enables HDFS deployment on a wide range of machines. A typical HDFS deployment has a dedicated machine that runs only the NameNode software, and all other machines in the cluster run one instance of the DataNode software.

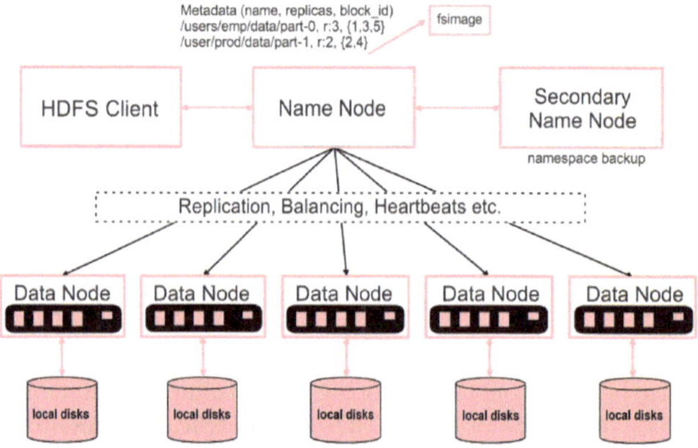

Figure 3.4: *HDFS architecture*

The primary functions of NameNode and DataNode are as follows:

- **Namespace management**: The NameNode manages the file system namespace, including the hierarchy of directories and files. It also stores metadata such as file names, permissions, and directory structure.
- **File-to-block mapping**: Internally, NameNode splits every file into one or more blocks, which are stored in a set of DataNodes. The size of the block varies according to the Hadoop version. For example, in Hadoop 1.x, the default block size was 64 MB; in Hadoop 2.x, the block size was 128 MB; and in Hadoop 3.x, the block size is 128 MB or 256 MB, depending on the configuration. The NameNode maintains the mapping of files to the blocks. It keeps track of which blocks belong to which files; for example, if a file is split into four blocks, NameNode maintains all the information about their count and corresponding names of blocks. The DataNodes also perform block creation, deletion, and replication based on instructions from the NameNode.
- **Metadata storage**: The metadata about files and directories, including their attributes and block locations, is stored in the memory of the NameNode. This metadata is crucial for the proper functioning of the distributed file system.
- **Ensuring data integrity**: The NameNode plays an important role in maintaining data integrity by tracking the location and health of data blocks. If a DataNode reports a block as corrupt, the NameNode will take appropriate action accordingly.
- **Checkpointing**: NameNode is a single point of failure in HDFS. To address this problem, the concept of **high availability** (**HA**) was introduced in Hadoop 2.x with the addition of a Secondary NameNode. In this architecture, there are two separate machines, one serves as the active NameNode, handling all read and write requests, while the secondary node functions as the standby NameNode, ready to take over in case of a failure in the active NameNode. The NameNode creates periodic checkpoints to save its namespace state, known as **fsimage**, to the disk, as shown in *Figure 3.4*. The fsimage is considered a critical component in HDFS. It is a snapshot of the file system metadata at a particular point in time and is regularly updated through the checkpointing process to maintain an accurate representation of the HDFS. Checkpointing helps in recovering the file system metadata from fsimage in case of a NameNode failure.
- **Heartbeat and block report processing**: In HDFS, NameNode keeps track of the working condition of the DataNodes, which store the actual data blocks. DataNodes periodically send heartbeat signals to the NameNode for the same. The receipt of the heartbeat signal indicates that the DataNode is alive. DataNodes also send block reports with information about the blocks they store to the NameNode.
- **Block replication**: In Hadoop, NameNode determines the replication factor for each block based on the configured settings. Users can update the replication factor as per their application requirements. It ensures that the required number of replicas for each block is maintained across the cluster. For example NameNode stores metadata about two files named as **`Emp.txt`** and **`Prod.txt`**. **`Emp.txt`** is split into three blocks: **`blk_001`**, **`blk_002`**, and **`blk_003`** and **`Prod.txt`** is split into **`blk_004`** and **`blk_005`**. All the data blocks are stored in DataNodes, and their replicas are stored in different nodes. It can be observed in *Figure 3.5* for replication factor=3, three copies of each block are stored on the DataNodes:

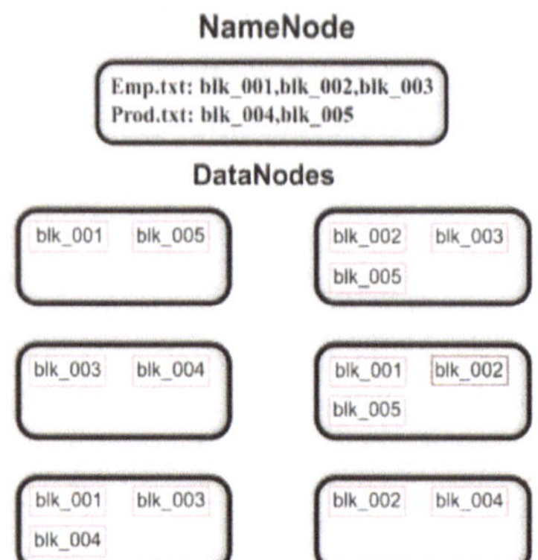

Figure 3.5: *Block replication*

- **Handling client's read/write requests**: When a client requests to read or write a file from the HDFS, it communicates primarily with the NameNode. For read requests, NameNode provides the client with the necessary information about the file's block locations. Next, the client's read requests are executed by the DataNode. Since all file blocks are replicated, the question arises, which DataNode will serve the client.

In Hadoop, large HDFS instances often run on a computer cluster that is commonly distributed across many racks, as illustrated in *Figure 3.6*. The network connectivity is more robust and offers higher bandwidth when machines are situated within the same rack than when they are located in separate racks. The main objective of the rack-aware replica placement strategy is to enhance data reliability, availability, and network bandwidth utilization in HDFS. It requires a lot of tuning and experience.

A simple but less efficient approach is to deploy replicas on different racks. This prevents data loss in case of an entire rack failure and facilitates bandwidth utilization for reading data from multiple racks. This policy ensures an even distribution of replicas across the cluster and supports load balancing in the event of component failures, but at the expense of increased write costs. This is because each write operation needs to transfer blocks to multiple racks.

Commonly, for the replication factor of three, HDFS's policy is to place one replica on one node in the local rack, another on a node in a different (remote) rack, and the third on a different node in the same remote rack.

This policy also helps in cutting down inter-rack write traffic and thus improves write performance. As the chances of rack failure are far lower than those of node failure, data reliability and availability guarantees are the least affected. However, with this policy, the replicas of a file are not distributed evenly across the racks. Overall, one-third of replicas are placed on one node, two-thirds are on one rack, and the rest are evenly distributed across the remaining racks. This policy improves write performance without compromising data reliability or read performance.

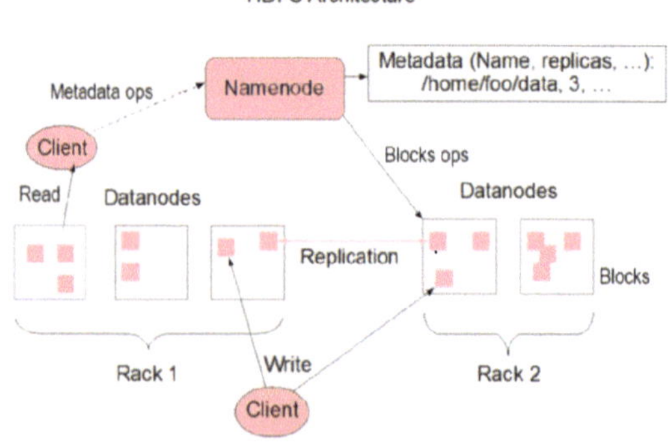

Figure 3.6: *Rack awareness*

To minimize, global bandwidth consumption and read latency, the first attempt of HDFS is to serve the read request from a replica closest to the client. Accordingly, if a replica exists on the same rack as the client node, it is prioritized to serve the read request. If the HDFS cluster spans multiple data centers, a replica residing in the local data center is chosen over any remote replica to complete the request.

In contrast, a client's request to create a file does not reach the NameNode directly. Primarily, client file data is cached into a temporary local file in HDFS. As soon as the local file accumulates data worth the size of one HDFS block, the NameNode is contacted. The NameNode puts the file's name into the file system hierarchy and allocates a data block for it. Next, NameNode redirects the client with the information about the destination data block and the allocated DataNode. Finally, the client's block of data is flushed from the local temporary file to the specified DataNode. As the client closes the file, the rest of the unflushed data is also transferred to the DataNode, and the NameNode is informed. At this stage, the NameNode commits the file creation operation to a persistent store.

Properties of Hadoop Distributed File System

HDFS is a key component of the Hadoop ecosystem. It is designed to store and manage large volumes of data across multiple machines in a distributed manner. The following sections discuss the key properties and features of HDFS.

Fault tolerance

HDFS is designed for reliable storage of big files across machines in a large cluster. It stores every file as a sequence of blocks. Each file is split into blocks of the same size, except the last block. In Hadoop 2.x, fault tolerance is attained via replication of blocks. All blocks are replicated and stored on different DataNodes. So, whenever a DataNode in the cluster goes down, users still have access to the data from other machines where the replica is stored. Optimal placement of replicas is a distinguishing factor of HDFS as compared to other distributed file systems in Hadoop 2.x. For a better understanding, assume HDFS with four DataNodes, which include D1, D2, D3, and D4. A user stores a file named Emp.txt of size 384 MB. In Hadoop 2.x, HDFS splits this file into three blocks as X, Y, and Z, each of 128 MB (default block size). HDFS creates replicas of all blocks (default replication factor of three) and stores them on different nodes to attain fault tolerance, as shown in *Figure 3.7*. Assume that block X is stored on DataNodes D1, D2, and D4, block Y is stored on DataNodes D2, D3, and D4, and block Z is stored on DataNodes D1, D2, and D3. If DataNode D1 fails, the data of blocks X and Z present in D1 is not lost as their replicas are still available to the user from DataNodes (D2, D4 for X) and (D2, D3 for Z). Hence, due to replication, there is no data loss, even in unfavorable conditions.

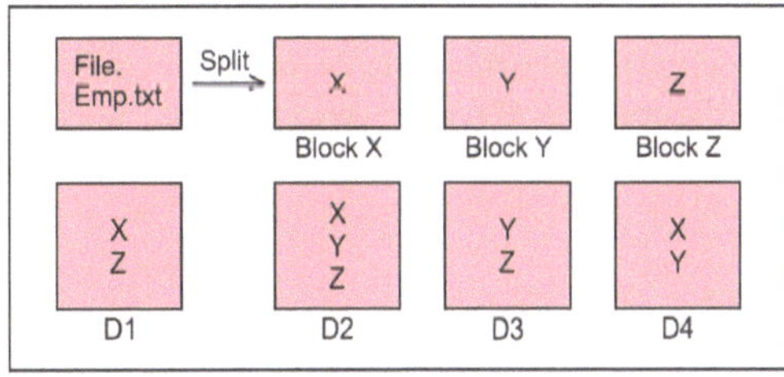

***Figure 3.7**: Replication mechanism*

However, the replication mechanism used for fault tolerance in Hadoop 2.x is expensive. The default replication factor of three in HDFS has 200% overhead in storage space and other resources (e.g., network bandwidth). As per experts, additional block replicas are rarely accessed during normal operations in warm and cold datasets with relatively low I/O activities. Nevertheless, they still consume the same number of resources as the first replica.

Erasure coding

In Hadoop 3.x, the resource usage problem is resolved by introducing **erasure coding (EC)** instead of replication. EC provides the same level of fault tolerance but with reduced storage space. In EC, a file or dataset is broken down into smaller units called **stripes**, and these stripes are distributed across multiple disks or storage nodes. For each stripe of the original dataset, a certain number of parity cells are generated. Unlike replication, in which identical copies of data are stored on separate machines, EC reduces storage overhead by calculating and storing parity information only. The information contained in parity cells is used to reconstruct the original data if some of the storage nodes or disks fail. The number of parity cells generated is customizable and determines the level of fault tolerance. Some common configurations widely used in EC are Reed-Solomon codes. EC is a resilient and efficient method for data protection that provides fault tolerance and reduced storage overhead as compared to traditional replication strategies. It also reduces the storage overhead by up to 50%.

Robustness

To provide reliable data storage in the presence of failures is the prime objective of HDFS. The three common types of failures include NameNode failures, DataNode failures, and network partitions. In Hadoop 2.x, NameNode failure is handled via checkpointing. DataNode failures and problems in network partitions are detected by NameNode via the absence of a heartbeat message. Periodically, all DataNodes send a heartbeat message to the NameNode. The absence of a heartbeat may be due to a loss of connection with a DataNode in a network partition or failure of the DataNode itself. The NameNode keeps track of DataNodes without recent heartbeats, marking them dead. Further, no new I/O requests are forwarded to the dead DataNodes. As the death of a DataNode disturbs the replication factor of some blocks, NameNode automatically performs replication whenever necessary.

Scalability

HDFS supports seamless scalability to meet the growing data requirements. The two primary scalability mechanisms available are **vertical scalability** (**VS**) and **horizontal scalability** (**HS**). VS involves adding more resources, such as CPU, memory, and disk space, to the existing nodes in the cluster, whereas the HS method entails adding more machines to the cluster. HS is generally preferred because it enables the cluster to expand from tens to hundreds of nodes dynamically without any downtime.

Processing data using MapReduce

Hadoop MapReduce is a Java-based framework for distributed processing within the Apache Hadoop ecosystem. It is one of the core components of Hadoop. MapReduce is a software framework and a programming model that enables a user to write simple applications that can process huge amounts of data in parallel via large clusters of commodity hardware in a reliable and fault-tolerant way. The MapReduce concept was initially motivated by functional programming languages such as LISP, particularly its map and reduce primitives used for list processing. It also shares a close connection with the scatter and reduce concepts of the **message-passing interface** (**MPI**) used in distributed-memory architectures. Nevertheless, MapReduce in Hadoop hides the underlying complexity of distributed and parallel processing, making it easier for programmers to use.

Working of MapReduce

A MapReduce system splits the data processing job into two tasks: the map task and the reduce task. It divides the input data into independent chunks of key-value pairs. Each chunk of data is processed in parallel by the map tasks. After sorting the output of the map tasks, the framework passes it as input to the reduce tasks. *Figure 3.8* depicts the input and the output of the job stored in HDFS:

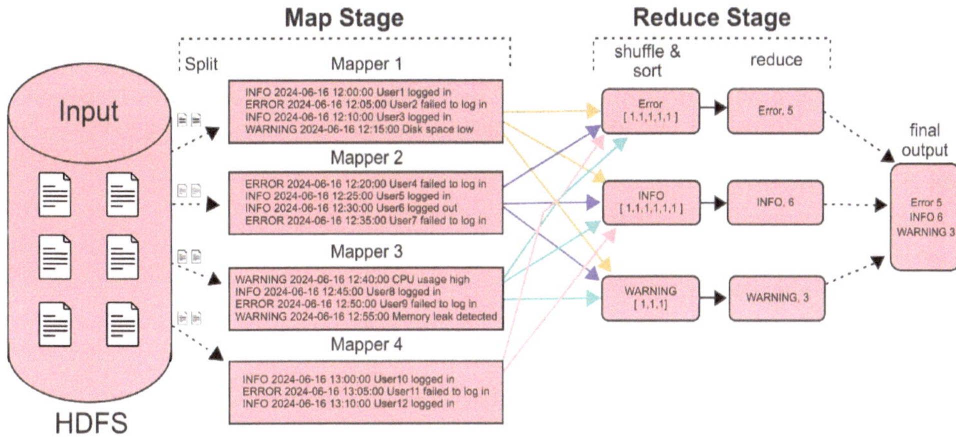

Figure 3.8: Working of MapReduce

- **MapReduce logical data flow pipeline:** In Hadoop's MapReduce framework, data processing is structured around key-value pairs, denoted as (K, V), where K is the key and V is the value associated with it. Let us understand the workings of the MapReduce process with the help of an example (*refer figure 3.8*). Assume we have log data stored in a file called **`logs.txt`**, also shown in *Table 3.1*, with the following details:
    - **Log level**: It represents the severity or type of the log message, such as INFO, ERROR, or WARNING.
    - **Date**: This column indicates the log entry date, formatted as YYYY-MM-DD.
    - **Time**: It shows the log entry time, formatted as HH:MM.
    - **User**: It refers to the user associated with the log entry, such as User1, User2, etc.
    - **Message**: It indicates the actual log message, describing the event or action, such as logged in, failed to log in, or disk space is low:

```
INFO 2024-06-16 12:00:00 User1 logged in
ERROR 2024-06-16 12:05:00 User2 failed to log in
INFO 2024-06-16 12:10:00 User3 logged in
WARNING 2024-06-16 12:15:00 Disk space low
ERROR 2024-06-16 12:20:00 User4 failed to log in
INFO 2024-06-16 12:25:00 User5 logged in
INFO 2024-06-16 12:30:00 User6 logged out
ERROR 2024-06-16 12:35:00 User7 failed to log in
WARNING 2024-06-16 12:40:00 CPU usage high
INFO 2024-06-16 12:45:00 User8 logged in
ERROR 2024-06-16 12:50:00 User9 failed to log in
WARNING 2024-06-16 12:55:00 Memory leak detected
INFO 2024-06-16 13:00:00 User10 logged in
ERROR 2024-06-16 13:05:00 User11 failed to log in
INFO 2024-06-16 13:10:00 User12 logged in
```

***Table 3.1**: Input log.txt file*

- **Job input and map tasks**: The input data is divided into multiple splits, and an individual map task processes each split. The number of map tasks is determined based on the size of the input data, and each map task processes a portion of the overall dataset in parallel. For example, if a user provides a log file of 1 terabyte in size as input, Hadoop may decide to split this file into smaller blocks. By default, Hadoop splits files into blocks of 128 megabytes (or 256 megabytes, depending on the configuration). Thus, a one-terabyte file would typically be divided into 8,192 blocks of 128 megabytes each, assuming a default block size of 128 megabytes.

  1 **terabyte** (**TB**) is equal to 1,024 **gigabytes** (**GB**).

  1 GB is equal to 1,024 **megabytes** (**MB**).

  Therefore, 1 TB is equal to:

  $$1\ TB=1{,}024\times 1{,}024\ MB=1{,}048{,}576\ MB$$

  Now, divide this by the block size of 128 MB to find the number of blocks:

  $$Number\ of\ blocks=1{,}048{,}576\ MB/128\ MB=8{,}192$$

  So, 1 TB is equal to 8,192 blocks of size 128 MB.

  Assume that the size of the sample **`log.txt`** file is 512 MB. HDFS creates four splits of this file (assuming a default block size of 128 MB). Each split is processed by one map task.

Map function

The programmer implements the map and reduce tasks by writing a **`map`** and **`reduce`** function in the Java programming language (supported by default) that processes each input record independently. The map function takes a set of records from a split as input and emits zero or more key-value pairs as output. The emitted key-value pairs are intermediate data, which are shuffled and sorted before being passed to the reduce phase. In the log file example, there are four Mappers; each Mapper takes input records as shown in *Figure 3.8*. The **`map`** function extracts the log level from each log entry and emits key-value pairs. The key is the log level, and the value is 1 (indicating the frequency of occurrence of a particular log level), as outlined in *Table 3.2*:

Mappers	Input	Output (key, value)

Mapper1	`INFO 2024-06-16 12:00:00 User1 logged in`
	`ERROR 2024-06-16 12:05:00 User2 failed to log in`
	`INFO 2024-06-16 12:10:00 User3 logged in`
	`WARNING 2024-06-16 12:15:00 Disk space low`
		`(INFO, 1)`
		`(ERROR, 1)`
		`(INFO, 1)`
		`(WARNING, 1)`

Mapper2	`ERROR 2024-06-16 12:20:00 User4 failed to log in`
	`INFO 2024-06-16 12:25:00 User5 logged in`
	`INFO 2024-06-16 12:30:00 User6 logged out`
	`ERROR 2024-06-16 12:35:00 User7 failed to log in`
		`(ERROR, 1)`
		`(INFO, 1)`
		`(INFO, 1)`
		`(ERROR, 1)`

Mapper3	`WARNING 2024-06-16 12:40:00 CPU usage high`
	`INFO 2024-06-16 12:45:00 User8 logged in`
	`ERROR 2024-06-16 12:50:00 User9 failed to log in`
	`WARNING 2024-06-16 12:55:00 Memory leak detected`
		`(WARNING, 1)`
		`(INFO, 1)`
		`(ERROR, 1)`
		`(WARNING, 1)`

Mapper4	`INFO 2024-06-16 13:00:00 User10 logged in`
	`ERROR 2024-06-16 13:05:00 User11 failed to log in`
	`INFO 2024-06-16 13:10:00 User12 logged in`
		`(INFO, 1)`
		`(ERROR, 1)`
		`(INFO, 1)`

Table 3.2: *Map phase with 4 Mappers*

Shuffling and sorting

In this step, the MapReduce framework groups all the intermediate key-value pairs with the same key from different map tasks. These groups are then sorted by key, and each group is sent to a specific reducer based on the key, as shown in *Table 3.3*:

Input (key, value) pairs	Output-shuffle and sort (key, list of values)
(INFO, 1) (ERROR, 1) (INFO, 1) (WARNING, 1)	(ERROR, [1, 1, 1, 1, 1]) (INFO, [1, 1, 1, 1, 1, 1]) (WARNING, [1, 1, 1])
(ERROR, 1) (INFO, 1) (INFO, 1) (ERROR, 1)	
(WARNING, 1) (INFO, 1) (ERROR, 1) (WARNING, 1)	
(INFO, 1) (ERROR, 1) (INFO, 1)	

Table 3.3: *Intermediate shuffled and sorted output*

Reduce function

The programmer also defines a **`reduce`** function, implemented as the reducer, which processes the grouped and sorted key-value pairs. Each reducer receives all the records associated with a specific key, and it processes them one at a time. The reduce function emits zero or more key-value pairs as output. The reduce phase's output is the MapReduce job's final result. The output key-value pairs can be written to a file or used as input for subsequent MapReduce jobs. In the log data example, the reducer processes each grouped key-value pair and sums up the values for each log level, as shown in *Table 3.4*:

Input (key, list of values)	Output (key, value (total count/sum)
(ERROR, [1, 1, 1, 1, 1])	(ERROR, 5)
(INFO, [1, 1, 1, 1, 1, 1])	(INFO, 6)
(WARNING, [1, 1, 1])	(WARNING, 3)

Table 3.4: *Reduce phase*

Throughout this process, the key-value pair abstraction (K, V) is maintained. Both the map and reduce functions receive input in the form of (K, V) pairs, and they emit (K, V) pairs as well. This consistent structure simplifies the programming model and allows for the parallel and distributed processing of large datasets. The programmer's responsibility is to define the logic for the map and reduce functions to achieve the desired data processing tasks. This division of the input data into smaller splits allows Hadoop to process the large dataset in parallel, taking advantage of the distributed nature of the computing cluster. The number of map tasks and their parallel execution make it possible to handle massive datasets efficiently.

Job scheduling and monitoring in MapReduce

The MapReduce framework is also responsible for task scheduling, monitoring, and re-executing the failed tasks. Normally, the MapReduce framework and HDFS reside on the same nodes, i.e., both the compute nodes and the storage nodes are the same. This setup allows the framework to efficiently schedule tasks on nodes where the relevant data is already available. This leads to high aggregate bandwidth across the entire cluster.

In Hadoop 1.x, the MapReduce task was done by the TaskTracker and JobTracker daemons, which were installed on each machine in the cluster. These daemons are superseded by the ResourceManager and NodeManager components of **Yet Another Resource Negotiator (YARN)** in Hadoop 2.x, also illustrated in *Figure 3.9*. The basic idea of YARN is to split up the functionalities of resource management and scheduling/monitoring of jobs into separate daemons. In the MapReduce framework, there is a single master or global ResourceManager, an **ApplicationMaster (AM)** per-application, and the worker NodeManager. Here, an application may be a single job or a **direct acyclic graph (DAG)** of jobs. Both the ResourceManager and the NodeManager together form the data-computation framework.

The ResourceManager is the prime authority to manage and distribute resources among all the applications in the system. The ResourceManager has two main components—Scheduler and ApplicationsManager. Scheduler purely performs the task of allocating resources to the various applications based on the available capacities, queues, etc. It does not perform monitoring or status tracking for the application. The scheduler has pluggables (e.g., CapacityScheduler, FairScheduler, etc.) that partition the cluster resources among the various queues, applications, etc. On the other hand, the role of an ApplicationsManager is to accept job-submissions, negotiate the first container to execute the application specific ApplicationMaster, and to restart the ApplicationMaster container on failure, etc. The per-application ApplicationMaster is also responsible for negotiating appropriate resource containers from the ResourceManager/Scheduler and works with the NodeManager(s) to execute and monitor the progress of tasks.

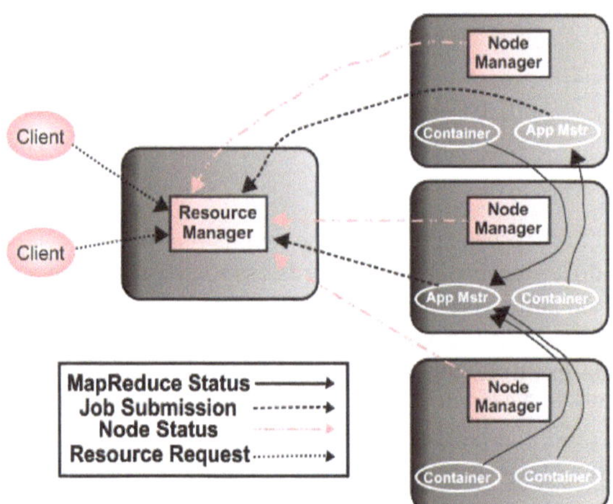

Figure 3.9: YARN architecture

The NodeManager is the per-machine framework agent that manages the containers, monitors their resource usage (CPU, memory, disk, network), and reports the same to the ResourceManager/Scheduler.

File formats

A file format refers to the structure and organization of data stored within files. It defines how data is encoded, stored, and represented in a file. The type of file format determines the storage efficiency, data processing speed, and compatibility of files with various tools and systems. In the realm of big data, where datasets can be massive and diverse, selecting an appropriate file format is crucial. The various file formats designed to address the specific needs of various real-world applications are illustrated in the following figure:

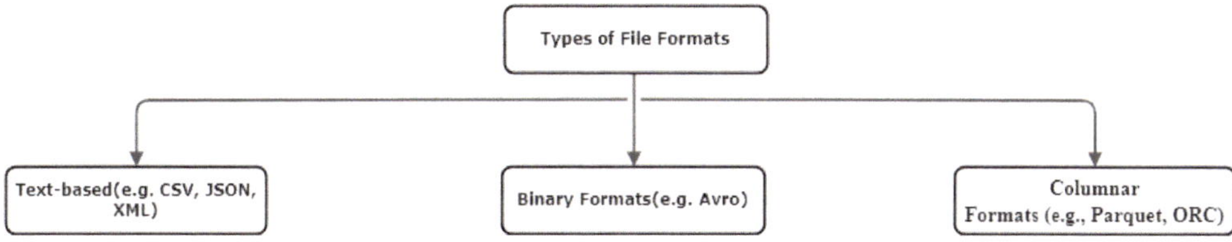

***Figure 3.10**: Types of file formats*

Given the diversity in data, such as structured, semi-structured, or unstructured data, movement and storage strategies must be adapted, considering the impact on overall performance. Hadoop supports various file formats to cater to different types of data and use cases, ensuring optimal performance and flexibility. The following section provides the details.

Text input

Text input format is a text-based file in which each row can be represented as a line delimited by a new line delimiter, and each field can be delimited based on the specified delimiter.

Pros:

- It is simple and easy to interpret and read.
- It supports compression but only on the **file level** (**BZIP2**).
- The commonly used formats are **comma-separated values** (**CSV**), text, and **JavaScript Object Notation** (**JSON**).
- Text files can be easily split based on the new-line delimiter

Cons:

- A compressed file cannot be read directly. The file needs to be decompressed before reading, which can have a significant read performance cost.
- Metadata must be stored separately and properly tracked.
- It has limited support for schema evolution, so changing the order of fields is not possible, but appending new fields at the end of the line is allowed.
- It does not support record or block-level compression.

CSV file format

CSV is a text-based, lightweight, and easily readable format. It is a commonly used format to export and import data between different applications and systems. A CSV file is organized into rows and columns, where each line represents a row of data separated by commas. These files can be easily mapped to relational data models, with each CSV file functioning as a table: rows in the CSV file correspond to records in the table, and columns correspond to attributes.

While CSV files are convenient for data exchange, relational data models offer significant advantages. They provide better structuring of data and support complex queries. Additionally, relational databases are highly efficient for managing large datasets and can easily integrate with various software systems.

JavaScript Object Notation file format

JSON is a lightweight, human-readable data interchange format. It features a semi-structured data model, meaning it does not require a predefined schema and allows flexible data representation. It was originally specified by *Douglas Crockford* in 2001. JSON has its roots in the JavaScript scripting language and is widely used across various programming languages, including C, C++, Java, Python, and Perl. The official internet media type for JSON is application/json, and files using this format have a `.json` extension. JSON's simplicity and versatility make it a popular choice for developers working on various applications across different programming environments. The following code shows an example of a JSON document to store information related to books based on their topic and edition:

```
{
  "books": [
    {
      "title": "JavaScript: The Good Parts",
      "author": "Douglas Crockford",
      "topics": ["Programming", "JavaScript"],
      "editions": [
        {
          "edition": 1,
          "year": 2008,
          "ISBN": "978-0596517748"
        }
      ]
    }
```

Cons:

- JSON supports a limited set of data types (strings, numbers, objects, arrays, Booleans, null), which may not be sufficient for all applications.
- For very large datasets, JSON can become verbose and less efficient compared to binary formats.
- The flexibility of not requiring a predefined schema sometimes leads to inconsistent data structures.
- JSON is susceptible to injection attacks if not properly sanitized, especially when used with JavaScript.
- JSON does not support comments, which can make it harder to document data structures directly within the file.

Applications of JSON:

- JSON is extensively used in RESTful web services and APIs for data interchange between clients and servers.
- Many applications and frameworks use JSON for configuration settings due to its readability and simplicity.
- JSON is often used for storing structured data in NoSQL databases like MongoDB.
- JSON is a popular choice for exchanging data between systems, especially in web development.
- Mobile applications frequently use JSON to communicate with backend services.

Sequence file format

A sequence file is a key-value binary file format that has a structure similar to a CSV file but with several differences. Each row can be delimited and split. Due to its binary format, it is often used as intermediate storage. Sequence files are more compact than text files.

Pros:

- Sequence files are more compact than plain text files, which helps in saving storage space.
- These files can be split and merged easily, which is beneficial for distributed processing systems like Hadoop.
- Sequence files support the merging of small files, which helps in reducing the number of files and improving processing efficiency.
- This file format supports record or block compression, which further reduces the file size and speeds up data transfer.

- The binary format allows for faster read / write operations as compared to text formats.

Cons:

- As the data is not in a human-readable format, it is harder to debug and inspect without proper tools.
- This format has limited support for schema evolution. Changing the order of fields is not possible, but appending new fields at the end of the record is feasible.
- It requires specific tools or libraries to read and write data, which can add complexity to the data processing pipeline.
- This format may lead to compatibility issues with systems or applications that do not support the binary format natively.

Applications of sequence files:

- It is widely used in the Hadoop ecosystem for storing intermediate data between MapReduce jobs.
- It is used in data warehousing solutions where large volumes of data need to be processed efficiently.
- It is suitable for backup and archiving purposes where data retrieval speed is more critical than readability.
- It is used in distributed systems to handle large datasets due to its compact and efficient storage capabilities.

  Sequence files balance storage efficiency and processing speed, making them a suitable choice for large-scale data processing tasks where human readability is not a primary concern.

Row columnar file formats

The **row columnar** (**RC**) file was first introduced in Hive 0.6.0. This format stores table data as binary key-value pairs in rows and columns. Initially, the data in the table is divided into groups of rows, and within each row group, the data is stored in columns. The RC file format first stores the metadata of a row group as part of the key and all the row group data as the value. This structure can be seen as similar to the sequence file format, but with additional advantages. An example illustrating the structure of an RC file format is as follows:

Example: Suppose we have a table of employees with the following columns: **`id`** (integer), **`name`** (string), **`age`** (integer), **`department`** (string), and the following records:

id	name	age	department
1	Alice	30	HR
2	Bob	25	Engineering
3	Charlie	35	Sales
4	David	28	Marketing

Refer to the following details to understand the RC file format structure:

- **Row groups**: Data is first divided into groups of rows. For simplicity, let us assume we have one row group with all four rows.
- **Column storage within row groups**: Within each row group, data is stored by columns.
- **Metadata**: It contains information about the row group, including the number of rows, the number of columns, and the schema (column names and types).
- **Data**: It contains the actual data stored in a columnar format within the row group. Each column's data is stored as an array of values. The RC file contains both metadata and data, combined, as shown in *Table 3.5*:

<table>
<tr><th>Row group metadata (Key)</th><th>Row group data (Value)</th></tr>
<tr><td><pre>{
  "row_count": 4,
  "column_count": 4,
  "columns": [
    {"name": "id", "type": "int"},
    {"name": "name", "type": "string"},
    {"name": "age", "type": "int"},
    {"name": "department", "type": "string"}
  ]
}</pre></td><td><pre>{
  "id": [1, 2, 3, 4],
  "name": ["Alice", "Bob", "Charlie", "David"],
  "age": [30, 25, 35, 28],
  "department": ["HR", "Engineering", "Sales",
"Marketing"]
}</pre></td></tr>
<tr><th colspan="2">Combined RC file</th></tr>
<tr><td colspan="2"><pre>{
  "row_group": {
    "metadata": {
      "row_count": 4,
      "column_count": 4,
      "columns": [
        {"name": "id", "type": "int"},
        {"name": "name", "type": "string"},
        {"name": "age", "type": "int"},
        {"name": "department", "type": "string"}
      ]
    },
    "data": {
      "id": [1, 2, 3, 4],
      "name": ["Alice", "Bob", "Charlie", "David"],
      "age": [30, 25, 35, 28],
      "department": ["HR", "Engineering", "Sales", "Marketing"]
    }
  }
}</pre></td></tr>
</table>

***Table 3.5**: RC file data*

Pros of RC files:

- By combining row and column storage, RC files enable efficient data retrieval and processing, especially in analytical workloads where columnar access is beneficial.
- It supports compression at both row and column levels, which helps to save storage space and improve I/O performance.
- This format is specifically optimized for use with Apache Hive, making it a suitable choice for data warehousing solutions that rely on Hive.
- This format provides performance improvements over traditional sequence files, especially for read-intensive operations.

Cons of RC files:

- The combination of row and column storage adds complexity to the file format, which can make implementation and debugging more challenging.
- It requires specific tools or libraries to read and write RC files, limiting its use to systems that support this format.
- Like sequence files, RC files have limited support for schema evolution. Changing the order of fields can be problematic, but appending new fields is possible.

Applications of RC files:

- This format is widely used in data warehousing solutions, particularly with Apache Hive, where large volumes of data need to be processed and analyzed efficiently.
- It is suitable for big data analytics workloads that benefit from columnar data access patterns, such as OLAP queries.
- It is often used in the Hadoop ecosystem for storing intermediate data between processing stages, leveraging its compression and storage efficiency features.
- RC files provide a versatile and efficient storage format that leverages the benefits of both row and columnar storage, making them an excellent choice for data-intensive applications in the Hadoop ecosystem.

ORC file formats

The **optimized row columnar** (**ORC**) file format is mainly designed for optimizing Hadoop workloads as it provides enhanced compression and performance benefits compared to older formats like RC File. An example representation of data in ORC format is as follows:

Assume we have the following dataset in CSV format:

TransactionID,CustomerID,ProductID,Quantity,Price,Date

101,1001,2001,2,10.99,2023-01-01

102,1002,2003,1,5.75,2023-01-02

103,1001,2002,3,8.50,2023-01-02

In ORC format, the data would be structured and stored as follows:

Columnar storage: Each column is stored separately. So, the data would look like:

Column 1 (TransactionID): [101, 102, 103]

Column 2 (CustomerID): [1001, 1002, 1001]

Column 3 (ProductID): [2001, 2003, 2002]

Column 4 (Quantity): [2, 1, 3]

Column 5 (Price): [10.99, 5.75, 8.50]

Column 6 (Date): ["2023-01-01", "2023-01-02", "2023-01-02"]

This example illustrates the basic concept of how data is organized in a columnar fashion and compressed in ORC format. The actual storage in ORC format involves more sophisticated handling of data types, compression algorithms, and metadata.

The key features and advantages of the ORC file format are:

- ORC stores data in a columnar manner, where values from each column are stored together. This design is particularly advantageous for analytics workloads involving operations like filtering and aggregation, as it allows for efficient access to specific columns without needing to read entire rows.
- ORC typically achieves high levels of compression, often around 75% or more. This compression is beneficial in reducing storage costs and improving query performance by minimizing the amount of data that needs to be read from disk.

- ORC is optimized to work efficiently within the Hadoop ecosystem. It supports features that are essential for Hadoop-based processing frameworks like Apache Hive, Apache Pig, and Apache Spark. This includes support for parallel processing and efficient data serialization/deserialization.
- ORC supports various compression algorithms that are optimized for different types of data and performance requirements. This flexibility allows users to choose the compression method that best suits their specific use case.
- Due to its columnar storage and efficient compression techniques, ORC can significantly improve query performance for analytical workloads. Operations such as scanning specific columns, applying predicates, and aggregating data are typically faster compared to row-oriented formats.

Overall, ORC is a popular choice for storing large datasets in Hadoop environments where efficient data processing and storage optimization are critical requirements. Its combination of columnar storage, high compression rates, and Hadoop integration makes it well-suited for data warehousing, data lakes, and other big data applications.

Avro file format

Avro is a data serialization framework developed within the Apache Hadoop project. It is designed to store data in a compact binary format and provides capabilities for schema evolution and data serialization. The key characteristics of the Avro file format are:

- Avro serializes data into a binary format, which makes it efficient for storage and transmission in Hadoop and other distributed systems.
- Avro uses JSON to define schemas, which describe the structure of the data being serialized. This schema is essential to interpret the data and enables interoperability across different programming languages.
- One of Avro's strengths is its support for schema evolution. This means developers can evolve data schema over time by adding, deleting, or modifying fields while ensuring backward and forward compatibility. Avro allows multiple versions of schemas to coexist, thereby enabling applications to read data written with different schema versions.
- Avro supports complex data types such as nested records, arrays, maps, and unions, which makes it suitable for storing diverse and hierarchical data structures.

Let us understand how data can be structured and serialized in Avro format with the help of an example. Assume a schema for storing information about books as shown in *Table 3.6*. In Avro, this schema defines a record type named **`Book`** with four fields, including **`title`** (**`string`**), **`author`** (**`string`**), **`publish_year`** (**`integer`**), **`price`** (**`float`**), and the sample data. Each record is encoded using the defined schema when the data is serialized into Avro format. Avro typically stores data in a binary format; however, for better understanding, *Table 3.6* shows how the data might appear when encoded in a JSON-like Avro format:

<table>
<tr><th>Schema for books</th><th>Sample data</th></tr>
<tr><td><pre>
{
  "type": "record",
  "name": "Book",
  "fields": [
    {"name": "title", "type": "string"},
    {"name": "author", "type": "string"},
    {"name": "publish_year", "type": "int"},
    {"name": "price", "type": "float"}
  ]
}
</pre></td><td><pre>
[
  {
    "title": "The White Tiger",
    "author": "Aravind Adiga",
    "publish_year": 2008,
    "price": 15.99
  },
  {
    "title": "The God of Small Things",
    "author": "Arundhati Roy",
    "publish_year": 1997,
    "price": 12.50
  },
  {
    "title": "Midnight's Children",
    "author": "Salman Rushdie",
    "publish_year": 1981,
    "price": 14.75
  }
]
</pre></td></tr>
<tr><th colspan="2">JSON like Avro format</th></tr>
<tr><td colspan="2"><pre>
[
  {"title": {"string": "The Great Gatsby"}, "author": {"string": "F. Scott Fitzgerald"}, "publish_year": {"int": 1925}, "price": {"float": 12.99}},
  {"title": {"string": "To Kill a Mockingbird"}, "author": {"string": "Harper Lee"}, "publish_year": {"int": 1960}, "price": {"float": 10.50}},
  {"title": {"string": "1984"}, "author": {"string": "George Orwell"}, "publish_year": {"int": 1949}, "price": {"float": 9.99}}
]
</pre></td></tr>
</table>

Table 3.6: Avro file format

Pros:

- It provides efficient storage and transmission due to its binary encoding.
- It supports evolving data schemas, enabling flexible changes to the data model over time.
- It is capable of handling nested or complex data structures.
- It is well-integrated with Hadoop ecosystem tools like Hive, Pig, and Spark.

Cons:

- As the binary format is not human readable, debugging and manual inspection become more challenging.
- When compared to some other formats like JSON, Avro's serialization may be slower due to its focus on compact binary representation.

- Avro requires schema information to read or write data, which means each record needs to include schema information or reference a schema stored separately.

Overall, Avro is mainly suitable for applications where schema flexibility, efficient storage, and support for evolving data structures are critical requirements, such as in big data analytics and data lake environments. Its integration with Hadoop and support for schema evolution make it a popular choice for data serialization and storage.

Parquet file format

Parquet is a columnar storage file format that is optimized for storing and processing large amounts of data in a highly efficient manner. It is widely used in big data processing frameworks like Apache Hadoop, Apache Spark, and others that support Hadoop-based file formats. The key features of Parquet are as follows:

- Parquet stores data column-wise rather than row-wise. This means that all values for a particular column are stored together, which is advantageous for analytical queries that often access specific columns rather than entire rows. This storage layout minimizes I/O operations and reduces disk seeks, improving query performance.
- Parquet supports various compression algorithms such as Snappy, GZIP, and others. Compression is applied to each column individually, which further reduces storage requirements and improves read performance. High compression ratios are achievable using this format, making it economical for storing large datasets.
- Similar to Avro, Parquet also supports schema evolution, which implies the schema of data can evolve over time by adding, removing, or modifying columns, along with ensuring backward and forward compatibility. This flexibility is crucial in data warehousing and analytics, where data schemas can change frequently.
- Parquet supports a wide range of data types, including primitive types (integers, floats, strings, etc.) as well as complex types like nested structures, arrays, and maps. This flexibility helps in modelling complex data hierarchies and relationships.
- Parquet supports predicate pushdown and column projection, which are optimization techniques used by query engines. Predicate pushdown allows filtering to be applied during the read operation, which reduces the amount of data read from disk. Column projection supports only the necessary columns to be read from disk, further optimizing query performance.
- Parquet files can be split into row groups and stored in a way that allows for parallel processing. Each row group can be processed independently, enabling efficient parallelism in distributed computing environments like Hadoop.
- Parquet is designed to integrate seamlessly with Apache Hadoop and other big data processing frameworks. It is the preferred file format for many distributed computing platforms like Apache Spark, Impala, Hive, and others due to its efficiency and performance characteristics.

On the whole, Parquet is a highly efficient columnar storage format designed for big data processing and analytics. Its features, such as columnar storage, compression, schema evolution, and integration with distributed computing frameworks, make it a preferred choice for handling large-scale data in modern data architectures.

Note: **Choosing the right file format depends on the nature of the data, the types of queries and analyses to be performed, and the overall architecture of the data processing pipeline. Each format brings its own set of advantages in terms of storage efficiency, query performance, schema flexibility, and integration capabilities with existing data tools and platforms.**

Conclusion

This chapter focused on the limitations of traditional file systems in managing big data challenges and the necessity for distributed file systems. You have explored the various types of distributed file systems and gained a detailed understanding of the architecture, properties, and functioning of the HDFS. Additionally, you learned how to write MapReduce programs to analyze data stored in HDFS and gained insights into job scheduling and monitoring within the MapReduce framework. The chapter also covered the various file formats supported by Hadoop, including text-based, binary, and columnar formats, and their pros, cons, and applications. By mastering these concepts, you are now equipped to effectively manage, process, and analyze large datasets using Hadoop and its associated tools and file formats.

In the next chapter, you will explore how commercial Hadoop distributions enhance the capabilities of open-source Hadoop, with a focus on the Cloudera framework. You will learn how to install the Cloudera QuickStart VMand practice essential HDFS commands in the Cloudera shell for basic data analysis.

Points to remember

The following list outlines the key takeaways from this chapter:

- Traditional file systems are designed for individual computers, so they lack the scalability and robustness needed to manage big data effectively.
- Distributed file systems spread data across multiple machines. Thus, they provide better scalability, fault tolerance, and data availability for handling large datasets.
- HDFS is a scalable and fault-tolerant distributed file system specifically designed for big data storage and processing in Hadoop.
- HDFS architecture consists of NameNode and DataNodes. NameNode represents the central server in HDFS that manages the metadata and directory structure of the file system. DataNodes are the servers where actual data is stored, managed, and retrieved based on instructions from the NameNode.
- HDFS offers high fault tolerance, scalability, and the ability to store very large files reliably across a distributed environment.
- The fundamental data structure used in MapReduce to facilitate distributed processing is key-value pairs. Map Phase is the initial phase where input data is transformed into key-value pairs. Shuffling and sorting is the process of transferring and sorting intermediate data between the map and reduce phases. In the Reduce phase, intermediate key-value pairs are aggregated and processed to produce the final output.
- Job scheduling and monitoring in MapReduce is the mechanism for managing, scheduling, and tracking the progress of MapReduce tasks across the distributed system.
- Different file formats supported by Hadoop are text-based, binary, and columnar. All formats have their own advantages, disadvantages, and suitable applications for efficient data storage and processing.

Multiple choice questions

1. **What is a characteristic of a traditional file system?**
   a. Scalability
   b. Fault tolerance
   c. Centralized storage
   d. MapReduce processing
2. **Which of the following is a key advantage of a DFS over a traditional file system?**
   a. Centralized management
   b. High scalability
   c. Limited storage capacity
   d. Sequential processing

3. **In a DFS, data is stored across multiple:**
   a. Drives
   b. Folders
   c. Servers
   d. Partitions
4. **What is the primary purpose of HDFS in the Hadoop ecosystem?**
   a. Real-time data processing
   b. Batch processing of large data sets
   c. SQL operations
   d. OLTP
5. **In HDFS, which component is responsible for storing metadata about the file system namespace and the blockmap?**
   a. NameNode
   b. DataNode
   c. Job tracker
   d. Task tracker
6. **In HDFS architecture, what component is responsible for storing the actual data blocks?**
   a. NameNode
   b. DataNode
   c. Job tracker
   d. Task tracker
7. **The role of the NameNode in HDFS is primarily:**
   a. Storing data blocks
   b. Managing metadata
   c. Executing MapReduce jobs
   d. Sorting and shuffling
8. **What is a key property of HDFS that ensures fault tolerance?**
   a. Data replication
   b. Data compression
   c. In-memory processing
   d. Centralized storage
9. **In MapReduce, what is a fundamental unit of data processed by the Mapper?**
   a. File
   b. Block
   c. Key-value pair
   d. Record
10. **The map phase in MapReduce involves:**
    a. Data sorting
    b. Data shuffling
    c. Data storage
    d. Data replication
11. **What is the primary purpose of the reduce phase in MapReduce?**
    a. Data sorting
    b. Data shuffling
    c. Aggregation
    d. Data replication
12. **In MapReduce, what does the shuffling phase involve?**
    a. Sorting and transferring map outputs
    b. Replicating data blocks
    c. Executing reduce tasks
    d. Aggregating key-value pairs
13. **Which file format is specifically designed for efficient columnar storage and is ideal for analytical queries that require high compression and fast data retrieval?**
    a. CSV
    b. Avro
    c. JSON
    d. Parquet

14. **What is the primary role of the ResourceManager in YARN architecture?**
    a. Manage data storage in HDFS
    b. Execute MapReduce jobs
    c. Manage resources and schedule applications
    d. Store metadata about Hadoop clusters
15. **Which of the following file formats is known for its compact binary encoding and includes schema information, making it suitable for complex data structures and schema evolution?**
    a. XML
    b. ORC
    c. Avro
    d. Text-based

Answers

1. c.	2. b.	3. c.	4. b.	5. a.
6. b.	7. b.	8. a.	9. c.	10. a.
11. c.	12. c.	13. d.	14. c.	15. c.

Questions

1. Explain the limitations of a traditional file system in handling large-scale data and how distributed file systems address these limitations.
2. Discuss the role of the NameNode and DataNodes in HDFS architecture. How does data replication contribute to fault tolerance in HDFS?
3. Describe the key phases involved in processing data using MapReduce. How does the MapReduce programming model handle parallel processing of large datasets?
4. Assume you have an HDFS cluster with a replication factor of 3. The total size of your data is 15 TB. Calculate the total storage capacity required in the HDFS cluster, considering the replication factor.
5. A tech startup needs to implement HDFS for its growing dataset. Outline the steps they should take to set up HDFS, distribute data across nodes, and ensure fault tolerance.
6. If a single data block in HDFS is 128 MB, calculate the number of data blocks the file will be divided into in the HDFS cluster for a file of 1 GB in size.
7. In a MapReduce job, the Mapper processes 100,000 input records, and each record emits 3 key-value pairs. If the MapReduce job has 5 Mappers, calculate the total number of key-value pairs emitted by all Mappers during the Map phase.
8. In a MapReduce job, the reducer receives input from 10 Mappers, and each Mapper sends 500 key-value pairs. If the reducer output has a total of 2,000 key-value pairs, calculate the average number of key-value pairs processed by each reducer.
9. An organization heavily relies on HDFS for data storage. Develop a case study highlighting a scenario where a DataNode fails, and discuss how HDFS ensures fault tolerance and data recovery in such situations.
10. Given a scenario where a company needs to store and analyze large volumes of web server logs, determine which file format (text-based, binary, or columnar) would be the most appropriate to use. Justify your choice based on factors such as data retrieval speed, storage efficiency, ease of use, and compatibility with big data processing frameworks. Provide a detailed explanation of how your chosen format would optimize the storage and analysis of the data.

Join our Discord space

Join our Discord workspace for latest updates, offers, tech happenings around the world, new releases, and sessions with the authors:

https://discord.bpbonline.com

CHAPTER 4
Big Data Analysis with Cloudera

Without big data analytics, companies are blind and deaf.

— Geoffrey Moore

Introduction

This chapter provides an introduction to commercial Hadoop distributions and their ability to enhance the capabilities of the open-source Hadoop platform. It explains in detail the Cloudera framework, a leading commercial Hadoop distribution that is widely used in the industry. It provides a step-by-step guide to download and install the Cloudera Quickstart VM, a pre-configured virtual machine that allows one to set up a Hadoop environment on local machines. Next, it provides practical demonstrations of basic HDFS commands in the Cloudera shell, which are required for data analysis.

Structure

In this chapter, we will cover the following topics:

- Commercial Hadoop distributions
- Introduction to Cloudera framework
- Basic HDFS shell commands

Objectives

By the end of this chapter, the readers will gain a comprehensive understanding of how commercial Hadoop distributions extend and enhance the capabilities of the open-source Hadoop ecosystem. Readers will specifically explore the Cloudera framework, one of the most widely adopted enterprise-grade Hadoop distributions, and will understand why it has become a preferred choice in the industry for scalable data management and analytics. Through a guided, step-by-step setup of the Cloudera Quickstart VM, they will learn how to easily deploy a pre-configured Hadoop environment on their local machine that enables hands-on practice without the complexity of manual configuration. Additionally, they will work with essential HDFS shell commands in the Cloudera terminal, which will help them to develop the foundational skills required to store, navigate, and manage data within the Hadoop Distributed File System. By mastering these concepts and skills, readers will be well-equipped to leverage Cloudera for practical data analysis tasks.

Commercial Hadoop distributions

Hadoop is an open-source framework for distributed storage and processing of large data sets. To overcome the inherent challenges in the installation of Hadoop, several commercial distributions of Hadoop are made available, which often include additional tools, management features, and support services to enhance the usability and performance of Hadoop. They provide scalable and distributed computing capabilities across on-premises and cloud-based storage systems. They also provide access to query/reporting tools, machine learning, and data management infrastructure components in Hadoop. Some popular commercial Hadoop vendors are as follows:

- Cloudera CDH Hadoop Distribution
- **Hortonworks Data Platform** (**HDP**)
- MapR Hadoop Distribution
- Amazon Elastic MapReduce
- IBM Open Platform
- Microsoft Azure's HDInsight—Cloud-based Hadoop Distribution
- DataStax Enterprise analytics
- EMC[2]
- Dell—Cloudera Apache Hadoop Solution

Refer to the following figure for an illustrated example:

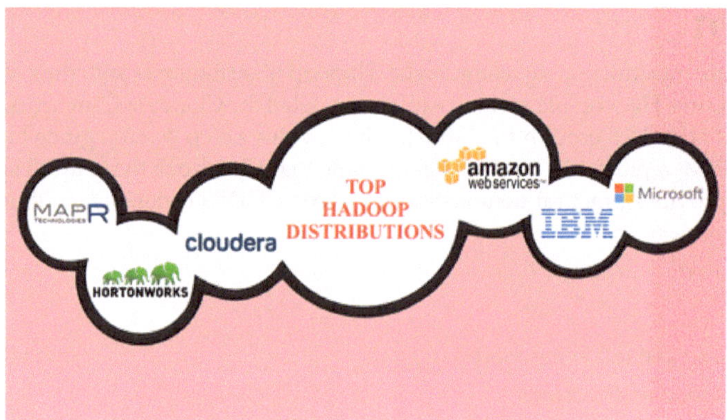

***Figure 4.1**: Commercial distributions of Hadoop*

Introduction to Cloudera framework

Cloudera offers its own distribution of Apache Hadoop, known as **Cloudera Distribution for Hadoop** (**CDH**). Cloudera was founded in 2008 by a group of engineers from *Yahoo, Google,* and *Facebook*. CDH provides all core components of Hadoop along with additional tools and services that enhance the functionality and ease of use. It is an integrated platform that incorporates various components of the Hadoop ecosystem, such as Apache Hive, Apache HBase, Apache Spark, Apache Impala, and more.

This integrated platform aims to simplify the deployment and management of big data solutions. It is designed to address various data management needs, including data storage, processing, and analytics. It supports both batch and real-time processing of large datasets. It also includes tools for data encryption, access control, auditing, and policy enforcement, helping organizations maintain compliance and secure their data. It allows organizations to perform advanced analytics and build **machine learning** (**ML**) models on top of their big data infrastructure. Cloudera provides virtual machine images of complete Apache Hadoop clusters, which make it easy for anyone to start with Cloudera CDH. In this book, all examples of big data analysis are executed using the Cloudera distribution of Hadoop.

CDH is typically installed using Cloudera QuickStart VM, which includes everything required for using CDH, such as Impala, Cloudera Search, and Cloudera Manager. It uses a package-based installer that allows you to work with or without the Cloudera Manager. The various steps to install Cloudera QuickStart VMare discussed in the following section.

Steps to download and install Cloudera QuickStart VM

Follow these steps to download and install Cloudera QuickStart VM:

1. Check system requirements:

   a. Hardware requirements:

      - **Memory (RAM)**: The amount of RAM required depends on the size of your data and the type of workload. Typically, Cloudera recommends a minimum of 8 GB RAM per node.
      - **Processor (CPU)**: Multi-core processors (quad-core or higher) are recommended.
      - **Disk space**: Sufficient disk space for VM and Cloudera operating system, Cloudera Manager, and Hadoop components. The exact requirements depend on your specific installation and usage.

   b. Software requirements:

      - **Operating system (OS)**: Cloudera supports various Linux distributions, including CentOS, **Red Hat Enterprise Linux** (**RHEL**), Ubuntu, and SUSE.
      - **Java**: Cloudera requires the **Java Development Kit** (**JDK**) to be installed on all nodes. The version may vary based on the Cloudera distribution, but it is typically Java 8 or later.
      - The prerequisite of Cloudera QuickStart VMInstallation is a virtualization platform such as Oracle VirtualBox or **VMware** (**VMW**). Download and install VirtualBox on your Windows machine from the website (**https://www.virtualbox.org/wiki/Downloads**).

2. **Download and install Cloudera QuickStart VM**: Visit the Cloudera website and download the Cloudera Manager package that matches your operating system. The Cloudera Manager can be downloaded from:

   https://www.cloudera.com/downloads.html

   a. Once the file is downloaded, go to the downloads folder and unzip these files, as shown in *Figure 4.2*. It can then be used to set up a single node Cloudera cluster:

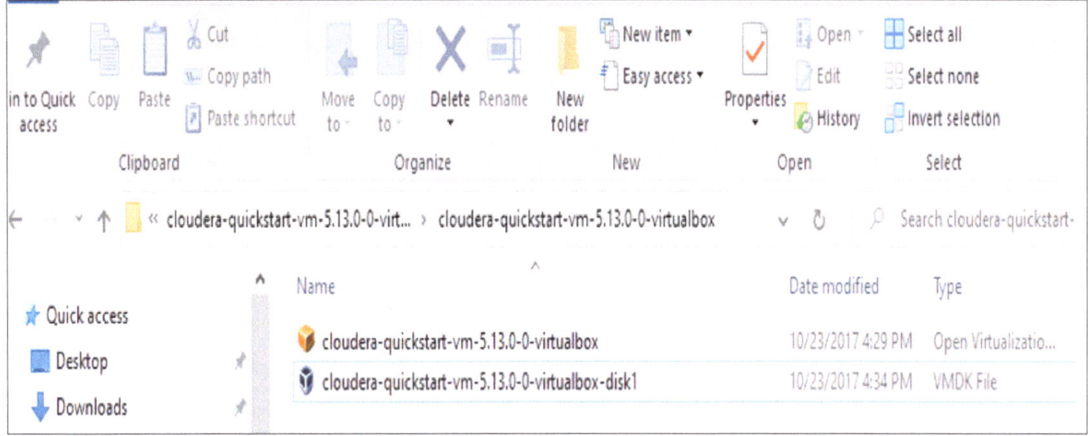

***Figure 4.2**: Cloudera QuickStart VMinstallation*

3. The next step is to install VirtualBox by double-clicking the **VirtualBox** icon available on the desktop, as shown in *Figure 4.3*:

***Figure 4.3**: Oracle VirtualBox icon on desktop*

4. Next, the VirtualBox window shown in *Figure 4.4* appears:

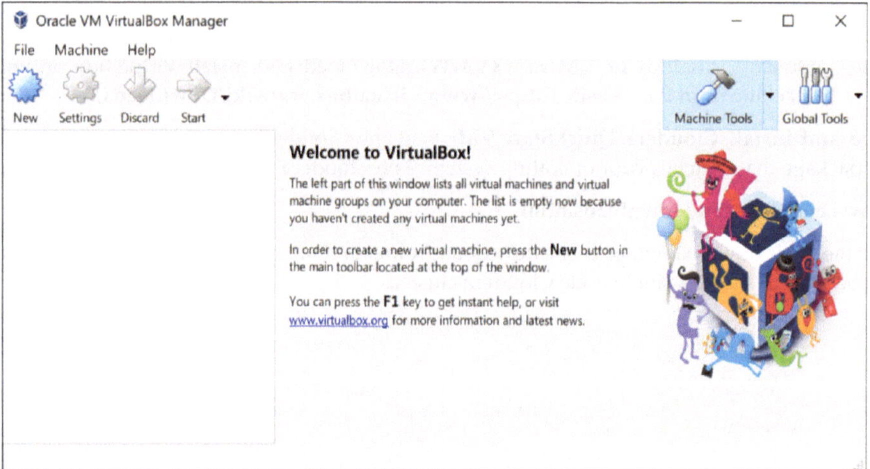

***Figure 4.4**: VirtualBox window*

5. Go to the **File** menu, and click on **Import Appliance**, as shown in *Figure 4.5*:

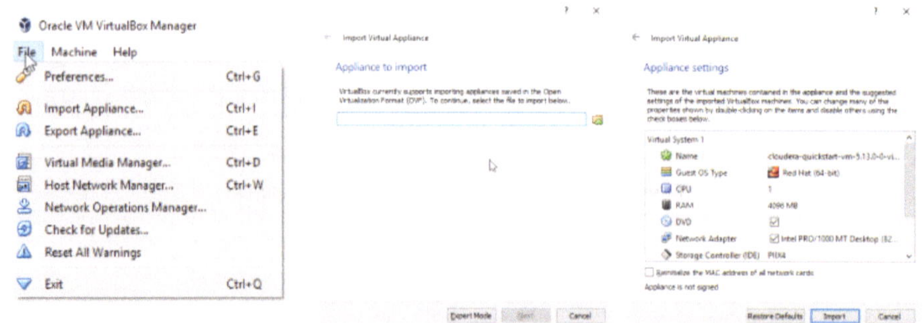

***Figure 4.5**: Import Appliance in VirtualBox window*

6. The next step is to browse and select the Cloudera QuickStart VMfrom the directory (wherever you have downloaded it in your system) by clicking on the encircled icon, as shown in *Figure 4.6*:

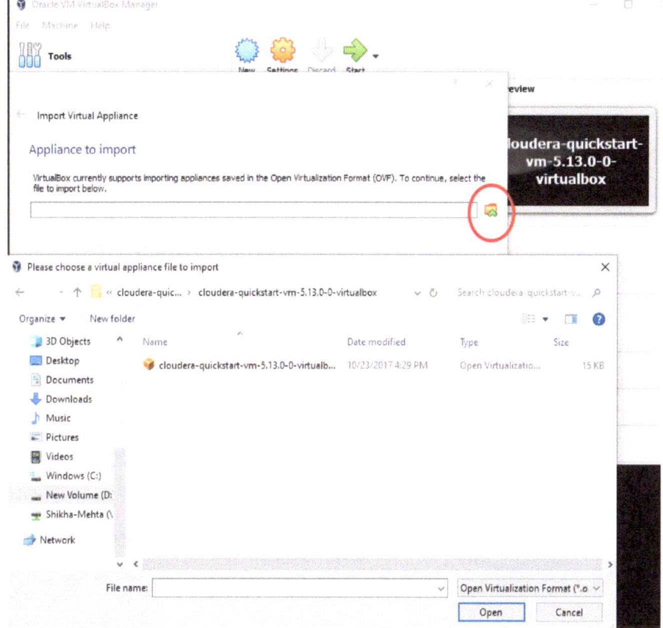

***Figure 4.6:** Browse Cloudera QuickStart VMin VirtualBox*

7. *Figure 4.7* shows the configuration settings of the chosen appliance, which can be changed as per requirement:

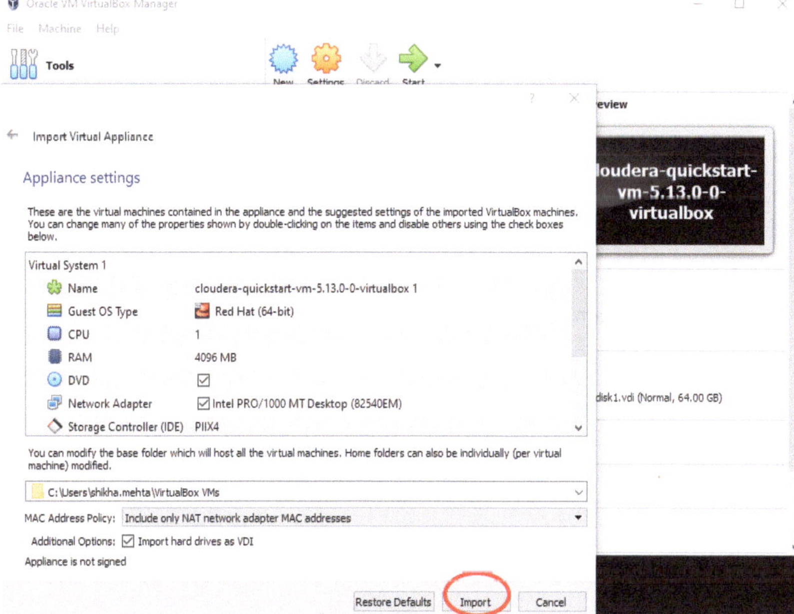

***Figure 4.7:** Appliance settings*

8. On clicking **Import**, the process of importing the Cloudera QuickStart VMin VirtualBox will begin, as shown in *Figure 4.8:*

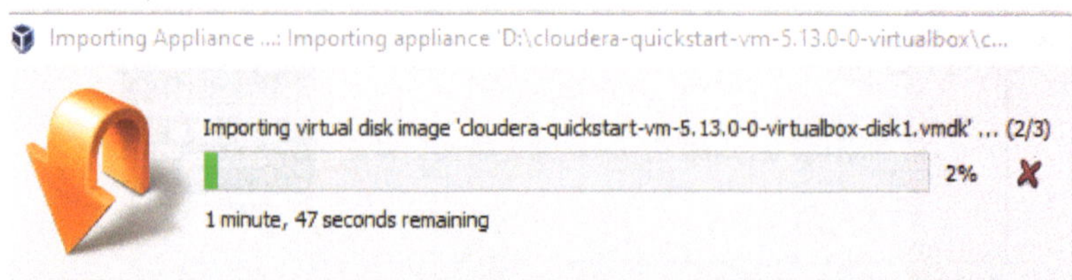

Figure 4.8: *Import Cloudera QuickStart VMin VirtualBox*

9. After importing, the Cloudera QuickStart VMis ready to launch, as shown in *Figure 4.9*. You can change the configurations by clicking on the **Settings** icon or directly launching Cloudera by clicking on the **Start** icon:

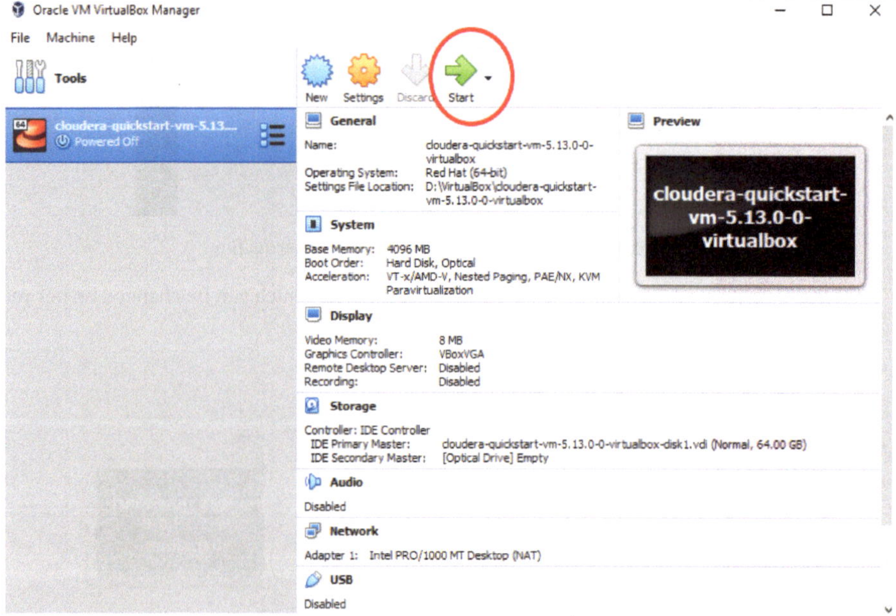

Figure 4.9: *Cloudera QuickStart VMin VirtualBox*

10. In settings, you may change the **General**, as shown in *Figure 4.10:*

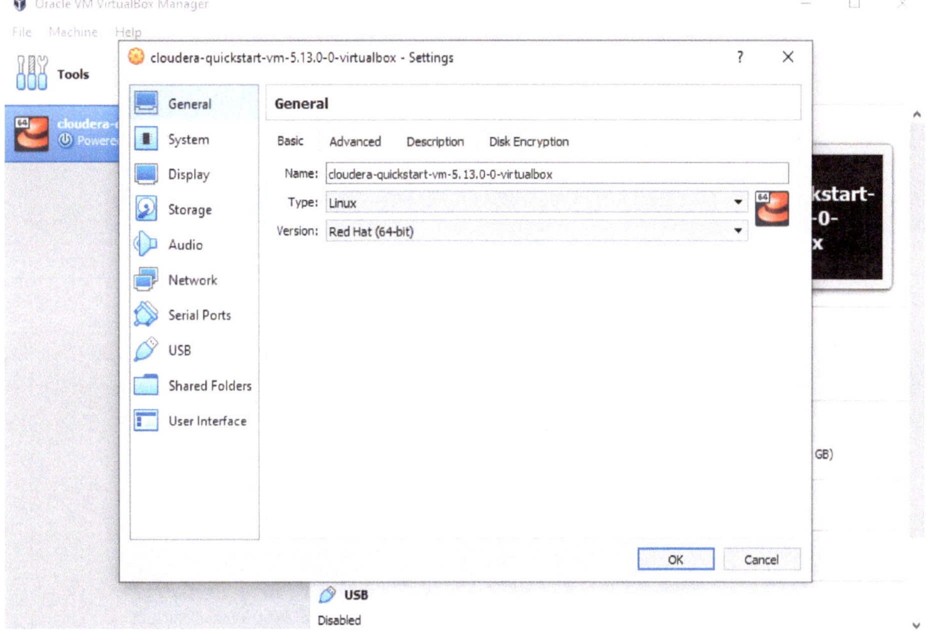

***Figure 4.10**: General configuration settings*

11. Similarly, other settings, such as **System**, **Display**, **Storage**, etc, as shown in *Figure 4.11*, can be changed by clicking on the respective icons:

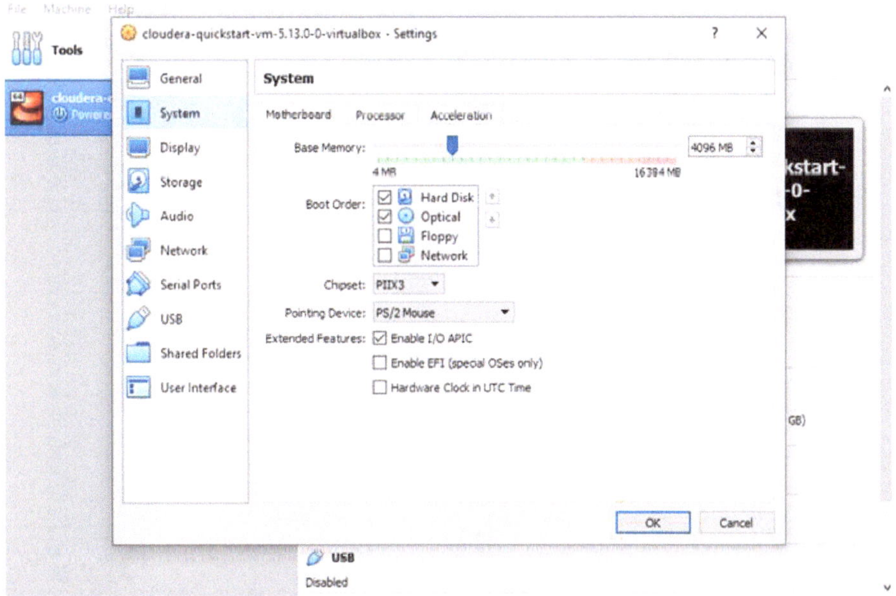

***Figure 4.11**: System configuration settings*

12. Click on the start icon as shown in *Figure 4.9,* and Cloudera starts booting. It will take some time, and finally, the window, as shown in *Figure 4.12,* appears. It indicates that Cloudera is installed properly and running. By default:
    a. **Username**: **`cloudera`**
    b. **Password**: **`cloudera`**

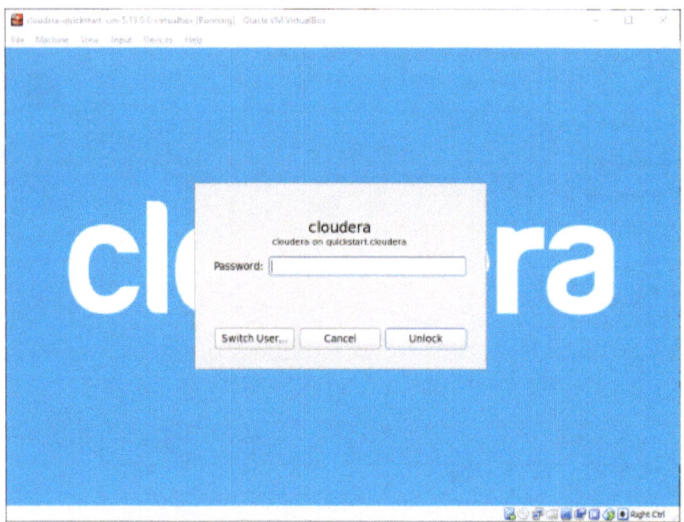

***Figure 4.12:** Cloudera QuickStart VMrunning*

13. After a successful login, Cloudera is ready for big data processing, as shown in *Figure 4.13:*

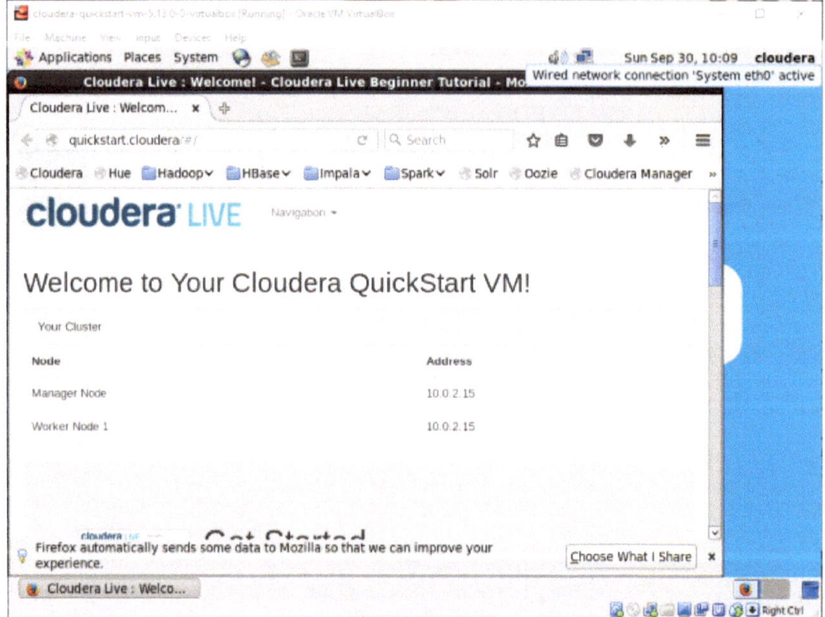

***Figure 4.13:** Cloudera QuickStart VMrunning*

Basic HDFS shell commands

As the data is stored in HDFS, there are a number of commonly used Hadoop fs commands that are used to manage files on a Hadoop cluster. These Hadoop **`hdfs`** commands can be run in the Cloudera shell. All these commands are case sensitive and must be written in small case. To start the Cloudera shell, follow the steps, as shown in *Figure 4.14:*

1. Go to **Applications** (in the top left corner) | **System Tools** | **Terminal**.
2. In the terminal all Hadoop commands can be executed either by using **`hadoop fs`** or **`hdfs dfs`**, as shown in all the following examples. **Example**: **`hadoop fs -help`**.

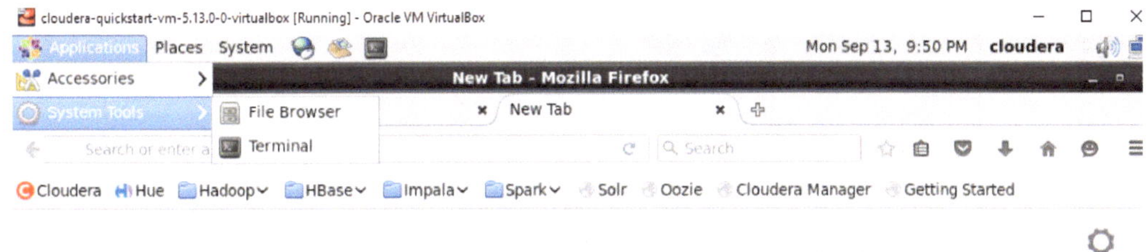

***Figure 4.14**: Steps to start Cloudera shell*

The various shell commands used for managing the HDFS are:

- **help**: This shell command provides information about all the available Hadoop commands and how to use them, as shown in *Figure 4.15:*
  - **Example**: **`hadoop fs -help`**

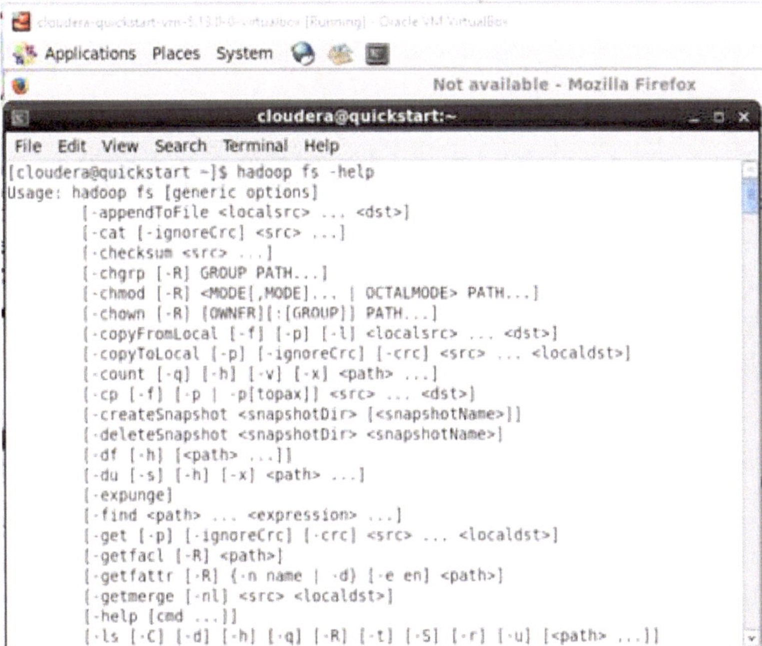

***Figure 4.15**: Output of the help command in the shell*

  - Using help along with other shell commands provides information specific to the given shell command e.g **`hadoop fs -help ls`** provides information on the usage of **`ls`**, as shown in *Figure 4.16:*

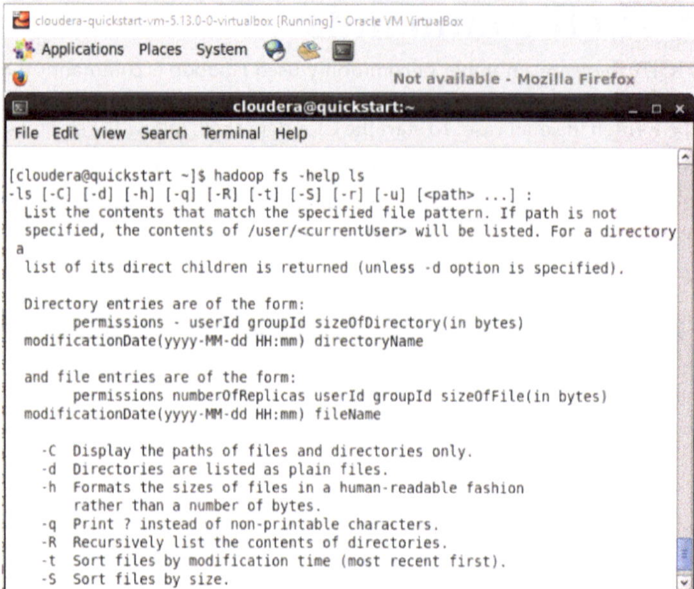

Figure 4.16: Output of Hadoop fs help ls command in shell

- **usage**: This command provides all the options that can be used with a particular `hdfs` command, as shown in *Figure 4.17*. Here, this command gives all the options that can be used with the `ls` command.
  - **Example**: `hadoop fs -usage ls`

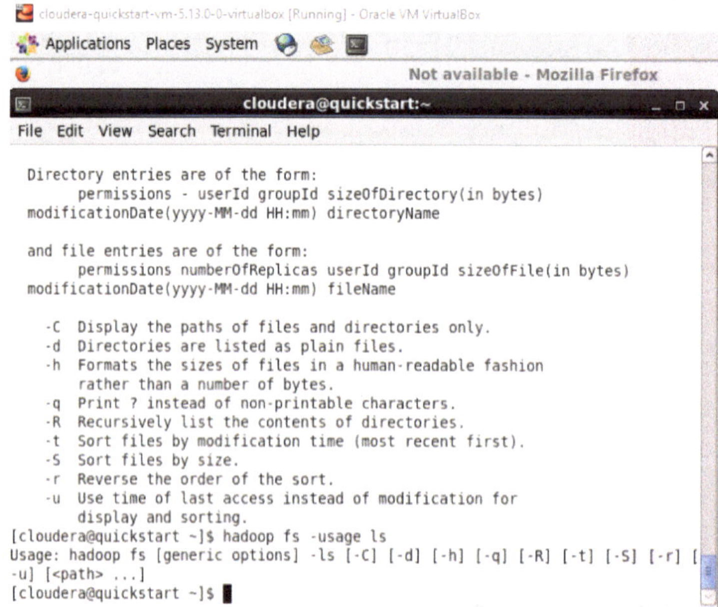

Figure 4.17: Output of the usage command in the shell

- **ls**: This command lists all the files and subdirectories under the default directory. In this example, as shown in *Figure 4.18,* the default directory for the Cloudera VM is **`/user/Cloudera`**.
  - **Example**: **`hadoop fs -ls`**

  To explore all the files and subdirectories available in the root directory, update the preceding command as: **`hadoop fs -ls /`**

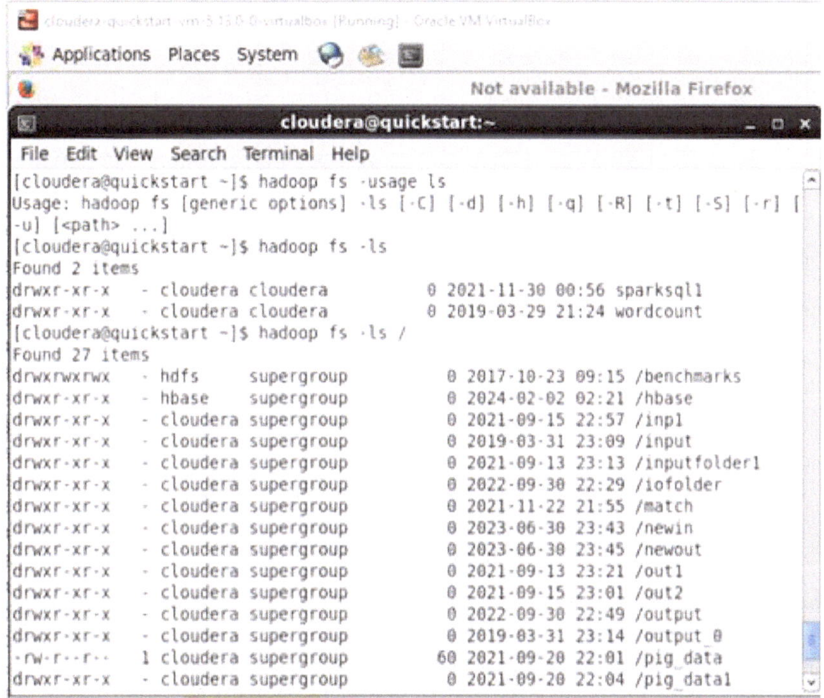

***Figure 4.18**: Output of ls command and its variation*

- **mkdir**: This command is used to create a new directory at a specified location. For example, the following command will create a new directory named **`mydir`** under the location **`/user/Cloudera`**, as shown in *Figure 4.19*.

- **Example**: `hadoop fs -mkdir /user/cloudera/mydir`

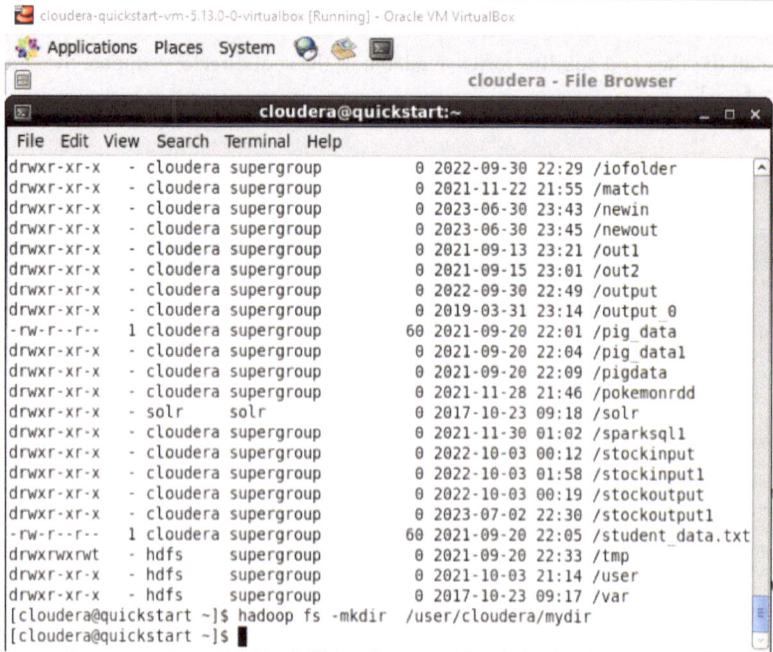

Figure 4.19: Output of mkdir command

- **copyFromLocal and put**: Both these commands help to copy the file from one location to another. The difference between commands is that the **`CopyFromLocal`** command copies the file from the local file system to HDFS, as shown in *Figure 4.20,* while the **`put`** command can be used to copy multiple files from anywhere (local or network) to anywhere (HDFS or local file system), as shown in *Figure 4.21*.

  The following example copies the **`Bsample.txt`** file from the local file system to the specified location - **`/user/cloudera/myfirstdir`**. Remember that the **`Bsample.txt`** file and the myfirstdir must be created before executing this command.

  - Example: `hadoop fs -copyFromLocal Bsample1.txt /user/cloudera/myfirstdir`

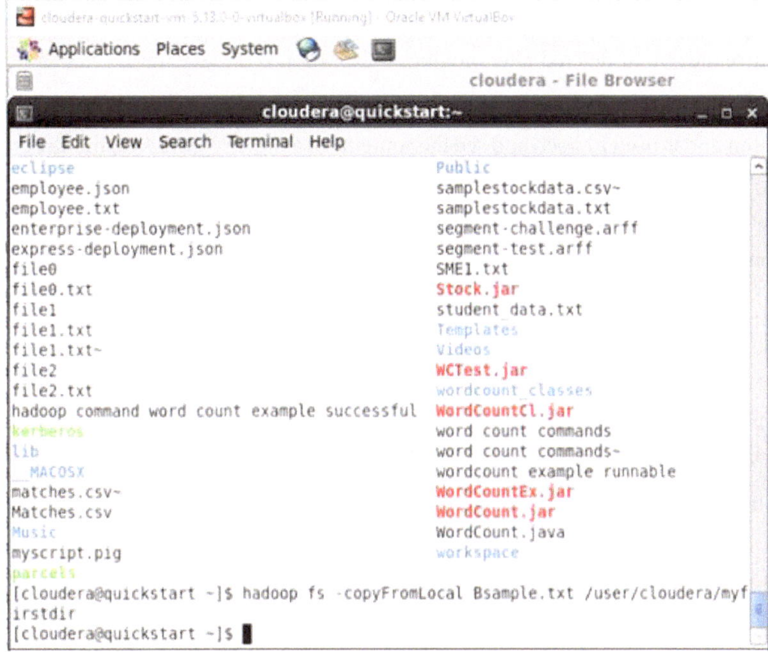

Figure 4.20: Example of copyFromLocal command

The following example, as shown in *Figure 4.21*, copies the **`Newsample.txt`** file from the local file system to the specified directory using the **`put`** command (**`mydir1`**). The figure shows that the file has been successfully copied, and the same is verified by executing the **`hadoop fs -cat /user/cloudera/mydir1/Newsample.txt`** command.

- Example: **`hadoop fs -put Newsample.txt /user/cloudera/mydir1`**

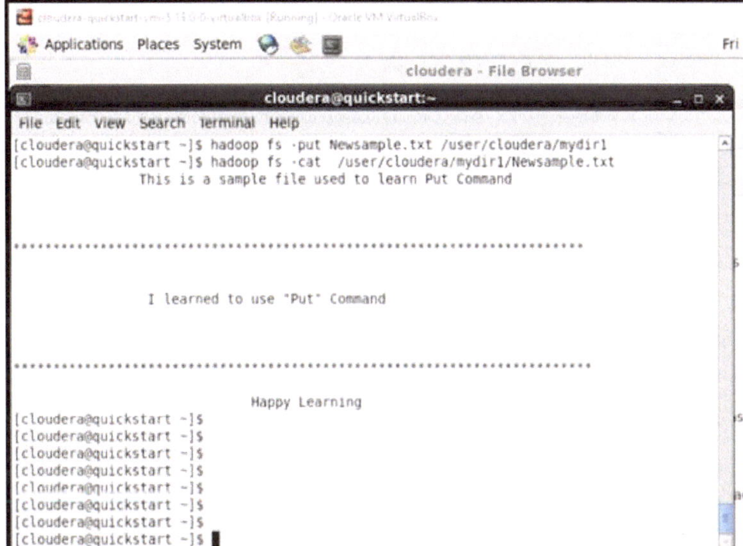

Figure 4.21: Example of putcommand

- **moveFromLocal**: This command's functionality is similar to the put command, but the source file is deleted after copying. The following example will move the file from the local file system to the desired location, and the source file will be deleted after moving.
    - **Example**: `hadoop fs -moveFromLocal Newsample3.txt /user/cloudera/dir3`
- **cat**: This command is used to open and see the contents of a file. In *Figure 4.21*, the **`cat`** command is used to display the contents of the **`Newsample.txt`** file located in **`/user/cloudera/mydir1/`**.
    - **Example**: `hadoop fs -cat /user/cloudera/mydir1/Newsample.txt`
- **du**: This command is used to check the disk usage (**`du`**) for all the files available under a given directory, as shown in *Figure 4.22*. In the output, the first column indicates the base size (in bytes) of the file or directory before replication. As HDFS replicates files, the second field provides information about the total disk space consumed by the respective file or directory after it has been replicated. Since both numbers are the same, it likely means replication factor = 1 in your QuickStart setup (which is normal).
    - **Example**:

```
hadoop fs -du                                    //for home directory
hadoop fs -du /user/cloudera/firstdir          //for  particular directory
```

- **df**: This command is used to check the capacity, size, and free space available on the HDFS file system. Optionally **-h** can be used to see the output in human readable format, as shown in *Figure 4.22*. The Size field represents the total storage capacity available in the HDFS cluster. The Used field indicates the amount of storage space currently consumed by data stored in HDFS. The Available field shows the remaining free storage space that can still be utilized. The Use% field reflects the percentage of the total storage capacity that is currently in use.

    In this case, the total HDFS capacity is 54.5 GB, out of which 833.7 MB is being used. This corresponds to only 1% of the total storage, indicating very light usage. Such low utilization is completely normal in a freshly configured QuickStart VM, where minimal data has been loaded into the system.
    - **Example**:

```
hadoop fs -df
hadoop fs -df -h
```

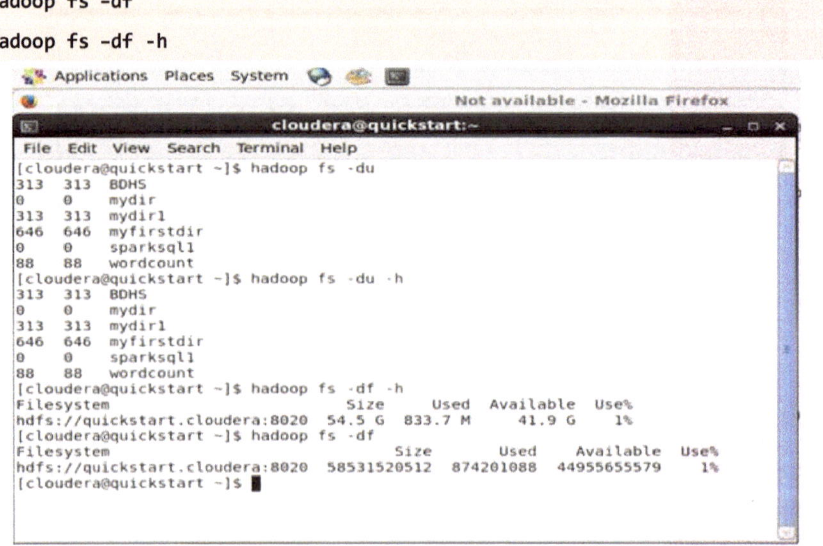

Figure 4.22: Example of the du and df command

- **copyToLocal and get**: The **get** command is used to copy files from HDFS to the local file system. However, the destination is restricted to a local file reference when we use **copyToLocal**. While using **get** there are no such restrictions.
  - **Example**:

```
hadoop fs -copyToLocal /wou1/part-r-00000  /home/cloudera/
hadoop fs -get /wou1/part-r-00000 /home/cloudera/
```

In the preceding example, a file named **part-r-00000** is copied from the **wou1** directory in the **hdfs** to **cloudera** home directory. *Figure 4.23* depicts the contents of the **part-r-00000** file available in **hdfs**:

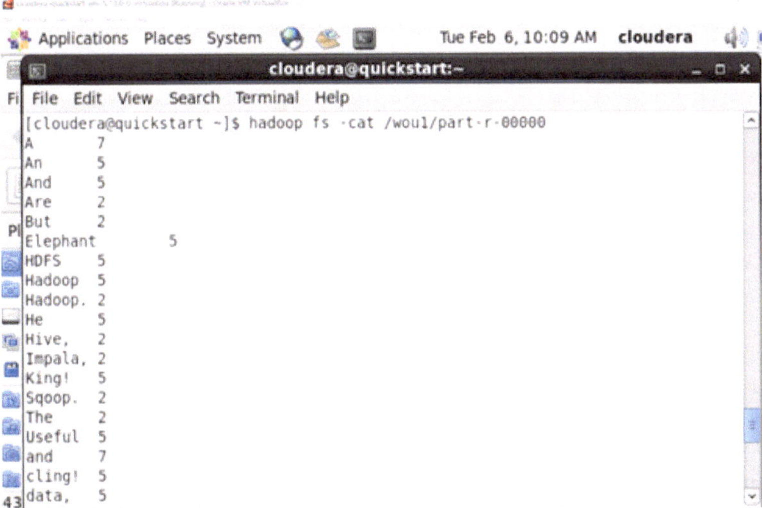

***Figure 4.23**: part-r-00000 file available in hdfs*

Figure 4.24 shows the usage of **get** command:

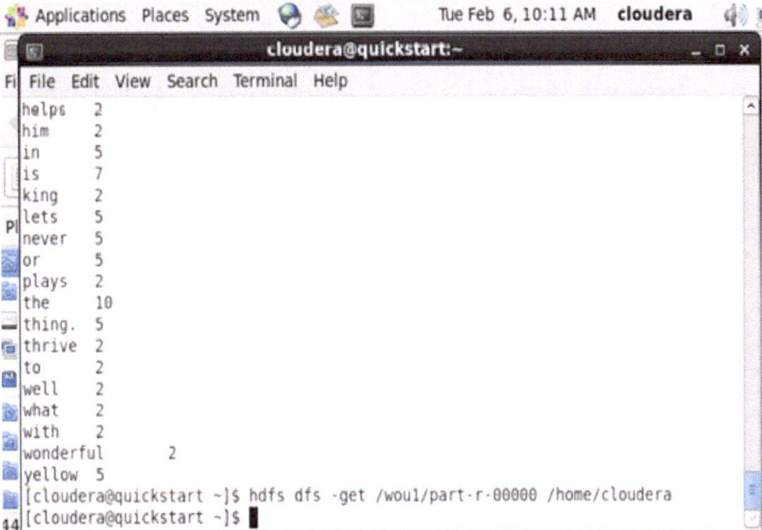

***Figure 4.24**:Usage of the get command*

It can be verified from the Cloudera home directly that the desired file is copied from **hdfs** to the local file system, as shown in *Figure 4.25:*

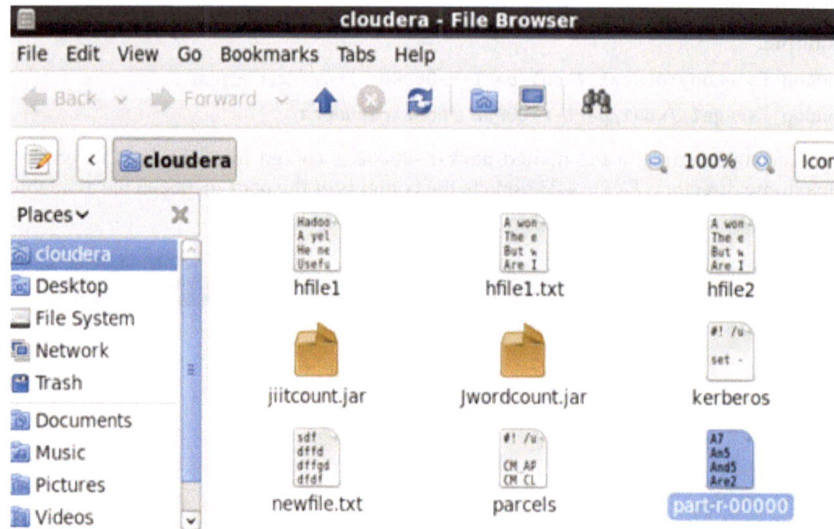

Figure 4.25:part-r-00000 file copied

- **touchz**: It is used to create an empty file at the specified location. The given example, as shown in *Figure 4.26*, creates an empty file named **bdhs1.txt** at the location **/user/cloudera**. The same can be verified using the **ls** command, as shown in *Figure 4.26:*
  - **Example**: **hadoop fs -touchz /user/cloudera/bdhs1.txt**

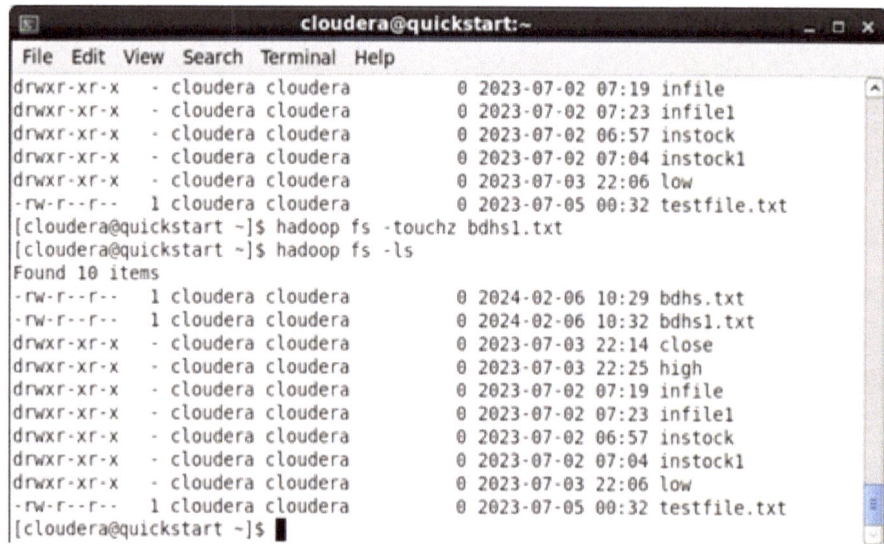

Figure 4.26: Example of touchz command

- **setrep**: This command can be used to set the replication for a specific file. The given example will set the replication factor of **bdhs.txt** file to 2, as shown in *Figure 4.27*. The same can be verified by using the **ls** command, which shows the replication factor of the **bdhs.txt** file as 2 in the second column of the output.

- **Example:** **`hadoop fs -setrep -w 2 /user/cloudera/bdhs.txt`**

```
Applications Places System    Tue Feb 6, 10:50 AM cloudera
cloudera@quickstart:~
File Edit View Search Terminal Help
drwxr-xr-x   - cloudera cloudera          0 2023-07-02 06:57 instock
drwxr-xr-x   - cloudera cloudera          0 2023-07-02 07:04 instock1
drwxr-xr-x   - cloudera cloudera          0 2023-07-03 22:06 low
-rw-r--r--   1 cloudera cloudera          0 2023-07-05 00:32 testfile.txt
[cloudera@quickstart ~]$ hadoop fs -setrep -w 2 /user/cloudera/bdhs.txt
Replication 2 set: /user/cloudera/bdhs.txt
Waiting for /user/cloudera/bdhs.txt ... done
[cloudera@quickstart ~]$ hadoop fs -ls
Found 10 items
-rw-r--r--   2 cloudera cloudera          0 2024-02-06 10:29 bdhs.txt
-rw-r--r--   1 cloudera cloudera          0 2024-02-06 10:32 bdhs1.txt
drwxr-xr-x   - cloudera cloudera          0 2023-07-03 22:14 close
drwxr-xr-x   - cloudera cloudera          0 2023-07-03 22:25 high
drwxr-xr-x   - cloudera cloudera          0 2023-07-02 07:19 infile
drwxr-xr-x   - cloudera cloudera          0 2023-07-02 07:23 infile1
drwxr-xr-x   - cloudera cloudera          0 2023-07-02 06:57 instock
drwxr-xr-x   - cloudera cloudera          0 2023-07-02 07:04 instock1
drwxr-xr-x   - cloudera cloudera          0 2023-07-03 22:06 low
-rw-r--r--   1 cloudera cloudera          0 2023-07-05 00:32 testfile.txt
[cloudera@quickstart ~]$
```

***Figure 4.27**: Output of setrep command*

- **chgrp**: This command is used to change the group name of a file or a path. The user must be the owner of the files, or else a super-user, to execute this command.
  - **Example one**: **`hadoop fs -chgrp -R  newgroup/newin/file1.txt`**

    It will change the **`/newin/file1.txt`** directory group membership from a supergroup to a new group. Superuser permission is required to perform this operation. If superuser permission is not available, use the command (Example 2) as shown in *Figure 4.28*:
  - **Example two**: **`sudo -u hdfshadoop fs -chgrp -R  newgroup  /newin/file1.txt`**

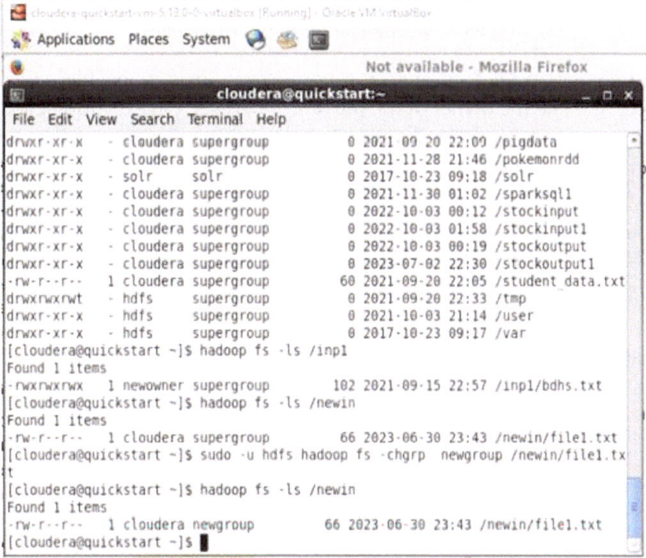

***Figure 4.28**: Output of chgrp command*

- **chown**: This command is used to change both the owner and group name simultaneously. To perform this operation, superuser permission is required. If permission is available, execute the command given in *example one*; else, run *example two*. This command will change the owner of **`/newin/file1.txt`** Cloudera to the new owner, as shown in *Figure 4.29*:
    - **Example one**: **`hdfs hadoop fs -chown newowner /newin/file1.txt`**
    - **Example two**: **`sudo -u hdfs Hadoop fs -chown newowner /newin/file1.txt`**

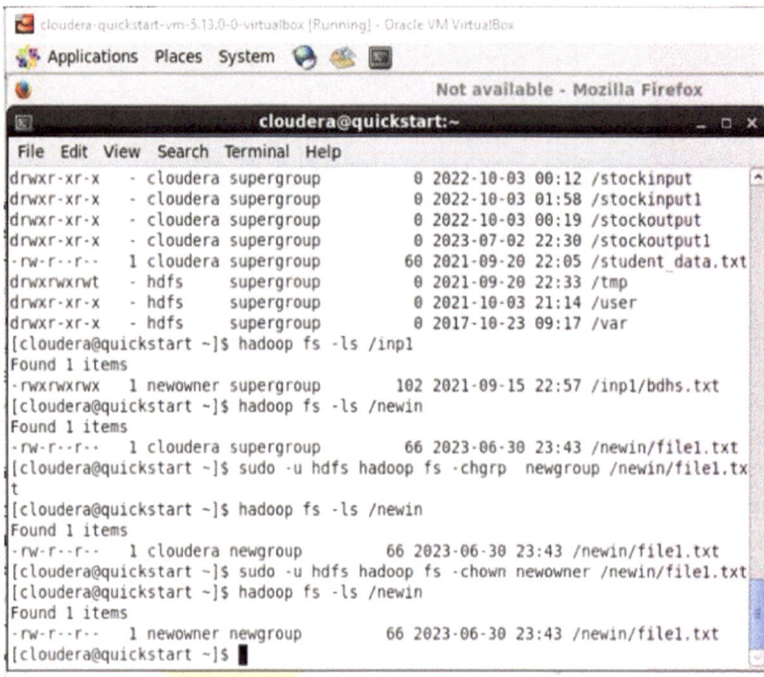

Figure4.29:Output of the chown command

- **chmod**: This command is used to change the permissions of a given file or directory. To execute this command, the user must be the owner of the file or a superuser. On executing **`chmod 777`**, all users will get read, write, and execute permission on the file. Granting all permissions to all users is usually discouraged in production environments because it can pose security risks. It is preferred to temporarily change full permissions on a file or directory in HDFS, as shown in *Figure 4.30*.

    It is important to restore the proper permissions once the required operation is completed or the security risk is mitigated. This can be done by running a similar **`chmod`** command with the appropriate permissions, such as **`chmod 755`** to grant read, write, and execute permissions to the owner and read-only access to others.
    - **Example**: **`hadoop fs -chmod777 /inp1/bdhs.txt`**

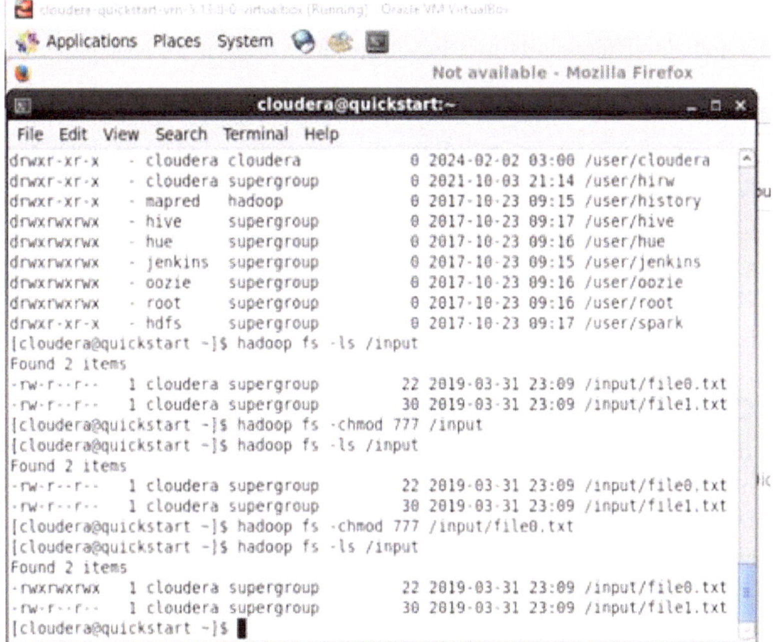

Figure 4.30*: Output of chmod command*

Conclusion

This chapter highlighted the power of commercial Hadoop distributions in enhancing the functionality of the open-source Hadoop platform. It provided a comprehensive introduction to working with Hadoop using Cloudera framework. It serves as a guide for readers through the process of setting up a Hadoop environment using the Cloudera Quickstart VM. Finally, various HDFS shell commands are demonstrated with practical examples, including their execution and corresponding results using the Cloudera shell.

In the next chapter, you will learn to perform stock data analysis using Hadoop. You will also learn to implement a MapReduce program using the Java programming language, store data in HDFS, and perform analysis.

Points to remember

The following list outlines the key takeaways from this chapter:

- **Commercial Hadoop**: Distributions are enterprise versions of Hadoop provided by companies like Cloudera, Hortonworks, MapR, etc. They offer additional tools, support, and enhancements over the standard open-source Hadoop to serve industrial needs better.
- Cloudera is a leading commercial Hadoop distribution that provides a comprehensive big data platform. It integrates Hadoop with enterprise features like security, management tools, and data analytics for large-scale data processing.
- Cloudera QuickStart VMis a pre-configured virtual machine provided by Cloudera that includes Hadoop and the necessary ecosystem tools (e.g., Hive, HBase, etc.). It enables users to quickly set up a Hadoop environment on their local machines for learning or testing.
- Some basic HDFS commands are as follows:
  - **hdfsdfs -ls**: Lists the files and directories in the specified HDFS path.

- **hdfsdfs -mkdir<directory>**: Creates a new directory in the HDFS file system.
- **hdfsdfs -put <local_file><hdfs_directory>**: Uploads a file from the local file system to a directory in HDFS.
- **hdfsdfs -get <hdfs_file><local_directory>**: Downloads a file from HDFS to the local file system.
- **hdfsdfs -copyFromLocal<local_file><hdfs_directory>**: Copies a file from the local file system to HDFS.
- **hdfsdfs -cat <hdfs_file>**: Displays the contents of a file stored in HDFS on the command line.
- **hdfsdfs -touchz<file>**: Creates an empty file in HDFS with zero bytes.
- **hdfsdfs -chmod<permissions><file>**: Changes the file or directory permissions in HDFS (similar to the UNIX chmod command).
- **hdfsdfs -chgrp<group><file>**: Changes the group ownership of a file or directory in HDFS.

Multiple choice questions

1. **What does the Cloudera framework primarily focus on?**
   a. Data analysis b. Cloud computing
   c. Big data management d. Artificial intelligence
2. **Which of the following is not a component of the Cloudera Quickstart VM?**
   a. HDFS b. Spark
   c. Hive d. MySQL
3. **What is the primary purpose of the Cloudera Quickstart VM?**
   a. To provide enterprise-level support for Hadoop
   b. To offer a cloud-based Hadoop environment for big data analysis
   c. To provide a pre-configured virtual machine for setting up a local Hadoop environment
   d. To replace the open-source Hadoop with a more advanced version
4. **What does the du command do in Hadoop shell?**
   a. Displays disk usage of files and directories in HDFS
   b. Deletes files and directories in HDFS
   c. Downloads files from HDFS to the local file system
   d. Uploads files from the local file system to HDFS
5. **Which virtualization platforms are supported by Cloudera Quickstart VM?**
   a. VMware and Hyper-V b. VirtualBox and VMware
   c. Docker and VirtualBox d. XenServer and Hyper-V
6. **Which command is used to list all files and directories in a specific HDFS path?**
   a. hdfsdfs -copyFromLocal b. hdfsdfs -ls
   c. hdfsdfs -mkdir d. hdfsdfs -rm
7. **Which command is used to change the replication factor of a file in HDFS?**
   a. replicate b. setrep
   c. changerep d. adjustrep
8. **What does the command hdfsdfs -touchz do?**
   a. Creates a non-empty file in HDFS
   b. Lists all zero-byte files in HDFS
   c. Creates an empty file with zero bytes in HDFS
   d. Removes a zero-byte file in HDFS

9. **Which of the following commands changes the group ownership of a file in HDFS?**
   a. hdfsdfs -chgrp
   b. hdfsdfs -chmod
   c. hdfsdfs -touchz
   d. hdfsdfs -rm
10. **Which command is used to upload a local file to HDFS?**
   a. hdfsdfs -get
   b. hdfsdfs -put
   c. hdfsdfs -cat
   d. hdfsdfs -rm

Answers

1. c.	2. d.	3. c.	4. b.	5. b.
6. b.	7. c.	8. c.	9. a.	10. b.

Questions

1. What are Commercial Hadoop Distributions, and how do they differ from the open-source Hadoop? Give examples of a few popular commercial distributions and explain what they offer over the open-source version.
2. Why do companies prefer using commercial Hadoop distributions for their big data processing needs?
3. Cloudera is known for its enterprise-level features. Explain the major components of Cloudera that make it stand out from other Hadoop distributions.
4. Identify the limitations of the Cloudera Quickstart VM. Why might it not be suitable for production environments?
5. Using Cloudera Quickstart VM, import a sample dataset into HDFS using the hdfsdfs -put command. Then, verify that the file has been uploaded using the hdfsdfs -ls command.
6. Perform the following operations in HDFS and provide the output:
   - Create a directory named bigdata in HDFS.
   - Upload a local file into the bigdata directory.
   - List all files in the bigdata directory.
   - Delete the file from HDFS.
7. Define HDFS and elaborate on its significance in handling Big Data. Provide examples of basic HDFS commands and their functionalities.
8. Explain the significance of file permissions in HDFS and how they are managed using the chmod and chown commands. Describe the syntax and options available for modifying permissions and ownership of files and directories in HDFS. Discuss the best practices for setting appropriate permissions to ensure data security and access control within a Hadoop cluster.
9. Discuss strategies for uploading, downloading, and manipulating data stored in HDFS using commands such as get, copyToLocal, and tail. Explain how users can transfer data between the local file system and HDFS, as well as extract or view specific portions of files using these commands.
10. Perform the following operations in HDFS and provide the output:
    - Create an empty file named sample.txt in the bigdata directory using the touchz command.
    - Change the permissions of sample.txt to 755 using the chmod command.
    - Change the group ownership of sample.txt to a new group named bigdata-group using the chgrp command.
    - Display the contents of the bigdata directory to verify the changes using the ls command.

Chapter 5
Stock Data Analysis with Cloudera

The world is one big data problem.

— Andrew McAfee

Introduction

This chapter focuses on analyzing big data using Hadoop in the Cloudera framework. It enables you to perform data analysis tasks and leverage the power of big data technology for real-world applications. It provides a step-by-step analysis of stock market data, which includes understanding the nature of stock market data, exporting the stock data into **Hadoop Distributed File System** (**HDFS**) for processing, and executing the map-reduce program in the Hadoop shell. By the end of the chapter, readers will have a complete understanding of storing data in HDFS and will be able to perform stock data analysis using the MapReduce in the Cloudera framework.

Structure

In this chapter, we will cover the following topics:

- Stock market data analysis using Hadoop in Cloudera framework
- Executing a MapReduce Java program to analyze stock data

Objectives

By the end of this chapter, readers will be able to understand the various aspects of stock market data in terms of volume, variety, and velocity. Next, they will learn to write a MapReduce program in the Java programming language for the analysis of stock market data. Readers also learn about the important libraries and implementation of Mapper and reducer functions to read and analyze stock market data. Subsequently, they will understand the process to import jar files and analyze data in the Hadoop shell. They will also have a complete understanding of storing data in HDFS and will be able to perform stock data analysis using the MapReduce framework in the Cloudera framework.

Stock market data analysis using Hadoop in Cloudera framework

Stock market data consists of the information collected and recorded about a particular stock traded on a stock exchange. This data typically includes various metrics and attributes that describe the performance and characteristics of the stock. Stock data is considered big data, as it deals with large volumes of historical data from multiple stocks traded on various exchanges over extended periods. This happens due to the following reasons:

- **Volume**: The total volume of stock market data generated daily is massive, with millions of transactions occurring on exchanges worldwide.

- **Variety:** Stock market data comes in various formats, including structured data (e.g., price and volume data) and unstructured data (e.g., news articles, social media sentiment).
- **Velocity:** Stock market data is quickly generated and updated, especially during trading hours when transactions occur in real time.

Stock data analysis often involves complex computations, statistical modeling, and **machine learning** (**ML**) algorithms to extract insights and predict market movements. Despite the challenges of handling big data, the insights derived from analyzing stock market data are highly valuable for investors, traders, financial institutions, and policymakers. Harnessing the power of big data analytics enables better decision-making and risk management in the financial markets. Therefore, stock market data is used here to answer the following queries for traders:

- *What is the maximum value of the closing price for a company from Feb 20, 2006, to Oct 9,2015?*
- *What is the minimum closing price value for a company from Feb 20, 2006 to Oct 9,2015?*
- *What is the maximum value of the opening price for a company from Feb 20, 2006 to Oct 9,2015?*
- *What is the minimum closing price value for a company from Feb 20, 2006 to Oct 9,2015?*

Figure 5.1 shows the sample data that is analyzed to answer the queries provided:

```
samplestockdata - Notepad
File  Edit  Format  View  Help
A,1999-11-18,45.5,50.0,40.0,44.0,44739900.0,0.0,1.0,43.365904292779,47.654839882174,38.12387190574,41.936259096314,44739900.0
A,1999-11-19,42.94,43.0,39.81,40.38,10897100.0,0.0,1.0,40.925976490811,40.98316229867,37.942783514187,38.486048688844,10897100.0
A,1999-11-22,41.31,44.0,40.06,44.0,4705200.0,0.0,1.0,39.372428710653,41.936259096314,38.181057713598,41.936259096314,4705200.0
A,1999-11-23,42.5,43.63,40.25,40.25,4274400.0,0.0,1.0,40.506613899848,41.583613281185,38.36214610515,38.36214610515,4274400.0
A,1999-11-24,40.13,41.94,40.0,41.06,3464400.0,0.0,1.0,38.247774489433,39.972879693168,38.12387190574,39.13415451124,3464400.0
A,1999-11-26,40.88,41.5,40.75,41.19,1237100.0,0.0,1.0,38.962597087666,39.553517102205,38.838694503972,39.258057094935,1237100.0
A,1999-11-29,41.0,42.44,40.56,42.13,2914700.0,0.0,1.0,39.076968703383,40.44942809199,38.65760611242,40.15396808472,2914700.0
A,1999-11-30,42.0,42.94,40.94,42.19,3083000.0,0.0,1.0,40.030065501027,40.925976490811,39.019782895524,40.211153892579,3083000.0
A,1999-12-01,42.19,43.44,41.88,42.94,2115400.0,0.0,1.0,40.211153892579,41.402524889633,39.915693885309,40.925976490811,2115400.0
A,1999-12-02,43.75,45.0,43.19,44.13,2195900.0,0.0,1.0,41.697984896903,42.889355893957,41.164250690222,42.060161680007,2195900.0
A,1999-12-03,44.94,45.69,44.31,44.5,2175700.0,0.0,1.0,42.832170086098,43.546992684331,42.231719103583,42.412807495135,2175700.0
A,1999-12-06,45.25,46.44,45.19,45.75,1610000.0,0.0,1.0,43.127630093368,44.261815282564,43.070444285509,43.60417849219,1610000.0
A,1999-12-07,45.75,46.0,44.31,45.25,1585100.0,0.0,1.0,43.60417849219,43.842452691601,42.231719103583,43.127630093368,1585100.0
A,1999-12-08,45.25,45.63,44.81,45.19,1350400.0,0.0,1.0,43.127630093368,43.489806876472,42.708267502405,43.070444285509,1350400.0
A,1999-12-09,45.25,45.94,45.25,45.81,1451400.0,0.0,1.0,43.127630093368,43.785266883742,43.127630093368,43.661364300048,1451400.0
A,1999-12-10,45.69,45.94,44.75,44.75,1190800.0,0.0,1.0,43.546992684331,43.785266883742,42.651081694546,42.651081694546,1190800.0
A,1999-12-13,45.5,46.25,44.38,45.5,2875900.0,0.0,1.0,43.365904292779,44.080726891011,42.298435879418,43.365904292779,2875900.0
A,1999-12-14,45.38,45.38,42.06,43.0,1665900.0,0.0,1.0,43.251532677062,43.251532677062,40.087251308885,40.98316229867,1665900.0
A,1999-12-15,42.0,42.31,41.0,41.69,2087100.0,0.0,1.0,40.030065501027,40.325525508296,39.076968703383,39.734605493757,2087100.0
A,1999-12-16,42.0,48.0,42.0,47.25,1848300.0,0.0,1.0,40.030065501027,45.748646286887,40.030065501027,45.033823688655,1848300.0
A,2000-02-15,76.56,83.0,76.56,81.88,1443200.0,0.0,1.0,72.969090827586,79.10703420441,72.969090827586,78.039565791049,1443200.0
A,2000-02-16,80.0,81.88,79.38,81.0,1288800.0,0.0,1.0,76.247743811479,78.039565791049,75.65682379694,77.200840609123,1288800.0
A,2000-02-17,81.0,97.0,77.63,97.0,675900.0,0.0,1.0,77.200840609123,92.450389371418,73.988904401064,92.450389371418,675900.0
A,2000-02-18,88.5,95.88,88.06,93.75,2904200.0,0.0,1.0,84.349066591449,91.382920958058,83.929704000486,89.35282477907,2904200.0
A,2000-02-22,96.0,97.38,90.0,91.5,1593700.0,0.0,1.0,91.497292573775,92.812566154523,85.778711787914,87.208356984379,1593700.0
```

***Figure 5.1**: Sample stock market data*

MapReduce program in Java for stock data analysis

This Java program leverages Hadoop MapReduce to analyze stock data by performing aggregation operations such as average, minimum, or maximum on specified fields within a given date range. It is designed to be executed on a Hadoop cluster, processing large volumes of stock data efficiently in a distributed manner. The following points explain the way to implement mapper and reducer functions for implementing a MapReduce program in Java. The program is written to answer the queries mentioned in the preceding section:

- **Import libraries:** This section imports necessary Java and Hadoop libraries for file handling, date parsing, configuration, mapping, reducing, **input/output** (**I/O**) handling, exception handling, data parsing, string manipulation, Hadoop configuration, and MapReduce job setup. Refer to the following code:

```
import java.io.File;
import java.io.IOException;
import java.text.ParseException;
import java.text.SimpleDateFormat;
import java.util.ArrayList;
import java.util.Arrays;
import java.util.Date;
import java.util.List;
import java.util.Scanner;
import java.util.StringTokenizer;

import org.apache.hadoop.conf.Configuration;
import org.apache.hadoop.fs.File system;
import org.apache.hadoop.fs.Path;
import org.apache.hadoop.io.FloatWritable;
import org.apache.hadoop.io.Text;
import org.apache.hadoop.mapreduce.Job;
import org.apache.hadoop.mapreduce.Mapper;
import org.apache.hadoop.mapreduce.Reducer;
import org.apache.hadoop.mapreduce.lib.input.FileInputFormat;
import org.apache.hadoop.mapreduce.lib.output.FileOutputFormat;
```

- **Mapper class -StockAnalyzerMapper:** This class extends the Mapper class, where it takes key-value pairs (input key type `Object`, input value type `Text`) and emits intermediate key-value pairs (`Text`, `FloatWritable`). This class contains the following methods:
  - **Mapper- setup() method**: This method is called once at the beginning of the mapper task. It retrieves configuration parameters such as the field name, start date, and end date. Here, the field name refers to the closing or opening price, and the start and end dates refer to the duration for which the user wants to analyze the data from the given dataset.
  - **Map function**: This method processes each input record and emits key-value pairs based on specified criteria. This method is called for each key value pair in the input data. It parses the input data, extracts the required fields (close, low, high), and emits intermediate key-value pairs based on the specified date range.

    Refer to the following code:

```
public static class StockAnalyzerMapper
   extends Mapper<Object, Text, Text, FloatWritable>{

private static FloatWritablemappedValue = null;
private Text ticker = new Text();
private String startDate, endDate, fieldName;

@Override
protected void setup(Mapper<Object, Text, Text,
FloatWritable>.Context context)
```

```
                    throws IOException, InterruptedException {
                Configuration conf = context.getConfiguration();
        this.fieldName = conf.get("field_name");
        this.startDate = conf.get("start_date");
        this.endDate = conf.get("end_date");
        super.setup(context);
              }

                    public void map(Object key, Text value, Context context
                        ) throwsIOException, InterruptedException {
                String inputString = value.toString();
        String[] inputRecord = inputString.split(",");
                int columnIndex = 0;
                if (fieldName.equals("close")) {
        columnIndex = 5;
                }
                if (fieldName.equals("low")) {
        columnIndex = 4;
                }
                if (fieldName.equals("high")) {
        columnIndex = 3;
                }
        SimpleDateFormatcsvDateFormat = new SimpleDateFormat("yyyy-MM-dd");
        SimpleDateFormatuserInputDateFormat = new
        SimpleDateFormat("MM/dd/yyyy");
                Date start = null, end = null, current = null;
                try {
                        start = userInputDateFormat.parse(startDate);
                        end = userInputDateFormat.parse(endDate);
                        current = csvDateFormat.parse(inputRecord[1]);
                    } catch (ParseException e) {
        e.printStackTrace();
                    }

                if ((current.after(start) &&current.before(end)) ||
        current.equals(start) || current.equals(end)) {
        ticker.set(inputRecord[0]);
        mappedValue = new
        FloatWritable(Float.parseFloat(inputRecord[columnIndex]));
        context.write(ticker, mappedValue);
                }
          }
```

- **Reducer class-AggregatorReducer**: This class extends Hadoop's Reducer class and defines the logic for the reducing phase of MapReduce. It receives key-value pairs (input key type **`Text`**, input value type **`FloatWritable`**) from mappers, aggregates them based on keys, and emits final output key-value pairs (**`Text`**, **`FloatWritable`**). This class contains:
  - **Reducer setup:** Similar to the Mapper setup, this method initializes variables and configurations before the reducing task begins.
  - **Reduce function:** This method processes key-value pairs received from mappers and performs aggregation operations based on the specified aggregation operator (e.g., average, minimum, maximum). This method aggregates the values based on the aggregation operator for each key (stock ticker) specified at run time by the user.

  Refer to the following code to understand the same:

```
public static class AggregatorReducer
                extends Reducer<Text,FloatWritable,Text,FloatWritable> {
            private FloatWritable result = new FloatWritable();
            private String aggregationOperator;

            @Override
            protected void setup(
                        Reducer<Text, FloatWritable, Text, FloatWritable>.Context
context)
                        throws IOException, InterruptedException {
                Configuration conf = context.getConfiguration();
this.aggregationOperator = conf.get("aggregation_operator");
super.setup(context);
            }

            public void reduce(Text key, Iterable<FloatWritable> values,
                                Context context
                                ) throwsIOException, InterruptedException {
              if (aggregationOperator == "avg") {
                  float sum = 0.0f;
                  int count = 0;
                  for (FloatWritableval : values) {
                        sum += val.get();
                        count++;
                    }
                  sum /= count;
System.out.println("avg"+sum);
result.set(sum);
context.write(key, result);

              }
              if (aggregationOperator == "min") {
```

```
                float min = Float.MAX_VALUE;
                for (FloatWritableval : values) {
                      min = Math.min(min, val.get());
                    }
System.out.println("min"+min);
result.set(min);
context.write(key, result);
            }
            if (aggregationOperator == "max") {
                float max = Float.MIN_VALUE;
                for (FloatWritableval : values) {
                      max = Math.max(max, val.get());
                    }
System.out.println("max"+max);
result.set(max);
context.write(key, result);
            }
        }
```

- **Main method:** This is the entry point of the program. It sets up the Hadoop job, configures it, and executes it. It contains:
  - **Configuration setup:** It sets up configuration parameters based on the command-line arguments. It also configures the MapReduce job with appropriate classes, input/output key-value types, and a number of reduced tasks. It loads the Hadoop configuration from **`core-site.xml`** and **`hdfs-site.xml`**.
  - **Command line arguments parsing:** This code checks the number and validity of command-line arguments passed by the user at run time.
  - **Job setup:** It is used to create a new MapReduce job **`instance(Job job = Job.getInstance(conf, "analyze stock"))`**.
    - **Mapper class (StockAnalyzerMapper.class):** It defines the logic for processing input records. Each record is processed and transformed into key-value pairs.
    - **Combiner (AggregatorReducer.class):** The combiner is an optional optimization step. It performs partial aggregation of the mapper output before sending it to the reducer. This reduces the amount of data to be shuffled across the network.
    - **Reducer class (AggregatorReducer.class):** It performs the final aggregation of key-value pairs and outputs the final processed result.
- **Input and output format setup**: This code specifies the output key and value classes:
  - **`FileInputFormat.addInputPath(job, new Path(inputPath))`:**
    - It sets the **input path** where the job will read data from.
    - **`inputPath`** is a variable containing the location of the input dataset (e.g., HDFS path: **`"hdfs://namenode:9000/input/stocks.csv"`**).
  - **`FileOutputFormat.setOutputPath(job, new Path(args[2]))`:**
    - It defines the output path where the processed results will be stored. It is important to note that the output directory must not exist before running the job, or Hadoop will throw an error.

  - `args[2]` represents a command-line argument provided when running the job (e.g., `"hdfs://namenode:9000/output/results"`).

- **Hadoop file system setup**: This retrieves the Hadoop file system instance associated with the job's configuration (`conf`). It enables you to interact with HDFS, such as checking if a file exists, deleting an existing output directory before running the job, and reading/writing files in HDFS.
- **Job execution**: This code submits the job to the Hadoop cluster for execution and waits for it to complete. It returns `true` if the job executes successfully, otherwise `false`.

  Refer to the following code:

```
                public static void main(String[] args) throws Exception
{
                Configuration conf = new Configuration(); // Creates a Hadoop configuration
object.
for(int i=0; i<args.length;i++)
System.out.println(args[i]+" arguments."+ i);
                if (args.length< 7) {
            for(int i=0; i<args.length;i++)
System.out.println(args[i]+"Insufficient arguments.");
System.exit(1);
                }
// Command Line arguments parsing
                if (args.length> 7) {
            for(int i=0; i<args.length;i++)
System.out.println(args[i]+"too many arguments.");
System.exit(1);
                }
                if (!(args[5].equals("min") || args[5].equals("max") ||
args[5].equals("avg"))) {
System.out.println("Invalid arguments.");
System.exit(1);
                }
                if (!(args[6].equals("close") || args[6].equals("low") ||
args[6].equals("high"))) {
System.out.println("Invalid arguments.");
System.exit(1);
                }
// Configuration setup
conf.set("start_date", args[3]);
conf.set("end_date", args[4]);
conf.set("aggregation_operator", args[5]);
conf.set("field_name", args[6]);
// This code sets up a Hadoop MapReduce job to analyze stock data.
                Job job = Job.getInstance(conf, "analyze stock");
job.setJarByClass(AnalyzeStock.class);
```

```
// Mapper, Combiner, and Reducer Setup
job.setMapperClass(StockAnalyzerMapper.class);
job.setCombinerClass(AggregatorReducer.class);
job.setReducerClass(AggregatorReducer.class);
// Input and Output Key-Value Format
job.setOutputKeyClass(Text.class);
job.setOutputValueClass(FloatWritable.class);
// Setting the Number of Reducers
job.setNumReduceTasks(1);

// Hadoop File System Setup
File system hdfs = File system.get(conf);
            String inputPath = args[1];
            if (hdfs.exists(new Path(inputPath))) {
FileInputFormat.addInputPath(job, new Path(inputPath));
                }
                else {  System.out.println(inputPath + " doesn't exist.");
System.exit(1);
                }
FileOutputFormat.setOutputPath(job, new Path(args[2]));
            if (hdfs.exists(new Path(args[5])))
hdfs.delete(new Path(args[5]), true);
// Job Execution
System.exit(job.waitForCompletion(true) ? 0 : 1);}}

    // Command line arguments validation
System.exit(1);
}
```

Executing a MapReduce Java program to analyze stock data

Follow these steps to execute a MapReduce Java program to analyze stock data:

1. Go to **Applications** | **System Tools** | **File Browser**, as shown in *Figure 5.2*:

Figure 5.2: *Steps to open file browser in Cloudera*

2. Go to the desktop; double-click on the Eclipse icon, and the Eclipse IDE appears, as shown in *Figure 5.3*:

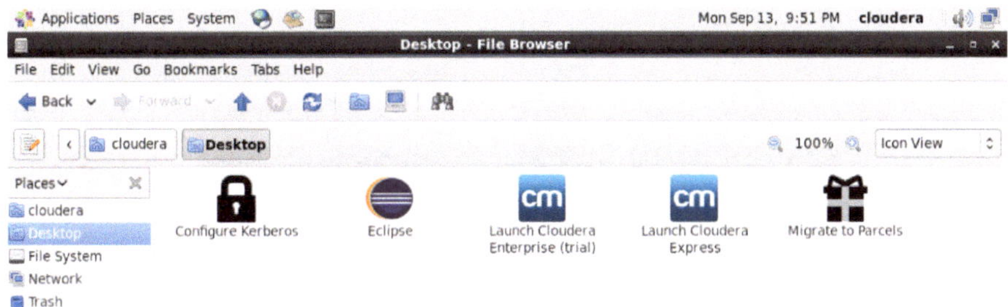

***Figure 5.3**: Location to open Eclipse in Cloudera*

3. **File | New | Java Project |** specify any name for the project **`StockAnalysis`** and click on **Next**. The same is illustrated in *Figure 5.4*:

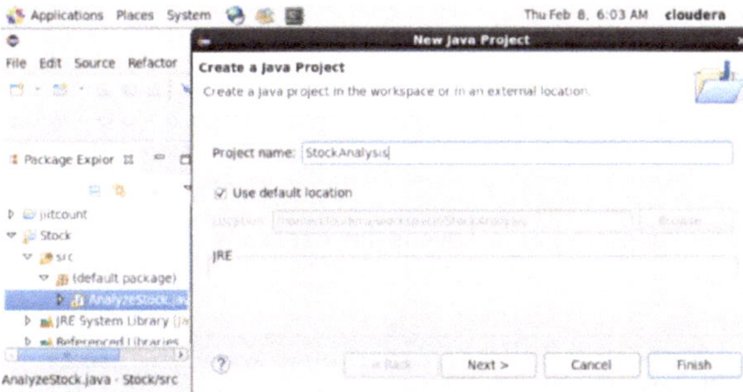

***Figure 5.4**: Create Java project in Eclipse*

4. Click **Next**, and a new window will appear; click on **Libraries | Add External JARs**, as shown in *Figure 5.5*:

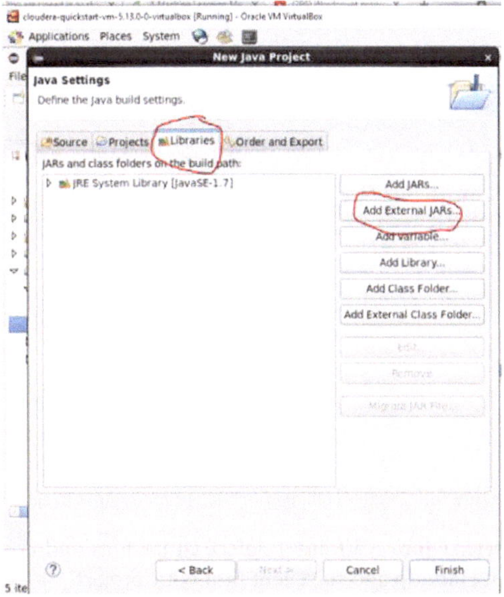

***Figure 5.5**: Import libraries in an Eclipse project*

5. Refer to *Figure 5.6* to import files, go to **File System** | **usr** | **lib** | **hadoop**:

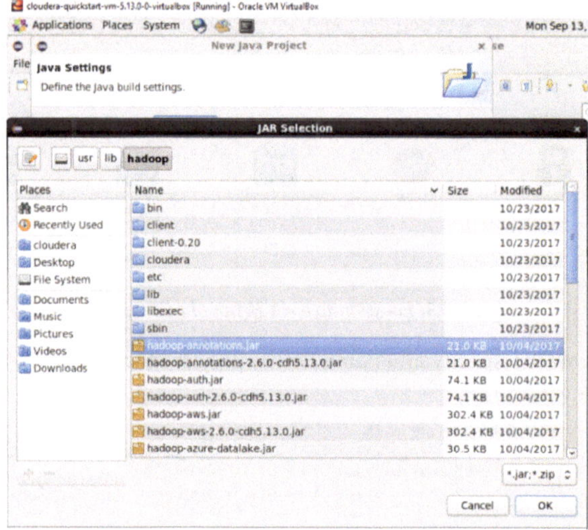

Figure 5.6: Import Hadoop libraries in the Eclipse project

6. Next, select all JAR files beginning from **`hadoop-annotations.jar`** till the end and click **Ok**, as shown in *Figure 5.7*:

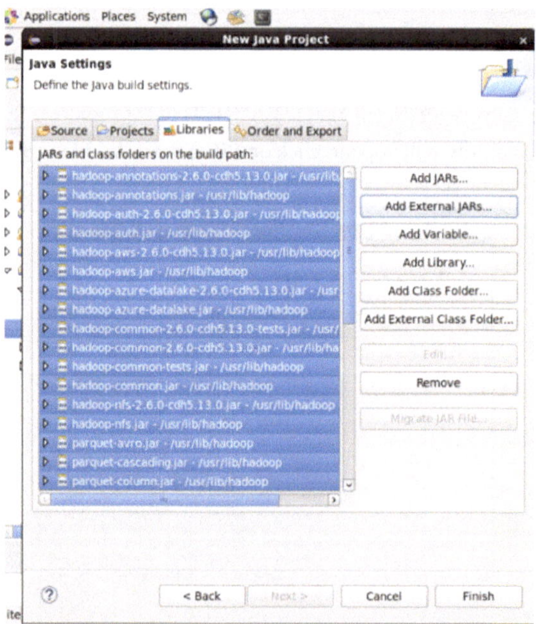

Figure 5.7: Import Hadoop libraries in the Eclipse project

7. Again, click on **Add External Jars** | **Client** | select all jar files and click **OK**, and then click **Finish**. It includes all JAR files from Hadoop and the client into your project.

8. Next, to create a class for writing the Java program, click on **AnalyzeStock** | **Src** | **New** | **Class**, as shown in *Figure 5.8*:

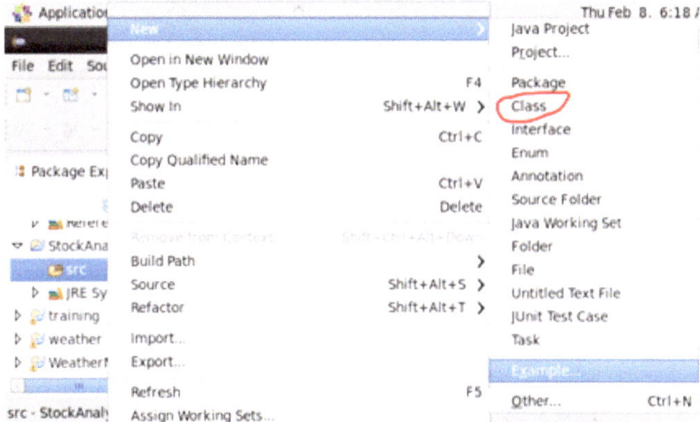

***Figure 5.8**: Create a Java class in an Eclipse project*

9. Assign a name to your class; you can specify any name and click **Finish**, as shown in *Figure 5.9*:

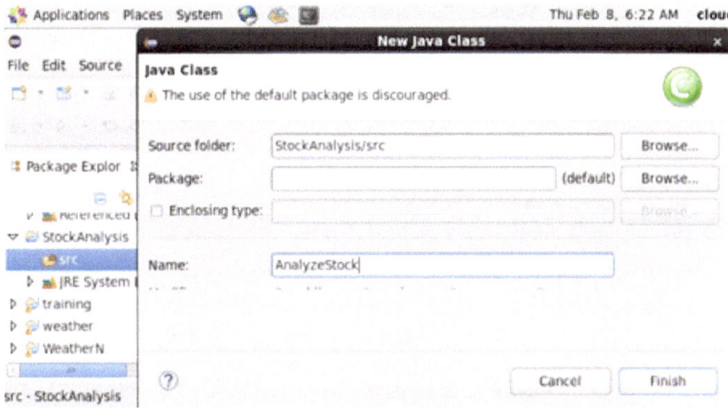

***Figure 5.9**: Assign a class name in an Eclipse project*

10. As shown in *Figure 5.10*, you are ready to write a MapReduce program for analyzing the stock data:

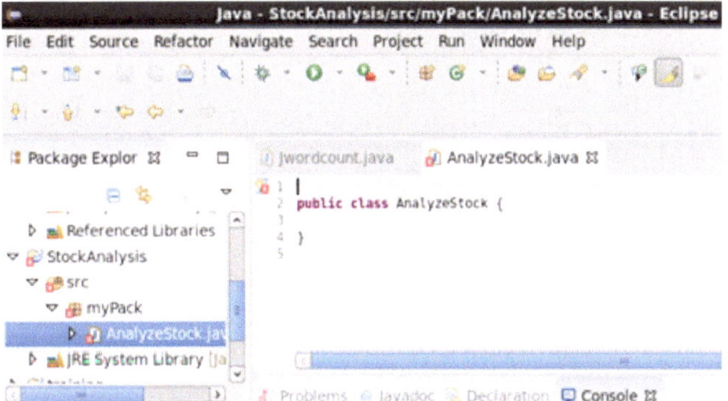

***Figure 5.10**: Window to write a Java program for data analysis*

11. After writing the Java program, compile and export the JAR file of your code in the Cloudera environment, as shown in *Figure 5.11*:

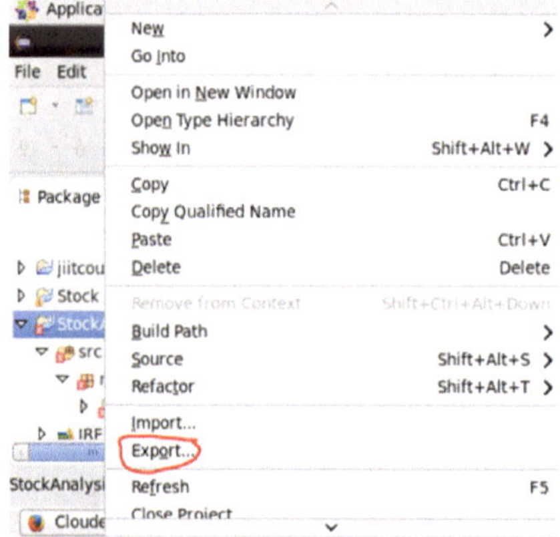

***Figure 5.11**: Steps to export the project*

12. After clicking on **Export**, a new window appears, which is also illustrated in the following figure:

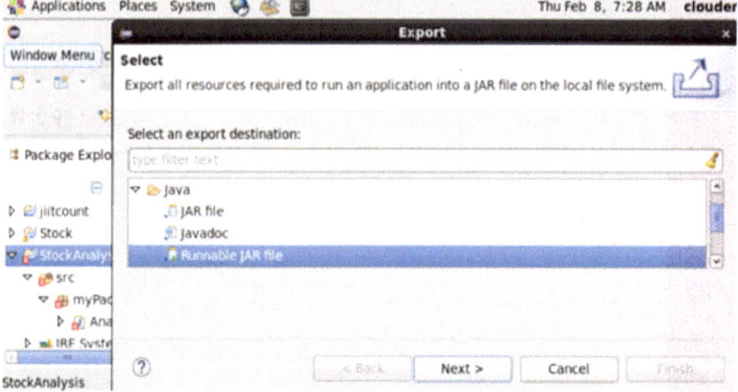

***Figure 5.12**: Steps to choose a JAR file*

13. Select the runnable JAR file and click **Next**, and the new window appears, as illustrated in *Figure 5.13*. In the new window, select **AnalyzeStock** and **Browse**:

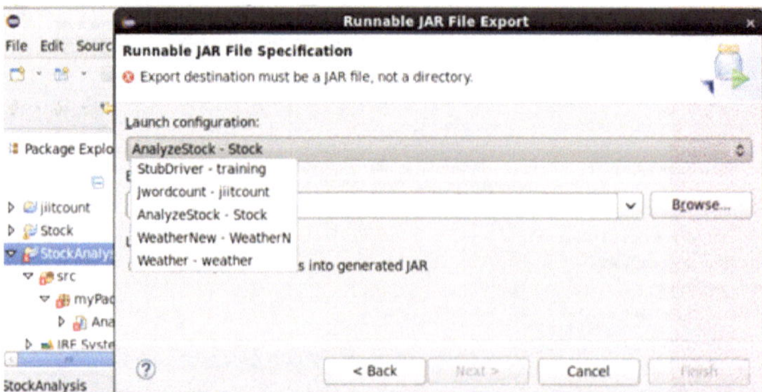

***Figure 5.13**: Select AnalyzeStock project*

14. Once you click on **Browse**, a new window appears. Select **Cloudera** | change the name of the JAR file to **Stock** (in this example), click **OK**, and click **Finish**:

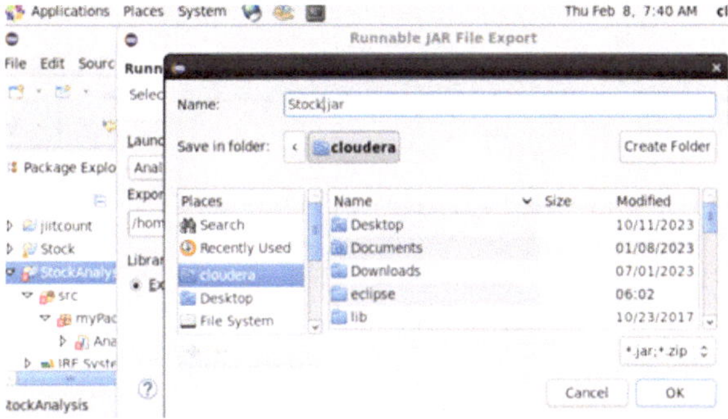

Figure 5.14: Stock.jar file of AnalyzeStock project in the Cloudera file system

15. Next, to verify that the JAR file created by you is exported in the Cloudera folder, go to **File System** | **Home** | **cloudera** | **Stock.jar** is imported:

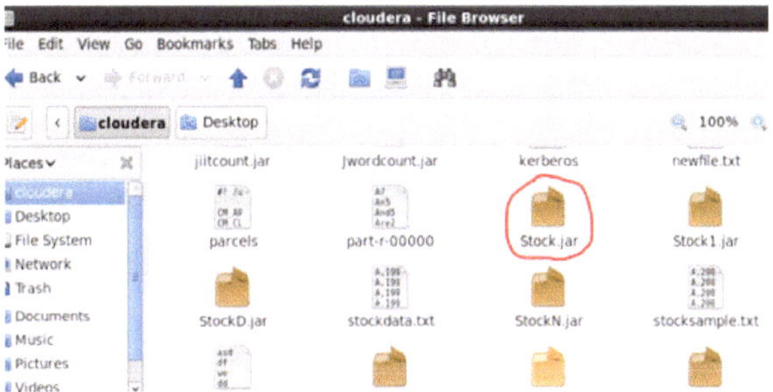

Figure 5.15: Steps to verify the export of the Stock.jar file to the Hadoop file system in Cloudera

Export stock data in HDFS

Follow these steps to export stock data in HDFS:

1. The next step is to export stock data to HDFS. The stock data may be downloaded from the **World Wide Web (WWW)**.
2. Open the terminal, as illustrated in *Figure 5.16*, of Cloudera (given on top) and just click to open:

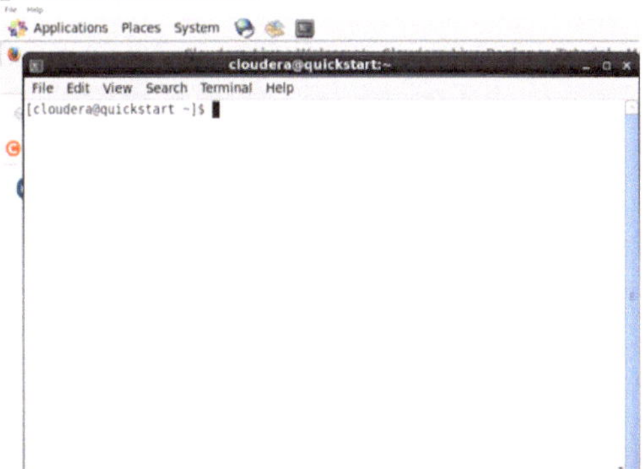

Figure 5.16: Steps to open Shell in Cloudera

a. Use the **`ls`** command (**`hdfs dfs -ls/`** to see the files and directories in Cloudera, **`stock.jar`** file, and the **`samplestockdata.txt`**). Refer to *Figure 5.17:*

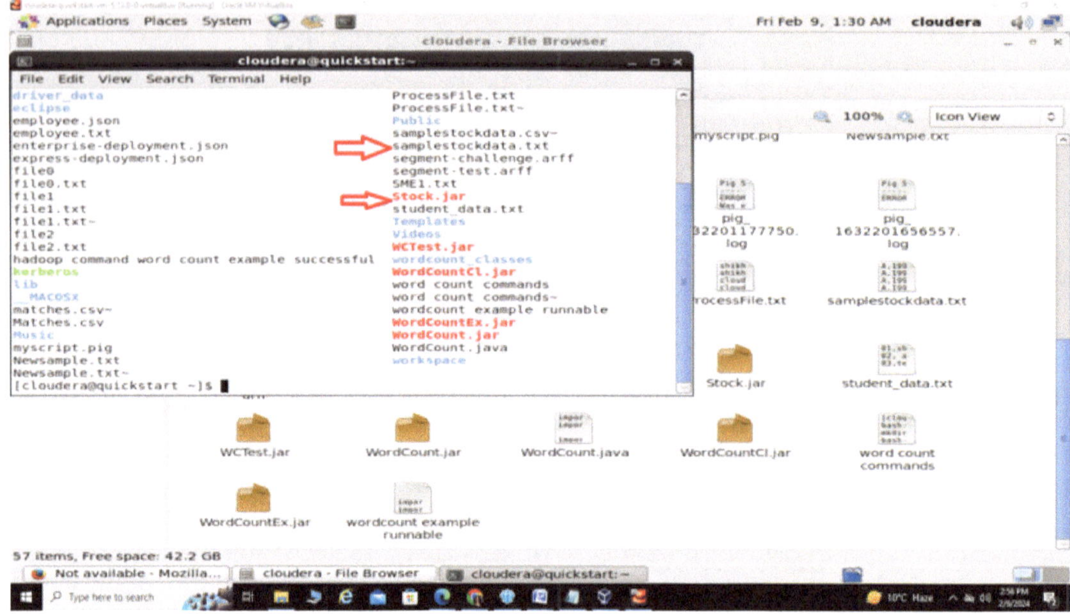

Figure 5.17: List of files and directories in Hadoop file system

3. Next, create two folders, one for the input file and another for the output file, as **`stockinput`** and **`stockoutput`**. Move the **`samplestockdata.txt`** file from the local file system to **`stockinput`** directory. The same can be verified by using **`ls`** command, as shown in *Figure 5.18*.

   Refer to the following code:

```
hdfs dfs -mkdir /stockinput
hdfs dfs -mkdir /stockoutput
hdfs dfs -put  samplestockdata.txt /stockinput
hdfs dfs -ls  /stockinput
```

   Note: If you get safe mode errors, run this command and then create a directory: `hdfs  dfsadmin -safemode leave`

4. If access is denied for the **`root`** user. Superuser privilege is required; try the following code:

   Login as root service

   Password: **`cloudera`**

   Next execute

```
sudo -u hdfs hdfs dfsadmin -safemode leave
sudo -u hdfs Hadoop fs -mkdir /stockinput
```

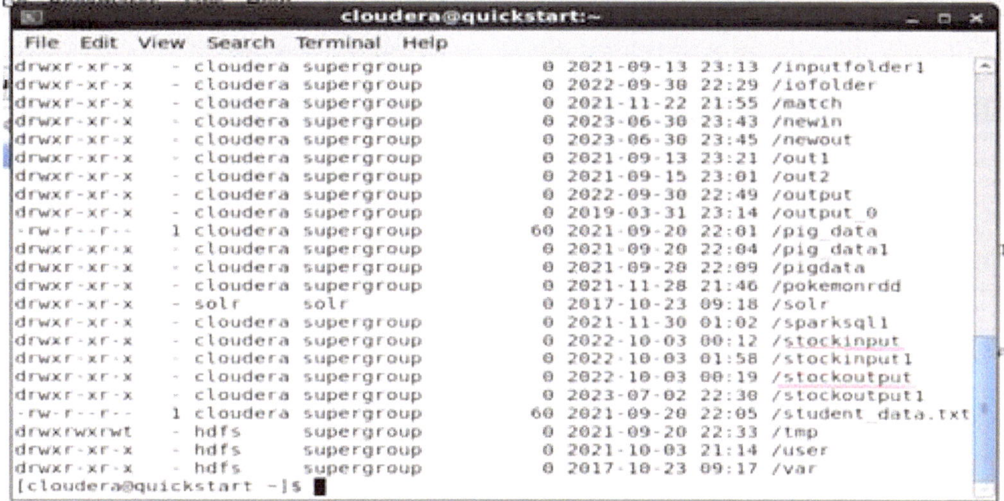

Figure 5.18: Verification in stockinput and stockoutput folders of the Hadoop file system

5. Next, execute the **Hadoop jar command,** as shown in *Figure 5.19*. It is used to run a Hadoop MapReduce job packaged as a JAR file. The following list provides a breakdown of each part of the command and its function:

```
hadoop jar /home/cloudera/Stock.jar AnalyzeStock 02/20/2006 10/09/2015 min close /stockinput/
samplestockdata.txt /stockoutput1
```

- **hadoop jar**: This is the command to execute a JAR file that contains a Hadoop MapReduce job.
- **/home/cloudera/Stock.jar**: The path to the JAR file that contains the compiled MapReduce program.
- **AnalyzeStock**: The main class inside the JAR file that contains the `main()` method and executes the MapReduce job.
- **02/20/2006 10/09/2015**: These are arguments passed to the program that define the date range for filtering stock data.
- **min close**: These two arguments specify that the program should analyze the minimum closing price of stocks.
- **/stockinput/samplestockdata.txt**: The input file path in HDFS where the stock market data is stored.
- **/stockoutput1**: The output directory in HDFS where the results of the analysis will be saved.

Figure 5.19 shows the different stages of MapReduce jobs completed over time, and finally, the job is completed successfully:

```
Applications Places System
cloudera@quickstart:~
File Edit View Search Terminal Help
[cloudera@quickstart ~]$ hadoop jar /home/cloudera/Stock.jar AnalyzeStock 02/20/
2006 10/09/2015 min close /stockinput1/samplestockdata.txt /stockoutput1
23/07/02 22:28:30 INFO client.RMProxy: Connecting to ResourceManager at /0.0.0.0
:8032
23/07/02 22:28:31 WARN mapreduce.JobResourceUploader: Hadoop command-line option
 parsing not performed. Implement the Tool interface and execute your applicatio
n with ToolRunner to remedy this.
23/07/02 22:28:31 INFO input.FileInputFormat: Total input paths to process : 1
23/07/02 22:28:31 WARN hdfs.DFSClient: Caught exception
java.lang.InterruptedException
        at java.lang.Object.wait(Native Method)
        at java.lang.Thread.join(Thread.java:1281)
        at java.lang.Thread.join(Thread.java:1355)
        at org.apache.hadoop.hdfs.DFSOutputStream$DataStreamer.closeResponder(DF
SOutputStream.java:967)
        at org.apache.hadoop.hdfs.DFSOutputStream$DataStreamer.endBlock(DFSOutpu
tStream.java:705)
        at org.apache.hadoop.hdfs.DFSOutputStream$DataStreamer.run(DFSOutputStre
am.java:894)
23/07/02 22:28:31 INFO mapreduce.JobSubmitter: number of splits:1
23/07/02 22:28:31 INFO mapreduce.JobSubmitter: Submitting tokens for job: job_16
88360848437_0001
23/07/02 22:28:32 INFO impl.YarnClientImpl: Submitted application application_16
88360848437_0001
23/07/02 22:28:32 INFO mapreduce.Job: The url to track the job: http://quickstar
t.cloudera:8088/proxy/application_1688360848437_0001/
23/07/02 22:28:32 INFO mapreduce.Job: Running job: job_1688360848437_0001
23/07/02 22:28:43 INFO mapreduce.Job: Job job_1688360848437_0001 running in uber
 mode : false
23/07/02 22:28:43 INFO mapreduce.Job:  map 0% reduce 0%
23/07/02 22:28:52 INFO mapreduce.Job:  map 100% reduce 0%
23/07/02 22:29:01 INFO mapreduce.Job:  map 100% reduce 100%
23/07/02 22:29:02 INFO mapreduce.Job: Job job_1688360848437_0001 completed succe
ssfully
```

***Figure 5.19**: MapReduce program execution for stock data analysis*

6. This is a Hadoop MapReduce job execution command. It executes a MapReduce program that processes large-scale stock market data in a distributed environment. The JAR file contains compiled Java code, including the Mapper and Reducer functions, which process the stock data to extract meaningful insights (such as the minimum closing price within a given date range).
7. *Figure 5.20* shows the volume of stock data read from HDFS and the amount of time spent completing the map-reduce jobs. It also provides information about the number of map input records, combiners, shuffle size, and reduced output records:

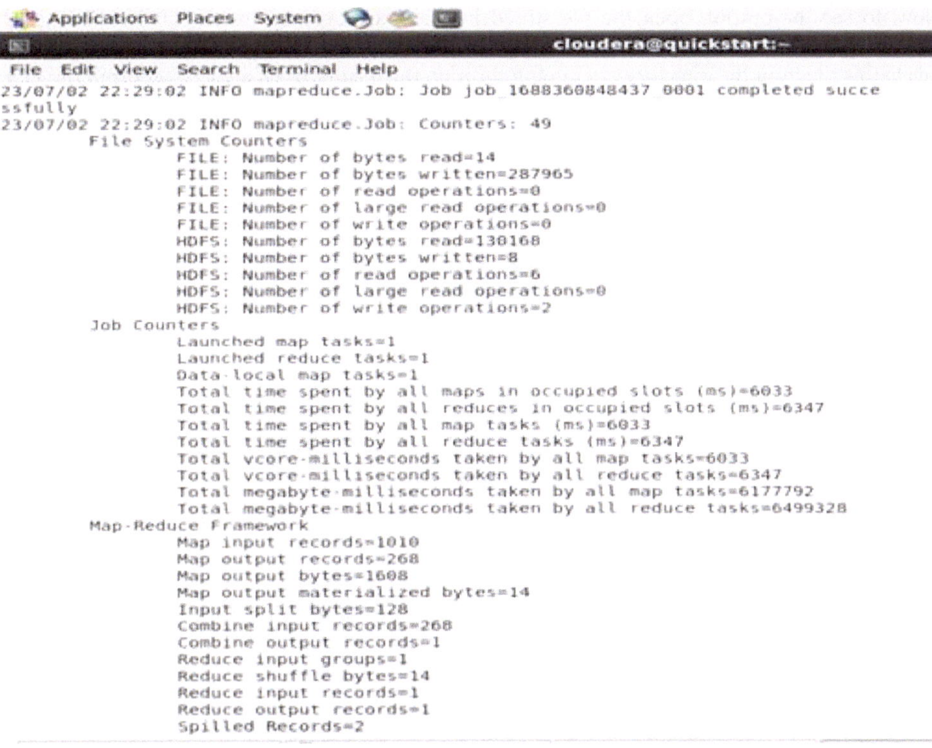

***Figure 5.20**: HDFS data readand MapReduce job processing*

8. *Figure 5.21* shows the final stage of Hadoop job processing with details on memory utilization, errors (if any) that occurred at any stage:

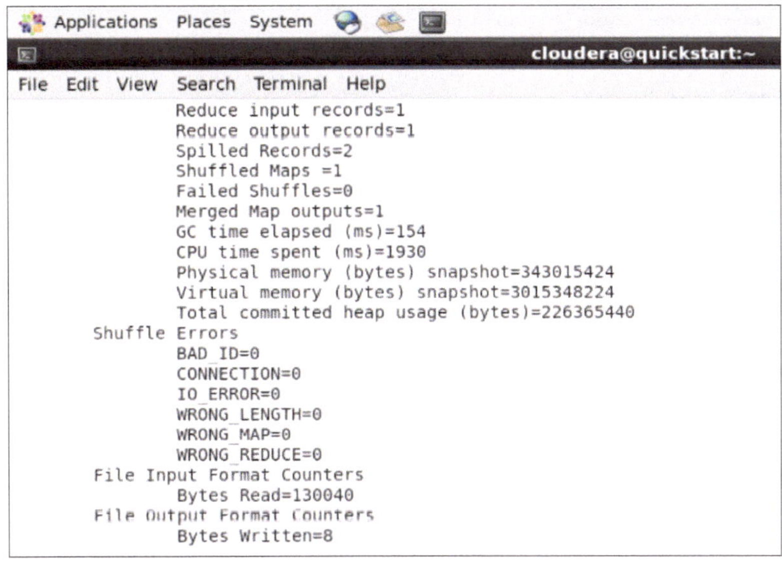

***Figure 5.21**: MapReduce program execution for stock data analysis*

9. Now, to see the output, open the file stored in the stockoutput1 directory. It is to be noted that the **part-r-00000** file is created automatically by the file system and always with the same name. Therefore, delete this file from the directory after going through the results, or create a new output directory to store the output for the subsequent execution.
10. *Figure 5.22* shows the minimum closing price of stock after execution. Execute the following command to see the output:

```
hdfs dfs -cat /stockoutput1/part-r-00000
```

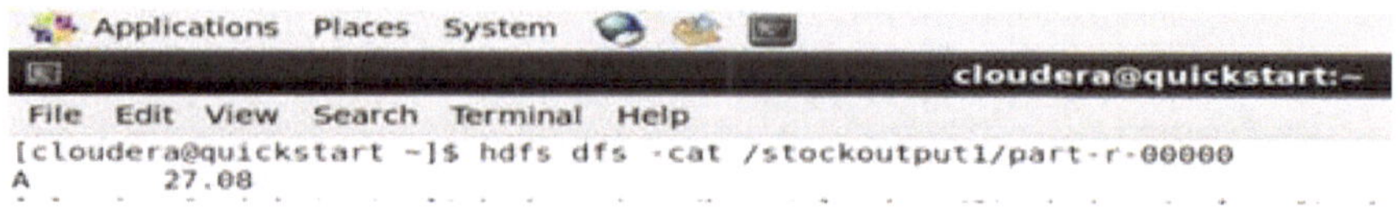

***Figure 5.22**: Output of the minimum closing price of the stock during the given period*

11. You can execute the same program any number of times for different queries, e.g., to find the maximum closing price of stock during the same period as shown in *Figure 5.23*.

```
hadoop jar /home/cloudera/Stock.jar AnalyzeStock 02/20/2006 10/09/2015 min close /
stockinput/samplestockdata.txt /stockoutput1
```

***Figure 5.23**: Program execution for the maximum closing price*

12. The output for this query can be seen by executing the same command (**hdfs dfs -cat /stockoutput1/part-r-00000**) as shown in *Figure 5.24*:

***Figure 5.24**: Output for the maximum closing price of the stock during the given period*

Conclusion

In this chapter, you learned to analyze big data using Hadoop within the Cloudera framework. By following a structured approach, you gained hands-on experience handling stock market data, from data ingestion into HDFS to executing MapReduce programs for analysis. You have developed the ability to write MapReduce programs in the Java programming language, which enables you to leverage big data technologies for real-world scenarios.

In the next chapter, you will learn about Apache Pig, a high-level scripting language for analyzing large datasets in Apache Hadoop. It provides a straightforward way to process and analyze big data without the need for complex MapReduce code.

Points to remember

The following list outlines the key takeaways from this chapter:

- Utilize Cloudera's suite of tools to manage and analyze large datasets, allowing for scalable and efficient stock market data processing.

- Understand the data's structure, including key metrics like prices, volume, and timestamps, to identify trends and patterns relevant to trading strategies.
- Use HDFS commands like hdfs dfs -ls, hdfs dfs -put, and hdfs dfs -get to navigate, upload, and download data within the HDFS.
- Submit and monitor jobs using tools like Hadoop jars to process data through distributed computing frameworks, optimizing performance for large-scale stock data analysis.
- Write and compile a Java program that uses the MapReduce paradigm to filter, sort, and summarize stock data across multiple nodes.
- Load stock data into HDFS using commands and enable it to be processed in a distributed environment.
- Step includes compiling the Java program, creating a jar file, submitting it to the Hadoop cluster using the Hadoop jar command, and analyzing the output to gain insights into stock trends.

Multiple choice questions

1. **What is the first step in analyzing stock data using Cloudera's Hadoop ecosystem?**
   a. Visualizing the data
   b. Exporting data into HDFS
   c. Running a MapReduce job
   d. Writing SQL queries
2. **Which component of Cloudera is primarily used for managing and analyzing large datasets?**
   a. Cloudera Navigator
   b. Cloudera Impala
   c. Cloudera Manager
   d. Cloudera Data Science Workbench
3. **Which command is used to list files in a Hadoop Distributed File System (HDFS) directory?**
   a. hdfs dfs -put
   b. hdfs dfs -get
   c. hdfs dfs -ls
   d. hdfs dfs -copyFromLocal
4. **What is the purpose of a MapReduce program in stock data analysis?**
   a. To visualize stock data
   b. To store stock data
   c. To process and analyze large volumes of stock data
   d. To clean and format stock data
5. **Which Java class is essential for writing a MapReduce program in Hadoop?**
   a. Mapper
   b. Collector
   c. Analyzer
   d. Sorter
6. **In a Java MapReduce program, how do you specify the input and output paths for the job?**
   a. Using the Job.setMapperClass() method
   b. Using the FileInputFormat.setInputPaths() and FileOutputFormat.setOutputPath() methods
   c. Using the Job.setReducerClass() method
   d. Using the Job.setJarByClass() method
7. **Which command is used to submit a MapReduce job in a Hadoop cluster?**
   a. hadoop run
   b. hadoop execute
   c. hadoop job
   d. hadoop jar

8. **What is the role of the Reducer in a MapReduce job?**
   a. Splits the input data into smaller chunks
   b. Aggregates and summarizes the output of the Mapper
   c. Formats the final output data
   d. Transfers data into HDFS
9. **Which tool in Cloudera can be used to perform SQL-like queries on large datasets stored in HDFS?**
   a. Cloudera Impala
   b. Cloudera Navigator
   c. Cloudera Hue
   d. Cloudera Director
10. **What is the primary advantage of using Hadoop for stock data analysis?**
    a. It is easier to set up than other systems
    b. It provides real-time data processing
    c. It allows scalable processing of large datasets across a distributed network
    d. It automatically generates trading signals

Answers

1.	b.	2.	c.	3.	c.	4.	c.	5.	a.
6.	b.	7.	d.	8.	b.	9.	a.	10.	c.

Questions

1. **Case study**: Real-time traffic data analysis using Hadoop in Cloudera

   A city transportation department wants to improve traffic management and reduce congestion by analyzing real-time traffic data from various sensors and cameras installed across the city. The goal is to optimize traffic flow, predict congestion points, and enhance public safety.
2. Discuss the advantages of using Hadoop in Cloudera for analyzing real-time traffic data compared to traditional data processing systems.
3. How can MapReduce be utilized in this scenario to identify traffic congestion patterns, and what would be the role of the Mapper and Reducer functions?
4. What challenges might arise when integrating multiple data sources (e.g., traffic sensors, GPS data, and social media feeds) for real-time analysis, and how can Cloudera's ecosystem help address these challenges?
5. Explain how machine learning algorithms could be applied to the processed traffic data to enhance predictive analytics capabilities, and suggest some specific use cases.
6. How can Cloudera's data security features be leveraged to ensure the privacy and security of sensitive traffic data, especially when dealing with PII?
7. Write a detailed guide on how to write and execute a MapReduce program in Java for analyzing stock market data. Include code snippets and explanations.
8. Describe the process of exporting stock market data into HDFS. Discuss the various methods and tools available for this task.
9. Explain the role of the Mapper function and Reducer functions in log data analysis. Describe the input and output formats expected from the Mapper and Reducer. Provide pseudocode or an algorithm to illustrate how the Mapper extracts relevant information from log data.

CHAPTER 6
Understanding Pig for Big Data Processing

Data is a precious thing and will last longer than the systems themselves.

— *Tim Berners-Lee*

Introduction

This chapter looks into the fundamentals of Apache Pig, a high-level platform used for processing and analyzing large datasets in Apache Hadoop. It begins with an overview of Pig, its significance in the big data ecosystem, and the reasons for its popularity. Next, the architecture of Apache Pig is explained, highlighting its core components and their roles in data processing. The rest of the chapter focuses on the practical aspects of running Pig in Cloudera, a widely used Hadoop distribution. It explores the different execution modes available in Pig to understand how to optimize performance based on specific use cases. In the last part, the readers learn about Pig Latin, the scripting language used in Pig. Readers are familiarized with the Pig Latin data model, data types, and various types of operators with practical demonstrations in Cloudera.

Structure

In this chapter, we will cover the following topics:

- Introduction to Apache Pig
- Architecture of Apache Pig
- Running Pig in Cloudera
- Pig Latin data model
- Pig Latin relational operators

Objectives

By the end of this chapter, readers will be able to understand the fundamentals of Apache Pig and its role in the big data ecosystem. They will gain insights into the architecture of Apache Pig, including its core components and their functions in data processing. Readers will also learn to run Pig in Cloudera, exploring its different execution modes to optimize performance based on specific use cases. Additionally, they will develop proficiency in Pig Latin, the scripting language used in Pig, by understanding its data model, data types, and various operators through practical demonstrations in Cloudera.

Introduction to Apache Pig

Apache Pig is a scripting platform that processes and analyzes large data sets on Hadoop clusters. It can ingest any type of data, be it structured, semi-structured, or unstructured, and stores the results using HDFS. *Yahoo* researchers developed Apache Pig in late 2006. It later became an Apache open-source project.

Need for Apache Pig

Before 2006, programs were written only on MapReduce using Java. Developers had to understand the map, sort, shuffle, and reduce fundamentals for writing a program for which they needed everyday operations, such as joining, filtering, etc. Writing and managing the map-reduce code consumed a significant amount of time for the developers. To overcome these issues, Pig was developed. It provides an interface to the users for data processing and analysis without understanding the MapReduce programming, thereby reducing production time. Internally, Pig's infrastructure layer consists of a compiler that produces sequences of MapReduce programs, for which large-scale parallel implementations already exist (e.g., the Hadoop subproject). It provides a high-level textual language called **Pig Latin** to write complex data analysis programs and the infrastructure to evaluate these programs. Pig Latin is designed to perform data transformation operations such as **extract, transform, and load** (**ETL**).

Some key characteristics of Apache Pig are as follows:

- **Ease of programming**: Pig Latin is a simple, procedural language that is easy to learn and use, especially for those familiar with scripting languages like SQL or Python. It is designed to be declarative, which allows users to specify what operations they want to perform on their data rather than how those operations should be executed. It provides a layer of abstraction that hides the complexities of Hadoop MapReduce programming so that users can focus on data processing logic rather than low-level implementation details. The Pig execution engine automatically translates Pig Latin statements into MapReduce jobs. The engine optimizes these jobs internally based on factors like data locality, job chaining, and parallel execution. Apache Pig optimizes data processing by executing operations in a pipeline fashion, which reduces the need for intermediate storage and minimizes data movement across the cluster.
- **Data processing flexibility**: Pig supports many data types, including primitive types (integers, floats, strings, etc.), complex types (tuples, bags, maps), and user-defined types. This flexibility enables users to handle diverse data formats and structures efficiently.
- **Rich set of operators and functions**: Pig provides a rich library of built-in operators and functions for string manipulation, mathematical operations, date-time functions, data manipulation, transformation, filtering, aggregation, etc. These operators can also be combined to perform complex data processing tasks within Pig Latin scripts.
- **Parallel execution**: Pig executes the data processing tasks in parallel across a Hadoop cluster, leveraging the scalability and fault tolerance of Hadoop MapReduce. This helps to efficiently process large data sets by distributing the workload across multiple nodes in the cluster.
- **Optimization capabilities**: Pig optimizes data processing workflows by generating efficient execution plans based on the structure of Pig Latin scripts. It performs various types of optimizations, such as query reordering, predicate pushdown, column pruning, etc., to minimize data movement and improve performance.
- **Extensibility**: Users can extend Pig's functionality by writing their own **user-defined functions** (**UDFs**) in Java, Python, or other **Java Virtual Machine** (**JVM**) compatible languages. UDFs can be seamlessly integrated into Pig Latin scripts to perform user-defined tasks.
- **Interoperability**: Pig can be easily integrated with other components of the Hadoop ecosystem, including HDFS, HBase (NoSQL database), Hive (data warehouse infrastructure), etc. This interoperability facilitates smooth data integration and workflow orchestration within Hadoop environments.
- **Debugging and scripting tools**: Pig provides tools for debugging and testing Pig Latin scripts, including scripts running in local mode for development and testing purposes. It also supports script embedding, which helps users incorporate Pig scripts within larger workflows or applications.
- **Community and ecosystem**: Apache Pig is an open-source project with an active community of developers and users. Therefore, Pig users benefit from ongoing community development, support, and contributions, as well as a growing ecosystem of tools and libraries built around Pig for various use cases.

Overall, Apache Pig is a powerful platform for scalable, flexible, and efficient data processing in Hadoop environments for big data analytics and ETL.

Architecture of Apache Pig

Apache Pig is a high-level platform for analyzing large data sets with a high-level language for writing data analysis programs. It utilizes the Hadoop Ecosystem's infrastructure to evaluate these programs.

The architecture of Apache Pig consists of two main layers:

- **Pig Latin**: It is a high-level data flow language used in Apache Pig. It is a scripting language that allows users to express data processing tasks straightforwardly. It is similar to SQL but explicitly designed for Hadoop. Users write Pig Latin scripts to specify how data should be loaded, transformed, and stored. Pig Latin abstracts the complexities of MapReduce programming, making it easier to write data processing tasks.
- **Pig engine**: It provides the runtime environment for Pig Latin scripts. It takes Pig Latin scripts as input and processes them using various components, as shown in *Figure 6.1*:

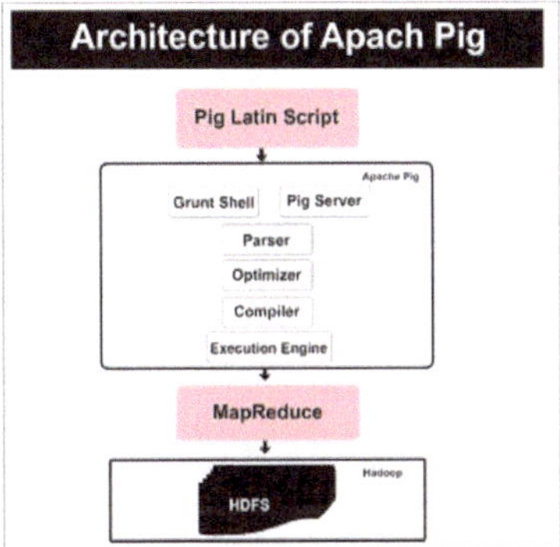

***Figure 6.1**: Architecture of Apache Pig*

- **Parser**: It takes Pig Latin scripts as input, checks the script's syntax, does type checking, and performs other miscellaneous checks. The output of this step is a **directed acyclic graph** (**DAG**) that represents the Pig Latin statements and logical operators. In DAG, the logical operators are represented as the nodes, and the data flows are represented as edges (the logical plan).

  The logical plan represents the sequence of operations specified in the Pig Latin script in terms of algebraic operations such as projections, filters, joins, etc. It is an abstract representation of the script's intent.
- **Optimizer**: Next, the logical plan (DAG) is passed to the optimizer. It analyzes the script to perform logical optimizations, such as removing redundancy or expressions, to streamline the data processing flow. It also performs pushdown optimizations by performing operations like filtering or data type conversion closer to the data source (e.g., HDFS) for earlier processing and thereby reducing data volume to ensure that data is processed faster and more efficiently.
- **Compiler**: After optimization, the compiler translates a logical plan into a physical plan. The physical plan represents how the logical operations regarding MapReduce jobs will be executed. Each operator in the physical plan refers to a MapReduce job or a series of jobs.
- **Execution engine**: Finally, all the MapReduce jobs are submitted to Hadoop in a sorted order to produce the desired results. The jobs are executed by the execution engine using the appropriate execution environment.

Thus, the Pig engine simplifies working with Hadoop by handling parsing, optimization, compilation, and execution. Translating high-level Pig Latin script into low-level MapReduce code by the Pig engine makes it easier for data analysts to focus on data transformations without having expertise in MapReduce.

Running Pig in Cloudera

There are three ways to execute Pig Latin programs, which are illustrated in *Figure 6.2*, and all of which work in local and MapReduce modes:

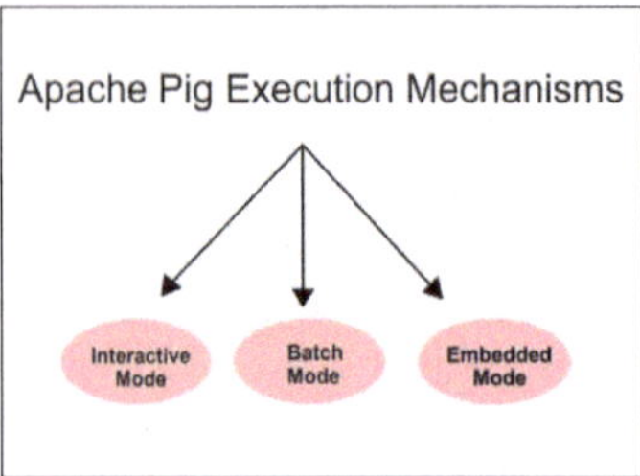

***Figure 6.2**: Pig Latin execution modes*

Interactive mode, the Grunt shell

It is an interactive shell for running Pig commands. Grunt starts by simply writing Pig in the Cloudera terminal, as shown in *Figure 6.3*. This command initiates the environment for running Pig scripts and starts the Grunt shell:

***Figure 6.3**: Cloudera terminal to start the Grunt shell for Pig Latin*

Pig allows execution of the Grunt shell in two modes: local and MapReduce mode. The same is illustrated in *Figure 6.4*:

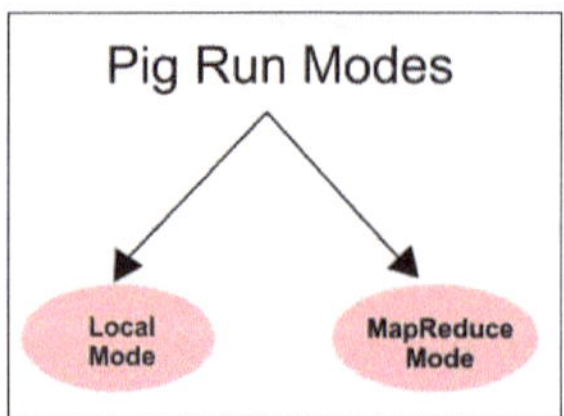

***Figure 6.4**: Execution modes in Pig*

Local mode

In the local mode, the engine runs the MapReduce jobs within a single JVM on the local machine. All the available files are installed and run on the localhost and the file system. This is suitable for small datasets or testing purposes. The execution type is set using the **-x** or **-exec** type option.

The command to start the Grunt, the Pig interactive shell in local mode, is as follows:

```
$ pig -x local
 grunt>
```

The same is illustrated in the following figure:

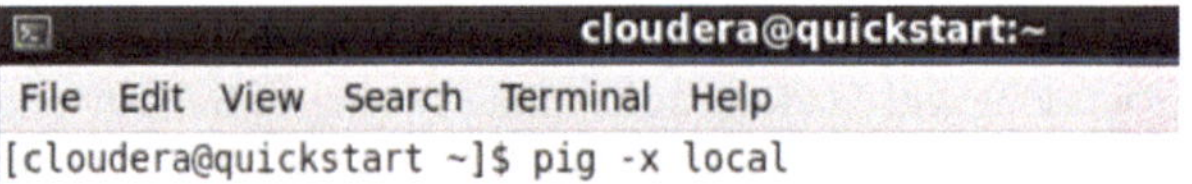

***Figure 6.5**: Local execution mode in Pig*

After typing the command depicted in *Figure 6.5* in the terminal, press enter. It starts configuring the execution environment and starts with the **grunt** shell, as shown in *Figure 6.6:*

```
grunt>
```

***Figure 6.6:** Grunt shell for local execution mode in Pig*

Distributed mode

It is also called **Hadoop** or **MapReduce mode**. The execution engine leverages the Hadoop cluster to analyze the large datasets. It submits the MapReduce jobs to the Hadoop YARN for distributed processing across the cluster nodes. This helps Pig to handle massive data volumes efficiently. It can be executed against a fully-distributed Hadoop installation as well as a semi-distributed Hadoop installation. It presents the input and output data on HDFS. It is a recommended mode for production environments. The command for MapReduce mode, as shown in *Figure 6.7:*

Syntax:

```
$ pig
```

Or,

```
$ pig -x mapreduce
```

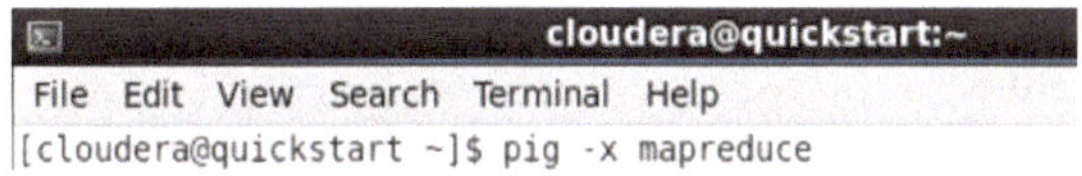

***Figure 6.7:** MapReduce execution mode in Pig*

After invoking the Grunt shell, you may start executing your Pig script directly. You can exit the Grunt shell using *ctrl + d*.

Batch mode script

Pig allows the execution of a group of commands together in batch mode. A Latin script can be written in a file to solve a particular problem. For example, you may create a file with the name **plscript.pig** and write all commands in this file required to perform the analysis.

Next, write the following commands to execute the script:

```
grunt> pig -x local plscript.pig
```

Or,

```
grunt> pig -x mapreduce plscript.pig
```

Embedded mode UDF

Apache Pig allows users to define customized functions UDFs in programming languages such as Java and use them in the script.

Pig Latin data model

In Pig, data modeling involves defining the structure and relationships within the data to facilitate analysis. This includes defining data types in Pig and describing the data for analysis.

In Apache Pig, data types are divided into two categories: Scalar types and Complex types. The details are as follows:

- **Scalar types**: These data types are simple and contain only a single value, similar to those in most programming languages, as shown in *Table 5.1*. Except for byte array, all these types are represented in Pig interfaces by **java.lang** classes, which makes it easy to work within UDFs.

If no data type is specified during data loading, Pig assigns the data to a byte array. While loading data, Pig tries to infer the schema (data types of columns) based on the data. If there is a mismatch between the data type and the schema, Pig attempts to coerce the data to match the schema. For example, loading a string value into an integer column might result in a null value or an error depending on the data.

Pig does not have a built-in mechanism for explicitly casting between scalar data types. Therefore, these conversions need to be handled explicitly in Pig Latin scripts through manipulation functions.

Scalar data type	Interface	Example
`int`	They store a four-byte/32-bit signed integer. Constant integers are expressed as integer numbers.	`26`
`long`	A long integer. They store an eight-byte/64-bit signed integer. Constant longs are expressed as integer numbers with an `L` appended.	`26L` (capital or lowercase L)
`float`	It represents a 32-bit floating-point number for decimal values. Floats are represented in interfaces by `java.lang`.	`26.5F` (capital or lowercase F)
`double`	It represents a 64-bit floating-point number for more precise decimals.	`26.5`
`chararray`	It represents a variable-length string of characters in UTF-8 format. In addition to standard alphanumeric and symbolic characters, you can express certain characters in `chararrays` by using backslash codes, such as `\t` for tab and `\n` for return.	`"hello world"`
`bytearray`	It represents a variable-length array of bytes. `bytearrays` are represented in interfaces by a Java class `DataByteArray` that wraps a Java `byte[]`. There is no way to specify a constant `bytearray`.	
`boolean`	It represents a logical value, either true or false.	

Table 6.1: Scalar data types in Pig

Understanding these scalar data types will help you to effectively store, process, and analyze various data elements within your Apache Pig programs.

- **Complex types**: Apache Pig has several complex data types beyond storing single values. Pig has three complex data types: maps, tuples, and bags. These types can contain data of any type, including other complex types. This allows the creation of rich data structures to model complex relationships within real-world data. Detailed explanation of each complex data type in Pig is as follows:
  - **Tuples**: A tuple represents an ordered list of values similar to structs in C or named tuples in Python. A tuple is a row with one or more fields, where each field can be any data type. A tuple contains a fixed number of elements, each with its position (index) starting from 0. The data type of each element can be any Pig data type.

    Syntax: `( field [, field …] )`

    A tuple is enclosed in parentheses `( )`. `'field'` represents a piece of data . A field can be any data type (including tuple and bag).

    Example: `(16, 'Aayush', 5.14)`

    This tuple has three elements: an integer (`16`), a string (`"Aayush"`), and a double (`5.14`).

    In tuples, a field may or may not have data. If a field has no data, then, in a load statement, the loader will inject null into the tuple. The actual value substituted for null is loader-specific; for example, PigStorage substitutes an empty field for null. In case of a non-load statement, if a requested field is missing from a tuple, Pig will inject null.

Tuples represent data records with multiple fields, like sensor readings (timestamp, temperature, humidity) or customer purchase details (`id`, `product_id`, `quantity`).

- **Map**: In Pig, a map represents a key-value pair collection, similar to dictionaries in Python or hash maps in Java. Each element in a map consists of a key (`chararray`) and a value, which can be any Pig data type, including another complex type:

```
[ key#value, <key#value …>]
```

Syntax (<> denotes optional). Maps are enclosed in straight brackets `[ ]`. Key value pairs are separated by the hash sign `#` and a comma between key-value pairs. In Pig, the `key` must be the char array data type, and the `value` must be a unique value of any data type (which defaults to a byte array).

Example: `{('name'#'Aayush', 'age'#18), ('city'#'Noida', 'country'#'India')}`

This map has two key-value pairs, where "`name`," "`city`," and "`country`" are keys (strings), and `Aayush`, `Noida`, and `India` are values (strings), respectively. The age is a key with an integer value (25). These keys are used as indices to find the values from the data.

Maps are helpful with JSON-like data, where they can store attributes like user profiles with attributes (name, age, location) or product details with properties (name, price, category).

- **Bags**: In Pig, a bag represents an unordered collection of elements similar to lists in Python or arrays in Java. A bag can contain any number of duplicate elements, and the order of elements is not significant. The data type of each element can be any Pig data type.

Syntax: `{ tuple [, tuple …] }`

A bag is enclosed in curly brackets `{ }`, and a `tuple` represents a tuple.

Example: `{'apple', 'banana', 'apple'}`

This bag contains three elements: two strings (`apple`) and one string (`banana`).

A bag can have tuples with differing numbers of fields and fields with different data types. Therefore, if Pig attempts to access a field that does not exist, a null value is substituted.

For effective processing of bags, the schemas of the tuples within those bags should be the same. For example, if half of the tuples include char array fields and the other half include float fields, only half will participate in the computation because the `chararray` fields will be converted to null.

Bags are used to represent collections without a specific order, such as a list of product tags, a shopping cart with multiple items, or a log file with various events.

Understanding complex data types effectively helps to represent and manipulate hierarchical data structures within the Apache Pig programs, which are used for powerful data analysis tasks.

- **Relation**: In Apache Pig, Pig Latin statements work with relations. Relations are used to represent datasets. A relation, as shown in *Figure 6.8*, is basically a bag of tuples, where each tuple is a collection of fields. A field represents a piece of data.

Relations in Pig are similar to relations/tables in relational databases, where the tuples in the bag correspond to the rows in a table.

However, unlike relational databases, Pig relations have a dynamic schema; each tuple can have a varied number of fields. Also, Pig relations are unordered, which implies that tuples may be processed in any order. Moreover, processing can be parallelized, meaning that the processing may not happen according to total ordering. Relations are referred to by the name or alias. These names are assigned by developers as part of a Pig Latin statement.

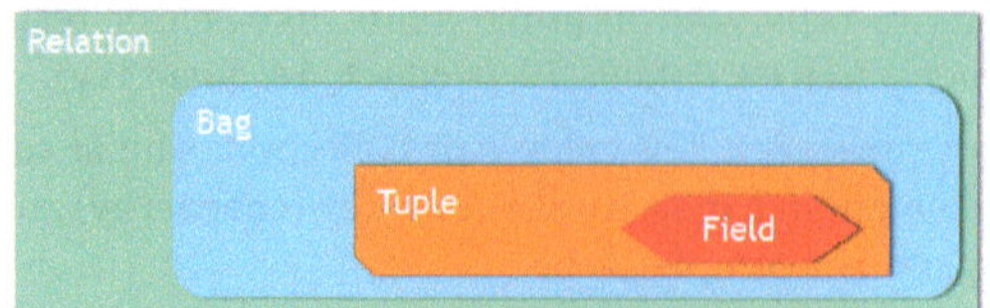

***Figure 6.8:** Structure of a relation in Pig*

Pig Latin relational operators

Apache Pig is an analytical tool that analyzes large datasets that exist in the **Hadoop Distributed File System** (**HDFS**). The various operators used to load, store, and analyze the data to fulfill the analytical needs of the organizations are illustrated in *Figure 6.9*:

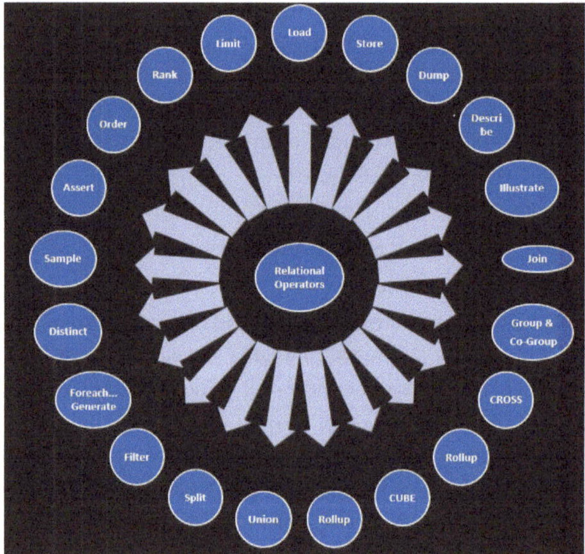

***Figure 6.9:** Operators in Pig*

To understand the working of various operators, let us consider a case study where we have a dataset containing information about sales transactions from an e-commerce platform stored in a **`sales_trans.txt`** file. The dataset consists of the following fields:

- **Transaction ID(Tran_ID)**: Unique identifier for each transaction.
- **Customer ID(Cust_ID)**: Unique identifier for each customer.
- **Product ID(Prod_ID)**: Unique identifier for each product.
- **Product Name(Prod_Name)**: Name of the product.
- **Quantity(Qty)**: The quantity of the product purchased in each transaction.
- **Price**: The price of each unit of the product.
- **Timestamp**: The timestamp of the transaction.

The sample of data stored in the **`sales_trans.txt`** file is as follows:

- Tran_ID, Cust_ID, Prod_ID, Prod_Name, Qty, Price, Timestamp
- 1, 101, 1, "Laptop", 2, 800, "2024-03-01 10:00:00"

- 2, 102, 3, "Smartphone", 1, 600, "2024-03-01 10:05:00"
- 3, 103, 2, "Tablet", 1, 400, "2024-03-01 10:10:00"
- 4, 104, 1, "Laptop", 1, 800, "2024-03-01 10:15:00"
- 5, 105, 3, "Smartphone", 3, 600, "2024-03-01 10:20:00"
- 6, 106, 4, "Headphones", 2, 100, "2024-03-01 10:25:00"

Detailed explanation of relational operators in Pig is as follows:

- **LOAD operator**: It loads data into Apache Pig from the HDFS/ Local file system.

  The syntax of the load statement is as follows:

  ```
  Relation_name = LOAD 'Input file path' USING function as schema;
  ```

  Here, `Relation_name` is the name of the relation to store the data. The user specifies it. In the `Input file path`, you need to mention the complete path where the file is stored. A schema refers to the schema of the data that needs to be defined by the developer to load data into the relation. We can define the required schema as follows:

  ```
  (column1 : data type, column2 : data type, column3 : data type);
  ```

  The *function* refers to the name of the function. The function name varies depending on the type of file format from which data needs to be loaded. The set of functions supported by Pig Latin is given in *Figure 6.10:*

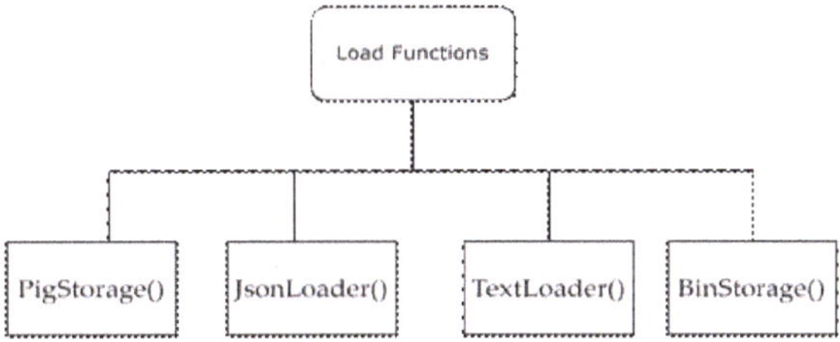

***Figure 6.10**: Types of loader functions*

- **PigStorage()**: It is the default function used to load /store the data. It supports structured text files (in human-readable UTF-8 format) in compressed or uncompressed form. The input data to the load can be a file, a directory, or a glob. Both simple and complex data types can be read/written using this function. This function requires data to be formatted using a field delimiter such as the tab character ('\t'), (','), or other specified character.

  Syntax: `PigStorage ([field_delimiter] , ['options'] )`

  For example:

  ```
  grunt>sales_data = LOAD 'sales_trans.txt' USING PigStorage(',') AS ( Transaction_ID: int, Customer_ID: int,  Product_ID: int, Product_Name: chararray,    Quantity: int,    Price: float,    Timestamp: chararray );
  ```

  Here, `sales_data` is the name of the relation. In this example, data is stored in a .txt file, and data is separated by a comma, so the `PigStorage` function is used to load the data, and the comma delimiter is passed as a parameter to the function. Next, the schema for the relation is specified with field names and data types corresponding to the `sales_trans.txt` file, which stores the dataset. The same command is written in the Grunt shell in Cloudera, as shown in *Figure 6.11:*

```
grunt> sales_data = LOAD '/chap5Pig/sales_trans.txt' USING Pig
Storage(',') as (Trans_ID:int, Cust_ID:int,Prod_ID:int,Prod_Na
me:chararray,Qty:int,Price:float,Timestamp:chararray);
```

***Figure 6.11**: PigStorage() load function*

- **JsonLoader()**: It is used to load data stored in JSON format. Assume the above sales transaction data is stored in a JSON file as **sales_trans.json**.

  To load the preceding data, use the following code:

```
grunt>sales_data = LOAD 'sales_trans.json' USING JsonLoader();
```

  The preceding Pig Latin statement loads the data from the input(**sales_trans.json**) JSON file using the JsonLoader, which automatically parses the JSON data into Pig relations. When you run this script, Pig will load the JSON data from the input file and process it according to the specified script.

  > Note: **Ensure that the input data is a properly formatted JSON file before loading it using the JSON loader in Pig.**

  The following code shows **Sales_trans.json** file:

```
[
  {
    "Tran_ID": 1,
    "Cust_ID": 101,
    "Prod_ID": 1,
    "Prod_Name": "Laptop",
    "Qty": 2,
    "Price": 800,
    "Timestamp": "2024-03-01 10:00:00"
  },
  {
    "Tran_ID": 2,
    "Cust_ID": 102,
    "Prod_ID": 3,
    "Prod_Name": "Smartphone",
    "Qty": 1,
    "Price": 600,
    "Timestamp": "2024-03-01 10:05:00"
  },
  {
    ............................
  }
]
```

- **TextLoader()**: This built-in function loads data from a text file. It reads each line of the file as a string. This can be used to load unstructured or semi-structured datasets. It also supports compression. The following script loads the data from the **sales_trans.txt** file using **TextLoader()**. It reads each line of the text file as a string:

```
grunt>sales_data = LOAD 'sales_trans.txt' USING TextLoader();
```

  After running the script, each line from the input text file (**sales_trans.txt**) is loaded as a separate record in Pig, and the fields within each record are separated by commas. This data can be further processed or manipulated as per the requirements using Pig Latin transformations and operations.

STORE operator

In Apache Pig, after loading data into a relation or the result of a computation or transformation, it is stored in a storage system like HDFS, Amazon S3, or any other supported storage system. The STORE statement is used to accomplish this task.

Here is the syntax for using the STORE statement in Pig:

```
STORE <relation> INTO '<output_location>' [USING <storage_function>];
```

Where, **<relation>** is the name of the relation you want to store, **<output_location>** is the location where you want to store the data and, **<storage_function>** (optional) specifies how the data should be stored. If not specified, Pig uses the default storage function, which is usually used for storing data in HDFS.

For example:

```
grunt>STORE sales_data INTO '/chapt5out/';
```

Or,

```
grunt>STORE sales_data INTO '/chapt5out/' USING PigStorage(',');
```

The preceding example stores the relation **sales_data** in the HDFS directory **"/chap5out/"** as shown in *Figure 6.12*. The second statement will store the data in the desired format (comma-separated). After executing the above STORE statement, a directory is created with the specified name (here chap5out), and the data is stored there. To verify the data stored in the output directory, first list the files in the directory named output using the ls command, as shown in the following example:

```
Cloudera>hdfsdfs -ls 'chap5out'
```

You will observe two files with the name **part-r-00000** in the output folder. The STORE statement stores the data in this file. The contents of this file can be seen using the cat command:

```
Cloudera>hdfsdfs  -cat chap5out part-r-00000
```

Figures 6.12, 6.13, and *6.14* show the execution and results of STORE operators in the Cloudera **grunt** shell.

Following figure shows the execution of the STORE command and the intermediate outputs, respectively:

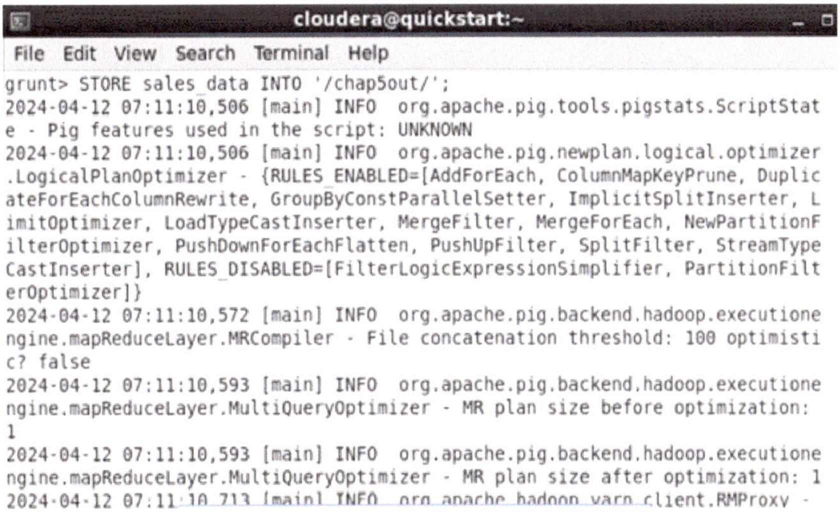

```
cloudera@quickstart:~
File Edit View Search Terminal Help
grunt> STORE sales_data INTO '/chap5out/';
2024-04-12 07:11:10,506 [main] INFO  org.apache.pig.tools.pigstats.ScriptStat
e - Pig features used in the script: UNKNOWN
2024-04-12 07:11:10,506 [main] INFO  org.apache.pig.newplan.logical.optimizer
.LogicalPlanOptimizer - {RULES_ENABLED=[AddForEach, ColumnMapKeyPrune, Duplic
ateForEachColumnRewrite, GroupByConstParallelSetter, ImplicitSplitInserter, L
imitOptimizer, LoadTypeCastInserter, MergeFilter, MergeForEach, NewPartitionF
ilterOptimizer, PushDownForEachFlatten, PushUpFilter, SplitFilter, StreamType
CastInserter], RULES_DISABLED=[FilterLogicExpressionSimplifier, PartitionFilt
erOptimizer]}
2024-04-12 07:11:10,572 [main] INFO  org.apache.pig.backend.hadoop.executione
ngine.mapReduceLayer.MRCompiler - File concatenation threshold: 100 optimisti
c? false
2024-04-12 07:11:10,593 [main] INFO  org.apache.pig.backend.hadoop.executione
ngine.mapReduceLayer.MultiQueryOptimizer - MR plan size before optimization:
1
2024-04-12 07:11:10,593 [main] INFO  org.apache.pig.backend.hadoop.executione
ngine.mapReduceLayer.MultiQueryOptimizer - MR plan size after optimization: 1
2024-04-12 07:11:10,713 [main] INFO  org.apache.hadoop.yarn.client.RMProxy -
```

***Figure 6.12**: STORE operator*

This figure shows the execution of the **STORE** command and the intermediate outputs:

```
Input(s):
Successfully read 5 records (608 bytes) from: "/chap5Pig/sales_trans.txt"

Output(s):
Successfully stored 5 records (243 bytes) in: "/chap5out"

Counters:
Total records written : 5
Total bytes written : 243
Spillable Memory Manager spill count : 0
Total bags proactively spilled: 0
Total records proactively spilled: 0

Job DAG:
job_1712927833390_0001


2024-04-12 07:11:30,242 [main] INFO  org.apache.pig.backend.hadoop.executione
ngine.mapReduceLayer.MapReduceLauncher - Success!
```

***Figure 6.13**: STORE operator intermediate output*

This figure shows the execution and results of STORE operators in the Cloudera Grunt shell:

```
File  Edit  View  Search  Terminal  Help
[cloudera@quickstart ~]$ hdfs dfs -cat /chap5out/
cat: `/chap5out': Is a directory
[cloudera@quickstart ~]$ hdfs dfs -ls  /chap5out/
Found 2 items
-rw-r--r--   1 cloudera supergroup          0 2024-04-12 07:11 /chap5out/_SUCCES
S
-rw-r--r--   1 cloudera supergroup        243 2024-04-12 07:11 /chap5out/part-m-
00000
[cloudera@quickstart ~]$ hdfs dfs -cat /chap5out/part-m-00000
1       101     1       "LapTop"        2       800.0   "2024-03-01 10:00:00"
2       102     3       "Smartphone"    1       600.0   "2024-03-01 10:05:00"
3       103     2       "Tablet"        1       400.0   "2024-03-01 10:10:00"
4       104     1       "LapTop"        1       800.0   "2024-03-01 10:15:00"
5       105     3       "Smartphone"    3       600.0   "2024-03-01 10:20:00"
[cloudera@quickstart ~]$
```

***Figure 6.14**: Final output of STORE operator*

Conclusion

This chapter introduced Apache Pig, a high-level language platform used by organizations to analyze large data sets. Pig's architecture has two main components: Pig Latin and Pig Engine. Pig Latin writes the scripts for data analysis tasks, and Pig Engine executes the scripts. The chapter further explained how to execute Pig scripts within the Cloudera framework. It covered both simple and complex data types supported in Pig Latin, along with various relational operators. These operators include commands for loading data from different file formats, processing it, and storing the results in specified locations. Detailed syntax, explanations, and practical applications of these operators were demonstrated using the Grunt shell in the Cloudera environment.

The next chapter will explore built-in functions, UDFs, and case studies on data analysis using Pig.

Points to remember

The following list outlines the key takeaways from this chapter:

- Apache Pig is a platform for analyzing large datasets in Hadoop using a high-level scripting language.
- It simplifies complex data processing tasks on Hadoop by providing an abstraction over MapReduce.

- The architecture of Apache Pig comprises a language parser, optimizer, and execution engine for transforming Pig Latin scripts into MapReduce jobs.
- Pig can be run in Cloudera by installing it on the cluster and submitting Pig scripts through the command line or UI.
- Pig supports local mode for development and MapReduce mode for distributed processing on Hadoop clusters.
- Pig scripts are executed using the Pig interpreter, either interactively or by submitting script files.
- Pig Latin is a scripting language used for expressing data transformations and processing in Apache Pig.
- It follows a relational data model, where data is represented as relations (tables) consisting of tuples (rows) and fields (columns).
- Data types in Pig: Pig supports various data types such as int, long, float, double, chararray, bytearray, tuple, bag, and map for representing different kinds of data.
- Pig Latin relational operators include LOAD, and STORE, for data manipulation and transformation.

Multiple choice questions

1. **What is the primary purpose of Apache Pig?**
   a. To process structured data in Hadoop
   b. To process unstructured data in Hadoop
   c. To visualize data stored in Hadoop
   d. To query data in Hadoop using SQL
2. **Which of the following best describes the architecture of Apache Pig?**
   a. Pig consists of a single component that processes data
   b. Pig is built on top of MapReduce and executes jobs in Hadoop
   c. Pig executes jobs independently of Hadoop
   d. Pig uses SQL queries to interact with data
3. **Which of the following is a data modelling approach used in Pig?**
   a. Relational model
   b. Document model
   c. Columnar model
   d. Schemaless model
4. **Which Pig operator is used to load data from HDFS into Pig?**
   a. LOAD
   b. STORE
   c. FETCH
   d. RETRIEVE
5. **Which loader function is used to load JSON data in Pig?**
   a. PigStorage()
   b. JsonLoader()
   c. TextLoader()
   d. LoadJson()
6. **Which operator is used to store data from Pig to HDFS?**
   a. SAVE
   b. STORE
   c. SAVEAS
   d. DUMP
7. **Which of the following diagnostic operators displays the schema of a relation?**
   a. DUMP
   b. DESCRIBE
   c. ILLUSTRATE
   d. SCHEMA

8. **Which Pig operator is used for filtering data based on a condition?**
   a. FILTER
   b. SELECT
   c. EXTRACT
   d. SEARCH
9. **Which operator is used for performing aggregation in Pig?**
   a. AGGREGATE
   b. SUMMARIZE
   c. GROUP
   d. COLLECT
10. **Which operator is used to perform a self-join in Pig?**
    a. JOIN
    b. COGROUP
    c. CROSS
    d. SPLIT

Answers

1. b.	2. b.	3. d.	4. a.	5. b.
6. b.	7. b.	8. a.	9. c.	10. a.

Questions

1. Explain the architecture of Apache Pig and how it differs from traditional MapReduce processing in Hadoop.
2. Discuss the advantages and disadvantages of using a schemaless data model in Apache Pig for data processing.
3. Describe the purpose and functionality of the LOAD and STORE operators in Apache Pig. Provide examples to illustrate their usage.
4. Compare and contrast the usage of the GROUP and COGROUP operators in Apache Pig. Provide scenarios where each operator would be most appropriate.
5. Explain how the FILTER operator works in Apache Pig. Provide examples of different filtering conditions and their effects on data processing.
6. Given a dataset transaction stored in HDFS with the following schema: (customer_id: int, item_id: int, quantity: int, total_price: float), write a Pig Latin script to load this data into a relation named sales_data.
7. Using Pig Latin, perform a JOIN operation between two datasets: customers and orders. The customers dataset has the schema (customer_id: int, name: chararray, city: chararray), and the orders dataset has the schema (order_id: int, customer_id: int, order_date: chararray, total_amount: float).
8. Write a Pig Latin script to calculate the total sales for each customer from the sales_data relation created earlier. Display the results sorted by total sales in descending order.
9. Given a dataset logs containing server log data with the schema (timestamp: chararray, ip_address: chararray, request_type: chararray, status_code: int), write a Pig Latin script to filter out log entries with status code 404 (Not Found).
10. Using Pig Latin, perform a GROUP BY operation on the sales_data relation to find the total quantity sold for each item. Additionally, filter out items with a total quantity less than 100, and display the results sorted by total quantity in descending order.

Chapter 7
Operators in Pig Latin

Big data is at the foundation of all of the megatrends that are happening today.

– Chris Lynch

Introduction

Apache Pig is a high-level platform for processing large-scale datasets in Hadoop. It provides a scripting language called **Pig Latin**, which simplifies complex data transformations using a set of relational and procedural operators. This chapter introduces key Apache Pig operators that help in data processing, including debugging, relational operations, filtering, transformations, sorting, and ranking. It is essential to understand these operators for handling big data flows efficiently. Apache Pig simplifies tasks like joins, grouping, filtering, or sampling, as compared to traditional MapReduce programming. By the end of this chapter, you will be able to apply these operators effectively to process, analyze, and transform large datasets in a Hadoop ecosystem.

Structure

In this chapter, we will cover the following topics:

- Debugging and inspection operators
- Relational operators
- Sorting and ranking operators

Objectives

By the end of this chapter, the readers will have a solid understanding of various Apache Pig operators used for data processing. Readers will learn how to debug and inspect data using DUMP, DESCRIBE, and ILLUSTRATE operators. They will also be able to perform relational operations such as different types of joins (JOIN, SELF JOIN, INNER JOIN, OUTER JOIN), COGROUP, and CROSS. Additionally, they will explore advanced aggregation techniques like CUBE and ROLLUP for multidimensional analysis. Finally, they will learn to organize and manage data efficiently through sorting, ranking, and limiting operations with ORDER, RANK, and LIMIT, as well as combining datasets using UNION. These concepts will equip readers with the necessary skills to efficiently process and analyze large datasets in a Hadoop ecosystem using Apache Pig.

Debugging and inspection operators

In Apache Pig, these operators are used to debug and understand the data flow within a Pig script. They provide insights into the data at various processing stages and are explained in detail in the upcoming subsections.

DUMP

This operator displays the contents of a relation (bag of tuples) in the console. It is useful for quick inspection of the data at a particular point in the script.

Syntax: `DUMP <relation>;`

Example: `grunt>DUMP sales_data;`

The **`sales_data`** relation stores the data stored in **`sales_trans.txt`** file is as follows:

- Tran_ID, Cust_ID, Prod_ID, Prod_Name, Qty, Price, Timestamp
- 1, 101, 1, "Laptop", 2, 800, "2024-03-01 10:00:00"
- 2, 102, 3, "Smartphone", 1, 600, "2024-03-01 10:05:00"
- 3, 103, 2, "Tablet", 1, 400, "2024-03-01 10:10:00"
- 4, 104, 1, "Laptop", 1, 800, "2024-03-01 10:15:00"
- 5, 105, 3, "Smartphone", 3, 600, "2024-03-01 10:20:00"
- 6, 106, 4, "Headphones", 2, 100, "2024-03-01 10:25:00"

Figure 7.1 shows that primarily, data of **`sales_trans.txt`** file is stored in relation **`sales_data,`** and then the DUMP operator is used to display the data in the grunt shell in Cloudera:

```
File Edit View Search Terminal Help
grunt> sales_data = LOAD '/chap5Pig/sales_trans.txt' USING PigStorage(',') as (Trans_I
D:int, Cust_ID:int,Prod_ID:int,Prod_Name:chararray,Qty:int,Price:float,Timestamp:chara
rray);
grunt> Dump sales_data;
2024-04-16 10:37:37,856 [main] INFO  org.apache.pig.tools.pigstats.ScriptState - Pig f
eatures used in the script: UNKNOWN
2024-04-16 10:37:37,891 [main] INFO  org.apache.pig.newplan.logical.optimizer.LogicalP
lanOptimizer - {RULES_ENABLED=[AddForEach, ColumnMapKeyPrune, DuplicateForEachColumnRe
write, GroupByConstParallelSetter, ImplicitSplitInserter, LimitOptimizer, LoadTypeCast
Inserter, MergeFilter, MergeForEach, NewPartitionFilterOptimizer, PushDownForEachFlatt
en, PushUpFilter, SplitFilter, StreamTypeCastInserter], RULES_DISABLED=[FilterLogicExp
ressionSimplifier, PartitionFilterOptimizer]}
2024-04-16 10:37:37,990 [main] INFO  org.apache.pig.backend.hadoop.executionengine.map
ReduceLayer.MRCompiler - File concatenation threshold: 100 optimistic? false
2024-04-16 10:37:38,004 [main] INFO  org.apache.pig.backend.hadoop.executionengine.map
ReduceLayer.MultiQueryOptimizer - MR plan size before optimization: 1
2024-04-16 10:37:38,004 [main] INFO  org.apache.pig.backend.hadoop.executionengine.map
ReduceLayer.MultiQueryOptimizer - MR plan size after optimization: 1
2024-04-16 10:37:38,112 [main] INFO  org.apache.hadoop.yarn.client.RMProxy - Connectin
```

Figure 7.1: *DUMP operators' execution*

Refer to the following figure for the execution and output of DUMP operators in the Grunt shell in Cloudera:

```
File Edit View Search Terminal Help

2024-04-11 09:04:26,632 [main] INFO  org.apache.pig.backend.hadoop.executionengi
ne.mapReduceLayer.MapReduceLauncher - Success!
2024-04-11 09:04:26,635 [main] INFO  org.apache.hadoop.conf.Configuration.deprec
ation - fs.default.name is deprecated. Instead, use fs.defaultFS
2024-04-11 09:04:26,635 [main] INFO  org.apache.hadoop.conf.Configuration.deprec
ation - mapred.job.tracker is deprecated. Instead, use mapreduce.jobtracker.addr
ess
2024-04-11 09:04:26,636 [main] INFO  org.apache.pig.data.SchemaTupleBackend - Ke
y [pig.schematuple] was not set... will not generate code.
2024-04-11 09:04:26,652 [main] INFO  org.apache.hadoop.mapreduce.lib.input.FileI
nputFormat - Total input paths to process : 1
2024-04-11 09:04:26,652 [main] INFO  org.apache.pig.backend.hadoop.executionengi
ne.util.MapRedUtil - Total input paths to process : 1
(1,101,1,"LapTop",2,800.0,"2024-03-01 10:00:00")
(2,102,3,"Smartphone",1,600.0,"2024-03-01 10:05:00")
(3,103,2,"Tablet",1,400.0,"2024-03-01 10:10:00")
(4,104,1,"LapTop",1,800.0,"2024-03-01 10:15:00")
(5,105,3,"Smartphone",3,600.0,"2024-03-01 10:20:00")
grunt> ▌
```

Figure 7.2: *DUMP operator output*

DESCRIBE

This operator is used to view a relation's schema. It shows the names and types of fields in the relation as shown in *Figure 7.3*.

Syntax: **`DESCRIBE <relation>;`**

Example: `grunt> DESCRIBE sales_data;`

Figure 7.3 shows the names and types of fields in the relation:

```
grunt> DESCRIBE sales_data
sales_data: {Trans_ID: int,Cust_ID: int,Prod_ID: int,Prod_Name: chararray,Qty: i
nt,Price: float,Timestamp: chararray}
```

***Figure 7.3**: Output of DESCRIBE operator*

ILLUSTRATE

This operator provides a step-by-step execution plan of a Pig script:

Syntax: **`ILLUSTRATE <relation>;`**

Example: `grunt>ILLUSTRATE sales_data;`

Figure 7.4 shows how the data flows through each operation in the script:

```
File  Edit  View  Search  Terminal  Help
grunt> ILLUSTRATE sales_data;
2024-04-12 07:25:46,765 [main] INFO  org.apache.hadoop.conf.Configuration.dep
recation - fs.default.name is deprecated. Instead, use fs.defaultFS
2024-04-12 07:25:46,765 [main] INFO  org.apache.hadoop.conf.Configuration.dep
recation - mapred.job.tracker is deprecated. Instead, use mapreduce.jobtracke
r.address
2024-04-12 07:25:46,818 [main] INFO  org.apache.hadoop.conf.Configuration.dep
recation - fs.default.name is deprecated. Instead, use fs.defaultFS
2024-04-12 07:25:46,818 [main] INFO  org.apache.hadoop.conf.Configuration.dep
recation - mapred.job.tracker is deprecated. Instead, use mapreduce.jobtracke
r.address
2024-04-12 07:25:46,818 [main] INFO  org.apache.pig.backend.hadoop.executione
ngine.HExecutionEngine - Connecting to hadoop file system at: hdfs://quicksta
rt.cloudera:8020
2024-04-12 07:25:46,819 [main] INFO  org.apache.pig.backend.hadoop.executione
ngine.HExecutionEngine - Connecting to map-reduce job tracker at: localhost:8
021
2024-04-12 07:25:46,824 [main] INFO  org.apache.pig.newplan.logical.optimizer
.LogicalPlanOptimizer - {RULES_ENABLED=[DuplicateForEachColumnRewrite, Implic
itSplitInserter, LoadTypeCastInserter, NewPartitionFilterOptimizer, StreamTyp
eCastInserter], RULES_DISABLED=[AddForEach, ColumnMapKeyPrune, FilterLogicExp
```

***Figure 7.4**: ILLUSTRATE operator execution*

Figure 7.5 shows the intermediate output of how the data flows through each operation in the script:

```
e - Pig script settings are added to the job
2024-04-12 07:25:47,195 [main] INFO  org.apache.pig.backend.hadoop.executione
ngine.mapReduceLayer.JobControlCompiler - mapred.job.reduce.markreset.buffer.
percent is not set, set to default 0.3
2024-04-12 07:25:47,205 [main] WARN  org.apache.pig.data.SchemaTupleBackend -
 SchemaTupleBackend has already been initialized
2024-04-12 07:25:47,210 [main] INFO  org.apache.pig.backend.hadoop.executione
ngine.mapReduceLayer.PigMapOnly$Map - Aliases being processed per job phase (
AliasName[line,offset]): M: sales_data[1,13] C:  R:
-----------------------------------------------------------------------------
------------------------------------------------------------------------
| sales_data      | Trans_ID:int     | Cust_ID:int     | Prod_ID:int     | Prod_N
ame:chararray     | Qty:int     | Price:float     | Timestamp:chararray     |
-----------------------------------------------------------------------------
------------------------------------------------------------------------
|                 | 3                | 103             | 2               | "Table
t"                | 1           | 400              | "2024-03-01 10:10:00"   |
-----------------------------------------------------------------------------
------------------------------------------------------------------------
```

Figure 7.5: ILLUSTRATE operator intermediate output

All these diagnostic operators help to understand the data's structure, verify the correctness of transformations, and identify any issues in the Pig script. They are essential tools for debugging and troubleshooting during the development of Pig scripts.

Relational operators

One of the key components of Pig Latin is relational operators, which allow you to manipulate and transform data efficiently. Relational operators enable you to perform fundamental operations such as filtering, grouping, joining, and sorting datasets. These operators help to process structured and semi-structured data with ease, making Pig a powerful tool for data analysts and engineers.

We will now explore the most commonly used relational operators in Pig Latin, their syntax, and practical use cases to help you leverage the full potential of Apache Pig in big data processing.

Join

This operator is used to combine records from two or more relations. It requires one (or a group of) tuples from each relation to be declared as keys. If the keys of tuples in two relations match, the tuples are combined; otherwise, they are dropped.

The various types of join operators in Pig Latin are discussed in the upcoming section.

Self join

It is used to join a relation with itself. Self joins in Pig are usually performed to load the same data multiple times. The same data/relation is loaded using two different aliases to avoid naming conflicts. The following code shows that the data of **sales_trans.txt** is stored in two relations, namely **sales_data** and **sales_data1**. The next join operator is used to join the relations by their **Prod_ID**:

```
grunt>sales_data = LOAD 'sales_trans.txt' USING PigStorage(',') AS ( Transaction_ID: int,   Customer_
ID: int,  Product_ID: int, Product_Name: chararray,    Quantity: int,    Price: float,   Timestamp:
chararray );

grunt>sales_data1  =  LOAD  'sales_trans.txt'  USING  PigStorage(',')  AS  (  Transaction_ID:  int,
Customer_ID: int,  Product_ID: int, Product_Name: chararray,    Quantity: int,    Price: float,
```

```
Timestamp: chararray );
grunt>self_joined_data = JOIN sales_data by Prod_ID, sales_data1 by Prod_ID;
```

Figure 7.6 shows the execution of the self join operator :

```
File  Edit  View  Search  Terminal  Help
grunt> self_join = JOIN sales_data by Prod_ID,sales_data1 by Prod_ID;
grunt> DUMP self_join;
2024-04-12 08:15:18,175 [main] INFO  org.apache.pig.tools.pigstats.ScriptStat
e - Pig features used in the script: HASH_JOIN
2024-04-12 08:15:18,176 [main] INFO  org.apache.pig.newplan.logical.optimizer
.LogicalPlanOptimizer - {RULES_ENABLED=[AddForEach, ColumnMapKeyPrune, Duplic
ateForEachColumnRewrite, GroupByConstParallelSetter, ImplicitSplitInserter, L
imitOptimizer, LoadTypeCastInserter, MergeFilter, MergeForEach, NewPartitionF
ilterOptimizer, PushDownForEachFlatten, PushUpFilter, SplitFilter, StreamType
CastInserter], RULES_DISABLED=[FilterLogicExpressionSimplifier, PartitionFilt
erOptimizer]}
2024-04-12 08:15:18,184 [main] INFO  org.apache.pig.backend.hadoop.executione
ngine.mapReduceLayer.MRCompiler - File concatenation threshold: 100 optimisti
c? false
2024-04-12 08:15:18,185 [main] INFO  org.apache.pig.backend.hadoop.executione
ngine.mapReduceLayer.MRCompiler$LastInputStreamingOptimizer - Rewrite: POPack
age->POForEach to POJoinPackage
2024-04-12 08:15:18,186 [main] INFO  org.apache.pig.backend.hadoop.executione
ngine.mapReduceLayer.MultiQueryOptimizer - MR plan size before optimization:
1
2024-04-12 08:15:18,186 [main] INFO  org.apache.pig.backend.hadoop.executione
```

***Figure 7.6**: Self join operator execution*

Refer to *Figure 7.7* to see the output of the self join operator :

```
File  Edit  View  Search  Terminal  Help
2024-04-12 08:15:46,583 [main] INFO  org.apache.pig.backend.hadoop.executione
ngine.util.MapRedUtil - Total input paths to process : 1
(4,104,1,"LapTop",1,800.0,"2024-03-01 10:15:00",4,104,1,"LapTop",1,800.0,"202
4-03-01 10:15:00")
(4,104,1,"LapTop",1,800.0,"2024-03-01 10:15:00",1,101,1,"LapTop",2,800.0,"202
4-03-01 10:00:00")
(1,101,1,"LapTop",2,800.0,"2024-03-01 10:00:00",4,104,1,"LapTop",1,800.0,"202
4-03-01 10:15:00")
(1,101,1,"LapTop",2,800.0,"2024-03-01 10:00:00",1,101,1,"LapTop",2,800.0,"202
4-03-01 10:00:00")
(3,103,2,"Tablet",1,400.0,"2024-03-01 10:10:00",3,103,2,"Tablet",1,400.0,"202
4-03-01 10:10:00")
(5,105,3,"Smartphone",3,600.0,"2024-03-01 10:20:00",5,105,3,"Smartphone",3,60
0.0,"2024-03-01 10:20:00")
(5,105,3,"Smartphone",3,600.0,"2024-03-01 10:20:00",2,102,3,"Smartphone",1,60
0.0,"2024-03-01 10:05:00")
(2,102,3,"Smartphone",1,600.0,"2024-03-01 10:05:00",5,105,3,"Smartphone",3,60
0.0,"2024-03-01 10:20:00")
(2,102,3,"Smartphone",1,600.0,"2024-03-01 10:05:00",2,102,3,"Smartphone",1,60
0.0,"2024-03-01 10:05:00")
```

***Figure 7.7**: Self join operator output*

Inner join

This join operator performs an inner or equi join of two or more relations based on common field values. It returns rows when a match is based on the common field in both relations. A new relation is created by combining column values of two relations based on a certain join predicate. Let us understand with the help of an example:

Consider the two relations as **sales_trans.txt** and **customers.txt** with the following details:

```
Cust_ID, Cust_Name, Age
101, "Mona", 30
102, "Rahul", 25
103, "Teana", 35
104, "Aayush", 28
105, "Nishu", 40
```

Syntax: **alias = JOIN alias BY {expression|'('expression [, expression …]')'} (, alias BY {expression|'('expression [, expression …]')'} …) [USING 'replicated' | 'skewed' | 'merge' | 'merge-sparse'] [PARTITION BY partitioner] [PARALLEL n];**

Here **BY** is a keyword, expression refers to a field expression (e.g. **X = JOIN relation1 BY field A, relation2 BY fieldB;**), **USING** is a keyword, **'replicated'** is used to perform replicated joins, **'skewed'** is used to perform skewed joins, **'merge'** is used to perform merge joins, **'merge-sparse'** is used to perform merge-sparse joins, **PARTITION BY** refers to the partitioner feature that is used to specify the Hadoop Partitioner. The partitioner controls the partitioning of the keys of the intermediate map-outputs:

Example: grunt>inner_join_result = JOIN sales_data BY Cust_ID, customers BY Cust_ID;

In the preceding example, the join-predicate is **Cust_ID**. Thus, an inner join returns only the rows with a match between the common columns (**Cust_ID**) in both relations:

```
grunt>DUMP inner_join_result;
```

Refer to *Figure 7.8*, to see the execution of the previous code in **grunt** shell:

```
File  Edit  View  Search  Terminal  Help
grunt> inner_join = JOIN sales_data BY Cust_ID, customer BY Cust_ID;
2024-04-12 07:42:20,402 [main] INFO  org.apache.hadoop.conf.Configuration.dep
recation - fs.default.name is deprecated. Instead, use fs.defaultFS
2024-04-12 07:42:20,402 [main] INFO  org.apache.hadoop.conf.Configuration.dep
recation - mapred.job.tracker is deprecated. Instead, use mapreduce.jobtracke
r.address
grunt> DUMP inner_join;
2024-04-12 07:43:06,908 [main] INFO  org.apache.pig.tools.pigstats.ScriptStat
e - Pig features used in the script: HASH_JOIN
2024-04-12 07:43:06,908 [main] INFO  org.apache.pig.newplan.logical.optimizer
.LogicalPlanOptimizer - {RULES_ENABLED=[AddForEach, ColumnMapKeyPrune, Duplic
ateForEachColumnRewrite, GroupByConstParallelSetter, ImplicitSplitInserter, L
imitOptimizer, LoadTypeCastInserter, MergeFilter, MergeForEach, NewPartitionF
ilterOptimizer, PushDownForEachFlatten, PushUpFilter, SplitFilter, StreamType
CastInserter], RULES_DISABLED=[FilterLogicExpressionSimplifier, PartitionFilt
erOptimizer]}
2024-04-12 07:43:06,918 [main] INFO  org.apache.pig.backend.hadoop.executione
ngine.mapReduceLayer.MRCompiler - File concatenation threshold: 100 optimisti
c? false
2024-04-12 07:43:06,922 [main] INFO  org.apache.pig.backend.hadoop.executione
ngine.mapReduceLayer.MRCompiler$LastInputStreamingOptimizer - Rewrite: POPack
```

***Figure** 7.8 :Inner-join operator execution*

It can be observed in *Figure 7.9* that for **Cust_ID=106**, results are not shown as this ID does not exist in the customers relation:

```
File  Edit  View  Search  Terminal  Help
job_1712927833390_0003


2024-04-12 07:43:35,267 [main] INFO  org.apache.pig.backend.hadoop.executione
ngine.mapReduceLayer.MapReduceLauncher - Success!
2024-04-12 07:43:35,268 [main] INFO  org.apache.hadoop.conf.Configuration.dep
recation - fs.default.name is deprecated. Instead, use fs.defaultFS
2024-04-12 07:43:35,268 [main] INFO  org.apache.hadoop.conf.Configuration.dep
recation - mapred.job.tracker is deprecated. Instead, use mapreduce.jobtracke
r.address
2024-04-12 07:43:35,268 [main] INFO  org.apache.pig.data.SchemaTupleBackend -
 Key [pig.schematuple] was not set... will not generate code.
2024-04-12 07:43:35,273 [main] INFO  org.apache.hadoop.mapreduce.lib.input.Fi
leInputFormat - Total input paths to process : 1
2024-04-12 07:43:35,273 [main] INFO  org.apache.pig.backend.hadoop.executione
ngine.util.MapRedUtil - Total input paths to process : 1
(1,101,1,"LapTop",2,800.0,"2024-03-01 10:00:00",101,"Mona",30)
(2,102,3,"Smartphone",1,600.0,"2024-03-01 10:05:00",102,"Rahul",25)
(3,103,2,"Tablet",1,400.0,"2024-03-01 10:10:00",103,"Teana",35)
(4,104,1,"LapTop",1,800.0,"2024-03-01 10:15:00",104,"Aayush",28)
```

Figure 7.9: *Inner-join operator output*

Join

This operator uses the keywords left, right, or full outer joins to perform the respective joins. In outer joins, the keyword OUTER is optional. In the absence of the OUTER keyword, the keywords LEFT, RIGHT, and FULL are interpreted as left outer, right outer, and full outer joins, respectively.

Note: Outer joins only work when the relations that need to produce nulls (in the case of non-matching keys) have schemas.

Outer joins only work for two-way joins; to perform a multi-way outer join, you will need to perform multiple two-way outer join statements.

Syntax:

```
alias = JOIN left-alias BY left-alias-column [LEFT|RIGHT|FULL] [OUTER], right-alias BY right-alias-column [USING 'replicated' | 'skewed' | 'merge'] [PARTITION BY partitioner] [PARALLEL n];
```

Where **BY** is a keyword, the expression refers to a field expression (e.g., **X = JOIN relation1 BY field A, relation2 BY field ;**), and alias-column refers to the name of the join column for the corresponding relation. It applies to the left-alias column and the right-alias column. **LEFT** is used for the left outer join; **RIGHT** is used for the right outer join, **FULL** for the full outer join, and **OUTER** (optional) keyword. All other features are optional as discussed in the preceding sections.

Left outer join

It returns all the rows from the left dataset and matching rows from the right dataset.

Example:

```
grunt>left_outer_join_result = JOIN sales_data BY Cust_ID LEFT OUTER, customers BY Cust_ID;
grunt>DUMP left_outer_join_result;
```

Refer to *Figure 7.14*, for the execution of the code:

```
File  Edit  View  Search  Terminal  Help
grunt> sales_data = LOAD '/chap5Pig/sales_trans.txt' USING PigStorage(',') as (T
rans_ID:int, Cust_ID:int,Prod_ID:int,Prod_Name:chararray,Qty:int,Price:float,Tim
estamp:chararray);
grunt> customer = LOAD '/chap5Pig/customers.txt' USING PigStorage(',') as (Cust_
ID:int,Cust_Name:chararray,Age:int);
grunt> left_outer_join = JOIN sales_data BY Cust_ID LEFT OUTER, customer BY Cust
_ID;
grunt> Dump left_outer_join;
2024-04-17 00:25:02,070 [main] INFO  org.apache.pig.tools.pigstats.ScriptState -
 Pig features used in the script: HASH_JOIN
2024-04-17 00:25:02,094 [main] INFO  org.apache.pig.newplan.logical.optimizer.Lo
gicalPlanOptimizer - {RULES_ENABLED=[AddForEach, ColumnMapKeyPrune, DuplicateFor
EachColumnRewrite, GroupByConstParallelSetter, ImplicitSplitInserter, LimitOptim
izer, LoadTypeCastInserter, MergeFilter, MergeForEach, NewPartitionFilterOptimiz
er, PushDownForEachFlatten, PushUpFilter, SplitFilter, StreamTypeCastInserter],
RULES_DISABLED=[FilterLogicExpressionSimplifier, PartitionFilterOptimizer]}
2024-04-17 00:25:02,171 [main] INFO  org.apache.pig.backend.hadoop.executionengi
ne.mapReduceLayer.MRCompiler - File concatenation threshold: 100 optimistic? fal
se
```

Figure 7.10: Left outer join

Refer to the following figure for output. It can be observed that **`Cust_ID=105`** is present in the left relation (**`sales_trans`**) but not in the right relation(customer). Therefore, the tuple with **`Cust_ID=105`** is also included in the output:

```
File  Edit  View  Search  Terminal  Help
job_1712927833390_0004


2024-04-12 07:50:37,138 [main] INFO  org.apache.pig.backend.hadoop.executionengine.mapReduceLayer.MapReduceLaunc
her - Success!
2024-04-12 07:50:37,138 [main] INFO  org.apache.hadoop.conf.Configuration.deprecation - fs.default.name is depre
cated. Instead, use fs.defaultFS
2024-04-12 07:50:37,138 [main] INFO  org.apache.hadoop.conf.Configuration.deprecation - mapred.job.tracker is de
precated. Instead, use mapreduce.jobtracker.address
2024-04-12 07:50:37,138 [main] INFO  org.apache.pig.data.SchemaTupleBackend - Key [pig.schematuple] was not set.
.. will not generate code.
2024-04-12 07:50:37,146 [main] INFO  org.apache.hadoop.mapreduce.lib.input.FileInputFormat - Total input paths t
o process : 1
2024-04-12 07:50:37,146 [main] INFO  org.apache.pig.backend.hadoop.executionengine.util.MapRedUtil - Total input
 paths to process : 1
(1,101,1,"LapTop",2,800.0,"2024-03-01 10:00:00",101,"Mona",30)
(2,102,3,"Smartphone",1,600.0,"2024-03-01 10:05:00",102,"Rahul",25)
(3,103,2,"Tablet",1,400.0,"2024-03-01 10:10:00",103,"Teana",35)
(4,104,1,"LapTop",1,800.0,"2024-03-01 10:15:00",104,"Aayush",28)
(5,105,3,"Smartphone",3,600.0,"2024-03-01 10:20:00",,,)
```

Figure 7.11: Left outer Join output

Right outer join

It returns all the rows from the right dataset and matching rows from the left dataset.

Example:

```
grunt>right_outer_join_result = JOIN transactions BY Cust_ID RIGHT OUTER, customers BY Cust_ID;
grunt>DUMP right_outer_join_result;
```

Refer to *Figure 7.12* for the execution of the code:

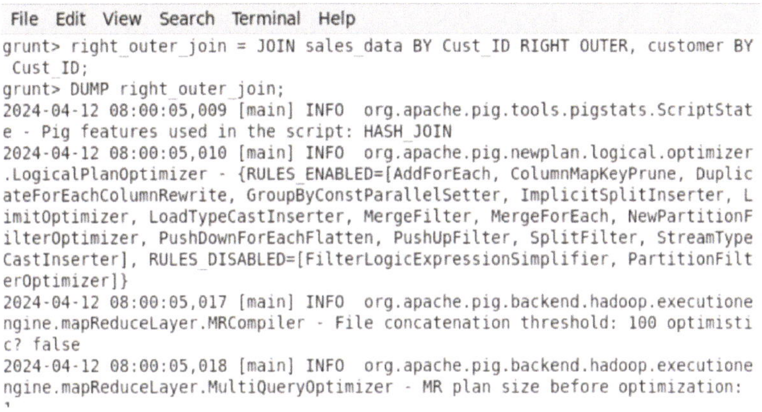

```
File Edit View Search Terminal Help
grunt> right_outer_join = JOIN sales_data BY Cust_ID RIGHT OUTER, customer BY
 Cust_ID;
grunt> DUMP right_outer_join;
2024-04-12 08:00:05,009 [main] INFO  org.apache.pig.tools.pigstats.ScriptStat
e - Pig features used in the script: HASH_JOIN
2024-04-12 08:00:05,010 [main] INFO  org.apache.pig.newplan.logical.optimizer
.LogicalPlanOptimizer - {RULES_ENABLED=[AddForEach, ColumnMapKeyPrune, Duplic
ateForEachColumnRewrite, GroupByConstParallelSetter, ImplicitSplitInserter, L
imitOptimizer, LoadTypeCastInserter, MergeFilter, MergeForEach, NewPartitionF
ilterOptimizer, PushDownForEachFlatten, PushUpFilter, SplitFilter, StreamType
CastInserter], RULES_DISABLED=[FilterLogicExpressionSimplifier, PartitionFilt
erOptimizer]}
2024-04-12 08:00:05,017 [main] INFO  org.apache.pig.backend.hadoop.executione
ngine.mapReduceLayer.MRCompiler - File concatenation threshold: 100 optimisti
c? false
2024-04-12 08:00:05,018 [main] INFO  org.apache.pig.backend.hadoop.executione
ngine.mapReduceLayer.MultiQueryOptimizer - MR plan size before optimization:
```

***Figure 7.12**:Right outer join*

Refer to *Figure 7.13* for output. As **`CustID =105`** is not present in right, it is not there in the output:

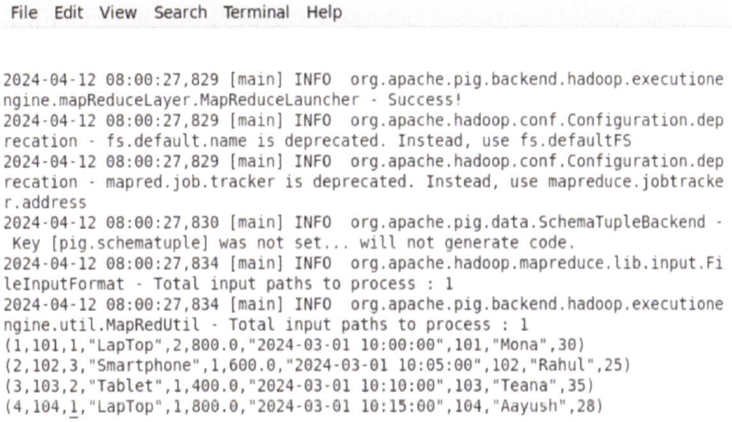

```
File Edit View Search Terminal Help

2024-04-12 08:00:27,829 [main] INFO  org.apache.pig.backend.hadoop.executione
ngine.mapReduceLayer.MapReduceLauncher - Success!
2024-04-12 08:00:27,829 [main] INFO  org.apache.hadoop.conf.Configuration.dep
recation - fs.default.name is deprecated. Instead, use fs.defaultFS
2024-04-12 08:00:27,829 [main] INFO  org.apache.hadoop.conf.Configuration.dep
recation - mapred.job.tracker is deprecated. Instead, use mapreduce.jobtracke
r.address
2024-04-12 08:00:27,830 [main] INFO  org.apache.pig.data.SchemaTupleBackend -
 Key [pig.schematuple] was not set... will not generate code.
2024-04-12 08:00:27,834 [main] INFO  org.apache.hadoop.mapreduce.lib.input.Fi
leInputFormat - Total input paths to process : 1
2024-04-12 08:00:27,834 [main] INFO  org.apache.pig.backend.hadoop.executione
ngine.util.MapRedUtil - Total input paths to process : 1
(1,101,1,"LapTop",2,800.0,"2024-03-01 10:00:00",101,"Mona",30)
(2,102,3,"Smartphone",1,600.0,"2024-03-01 10:05:00",102,"Rahul",25)
(3,103,2,"Tablet",1,400.0,"2024-03-01 10:10:00",103,"Teana",35)
(4,104,1,"LapTop",1,800.0,"2024-03-01 10:15:00",104,"Aayush",28)
```

***Figure 7.13**: Output of right outer join*

Full outer join

It returns all the rows when there is a match in the left or right dataset. The output of full outer join includes all records from both datasets:

```
grunt>full_outer_join_result = JOIN transactions BY Cust_ID FULL OUTER, customers BY Cust_ID;
grunt>DUMP full_outer_join_result;
```

Refer to *Figure 7.14* for execution of preceding code:

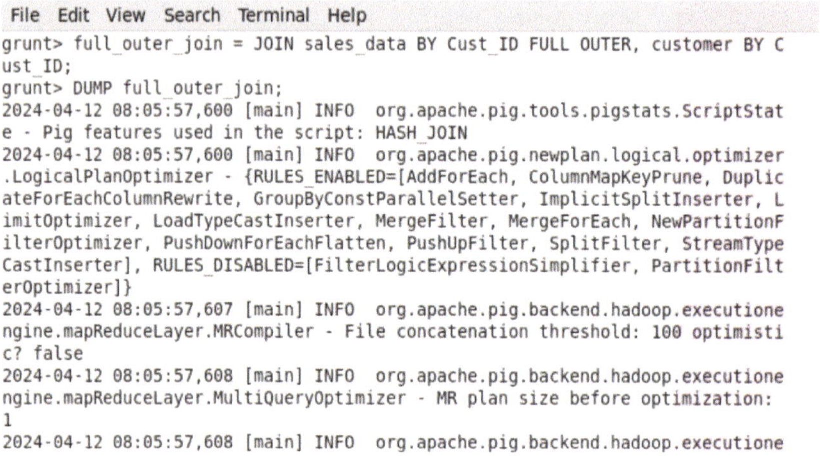

```
File  Edit  View  Search  Terminal  Help
grunt> full_outer_join = JOIN sales_data BY Cust_ID FULL OUTER, customer BY C
ust_ID;
grunt> DUMP full_outer_join;
2024-04-12 08:05:57,600 [main] INFO  org.apache.pig.tools.pigstats.ScriptStat
e - Pig features used in the script: HASH_JOIN
2024-04-12 08:05:57,600 [main] INFO  org.apache.pig.newplan.logical.optimizer
.LogicalPlanOptimizer - {RULES_ENABLED=[AddForEach, ColumnMapKeyPrune, Duplic
ateForEachColumnRewrite, GroupByConstParallelSetter, ImplicitSplitInserter, L
imitOptimizer, LoadTypeCastInserter, MergeFilter, MergeForEach, NewPartitionF
ilterOptimizer, PushDownForEachFlatten, PushUpFilter, SplitFilter, StreamType
CastInserter], RULES_DISABLED=[FilterLogicExpressionSimplifier, PartitionFilt
erOptimizer]}
2024-04-12 08:05:57,607 [main] INFO  org.apache.pig.backend.hadoop.executione
ngine.mapReduceLayer.MRCompiler - File concatenation threshold: 100 optimisti
c? false
2024-04-12 08:05:57,608 [main] INFO  org.apache.pig.backend.hadoop.executione
ngine.mapReduceLayer.MultiQueryOptimizer - MR plan size before optimization:
1
2024-04-12 08:05:57,608 [main] INFO  org.apache.pig.backend.hadoop.executione
```

***Figure 7.14**: Full outer join*

Refer to *Figure 7.15* to see the output. It combines the tuples if the match is found on the join predicate and null values where there is no match:

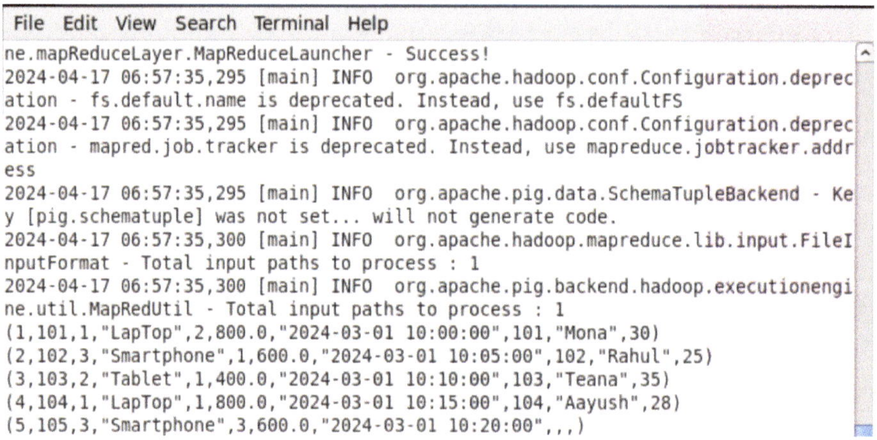

```
File  Edit  View  Search  Terminal  Help
ne.mapReduceLayer.MapReduceLauncher - Success!
2024-04-17 06:57:35,295 [main] INFO  org.apache.hadoop.conf.Configuration.deprec
ation - fs.default.name is deprecated. Instead, use fs.defaultFS
2024-04-17 06:57:35,295 [main] INFO  org.apache.hadoop.conf.Configuration.deprec
ation - mapred.job.tracker is deprecated. Instead, use mapreduce.jobtracker.addr
ess
2024-04-17 06:57:35,295 [main] INFO  org.apache.pig.data.SchemaTupleBackend - Ke
y [pig.schematuple] was not set... will not generate code.
2024-04-17 06:57:35,300 [main] INFO  org.apache.hadoop.mapreduce.lib.input.FileI
nputFormat - Total input paths to process : 1
2024-04-17 06:57:35,300 [main] INFO  org.apache.pig.backend.hadoop.executionengi
ne.util.MapRedUtil - Total input paths to process : 1
(1,101,1,"LapTop",2,800.0,"2024-03-01 10:00:00",101,"Mona",30)
(2,102,3,"Smartphone",1,600.0,"2024-03-01 10:05:00",102,"Rahul",25)
(3,103,2,"Tablet",1,400.0,"2024-03-01 10:10:00",103,"Teana",35)
(4,104,1,"LapTop",1,800.0,"2024-03-01 10:15:00",104,"Aayush",28)
(5,105,3,"Smartphone",3,600.0,"2024-03-01 10:20:00",,,)
```

***Figure 7.15**: Output of full outer join*

GROUP and COGROUP

Operators similar to each other. However, GROUP is applied to one relation, and COGROUP is used in statements involving two or more relations. Grouping is done based on a key. The COGROUP operator groups the data from multiple relations based on a common key. At one time, the COGROUP operator can be used with up to 127 relations. COGROUP can be used when you want to do operations like a semi join in Pig Latin.

Example:

Grouping transactions by `Cust_ID`:

```
grunt>group_sales= GROUP sales_data BY Cust_ID;
grunt>Dump group_sales;
```

Refer to *Figure 7.16* for execution of preceding code in Grunt shell:

```
File  Edit  View  Search  Terminal  Help
grunt> group_sales = GROUP sales_data BY Cust_ID;
grunt> DUMP group_sales;
2024-04-12 08:19:28,035 [main] INFO  org.apache.pig.tools.pigstats.ScriptStat
e - Pig features used in the script: GROUP_BY
2024-04-12 08:19:28,035 [main] INFO  org.apache.pig.newplan.logical.optimizer
.LogicalPlanOptimizer - {RULES_ENABLED=[AddForEach, ColumnMapKeyPrune, Duplic
ateForEachColumnRewrite, GroupByConstParallelSetter, ImplicitSplitInserter, L
imitOptimizer, LoadTypeCastInserter, MergeFilter, MergeForEach, NewPartitionF
ilterOptimizer, PushDownForEachFlatten, PushUpFilter, SplitFilter, StreamType
CastInserter], RULES_DISABLED=[FilterLogicExpressionSimplifier, PartitionFilt
erOptimizer]}
2024-04-12 08:19:28,041 [main] INFO  org.apache.pig.backend.hadoop.executione
ngine.mapReduceLayer.MRCompiler - File concatenation threshold: 100 optimisti
c? false
2024-04-12 08:19:28,043 [main] INFO  org.apache.pig.backend.hadoop.executione
ngine.mapReduceLayer.MultiQueryOptimizer - MR plan size before optimization:
1
2024-04-12 08:19:28,043 [main] INFO  org.apache.pig.backend.hadoop.executione
ngine.mapReduceLayer.MultiQueryOptimizer - MR plan size after optimization: 1
2024-04-12 08:19:28,061 [main] INFO  org.apache.hadoop.yarn.client.RMProxy -
```

***Figure 7.16**: Group sales data*

Refer to *Figure 7.17* for output. In the output, each tuple consists of **`Cust_ID`** and a bag of all transactions corresponding to that **`Cust_ID`**. Since in our dataset, each **`Cust_ID`** appears only once, each bag contains a single transaction. If a **`Cust_ID`** had multiple transactions, all its transactions would be nested in the same bag.

```
2024-04-12 08:19:51,116 [main] INFO  org.apache.pig.backend.hadoop.executione
ngine.mapReduceLayer.MapReduceLauncher - Success!
2024-04-12 08:19:51,116 [main] INFO  org.apache.hadoop.conf.Configuration.dep
recation - fs.default.name is deprecated. Instead, use fs.defaultFS
2024-04-12 08:19:51,116 [main] INFO  org.apache.hadoop.conf.Configuration.dep
recation - mapred.job.tracker is deprecated. Instead, use mapreduce.jobtracke
r.address
2024-04-12 08:19:51,117 [main] INFO  org.apache.pig.data.SchemaTupleBackend -
 Key [pig.schematuple] was not set... will not generate code.
2024-04-12 08:19:51,123 [main] INFO  org.apache.hadoop.mapreduce.lib.input.Fi
leInputFormat - Total input paths to process : 1
2024-04-12 08:19:51,123 [main] INFO  org.apache.pig.backend.hadoop.executione
ngine.util.MapRedUtil - Total input paths to process : 1
(101,{(1,101,1,"LapTop",2,800.0,"2024-03-01 10:00:00")})
(102,{(2,102,3,"Smartphone",1,600.0,"2024-03-01 10:05:00")})
(103,{(3,103,2,"Tablet",1,400.0,"2024-03-01 10:10:00")})
(104,{(4,104,1,"LapTop",1,800.0,"2024-03-01 10:15:00")})
(105,{(5,105,3,"Smartphone",3,600.0,"2024-03-01 10:20:00")})
```

***Figure 7.17**: Output of group sales data*

COGROUP transactions with customers data based on **`Cust_ID`**.

```
grunt>cogroup_sales = COGROUP sales_data BY Cust_ID, customer BY Cust_ID;
grunt>DUMP cogroup_sales;
```

Refer to *Figure 7.18* for execution of preceding code:

```
cloudera@quickstart:~
File Edit View Search Terminal Help
grunt> cogroup_sales = COGROUP sales_data BY Cust_ID, customer BY Cust_ID;
grunt> Dump cogroup_sales;
2024-04-17 07:07:35,204 [main] INFO  org.apache.pig.tools.pigstats.ScriptState -
 Pig features used in the script: COGROUP
2024-04-17 07:07:35,204 [main] INFO  org.apache.pig.newplan.logical.optimizer.Lo
gicalPlanOptimizer - {RULES_ENABLED=[AddForEach, ColumnMapKeyPrune, DuplicateFor
EachColumnRewrite, GroupByConstParallelSetter, ImplicitSplitInserter, LimitOptim
izer, LoadTypeCastInserter, MergeFilter, MergeForEach, NewPartitionFilterOptimiz
er, PushDownForEachFlatten, PushUpFilter, SplitFilter, StreamTypeCastInserter],
RULES_DISABLED=[FilterLogicExpressionSimplifier, PartitionFilterOptimizer]}
2024-04-17 07:07:35,212 [main] INFO  org.apache.pig.backend.hadoop.executionengi
ne.mapReduceLayer.MRCompiler - File concatenation threshold: 100 optimistic? fal
se
2024-04-17 07:07:35,214 [main] INFO  org.apache.pig.backend.hadoop.executionengi
ne.mapReduceLayer.MultiQueryOptimizer - MR plan size before optimization: 1
2024-04-17 07:07:35,214 [main] INFO  org.apache.pig.backend.hadoop.executionengi
ne.mapReduceLayer.MultiQueryOptimizer - MR plan size after optimization: 1
2024-04-17 07:07:35,227 [main] INFO  org.apache.hadoop.yarn.client.RMProxy - Con
necting to ResourceManager at /0.0.0.0:8032
```

Figure 7.18: *COGROUP sales data with customer data*

Refer to *Figure 7.19* for the output:

```
2024-04-12 08:24:51,055 [main] INFO  org.apache.pig.backend.hadoop.executione
ngine.mapReduceLayer.MapReduceLauncher - Success!
2024-04-12 08:24:51,056 [main] INFO  org.apache.hadoop.conf.Configuration.dep
recation - fs.default.name is deprecated. Instead, use fs.defaultFS
2024-04-12 08:24:51,056 [main] INFO  org.apache.hadoop.conf.Configuration.dep
recation - mapred.job.tracker is deprecated. Instead, use mapreduce.jobtracke
r.address
2024-04-12 08:24:51,056 [main] INFO  org.apache.pig.data.SchemaTupleBackend -
 Key [pig.schematuple] was not set... will not generate code.
2024-04-12 08:24:51,062 [main] INFO  org.apache.hadoop.mapreduce.lib.input.Fi
leInputFormat - Total input paths to process : 1
2024-04-12 08:24:51,062 [main] INFO  org.apache.pig.backend.hadoop.executione
ngine.util.MapRedUtil - Total input paths to process : 1
(101,{(1,101,1,"LapTop",2,800.0,"2024-03-01 10:00:00")},{(101,"Mona",30)})
(102,{(2,102,3,"Smartphone",1,600.0,"2024-03-01 10:05:00")},{(102,"Rahul",25)
})
(103,{(3,103,2,"Tablet",1,400.0,"2024-03-01 10:10:00")},{(103,"Teana",35)})
(104,{(4,104,1,"LapTop",1,800.0,"2024-03-01 10:15:00")},{(104,"Aayush",28)})
(105,{(5,105,3,"Smartphone",3,600.0,"2024-03-01 10:20:00")},{})
```

Figure 7.19: *Output of COGROUP*

CROSS

`CROSS` operator is used to compute the cross product or Cartesian product or cross join among two or more relations, refer to *Figure 7.20*.

Syntax: **`alias = CROSS alias, alias [, alias …] [PARTITION BY partitioner] [PARALLEL n];`**

An alias is the name of a relation. `PARTITION BY` partitioner specifies the Hadoop Partitioner. It controls the partitioning of the keys of the intermediate map outputs. `PARALLEL n`, can be used to increase a job's parallelism by specifying the number of reduce tasks.

For example:

```
grunt>cross_result = CROSS sales_data, customer;
grunt>DUMP cross_result;
```

Refer *to Figure 7.20* for the execution of the preceding code:

```
File  Edit  View  Search  Terminal  Help
grunt> cross_result = CROSS sales_data,customer;
grunt> DUMP cross_result;
2024-04-12 08:29:16,321 [main] INFO  org.apache.pig.tools.pigstats.ScriptStat
e - Pig features used in the script: CROSS
2024-04-12 08:29:16,321 [main] INFO  org.apache.pig.newplan.logical.optimizer
.LogicalPlanOptimizer - {RULES_ENABLED=[AddForEach, ColumnMapKeyPrune, Duplic
ateForEachColumnRewrite, GroupByConstParallelSetter, ImplicitSplitInserter, L
imitOptimizer, LoadTypeCastInserter, MergeFilter, MergeForEach, NewPartitionF
ilterOptimizer, PushDownForEachFlatten, PushUpFilter, SplitFilter, StreamType
CastInserter], RULES_DISABLED=[FilterLogicExpressionSimplifier, PartitionFilt
erOptimizer]}
2024-04-12 08:29:16,336 [main] INFO  org.apache.pig.backend.hadoop.executione
ngine.mapReduceLayer.MRCompiler - File concatenation threshold: 100 optimisti
c? false
2024-04-12 08:29:16,338 [main] INFO  org.apache.pig.backend.hadoop.executione
ngine.mapReduceLayer.MRCompiler$LastInputStreamingOptimizer - Rewrite: POPack
age->POForEach to POJoinPackage
2024-04-12 08:29:16,338 [main] INFO  org.apache.pig.backend.hadoop.executione
ngine.mapReduceLayer.MultiQueryOptimizer - MR plan size before optimization:
1
```

***Figure 7.20**: CROSS between sales data and customer data*

The result of the CROSS operation is a new relation containing all possible combinations of rows from the input relations, as shown in *Figure 7.21:*

```
cloudera@quickstart:~
File  Edit  View  Search  Terminal  Help
(5,105,3,"Smartphone",3,600.0,"2024-03-01 10:20:00",104,"Aayush",28)
(5,105,3,"Smartphone",3,600.0,"2024-03-01 10:20:00",103,"Teana",35)
(5,105,3,"Smartphone",3,600.0,"2024-03-01 10:20:00",102,"Rahul",25)
(5,105,3,"Smartphone",3,600.0,"2024-03-01 10:20:00",101,"Mona",30)
(4,104,1,"LapTop",1,800.0,"2024-03-01 10:15:00",104,"Aayush",28)
(4,104,1,"LapTop",1,800.0,"2024-03-01 10:15:00",103,"Teana",35)
(4,104,1,"LapTop",1,800.0,"2024-03-01 10:15:00",102,"Rahul",25)
(4,104,1,"LapTop",1,800.0,"2024-03-01 10:15:00",101,"Mona",30)
(3,103,2,"Tablet",1,400.0,"2024-03-01 10:10:00",104,"Aayush",28)
(3,103,2,"Tablet",1,400.0,"2024-03-01 10:10:00",103,"Teana",35)
(3,103,2,"Tablet",1,400.0,"2024-03-01 10:10:00",102,"Rahul",25)
(3,103,2,"Tablet",1,400.0,"2024-03-01 10:10:00",101,"Mona",30)
(2,102,3,"Smartphone",1,600.0,"2024-03-01 10:05:00",104,"Aayush",28)
(2,102,3,"Smartphone",1,600.0,"2024-03-01 10:05:00",103,"Teana",35)
(2,102,3,"Smartphone",1,600.0,"2024-03-01 10:05:00",102,"Rahul",25)
(2,102,3,"Smartphone",1,600.0,"2024-03-01 10:05:00",101,"Mona",30)
(1,101,1,"LapTop",2,800.0,"2024-03-01 10:00:00",104,"Aayush",28)
(1,101,1,"LapTop",2,800.0,"2024-03-01 10:00:00",103,"Teana",35)
(1,101,1,"LapTop",2,800.0,"2024-03-01 10:00:00",102,"Rahul",25)
(1,101,1,"LapTop",2,800.0,"2024-03-01 10:00:00",101,"Mona",30)
```

***Figure 7.21**: Output of CROSS operator*

This operator can be used to find all possible pairs of items from two datasets. Using CROSS on large datasets can be computationally expensive and result in a massive output relation. Therefore, it is important to consider other, more efficient ways to achieve the desired outcome, such as Pig Latin operators like JOIN, which can also achieve similar results without generating as much data.

CUBE

It is used to perform cube/rollup operations.

The CUBE operation is used to perform data aggregation for all possible combinations of specified groups by dimensions. It is used for multidimensional analysis of data. This is particularly useful to generate summary (like counts, sums, etc.) statistics or perform aggregation across multiple dimensions. The number of groups by combinations generated by the cube for n dimensions will be 2n.

Syntax: `alias = CUBE alias BY {CUBE expression | ROLLUP expression }, [ CUBE expression | ROLLUP expression ] [PARALLEL n];`

Where alias is the name of the relation, **CUBE**, **ROLLUP**, and **BY** are keywords, and expression refers to the projections (dimensions) of the relation. It supports field, star, and project-range expressions.

For example:

```
grunt>cube_data = CUBE sales_data BY CUBE(Prod_ID,Cust_ID,Qty);
grunt>summary_stat = FOREACH cube_data GENERATE group as cube_group, SUM(cube.Qty) AS total_qty, SUM(cube.Price) AS total_price;
grunt> Dump summary_stat;
```

Figure 7.22 shows the usage of the CUBE operator:

```
grunt> cube_data = CUBE sales_data BY CUBE(Prod_ID,Cu
st_ID,Qty);
grunt> summary_stat = FOREACH cube_data GENERATE grou
p as cube_group, SUM(cube.Qty) AS total_qty, SUM(cube
.Price) AS total_price;
grunt> Dump summary_stat;
```

***Figure 7.22:** CUBE operator on sales data*

Figure 7.23 shows the partial output of the **CUBE** operator, as the actual production has a large number of rows:

```
2024-04-17 07:24:37,531 [main] INFO  org.apache.hadoop.conf.Configuration.deprecation
- mapred.job.tracker is deprecated. Instead, use mapreduce.jobtracker.address
2024-04-17 07:24:37,532 [main] INFO  org.apache.pig.data.SchemaTupleBackend - Key [pig
.schematuple] was not set... will not generate code.
2024-04-17 07:24:37,540 [main] INFO  org.apache.hadoop.mapreduce.lib.input.FileInputFo
rmat - Total input paths to process : 1
2024-04-17 07:24:37,540 [main] INFO  org.apache.pig.backend.hadoop.executionengine.uti
l.MapRedUtil - Total input paths to process : 1
((1,101,2),2,800.0)
((1,101,),,800.0)
((1,104,1),1,800.0)
((1,104,),,800.0)
((1,,1),1,800.0)
((1,,2),2,800.0)
((1,,),,1600.0)
((2,103,1),1,400.0)
((2,103,),,400.0)
((2,,1),1,400.0)
((2,,),,400.0)
((3,102,1),1,600.0)
```

***Figure 7.23:** Output of the CUBE operator on sales data*

Let us understand this output in detail:

- Each line represents a grouping set along with its corresponding total quantity and total price. The **`cube_group`** column shows the dimensions involved in each grouping set.
- For example, ((1,101,2),2,800.0) indicates a grouping set where Prod_ID is 1, Cust_ID is 101, and Qty is 2.
- The **`total_quantity`** column represents the total quantity of products sold(here value is 2) for each grouping set, and the **`total_price`** column represents the total price of products (here value is 800.0) sold for each grouping set.

CUBE is useful for generating comprehensive reports or performing exploratory data analysis when you must simultaneously analyze data across multiple dimensions. However, CUBE can significantly increase the size of the result set, so it is essential to use it judiciously, especially with large datasets.

Rollup operation

The ROLLUP operation is used for multi-level aggregation, similar to the **GROUP BY** operation, but with the addition of generating subtotal rows for each level of aggregation. It computes a set of aggregations, including totals for a value hierarchy. The number of groups by combinations generated by rollup for n dimensions will be n+1.

The following statements are used to group by **Prod_ID** and **Cust_ID**, and perform **ROLLUP**:

```
grunt>rollup_data = CUBE sales_data BY ROLLUP(Prod_ID, Cust_ID);
grunt>summary_stat = FOREACH rollup_data GENERATE group AS rollup_group;
grunt> Dump summary_stat;
```

Refer to *Figure 7.24* for the execution of the preceding code in the shell. In *Figure 7.24*, the first line aggregates the **sales_data** relation by using the **CUBE** operator with the **ROLLUP** function on the columns **Prod_ID** and **Cust_ID**. It creates multiple levels of subtotals and a grand total based on combinations of these columns.

In the next statement, **FOREACH** is used to iterate over each record in the **rollup_data** relation, and the **GENERATE** keyword is used to specify the fields to be included in the output. In this case, it renames the grouping column generated by **ROLLUP** as **rollup_group** and assigns it to a new relation, **summary_stats**. The next command displays the summary statistics or aggregated data generated by the **ROLLUP** operation.

```
grunt> rollup_data = CUBE sales_data BY ROLLUP(Prod_ID,Cust_ID);
grunt> summary_stat = FOREACH rollup_data GENERATE group AS rollup_group;
grunt> Dump summary_stat;
```

***Figure 7.24**: Rollup operator*

After execution, the output generated by the preceding code is shown in *Figure 7.25*. In this output, each line represents a grouping set along with its corresponding total sales amount. The grouping sets are formed based on the **ROLLUP** operation, which generates subtotal rows for various levels of aggregation.

For example, (1,101) indicates the total sales amount for product 1 purchased by customer 101, (1,) means the total sales amount for product 1 across all customers, (101) refers to the total sales amount for all products purchased by customer 101, and (,) indicates the overall total sales amount across all products and customers.

This output provides a hierarchical summary of the total sales amount at different levels of aggregation, which provides a deeper analysis of the data. The **ROLLUP** operation thus helps to efficiently compute subtotal rows for various levels of aggregation to get a comprehensive summary of the data.

```
2024-04-17 09:49:03,349 [main] INFO  org.apache.hadoop.conf.Configuration.deprecation - fs.default.name is depre
cated. Instead, use fs.defaultFS
2024-04-17 09:49:03,349 [main] INFO  org.apache.hadoop.conf.Configuration.deprecation - mapred.job.tracker is de
precated. Instead, use mapreduce.jobtracker.address
2024-04-17 09:49:03,349 [main] INFO  org.apache.pig.data.SchemaTupleBackend - Key [pig.schematuple] was not set.
.. will not generate code.
2024-04-17 09:49:03,354 [main] INFO  org.apache.hadoop.mapreduce.lib.input.FileInputFormat - Total input paths t
o process : 1
2024-04-17 09:49:03,354 [main] INFO  org.apache.pig.backend.hadoop.executionengine.util.MapRedUtil - Total input
 paths to process : 1
((1,101))
((1,104))
((1,))
((2,103))
((2,))
((3,102))
((3,105))
((3,))
((,))
grunt>
```

***Figure 7.25**: Output of rollup operator*

Refer to the following table, which compares **CUBE** with **ROLLUP** operators:

Feature	CUBE	ROLLUP
Purpose	It generates all possible combinations.	It generates hierarchical summarization.
No. of groups	2^n(exponential)	n+1(linear)
Complexity	More expensive	Less expensive
Use case	Multidimensional analysis	Hierarchical drill downs

***Table 7.1:** Comparison table*

If **CUBE** and **ROLLUP** operations are used together, the output groups will be the cross product of all groups generated by the cube and rollup operations. If there are m dimensions in cube operations and n dimensions in rollup operation, then the overall number of combinations will be *(2^m) * (n+1)*.

UNION operator

It is used to merge the contents of two or more relations. It does not preserve the order of tuples. Both the input and output relations are interpreted as unordered bags of tuples. Like other databases, it is the user's responsibility to either ensure that the tuples in the input relations have the same schema or be able to process varying tuples in the output relation. It does not eliminate duplicate tuples either.

Syntax: `alias = UNION [ONSCHEMA] alias, alias [, alias …] [PARALLEL n];`

Where an alias is the name of a relation, **ONSCHEMA** is a clause used to base the union on named fields (rather than positional notation). All inputs to the union must have a non-unknown (non-null) schema. **PARALLEL n** option is only applicable for tez execution mode and does not work with MapReduce mode. Specifying **PARALLEL** introduces an extra reduce step, which degrades the performance. Here, the main purpose is to control the number of output files.

For example:

```
-- UNION operation to combine two datasets
grunt>union_result = UNION sales_data, customer;
grunt>Dump union_result;
```

Refer to *Figure 7.26* for the execution of the code:

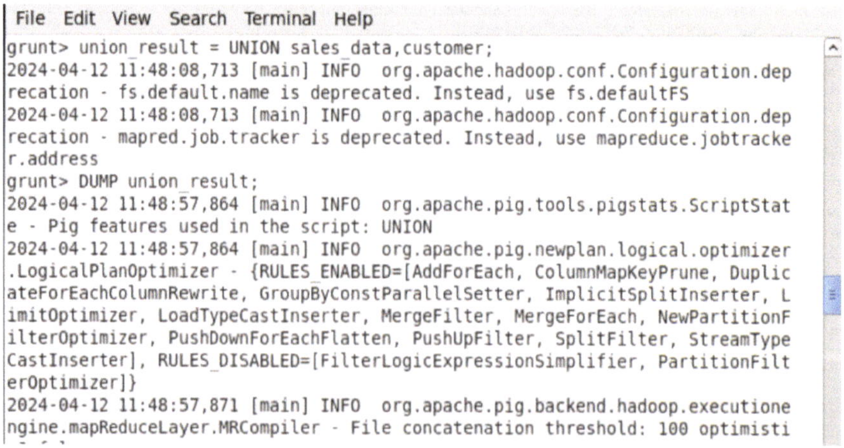

```
File Edit View Search Terminal Help
grunt> union_result = UNION sales_data,customer;
2024-04-12 11:48:08,713 [main] INFO  org.apache.hadoop.conf.Configuration.dep
recation - fs.default.name is deprecated. Instead, use fs.defaultFS
2024-04-12 11:48:08,713 [main] INFO  org.apache.hadoop.conf.Configuration.dep
recation - mapred.job.tracker is deprecated. Instead, use mapreduce.jobtracke
r.address
grunt> DUMP union_result;
2024-04-12 11:48:57,864 [main] INFO  org.apache.pig.tools.pigstats.ScriptStat
e - Pig features used in the script: UNION
2024-04-12 11:48:57,864 [main] INFO  org.apache.pig.newplan.logical.optimizer
.LogicalPlanOptimizer - {RULES_ENABLED=[AddForEach, ColumnMapKeyPrune, Duplic
ateForEachColumnRewrite, GroupByConstParallelSetter, ImplicitSplitInserter, L
imitOptimizer, LoadTypeCastInserter, MergeFilter, MergeForEach, NewPartitionF
ilterOptimizer, PushDownForEachFlatten, PushUpFilter, SplitFilter, StreamType
CastInserter], RULES_DISABLED=[FilterLogicExpressionSimplifier, PartitionFilt
erOptimizer]}
2024-04-12 11:48:57,871 [main] INFO  org.apache.pig.backend.hadoop.executione
ngine.mapReduceLayer.MRCompiler - File concatenation threshold: 100 optimisti
```

***Figure 7.26:** Usage of UNION operator*

Figure 7.27 shows the output of the **UNION** operator. It precisely depicts the combined output of both relations:

```
File Edit View Search Terminal Help
2024-04-12 11:49:21,331 [main] INFO  org.apache.hadoop.conf.Configuration.dep
recation - mapred.job.tracker is deprecated. Instead, use mapreduce.jobtracke
r.address
2024-04-12 11:49:21,332 [main] INFO  org.apache.pig.data.SchemaTupleBackend -
 Key [pig.schematuple] was not set... will not generate code.
2024-04-12 11:49:21,340 [main] INFO  org.apache.hadoop.mapreduce.lib.input.Fi
leInputFormat - Total input paths to process : 2
2024-04-12 11:49:21,340 [main] INFO  org.apache.pig.backend.hadoop.executione
ngine.util.MapRedUtil - Total input paths to process : 2
(1,101,1,"LapTop",2,800.0,"2024-03-01 10:00:00")
(2,102,3,"Smartphone",1,600.0,"2024-03-01 10:05:00")
(3,103,2,"Tablet",1,400.0,"2024-03-01 10:10:00")
(4,104,1,"LapTop",1,800.0,"2024-03-01 10:15:00")
(5,105,3,"Smartphone",3,600.0,"2024-03-01 10:20:00")
(101,"Mona",30)
(102,"Rahul",25)
(103,"Teana",35)
(104,"Aayush",28)
```

***Figure 7.27:** Output of the UNION operator*

SPLIT

The SPLIT operator is used to partition the contents of a relation into two or more relations based on some given expression. Based on the conditions stated in the expression, a tuple may be assigned to more than one relation or may not be assigned to any relation.

Syntax: **`SPLIT alias INTO alias IF expression, alias IF expression [, alias IF expression …] [, alias OTHERWISE];`**

Where alias is the name of a relation, **`INTO`** and **`IF`** are the required keywords, expression is an expression, and **`OTHERWISE`** is an optional keyword that designates a default relation.

Example:

```
grunt>SPLIT customer INTO cust_details1 IF Age < 30, cust_details2 OTHERWISE;
grunt> Dump cust_details1;
```

As shown in *Figure 7.28,* **`SPLIT`** operators can be used to split the dataset based on certain conditions. Here, the customer dataset is split based on age; the dataset with age less than 30 is stored in **`cust_details1,`** and the rest is stored in **`cust_details2`**:

```
grunt> SPLIT customer into cust_details1 if Age < 30, cust_details2 OTHERWISE;
grunt> DUMP cust_details2;
```

***Figure 7.28:** Use of the SPLIT operator*

The output of **cust_details1**, as shown in *Figure 7.29*, has records with ages less than 30:

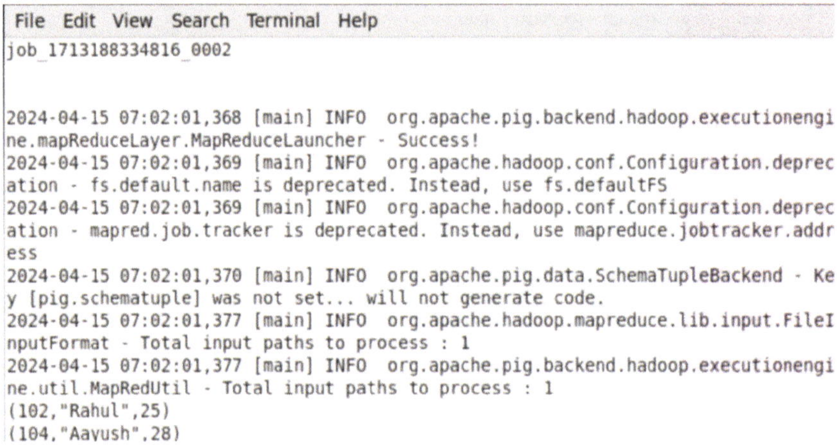

```
File  Edit  View  Search  Terminal  Help
job_1713188334816_0002


2024-04-15 07:02:01,368 [main] INFO  org.apache.pig.backend.hadoop.executionengi
ne.mapReduceLayer.MapReduceLauncher - Success!
2024-04-15 07:02:01,369 [main] INFO  org.apache.hadoop.conf.Configuration.deprec
ation - fs.default.name is deprecated. Instead, use fs.defaultFS
2024-04-15 07:02:01,369 [main] INFO  org.apache.hadoop.conf.Configuration.deprec
ation - mapred.job.tracker is deprecated. Instead, use mapreduce.jobtracker.addr
ess
2024-04-15 07:02:01,370 [main] INFO  org.apache.pig.data.SchemaTupleBackend - Ke
y [pig.schematuple] was not set... will not generate code.
2024-04-15 07:02:01,377 [main] INFO  org.apache.hadoop.mapreduce.lib.input.FileI
nputFormat - Total input paths to process : 1
2024-04-15 07:02:01,377 [main] INFO  org.apache.pig.backend.hadoop.executionengi
ne.util.MapRedUtil - Total input paths to process : 1
(102,"Rahul",25)
(104,"Aayush",28)
```

***Figure 7.29**: Output of SPLIT operator*

Filtering and transformation operators

In Apache Pig, filtering and transformation operators play a crucial role in processing large datasets efficiently. Filtering operators are used to extract specific subsets of data based on conditions. The most commonly used filtering operator is **FILTER**, which removes unwanted records based on a given condition. Other useful operators include **DISTINCT** (removes duplicates) and **LIMIT** (restricts the number of records). On the other hand, transformation operators help to modify and reshape data. Common transformation operators include **FOREACH** ... **GENERATE** (used for column selection and computations), **FLATTEN** (to unnest nested data), and **JOIN** (to combine multiple datasets). By leveraging these operators, you can clean, refine, and transform raw data into meaningful insights efficiently in a Hadoop-based big data environment.

FILTER operator

It is used to extract the subset of data that meets the desired criteria. It is a core concept for data manipulation and analysis tasks in Pig Latin. The **FILTER** operator can be used to remove unwanted or irrelevant data from the datasets for analysis. It is also used along with **JOIN** or **SPLIT** operators to achieve the desired data selection. However, the **FILTER** operation's efficiency depends on the condition's complexity and the input data's size. Simple conditions are usually faster to evaluate.

Syntax: alias = FILTER alias BY expression;

Where alias is the name of the relation, **BY** is the required keyword, and expression refers to the Boolean expression.

For example:

```
grunt>filtered_transactions = FILTER sales_data BY Qty > 1;

grunt> Dump filtered_transactions;
```

Figure 7.30 shows the use **FILTER** operator to filter the sales data where **Qty** is greater than 1:

```
File Edit View Search Terminal Help
grunt> filtered_transactions = FILTER sales_data BY Qty > 1;
grunt> Dump filtered_transactions;
2024-04-15 07:12:06,335 [main] INFO  org.apache.pig.tools.pigstats.ScriptState -
 Pig features used in the script: FILTER
2024-04-15 07:12:06,335 [main] INFO  org.apache.pig.newplan.logical.optimizer.Lo
gicalPlanOptimizer - {RULES_ENABLED=[AddForEach, ColumnMapKeyPrune, DuplicateFor
EachColumnRewrite, GroupByConstParallelSetter, ImplicitSplitInserter, LimitOptim
izer, LoadTypeCastInserter, MergeFilter, MergeForEach, NewPartitionFilterOptimiz
er, PushDownForEachFlatten, PushUpFilter, SplitFilter, StreamTypeCastInserter],
RULES_DISABLED=[FilterLogicExpressionSimplifier, PartitionFilterOptimizer]}
2024-04-15 07:12:06,341 [main] INFO  org.apache.pig.backend.hadoop.executionengi
ne.mapReduceLayer.MRCompiler - File concatenation threshold: 100 optimistic? fal
se
2024-04-15 07:12:06,342 [main] INFO  org.apache.pig.backend.hadoop.executionengi
ne.mapReduceLayer.MultiQueryOptimizer - MR plan size before optimization: 1
2024-04-15 07:12:06,342 [main] INFO  org.apache.pig.backend.hadoop.executionengi
ne.mapReduceLayer.MultiQueryOptimizer - MR plan size after optimization: 1
2024-04-15 07:12:06,356 [main] INFO  org.apache.hadoop.yarn.client.RMProxy - Con
necting to ResourceManager at /0.0.0.0:8032
2024-04-15 07:12:06,358 [main] INFO  org.apache.pig.tools.pigstats.ScriptState -
```

***Figure 7.30**: Use of FILTER operator*

In the output, refer to *Figure 7.31*, which illustrates that only tuples with a quantity greater than 1 are retained, which are transaction IDs 1 and 5. The **`FILTER`** operator effectively selects rows from the input relation (**`sales_data`**) that satisfy the specified condition (Qty > 1). These selected rows form the output relation (**`filtered_transactions`**):

```
Job DAG:
job_1713188334816_0004


2024-04-15 07:12:24,257 [main] INFO  org.apache.pig.backend.hadoop.executionengi
ne.mapReduceLayer.MapReduceLauncher - Success!
2024-04-15 07:12:24,257 [main] INFO  org.apache.hadoop.conf.Configuration.deprec
ation - fs.default.name is deprecated. Instead, use fs.defaultFS
2024-04-15 07:12:24,257 [main] INFO  org.apache.hadoop.conf.Configuration.deprec
ation - mapred.job.tracker is deprecated. Instead, use mapreduce.jobtracker.addr
ess
2024-04-15 07:12:24,258 [main] INFO  org.apache.pig.data.SchemaTupleBackend - Ke
y [pig.schematuple] was not set... will not generate code.
2024-04-15 07:12:24,267 [main] INFO  org.apache.hadoop.mapreduce.lib.input.FileI
nputFormat - Total input paths to process : 1
2024-04-15 07:12:24,267 [main] INFO  org.apache.pig.backend.hadoop.executionengi
ne.util.MapRedUtil - Total input paths to process : 1
(1,101,1,"LapTop",2,800.0,"2024-03-01 10:00:00")
(5,105,3,"Smartphone",3,600.0,"2024-03-01 10:20:00")
```

***Figure 7.31**: Output of FILTER operator*

FOREACH GENERATE

The FOREACH operator is used to iterate over each element (tuple or bag(inner bags and outer bags) within a relation and perform specific transformations on them. It works with columns of data. **`FOREACH`** processes each row (tuple) or element within a bag (collection of values) individually within a relation. Inside the **`FOREACH`** block, transformations are defined using Pig Latin statements to modify or generate new data, based on the current element. These statements can be project, filter, UDFs. The output of **`FOREACH`** can be a new relation containing modified elements or a completely new structure based on the applied transformations. It is similar to the **`SELECT`** statement in SQL.

Syntax:

```
alias  = FOREACH { block | nested_block };
```

Where alias is the name of the relation (outer bag), block refers to **FOREACH...GENERATE** block used with a relation (outer bag).

Note: FOREACH statements can be nested to two levels only. FOREACH statements that are nested to three or more levels will result in a grammar error.

For example:

```
grunt>trans_data = FOREACH sales_data GENERATE Trans_ID as T_ID, QTY AS Qnt, Price AS Unit_price, Qty*Price AS Total_cost;
grunt> Dump trans_data;
```

Figure 7.32 shows the use of the **FOREACH** ...**GENERATE** operator to calculate the total cost for each transaction and select relevant columns.

The **FOREACH** operator iterates over each tuple in the input relation (**sales_data**), calculates the total cost by multiplying the quantity (**Qty**) by the unit price (**Price**), and selects the relevant columns for the output relation (**trans_data**).

```
File Edit View Search Terminal Help
grunt> trans_data = FOREACH sales_data GENERATE Trans_ID AS T_ID, Qty AS Qnt,Pri
ce AS Unit_price, Qty*Price AS Total_cost;
2024-04-15 07:21:45,871 [main] WARN  org.apache.pig.PigServer - Encountered Warn
ing IMPLICIT_CAST_TO_FLOAT 1 time(s).
grunt> Dump trans_data;
2024-04-15 07:22:06,901 [main] WARN  org.apache.pig.PigServer - Encountered Warn
ing IMPLICIT_CAST_TO_FLOAT 1 time(s).
2024-04-15 07:22:06,902 [main] INFO  org.apache.pig.tools.pigstats.ScriptState -
 Pig features used in the script: UNKNOWN
2024-04-15 07:22:06,903 [main] INFO  org.apache.pig.newplan.logical.optimizer.Lo
gicalPlanOptimizer - {RULES_ENABLED=[AddForEach, ColumnMapKeyPrune, DuplicateFor
EachColumnRewrite, GroupByConstParallelSetter, ImplicitSplitInserter, LimitOptim
izer, LoadTypeCastInserter, MergeFilter, MergeForEach, NewPartitionFilterOptimiz
er, PushDownForEachFlatten, PushUpFilter, SplitFilter, StreamTypeCastInserter],
RULES_DISABLED=[FilterLogicExpressionSimplifier, PartitionFilterOptimizer]}
2024-04-15 07:22:06,905 [main] INFO  org.apache.pig.newplan.logical.rules.Column
PruneVisitor - Columns pruned for sales_data: $1, $2, $3, $6
2024-04-15 07:22:06,909 [main] INFO  org.apache.pig.backend.hadoop.executionengi
ne.mapReduceLayer.MRCompiler - File concatenation threshold: 100 optimistic? fal
```

Figure 7.32: *Use of FOREACH ...GENERATE operator*

Figure 7.33 shows the output generated after execution of the preceding code. In the output, each tuple represents a transaction with the following columns: **Transaction_ID**, **Quantity**, **Unit_Price**, and **Total_Cost**:

```
cloudera@quickstart:~
File Edit View Search Terminal Help
2024-04-15 07:22:25,158 [main] INFO  org.apache.pig.backend.hadoop.executionengi
ne.mapReduceLayer.MapReduceLauncher - Success!
2024-04-15 07:22:25,158 [main] INFO  org.apache.hadoop.conf.Configuration.deprec
ation - fs.default.name is deprecated. Instead, use fs.defaultFS
2024-04-15 07:22:25,158 [main] INFO  org.apache.hadoop.conf.Configuration.deprec
ation - mapred.job.tracker is deprecated. Instead, use mapreduce.jobtracker.addr
ess
2024-04-15 07:22:25,159 [main] INFO  org.apache.pig.data.SchemaTupleBackend - Ke
y [pig.schematuple] was not set... will not generate code.
2024-04-15 07:22:25,168 [main] INFO  org.apache.hadoop.mapreduce.lib.input.FileI
nputFormat - Total input paths to process : 1
2024-04-15 07:22:25,168 [main] INFO  org.apache.pig.backend.hadoop.executionengi
ne.util.MapRedUtil - Total input paths to process : 1
(1,2,800.0,1600.0)
(2,1,600.0,600.0)
(3,1,400.0,400.0)
(4,1,800.0,800.0)
(5,3,600.0,1800.0)
```

Figure 7.33: *Output of FOREACH ...GENERATE operator*

DISTINCT

DISTINCT operator is used to remove duplicate tuples in a relation. It does not retain the original order of the contents (to eliminate duplicates, Pig must first sort the data). **DISTINCT** cannot be used on a subset of fields. To perform this task, use **FOREACH** and a nested block to select the fields and then apply **DISTINCT**.

Syntax: alias = DISTINCT alias [PARTITION BY partitioner] [PARALLEL n];

Where alias is the name of the relation, **PARTITION BY** feature is used to specify the Hadoop Partitioner.

For example: Let us create another dataset with redundant product data, as **prod.txt** as follows:

```
prod_ID Qty
AA 34
BB 45
CC 23
AA 78
AA 34
BB 45
DD 89
DD 89
grunt>dist_result= DISTINCT product;
```

Figure 7.34 shows the loading of the **prod.txt** dataset in a product relation and then the application of the **DISTINCT** operator to that relation:

```
File Edit View Search Terminal Help
grunt> product = LOAD '/chap5Pig/prod.txt' USING PigStorage(',') as (Prod_I
D:chararray,Qty:int);
grunt> dist_result = DISTINCT product;
grunt> Dump dist_result;
```

***Figure 7.34**: Use of the DISTINCT operator*

In the output, refer to *Figure 7.35;* each line represents a distinct product ID present in the **prod.txt** file. The **DISTINCT** operator ensures that unique data values are retained, eliminating duplicates:

```
2024-04-18 06:40:36,942 [main] INFO  org.apache.pig.backend.hadoop.executio
nengine.mapReduceLayer.MapReduceLauncher - Success!
2024-04-18 06:40:36,943 [main] INFO  org.apache.hadoop.conf.Configuration.d
eprecation - fs.default.name is deprecated. Instead, use fs.defaultFS
2024-04-18 06:40:36,943 [main] INFO  org.apache.hadoop.conf.Configuration.d
eprecation - mapred.job.tracker is deprecated. Instead, use mapreduce.jobtr
acker.address
2024-04-18 06:40:36,943 [main] INFO  org.apache.pig.data.SchemaTupleBackend
 - Key [pig.schematuple] was not set... will not generate code.
2024-04-18 06:40:36,948 [main] INFO  org.apache.hadoop.mapreduce.lib.input.
FileInputFormat - Total input paths to process : 1
2024-04-18 06:40:36,948 [main] INFO  org.apache.pig.backend.hadoop.executio
nengine.util.MapRedUtil - Total input paths to process : 1
(AA 34,)
(AA 78,)
(BB 45,)
(CC 23,)
(DD 89,)
```

***Figure 7.35**: Output of DISTINCT operator*

SAMPLE

The **SAMPLE** operator in Pig is used to obtain a random sample of data from a relation. It allows you to specify the fraction of data you want to sample or the number of tuples you want to retrieve. When working with large datasets, sampling is useful for data exploration, testing, and analysis. By taking a sample, you can gain insights into the characteristics of your data without processing the entire dataset.

Example :

```
grunt>Sample_data = SAMPLE sales_data 0.2;

grunt>DUMP Sample_data;
```

Figure 7.36 shows the use of the **SAMPLE** operator to get 20% sample of the data:

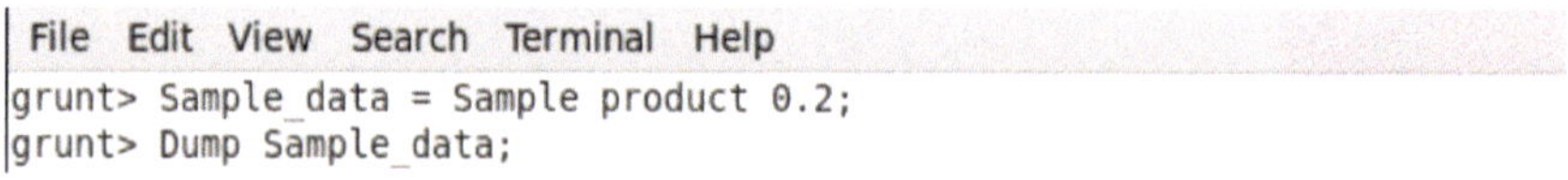

```
File  Edit  View  Search  Terminal  Help
grunt> Sample_data = Sample product 0.2;
grunt> Dump Sample_data;
```

***Figure 7.36**: Execution of the SAMPLE operator*

Refer to *Figure 7.37*. As the product relation has only eight tuples, it displays one record in the output:

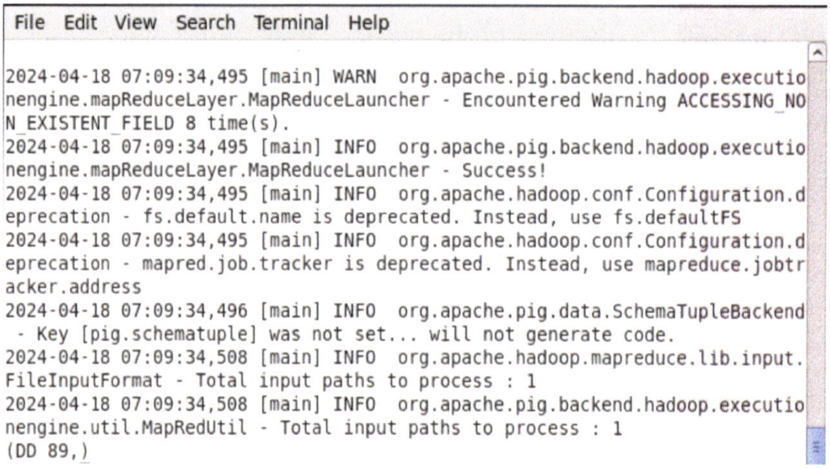

```
File  Edit  View  Search  Terminal  Help

2024-04-18 07:09:34,495 [main] WARN  org.apache.pig.backend.hadoop.executio
nengine.mapReduceLayer.MapReduceLauncher - Encountered Warning ACCESSING_NO
N_EXISTENT_FIELD 8 time(s).
2024-04-18 07:09:34,495 [main] INFO  org.apache.pig.backend.hadoop.executio
nengine.mapReduceLayer.MapReduceLauncher - Success!
2024-04-18 07:09:34,495 [main] INFO  org.apache.hadoop.conf.Configuration.d
eprecation - fs.default.name is deprecated. Instead, use fs.defaultFS
2024-04-18 07:09:34,495 [main] INFO  org.apache.hadoop.conf.Configuration.d
eprecation - mapred.job.tracker is deprecated. Instead, use mapreduce.jobtr
acker.address
2024-04-18 07:09:34,496 [main] INFO  org.apache.pig.data.SchemaTupleBackend
 - Key [pig.schematuple] was not set... will not generate code.
2024-04-18 07:09:34,508 [main] INFO  org.apache.hadoop.mapreduce.lib.input.
FileInputFormat - Total input paths to process : 1
2024-04-18 07:09:34,508 [main] INFO  org.apache.pig.backend.hadoop.executio
nengine.util.MapRedUtil - Total input paths to process : 1
(DD 89,)
```

***Figure 7.37**: Output of the SAMPLE operator*

ASSERT operator

The ASSERT operator in Pig is used to validate the structure and content of data at runtime. It allows you to define conditions that the data must meet, and if any tuple violates those conditions, an error is raised, and the script's execution is halted.

ASSERT statements are helpful for data quality assurance and debugging, ensuring that the data conforms to your expectations before further processing:

```
grunt> ASSERT sales_data BY (Qty > 0);
```

This command, as shown in *Figure 7.38*, ensures that the value in the "**Qty**" column is greater than 0 for every row in the "**sales_data**" relation. If any row fails to meet this condition, an error will be raised, indicating a violation of the assertion:

```
grunt> ASSERT sales_data BY (Qty > 0);
2024-04-15 07:43:56,164 [main] WARN  org.apache.pig.PigServer - Encountered Warn
ing IMPLICIT_CAST_TO_FLOAT 1 time(s).
grunt> █
```

***Figure 7.38**: Use of assert operator*

Sorting and ranking operators

Apache Pig provides sorting and ranking operators to organize and analyze data efficiently. These operators help arrange data in a specific order and assign ranks based on specified criteria.

ORDER

The ORDER operator in Pig is used to sort the data based on one or more fields in ascending or descending order. It rearranges the tuples in the relation according to the specified sorting criteria.

For example:

```
grunt>order_data = ORDER sales_data BY Qty;
grunt>DUMP order_data;
```

Figure 7.39 shows the use of **ORDER** command to sort data stored in **sales_data** relation in ascending order:

```
grunt> order_data = ORDER sales_data BY Qty;█
```

***Figure 7.39**: Use of ORDER operator*

After execution, the dataset stored in **sales_data** relation is sorted in ascending order based on quantity, as shown in *Figure 7.40:*

```
2024-04-15 07:48:39,473 [main] INFO  org.apache.pig.backend.hadoop.executionengi
ne.mapReduceLayer.MapReduceLauncher - Success!
2024-04-15 07:48:39,473 [main] INFO  org.apache.hadoop.conf.Configuration.deprec
ation - fs.default.name is deprecated. Instead, use fs.defaultFS
2024-04-15 07:48:39,473 [main] INFO  org.apache.hadoop.conf.Configuration.deprec
ation - mapred.job.tracker is deprecated. Instead, use mapreduce.jobtracker.addr
ess
2024-04-15 07:48:39,474 [main] INFO  org.apache.pig.data.SchemaTupleBackend - Ke
y [pig.schematuple] was not set... will not generate code.
2024-04-15 07:48:39,476 [main] INFO  org.apache.hadoop.mapreduce.lib.input.FileI
nputFormat - Total input paths to process : 1
2024-04-15 07:48:39,476 [main] INFO  org.apache.pig.backend.hadoop.executionengi
ne.util.MapRedUtil - Total input paths to process : 1
(4,104,1,"LapTop",1,800.0,"2024-03-01 10:15:00")
(3,103,2,"Tablet",1,400.0,"2024-03-01 10:10:00")
(2,102,3,"Smartphone",1,600.0,"2024-03-01 10:05:00")
(1,101,1,"LapTop",2,800.0,"2024-03-01 10:00:00")
```

***Figure 7.40**: Output of ORDER operator*

RANK

The RANK operator in Pig assigns a rank to all tuples based on a specified sorting criterion.

Example:

```
grunt>rank_data = RANK sales_data BY Qty DESC;

grunt>DUMP ranked_data;
```

It is similar to **ORDER** but adds a rank value to each tuple, indicating its position in the sorted result, as shown in *Figure 7.41:*

```
grunt> rank_data = RANK sales_data BY Qty DESC;
2024-04-15 07:58:21,294 [main] WARN  org.apache.pig.PigServer - Encountered Warn
ing IMPLICIT_CAST_TO_FLOAT 1 time(s).
grunt> Dump rank_data;
2024-04-15 07:58:37,019 [main] INFO  org.apache.pig.tools.pigstats.ScriptState -
 Pig features used in the script: RANK,FILTER
2024-04-15 07:58:37,019 [main] INFO  org.apache.pig.newplan.logical.optimizer.Lo
gicalPlanOptimizer - {RULES_ENABLED=[AddForEach, ColumnMapKeyPrune, DuplicateFor
EachColumnRewrite, GroupByConstParallelSetter, ImplicitSplitInserter, LimitOptim
izer, LoadTypeCastInserter, MergeFilter, MergeForEach, NewPartitionFilterOptimiz
er, PushDownForEachFlatten, PushUpFilter, SplitFilter, StreamTypeCastInserter],
RULES_DISABLED=[FilterLogicExpressionSimplifier, PartitionFilterOptimizer]}
2024-04-15 07:58:37,026 [main] INFO  org.apache.pig.backend.hadoop.executionengi
ne.mapReduceLayer.MRCompiler - File concatenation threshold: 100 optimistic? fal
se
2024-04-15 07:58:37,031 [main] INFO  org.apache.pig.backend.hadoop.executionengi
ne.mapReduceLayer.MultiQueryOptimizer - MR plan size before optimization: 4
2024-04-15 07:58:37,031 [main] INFO  org.apache.pig.backend.hadoop.executionengi
ne.mapReduceLayer.MultiQueryOptimizer - MR plan size after optimization: 4
```

***Figure 7.41**: Use of RANK operators*

In *Figure 7.42,* the first column represents the rank assigned based on quantity. Columns with higher quantities are assigned Rank 1 and 2, and as the amount is the same for the next three tuples, all are assigned the same Rank:

```
2024-04-15 08:00:16,157 [main] INFO  org.apache.pig.backend.hadoop.executionengi
ne.mapReduceLayer.MapReduceLauncher - Success!
2024-04-15 08:00:16,158 [main] INFO  org.apache.hadoop.conf.Configuration.deprec
ation - fs.default.name is deprecated. Instead, use fs.defaultFS
2024-04-15 08:00:16,158 [main] INFO  org.apache.hadoop.conf.Configuration.deprec
ation - mapred.job.tracker is deprecated. Instead, use mapreduce.jobtracker.addr
ess
2024-04-15 08:00:16,158 [main] INFO  org.apache.pig.data.SchemaTupleBackend - Ke
y [pig.schematuple] was not set... will not generate code.
2024-04-15 08:00:16,161 [main] INFO  org.apache.hadoop.mapreduce.lib.input.FileI
nputFormat - Total input paths to process : 1
2024-04-15 08:00:16,161 [main] INFO  org.apache.pig.backend.hadoop.executionengi
ne.util.MapRedUtil - Total input paths to process : 1
(1,5,105,3,"Smartphone",3,600.0,"2024-03-01 10:20:00")
(2,1,101,1,"LapTop",2,800.0,"2024-03-01 10:00:00")
(3,4,104,1,"LapTop",1,800.0,"2024-03-01 10:15:00")
(3,3,103,2,"Tablet",1,400.0,"2024-03-01 10:10:00")
(3,2,102,3,"Smartphone",1,600.0,"2024-03-01 10:05:00")
```

***Figure 7.42**: Output of RANK Operator*

LIMIT

The **LIMIT** operator in Pig is used to restrict the number of tuples in the relation to a specified limit. It is generally used in conjunction with **ORDER** or **RANK** to select a subset of the sorted or ranked data.

Example:

```
grunt>limit_data = Limit sales_data 2;
grunt>Dump limit_data;
```

Refer to *Figure 7.43* for the execution of the preceding code:

```
grunt> limit_data = Limit sales_data 2;
grunt> Dump limit_data;
```

***Figure 7.43**: Use of the LIMIT operator*

Figure 7.44 shows the output data limited to only two tuples from the **`sales_data`** relation:

```
2024-04-15 08:04:16,635 [main] INFO  org.apache.hadoop.mapred.ClientServiceDeleg
ate - Application state is completed. FinalApplicationStatus=SUCCEEDED. Redirect
ing to job history server
2024-04-15 08:04:16,773 [main] INFO  org.apache.pig.backend.hadoop.executionengi
ne.mapReduceLayer.MapReduceLauncher - Success!
2024-04-15 08:04:16,773 [main] INFO  org.apache.hadoop.conf.Configuration.deprec
ation - fs.default.name is deprecated. Instead, use fs.defaultFS
2024-04-15 08:04:16,773 [main] INFO  org.apache.hadoop.conf.Configuration.deprec
ation - mapred.job.tracker is deprecated. Instead, use mapreduce.jobtracker.addr
ess
2024-04-15 08:04:16,774 [main] INFO  org.apache.pig.data.SchemaTupleBackend - Ke
y [pig.schematuple] was not set... will not generate code.
2024-04-15 08:04:16,776 [main] INFO  org.apache.hadoop.mapreduce.lib.input.FileI
nputFormat - Total input paths to process : 1
2024-04-15 08:04:16,776 [main] INFO  org.apache.pig.backend.hadoop.executionengi
ne.util.MapRedUtil - Total input paths to process : 1
(1,101,1,"LapTop",2,800.0,"2024-03-01 10:00:00")
(2,102,3,"Smartphone",1,600.0,"2024-03-01 10:05:00")
```

***Figure 7.44**: Output of LIMIT operator*

Conclusion

The chapter detailed the various simple and complex data types supported in Pig Latin script and types of relational operators such as loading, filtering, grouping and joining, sorting, combining, and splitting. It also provided detailed syntax, explanation, and application of operators in the Cloudera framework via the Grunt shell.

In the next chapter, we will explore built-in functions, UDFs, and a case study on data analysis using Pig.

Points to remember

The following list outlines the key takeaways from this chapter:

- **Debugging and inspection operators**:
  - **DUMP**: Prints the contents of a relation to the console.
  - **DESCRIBE**: Shows the schema of a relation.
  - **ILLUSTRATE**: Displays sample data to demonstrate how a script processes data.
- **Relational operators**:
  - **Join**: Combines records from two or more relations based on a common field.
  - **Self join**: A join where a relation is joined with itself.
  - **Inner join**: Returns only matching records from both relations.
  - **Outer join (Includes variations below)**: Returns matching and non-matching records based on join type:

    - **Left outer join**: Returns all records from the left relation and matching records from the right relation.
    - **Right outer join**: Returns all records from the right relation and matching records from the left relation.
    - **Full outer join**: Returns all records from both relations, filling unmatched values with NULLs.
- **Cogroup**: Groups records from multiple relations based on a common key.
- **Cross**: Performs a Cartesian product (cross join) of two relations.
- **Cube**: Used for multi-dimensional aggregations in OLAP-style queries.
- **Rollup**: A specialized form of CUBE used for hierarchical aggregation.
- **Union**: Merges the contents of two or more relations.
- **Split**: Splits a relation into two or more relations based on a condition.
- **Filtering and transformation operators**
    - **FILTER**: Selects records based on a condition.
    - **FOREACH ... GENERATE**: Applies transformations on each record of a relation and produces new records.
    - **DISTINCT**: Removes duplicate records from a relation.
    - **SAMPLE**: Selects a random sample of data from a relation.
    - **ASSERT**: Validates data and throws an error if a condition is not met.
- **Sorting and ranking operators**
    - **ORDER**: Sorts records based on specified fields.
    - **RANK**: Assigns rank to records based on a given field.
    - **LIMIT**: Restricts the number of output records.

Multiple choice questions

1. **Which debugging operator prints the contents of a relation to the console in Apache Pig?**
    a. DESCRIBE
    b. DUMP
    c. ILLUSTRATE
    d. FILTER
2. **What does the DESCRIBE operator do in Apache Pig?**
    a. Prints the schema of a relation
    b. Displays sample data to illustrate data flow
    c. Joins two relations
    d. Sorts data in ascending order
3. **Which operator helps visualize how a Pig script processes data by showing intermediate steps?**
    a. CROSS
    b. COGROUP
    c. ILLUSTRATE
    d. ORDER
4. **What type of join returns only matching records from both relations?**
    a. Left outer join
    b. Right outer join
    c. Inner join
    d. Full outer join

5. **In a left outer join, which records are included in the result?**
   a. Only matching records from both relations
   b. All records from the left relation and matching records from the right relation
   c. All records from the right relation and matching records from the left relation
   d. All records from both relations, filling unmatched values with NULLs
6. **Which operator performs a Cartesian product of two relations?**
   a. CROSS
   b. COGROUP
   c. UNION
   d. SPLIT
7. **What does the DISTINCT operator do?**
   a. Sorts data in ascending order
   b. Removes duplicate records from a relation
   c. Selects a subset of records randomly
   d. Assigns rank to records
8. **Which operator allows hierarchical aggregation, often used for OLAP queries?**
   a. CUBE
   b. ROLLUP
   c. SAMPLE
   d. UNION
9. **The LIMIT operator in Apache Pig is used to:**
   a. Sort records based on a specified field
   b. Restrict the number of output records
   c. Assign rank to records
   d. Remove duplicate records
10. **What does the SPLIT operator do?**
   a. Joins two or more relations based on a common key
   b. Separates a relation into multiple relations based on a condition
   c. Merges multiple relations into one
   d. Assigns a sequential number to each record

Answers

1. b.	2. a.	3. c.	4. c.	5. b.
6. a.	7. b.	8. b.	9. b.	10. b.

Questions

1. A data processing team is analyzing a dataset containing customer transactions. Their Pig script is producing unexpected results, and they suspect a problem in how data is flowing through transformations. How would you use DUMP, DESCRIBE, and ILLUSTRATE to debug this issue? In what scenarios would ILLUSTRATE be more useful than DUMP?
2. A retail company has two datasets:

   customers (customer_id, name, city)

   orders (order_id, customer_id, amount)

The company wants to analyze orders placed by customers while ensuring all customers are included, even if they haven't placed an order. Which **join** strategy should be used and why?

3. A sensor network collects temperature data every second, but some readings are corrupted (e.g., negative values). You have a dataset: sensor_data (sensor_id, timestamp, temperature). How can you use the FILTER operator to remove invalid temperature readings? If you want to apply a transformation to convert Celsius to Fahrenheit for valid readings, how would you achieve it using FOREACH ... GENERATE?
4. An e-commerce company wants to analyze customer spending behavior and rank them by total spending. They also need a random sample of 10% of customers for a pilot study. How can you rank customers using the RANK operator?
5. A bank wants to run separate marketing campaigns for high-value and low-value customers. The dataset contains: customers (customer_id, name, account_balance). How can you use SPLIT to separate customers with balances above and below $10,000 into different relations? What are the advantages of using SPLIT instead of multiple FILTER operations?
6. A retailer wants to find the top 5 customers who have spent the most money. **Dataset**: customers (customer_id, name), transactions (transaction_id, customer_id, amount). Use appropriate commands to perform the given task.
7. A data scientist is processing web log data but getting unexpected results in an aggregation query. **Dataset**: web_logs (user_id, timestamp, page_viewed). Discuss the commands that can be used to resolve the given problem.
8. A financial institution receives transaction logs from multiple sources. Duplicates and missing values exist. **Dataset**: transactions (trans_id, user_id, amount, transaction_date). Show the use of DISTINCT and Filter operators to remove duplicate transactions and exclude records where the amount is NULL or negative.
9. A media company wants to divide users into two groups for ad testing and extract a random sample. **Dataset**: users (user_id, age, location, interests). Write commands to divide users into young_users (age < 30) and older_users (age >= 30) and to randomly pick 20% of users for an experimental ad campaign.
10. Use FOREACH ... GENERATE to format the output to only include user_id and interests.
11. A supermarket wants sales reports across multiple dimensions: product category and region. **Dataset**: sales (sale_id, product_category, region, revenue). Write queries to generate aggregated revenue across all possible combinations of product_category and region.

CHAPTER 8
Functions in Apache Pig

Torture the data, and it will confess to anything.

— *Ronald Coase*

Introduction

In this chapter, readers will learn to develop practical applications of Pig Latin. One of the key advantages of Pig is its extensive set of built-in functions and the ability to define custom functions. These functions enable users to perform a wide range of data transformations and analyses. This chapter demonstrates how these functions can be leveraged to process and manipulate data efficiently using Cloudera. Next, the chapter presents the process of creating and using **user-defined functions** (**UDFs**) in Pig. UDFs demonstrate how custom logic can be encapsulated into reusable functions. By developing UDFs, users can extend Pig's functionality to meet specific requirements, such as implementing complex business rules, performing advanced analytics, or integrating with external systems.

Structure

In this chapter, we will cover the following topics:

- Built-in functions
- Eval functions
- String functions
- User-defined functions

Objectives

By the end of this chapter, the readers will be able to understand the capabilities of Pig, focusing specifically on its built-in functions and UDFs. They will be able to leverage the built-in functions like eval functions (max(), count(), avg(), BagToString(), PluckTuple(), etc.), string functions (ENDSWITH(), SUBSTRING(), LAST_INDEX_OF(), etc.) of Pig Latin with practical understanding to solve real-world problems. They will also be able to design and develop UDFs to meet growing business needs or to perform advanced analytics, and will learn to perform big data analytics with the help of a case study on Stock data using Pig Latin in the Cloudera framework.

Built-in functions

Pig is a high-level scripting language for analyzing large datasets in Apache Hadoop. It provides an easy way to process and analyze large datasets without the need for complex MapReduce code. One of the key benefits of Pig is its extensive set of built-in functions and the ability to define custom functions, which help users to perform a wide range of data transformations and analyses.

Pig provides a rich library of built-in functions that can be used to perform a wide range of data processing tasks, including string manipulation, mathematical operations, date/time functions, and much more. These functions provide a convenient way to perform common data transformations without requiring custom coding.

To understand the working of various operators, we have used the sales (**`sales_trans.txt`**) and customers (**`customer.txt`**) datasets from an e-commerce platform.

The **sales_trans.txt** dataset consists of the following fields:

- **Transaction ID (Tran_ID)**: Unique identifier for each transaction.
- **Customer ID (Cust_ID)**: Unique identifier for each customer.
- **Product ID (Prod_ID)**: Unique identifier for each product.
- **Product Name (Prod_Name)**: Name of the product.
- **Quantity (Qty)**: The quantity of the product purchased in each transaction.
- **Price**: The price of each unit of the product.
- **Timestamp**: The timestamp of the transaction.

The **customer.txt** dataset consists of the following fields:

- **Customer ID (Cust_ID)**: Unique identifier for each customer.
- **Customer Name (Cust_Name)**: Name of customer.
- **Age**: Age of customer.

The sample of data stored in the **sales_trans.txt** file is as follows:

- Tran_ID, Cust_ID, Prod_ID, Prod_Name, Qty, Price, Timestamp
- 1, 101, 1, "Laptop", 2, 800, "2024-03-01 10:00:00"
- 2, 102, 3, "Smartphone", 1, 600, "2024-03-01 10:05:00"
- 3, 103, 2, "Tablet", 1, 400, "2024-03-01 10:10:00"
- 4, 104, 1, "Laptop", 1, 800, "2024-03-01 10:15:00"
- 5, 105, 3, "Smartphone", 3, 600, "2024-03-01 10:20:00"
- 6, 106, 4, "Headphones", 2, 100, "2024-03-01 10:25:00"

The sample of data stored in the **customers.txt** file is as follows:

- Cust_ID, Cust_Name, Age
- 101, "Mona", 30
- 102, "Rahul", 25
- 103, "Teana", 35
- 104, "Aayush", 28
- 105, "Nishu", 40

Both datasets are stored in the **sales_data** and **customer** relations as follows before applying evaluation functions, as shown in the following code:

```
grunt>sales_data = LOAD 'sales_trans.txt' USING PigStorage(',') AS ( Transaction_ID: int, Customer_ID: int,  Product_ID: int, Product_Name: chararray,    Quantity: int,     Price: float, Timestamp: chararray );

grunt>customer = LOAD 'customers.txt' USING PigStorage(',') AS ( Cust_ID: int,  Cust_Name: chararray,    Age: int );
```

Eval functions

In Pig Latin, evaluation functions are powerful tools that allow users to perform computations and transformations on data. These functions are similar to functions in traditional programming languages and help simplify data processing tasks within a Pig script. Evaluation functions are typically used within **FOREACH** and **GROUP** operations in Pig Latin scripts to apply transformations or aggregations to data. Evaluation functions in Pig are mainly used in the following two ways:

- **Built-in functions (BIFs)**: These are ready-to-use functions provided by Pig for common operations such as mathematical computations, string manipulation, date processing, and more. For example, **`SUM()`** to add numbers, **`CONCAT()`** to join strings, **`UPPER()`** to convert text to uppercase, etc.
- **UDFs**: When built-in functions are not enough, users can create their own functions using Java, Python, or other languages supported by Pig. UDFs allow custom logic and are especially useful for complex transformations.

In this section, we will be looking at some eval functions:

- **AVG()**: It is used to compute the average of the numeric values in a single-column bag. This function requires a preceding **`GROUP ALL`** statement for global averages and a **`GROUP BY`** statement for group averages, as shown in *Figure 8.1*.

  Here, the **`AVG()`** function is used to compute the average age of customers in the customer relation. The **`AVG`** function ignores **`NULL`** values:

  - **Syntax: `AVG(expression)`**

    Here, expression is any expression whose result is a bag. The elements of the bag should be of numeric data type only.

  - **Example**:

    ```
    grunt>avg_age = FOREACH (GROUP customer ALL) GENERATE AVG(customer.Age);
    grunt> Dump avg_age;
    ```

    In *Figure 8.1*, the statement **`GROUP`** customer **`ALL`** groups all tuples in the customer relation into a single group. The **`ALL`** keyword indicates that we want to group all tuples together. The **`FOREACH`** statement iterates over each group generated by the **`GROUP`** operation. **`GENERATE AVG(customer.Age)`** statement calculates the average of the Age field for all tuples in the customer relation.

    Hence, this script computes the average age of all customers by grouping them all together and then calculating the average of their ages, as shown in *Figure 8.1*:

    ```
    grunt> avg_age = FOREACH (GROUP customer ALL) GENERATE AVG(customer
    .Age);
    grunt> Dump avg_age
    ```

    ***Figure 8.1**: Use of AVG() function*

    Figure 8.2 shows the output of executing the **`AVG()`** function:

    ```
    2024-05-04 04:46:17,580 [main] INFO  org.apache.hadoop.mapreduce.li
    b.input.FileInputFormat - Total input paths to process : 1
    2024-05-04 04:46:17,580 [main] INFO  org.apache.pig.backend.hadoop.
    executionengine.util.MapRedUtil - Total input paths to process : 1
    (29.5)
    grunt>
    ```

    ***Figure 8.2**: Output of AVG() function*

- **BagToString()**: This function is used to concatenate the elements of a bag into a single char array string. The string is created by placing an optional delimiter between all values.

  To perform the same, refer to *Figure 8.3*, **`customers.text`** data is first loaded in a relation named as customer. Next, the GROUP operation groups all the records in the customer relation into a single group. The ALL keyword indicates that all records will be grouped. This results in a single tuple containing a bag of all customer records. A dump statement is used to verify the operations at various stages.

  - **Syntax: `BagToString(vals:bag [, delimiter:chararray])`**

    Here, **`vals`** refers to a bag of arbitrary values. All these values are cast to **`chararray`** if they are not already. **`delimiter`** refers to a **`chararray`** value which is placed between elements of the bag, e.g., the default delimiter is underscore _.

- **Example**:

```
grunt> customer = LOAD '/chap5Pig/customers.txt' USING PigStorage(',') as (Cust_
ID:int,Cust_Name:chararray,Age:int);
grunt>group_cust = Group customer All;
grunt> Dump group_cust;
grunt>cust_string = Foreach group_cust Generate BagToString(customer);
Dump cust_string;
```

Figure 8.3 shows the execution of the preceding code:

```
grunt> customer = LOAD '/chap5Pig/customers.txt' USING PigStorage(',') as
st_ID:int,Cust_Name:chararray,Age:int);
grunt> group_cust = Group customer All;
grunt> cust_string = Foreach group_cust Generate BagToString(customer);
grunt> Dump cust_string;
```

Figure 8.3: *Usage of BagToString() function*

Figure 8.4 shows the output after execution of the aforementioned code:

```
(104_"Aayush"_28_103_"Teana"_35_102_"Rahul"_25_101_"Mona"_30)
grunt>
```

Figure 8.4: *Final output of BagToString() function*

- **CONCAT()**: This function is used to combine two or more expressions of the same type. If any subexpression is null, the resulting expression is also null.
  - **Syntax**:

```
CONCAT (expression, expression, [...expression])
```

Here, **expression** can be any expression.

- **Example**:

```
grunt>concat_names = FOREACH customer GENERATE CONCAT(Cust_Name, 'is' ,(charrarray)Age,
'years old') AS info;
grunt> Dump concat_names;
```

Here, the **CONCAT()** function is used to concatenate the name and age of the customer relation with the string **is** and **years old**, as shown in *Figure 8.5*:

```
grunt> concat_names = FOREACH customer GENERATE CONCAT(Cust_Name, '
 is ', (chararray)Age, ' years old') AS info;
grunt> Dump concat_names;
```

Figure 8.5: *Use of the CONCAT() function*

As shown in *Figure 8.5*, **FOREACH** customer **GENERATE** statement iterates over each tuple in the customer relation and applies a **CONCAT** transformation to it. Next, **CONCAT(Cust_Name, 'is', (chararray) Age, 'years old') AS info** statement concatenates the **Cust_Name**, the string **'is'**, the value of **Age** (converted to a character array using (**chararray**), and the string **'years old'**. This concatenated string is then named info and is included in the resulting relation.

As shown in *Figure 8.6*, for a tuple in the customer relation with **Cust_Name** as **"Rahul"** and **Age** as **25**, after running this script, we get a new relation with a field info containing the string **Rahul is 25 years old** along with others.

```
2024-05-04 04:53:19,354 [main] INFO  org.apache.hadoop.mapreduce.li
b.input.FileInputFormat - Total input paths to process : 1
2024-05-04 04:53:19,354 [main] INFO  org.apache.pig.backend.hadoop.
executionengine.util.MapRedUtil - Total input paths to process : 1
("Mona" is 30 years old)
("Rahul" is 25 years old)
("Teana" is 35 years old)
("Aayush" is 28 years old)
grunt>
```

***Figure 8.6:** Output of the CONCAT() function*

- **COUNT() and COUNT_STAR()**: These functions are used to count the number of elements in a bag or dataset, but they behave differently for **NULL** values. The **COUNT()** function counts the number of non-null tuples in a bag. However, if the first field of a tuple is **NULL**, that tuple is not counted. Unlike **COUNT()**, the **COUNT_STAR()** function includes tuples even if their fields are **NULL**. These functions require a preceding **GROUP ALL** (*Figure 8.7*) statement for global counts and a **GROUP BY** statement for group-level counts.

Note: The tuple designator (*) does not work with COUNT() in Apache Pig. That is, COUNT(*) is invalid and will result in an error. Use COUNT(bag) or COUNT_STAR(bag) instead, depending on whether you want to exclude or include NULL values.

- **Syntax**:

  COUNT(expression)

  Or:

  COUNT_STAR(expression)

  Here, expression refers to an expression with a data type bag.

- **Example**:

  ```
  grunt>customer_count=  FOREACH (GROUP customer ALL) GENERATE COUNT(customer);
  grunt> Dump customer_count;
  ```

  As shown in *Figure 8.7*, **GROUP** customer groups all tuples in the customer relation into a single group. The **FOREACH** statement iterates over a single group and uses **COUNT(customer)** to count the number of tuples in the customer bag.

```
grunt> customer_count = FOREACH (GROUP customer ALL) GENERATE COUNT
(customer);
grunt>
grunt> Dump customer_count;
```

***Figure 8.7:** Usage of the COUNT () function*

Figure 8.8 shows the output for the **COUNT()** function:

```
2024-05-04 04:57:22,866 [main] INFO  org.apache.pig.data.SchemaTupl
eBackend - Key [pig.schematuple] was not set... will not generate c
ode.
2024-05-04 04:57:22,871 [main] INFO  org.apache.hadoop.mapreduce.li
b.input.FileInputFormat - Total input paths to process : 1
2024-05-04 04:57:22,871 [main] INFO  org.apache.pig.backend.hadoop.
executionengine.util.MapRedUtil - Total input paths to process : 1
(4)
```

***Figure 8.8:** Output of COUNT() function*

The following code shows an example of **COUNT_STAR()**. Here, **GROUP sales_data ALL** groups all records in the **sales_data** relation into one group and then **COUNT_STAR(sales_data.Price)**, returns the total number of tuples, regardless of whether the **Price** field is **NULL**:

```
grunt>cnt_star=  FOREACH (GROUP sales_data ALL) GENERATE COUNT_STAR(sales_data.Price);
grunt> Dump cnt_star;
```

Figure 8.9 shows the **COUNT_STAR()** example in grunt shell:

```
grunt> cnt_star = FOREACH (GROUP sales_data ALL) GENERATE COUNT_STAR(sales_data.
Price);_
```

Figure 8.9: *Usage of the COUNT_STAR() function*

Figure *8.10* shows the output after executing the example of the **COUNT_START()** function:

```
2024-05-04 08:13:47,718 [main] INFO  org.apache.pig.backend.hadoop.executionengi
ne.util.MapRedUtil - Total input paths to process : 1
(5)
```

Figure 8.10: *Output of the COUNT () function*

- **DIFF()**: The **DIFF()** function is designed to compare two bags and return the tuples that are not common between them. It takes two bags as inputs, compares their contents, and returns a bag containing the differences. If both bags are identical, the function returns an empty bag. If inputs are not bags, Pig wraps them into single-tuple bags and then performs the comparison. Note that the function is optimized only when both bags fit into memory.

  If not, performance degrades significantly:

  - **Syntax:** **DIFF(bag_expression1, bag_expression2)**

    Here, both expressions should evaluate to **bags** (ideally).

    Example:

    ```
    grunt> product = LOAD '/chap5Pig/prod.txt' USING PigStorage(',') as (Prod_
    ID:chararray,Qty:int);
    product1 = LOAD '/chap5Pig/prod1.txt' USING PigStorage(',') as (Prod_
    ID:chararray,Qty:int);
    grunt>cogroup_data = COGROUP product by Prod_ID, product1 by Prod_ID;
    grunt> Dump cogroup_data;
    grunt>diff_data = FOREACH cogroup_data GENERATE DIFF(product, product1) AS diff_
    data;

    grunt> Dump diff_data;
    ```

    As shown in *Figure 8.11*, **LOAD** statements read data from files **/chap5Pig/prod.txt and /chap5Pig/prod1.txt** in the relations product and product 1. The **COGROUP** statement groups the two datasets, **product** and **product1**, by the **Prod_ID** field:

    ```
    grunt> product = LOAD '/chap5Pig/prod.txt' USING PigStorage(',') as (Prod_ID:
    chararray,Qty:int);
    grunt> product1 = LOAD '/chap5Pig/prod1.txt' USING PigStorage(',') as (Prod_I
    D:chararray,Qty:int);
    grunt> cogroup_data = COGROUP product by Prod_ID, product1 by Prod_ID;
    grunt> Dump cogroup_data;
    ```

    Figure 8.11: *Usage of the Diff() function*

    This results in a relation where each group contains the tuples from both **product** and **product1** that have the same **Prod_ID**, as shown in *Figure 8.12*:

```
(AA 34,{(AA 34,),(AA 34,)},{(AA 34,)})
(AA 78,{(AA 78,)},{(AA 78,)})
(BB 45,{(BB 45,),(BB 45,)},{(BB 45,),(BB 45,)})
(CC 23,{(CC 23,)},{})
(DD 89,{(DD 89,),(DD 89,)},{})
(PP 89,{},{(PP 89,)})
(XX 23,{},{(XX 23,)})
(YY 34,{},{(YY 34,)})
```

Figure 8.12: *Output of cogroup_data*

Finally, the **DIFF()** function is applied to the cogrouped data, as shown in *Figure 8.13*:

```
grunt> diff_data = FOREACH cogroup_data GENERATE DIFF(product,product1);
grunt> Dump diff_data;
```

Figure 8.13: *Output of Diff () function*

It generates a new relation, **diff_data**, that contains the differences between the two bags for each group, as shown in *Figure 8.14*. In the result, the first three empty bags indicate that both bags had the same data.

```
({})
({})
({})
({(CC 23,)})
({(DD 89,)})
({(PP 89,)})
({(XX 23,)})
({(YY 34,)})
```

Figure 8.14: *Output of Diff() function*

- **IsEmpty()**: This function checks if a bag or map is empty (has no data). It can be used to filter data.
  - **Syntax**:

    IsEmpty(expression)

    Here, expression refers to an expression with any data type.
  - **Example**:

    ```
    grunt>Cogroup_data = COGROUP sales_data By Cust_ID, customer BY Cust_ID;
    grunt>isempty_data = filter cogroup_data by Isempty(customer);
    grunt> Dump isempty_data;
    ```

    As shown in *Figure 8.15*, the **COGROUP** statement groups the **sales_data** and **customer** datasets by the **Cust_ID** field:

    ```
    grunt> cogroup_data = COGROUP sales_data BY Cust_ID, customer BY Cust_ID;
    grunt>  isempty_data = filter cogroup_data by IsEmpty(customer);
    grunt> Dump isempty_data;
    ```

    Figure 8.15: *Usage of the IsEmpty() function*

    This results in a group that contains tuples from both datasets that share the same **Cust_ID**. The next statement filters the **Cogroup_data** to include only the groups where the customer dataset is empty. Here, **IsEmpty(customer)** checks if the customer bag in the group is empty.

    Hence, the output, as shown in *Figure 8.16*, filters out the tuple with **Cust_ID = 105** where customer data is empty:

```
2024-05-05 00:17:37,196 [main] INFO  org.apache.pig.backend.hadoop.execut
ionengine.util.MapRedUtil - Total input paths to process : 1
(105,{(5,105,3,"Smartphone",3,600.0,"2024-03-01 10:20:00")},{})
```

Figure 8.16: Output of the IsEmpty() function

- **MAX()**: This function is used to find the maximum of the numeric values or **chararrays** in a single-column bag.

  It requires a preceding **GROUP ALL** statement for global maximums (*Figure 8.18*) and a **GROUP BY** statement for group maximums.

  The **MAX** function ignores **NULL** values.

  - **Syntax:**

    ```
    MAX(expression)
    ```

    Here, an expression should be numeric with data types as **int**, **long**, **float**, **double**, **bigdecimal**, **biginteger**, **chararray**, **datetime**, or **bytearray**.

  Figure 8.17 shows the execution of the **MAX()** function:

```
grunt> max_Age = FOREACH (GROUP customer ALL) GENERATE MAX(customer.Age);
grunt> Dump max_Age;
```

Figure 8.17: Usage of MAX() function

Figure 8.18 shows the maximum value of customer age from the customer relation:

```
2024-05-04 06:00:47,464 [main] INFO  org.apache.pig.data.SchemaTupleBackend - Ke
y [pig.schematuple] was not set... will not generate code.
2024-05-04 06:00:47,472 [main] INFO  org.apache.hadoop.mapreduce.lib.input.FileI
nputFormat - Total input paths to process : 1
2024-05-04 06:00:47,472 [main] INFO  org.apache.pig.backend.hadoop.executionengi
ne.util.MapRedUtil - Total input paths to process : 1
(35)
grunt>
```

Figure 8.18: Output of MAX() function

- **MIN()**: This function is designed to calculate the minimum of the numeric values or **chararrays** in a single-column bag.

  It requires a preceding **GROUPALL** statement for global minimums, as shown in *Figure 8.19*, and a **GROUP BY** statement for group minimums.

  - **Syntax: MIN(expression)**

    Here, expression refers to the data types such as **int**, **long**, **float**, **double**, **bigdecimal**, **biginteger**, **chararray**, **datetime**, or **bytearray**.

    Figure 8.19 shows the execution of the **MIN()** function:

```
grunt> min_Age = FOREACH (GROUP customer ALL) GENERATE MIN(customer.Age);
grunt> Dump min_Age;
```

Figure 8.19: Usage of MIN() function

It ignores NULL values. *Figure 8.20* shows the minimum value of customer age from the customer relation:

```
2024-05-04 06:05:59,804 [main] INFO  org.apache.pig.data.SchemaTupleBackend - Ke
y [pig.schematuple] was not set... will not generate code.
2024-05-04 06:05:59,808 [main] INFO  org.apache.hadoop.mapreduce.lib.input.FileI
nputFormat - Total input paths to process : 1
2024-05-04 06:05:59,808 [main] INFO  org.apache.pig.backend.hadoop.executionengi
ne.util.MapRedUtil - Total input paths to process : 1
(25)
```

***Figure 8.20**: Output of MIN() function*

- **SIZE()**: This function computes the number of elements based on any Pig data type (**`int`**, **`long`**, **`float`**, **`double`**, **`chararray`**, **`bytearray`**, **`Tuple`**, **`map`**, **`bag`**, etc.). **`SIZE`** includes **`NULL`** values in the size computation, and it is not algebraic.

  If the object mentioned in the expression is null, the **`SIZE`** function returns null.

  - **Syntax: `SIZE(expression)`**

    Here, expression with any data type.

  - **Example:**

```
grunt>size_sales = FOREACH  sales_data Generate SIZE(Prod_Name);
grunt>Dump size_sales;
```

  Figure 8.21 shows that the **`SIZE()`** function is used to calculate the size of the name column:

```
grunt> size_sales = FOREACH sales_data GENERATE SIZE(Prod_Na
me);
grunt> Dump size_sales;
```

***Figure 8.21**: Usage of the SIZE() function*

  Since it is of varchar type, the **`SIZE()`** function gives you the number of characters in the name of each product. Refer to *Figure 8.22* for output:

```
2024-05-05 07:52:22,025 [main] INFO  org.apache.pig.backend.
hadoop.executionengine.util.MapRedUtil - Total input paths t
o process : 1
(8)
(12)
(8)
(8)
(12)
```

***Figure 8.22**: Output of the SIZE() function*

- **SUBTRACT()**: The **`SUBTRACT()`** function in Pig is used to subtract one bag from another, resulting in a bag that contains elements from the first bag that are not present in the second bag. This operation is useful for filtering out common elements and finding unique elements in the first bag.

  The **`SUBTRACT`** function takes two bags as arguments.

  - **Syntax: `SUBTRACT(expression, expression)`**

    Here, expression is a bag with any data type.

  - **Example**:

```
grunt> product = LOAD '/chap5Pig/prod.txt' USING PigStorage(',') as (Prod_
ID:chararray,Qty:int);
grunt> product1 = LOAD '/chap5Pig/prod1.txt' USING PigStorage(',') as (Prod_
ID:chararray,Qty:int);
grunt>cogroup_data = COGROUP product BY Prod_ID, product1 BY Prod_ID;
grunt>sub_data = FOREACH cogroup_data GENERATE SUBTRACT(product,product1);
grunt> Dump sub_data;
```

As shown in *Figure 8.23*, after loading the data in **product** and **product1**, they are **cogrouped** by the **Prod_ID** field. It results in a relation named **cogroup_data** where each group contains records from both product and product1 that share the same **Prod_ID**. Next, the **cogrouped** data is iterated for each group, such that the **SUBTRACT** function removes tuples in **product1** that are present in the product relation. The **SUBTRACT** function essentially performs a set difference operation.

```
grunt> product = LOAD '/chap5Pig/prod.txt' USING PigStorage(',') as (Prod_ID:
rarray,Qty:int);
grunt> product1 = LOAD '/chap5Pig/prod1.txt' USING PigStorage(',') as (Prod_I
hararray,Qty:int);
grunt> cogroup_data = COGROUP product BY Prod_ID, product1 BY Prod_ID;
grunt> sub_data = FOREACH cogroup_data GENERATE SUBTRACT(product,product1);
grunt> Dump sub_data;
```

Figure 8.23: *Usage of SUBTRACT() function*

It returns a new bag with tuples of the first bag that are not in the second bag, as shown in *Figure 8.24:*

```
({})
({})
({})
({(CC 23,)})
({(DD 89,)})
({})
({})
({})
```

Figure 8.24: *Output of SUBTRACT() function*

- **SUM()**: This function is used to compute the sum of the numeric values in a single-column bag. It requires a preceding **GROUP ALL** statement for global sums and a **GROUP BY** statement for group sums. The **SUM** function ignores **NULL** values.
  - **Syntax: SUM(expression)**
  - **Example**:

```
grunt>Sum_qty = FOREACH (GROUP sales_data ALL) GENERATE SUM(sales_data.Qty);
grunt> Dump Sum_qty;
```

As shown in *Figure 8.25*, sales data is grouped using **GROUP ALL** before computing the sum:

```
grunt> sum_qty = FOREACH (GROUP sales_data ALL) GENERATE SUM(sales_data.Qty);
grunt> Dump sum_qty;
```

Figure 8.25: *Usage of SUM() function*

Then, the **SUM()** function is applied to compute the sum of the quantity column in the **sales_data** relation, as shown in *Figure 8.26:*

```
2024-05-04 08:03:25,874 [main] INFO  org.apache.pig.backend.hadoop.executionengi
ne.util.MapRedUtil - Total input paths to process : 1
(8)
grunt>
```

Figure 8.26: *Output of SUM() function*

- **TOKENIZE()**: This function is used to split a string (all words in a single tuple) into a bag of words, with each word in a single tuple.
  - **Syntax: TOKENIZE(expression [, 'field_delimiter'])**

  Here, expression is of **chararray** data type, and **'field_delimiter'** is an optional field delimiter (in single quotes). If **field_delimiter** is null or not passed, the delimiters will be: space [ ], double quote ["], comma [,], parenthesis [()], and star [*].

- **Example**: Assume a product dataset with product name and quantity as follows, to understand the working of the `TOKENIZE()` function:

  Example: apple phone, 23

  samsung mobile, 34

  sony TV, 87

  Lg refrigerator, 76

  lg microwave, 65

```
grunt> product3 = LOAD '/chap5Pig/prod3.txt' USING PigStorage(',') as (Prod_
Name:chararray,Qty:int);
grunt>prod_token = FOREACH product3 GENERATE TOKENIZE(Prod_Name);
grunt>Dump prod_token;
```

  As shown in *Figure 8.27*, `TOKENIZE()` function is applied to product name:

```
grunt> prod_token = FOREACH product3 GENERATE TOKENIZE(Prod_Name);
grunt> Dump prod_token;
```

***Figure 8.27**: Usage of the TOKENIZE() function*

In the output, as shown in *Figure 8.28*, it splits the name string (all words in a single tuple) into a bag of words with each word in a single tuple:

```
2024-05-26 11:05:38,375 [main] INFO  org.apache.pig.backend.hadoop.executione
ngine.util.MapRedUtil - Total input paths to process : 1
({(apple),(phone)})
({(samsung),(mobile)})
({(sony),(TV)})
({(Lg),(refrigerator)})
({(lg),(microwave)})
```

***Figure 8.28**: Output of the TOKENIZE() function*

- **TOBAG()**: This function is used to convert one or more expressions to individual tuples, which are then placed in a bag.
  - **Syntax:** `TOBAG(expression [, expression ...])`
  - **Example**:

```
grunt>sales_data = LOAD '/chap5Pig/sales_trans.txt' USING PigStorage(',') as
(Trans_ID:int, Cust_ID:int, Prod_ID:int, Prod_Name:chararray, Qty:int, Price:float,
Timestamp:chararray);
grunt>tobag = FOREACH sales_data GENERATE TOBAG (Trans_ID, Cust_ID, Prod_ID, Prod_
Name);
grunt> Dump tobag;
```

  Here, expression can be of any data type. `FOREACH` statement is used to iterate over the sales data to create a bag containing the fields `Trans_ID`, `Cust_ID`, `Prod_ID`, and `Prod_Name` using the `TOBAG()` function, as shown in *Figure 8.29:*

```
grunt> tobag = FOREACH sales_data GENERATE TOBAG (Trans_ID, Cust_ID, Prod_ID,
 Prod_Name);
grunt> Dump tobag;
```

***Figure 8.29**: Usage of the TOBAG() function*

The output in *Figure 8.30* shows that every tuple of sales data is converted to a bag with the specified fields:

```
2024-05-04 08:20:36,193 [main] INFO  org.apache.pig.backend.hadoop.executionengi
ne.util.MapRedUtil - Total input paths to process : 1
({(1),(101),(1),("LapTop")})
({(2),(102),(3),("Smartphone")})
({(3),(103),(2),("Tablet")})
({(4),(104),(1),("LapTop")})
({(5),(105),(3),("Smartphone")})
```

Figure 8.30: Output of the TOBAG() function

- **TOMAP()**: The **TOMAP** function in Apache Pig is used to create a map (dictionary-like data structure) from specified fields in a relation.

  Each key-value pair in the map is generated from the input fields.

  It is important to note that the user must provide an even number of expressions as parameters, and these elements must comply with the map type rule, i.e., every odd element that is a key-expression must be a **chararray** since only **chararrays** can be keys into the map, whereas every even element that is a value-expression can be of any type supported by a map.

  - **Syntax:** **TOMAP(key-expression, value-expression [, key-expression, value-expression ...])**

    Here, key expressions are of type **chararray**, and value expressions can be expressions of any type supported by a map.

  - **Example**:

    ```
    grunt>tomap = FOREACH sales_data GENERATE TOMAP (Cust_ID, Prod_ID);
    grunt>Dump tomap;
    ```

    As shown in *Figure 8.31*, the **FOREACH** statement is used to iterate over the sales data to convert the columns **Prod_Name** and **Prod_ID** into key-value pairs using the **TOMAP** function:

    ```
    grunt> tomap = FOREACH sales_data GENERATE TOMAP ( Prod_Name, Prod_ID);
    ```

    Figure 8.31: Usage of TOMAP() function

    Figure 8.32 shows that each record from the **sales_data** is transformed into a map containing the specified key-value pairs:

    ```
    2024-05-04 08:50:08,148 [main] INFO  org.apache.pig.backend.hadoop.execut
    ionengine.util.MapRedUtil - Total input paths to process : 1
    (["LapTop"#1])
    (["Smartphone"#3])
    (["Tablet"#2])
    (["LapTop"#1])
    (["Smartphone"#3])
    ```

    Figure 8.32: Output of TOMAP() function

- **TOP()**: The **TOP** function in Apache Pig is used to find the top N tuples from a dataset based on a specified field and sorting order. This can be useful when you need to retrieve the highest or lowest values from your data.

  - **Syntax:** **TOP(topN,column,relation)**

    Here, **topN** refers to the number of top tuples to return. It is of type integer, column in the tuple refers to the column whose values are being compared.

    Note: 0 denotes the first column, and relation is the name of the relation with the desired dataset containing the column.

The function assumes that all tuples in the bag contain an element of the same type in the compared column.

By default, the **TOP** function uses descending order. However, it can be configured via the **DEFINE** statement.

- **Example**:

```
DEFINE asc TOP('ASC'); -- ascending order
DEFINE desc TOP('DESC'); -- descending order
grunt> sales = Group sales_data By ALL;
grunt> top_sales = Foreach sales { top = TOP(2, 0, sales_data); Generate top; }
grunt>Dump top_sales;
```

As shown in *Figure 8.33*, the first step is to group all records in the **sales_data** relation into a single group:

```
grunt> sales = Group sales_data ALL;
grunt> top_sales = Foreach sales {
>> top = TOP(2,0,sales_data);
>> Generate top;}
grunt> Dump top_sales;
```

***Figure 8.33**: Usage of TOP() function*

The **ALL** keyword is used to group the entire dataset into one bag. The **FOREACH** loop processes the single group created by the **GROUP** operation. The **TOP** function is used to find the top 2 records within the entire dataset based on **Trans_ID** in ascending order, as shown in *Figure 8.34:*

```
2024-05-26 11:34:23,483 [main] INFO  org.apache.pig.backend.hadoop.executione
ngine.util.MapRedUtil - Total input paths to process : 1
({(4,104,1,"LapTop",1,800.0,"2024-03-01 10:15:00"),(5,105,3,"Smartphone",3,60
0.0,"2024-03-01 10:20:00")})
```

***Figure 8.34**: Output of TOP() function*

- **TOTUPLE():** In Apache Pig, the **TOTUPLE** function groups multiple fields together into a single tuple, which can then be processed as a unit.
  - **Syntax: TOTUPLE(expression [, expression ...])**

    Here, expression can be of any datatype.
  - **Example**:

```
grunt> totuple = FOREACH sales_data GENERATE TOTUPLE (Trans_ID, Cust_ID, Prod_ID, Prod_Name);
grunt> Dump totuple;
```

As shown in *Figure 8.35*, the **FOREACH ... GENERATE** statement iterates over the **sales_data** and creates a tuple using the **TOTUPLE** function from the **Trans_ID, Cust_ID, Prod_ID**, and **Prod_Name** fields:

```
grunt> totuple = FOREACH sales_data GENERATE TOTUPLE (Trans_ID, Cust_ID,
Prod_ID, Prod_Name);
```

***Figure 8.35**: Usage of TOTUPLE() function*

The output indicates that all fields are combined into a single tuple for each record. The resulting relation is shown in *Figure 8.36*:

```
2024-05-04 08:45:23,469 [main] INFO  org.apache.pig.backend.hadoop.execut
ionengine.util.MapRedUtil - Total input paths to process : 1
((1,101,1,"LapTop"))
((2,102,3,"Smartphone"))
((3,103,2,"Tablet"))
((4,104,1,"LapTop"))
((5,105,3,"Smartphone"))
```

***Figure 8.36**: Output of TOTUPLE() function*

String functions

One of the key strengths of Apache Pig lies in its rich set of built-in functions, particularly those designed for string manipulation. String functions in Apache Pig are used to perform operations such as searching, extracting, modifying, or comparing string values within data pipelines. These functions are essential when working with textual data for cleaning messy input, formatting output, or parsing values for analysis. In Apache Pig, all function names are case sensitive and upper case. Pig string functions take an extra first parameter, and the string to which all the operations are applied. If any of the input parameters are null or if an insufficient number of parameters are supplied, `NULL` is returned. Some of the commonly used string functions in Apache Pig are shown in *Table 8.1*:

Function name and syntax	Usage	Example

`SUBSTRING(string, startIndex, stopIndex)`	Use the SUBSTRING function to return a substring from a given string.	`grunt> A = LOAD 'data.txt' AS (line:chararray);`
		`grunt> B = FOREACH A GENERATE SUBSTRING(line, 0, 4);`
		If line = 'PigLatin' SUBSTRING('PigLatin', 0, 4) | 'PigL'

`ENDSWITH(string, teststring)/ STARTSWITH(string, testAgainst)`	It is used to check if the argument in the first parameter ends with the string in the second.	`grunt> A = LOAD 'data.txt' AS (line:chararray);`
		`grunt> B = FOREACH A GENERATE ENDSWITH(line, 'Pig'), ENDSWITH(line, 'Latin');`
		If line = 'PigLatin':
		• ENDSWITH('PigLatin', 'Pig') | false
		• ENDSWITH('PigLatin', 'Latin') | true
		`grunt> A = LOAD 'data.txt' AS (line:chararray);`
		`grunt> B = FOREACH A GENERATE STARTSWITH(line, 'Pig'), STARTSWITH(line, 'Latin');`
		If line = 'PigLatin':
		• STARTSWITH('PigLatin', 'Pig') | true
		• STARTSWITH('PigLatin', 'Latin') | false

`EqualsIgnoreCase(string1, string2)`	It is used to determine if two strings are equal, ignoring case.	`grunt> A = LOAD 'data.txt' AS (col1:chararray, col2:chararray);`
		`grunt> B = FOREACH A GENERATE EqualsIgnoreCase(col1, col2);`
		If col1 = 'PIGLATIN' and col2 = 'piglatin'
		• EqualsIgnoreCase('PIGLATIN', 'piglatin') | true

`INDEXOF(string, 'character', startIndex)`	This function returns the index of the first occurrence of a character in a string. It searches forward from a start index. The forward search for the character begins at the designated start index.	**grunt> A = LOAD 'data.txt' AS (line:chararray);** **grunt> B = FOREACH A GENERATE INDEXOF(line, 'a', 2);** Suppose line = 'banana', INDEXOF('banana', 'a', 2) | 3 (First 'a' after index 2 is at index 3)
`LAST_INDEX_OF(string, 'character')`	It returns the index of the last occurrence of a character in a string. It searches backward from the end of the string. The backward search for the character begins at the end of the string.	**grunt> A = LOAD 'data.txt' AS (line:chararray);** **grunt> B = FOREACH A GENERATE LAST_INDEX_OF(line, 'a');** Suppose line = 'banana', LAST_INDEX_OF('banana', 'a') → 5 (The last 'a' is at index 5)
`LCFIRST(expression)/ UCFIRST(expression)`	These functions are used to convert only the first character in a string to lower (LCFIRST) / upper (UCFIRST case.	**grunt> A = LOAD 'data.txt' AS (line:chararray);** **grunt> B = FOREACH A GENERATE LCFIRST(line);** Suppose line = 'Apple', LCFIRST('Apple') | 'apple' **grunt> A = LOAD 'data.txt' AS (line:chararray);** **grunt> B = FOREACH A GENERATE UCFIRST(line);** Suppose line = 'banana', UCFIRST('banana') | 'Banana'
`LOWER(expression)/ UPPER(expression)`	These functions are used to convert all characters in a string to lower (LOWER) case andor upper (UPPER) case.	**grunt> A = LOAD 'data.txt' AS (line:chararray);** **grunt> B = FOREACH A GENERATE LOWER(line), UPPER(line);** If line = 'PigLatin' Output | 'piglatin' and 'PIGLATIN'
`LTRIM(expression)/ RTRIM(expression)/ TRIM(expression)`	These functions are used to remove leading (LTRIM) / trailing (RTRIM) white space from a string, whereas TRIM removes both leading and trailing spaces.	**grunt> A = LOAD 'data.txt' AS (line:chararray);** **grunt> B = FOREACH A GENERATE LTRIM(line), RTRIM(line), TRIM(line);** If line = ' Hello World ' **Output**: • LTRIM | 'Hello World ' • RTRIM | ' Hello World' • TRIM | 'Hello World'

REGEX_EXTRACT (string, regex, index)/ REGEX_EXTRACT_ALL (string, regex)	The REGEX_EXTRACT function is used to extract the matched group defined by the index parameter (where the index is a 1-based parameter), where matching is performed using a regular expression. The function returns a string that corresponds to the matched group in the position specified by the index. If there is no matched expression at that position, NULL is returned. Whereas the REGEX_EXTRACT_ALL function is used to extract all matched groups.	**grunt> A = LOAD 'data.txt' AS (line:chararray);** **grunt> B = FOREACH A GENERATE REGEX_EXTRACT(line, '(\\d+)', 1);** If line = 'Order1234Confirmed' Regex (\d+) captures numbers → Output: '1234' **grunt> A = LOAD 'data.txt' AS (line:chararray);** **grunt> B = FOREACH A GENERATE REGEX_EXTRACT_ALL(line, '\\d+');** If line = 'Item12Price34' Output → {(12),(34)}

***Table 8.1**: String functions*

User-defined functions

While Pig's built-in functions cover many use cases, there are times when custom logic is required to handle specialized data processing tasks. This is where UDFs are required. UDFs enable users to define their functions in Java, Python, or other programming languages and seamlessly integrate them into Pig scripts.

We will explore the process of creating and utilizing UDFs in Pig, demonstrating how to encapsulate custom logic into reusable functions. By developing UDFs, users can extend Pig's functionality to meet specific requirements, such as implementing complex business rules, performing advanced analytics, or integrating with external systems.

UDF in Pig Latin to convert data to lowercase

Among all the languages, Pig provides the most extensive support for Java functions. In this section, we will explore how to create a sample UDF using Eclipse in Cloudera.

Let us consider the data stored in the `prod.txt` file with `Prod_ID` and `Qty`, as shown in *Figure 8.37*:

```
[cloudera@quickstart ~]$ hdfs dfs -cat /chap5Pig/prod.txt
AA 34
BB 45
CC 23
AA 78
AA 34
BB 45
DD 89
DD 89
```

***Figure 8.37**: Data in the prod.txt file*

Next, let us write a UDF in Java to convert the `Prod_ID` to lowercase. Follow these steps to write a UDF function:

1. Open Eclipse in Cloudera.

2. Create a new project (say, **PigLudf**).
3. Create a package with the name com and create a Java class with the name **PigUDF**, as shown in *Figure 8.38*. The code is as follows:

```
package com;

import java.io.IOException;

import org.apache.pig.EvalFunc;
import org.apache.pig.data.Tuple;

public class PigUDF extends EvalFunc<String> {

public String exec(Tuple input) throws IOException {

if (input == null || input.size() == 0)
return null;

String prodID = (String) input.get(0);
String Qty = (String) input.get(1);

return prodID.toLowerCase() + " " + Qty;
}
}
```

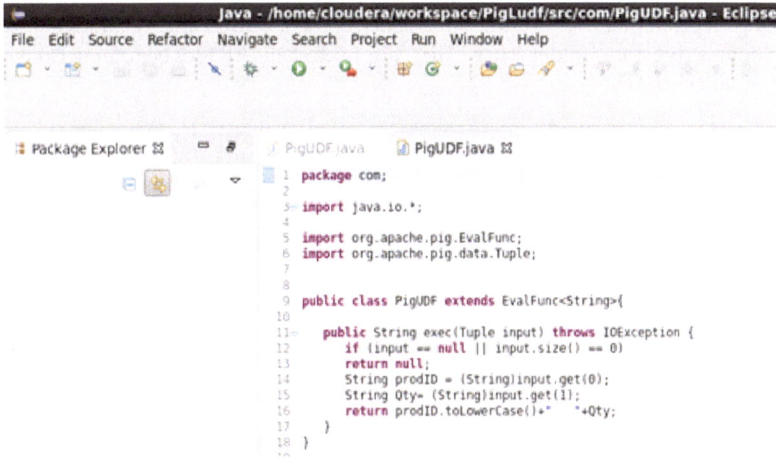

***Figure 8.38:** Java code*

Figure 8.38 shows Java code, which defines a UDF.

Let us break down the code step by step:

- **Package declaration**:
  - **package com**: Indicates this UDF belongs to the `com` package.

- **Imports**:
  - **java.io.***: Imports basic input-output classes.
  - **org.apache.pig.EvalFunc**: Imports the `EvalFunc` class from Apache Pig. `EvalFunc` is the base class for all UDFs in Pig.
  - **org.apache.pig.data.Tuple**: Imports the `Tuple` class from Pig's data package. A tuple represents a data record in Pig, similar to a row in a table.
- **Class declaration**:

```
public class PigUDF extends EvalFunc<String> {
```

  - **PigUDF**: This class extends `EvalFunc<String>`, indicating that it is a Pig UDF that returns a `String`.
- **exec method**: This method overrides the `exec` method defined in `EvalFunc`. It takes a `Tuple` (input) as a parameter and returns a `String`.

  The `if` statement checks if the input `Tuple` is null or empty. If so, it returns null. The next two statements retrieve the first and second fields (`prodID` and `Qty`) from the input Tuple. These statements assume both fields are of type `String`.
- Finally, in the return statement, `prodID.toLowerCase()` statement converts `prodID` to lowercase and concatenates it with a space (`" "`) and `Qty`, and returns the concatenated result as a single `String`. The output type of this UDF (`String`) should match the expected output type in your Pig script.

  Note: **Ensure that the input `Tuple` (input) matches the expected schema (at least two fields).**

4. After writing the Java code, it is important to import the Pig JAR files into the environment before compiling the program.
5. The jar files required for successful compilation can be imported by right-clicking the `PigLudf` project name in the Project Explorer, as shown in *Figure 8.38*, and choosing properties from the drop-down menu.
6. After clicking on properties, follow these steps. Click on **Java Build Path** | **Libraries** | **Add External JARs** | choose cloudera directory/folder | **usr** | **lib** | **pig** | select all JAR files beginning from `pig.jar` as shown in *Figure 8.39* and click **OK**:

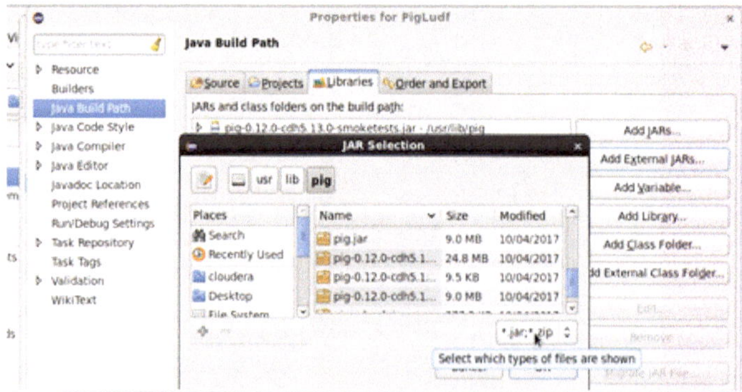

Figure 8.39: Steps to import JAR files for Pig

7. Next, compile the program.
8. After compiling the class without errors, the next step is to export the JAR file to the Cloudera home.

   For the same, right-click on the `PigLudf` project, which gives you a drop-down menu.

9. Select export from the menu, as shown in *Figure 8.40:*

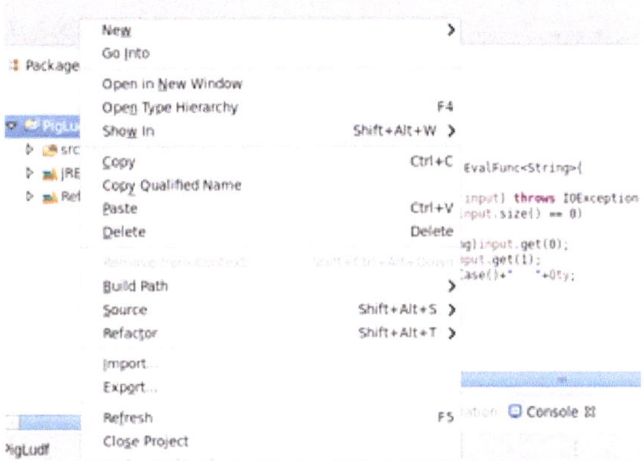

***Figure 8.40**: Export the JAR file of the project*

10. Next, select the **JAR file**, as shown in *Figure 8.41:*

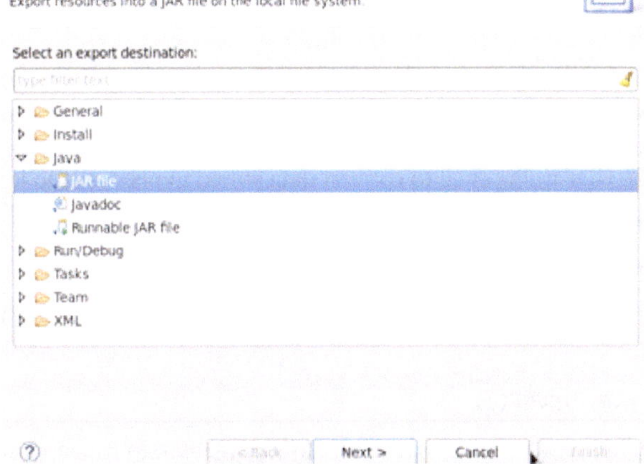

***Figure 8.41**: Selecting the JAR file of the project*

11. Next, a new window appears to browse the destination folder (choose home/cloudera here) and assign a name to the export JAR file, and click **OK**, as shown in *Figure 8.42:*

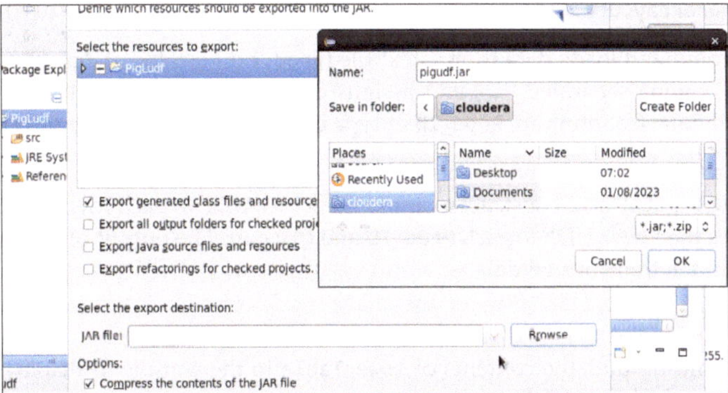

***Figure 8.42**: Export JAR file of the project*

12. Finally, a new window appears. Click **Finish**, and the JAR file will be exported in the destination folder, as shown in *Figure 8.43*:

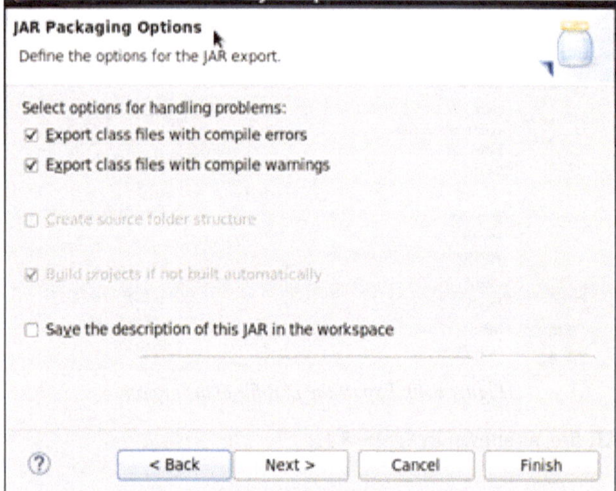

Figure 8.43*: Final window to export the jar file of the project*

In the specified folder, a JAR file is created. This can be verified by checking the **`path /home/cloudera`**. The JAR file contains the compiled Java class of the UDF. After writing the UDF and generating the JAR file, the next step is to use the UDF in Pig shell to convert data stored in **`prod.txt`** to lowercase.

13. Open the Pig shell and use the following commands:

   a. **`REGISTER /home/cloudera/pigudf.jar;`**

      This command registers an external JAR file (**`pigudf.jar`**) containing UDFs that you want to use in your Pig script.

   b. **`DEFINE lower com.PigUDF();`**

      This command defines an alias named lower for **`com.PigUDF()`** function defined within the Java class **`com.PigUDF`** to convert input data to lowercase.

   c. **LOAD command**:

      i. **`product = LOAD '/chap5Pig/prod.txt' USING PigStorage(',') as (Prod_ID:chararray,Qty:int);`**

         This command loads data from a text file (**`prod.txt`**) located at **`/chap5Pig/`**. It assumes that the file is comma-separated (**`','`**) and assigns column names (**`Prod_ID:chararray`**, **`Qty:int`**) to the loaded data. Columns are **`Prod_ID`** of type **`chararray`** and **`Qty`** of type **`int`**.

      ii. **`lowerTable = FOREACH product GENERATE lower(Prod_ID, Qty);`** This command uses the **`FOREACH`** ... **`GENERATE`** construct to apply the lower UDF to each row (product). Specifically, it applies the lower UDF to each **`Prod_ID`** and **`Qty`** pair. The output of this step (**`lowerTable`**) will contain the transformed data.

   d. **`DUMP lowerTable;`**

      This command outputs the contents of **`lowerTable`** to the console. It displays the transformed data after applying the lower UDF.

Figure 8.44 shows the execution of the preceding steps to register and execute the UDF:

```
grunt> REGISTER /home/cloudera/pigudf.jar;
2024-06-26 06:57:42,428 [main] INFO  org.apache.hadoop.conf.Configuration.deprec
ation - fs.default.name is deprecated. Instead, use fs.defaultFS
2024-06-26 06:57:42,428 [main] INFO  org.apache.hadoop.conf.Configuration.deprec
ation - mapred.job.tracker is deprecated. Instead, use mapreduce.jobtracker.addr
ess
grunt> DEFINE lower com.PigUDF();
grunt> product = LOAD '/chap5Pig/prod.txt' USING PigStorage(',') as (Prod_ID:cha
rarray,Qty:int);
grunt> lowerTable = Foreach product Generate lower(Prod_ID,Qty);
grunt> DUMP lowerTable;
2024-06-26 06:59:22,446 [main] INFO  org.apache.pig.tools.pigstats.ScriptState -
```

***Figure 8.44**: Steps to register and execute UDF*

Figure 8.45 shows the output of UDF, which has converted the product names to lowercase:

```
cloudera@quickstart:~
File  Edit  View  Search  Terminal  Help
ation - mapred.job.tracker is deprecated. Instead, use mapreduce.jobtracker.addr
ess
2024-06-26 06:59:42,518 [main] INFO  org.apache.pig.data.SchemaTupleBackend - Ke
y [pig.schematuple] was not set... will not generate code.
2024-06-26 06:59:42,531 [main] INFO  org.apache.hadoop.mapreduce.lib.input.FileI
nputFormat - Total input paths to process : 1
2024-06-26 06:59:42,531 [main] INFO  org.apache.pig.backend.hadoop.executionengi
ne.util.MapRedUtil - Total input paths to process : 1
(aa 34   null)
(bb 45   null)
(cc 23   null)
(aa 78   null)
(aa 34   null)
(bb 45   null)
(dd 89   null)
(dd 89   null)
grunt>
```

***Figure 8.45**: Output of UDF*

Conclusion

This chapter provided the practical applications of Pig Latin built-in functions, such as COUNT, MAX, MIN, TOKENIZE, and REGEX_EXTRACT_ALL, within the Cloudera ecosystem. These functions enable tasks ranging from basic data aggregation to complex text processing and pattern extraction. The chapter also highlighted the power of UDFs in extending Pig's functionality. By encapsulating custom logic into reusable functions, users can tailor data processing to specific business requirements.

This capability is crucial for implementing intricate business rules, conducting advanced analytics, or seamlessly integrating with external systems. In essence, Pig Latin is a pivotal tool for big data processing, offering both a rich library of built-in functions and the flexibility of custom UDFs. These capabilities empower users to tackle diverse data challenges with agility and precision within the Cloudera environment.

In the next chapter, we will learn Apache Hive, which is a powerful data warehousing and SQL-like querying tool used for summarizing, querying, and analyzing petabytes of data using SQL.

Points to remember

The following are some key takeaways from this chapter:

- Pig Latin functions serve a specific purpose within Pig Latin scripts, enabling data manipulation, transformation, and analysis on large datasets. Some of the functions discussed are:
  - **Eval functions**:
    - **Avg()**: Computes the average of numeric values in a relation.
    - **BagToString()**: Converts a bag (collection of tuples) to a string.
    - **CONCAT()**: Concatenates strings or bags.

  - **COUNT()**: Counts the number of elements in a bag.
  - **COUNT_STAR()**: Counts the number of tuples in a relation.
  - **DIFF()**: Finds the difference between two bags.
  - **IsEmpty()**: Checks if a bag or map is empty.
  - **MAX()**: Finds the maximum value in a bag.
  - **MIN()**: Finds the minimum value in a bag.
  - **PluckTuple()**: Extracts a tuple from a bag.
  - **SIZE()**: Returns the size of a bag, map, or tuple.
  - **SUBTRACT()**: Performs subtraction on numeric values.
  - **SUM()**: Computes the sum of numeric values in a bag.
  - **TOKENIZE()**: Splits a string into tokens (words).
  - **TOBAG()**: Converts a tuple or map into a bag.
  - **TOMAP()**: Converts a bag or tuple into a map.
  - **TOP()**: Finds the top N records based on a field.
  - **TOTUPLE()**: Converts a bag or map into a tuple.
- **String functions**:
  - **SUBSTRING()**: Extracts a substring from a string.
  - **ENDSWITH() / STARTSWITH()**: Checks if a string ends or starts with a specified substring.
  - **EqualsIgnoreCase()**: Compares two strings ignoring case.
  - **INDEXOF()**: Finds the position of a substring within a string.
  - **LAST_INDEX_OF()**: Finds the last occurrence of a substring within a string.
  - **LCFIRST() / UCFIRST()**: Converts the first character of a string to lowercase or uppercase.
  - **LOWER() / UPPER()**: Converts a string to lowercase or uppercase.
  - **LTRIM() / RTRIM() / TRIM()**: Trims whitespace from the left, right, or both sides of a string.
  - **REGEX_EXTRACT() / REGEX_EXTRACT_ALL()**: Extracts substrings using regular expressions.
  - **UDFs**: These are custom functions defined by users to perform specific operations not covered by built-in functions in Pig Latin. They extend the functionality of Pig Latin scripts by allowing users to write their logic using Java, Python, or other supported languages.

Multiple choice questions

1. **What does the Pig Latin function COUNT() do?**
   a. Counts the number of tuples in a relation
   b. Counts the number of elements in a bag
   c. Computes the average of numeric values
   d. Converts a bag to a string
2. **Which Pig Latin function is used to find the maximum value in a bag?**
   a. MAX()
   b. MIN()
   c. SUM()
   d. AVG()
3. **What does the TOKENIZE() function do in Pig Latin?**
   a. Converts a bag to a string
   b. Splits a string into tokens (words)
   c. Counts the number of elements in a bag
   d. Finds the difference between two bags

4. **Which function is used to convert a bag or tuple into a map in Pig Latin?**
   a. TOBAG()
   b. TOMAP()
   c. SIZE()
   d. COUNT_STAR()
5. **The REGEX_EXTRACT_ALL() function in Pig Latin is used for:**
   a. Extracting a single substring using regular expressions
   b. Extracting all substrings that match a regular expression
   c. Comparing two strings ignoring case
   d. Finding the position of a substring within a string
6. **What does the Pig Latin function IsEmpty() check?**
   a. If a bag or map is empty
   b. If a string ends with a specified substring
   c. If a string starts with a specified substring
   d. If a bag is empty
7. **Which function converts a tuple or map into a bag in Pig Latin?**
   a. TOBAG()
   b. TOMAP()
   c. TOTUPLE()
   d. PluckTuple()
8. **The function SUBSTRING() in Pig Latin is used for:**
   a. Concatenating strings or bags
   b. Extracting a substring from a string
   c. Converting a bag to a string
   d. Converting a string to lowercase
9. **What does the Pig Latin function UCFIRST() do?**
   a. Converts the first character of a string to uppercase
   b. Converts the first character of a string to lowercase
   c. Finds the last occurrence of a substring within a string
   d. Trims whitespace from both sides of a string
10. **Which function checks if a string starts with a specified substring in Pig Latin?**
    a. STARTSWITH()
    b. ENDSWITH()
    c. INDEXOF()
    d. LAST_INDEX_OF()
11. **The function DIFF() in Pig Latin is used for:**
    a. Finding the difference between two bags
    b. Counting the number of tuples in a relation
    c. Extracting all substrings that match a regular expression
    d. Checking if a bag or map is empty
12. **What does the Pig Latin function LCFIRST() do?**
    a. Converts the first character of a string to lowercase
    b. Converts the first character of a string to uppercase
    c. Trims whitespace from both sides of a string
    d. Converts a bag to a string
13. **Which function in Pig Latin is used to convert a bag or map into a tuple?**
    a. TOTUPLE()
    b. TOBAG()
    c. TOMAP()
    d. COUNT_STAR()

14. **The function REGEX_EXTRACT() in Pig Latin is used for:**
    a. Extracting a single substring using regular expressions
    b. Extracting all substrings that match a regular expression
    c. Comparing two strings ignoring case
    d. Finding the position of a substring within a string
15. **What is the purpose of the Pig Latin function SIZE()?**
    a. Converts a bag to a string
    b. Returns the size of a bag, map, or tuple
    c. Splits a string into tokens (words)
    d. Performs subtraction on numeric values

Answers

1. b.	2. a.	3. b.	4. b.	5. b.
6. a.	7. a.	8. b.	9. a.	10. a.
11. a.	12. a.	13. a.	14. a.	15. b.

Questions

1. Explain how the CONCAT() function works in Pig Latin. Provide an example scenario where concatenation might be useful in data processing.
2. Describe the difference between the functions COUNT() and COUNT_STAR() in Pig Latin. When would you use one over the other?
3. How does the REGEX_EXTRACT_ALL() function in Pig Latin handle regular expressions compared to REGEX_EXTRACT()? Provide an example of when you might prefer one over the other.
4. Illustrate the use of the TOTUPLE() function with an example. How does it differ from TOBAG() and TOMAP() in terms of data structure conversion in Pig Latin?
5. Compare and contrast the functions SUBSTRING() and REGEX_EXTRACT() in Pig Latin. When would you choose one over the other for extracting substrings, and why?
6. Examine the utility of the MAX() and MIN() functions in Pig Latin. Provide examples of scenarios where finding the maximum or minimum values in a dataset is crucial for analysis.
7. Describe how the functions UCFIRST() and LCFIRST() are used in Pig Latin. Provide examples where changing the case of the first character of strings is necessary in data processing tasks.
8. Explain the concept of UDFs in Pig Latin. What advantages do UDFs offer, and under what circumstances would you create and use a custom function?
9. You have a dataset containing information about sales transactions in a retail store. Each record includes fields such as transaction_id, customer_id, product_name, quantity, and unit_price. Write Pig Latin scripts to perform the following tasks using Pig Latin:
    a. Calculate the total sales amount for each customer.
    b. Find the top 5 customers with the highest total sales amount.
10. You are working with a dataset containing text documents. Each document is stored as a tuple with fields document_id and text_content. You need to perform text processing and analysis tasks using Pig Latin:
    a. Tokenize the text_content of each document into individual words.
    b. Count the frequency of each word across all documents.
    c. Find the top 10 most frequent words in the entire dataset.

CHAPTER 9
Hive-data Warehousing and SQL-like Queries

Torture the data, and it will confess to anything.

–Ronald Coase

Introduction

This chapter provides an extensive introduction to Apache Hive, a powerful data warehousing and SQL-like querying tool built on top of Hadoop. It begins by explaining the motivation behind using Hive, emphasizing its significance in simplifying big data processing tasks. Next, Hive's architecture is explained with precise details about the role of key components like the Thrift server, metastore, driver, and compiler in enabling efficient and scalable data processing. The chapter will introduce data types and the Hive data model, which revolves around tables, partitions, and buckets. The concept of tables in Hive is explored, along with partitioning techniques to improve query performance and data organization. Hive SerDe's are explained in the chapter, highlighting their importance in handling various data formats and enabling seamless integration with Hadoop ecosystem tools. The last section of the chapter compares the Hive with respect to Apache Pig and **relational database management systems** (**RDBMS**).

Structure

In this chapter, we will cover the following topics:

- Introduction to Hive
- Need for Hive
- Hive architecture
- Data types in Hive
- Hive serialization and deserialization
- Hive data model
- Hive vs. Pig
- Hive vs. RDBMS
- Hive Query Language

Objectives

By the end of this chapter, the readers will have a comprehensive understanding of Apache Hive, a robust tool for data warehousing and SQL-like querying built on Hadoop. They will grasp the motivation behind Hive's development and its role in simplifying big data processing tasks. The chapter will detail Hive's architecture, explaining the functions of key components such as the Thrift server, metastore, driver, and compiler, which contribute to efficient and scalable data processing. Readers will then be introduced to the data types and Hive data model, including concepts of tables, partitions, and buckets. Additionally, they will understand Hive SerDes and their crucial role in managing various data formats and integrating with the Hadoop ecosystem. Finally, the chapter will compare Hive with Apache Pig and traditional RDBMS, highlighting their differences and use cases.

Introduction to Hive

Hive is a distributed, fault-tolerant data warehousing tool for summarizing, querying, and analyzing petabytes of data residing in distributed storage. Hive is built on top of Apache Hadoop. It is an open-source data warehouse system that is designed to read, write, and manage large datasets stored in Apache **Hadoop Distributed File System** (**HDFS**). Hive provides a SQL-like interface to process and analyze data stored in HDFS. Apache Hive is not a complete database; it only stores metadata while the actual data resides in HDFS. Hive provides a query language called **HiveQL** (**HQL**) that is similar to SQL, making it accessible to engineers familiar with traditional databases. Hive creates a layer of abstraction such that when a user writes a query, HiveQL automatically translates SQL queries into MapReduce jobs that interact with HDFS. Additionally, Hive supports storage on S3, **Azure Data Lake Storage** (**ADLS**), and Google Cloud Storage. Hive functions as an **online analytical processing** (**OLAP**) system, making it ideal for analytics, report generation, and data mining operations in large data warehouses.

Need for Hive

Hive is a top-level Apache project conceived by Facebook. Before developing Apache Hive, Facebook was struggling with the growing volume of data for analytics and other inconsistencies in these large datasets to perform data-intensive tasks efficiently. The traditional RDBMS had limited capabilities to deal with a large amount of data. To solve these problems, Facebook initially introduced Hadoop. They were able to handle the large datasets using Hadoop HDFS. However, over a period of time, they found that they had to write MapReduce code in Java for every small task to be performed on data stored in HDFS. They had to write 50 to 60 lines of code in Java, even for the simple select command, which could be done by a single line query in SQL. Therefore, writing Java code to execute the complex jobs was the new challenge for engineers at Facebook, and this gave way to the creation of Hive. Over the years, Apache Hive emerged as a top-level Apache project as it saved a lot of development time for organizations. Hive simplified the tasks of summarization, analysis, query, and data exploration.

Apache Hive was created with the dual objectives:

- First, to design and develop a SQL-based declarative language that would allow developers to plug in their scripts and programs in Hive with minimal disruption when SQL does not serve.
- Second, to create a Hadoop-based centralized metadata store for all the datasets in the organization. Incepted by Facebook, Hive is widely used by companies like *Netflix*, *Twitter*, *Airbnb*, *LinkedIn*, *Yahoo*, *Uber*, *Spotify*, *Pinterest*, etc. for processing and analyzing vast amounts of data.

Hive architecture

Figure 9.1 shows the architecture of Hive, its components, and their interactions with Hadoop:

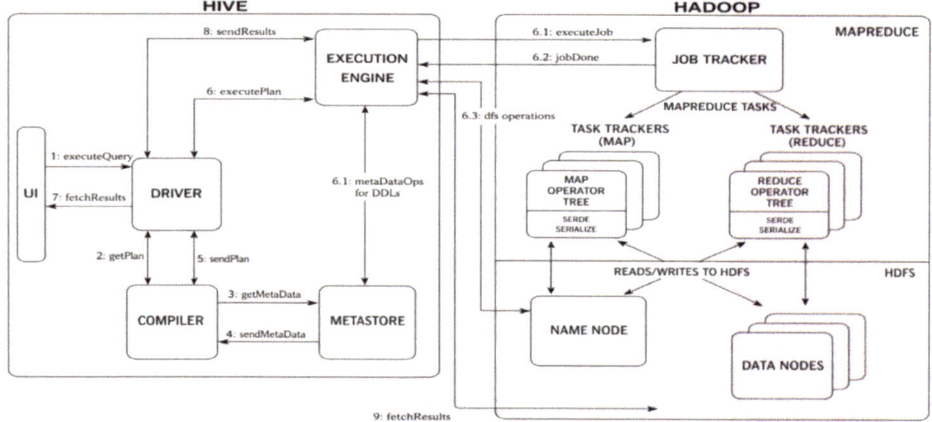

***Figure 9.1**: Hive architecture and query execution flow*

All these components work in unison to perform the data analysis tasks as follows:

- **User interface (UI)**: Users interact with Hive via an interface called **UI** to submit queries and perform other operations on the system. The various types of UI provided by Hive are as follows:
  - **Hive command line interface (CLI)**: It allows users to execute Hive queries and commands.
  - **Hive web interface (HWI)**: A web-based UI for submitting queries and managing the Hive environment.
  - **HiveServer2**: Provides a Thrift service that allows clients to execute queries remotely.
- **Driver**: The queries submitted by users are received by the driver. The driver in Apache Hive is responsible for managing the lifecycle of a Hive query. It handles the user sessions and interacts with the compiler to generate an execution plan for the query. The driver coordinates the execution of the plan using the appropriate execution engine (e.g., MapReduce, Tez). Finally, it fetches the results of the query execution and makes them available to the user. Thus, a driver manages the complete lifecycle of the query, from submission to retrieval of results.
- **Compiler**: The compiler in Apache Hive translates **Hive Query Language** (**HiveQL**) statements into a **directed acyclic graph** (**DAG**) of MapReduce or Tez tasks. It begins with the parsing of HiveQL query to generate an **abstract syntax tree** (**AST**). Next, it performs semantic analysis of the AST to check for semantic correctness (e.g., type checking, existence of tables/columns) and creates a logical plan from the AST. The logical plan is then converted into a physical plan with the help of the table and partition metadata looked up from the metastore, with details of the series of tasks to be executed. The compiler also applies optimizations to the execution plan to improve performance.
- **Metastore**: In Apache Hive, the metastore is a central repository that stores metadata about the data stored in Hive. The metastore plays an important role in managing and querying large datasets efficiently. Hive metastore has two main components, which include the metastore database, which is a relational database (e.g., MySQL, PostgreSQL, Oracle, and Derby) that stores all the metadata. The types of metadata stored in the metastore include database names, table names, column names and types, table partitions, storage formats (e.g., text, **optimized row columnar** (**ORC**), Parquet), the corresponding HDFS files where the data is stored, Table locations in the file system (e.g., HDFS, S3), the serializers and deserializers necessary to read and write data, etc. The other component is metastore service, which is a Thrift service that allows Hive and other applications to access the metadata stored in the metastore database. Thrift provides bindings in many popular languages. Thus, Hive metastore can be integrated with other big data tools and frameworks, such as Apache Spark, Apache Impala, and Presto, allowing them to leverage the metadata stored in Hive for efficient query execution.

  In Apache Hive, the Hive Metastore can operate in three configurations: Embedded, Local, and Remote mode.

  In Embedded Metastore Mode, Hive uses Apache Derby as the default metastore database. The metastore runs within the same JVM as the Hive application, meaning there is no separate service process. This configuration is simple to set up and requires minimal configuration. However, it supports only a single user at a time and is therefore not suitable for multi-user or production environments. It is primarily used for testing, learning, or small experimental setups.

  In Local Metastore Mode, the Hive client connects via JDBC to an external relational database such as MySQL or PostgreSQL. Although the metastore service runs locally on the same machine as Hive, the metadata is stored in an external RDBMS. This setup improves reliability compared to embedded mode and supports better concurrency, making it suitable for small-scale or departmental deployments.

  In Remote Metastore Mode, which is the most commonly used configuration in production environments, the metastore runs as a separate service exposed through Apache Thrift. Multiple Hive clients and other big data tools can connect to this service over the network. This architecture enables centralized metadata management, better scalability, and high concurrency support, making it ideal for distributed and enterprise-level environments.

- **Execution engine**: In Apache Hive, the execution engine is responsible for executing the plan created by the compiler. The plan is a DAG of stages. It manages the dependencies between the different stages of the plan and executes these stages on the appropriate system components. Hive runs these jobs on the Hadoop cluster and now provides support for different execution engines, for example, MapReduce, Tez, Spark, etc., to improve performance and flexibility. Hive relies on Hadoop's resource management capabilities. Hadoop's **Yet Another Resource Negotiator (YARN)** or Mesos manages the resources required for executing jobs.
- **Query execution in Hive**: *Figure 9.1* illustrates the detailed flow of a typical query in the system. The user interacts with the system via the UI for query execution. This query is received by the driver (*step 1* in *Figure 9.1*). The driver initiates a session for the query and sends it to the compiler for generating an execution plan (*step* 2). The compiler retrieves the required metadata from the metastore (*steps 3* and *4*). This metadata is essential for type-checking the expressions in the query tree and for pruning partitions based on query predicates. The plan generated by the compiler (*step 5*) forms a DAG of stages, with each stage representing either a map or reduce job, a metadata operation, or an operation on HDFS. For map or reduce stages, the plan includes map operator trees (executed on the mappers) and a reduce operator tree (for operations requiring reducers). The execution engine submits these stages to the appropriate components (*steps 6, 6.1, 6.2, and 6.3*). When a mapper starts, it reads raw data from HDFS (e.g., CSV lines). The deserializer (like LazySimpleSerDe) splits each record into columns, e.g., it converts `"101,John,IT"` into `[101,"John","IT"]`. Next, the mapper applies operations(e.g., filters, projections, etc). Then the serializer converts processed rows back to bytes and writes to a temporary HDFS file. For simple queries (no reducers), this temp file becomes the result.

  For **data manipulation language (DML)** operations, the final temporary file is moved to the table's location, ensuring that dirty data is not read, as file renaming is an atomic operation in HDFS. For queries, the execution engine reads the contents of the temporary file directly from HDFS as part of the fetch call from the driver (*steps 7, 8,* and *9*).

  This architecture allows Hive to provide a powerful and flexible data warehousing solution on top of Hadoop, enabling efficient querying and analysis of large datasets.

Data types in Hive

Hive supports a wide variety of data types that can be used to define the structure of tables and handle various kinds of data. These data types can be broadly categorized into primitive types, complex types, and user-defined types. The details of these data types are as follows:

- **Primitive data types**: These are the building blocks to define columns in Hive tables. Apache Hive provides numerous primitive data types, similar to those found in traditional SQL databases, but optimized for big data processing. The various primitive data types are as follows:
  - **Numeric types**: They are used when the column values represent numbers. Hive supports a variety of numeric types to balance storage efficiency and range of values, such as:
    - **TINYINT**: One-byte integer, ranges from -128 to 127.
    - **SMALLINT**: Two-byte integer, ranges from -32,768 to 32,767.
    - **INT**: Four-byte signed integer, ranges from -2,147,483,648 to 2,147,483,647.
    - **BIGINT**: Eight-byte integer, ranges from -9,223,372,036,854,775,808 to 9,223,372,036,854,775,807.
    - **FLOAT**: Four-byte single-precision floating point.
    - **DOUBLE**: Eight-byte double-precision floating point number.
  - **String types**: They are used when the column values represent textual data such as names, descriptions, or alphanumeric values.

    - **STRING**: It is a variable-length string. Its values can be enclosed within single quotes (') or double quotes ("). By default, **STRING** is mapped to **VARCHAR(32762)**.
    - **VARCHAR**: It is a variable-length string with a specified maximum length, defined as **VARCHAR(n)**.
    - **CHAR**: It is a fixed-length string, defined as **CHAR(n)**. Its maximum length is fixed at 255. One character takes one byte per character. **VARCHAR()** saves space as compared to **CHAR()**. For example, if value *XYZ* is stored in **VARCHAR(100)**, it occupies five bytes, whereas **CHAR(100)** with *XYZ* occupies 100 bytes.
  - **Date and time types**: They are used to represent temporal values such as dates and timestamps:
    - **TIMESTAMP**: It is used to specify date and time, including year, month, day, hour, minute, second, and fractional seconds.
    - **DATE**: It is used to specify a date value, including year, month, and day.
    - **INTERVAL**: It is used to represent intervals of time, such as **INTERVAL 1 DAY**.
    - **BOOLEAN**: It represents true or false values.
    - **BINARY**: It is used to store variable-length binary data.
- **Collection data types**: HiveQL has four collection data types. These data types can be used to embed a large amount of information in a single column as follows:
  - **ARRAY**: It is an ordered collection of the same type of elements. Let us consider that you want to store fruits that you like, e.g., *Mango, Banana, Apple, Orange*, etc. All these items have similar properties and belong to the same group, i.e., fruits. This group of data can be stored as an ARRAY. Arrays have a fixed size. Only arrays of primitive data types are supported in Hive. It is defined as **ARRAY<element_type>** e.g **ARRAY<STRING>**.
  - **MAP**: It is a collection of key-value pairs. It is defined as **MAP<key_type, value_type>**, e.g, **MAP<STRING, INT>**. Each key in **MAP** is unique and is mapped to a value. Both key and value can be of any data type. A dictionary is an example of a **MAP** data type, e.g., **{Word, Meaning}**, where the data type of the key is **STRING**, and the data type of the value is **ARRAY<VARCHAR>**, as meanings are usually sentences made of words.
  - **STRUCT**: It is a complex data type that groups multiple fields, each with its own type. It refers to a logical group of variables where a logical group can have the same or different data types. It is defined as **STRUCT<field_name1: type1, field_name2: type2, ...>**. For example, the **STRUCT** Student can be used to store the details about students, such as **Name(STRING)**, **Student_ID(INT)**, and **FEE(FLOAT)**.
  - **UNION**: It is a complex type that can hold one of several specified types at a time. It is used less frequently and requires explicit type handling.
- **User-defined types**: Hive allows the creation of user-defined types through the use of custom SerDes (serialization or deserialization libraries) or through the integration of external libraries. This flexibility extends Hive's capabilities to handle specific data types that may not be supported otherwise.

Hive serialization and deserialization

Serialization and deserialization (**SerDes**) formats are crucial in the Hive framework for processing data in various formats. SerDes facilitates the parsing of structured or unstructured data stored in HDFS according to the schema definitions of Hive tables. As users write data in tables, Hive uses HDFS storage, where data is stored in key-value pairs. Hive uses SerDe to convert the data from one file format to another for read and write operations as follows:

Reading from HDFS (Hive SELECT / query execution)

Hive internal Row object I Serializer I<key, value> I OutputFileFormat I HDFS files

Writing to HDFS (INSERT / CTAS / OVERWRITE)

Hive internal Row object | Serializer |<key, value> | OutputFileFormat | HDFS files

It is to be noted that here, the *key* part is ignored while reading and is always a constant when writing. Basically, the row object is stored in the *value*. Hive provides a set of built-in SerDes and also allows users to create custom SerDes to meet specific data requirements. These are as follows:

- **LazySimpleSerDe** is the default SerDe in Hive, primarily used for processing delimited text files, such as CSV or TSV files. It allows you to specify custom delimiters.
- **CSVSerDe** is an alternative to LazySimpleSerDe for reading and writing CSV files. It provides more flexibility and supports complex CSV parsing requirements.
- **RegexSerDe** is used for processing text files where each row is structured according to a regular expression. This SerDe is useful when data is not neatly delimited but follows a predictable pattern.
- **AvroSerDe** is used for reading and writing Avro data. Avro is a binary serialization format that is compact and efficient, making it a popular choice for data interchange.
- **OrcSerde** is used for reading and writing ORC files. ORC is a highly efficient file format that provides better compression and performance for Hive.
- **ParquetHiveSerDe** is used for working with Parquet files, which are columnar storage files optimized for analytical workloads.
- **JSONSerDe** is used for reading JSON data. This SerDe is helpful when working with data in JSON format.
- **ThriftSerDe** is a serialization or deserialization library in Hive that facilitates the reading and writing of data stored using the Apache Thrift framework. Thrift is a software framework for scalable cross-language services development, and it combines a software stack with a code generation engine to build services that work efficiently between different programming languages.
- **DynamicSerDe** is a Hive serialization or deserialization library designed to handle complex nested data structures, including those using **JavaScript Object Notation** (**JSON**) or **Extensible Markup Language** (**XML**). It is part of Hive's older set of SerDes and is often used in scenarios where the data format is not fixed or well-defined. DynamicSerDe can parse and process data dynamically based on the schema defined at runtime, which can be advantageous in flexible and evolving data environments.

Hive does not own the HDFS file format. Users have to use other tools to read and write directly from the HDFS. The current version of Hive provides the following file format classes to read and write HDFS files:

- **TextInputFormat/HiveIgnoreKeyTextOutputFormat**: These classes enable users to read/write data in plain text file format.
- **SequenceFileInputFormat/SequenceFileOutputFormat**: These are used for reading Hadoop Sequence Files, which are binary files containing key-value pairs.
- **RCFileInputFormat/RCFileOutputFormat**: These are used for reading or writing data in **Record Columnar File** (**RCFile**) format, which stores data column-wise within row groups.
- **OrcInputFormat / OrcOutputFormat**: These are used for reading or writing ORC files, a highly optimized columnar storage format.
- **ParquetInputFormat / ParquetOutputFormat**: These are used for reading Parquet files, which is another columnar storage format similar to ORC.
- **AvroContainerInputFormat / AvroContainerOutputFormat**: These are used for reading Avro files, a row-based storage format that supports schema evolution.
- **JSONInputFormat / JSONOutputFormat**: These are used for reading or writing JSON files, which provide flexibility and ease of use for semi-structured data.

Operators in Hive

Hive has all the important built-in operators, such as:

- **Relational operators**: These operators are used to compare two operands. They return Boolean data type (True/False), e.g, `>`,`<`,`==`, etc.
- **Arithmetic operators**: Hive supports all operators to perform arithmetic operations as well as bitwise operators, e.g, `+`,`-`,`*`, `&`, etc.
- **Logical operators**: They return either true or false, e.g, `AND`, `OR`, `NOT`, `&&`, `||`, `!`, etc.

Hive data model

Hive is an open-source data warehouse system that is built on top of Hadoop for querying and analysis of big data stored in HDFS. It is well-suited for processing structured and semi-structured data in Hadoop. Data in Apache Hive can be categorized into:

- Table
- Partition
- Bucket

Tables

Hive arranges data in the form of databases and tables. A database is a collection of tables. Apache Hive Tables are similar to the tables defined in relational databases. Logically, data is stored in the tables in Hive. A table is a collection of related data held in a structured format within a database. It consists of fields (columns) and rows. Let us consider a table with customer data, which includes customer demographics such as age, gender, location, and membership status. As shown in *Table 9.1*, columns are named **`customer_id`**, **`age`**, **`gender`**, **`location`**, and **`membership_status`**. The name of the table is **`customer`**. The data stored in the customer table resides in HDFS. This data is referred to as Hive data. Tables in Hive store two types of data: metadata and Hive data. As discussed in the preceding section, Hive metastore service stores the metadata for Hive tables and partitions. This data is stored in a relational database and can be accessed via the metastore service API. The information stored in metatore includes database IDs, table IDs, index IDs, index creation time, table creation time, etc.

customer_id	age	gender	location	Membership_status
C001	28	F	DELHI	Gold
C002	34	M	MUMBAI	Silver
C003	22	F	BANGLURU	Bronze
C004	45	M	HYDERABAD	Gold
C005	30	F	CHENNAI	silver

***Table 9.1**: Customer details*

Various operations like filter, projection, join, and union can be performed on tables. Hive tables are stored as directories under Hive's warehouse directory. This is the directory in HDFS, as illustrated in *Figure 9.2*:

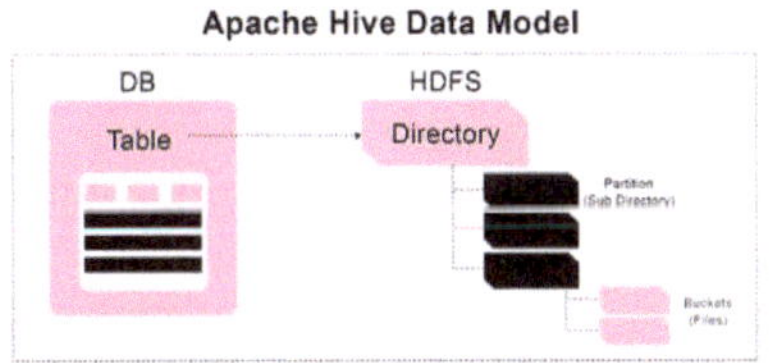

***Figure 9.2**: Hive data model*

In Hive, data can be stored in two types of tables. The details are as follows:

- **Managed table**: Managed tables are default tables in Hive. These are owned by Hive, such that the entire lifecycle of the tables' data is managed and controlled by Hive. Managed tables are also called internal tables. Hive owns the data for the internal tables. When the user creates a table in Hive, by default, it is managed or internal. An internal table is created in the specified path in HDFS. For creating external tables, users have to mention it explicitly. By default, an internal table is created in a folder path similar to **/user/hive/warehouse** directory of HDFS. This default path can be changed by the location property during table creation. When a managed table or partition is dropped, the data and the metadata associated with that table are also deleted from the HDFS. Let us understand the internal table with the help of an example. Assume your data is stored in a file named **customers.csv**. First, define the table structure (schema) and specify that it will store the data in a text format, as shown in *Table 9.2*. Hive will create this table and store its data in a directory under the Hive warehouse. Next, load the data into this internal table using the **LOAD DATA** command. The data is copied into the Hive-managed directory. Here, **LOCAL INPATH** means the file is located on the local file system. If it is on HDFS, you would omit **LOCAL.** Internally, Hive might store this table's data in a directory like **/user/hive/warehouse/customers_internal/**.

<table>
<tr><th>Create an internal table</th><th>Create an external table</th></tr>
<tr><td><pre>CREATE TABLE customers_internal (
    customer_id STRING,
    age INT,
    gender STRING,
    location STRING,
    membership_status STRING
)
ROW FORMAT DELIMITED
FIELDS TERMINATED BY ','
STORED AS TEXTFILE;</pre></td><td rowspan="3"><pre>CREATE EXTERNAL TABLE customers_external (
    customer_id STRING,
    age INT,
    gender STRING,
    location STRING,
    membership_status STRING
)
ROW FORMAT DELIMITED
FIELDS TERMINATED BY ','
STORED AS TEXTFILE
LOCATION '/path/to/external/customers';</pre></td></tr>
<tr><th>Load data into the internal table</th></tr>
<tr><td><pre>LOAD DATA LOCAL INPATH
'/path/to/customers.csv'
INTO TABLE customers_internal;</pre></td></tr>
</table>

Table 9.2: Internal vs. external tables in Hive

- **External table**: External tables are created by specifying the **EXTERNAL** keyword in the Hive create table statement. These tables are created for external use, such as when we want to use the data outside the Hive. The data in these tables is not managed by Hive, as these tables are stored outside the warehouse directory. These tables can access data stored in remote sources like remote HDFS locations or Azure Storage Volumes, etc. When an external table is dropped, unlike a managed table, only the metadata associated with the table gets deleted; the table data remains untouched by Hive. As shown above, you define the table structure just like you do with an internal table, but you also specify a location where the data already resides using the **LOCATION** clause. This path could be on HDFS or a location on the local file system. Hive will not move or copy the data. It will only reference the data at the specified location. The **LOCATION** clause specifies where the data is stored, for example, **/path/to/external/customers/**. Since the data already exists at the specified location, you do not need to load data separately. Hive will use the data directly from that location.

Partition

Hive was developed to reduce the query burden (posed by MapReduce) of Hadoop users. Apache Hive transforms the HiveQL queries into MapReduce jobs, and these jobs are submitted to the Hadoop cluster. However, whenever a HiveQL query is submitted, Hive reads the entire dataset, which leads to inefficient execution of MapReduce jobs over a large table. This problem is resolved by partitioning the data into tables.

In Apache Hive, table data is organized into partitions. Partitioning is a method to split the table into multiple parts based on partition keys. The partition keys can be the values of particular columns, like date, city, department, etc. Partitioning provides efficient querying of data slices.

In Apache Hive, partitioning is performed automatically at the time of table creation. Each partition is stored as a sub-record within the table's record present in the HDFS, which can improve query performance by limiting the amount of data scanned. Thus, whenever a particular table is queried, it is directed to the appropriate partition of the table containing the query values. As a result, the **input/output** (**I/O**) time required for processing the query is reduced, which ultimately improves the performance speed.

Types of partitioning

In Hive, partitioning is performed in the following two ways:

- Static partitioning
- Dynamic partitioning

Both these techniques aim to improve the query performance by dividing the data into manageable chunks; however, they differ in how the partitions are created and managed. The details are as follows:

- **Static partitioning**: In this technique, table partitions are created manually by the user. Users need to specify the partition key and values explicitly while loading the data into the table. This approach is simple but requires the data to be pre-organized according to the partition scheme before being loaded. It is more efficient for small datasets or when the number of partitions is small.

  For example, suppose you have customer data stored in a file organized by gender. To load this data into a Hive table and partition it by gender is done as follows:

  - **Create the Hive table with a partition**:

    ```
    CREATE TABLE customer_data_static (
      customer_id STRING,
      age INT,
      gender STRING,
      location STRING,
      Membership_status STRING
    )
    PARTITIONED BY (gender STRING);
    ```

  - **Load data into a static partition for each gender**:

    ```
    -- For Female partition
    LOAD DATA LOCAL INPATH 'path_to_data/customer_data.csv'
    INTO TABLE customer_data_static
    PARTITION (gender='F');

    -- For Male partition
    LOAD DATA LOCAL INPATH 'path_to_data/customer_data.csv'
    INTO TABLE customer_data_static
    PARTITION (gender='M');
    ```

As shown in the example, in static partitioning, you need to manually specify the partition column value, with gender='F' and gender='M'.

- **Dynamic partitioning**: In this method, Hive automatically determines the partition keys and values from the data being loaded. This approach is more flexible and can handle cases where the partition values are not known earlier. It is more efficient for large datasets with many partitions, as it automates the partitioning process. The following example explains how dynamic partitioning can be applied to stock data:
  - **Create the table**:

```
CREATE TABLE customer_data_dynamic (
  customer_id STRING,
  age INT,
  location STRING,
  Membership_status STRING
)
PARTITIONED BY (gender STRING);
```

  - **Configure Hive for dynamic partitioning**:

```
SET hive.exec.dynamic.partition = true;
SET hive.exec.dynamic.partition.mode = nonstrict;
```

  - **Insert data into a dynamic partition**:

```
INSERT OVERWRITE TABLE customer_data_dynamic
PARTITION (gender)
SELECT customer_id, age, location, Membership_status, gender
FROM customer_data;
```

  In this example, Hive automatically creates partitions based on the gender column values (F and M), and data will be stored in respective partitions without manually specifying the partition value. Here, the partition values need not be specified manually, which makes it easier to load large and varied datasets.

In summary, static partitioning is simpler and more controlled but requires more upfront data organization, while dynamic partitioning is more flexible and automated, making it better suited for handling large and varied datasets in Hive.

The following are the advantages of partitions:

- Partitioning helps in distributing the execution load horizontally.
- Partitioning speeds up the execution of queries with a low volume of data.

The following are the disadvantages of partitions:

- Too many partitions may lead to the creation of too many directories.
- It is more effective for low-volume data. Certain queries, like group by, may take a long time to execute on big data. For example, grouping the population of India will take a long time as compared to grouping the population of Delhi.

Buckets

In Hive, tables or partitions are further subdivided into buckets. Bucketing helps to overcome the limitations of partitioning. Partitioning is effective only in case scenarios, when the number of partitions is small or of comparatively equal size. For example, when partitioning of tables is based on geographic locations like country, bigger countries will have large partitions as compared to smaller countries, leading to unequal distribution of data.

Bucketing divides data into a fixed number of buckets based on a hashing function, which is applied to a bucket column. Each bucket is stored as a separate file. These buckets are essentially smaller, more manageable files within a larger dataset. This is similar to partitioning, but while partitioning divides data into separate directories, bucketing divides data within each partition or table. You must specify the number of buckets when creating a bucketed table. This number should be chosen based on the data size and expected query patterns. Bucketing can improve query performance, especially for queries that involve joins and aggregations, by reducing the amount of data scanned. This is particularly useful when working with large datasets and when you need efficient querying and data processing.

Partitioning and bucketing in customer data

Let us understand the concept of partition and bucket with the help of an example data from the customer.csv file. We will create a table partitioned by gender and bucketed by `customer_id`.

To create a bucketed table in Hive, you need to specify the number of buckets and the column on which you want to bucket the data, as shown in the following codes:

- **Create a bucketed table**:

```
CREATE TABLE customer_data_bucketed (
  customer_id STRING,
  age INT,
  location STRING,
  Membership_status STRING
)
PARTITIONED BY (gender STRING)
CLUSTERED BY (customer_id) INTO 4 BUCKETS;
```

- **Load data into the bucketed table**:

```
SET hive.enforce.bucketing = true;

INSERT INTO TABLE customer_data_bucketed
PARTITION (gender)
SELECT customer_id, age, location, membership_status, gender
FROM some_source_table;
```

As shown, Hive is created with the sample data, partitioned by `gender`, and `CLUSTERED BY` (`customer_id`) divides the data within each partition into four buckets based on the `customer_id`. Partitioning creates separate directories for each partition column value. Here, the partition column is gender, so two directories will be created: one for F and one for M:

- **Directory structure on HDFS**:

```
/user/hive/warehouse/customer_data_bucketed/
|
├── gender=F/
|   ├── 000000_0 (Bucket 1 for gender F)
|   ├── 000001_0 (Bucket 2 for gender F)
|   ├── 000002_0 (Bucket 3 for gender F)
|   └── 000003_0 (Bucket 4 for gender F)
|
└── gender=M/
    ├── 000000_0 (Bucket 1 for gender M)
```

```
├── 000001_0 (Bucket 2 for gender M)
├── 000002_0 (Bucket 3 for gender M)
└── 000003_0 (Bucket 4 for gender M)
```

Here, **gender=F/:** represents the directory containing data for female customers, while **gender=M/:** refers to the directory containing data for male customers. Within each gender directory, there are four files representing the buckets.

Bucketing further divides the data within each partition into N buckets, where N is the number of buckets specified (four in this case).

- **Data distribution into buckets**:
  - The bucket number is determined by the hash of the **customer_id** module, the number of buckets (four in this case).
  - Each bucket file (e.g., 000000_0, 000001_0, etc.) within a partition directory will contain data for specific customer IDs.

For example, let us assume the following simple hash function (**hash(customer_id) % 4**):

- C001 (hash % 4 = 1) | Bucket 1
- C002 (hash % 4 = 2) | Bucket 2
- C003 (hash % 4 = 3) | Bucket 3
- C004 (hash % 4 = 0) | Bucket 0
- C005 (hash % 4 = 1) | Bucket 1

Bucketing is different from partitioning in that it physically divides the data within each partition into smaller files (buckets). For every partition, a folder is created in the specified path, and every bucket represents one file in the specified format. So, physically, the data may be arranged as follows:

```
/user/hive/warehouse/customer_data_bucketed/
|
├── gender=F/
|  ├── 000000_0 (Empty or contains other IDs)
|  ├── 000001_0 (C001, C005)
|  ├── 000002_0 (Empty or contains other IDs)
|  └── 000003_0 (C003)
|
└── gender=M/
    ├──000000_0 (C004)
    ├── 000001_0 (C002)
    ├── 000002_0 (Empty or contains other IDs)
    └── 000003_0 (Empty or contains other IDs)
```

Here, the **gender=F/000001_0** file contains the rows for C001 and C005 because both hash to the same bucket. The **gender=F/000003_0** file contains the row for C003. The **gender=M/000000_0** file contains the row for C004, and the **gender=M/000001_0** file contains the row for C002.

Overall, partitioning splits the data into different directories (e.g., **gender=F** and **gender=M**). *Bucketing* further divides the data within each partition into files (buckets) based on the **customer_id** hash. When querying, Hive first selects the appropriate partition directory based on the partition column (gender), and then the correct bucket file(s) based on the bucket column (**customer_id**). This significantly reduces the amount of data scanned, improving query performance.

Hive vs. Pig

Apache Hive and Apache Pig are both tools used to process and analyze large datasets stored in Hadoop, but they have different use cases, features, and strengths as discussed in *Table 9.3*:

	Apache Hive	Apache Pig
Purpose	Hive is primarily designed for data warehousing applications and provides a SQL-like query language called HiveQL. It is best suited for structured data.	Pig is a high-level platform for creating MapReduce programs used with Hadoop. It is designed to handle both structured and semi-structured data.
Language	HiveQL (similar to SQL), which makes it accessible to users familiar with traditional databases.	Pig Latin is a procedural data flow language. It allows more complex data transformations and operations.
Data model	The relational model works best with structured data.	Flexible data model, works with structured, semi-structured, and unstructured data.
Performance	It is not as fast as real-time data processing systems, but it is optimized for read-heavy operations.	Good for complex data transformations and iterative data processing tasks.
Use case	Ideal for batch processing, reporting, and querying large datasets. It's suitable for those who want to use SQL-like syntax to interact with Hadoop.	Useful for **extract, transform, load** (ELT) data pipelines, and for data processing tasks that require custom transformations.

***Table 9.3**: Comparison of Hive with Pig*

Both Hive and Pig run on top of Hadoop and leverage HDFS for storing data. They are often used together in a data processing pipeline, with Pig handling the data transformation and Hive performing the final data analysis and querying.

Hive vs. RDBMS

Apache Hive and traditional RDBMS are both used for managing and querying data, but they are designed for different purposes and have distinct features, as discussed in *Table 9.4*:

	Apache Hive	RDBMS
Purpose	Hive is primarily designed for data warehousing applications and provides a SQL-like query language called **HiveQL**. It is best suited for structured data.	RDBMS is designed for managing and querying structured data using a predefined schema. It is widely used for transaction processing and operational databases.
Data storage	Uses HDFS for storing data, which is ideal for handling vast amounts of data across distributed systems.	Uses a more traditional storage system with tables, rows, and columns, typically on a single server or small cluster.
Schema on read	Data is interpreted when it is read, which allows for greater flexibility in handling unstructured or semi-structured data.	Data is structured and enforced during the write process, requiring a predefined schema.
Query language	Uses HiveQL, which is similar to SQL, but not fully compliant. HiveQL queries are converted into MapReduce jobs or executed using Apache Tez or Apache Spark for faster performance.	Uses standard SQL, which is fully compliant and widely used for database operations.

	Apache Hive	RDBMS
Scalability	Highly scalable and can handle petabytes of data across many nodes.	Limited scalability compared to Hive. Generally suited for smaller datasets and vertical scaling.
Performance	Not suitable for real-time processing. Hive is optimized for read-heavy operations and batch processing with high throughput.	Excellent for real-time processing and quick transactions. Provides **atomicity, consistency, isolation, and durability** (**ACID**) properties for data integrity.
Use case	Ideal for ETL processes, data warehousing, and big data analytics.	Suitable for **online transaction processing** (**OLTP**), business applications, and situations where data integrity and real-time performance are crucial.

***Table 9.4**: Comparison of Hive with Pig*

Each system has its strengths and is chosen based on the specific requirements of the data processing tasks at hand.

Hive Query Language

HiveQL is a query language used in Apache Hive. It is very similar to **structured query language** (**SQL**) but is designed to query and manage large datasets in a distributed environment.

The following are the key features of HiveQL:

- Hive does not require data to be structured in a particular format before storing it. The schema is applied when the data is read, not when it is written.
- HiveQL is very similar to SQL, making it easier for users familiar with SQL to use Hive.
- HiveQL queries are compiled into MapReduce, Tez, or Spark jobs, which run on Hadoop.

In Cloudera, to use the Hive CLI from the shell, open a terminal in CLOUDERA and type **`hive`** as shown in *Figure 9.3*, **`$ $HIVE_HOME/bin/hive`**:

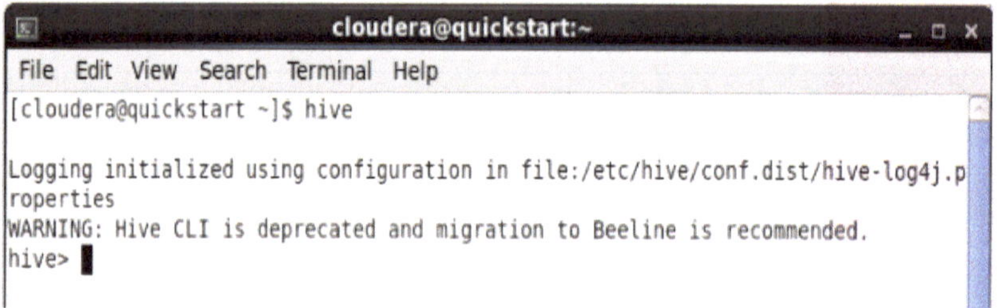

***Figure 9.3**: Running Hive in CLI*

Running HiveServer2 and Beeline

HiveServer2, as introduced in *Hive 0.11*, has its own CLI called **Beeline**. Hive CLI is now deprecated, as shown in *Figure 9.3*, because it lacks the multi-user, security, and other capabilities of HiveServer2. Beeline starts with the JDBC URL of the HiveServer2, which depends on the address and port where HiveServer2 was started. By default, it will be (localhost:10000), so the address will look like **`jdbc:hive2://localhost:10000`**. To start Beeline and HiveServer2 in the same process for testing purposes, to have a similar user experience in Hive CLI, type the command **`[cloudera@quickstart-]$ beeline -u jdbc:hive2://localhost:10000`** in the Cloudera terminal. The same is illustrated in *Figure 9.4*:

```
cloudera@quickstart:~
File Edit View Search Terminal Help
[cloudera@quickstart ~]$ beeline -u jdbc:hive2://localhost:10000
scan complete in 2ms
Connecting to jdbc:hive2://localhost:10000
Connected to: Apache Hive (version 1.1.0-cdh5.13.0)
Driver: Hive JDBC (version 1.1.0-cdh5.13.0)
Transaction isolation: TRANSACTION_REPEATABLE_READ
Beeline version 1.1.0-cdh5.13.0 by Apache Hive
0: jdbc:hive2://localhost:10000>
```

***Figure 9.4**: Run Beeline*

Now Hive is running. However, before creating the tables, it is important to check if the following directories (**/tmp and /user/hive/warehouse** (aka **hive.metastore.warehouse.dir**) and permissions (**chmod g+w**) which are already set; otherwise, execute the following HDFS commands to create directories, as illustrated in *Figure 9.5* and *Figure 9.6* and refer to *Figure 9.7* to set permissions:

```
[cloudera@quickstart-]$ hadoop fs -mkdir      /tmp
[cloudera@quickstart-]$ hadoop fs -mkdir      /user/hive/warehouse
[cloudera@quickstart-]$ hadoop fs -chmod g+w   /tmp
[cloudera@quickstart-]$ hadoop fs -chmod g+w   /user/hive/warehouse
```

Figure 9.5 shows the temp directory in HDFS:

```
cloudera@quickstart:~
File Edit View Search Terminal Help
[cloudera@quickstart ~]$ hadoop fs -ls /
Found 27 items
drwxrwxrwx   - hdfs     supergroup          0 2017-10-23 09:15 /benchmarks
drwxr-xr-x   - hbase    supergroup          0 2024-08-11 21:24 /hbase
drwxr-xr-x   - cloudera supergroup          0 2021-09-15 22:57 /inp1
drwxrwxrwx   - cloudera supergroup          0 2019-03-31 23:09 /input
drwxr-xr-x   - cloudera supergroup          0 2021-09-13 23:13 /inputfolder1
drwxr-xr-x   - cloudera supergroup          0 2022-09-30 22:29 /iofolder
drwxr-xr-x   - cloudera supergroup          0 2021-11-22 21:55 /match
drwxr-xr-x   - cloudera supergroup          0 2023-06-30 23:43 /newin
drwxr-xr-x   - cloudera supergroup          0 2023-06-30 23:45 /newout
drwxr-xr-x   - cloudera supergroup          0 2021-09-13 23:21 /out1
drwxr-xr-x   - cloudera supergroup          0 2021-09-15 23:01 /out2
drwxr-xr-x   - cloudera supergroup          0 2022-09-30 22:49 /output
drwxr-xr-x   - cloudera supergroup          0 2019-03-31 23:14 /output_0
-rw-r--r--   1 cloudera supergroup         60 2021-09-20 22:01 /pig_data
drwxr-xr-x   - cloudera supergroup          0 2021-09-20 22:04 /pig_data1
drwxr-xr-x   - cloudera supergroup          0 2021-09-20 22:09 /pigdata
drwxr-xr-x   - cloudera supergroup          0 2021-11-28 21:46 /pokemonrdd
drwxr-xr-x   - solr     solr                0 2017-10-23 09:18 /solr
drwxr-xr-x   - cloudera supergroup          0 2021-11-30 01:02 /sparksql1
drwxr-xr-x   - cloudera supergroup          0 2022-10-03 00:12 /stockinput
drwxr-xr-x   - cloudera supergroup          0 2022-10-03 01:58 /stockinput1
drwxr-xr-x   - cloudera supergroup          0 2022-10-03 00:19 /stockoutput
drwxr-xr-x   - cloudera supergroup          0 2023-07-02 22:30 /stockoutput1
-rw-r--r--   1 cloudera supergroup         60 2021-09-20 22:05 /student_data.txt
drwxrwxrwt   - hdfs     supergroup          0 2024-05-14 00:50 /tmp
```

***Figure 9.5**: tmp directory in hdfs*

Figure 9.6 shows the warehouse directory created in Hive:

```
[cloudera@quickstart ~]$ hadoop fs -ls /user/hive
Found 1 items
drwxrwxrwx   - hive supergroup          0 2021-09-29 20:55 /user/hive/warehouse
[cloudera@quickstart ~]$ 
```

***Figure 9.6**: user/hive/warehouse directory in Hive*

Figure 9.7 shows commands to set permissions:

```
[cloudera@quickstart ~]$ hadoop fs -chmod g+w /tmp
[cloudera@quickstart ~]$ hadoop fs -chmod g+w /user/hive/warehouse
[cloudera@quickstart ~]$ 
```

***Figure 9.7**: Setting permissions*

Hive, MapReduce, and local mode

Hive typically generates MapReduce jobs for executing queries, which are then submitted to a distributed MapReduce cluster. By default, Hive submits MapReduce jobs to a cluster defined by the **`mapred.job.tracker`** variable. This is suitable for processing large datasets across multiple nodes in a cluster.

However, Hive also supports running these jobs in local mode on the user's machine, which can be more efficient for small datasets. Local mode allows MapReduce jobs to run on the local machine instead of a cluster. It is enabled by setting **`mapreduce.framework.name=local`** in Hive. The user should ensure that the **`mapred.local.dir`** points to a valid local directory for temporary data storage. *Figure 9.8* shows the execution of Hive in local mode:

```
0: jdbc:hive2://localhost:10000> SET mapreduce.framework.name=local;
No rows affected (0.005 seconds)
```

***Figure 9.8**: Running Hive in local mode*

Hive can also automatically decide to run jobs in local mode based on the size and complexity of the job. It is managed by setting:

- **hive.exec.mode.local.auto**: To enable or disable automatic local mode (disabled by default).
- **hive.exec.mode.local.auto.inputbytes-max**: To maximum input size for local mode (default 128MB).
- **hive.exec.mode.local.auto.tasks.max**: Maximum number of map tasks for local mode (default four).

Figure 9.9 shows a command to run Hive in automatic mode:

```
0: jdbc:hive2://localhost:10000> SET hive.exec.mode.local.auto=false;
No rows affected (0.156 seconds)
```

***Figure 9.9**: Running Hive in automatic mode*

Jobs may run locally if the input size is small, there are few map tasks, and only one or zero reduce tasks are needed. Besides, differences in runtime environments between the local machine and Hadoop nodes can lead to inconsistencies. Thus, local mode jobs run in a separate **Java Virtual Machine (JVM)**, and the memory allocation for this JVM can be controlled via **`hive.mapred.local.mem`**.

Conclusion

This chapter focused on providing a thorough introduction to Apache Hive, elucidating its role as a powerful tool for data warehousing and SQL-like querying within the Hadoop ecosystem. It covered the motivations behind Hive's use, detailing how it simplifies big data processing tasks. The chapter further delved into Hive's architecture, highlighting the roles of critical components such as the Thrift server, metastore, driver, and compiler in facilitating efficient and scalable data handling. It also explored the Hive data model, emphasizing the significance of tables, partitions, and buckets for optimizing query performance and data organization. Additionally, the chapter explained Hive SerDes and their importance in managing diverse data formats and integrating with other Hadoop tools. It introduced the steps to execute HiveQL for creating tables and performing data analysis tasks. Finally, it provided a comparative analysis of Hive with Apache Pig and traditional RDBMS, clarifying their respective advantages and applications.

The next chapter will focus on data definition and data manipulation using HiveQL and a practical demonstration of big data processing using HiveQL in Cloudera.

Points to remember

The following list outlines the key takeaways from this chapter:

- Hive is a data warehousing tool built on top of Hadoop that allows for querying and managing large datasets using a SQL-like language called HiveQL.
- Hive simplifies data processing on Hadoop by providing an SQL-like interface, making it easier for users familiar with SQL to perform complex data analysis without needing deep knowledge of Hadoop's underlying technologies.
- **Hive architecture**:
    - **Thrift server**: A service that allows remote clients to submit Hive queries and retrieve results over a network.
    - **Metastore**: A central repository that stores metadata about Hive tables, such as their schema and location.
    - **Driver**: Manages the lifecycle of a Hive query by coordinating between the various components, from parsing the query to executing it.
    - **Compiler**: Converts HiveQL queries into a series of MapReduce jobs or Tez/DAG tasks for execution on Hadoop.
- **Hive data model**:
    - **Tables**: The primary unit of data storage in Hive, similar to tables in a traditional database, consisting of rows and columns.
    - **Partitions**: A way to divide tables into smaller, more manageable pieces based on column values, improving query performance.
    - **Buckets**: Sub-divisions of data within partitions that allow more efficient sampling and joins.
- Hive supports a variety of primitive and complex data types, including integers, strings, arrays, maps, and structs, to facilitate diverse data operations.
- SerDe is a framework in Hive that allows it to read and write data in different formats, enabling the use of custom data formats.
- Hive provides a SQL-like interface for data querying and is suitable for structured data, while Pig uses a procedural data flow language (Pig Latin) and is more flexible for processing semi-structured data.
- Hive is designed for large-scale data warehousing on Hadoop and supports batch processing, whereas traditional RDBMS systems are optimized for transactional processing and support ACID properties for real-time operations.

Multiple choice questions

1. **What is Hive primarily used for?**
   a. Real-time transaction processing
   b. Managing and querying large datasets using a SQL-like interface
   c. Machine learning model training
   d. Real-time data streaming
2. **Which component of Hive stores metadata about tables, such as their schema and location?**
   a. Thrift server
   b. Metastore
   c. Driver
   d. Compiler
3. **In Hive, what is the primary purpose of partitions?**
   a. To divide tables into smaller, more manageable pieces
   b. To store metadata about tables
   c. To compile Hive queries
   d. To execute HiveQL statements
4. **What is the function of the Hive Thrift server?**
   a. To store Hive tables and their metadata
   b. To handle the execution of MapReduce jobs
   c. To allow remote clients to submit queries and retrieve results
   d. To serialize and deserialize data in Hive
5. **Which of the following statements is true about static partitioning in Hive?**
   a. Partition values are dynamically determined at runtime
   b. Partition values are explicitly specified in the query
   c. Partitioning is done based on complex data types
   d. Partitioning is automatically managed by Hive
6. **What is the key difference between Hive and traditional RDBMS?**
   a. Hive supports ACID transactions, RDBMS does not
   b. Hive is optimized for real-time processing, RDBMS is not
   c. Hive is designed for large-scale batch processing, while RDBMS is optimized for transactional processing
   d. Hive only supports structured data, while RDBMS supports both structured and unstructured data
7. **Which of the following is a correct statement about Hive buckets?**
   a. Buckets are used to divide tables into partitions
   b. Buckets are used to further divide data within partitions for efficient sampling and joins
   c. Buckets are used to store metadata in Hive
   d. Buckets are a type of data type in Hive
8. **What is a key advantage of using Hive SerDe's?**
   a. They allow Hive to integrate with real-time streaming data
   b. They enable Hive to read and write data in various custom formats
   c. They compile HiveQL queries into MapReduce jobs
   d. They store metadata about Hive tables

9. **Which of the following best describes dynamic partitioning in Hive?**
   a. Partition values are determined at runtime based on data
   b. Partition values must be explicitly provided in the query
   c. Partitions are created for each distinct value in the table
   d. Partitions are merged automatically during query execution
10. **How does Hive differ from Pig in terms of data processing?**
   a. Hive uses a procedural language, while Pig uses a declarative SQL-like language
   b. Hive is more suited for semi-structured data, while Pig is better for structured data
   c. Hive provides a SQL-like interface, while Pig uses a data flow language called Pig Latin
   d. Hive is optimized for real-time data streaming, while Pig is for batch processing

Answers

1. b.	2. b.	3. a.	4. c.	5. b.
6. c.	7. b.	8. b.	9. a.	10. c.

Questions

1. Explain the architecture of Apache Hive, detailing the role of the Thrift server, metastore, driver, and compiler. How do these components work together to execute a Hive query?
2. Discuss the advantages of using Hive in a big data ecosystem. Why would an organization choose Hive over other data processing tools like Pig or traditional RDBMS?
3. What are partitions and buckets in Hive? Explain how they can improve query performance with an example.
4. Compare and contrast static and dynamic partitioning in Hive. Provide a use case scenario where dynamic partitioning would be preferred over static partitioning.
5. Describe the Hive data model. How do tables, partitions, and buckets work together to organize large datasets? Include an example of how you would create a partitioned and bucketed table in Hive.
6. Hive SerDe's play a crucial role in Hive's data handling capabilities. Explain what SerDe's are and provide an example of how to use a custom SerDe to process a specific data format in Hive.
7. In what scenarios would you prefer using Hive over Pig for data processing, and vice versa? Give practical examples to support your answer.
8. Discuss the key differences between Hive and traditional RDBMS systems. How does Hive handle data processing differently, and what are the implications for data storage and retrieval?
9. Describe the various data types supported in Hive. How would you handle complex data types like arrays and maps in a Hive table? Provide a practical example of creating a table with these data types.
10. You are tasked with querying a large dataset stored in Hive. Explain how you would optimize the performance of your query using partitions and buckets. Provide a step-by-step guide on implementing these optimizations in a real-world scenario.

Chapter 10
Data Analysis Using Hive

With data collection, the sooner the better is always the best answer.

-Marissa Mayer

Introduction

In this chapter, readers will learn about practical aspects of working with Apache Hive with a primary focus on data manipulation and querying tasks. The chapter begins with step-by-step instructions on how to start the Hive shell, Beeline, or a graphical interface like Hue in Cloudera. The chapter then explains **data definition language** (**DDL**) commands, which will help readers to create and manage database objects like tables. The chapter further executes essential DDL commands like creating tables, displaying table information, altering table structures, describing tables, truncating data, and deleting unwanted data. Next, the chapter explores **data manipulation language** (**DML**) commands and how they work with data in Hive tables. It covers loading data, inserting records, performing joins and aggregations, and using partitioning and clustering to retrieve data efficiently. All DDL and DML commands are explained with practical examples for the Hive shell and the Hue **graphical user interface** (**GUI**).

Structure

In this chapter, we will cover the following topics:

- Working with Hive
- Working with Hive Beeline shell
- Running DDL commands
- DML commands

Objectives

By the end of this chapter, readers will be able to start the Hive shell, use Beeline, or navigate Hue in Cloudera. They will be able to utilize key DDL commands to create and manage tables. Readers will also be able to work with DML commands for loading data, inserting records, and performing joins. Furthermore, they will be able to apply partitioning and clustering techniques to optimize data retrieval in Hive.

Working with Hive

Hive is a powerful data warehouse system that is used to manage and query large datasets stored in Hadoop. Hive provides HiveQL, a SQL-like interface to write queries and perform data analysis on large-scale datasets without bothering about the underlying complexities of Hadoop. To work with Hive, the primary steps required involve installing Cloudera and performing necessary configurations, as discussed in *Chapter 9, Hive-data Warehousing and SQL-like Queries*. The next step is to create databases and tables in Hive through the Hive shell, Beeline, or a graphical interface like Hue. In Apache Hive, data manipulation and definition are handled through two key types of SQL commands, which are DML and DDL. These commands allow users to manage, query, and manipulate data stored in Hive. Apache Hive is case insensitive, which implies Hive commands may be written in capital or small letters, but the names of user-defined databases or tables, etc., are case sensitive.

DDL commands

DDL commands are used to define, modify, and delete database objects such as databases, tables, and views in Hive. These commands manage the structure of the data rather than the data itself. Let us learn to manage and analyse large datasets generated from the e-commerce platform with the help of a case study on *E-commerce customer behavior analysis*. The goal of this case study is to analyze customer behavior on an E-commerce platform to improve user experience, increase sales, and enhance customer retention strategies.

Figure 10.1 shows the sample data of the **`customer_data.csv`** file used for analyzing customer behaviour:

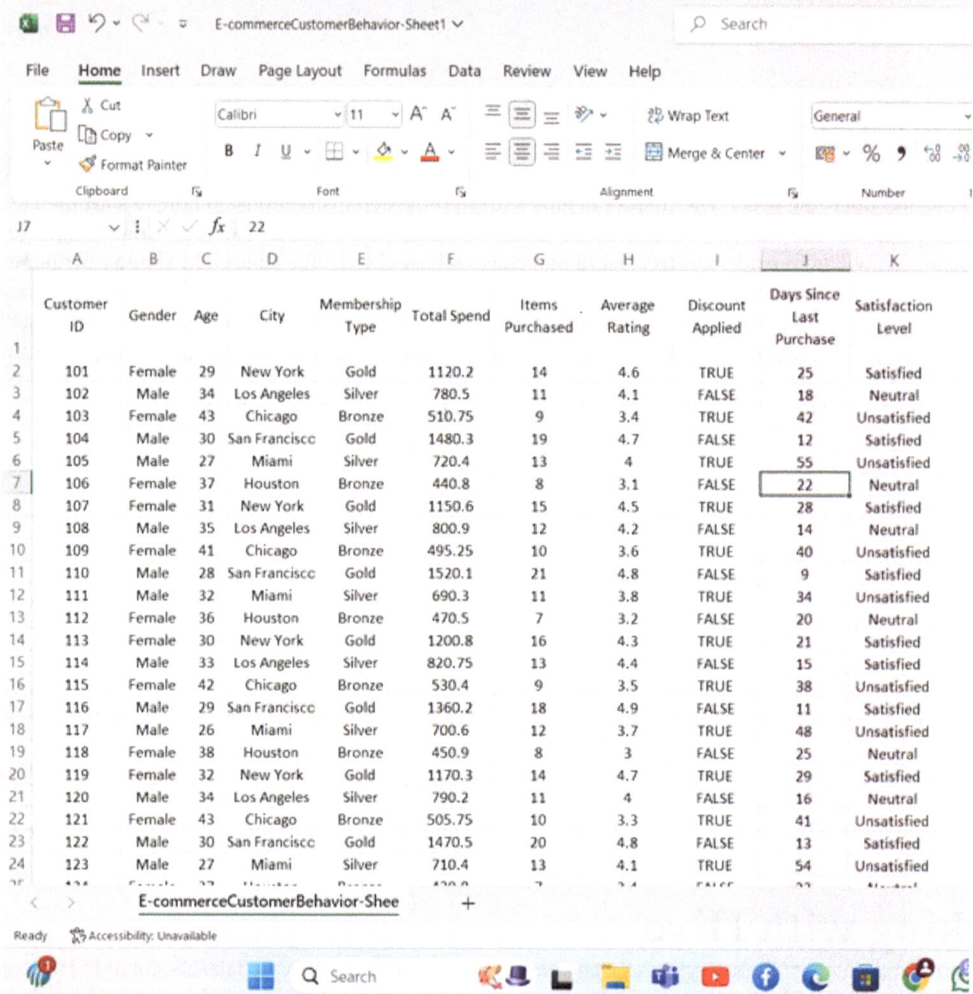

Customer ID	Gender	Age	City	Membership Type	Total Spend	Items Purchased	Average Rating	Discount Applied	Days Since Last Purchase	Satisfaction Level
101	Female	29	New York	Gold	1120.2	14	4.6	TRUE	25	Satisfied
102	Male	34	Los Angeles	Silver	780.5	11	4.1	FALSE	18	Neutral
103	Female	43	Chicago	Bronze	510.75	9	3.4	TRUE	42	Unsatisfied
104	Male	30	San Franciscc	Gold	1480.3	19	4.7	FALSE	12	Satisfied
105	Male	27	Miami	Silver	720.4	13	4	TRUE	55	Unsatisfied
106	Female	37	Houston	Bronze	440.8	8	3.1	FALSE	22	Neutral
107	Female	31	New York	Gold	1150.6	15	4.5	TRUE	28	Satisfied
108	Male	35	Los Angeles	Silver	800.9	12	4.2	FALSE	14	Neutral
109	Female	41	Chicago	Bronze	495.25	10	3.6	TRUE	40	Unsatisfied
110	Male	28	San Franciscc	Gold	1520.1	21	4.8	FALSE	9	Satisfied
111	Male	32	Miami	Silver	690.3	11	3.8	TRUE	34	Unsatisfied
112	Female	36	Houston	Bronze	470.5	7	3.2	FALSE	20	Neutral
113	Female	30	New York	Gold	1200.8	16	4.3	TRUE	21	Satisfied
114	Male	33	Los Angeles	Silver	820.75	13	4.4	FALSE	15	Satisfied
115	Female	42	Chicago	Bronze	530.4	9	3.5	TRUE	38	Unsatisfied
116	Male	29	San Franciscc	Gold	1360.2	18	4.9	FALSE	11	Satisfied
117	Male	26	Miami	Silver	700.6	12	3.7	TRUE	48	Unsatisfied
118	Female	38	Houston	Bronze	450.9	8	3	FALSE	25	Neutral
119	Female	32	New York	Gold	1170.3	14	4.7	TRUE	29	Satisfied
120	Male	34	Los Angeles	Silver	790.2	11	4	FALSE	16	Neutral
121	Female	43	Chicago	Bronze	505.75	10	3.3	TRUE	41	Unsatisfied
122	Male	30	San Franciscc	Gold	1470.5	20	4.8	FALSE	13	Satisfied
123	Male	27	Miami	Silver	710.4	13	4.1	TRUE	54	Unsatisfied

***Figure 10.1:** Customer behavior details*

Working with Hue GUI

To execute the Hive queries in Hue, follow these steps:

1. Once you have installed and initialized Cloudera, click on the **Hue** icon to start the Hue GUI, as shown in *Figure 10.2:*

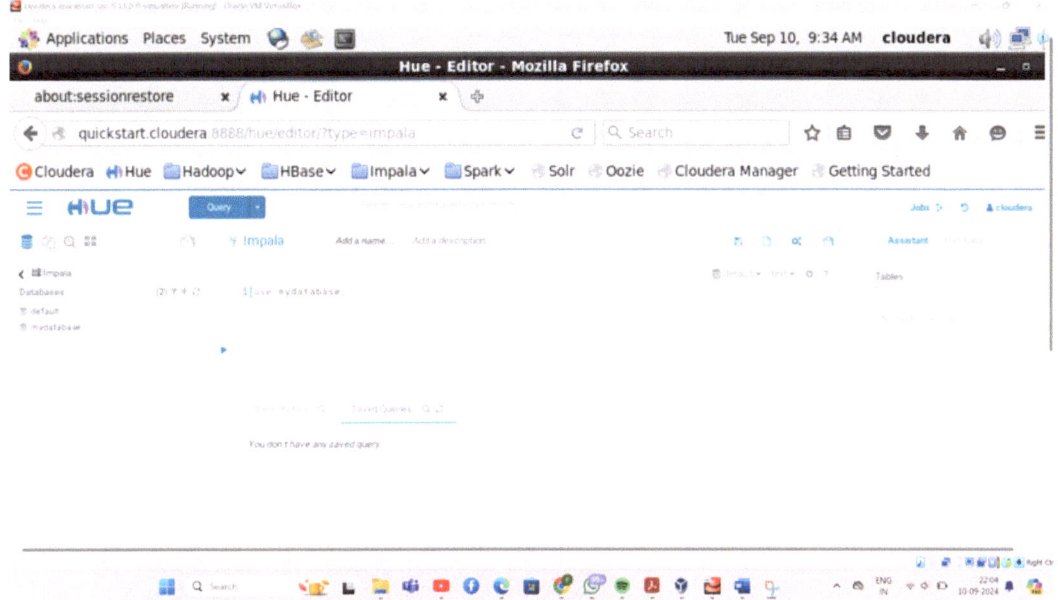

***Figure 10.2**: Hue icon in Cloudera*

2. In the left navigation panel of Hue, click on the encircled icon to see all directories and files stored in HDFS, as shown in *Figure 10.3:*

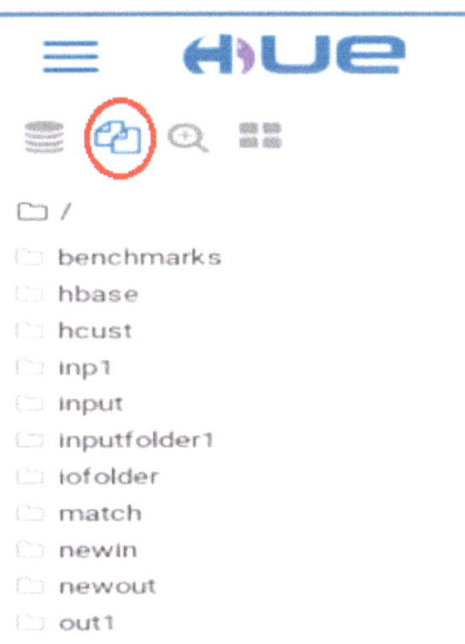

***Figure 10.3:** Icon to view all directories*

3. Similarly, to see the databases and tables created in Hive, click on the encircled icon, as shown in *Figure 10.4:*

***Figure 10.4:** HDFS icon in Hue*

4. By clicking on a particular database name, all tables under this database will be visible. After selecting the database in Hive, queries can be executed by opening the query editor, as shown in *Figure 10.5* and *Figure 10.6:*

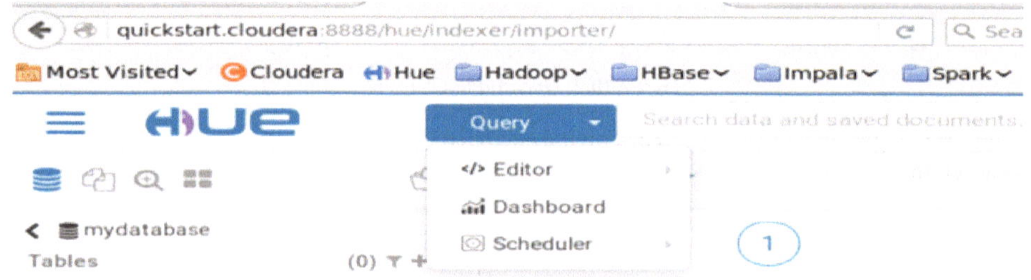

***Figure 10.5:** Hive query editor*

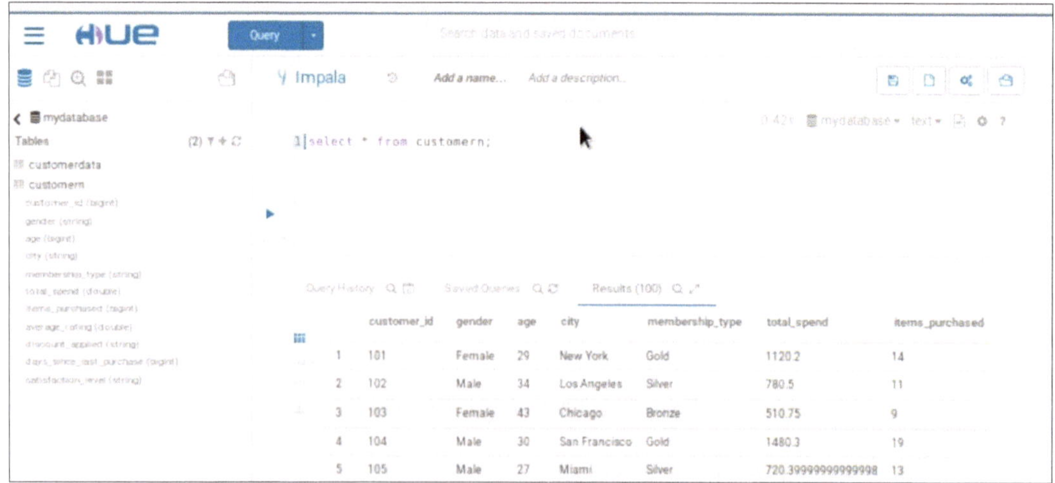

***Figure 10.6:** UI for query execution in Hive*

5. You can create tables and insert data directly using the query editor or load the data from existing files in a format supported by Hive.

6. In the left navigation panel of Hue, select the default database and click on the encircled icon (plus symbol) to create a table from the **`customer_data.csv`** file, as shown in *Figure 10.7*:

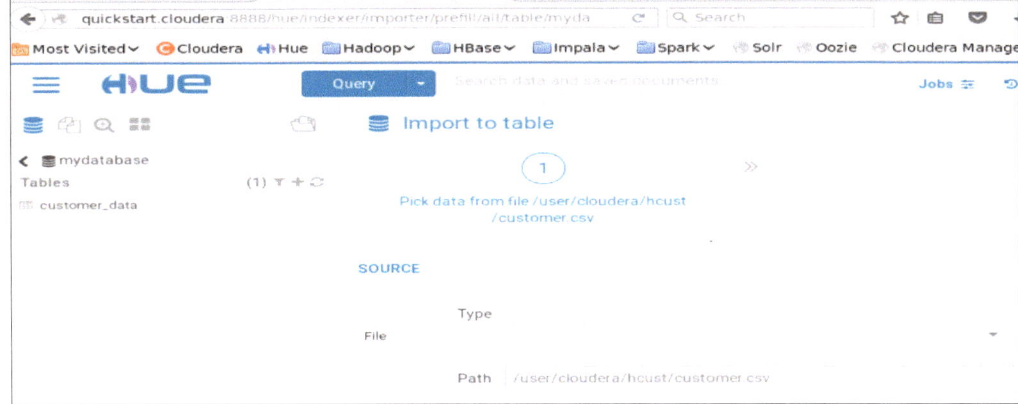

***Figure 10.7**: Loading existing data from a file in Hive*

7. In the middle panel importer user interface, choose **Type** as **`File`**. It will open a dialog box as shown in *Figure 10.8*, to upload the file from desired location:

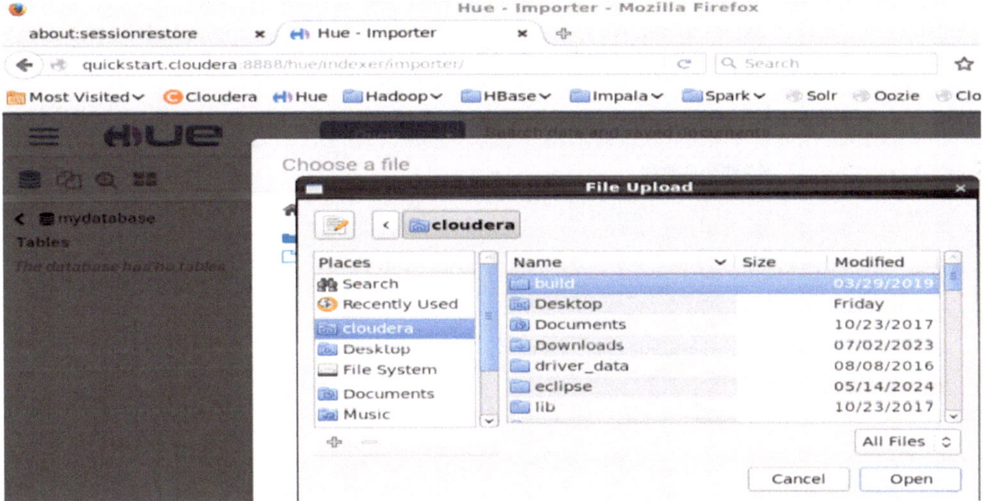

***Figure 10.8**: Dialog box to upload the data file*

8. Next, set the formats as—**Field Separator** as **`Comma (,)`** or **`Tab`**, **Record Separator** as **`New line`**, **Quote Character** as **`Double Quote`**, as shown in *Figure 10.9:*

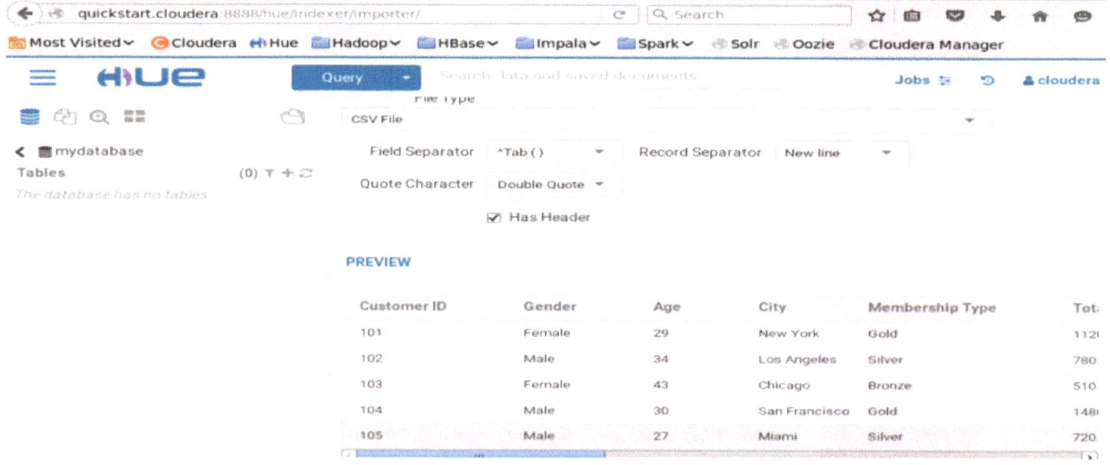

***Figure 10.9**: Format settings*

9. Then click **Next** at the bottom of the page and set the properties **Format** as **`Text`**.
10. Finally, edit the field names to remove spaces and change their data types appropriately, and click **Submit** at the bottom of the page, as shown in *Figure 10.10:*

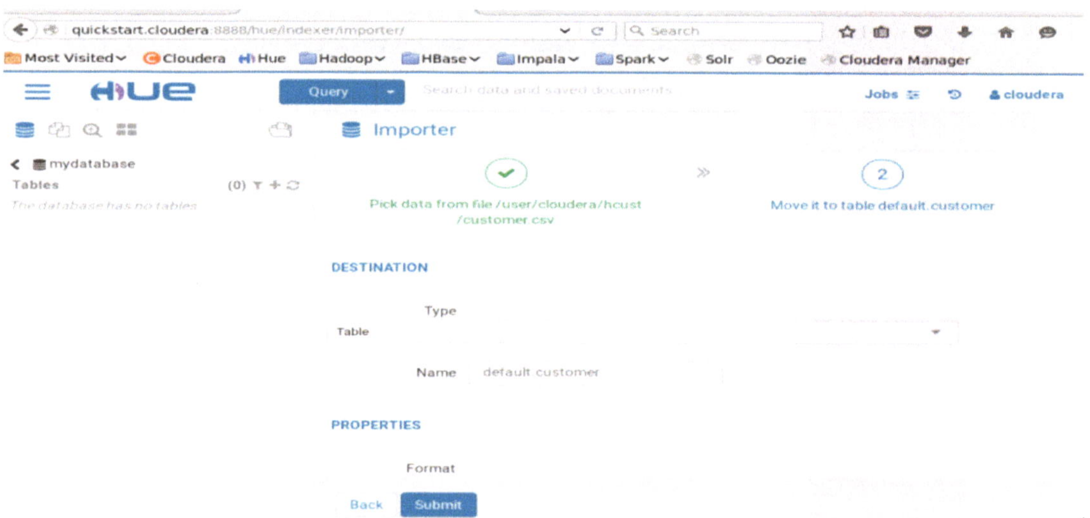

***Figure 10.10**: Change field names and types and submit*

11. It will create a table in the selected database (**mydatabase** here) as shown in *Figure 10.11*.

12. Now, click **Query** at the top of the page and select **Editor** | **Hive** to open the Hive editor and then execute the queries:

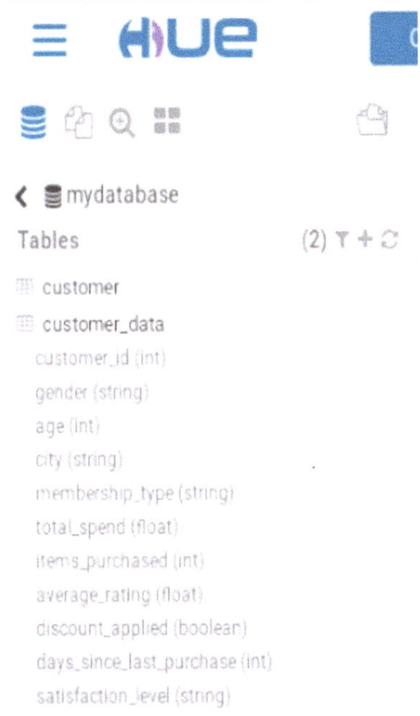

***Figure 10.11**: customer_data table created in mydatabase*

Working with Hive Beeline shell

To start the Beeline shell, follow these steps:

1. Open the terminal in Cloudera and type the following command: **`[cloudera@quickstart ~]$ beeline -u jdbc:hive2://localhost:10000`**
2. Refer to *Figure 10.12*, and the shell is ready to execute Hive queries:

***Figure 10.12**: Execute Hive queries*

Running DDL commands

Let us now learn to execute the DDL commands:

- **CREATE**: This command is used to create a database in Hive. A database here refers to a namespace where tables and their associated metadata are stored. Databases in Hive are logical containers that store tables, views, functions, etc. In the syntax, the **IF NOT EXISTS** option is used to prevent an error if the database already exists. *Figure 10.13* shows the execution of this command in Hive shell to create the database **`mydatabase`**.
    - **Syntax**: **`CREATE DATABASE [IF NOT EXISTS] database_name;`**
    - **Example**: **`CREATE DATABASE mydatabase;`**

```
0: jdbc:hive2://localhost:10000> CREATE DATABASE mydatabase;
INFO  : Compiling command(queryId=hive_20240904070202_f44e3267-6611-4dc0-ab99-a8
3cb6d2b92d): CREATE DATABASE mydatabase
INFO  : Semantic Analysis Completed
INFO  : Returning Hive schema: Schema(fieldSchemas:null, properties:null)
INFO  : Completed compiling command(queryId=hive_20240904070202_f44e3267-6611-4d
c0-ab99-a83cb6d2b92d); Time taken: 0.546 seconds
INFO  : Concurrency mode is disabled, not creating a lock manager
INFO  : Executing command(queryId=hive_20240904070202_f44e3267-6611-4dc0-ab99-a8
3cb6d2b92d): CREATE DATABASE mydatabase
INFO  : Starting task [Stage-0:DDL] in serial mode
INFO  : Completed executing command(queryId=hive_20240904070202_f44e3267-6611-4d
c0-ab99-a83cb6d2b92d); Time taken: 1.069 seconds
INFO  : OK
No rows affected (1.9 seconds)
0: jdbc:hive2://localhost:10000>
```

Figure 10.13: Execution of the CREATE command in the Hive shell

- **show databases**: This command is used to list all databases in Hive, as shown in the following *Figure 10.14*. On executing the given query, all existing databases are displayed:
    - **Syntax**: **`show databases;`**
    - **Example**: **`show databases;`**

```
4c77233cf6): show databases
INFO  : Semantic Analysis Completed
INFO  : Returning Hive schema: Schema(fieldSchemas:[FieldSchema(name:database_na
me, type:string, comment:from deserializer)], properties:null)
INFO  : Completed compiling command(queryId=hive_20240920190404_4fc9f6c7-1da0-47
ca-958b-5a4c77233cf6); Time taken: 0.574 seconds
INFO  : Concurrency mode is disabled, not creating a lock manager
INFO  : Executing command(queryId=hive_20240920190404_4fc9f6c7-1da0-47ca-958b-5a
4c77233cf6): show databases
INFO  : Starting task [Stage-0:DDL] in serial mode
INFO  : Completed executing command(queryId=hive_20240920190404_4fc9f6c7-1da0-47
ca-958b-5a4c77233cf6); Time taken: 0.022 seconds
INFO  : OK
+----------------+--+
| database_name  |
+----------------+--+
| default        |
| mydatabase     |
+----------------+--+
2 rows selected (0.908 seconds)
```

Figure 10.14: Show databases query execution

- **use database**: This command is used to set the current database for all operations. It changes the context of a particular database so that subsequent queries use this database.

- **Syntax**: `use database_name;`
- **Example**: `use mydatabase;`

In the shell, users need to use the particular database to execute subsequent queries, as shown in *Figure 10.15*:

```
2b49ce8947): Use mydatabase
INFO  : Semantic Analysis Completed
INFO  : Returning Hive schema: Schema(fieldSchemas:null, properties:null)
INFO  : Completed compiling command(queryId=hive_20240922004242_0c621206-7b91-49
52-bb1d-042b49ce8947); Time taken: 0.014 seconds
INFO  : Concurrency mode is disabled, not creating a lock manager
INFO  : Executing command(queryId=hive_20240922004242_0c621206-7b91-4952-bb1d-04
2b49ce8947): Use mydatabase
INFO  : Starting task [Stage-0:DDL] in serial mode
INFO  : Completed executing command(queryId=hive_20240922004242_0c621206-7b91-49
52-bb1d-042b49ce8947); Time taken: 0.005 seconds
INFO  : OK
No rows affected (0.029 seconds)
0: jdbc:hive2://localhost:10000>
```

Figure 10.15*: Query execution for use mydatabase*

Throughout the chapter, all the queries will be executed in the Hue graphical user interface:

- **DROP DATABASE**: This command deletes an entire database along with all its tables from hive.
  - **Syntax**: `DROP DATABASE [IF EXISTS] database_name [CASCADE | RESTRICT];`
  - **Example**: `DROP DATABASE IF EXISTS mydb;`

    Or,

    `DROP DATABASE IF EXISTS mydb CASCADE;`

    Or,

    `DROP DATABASE IF EXISTS mydb RESTRICT;`

    Here, `IF EXISTS` is used to prevent an error if the database does not exist. You can use `CASCADE` to delete all tables in the database before deleting the database, and `RESTRICT` to delete the database only if it is empty. To drop a database, we have created a database called `mydb`, as shown in *Figure 10.16:*

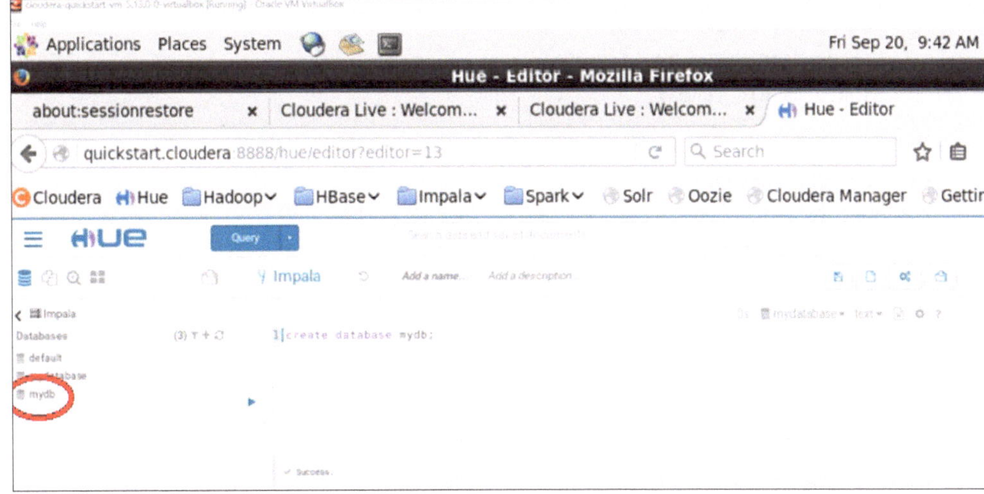

Figure 10.16*: Database created mydb*

Next, this database is dropped by executing the query as this database has no tables. The left navigation pane of *Figure 10.16* shows database creation, and *Figure 10.17* shows the deletion of the `mydb` database:

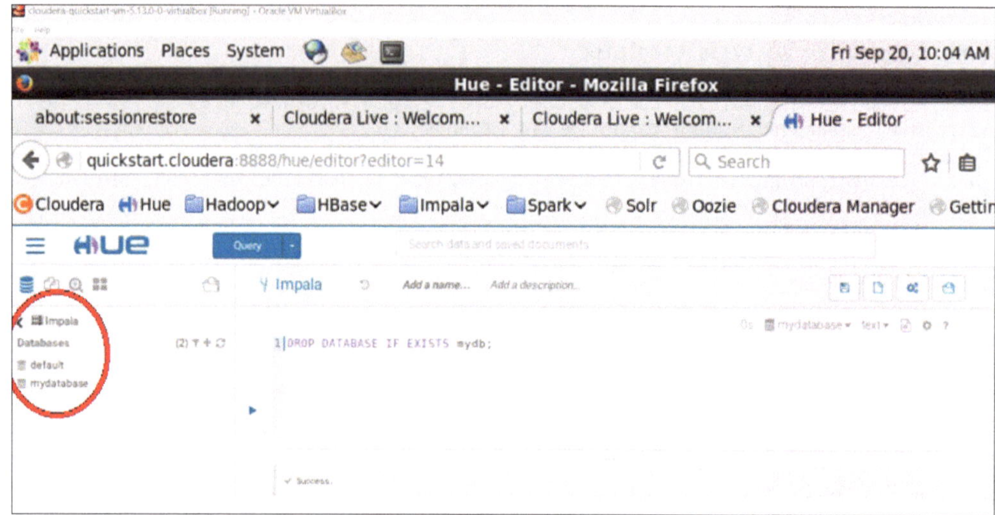

Figure 10.17: DROP Database 'mydb'

- **CREATE TABLE**: This command is used to define a new table within a database in Hive. To create a Hive table, you need to define the table schema and specify the format of the data. Refer to *Figure 10.18*.
  - **Syntax:**

```
CREATE TABLE [IF NOT EXISTS] table_name (
   column1 datatype,
   column2 datatype,
  ...
)
    ROW FORMAT DELIMITED
    FIELDS TERMINATED BY 'delimiter'
    STORED AS file_format;
```

  - **Example**:

```
CREATE TABLE custdata (
customer_id INT,
    gender STRING,
    age INT,
    city STRING,
membership_type STRING,
total_spend FLOAT,
items_purchased INT,
average_rating FLOAT,
discount_applied BOOLEAN,
days_since_last_purchase INT,
```

```
satisfaction_level STRING
)
ROW FORMAT DELIMITED
FIELDS TERMINATED BY','
STORED AS TEXTFILE;
```

The example shown in *Figure 10.18* creates a table named **custdata** with multiple columns (like **customer_id**, **gender**, **age**, etc.). In the query, **customer_id**, **items_purchased**, and **days_since_last_purchase** are declared as **INT** to store data as integer values, **gender**, **city**, **membership_type**, and **satisfaction_level** will store **STRING** type data, **total_spend**, **average_rating** will store decimal values, and **discount_applied** is a **BOOLEAN**. **ROW FORMAT DELIMITED** specifies the format for rows in the table, **FIELDS TERMINATED BY ','** indicates that fields (columns) will be separated by commas in the input file, and **STORED AS TEXTFILE** specifies that the data will be uploaded in this table from the plain text files.

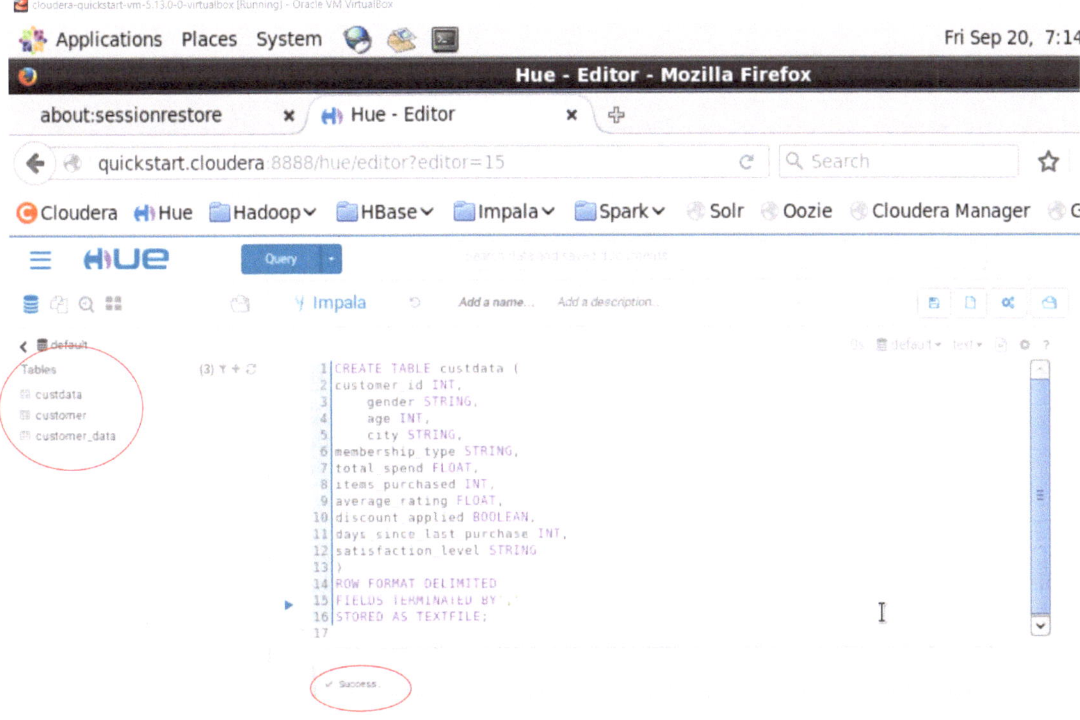

Figure 10.18: Create database query

As discussed in the preceding chapters, the two types of tables are supported in Hive: managed or internal tables and external tables. To create an external table, you need to specify the keyword **'EXTERNAL'** explicitly, as shown in the following example, as shown in code and *Figure 10.19*:

```
CREATE EXTERNAL TABLE customer_data_external ( customer_id INT, gender STRING, age INT, city
STRING, membership_type STRING, total_spend FLOAT, items_purchased INT, average_rating FLOAT,
discount_applied BOOLEAN, days_since_last_purchase INT, satisfaction_level STRING ) ROW FORMAT
DELIMITED FIELDS TERMINATED BY ',' STORED AS TEXTFILE LOCATION';
```

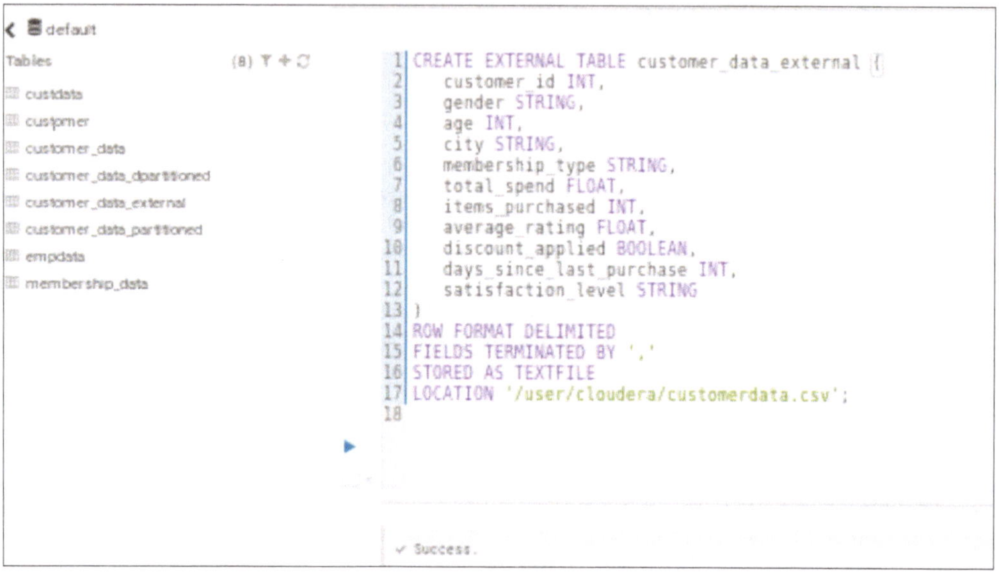
default
Tables
custdata
customer
customer_data
customer_data_dpartitioned
customer_data_external
customer_data_partitioned
empdata
membership_data
CREATE EXTERNAL TABLE customer_data_external (
customer_id INT,
gender STRING,
age INT,
city STRING,
membership_type STRING,
total_spend FLOAT,
items_purchased INT,
average_rating FLOAT,
discount_applied BOOLEAN,
days_since_last_purchase INT,
satisfaction_level STRING
)
ROW FORMAT DELIMITED
FIELDS TERMINATED BY ','
STORED AS TEXTFILE
LOCATION '/user/cloudera/customerdata.csv';
Success.

Figure 10.19: *Example of an external table*

The breakdown of the code is as follows:

- **CREATE EXTERNAL TABLE**: This keyword ensures that the table is created as an external table.
- **ROW FORMAT DELIMITED FIELDS TERMINATED BY ','**: Specifies that the fields in the data file are separated by commas.
- **STORED AS TEXTFILE**: Specifies the storage format (in this case, `TEXTFILE` format).
- **LOCATION '/path/to/external/data'**: Specifies the directory where the external data is located in HDFS (or a local file system if you are not using HDFS). You should replace /path/to/external/data with the actual path where your data is stored.

ALTER TABLE

This command is used to modify the structure of an existing table. You can add, change, or drop columns in the table using this command.

- **Syntax:** `ALTER TABLE table_name ADD|REPLACE|CHANGE COLUMNS (column_definition);`
- **Example (Add a column):** `ALTER TABLE custdata ADD COLUMNS (email STRING);`

This query will add a new column, email, to the `custdata` table created above. The output of the preceding query is shown in *Figure 10.20*. The left panel shows that the email column has been added to the `custdata` table after execution of the above query.

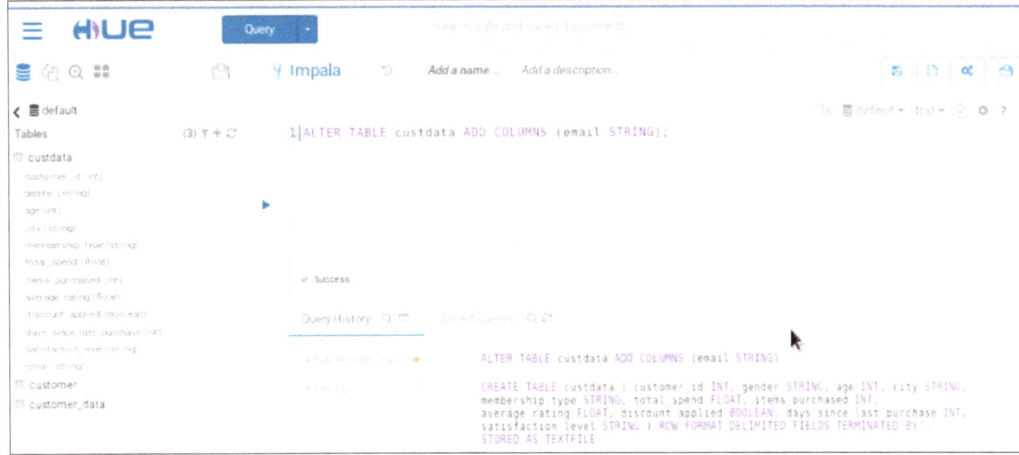

Figure 10.20: Execution and output of query with alter command

Refer to the following list to gain understanding:

- **DESCRIBE TABLE**: This command is used to retrieve the structure or metadata of a table, such as column names and data types.
  - **Syntax**: **`DESCRIBE [EXTENDED] table_name;`**
  - **Example**: **`DESCRIBE custdata;`**

  This query displays the structure (column names, data types) of the **`custdata`** table as shown in *Figure 10.21:*

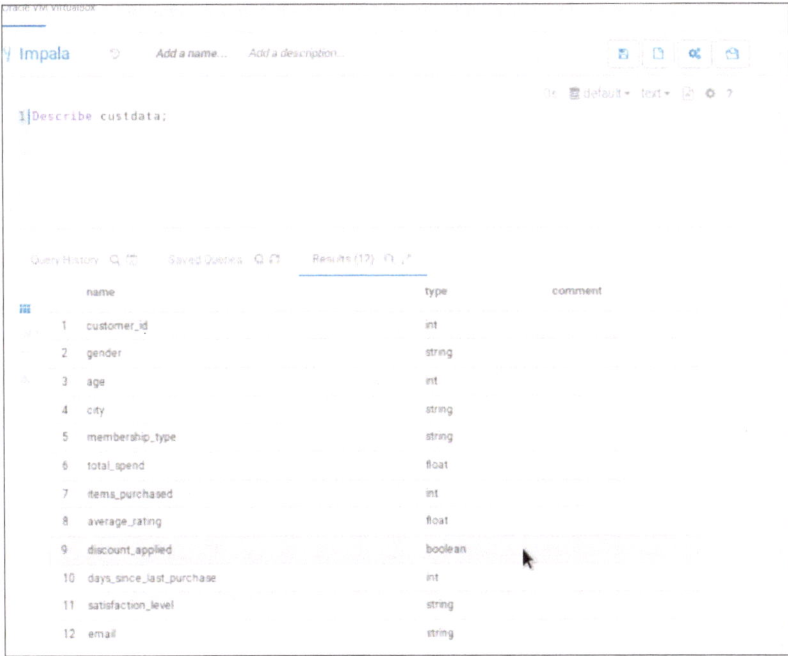

Figure 10.21: Execution and output of query with describe command

- **SHOW TABLES**: This command is used to list all tables in the current database (as set by the **`use`** command), as shown in list and *Figure 10.22:*
  - **Syntax**: **`SHOW TABLES;`**
  - **Example**: **`SHOW TABLES;`**

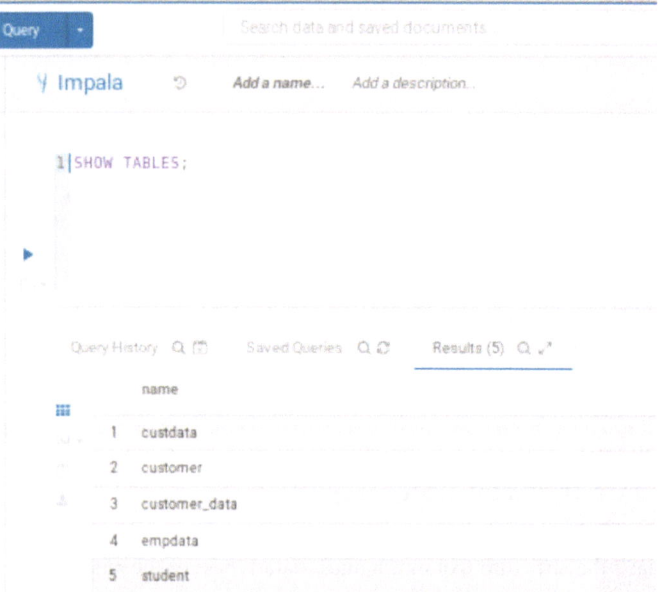

Figure 10.22: Execution and output of query with describe command

- **DROP TABLE**: This command deletes a table and its associated data from Hive. In the syntax IF EXISTS clause ensures that the command does not fail if the table does not exist. Here, the example query is used to delete the student table, as shown in *Figure 10.22*. The left pane in *Figure 10.23* shows only four tables out of five.
  - **Syntax**: **`DROP TABLE [IF EXISTS] table_name;`**
  - **Example**: **`DROP TABLE IF EXISTS student;`**

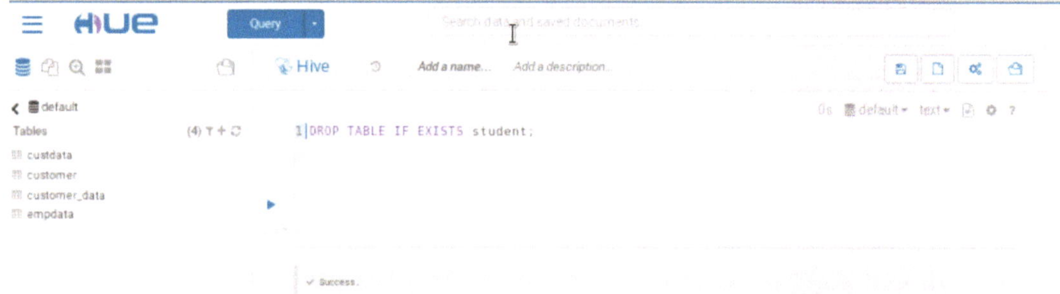

Figure 10.23: Execution and output of query with drop table command

- **TRUNCATE TABLE**: The **`TRUNCATE TABLE`** command is used to delete all rows from a table without deleting the table structure itself. The example removes all data from the emp table but keeps the table structure intact for future use.

- **Syntax**: `TRUNCATE TABLE table_name;`
- **Example**: `TRUNCATE TABLE empdata;`

  It can be seen in *Figure 10.24* that there are ten rows in the table **`empdata`**. On executing the example query, all these rows will be deleted:

***Figure 10.24**: Data stored in empdata table*

The **`TRUNCATE`** command retains the structure as compared to the **`DROP`** table command, as shown in the left panel in *Figure 10.25*. The same can also be confirmed by executing **`Describe table`** command.

***Figure 10.25**: Execution and output of query with the Truncate table command*

DML commands

Let us now understand the various DML commands:

- **LOAD DATA**: The **`LOAD DATA`** command loads data from a file into a Hive table. It can load data from the local file system or HDFS. In the syntax, if you specify **`LOCAL`**, Hive will look for the file on the local file system. Without **`LOCAL`**, Hive will look for the file in the **Hadoop Distributed File System** (HDFS). **`INPATH 'file_path'`** is the path of the file containing the data to be loaded, which means in this example, Hive will load data from the HDFS path **`/user/cloudera/customerdata.csv`**. If **`OVERWRITE`** is specified, Hive will overwrite the existing data in the table. If it is omitted, Hive will append the new data to the existing table data.

- **Syntax:** `LOAD DATA [LOCAL] INPATH 'file_path' [OVERWRITE] INTO TABLE table_name;`
- **Example:** `LOAD DATA INPATH '/user/cloudera/customerdata.csv' INTO TABLE mydatabase.customerdata;`

  The example query inserts data in **'cutomerdata'** table in **mydatabase** from the path **'/user/cloudera/customerdata.csv'** as shown in *Figure 10.26:*

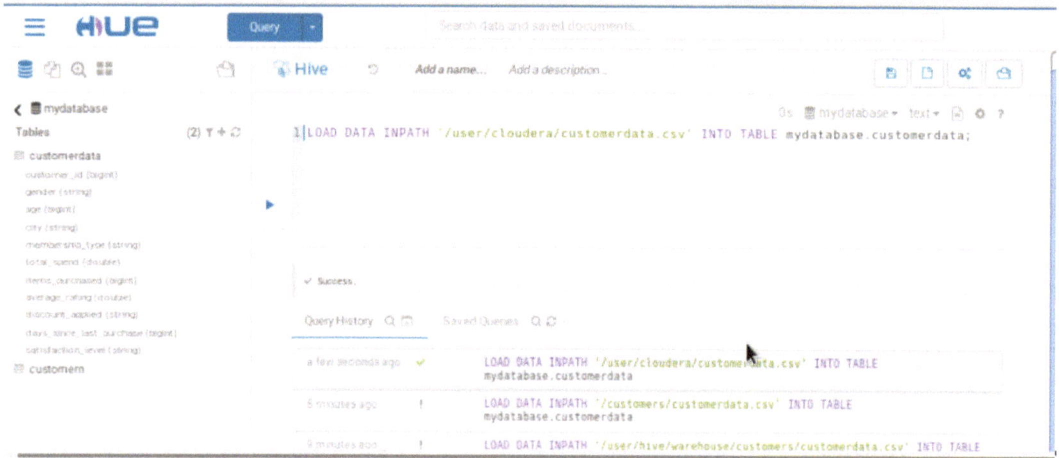

***Figure 10.26** : Execution and output of query with LOAD command*

- **INSERT INTO**: The **INSERT INTO** command inserts data into an existing table in Hive. You can insert values either by specifying them directly or by selecting from another table. Example for direct insertion of values:
  - **Syntax:** `INSERT INTO TABLE table_name VALUES (value1, value2, ...);`
  - **Example:** `INSERT INTO TABLE customer_data (VALUES (201, 'Male', 25, 'New York', 'Gold', 1000.5, 10, 4.5, TRUE, 5, 'Satisfied');`

    Figure 10.27 shows the example query for direct insertion of values. This inserts a single row of data into the **'customer_data'** table with values provided for each column.

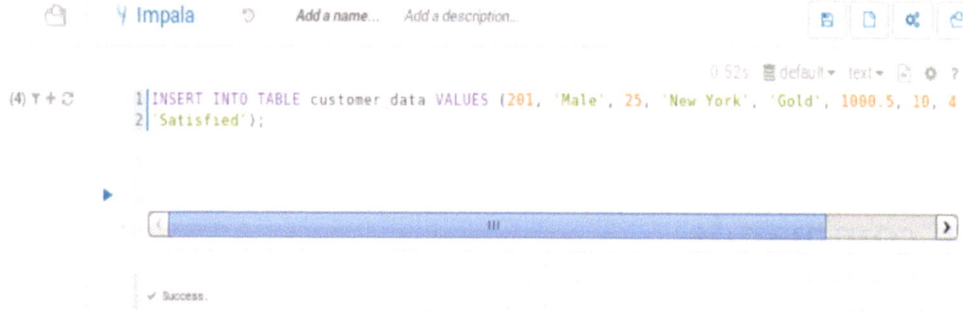

***Figure 10.27**: Execution and output of query with INSERT INTO command*

In *Figure 10.28*, a select query is executed to verify the insertion of a tuple with **customer_Id=201**:

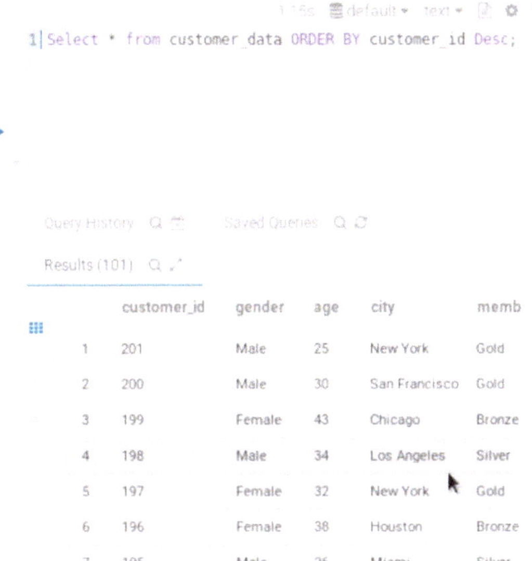

```
1| Select * from customer_data ORDER BY customer_id Desc;
```

Results (101)

	customer_id	gender	age	city	memb
1	201	Male	25	New York	Gold
2	200	Male	30	San Francisco	Gold
3	199	Female	43	Chicago	Bronze
4	198	Male	34	Los Angeles	Silver
5	197	Female	32	New York	Gold
6	196	Female	38	Houston	Bronze
7	195	Male	26	Miami	Silver

Figure 10.28: *Verification of execution insert query*

- Insertion of data from one table to another:
  - **Syntax:** **`INSERT INTO TABLE target_table SELECT * FROM source_table;`**
  - **Example:** **`INSERT INTO TABLE empdata SELECT customer_id, gender, age, city FROM customer_data;`**

  Figure 10.29 shows an example query where these selected column values from **'customer_data'** are inserted into the **'empdata'** table:

```
1| INSERT INTO TABLE empdata SELECT customer_id, gender, age, city FROM customer_data;
```

Figure 10.29: *Execution Insert query*

- **SELECT:** The **SELECT** command is used to query and retrieve data from one or more tables in Hive. The example query, as shown in *Figure 10.30*, retrieves customer data for all male customers, ordering the results by total spend in descending order.
  - **Syntax:** **`SELECT column1, column2, ... FROM table_name [WHERE condition] [GROUP BY column1, column2, ...] [ORDER BY column1 [ASC|DESC]];`**
  - **Example:** **`SELECT customer_id, total_spend FROM customer_data WHERE gender = 'Male' ORDER BY total_spend DESC;`**

0.49s default text

```
Select * from customer_data where gender='Male'ORDER BY total_spend Desc;
```

Query History Saved Queries Results (51)

	customer_id	gender	age	city	membership_type	total_spend	items_purchased
1	110	Male	28	San Francisco	Gold	1520.0999755[illegible]9375	21
2	158	Male	28	San Francisco	Gold	1500.0999755859375	21
3	188	Male	28	San Francisco	Gold	1500.0999755859375	21

***Figure 10.30**: Execution and output of the select command*

Join in Apache Hive

In Apache Hive, joins are used to combine rows from two or more tables based on a related column. Hive supports several types of joins, similar to SQL, including inner join, left outer join, right outer join, full outer join, cross join, and semi join.

To understand the various types of joins, let us create another table that stores membership-related information for customers, such as their membership type, status, and membership duration. *Figure 10.31* shows the table created with the given structure. The left panel shows that the table was created successfully.

- **Query**: `CREATE TABLE membership_data ( customer_id INT, membership_type STRING, membership_start_date DATE, membership_end_date DATE, membership_status STRING) ROW FORMAT DELIMITED FIELDS TERMINATED BY ',' STORED AS TEXTFILE;`

  In this table, `customer_id` is a unique identifier for each customer (linked to the `customer_data` table), `membership_type` refers to the type of membership (e.g., Gold, Platinum, etc.), `membership_start_date` indicates the date when the customer started their membership, `membership_end_date` is the date when the membership expires (or null if ongoing) and `membership_status` shows the status of the membership (e.g., Active, Expired).

***Figure 10.31** Creation of membership data table*

Next, sample data is inserted into the **`membership_data`** table, as shown in *Figure 10.32*, by executing the query given in the following figure. This query inserts five rows of sample data into the **`membership_data`** table. The data includes customer membership information with dates and membership status.

Example: `INSERT INTO TABLE membership_data VALUES (101, 'Gold', '2023-01-01', '2024-01-01', 'Active'), (102, 'Platinum', '2022-06-15', '2023-06-15', 'Expired'), (103, 'Silver', '2021-09-10', '2022-09-10', 'Expired'), (104, 'Gold', '2023-03-20', '2024-03-20', 'Active'), (105, 'Platinum', '2023-08-01', '2024-08-01', 'Active');`

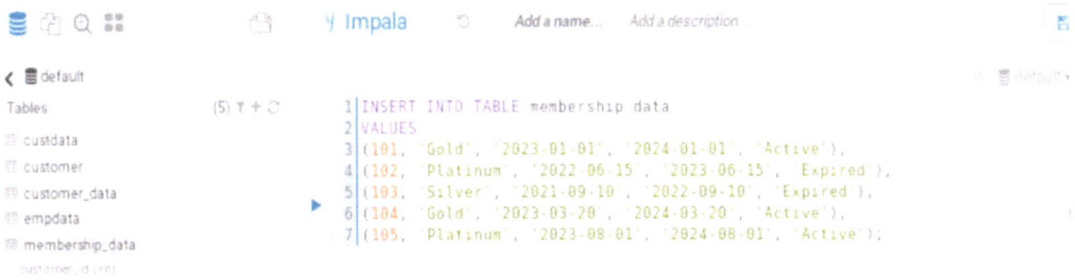

Figure 10.32: Insertion of data in membership data table

- **Inner join**: The inner join query retrieves rows that have matching values in both tables. The example query, as shown in *Figure 10.33*, retrieves matching rows based on **`customer_id`** from both **`customer_data`** and **`membership_data`**.
  - **Syntax:** `SELECT a.column1, b.column2, ... FROM table1 a JOIN table2 b ON a.common_column = b.common_column;`
  - **Example:** `SELECT a.customer_id, b.membership_type FROM customer_data a JOIN membership_data b ON a.customer_id = b.customer_id;`

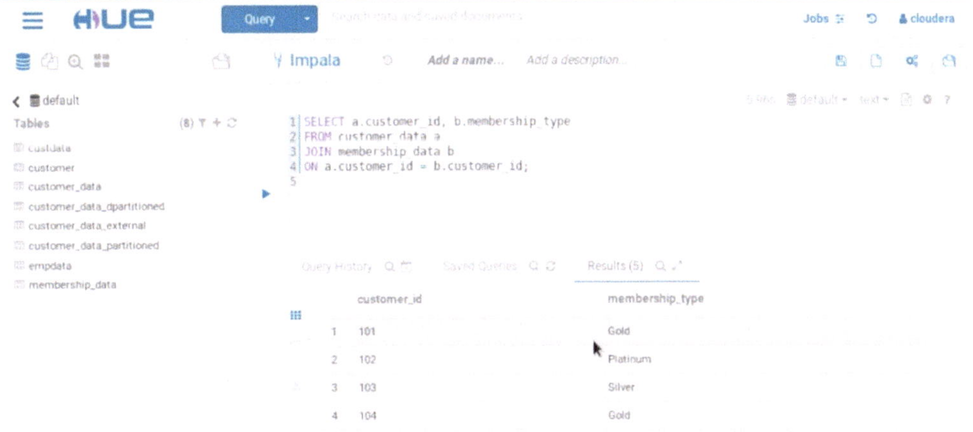

Figure 10.33: Query execution and results of the inner Join

- **LEFT OUTER JOIN**: The **`LEFT OUTER JOIN`** retrieves all rows from the left table and matching rows from the right table. If there is no match, NULL values are returned for columns of the right table. *Figure 10.34* shows the output of an example query that retrieves all customers from **`customer_data`** and their membership details, if available, from **`membership_data`**.

- Syntax: `SELECT a.column1, b.column2, ... FROM table1 a LEFT OUTER JOIN table2 b ON a.common_column = b.common_column;`
- Example: `SELECT a.customer_id, b.membership_type FROM customer_data a LEFT OUTER JOIN membership_data b ON a.customer_id = b.customer_id;`

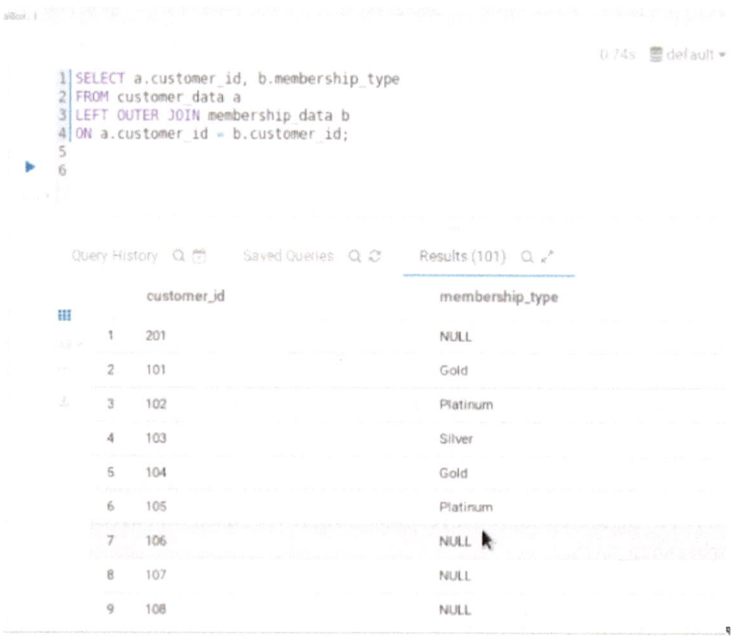

Figure 10.34: Results for LEFT OUTER JOIN

- **RIGHT OUTER JOIN**: The `RIGHT OUTER JOIN` retrieves all rows from the right table and matching rows from the left table. If no match is found, NULL values are returned for the columns of the left table. *Figure 10.35* shows that the `RIGHT OUTER JOIN` query retrieves all rows from `membership_data` and matching customer details from `customer_data`.
  - Syntax: `SELECT a.column1, b.column2, ... FROM table1 a RIGHT OUTER JOIN table2 b ON a.common_column = b.common_column;`
  - Example: `SELECT a.customer_id, b.membership_type FROM customer_data a RIGHT OUTER JOIN membership_data b ON a.customer_id = b.customer_id;`

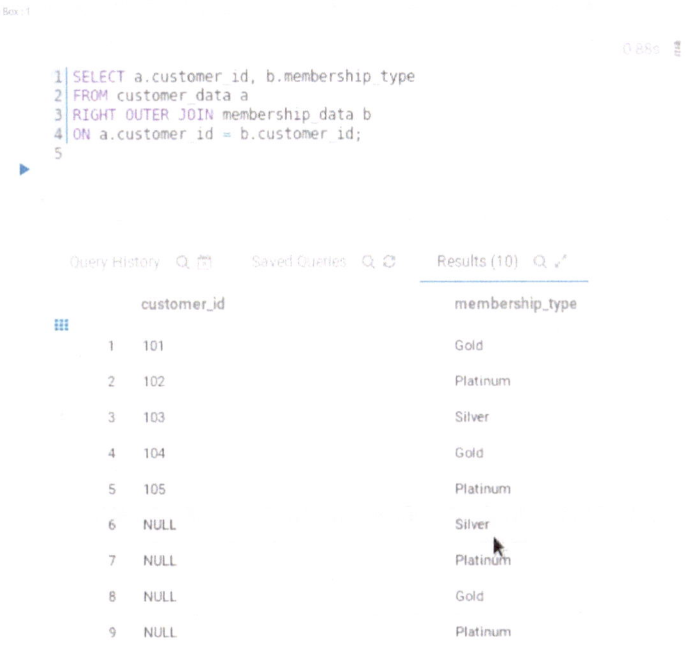

```
SELECT a.customer_id, b.membership_type
FROM customer_data a
RIGHT OUTER JOIN membership_data b
ON a.customer_id = b.customer_id;
```

Query History | Saved Queries | Results (10)

	customer_id	membership_type
1	101	Gold
2	102	Platinum
3	103	Silver
4	104	Gold
5	105	Platinum
6	NULL	Silver
7	NULL	Platinum
8	NULL	Gold
9	NULL	Platinum

***Figure 10.35:** Output of right outer join query*

Partitioning in Apache Hive

Partitioning in Hive improves query performance by organizing tables into smaller, manageable pieces (partitions) based on a column's values. Apache Hive provides two types of partitioning- static and dynamic. Using the **`customer_data`** example from above, let us learn to implement static and dynamic partitioning:

- **Static partitioning**: In static partitioning, the partition column's value is explicitly provided in the **`INSERT`** query, and Hive writes the data into that specific partition. This task is performed in two steps:
  1. Create a partitioned table.
  2. Load data into specific partitions.
- **Create a partitioned table (static partitioning)**: Let us partition the **`customer_data`** table by city. The following query (*Figure 10.36*) creates a partitioned table where each partition is created based on the city column. The left panel in the following figure shows the successful creation of a partitioned table.

  Query: **`CREATE TABLE customer_data_partitioned (customer_id INT, gender STRING, age INT, membership_type STRING, total_spend FLOAT, items_purchased INT, average_rating FLOAT, discount_applied BOOLEAN, days_since_last_purchase INT, satisfaction_level STRING) PARTITIONED BY (city STRING) ROW FORMAT DELIMITED FIELDS TERMINATED BY ',' STORED AS TEXTFILE;`**

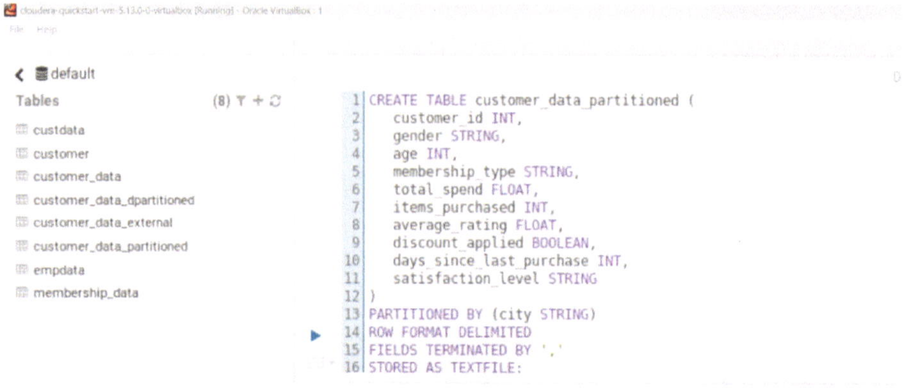
default
Tables
custdata
customer
customer_data
customer_data_dpartitioned
customer_data_external
customer_data_partitioned
empdata
membership_data
CREATE TABLE customer_data_partitioned (
customer_id INT,
gender STRING,
age INT,
membership_type STRING,
total_spend FLOAT,
items_purchased INT,
average_rating FLOAT,
discount_applied BOOLEAN,
days_since_last_purchase INT,
satisfaction_level STRING
)
PARTITIONED BY (city STRING)
ROW FORMAT DELIMITED
FIELDS TERMINATED BY ','
STORED AS TEXTFILE;

Figure 10.36: *Create partitioned table*

- **Static partition data loading**: In this method, you must explicitly specify the partition value when loading data into the partitioned table, as shown in the insert query given below. Refer to *Figure 10.37*. The data is inserted into the partition for `city='New York'` and the partition (city) is statically defined in the query.

  Query: **`INSERT INTO TABLE customer_data_partitioned PARTITION (city='New York') VALUES (1, 'Male', 25, 'Gold', 1000.5, 10, 4.5, TRUE, 5, 'Satisfied'), (2, 'Female', 30, 'Platinum', 2000.0, 15, 4.9, FALSE, 2, 'Very Satisfied');`**

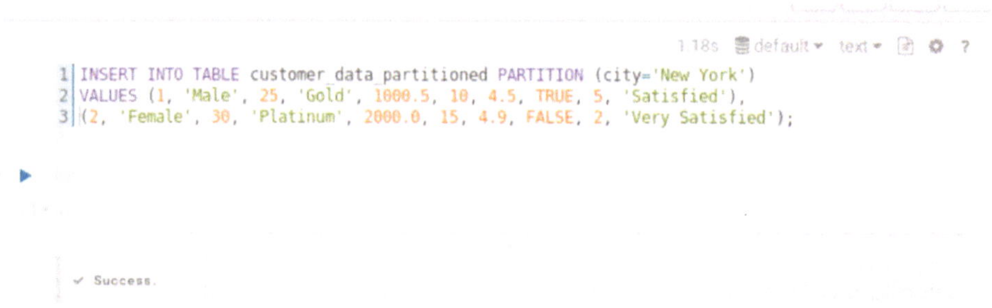
INSERT INTO TABLE customer_data_partitioned PARTITION (city='New York')
VALUES (1, 'Male', 25, 'Gold', 1000.5, 10, 4.5, TRUE, 5, 'Satisfied'),
(2, 'Female', 30, 'Platinum', 2000.0, 15, 4.9, FALSE, 2, 'Very Satisfied');
Success.

Figure 10.37: *Insertion of data in partitioned tables*

- **Dynamic partitioning**: In dynamic partitioning, Hive automatically determines the partition column's value based on the data being inserted. This is useful when you want to insert data into multiple partitions in one go. The various steps involved are:
  1. Enable dynamic partitioning in Hive
  2. Create a partitioned table
  3. Insert data dynamically:
     - **Enable dynamic partitioning**: Before using dynamic partitioning, you need to enable it in the Hive shell:

       ```
       SET hive.exec.dynamic.partition = true;
       SET hive.exec.dynamic.partition.mode = nonstrict;
       ```

       Here, **`hive.exec.dynamic.partition`**, enables dynamic partitioning and **`hive.exec.dynamic.partition.mode = nonstrict`** allows dynamic partitioning in all scenarios (default mode is strict, which requires at least one static partition).

- **Create a partitioned table (dynamic partitioning)**: The partitioned table structure remains the same as in static partitioning. *Figure 10.38* shows the creation of a table in the left panel after the execution of the query shown in the right panel.

  Query: **`CREATE TABLE customer_data_dpartitioned (customer_id INT, gender STRING, age INT, membership_type STRING, total_spend FLOAT, items_purchased INT, average_rating FLOAT, discount_applied BOOLEAN, days_since_last_purchase INT, satisfaction_level STRING) PARTITIONED BY (city STRING) ROW FORMAT DELIMITED FIELDS TERMINATED BY ',' STORED AS TEXTFILE;`**

Figure 10.38: *Create partitioned table for dynamic partitioning*

- **Dynamic partition data loading**: When loading data dynamically, you do not need to specify the partition value in the **`INSERT`** query. As shown in the following query, the city partition is determined dynamically based on the value of the city column from the **`customer_data`** table. This query, as illustrated in *Figure 10.39*, inserts data into appropriate partitions for different cities based on the data values.

Query: **`INSERT INTO TABLE customer_data_dpartitioned PARTITION (city) SELECT customer_id, gender, age, membership_type, total_spend, items_purchased, average_rating, discount_applied, days_since_last_purchase, satisfaction_level, city FROM customer_data;`**

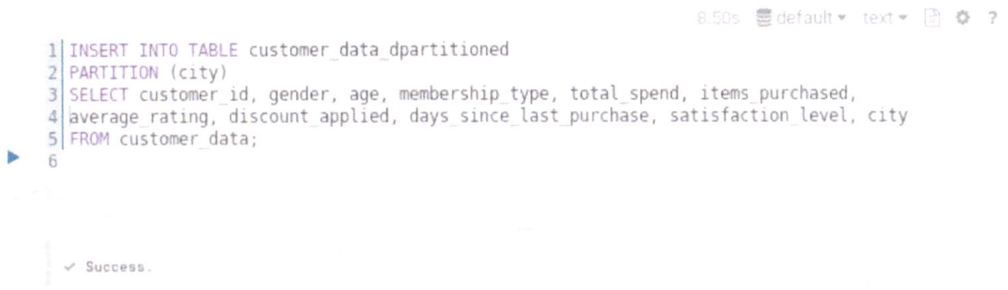

Figure 10.39: *Insert data partitioned table for dynamic partitioning*

- **Clustering in Hive (bucketing)**: Bucketing (or clustering) is another technique used to improve query performance by dividing data into buckets based on a hash of a column's value. It helps when partitioning is not sufficient to manage large datasets. Bucketing distributes the data more evenly, making querying more efficient. The steps to perform clustering in Hive are:
  1. Enable bucketing.
  2. Create a table with bucketing.
  3. Insert data into the bucketed table.

  - **Enable bucketing**: By default, bucketing is not enabled in Hive; the first step is to enable it by executing the command given below in the Hive shell. This ensures that Hive follows the bucketing during data insertion. Hue does not support bucketing in the current version. Hence, the example query is executed using the Beehive shell:

    ```
    hive.enforce.bucketing = true
    ```

  - **Create a bucketed table**: Next, create a table with bucketing by using the **`CLUSTERED BY`** clause.

    Query: **`CREATE TABLE customer_data_bucketed (customer_id INT, gender STRING, age INT, city STRING, membership_type STRING, total_spend FLOAT, items_purchased INT, average_rating FLOAT, discount_applied BOOLEAN, days_since_last_purchase INT, satisfaction_level STRING) CLUSTERED BY (customer_id) INTO 4 BUCKETS ROW FORMAT DELIMITED FIELDS TERMINATED BY ',' STORED AS TEXTFILE;`**

In this example (*Figure 10.40*), the table is bucketed by the **`customer_id`** column into four buckets. Here **`CLUSTERED BY (customer_id) INTO 4 BUCKETS`** divides the data into four buckets based on the hash value of **`customer_id`**.

```
INFO  : Executing command(queryId=hive_20240926084343_a8266bab-2ed2-4fcb-b004-7c
f6b3df5208): CREATE TABLE customer_data_bucketed (
customer_id INT,
gender STRING,
age INT,
city STRING,
membership_type STRING,
total_spend FLOAT,
items_purchased INT,
average_rating FLOAT,
discount_applied BOOLEAN,
days_since_last_purchase INT,
satisfaction_level STRING
)
CLUSTERED BY (customer_id) INTO 4 BUCKETS
ROW FORMAT DELIMITED
FIELDS TERMINATED BY ','
STORED AS TEXTFILE
INFO  : Starting task [Stage-0:DDL] in serial mode
INFO  : Completed executing command(queryId=hive_20240926084343_a8266bab-2ed2-4f
cb-b004-7cf6b3df5208); Time taken: 0.091 seconds
INFO  : OK
No rows affected (0.176 seconds)
0: jdbc:hive2://localhost:10000>
```

Figure 10.40*: Execution of query for creating table with bucketing*

  - **Insert data into the bucketed table**: The following query inserts data into the bucketed table. The data is distributed across four buckets based on the **`customer_id`** hash value.

Query: `INSERT INTO TABLE customer_data_bucketed VALUES (1, 'Male', 25, 'New York', 'Gold', 1000.5, 10, 4.5, TRUE, 5, 'Satisfied'), (2, 'Female', 30, 'Los Angeles', 'Platinum', 2000.0, 15, 4.9, FALSE, 2, 'Very Satisfied');`

Figure 10.41 shows the execution of the insert query:

```
File  Edit  View  Search  Terminal  Help
No rows affected (0.176 seconds)
0: jdbc:hive2://localhost:10000> INSERT INTO TABLE customer_data_bucketed
. . . . . . . . . . . . . . . .> VALUES
. . . . . . . . . . . . . . . .> (1, 'Male', 25, 'New York', 'Gold', 1000.5, 10,
 4.5, TRUE, 5, 'Satisfied'),
. . . . . . . . . . . . . . . .> (2, 'Female', 30, 'Los Angeles', 'Platinum', 20
00.0, 15, 4.9, FALSE, 2, 'Very Satisfied');
INFO  : Compiling command(queryId=hive_20240926084545_2ef30cb9-caa8-4b32-b0c3-8d
d5f4a84a34): INSERT INTO TABLE customer_data_bucketed
VALUES
(1, 'Male', 25, 'New York', 'Gold', 1000.5, 10, 4.5, TRUE, 5, 'Satisfied'),
(2, 'Female', 30, 'Los Angeles', 'Platinum', 2000.0, 15, 4.9, FALSE, 2, 'Very Sa
tisfied')
INFO  : Semantic Analysis Completed
INFO  : Returning Hive schema: Schema(fieldSchemas:[FieldSchema(name:_col0, type
:int, comment:null), FieldSchema(name:_col1, type:string, comment:null), FieldSc
hema(name:_col2, type:int, comment:null), FieldSchema(name:_col3, type:string, c
omment:null), FieldSchema(name:_col4, type:string, comment:null), FieldSchema(na
me:_col5, type:float, comment:null), FieldSchema(name:_col6, type:int, comment:n
ull), FieldSchema(name:_col7, type:float, comment:null), FieldSchema(name:_col8,
 type:boolean, comment:null), FieldSchema(name:_col9, type:int, comment:null), F
ieldSchema(name:_col10, type:string, comment:null)], properties:null)
INFO  : Completed compiling command(queryId=hive_20240926084545_2ef30cb9-caa8-4b
32-b0c3-8dd5f4a84a34); Time taken: 1.084 seconds
INFO  : Concurrency mode is disabled, not creating a lock manager
INFO  : Executing command(queryId=hive_20240926084545_2ef30cb9-caa8-4b32-b0c3-8d
```

***Figure 10.41**: Execution of insert query for bucketing*

Figure 10.41 shows that while executing the insert query, four files are created corresponding to the 4 buckets specified in the create query, as shown in *Figure 10.42*:

```
File  Edit  View  Search  Terminal  Help
INFO  : 2024-09-26 08:46:06,116 Stage-1 map = 100%,  reduce = 25%, Cumulative CP
U 2.34 sec
INFO  : 2024-09-26 08:46:08,479 Stage-1 map = 100%,  reduce = 50%, Cumulative CP
U 3.68 sec
INFO  : 2024-09-26 08:46:09,626 Stage-1 map = 100%,  reduce = 75%, Cumulative CP
U 5.03 sec
INFO  : 2024-09-26 08:46:10,694 Stage-1 map = 100%,  reduce = 100%, Cumulative C
PU 6.4 sec
INFO  : MapReduce Total cumulative CPU time: 6 seconds 400 msec
INFO  : Ended Job = job_1727335433913_0001
INFO  : Starting task [Stage-0:MOVE] in serial mode
INFO  : Loading data to table mydatabase.customer_data_bucketed from hdfs://quic
kstart.cloudera:8020/user/hive/warehouse/mydatabase.db/customer_data_bucketed/.h
ive-staging_hive_2024-09-26_08-45-28_880_960628356306835538-1/-ext-10000
INFO  : Starting task [Stage-2:STATS] in serial mode
INFO  : Table mydatabase.customer_data_bucketed stats: [numFiles=4, numRows=2, t
otalSize=125, rawDataSize=123]
INFO  : MapReduce Jobs Launched:
INFO  : Stage-Stage-1: Map: 1  Reduce: 4   Cumulative CPU: 6.4 sec   HDFS Read:
32371 HDFS Write: 421 SUCCESS
INFO  : Total MapReduce CPU Time Spent: 6 seconds 400 msec
INFO  : Completed executing command(queryId=hive_20240926084545_2ef30cb9-caa8-4b
32-b0c3-8dd5f4a84a34); Time taken: 42.119 seconds
INFO  : OK
No rows affected (43.221 seconds)
0: jdbc:hive2://localhost:10000>
```

***Figure 10.42** : Creation of 4 files corresponding to buckets*

- **Combining partitioning and bucketing**: You can also combine both **partitioning** and **bucketing** to achieve better data organization. The following query shows Partition by city and bucket by **customer_id**. In this query, data is first partitioned by city and then further distributed into four buckets within each partition based on **customer_id**. After creating the table, data may be inserted by executing the following insert query. The creation of these tables can be verified by executing the show tables query.

  Query: `CREATE TABLE customer_data_part_bucketed (customer_id INT, gender STRING, age INT, membership_type STRING, total_spend FLOAT, items_purchased INT, average_rating FLOAT, discount_applied BOOLEAN, days_since_last_purchase INT, satisfaction_level STRING) PARTITIONED BY (city STRING) CLUSTERED BY (customer_id) INTO 4 BUCKETS ROW FORMAT DELIMITED FIELDS TERMINATED BY ',' STORED AS TEXTFILE;`

- **Inserting data**: `Set hive.exec.dynamic.partition.mode=nonstrict;`

  `INSERT INTO TABLE customer_data_part_bucketed PARTITION (city) VALUES (1, 'Male', 25, 'Gold', 1000.5, 10, 4.5, TRUE, 5, 'Satisfied', 'New York'), (2, 'Female', 30, 'Platinum', 2000.0, 15, 4.9, FALSE, 2, 'Very Satisfied', 'Los Angeles');`

Aggregation and grouping functions

In Hive, you can use aggregation functions like **COUNT**, **SUM**, **AVG**, **MIN**, and **MAX** to summarize the data. Let us look at them in detail:

- **COUNT**: It is used to compute the count. The example query counts the total number of customers in the **customer_data** table, as shown in *Figure 10.43*.

  Example: `SELECT COUNT(customer_id) AS total_customers FROM customer_data;`

Figure 10.43: Execution and output of the COUNT function

- **SUM**: It is used to compute the sum. The example query (*Figure 10.44*) sums up the total amount spent by all customers, which is stored in the **total_spend** column.

  Example: `SELECT SUM(total_spend) AS total_revenue FROM customer_data;`

Impala Add a name... Add a description

```
1 SELECT SUM(total_spend) AS total_revenue FROM customer_data;
```

Results (1)

	total_revenue
1	85986.4501953125

***Figure 10.44**: Execution and output of the SUM function*

- **AVG**: It is used to compute the average. This query, as shown in *Figure 10.45*, calculates the average rating that customers gave (**`average_rating`**).

  Example: **`SELECT AVG(average_rating) AS avg_customer_rating FROM customer_data;`**

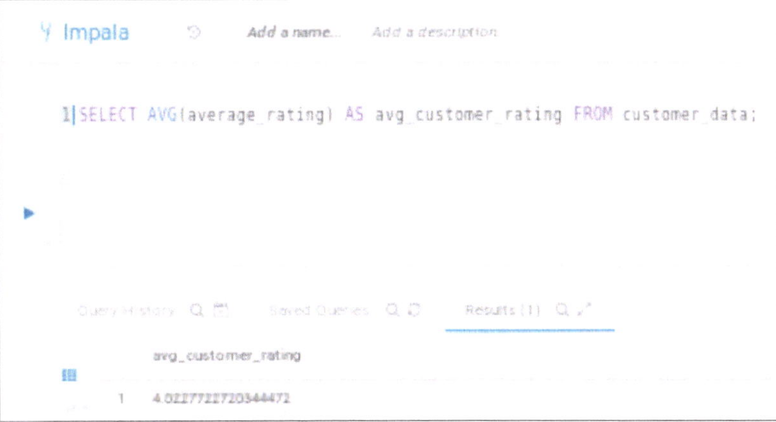

***Figure 10.45**: Execution and output of AVG function*

- **MIN and MAX**: It is used to compute the minimum and maximum values for a particular attribute. The example query, as shown in *Figure 10.46*, is used to find the minimum and maximum age of customers from the age column, showing the youngest and oldest customers.

  Example: **`SELECT MIN(age) AS youngest_customer_age, MAX(age) AS oldest_customer_age FROM customer_data;`**

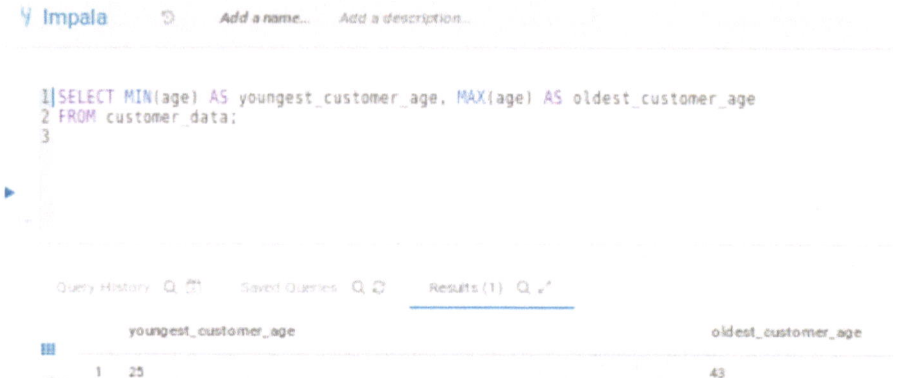

Figure 10.46: Execution and output of Min and Max functions

- **GROUP BY**: In Hive, the **`GROUP BY`** clause is used to group rows that have the same values in specified columns into aggregate data. This is commonly used in conjunction with aggregate functions like **`COUNT()`**, **`SUM()`**, **`AVG()`**, **`MAX()`**, and **`MIN()`** to summarize the grouped data. The example query, as shown in *Figure 10.47*, groups the data by city and calculates the total amount spent by customers in each city.

  Example query: **`SELECT city, SUM(total_spend) AS total_city_spend FROM customer_data GROUP BY city;`**

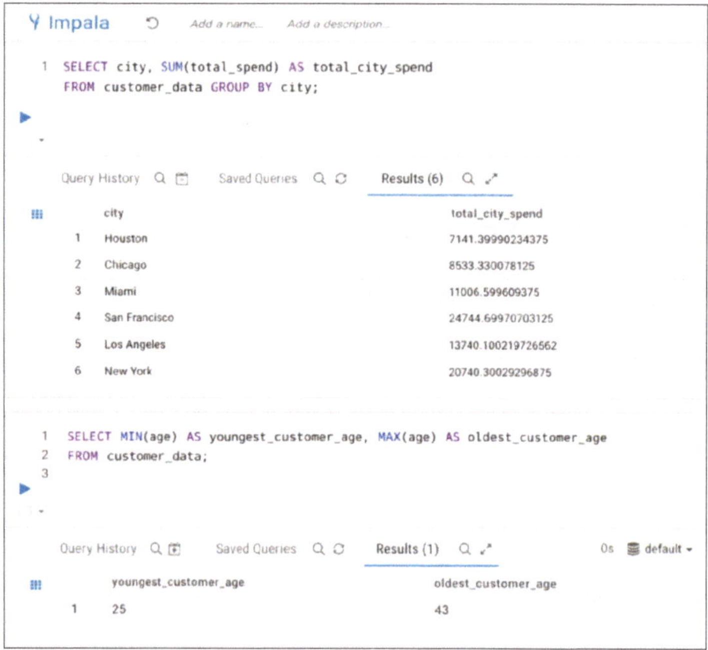

Figure 10.47: Execution and output of SUM function

- **GROUP BY with COUNT** is used to count the number of customers for each membership type (**`membership_type`**) by grouping the data, as shown in *Figure 10.48*.

  Example query: **`SELECT membership_type, COUNT(customer_id) AS num_customers FROM customer_data GROUP BY membership_type;`**

```
SELECT membership_type, COUNT(customer_id) AS num_customers
FROM customer_data GROUP BY membership_type;
```

Query History | Saved Queries | Results (3)

	membership_type	num_customers
1	Bronze	33
2	Silver	33
3	Gold	35

Figure 10.48: GROUP BY with COUNT

- **HAVING**: It is used to filter the result of a grouped query. You use the **HAVING** clause to filter groups after aggregation. The given query, as shown in *Figure 10.49*, groups the data by city, calculates the total amount spent per city, and then filters out cities where the total spend is less than or equal to 5000.

  Example query: **SELECT city, SUM(total_spend) AS total_city_spend FROM customer_data GROUP BY city HAVING SUM(total_spend) > 5000;**

10.32s default text

```
SELECT city, SUM(total_spend) AS total_city_spend FROM customer_data
GROUP BY city HAVING SUM(total_spend) > 5000;
```

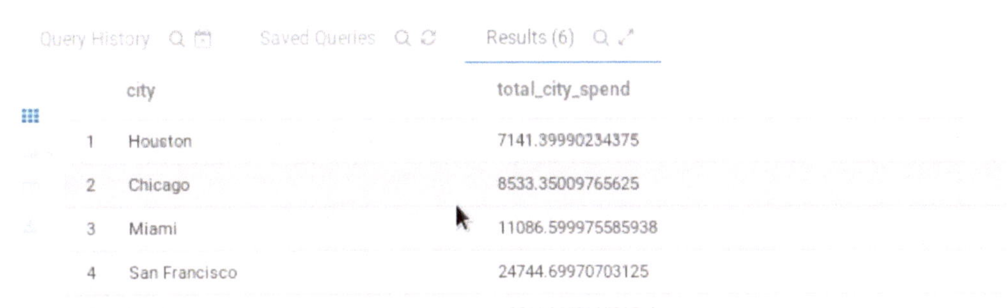

Query History | Saved Queries | Results (6)

	city	total_city_spend
1	Houston	7141.39990234375
2	Chicago	8533.35009765625
3	Miami	11086.599975585938
4	San Francisco	24744.69970703125

Figure 10.49: Group by with having

- **Multiple aggregations**: In Hive, you can perform multiple aggregations in a single **SELECT** query. This is useful when you want to calculate different aggregate values (such as **SUM()**, **COUNT()**, **AVG()**, etc.) for the same grouped data. This query, as shown in *Figure 10.50*, groups the data by **membership_type** and calculates both the average spend and the total number of items purchased for each membership type.

  Example query: **SELECT membership_type, AVG(total_spend) AS avg_spend, SUM(items_purchased) AS total_items FROM customer_data GROUP BY membership_type;**

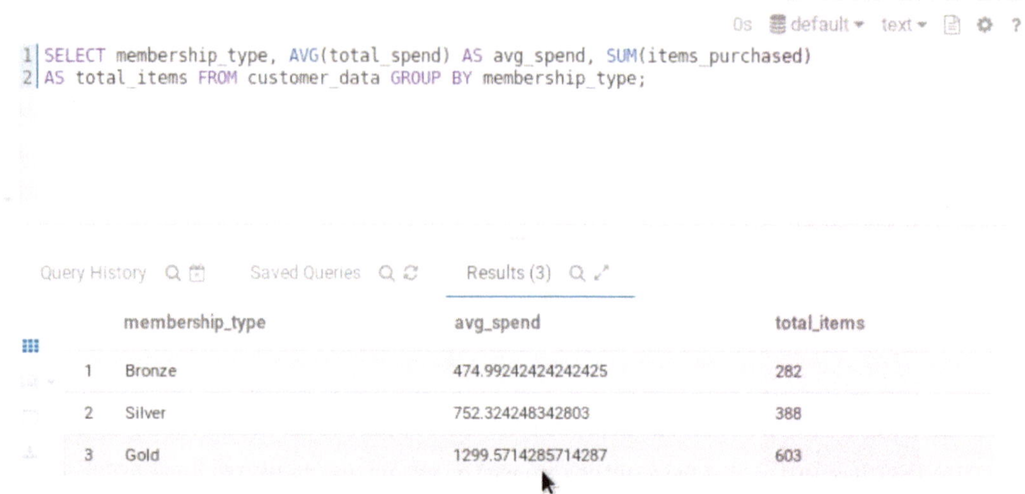

	membership_type	avg_spend	total_items
1	Bronze	474.99242424242425	282
2	Silver	752.324248342803	388
3	Gold	1299.5714285714287	603

Figure 10.50: *GROUP BY with multiple aggregations*

- **Nested aggregations with grouping** : You can also combine aggregate functions with the group by clause. The example query, as shown in *Figure 10.51,* groups the data by both city and **`membership_type`** and finds the maximum amount spent by a customer for each combination.

  Example query: **`SELECT city, membership_type, MAX(total_spend) AS max_city_membership_spend FROM customer_data GROUP BY city, membership_type;`**

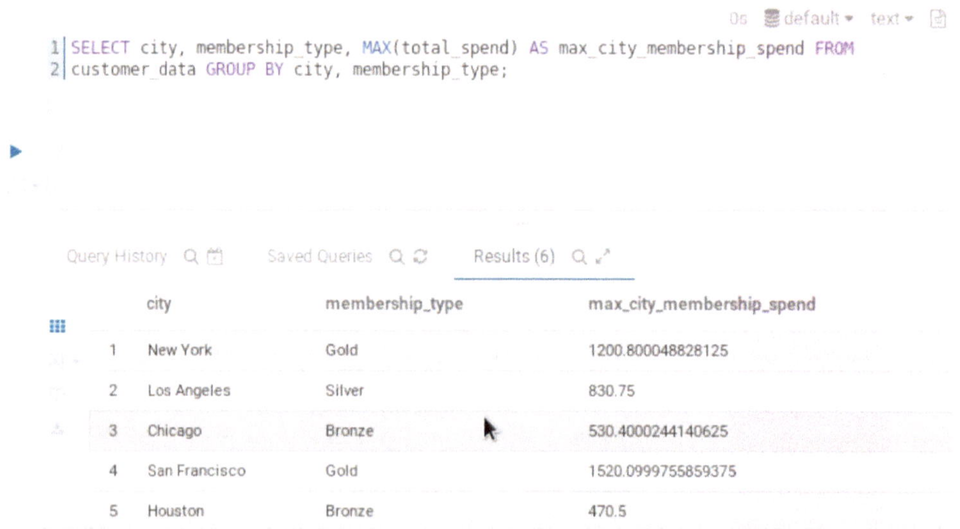

	city	membership_type	max_city_membership_spend
1	New York	Gold	1200.800048828125
2	Los Angeles	Silver	830.75
3	Chicago	Bronze	530.4000244140625
4	San Francisco	Gold	1520.0999755859375
5	Houston	Bronze	470.5

Figure 10.51: *Nested aggregation with grouping*

Conclusion

This chapter provided a practical guide to working with Apache Hive, focusing on data manipulation and querying tasks. It started with instructions on using the Hive shell, Beeline, and graphical interfaces like Hue in Cloudera, followed by an introduction to key DDL commands, such as creating, altering, and managing tables. The chapter also covered DML commands for loading data, inserting records, and performing joins. It also explained aggregation functions like COUNT, SUM, AVG, MIN, and MAX, which allow users to summarize data efficiently. The use of the GROUP BY clause to organize results and the HAVING clause to filter aggregated data was also discussed. Techniques like partitioning (static and dynamic) and clustering (bucketing) were discussed to optimize data storage and retrieval, with an emphasis on combining these techniques for better performance in large datasets.

In the next chapter, you will learn about Apache HBase, a non-relational (NoSQL) database that is designed to handle large amounts of structured data across many commodity servers.

Points to remember

The following list outlines the key takeaway from this chapter:

- Hive is a data warehousing tool built on top of Hadoop that allows users to query and manage large datasets using an SQL-like language.
- Hue is a web-based graphical interface that simplifies managing, querying, and visualizing Hive data without using the command line.
- In Cloudera, the Hive shell can be started from the terminal by executing the Hive command, allowing users to run Hive queries interactively.
- **Running DDL commands**:
    - **CREATE**: Used to create new tables or databases in Hive.
    - **SHOW**: Displays information such as available databases or tables.
    - **ALTER**: Modifies the structure of an existing table, such as adding or renaming columns.
    - **DESCRIBE**: Provides metadata information about a table or column.
    - **TRUNCATE**: Removes all data from a table without deleting the table itself.
    - **DELETE**: Deletes records from a table based on a condition.
- **Running DML commands**:
    - **LOAD**: Loads data into a Hive table from an external file.
    - **INSERT**: Inserts new records into an existing Hive table.
    - **COUNT**: Returns the number of rows in a table or matching a query condition.
    - **DROP**: Deletes tables, databases, or other objects from Hive.
    - **Partitioned By**: Organizes tables into partitions based on column values for efficient querying.
    - **Clustered By**: Divides data into buckets for faster data access and processing.
    - **AGGREGATION**: Summarizes data using functions like SUM(), AVG(), COUNT(), etc.
    - **GROUPING**: Groups data by specific columns to apply aggregate functions.
    - **JOIN**: Combines records from multiple tables based on a related column.

Multiple choice questions

1. **What is Apache Hive primarily used for?**
   a. Machine learning
   b. Real-time data processing
   c. Data warehousing and querying large datasets
   d. Web development
2. **Which command is used to start the Hive shell in Cloudera?**
   a. hive-shell
   b. hive
   c. start-hive
   d. run-hive
3. **Which of the following is a DDL command in Hive?**
   a. INSERT
   b. LOAD
   c. CREATE
   d. COUNT
4. **What does the TRUNCATE command do in Hive?**
   a. Deletes the entire table
   b. Removes all data from a table without deleting the table
   c. Deletes specific records from a table
   d. Drops a database
5. **In Hive, which command would you use to display metadata information about a table?**
   a. DESCRIBE
   b. SHOW
   c. ALTER
   d. COUNT
6. **What is the purpose of the PARTITIONED BY clause in Hive?**
   a. To delete partitions of a table
   b. To divide the table into logical partitions based on column values
   c. c) To cluster the table data into buckets
   d. To aggregate the data
7. **What is the purpose of the GROUP BY clause in Hive?**
   a. To join multiple tables
   b. To filter rows based on a condition
   c. To group rows with the same values in specified columns for aggregation
   d. To cluster data into buckets
8. **Which Hive command is used to combine records from multiple tables based on a related column?**
   a. GROUP BY
   b. JOIN
   c. AGGREGATION
   d. INSERT
9. **What does the AGGREGATION operation in Hive allow you to do?**
   a. Combine rows from two tables
   b. Summarize data using functions like SUM() or AVG()
   c. Load data into Hive tables
   d. Create partitions for efficient querying

10. **Which of the following is not a valid DML command in Hive?**
    a. INSERT
    b. LOAD
    c. SHOW
    d. DROP

Answers

1. c.	2. b.	3. c.	4. b.	5. a.
6. b.	7. c.	8. b.	9. b.	10. c.

Questions

1. Explain the difference between static and dynamic partitioning in Hive. In which scenarios would you prefer one over the other?
2. What is bucketing in Hive, and how does it differ from partitioning? How does combining partitioning and bucketing improve query performance?
3. Describe the role of the GROUP BY and HAVING clauses in Hive. How are they used together in querying large datasets?
4. Create a Hive table to store sales data with the following columns: order_id, customer_id, product_id, sales_amount, and order_date. Use the PARTITIONED BY clause to partition the table by order_date. Write a query to load sample data into this table.
5. Write a Hive query to calculate the total sales and the average sales amount per product from a table containing sales data. Use the GROUP BY clause to group the results by product_id.
6. Given a Hive table customer_transactions with columns customer_id, transaction_amount, and transaction_date, write a query to find the top 5 customers who have spent the most overall.
7. You are working with a large dataset that is both partitioned by year and bucketed by customer ID. Write a query that calculates the total revenue for a specific year while ensuring efficient querying using both partitioning and bucketing.
8. Write a Hive query that joins two tables: customers (with columns customer_id, customer_name) and orders (with columns order_id, customer_id, order_date, order_amount). Return a list of customers and their total order amount.
9. Write a query to delete all records from a Hive table where the order_date is earlier than January 1, 2022, without deleting the table itself. Ensure that only specific records are removed.
10. Create a Hive table employee_data and bucket it into 4 buckets based on employee_id. Write a query to load data into this table and verify that the data is properly distributed across buckets.

CHAPTER 11
Data Storage and Processing Using HBase

Numbers have an important story to tell. They rely on you to give them a clear and convincing voice.

-Stephen Few

Introduction

This chapter introduces HBase, a distributed and scalable database that can store large amounts of data in a column-oriented format. The chapter explains the need for HBase for big data analytics and the differences between HBase and traditional **relational database management systems** (**RDBMS**). It also covers the physical model, data organization, architecture, and data storage model of HBase. It describes the roles and functions of the main components of HBase, such as the HBase master, regions, region servers, and clients. It also explains how data is organized in tables, rows, columns, values, keys, and column families in HBase. The next part of the chapter demonstrates how to use the HBase shell in Cloudera to perform various data management operations, such as creating, listing, describing, altering, dropping, enabling, disabling, counting, putting, getting, deleting, truncating, and scanning tables. The chapter concludes with an example of designing and developing a stock market data application using HBase.

Structure

In this chapter, we will cover the following topics:

- Introduction to HBase
- HBase architecture
- HBase vs. RDBMS
- HBase applications and use cases

Objectives

At the end of this chapter, you will understand the fundamental concepts of HBase and will be able to differentiate between HBase and traditional RDBMS in terms of architecture, data organization, and scalability. Additionally, you will gain insights into HBase's physical data model, including how data is organized in tables, rows, columns, and column families. You will also comprehend the roles and functions of key HBase components such as the HBase master, regions, region servers, and clients. Furthermore, you will be equipped with the skills to use the HBase shell in Cloudera to perform various data management operations like creating, altering, and scanning tables. Lastly, you will be able to design and develop practical applications, such as a stock market data application, using HBase.

Introduction to HBase

HBase is a column-oriented, **non-relational database** (**NoSQL**), distributed database developed on top of the Hadoop file system. *NoSQL* here means it does not support **structured query language** (**SQL**) as its primary access language, like RDBMS. It is an open-source project that is modeled after *Google's Bigtable* and utilizes the **Hadoop Distributed File System** (**HDFS**) as its storage layer. It is designed to provide random, real-time read/write access to massive amounts of structured data. HBase is beneficial for handling large datasets in environments where scalability and fault tolerance are critical, such as data warehousing, search engines, and analytics applications. HBase is often integrated with various components of the Hadoop ecosystem, such as *MapReduce*, *Apache Hive*, and *Apache Spark*, for performing distributed data processing and analytics. The key characteristics of HBase are as follows:

- **Column-oriented storage**: HBase is a column-family-oriented database, which means data is stored in columns rather than rows (as in traditional relational databases like MySQL). In HBase, data is grouped into column families. Each column family can contain multiple columns, and each row in HBase can have a different number of columns. This type of structure is efficient for storing sparse datasets, where not every row has a value for every column, e.g., in a dataset about users, some users might have an email address, while others do not. With a column-oriented system, HBase only stores the email addresses that exist, rather than leaving empty fields (as you would in a relational table), which makes it storage efficient. This structure also provides efficient retrieval, for example, when querying for specific columns, HBase can quickly retrieve only the relevant data instead of scanning full rows. Consider a database of customer information outlined in *Table 11.1*. In a row-oriented system, all fields (ID, Name, Age, Email) for each customer are stored together in a row. This makes it efficient to retrieve all the information about a single customer, like *Teana*, since the entire row is stored contiguously. In a column-oriented database, data is stored column by column. Each column's values for all rows are stored together. This structure is more efficient when you often need to query just a few columns from large datasets. Thus, row-oriented databases are more efficient if you frequently access all details about individual customers (e.g., for user profiles), whereas column-oriented databases are best suited for analytics and reporting applications where you query specific columns like retrieving averages, sums, or filtering by specific fields, etc. Examples include *Apache HBase*, *Google Bigtable*, *Cassandra*, and *Amazon Redshift*, which are column oriented.

<table>
<tr><th>ID</th><th>Name</th><th>Age</th><th>Email</th></tr>
<tr><td>1</td><td>Ram</td><td>23</td><td>Ram@gmail.com</td></tr>
<tr><td>2</td><td>Teana</td><td>18</td><td>teana@gmail.com</td></tr>
<tr><td>3</td><td>Aayush</td><td>20</td><td>aayush@gmail.com</td></tr>
<tr><td>4</td><td>Rajesh</td><td>35</td><td>rajesh@gmail.com</td></tr>
<tr><th colspan="2">Row oriented</th><th colspan="2">Column oriented</th></tr>
<tr><td colspan="2">1. Ram, 23, Ram@gmail.com
2. Teana, 18, teana@gmail.com
3. Aayush,20, aayush@gmail.com</td><td colspan="2">Column: ID - [1, 2, 3]
Column: Name - [Ram, Teana, Aayush]
Column: Age - [23,18,20]
Column: Email - [teana@gmail.com, aayush@gmail.com, rajesh@gmail.com</td></tr>
</table>

***Table 11.1**: Database of customer information*

- **Real-time read/write access**: HBase provides low latency reads and writes, which implies data can be accessed and updated in near real-time. This is achieved by distributing the data across multiple nodes (servers), allowing parallel reads and writes. HBase stores data in memory (using memstore) before writing it to HDFS. HBase supports random reads/writes, which enables you to query or update any specific row or column without scanning through all data. For example, in a social media platform, you might want to update a user's profile in real-time or retrieve their latest messages as they arrive. HBase's real-time capabilities make this possible.

- **Scalability**: HBase is designed to scale horizontally, so as the data grows, you can add more servers (nodes) to the cluster, which is cost-effective, rather than upgrading existing machines (vertical scaling). HBase leverages region servers that manage different portions of the dataset. As data grows, it splits into regions, and these regions can be distributed across multiple servers. For example, imagine an e-commerce platform like *eBay* with millions of product listings. As more products are added, the system can scale horizontally by adding more nodes to store and serve the data.
- **Fault-tolerance**: HBase achieves fault tolerance by leveraging HDFS, which is designed to handle hardware failures without data loss. HDFS splits data into blocks and stores multiple copies (replicas) of each block across different nodes. Thus, if one node fails, another replica takes over to provide seamless access to the data. HBase's architecture also includes automatic failover mechanisms for region servers. If a region server fails, the data it manages can be redistributed to other servers, minimizing downtime. For example, in a financial trading system, where high availability is critical, even if a few servers fail, HBase ensures that the data is still accessible and transactions can continue uninterrupted.

Need for HBase

Apache HBase is part of the Hadoop ecosystem and is designed to overcome the various limitations of MapReduce for big data analysis. The details are as follows:

- **Real-time data access vs. batch processing**: The MapReduce framework is primarily used for batch processing and is suitable for large-scale, offline data processing tasks. It processes data in large batches, which can be time-consuming, and is not optimized for real-time interactions. On the other hand, HBase provides real-time random read/write access to large datasets. It supports quick, low-latency operations like inserting, reading, updating, and deleting data in real-time.
- **Random vs. sequential data access**: MapReduce is optimized for sequential access, where large chunks of data are processed from start to finish, which makes it ideal for batch processing tasks but not suitable for real-time data processing applications. HBase overcomes this challenge by providing random access to data, which means you can quickly retrieve specific rows or columns without scanning the entire dataset. This is particularly useful for applications like databases, where specific data needs to be accessed frequently.
- **Schema flexibility vs. defined data processing**: MapReduce requires predefined input and output formats, making it less flexible in terms of handling varying data structures. MapReduce jobs often need custom code to handle schema evolution or data format changes. On the other hand, HBase provides schema flexibility, which allows you to store semi-structured and unstructured data. It is well-suited for datasets where the structure may evolve over time.
- **Latency vs. throughput**: MapReduce prioritizes throughput over latency as it is designed to process large amounts of data efficiently rather than quickly responding to individual requests. The primary focus of HBase is on low-latency operations, which ensure fast data retrieval and updates. It is built for high-speed access and is well-suited for applications that require fast response times (e.g., querying a user's profile from millions of records).
- **Interactive applications vs. long-running jobs**: MapReduce is designed for long-running jobs that process large volumes of data at once, such as **extract, transform, load** (**ETL**) processes, large-scale data analysis, or data aggregation tasks. Whereas HBase is ideal for interactive applications that need to read/write data on demand, such as web applications, recommendation systems, or real-time dashboards.

- **Data storage model**: MapReduce relies on HDFS for storing the data. HDFS is optimized for storing large blocks of sequential data, which makes it less efficient for sparse datasets or scenarios where data needs to be retrieved in smaller pieces. HBase uses a column-family-oriented data storage model that makes it easy to store sparse datasets (where many columns may be empty) efficiently. This is highly beneficial for applications (recommender systems, social network analysis, etc) where many fields are blank in numerous records.
- **Handling high-volume and high-velocity data**: MapReduce is designed to work on batches of static data that have already been stored. This makes it unsuitable for high-velocity, continuously updating datasets. HBase can ingest high-velocity data in real-time, so it becomes an ideal choice for streaming data applications like social media feeds, **Internet of Things (IoT)** sensor data, or time-series data.

HBase data model

The HBase data model is a column-oriented, schema-less model designed for flexibility and scalability. It is suitable for handling large amounts of structured and semi-structured data. This model is specially designed to provide efficient reads and writes across massive datasets distributed over a cluster of servers. In HBase, data is stored in a table-based structure that is highly scalable and optimized for real-time read and write operations. Each table is made up of rows, uniquely identified by a row key, and each row contains multiple columns grouped into column families. This flexible schema allows HBase to efficiently manage large volumes of sparse, distributed, and semi-structured data across clusters of commodity servers.

Let us understand the key components of the HBase data model using a case study on a real-world example of a social media platform that stores user profiles, posts, and interactions (likes, comments, and shares) in HBase. It needs to handle a high volume of data with efficient real-time access for queries such as viewing a user's profile, retrieving recent posts, and checking interactions on each post, as discussed in the following list:

- **Tables**: In HBase, data is organized in the form of tables, similar to traditional databases. Each table is made up of rows and columns, but with a flexible, schema-less structure. Tables are stored in a distributed manner across a cluster of servers, which enables horizontal scalability and fault tolerance. While creating a table in HBase, you need to define the column families. Columns within these families can be added dynamically. This property makes HBase schema-less with respect to individual columns. In a social media application, assume we have three HBase tables, where *Table 11.2* stores basic information about each user:

Row key	Column family: info	Column family: settings
user_1234	**Name:** Teana	**privacy_level:** public
	Email: teana@gmail.com	**notification_preference:** email
	Age:18	
	Location: Delhi	

Table 11.2: *User_profiles*

Table 11.3, which contains the posts created by users:

Row key	Column family: content	Column family : metadata
user_1234_202401010830	**Text:** *Had a great time at the park!*	**Timestamp:** 2024-01-01 08:30
	Media_url: http://media.example.com/pic.jpg	**Location:** Central Park, NYC

Table 11.3: *user_posts*

Table 11.4 tracks interactions (like, comment, share) on each post:

Row key	Column family: content
post_5678_like_user_1234	**User_id**: user_1234
	Timestamp: 2024-01-02 10:45
post_5678_comment_user_4321	**User_id**: user_4321
	Timestamp: 2024-01-02 10:50
	Comment_text: *Great post!*

Table 11.4: *post_interactions*

- **Rows and row keys**: In HBase Table, each row is uniquely identified by a row key, which determines its position within the table. Row keys are byte arrays that allow arbitrary data (like integers, strings, or composite keys) to be used as keys. Row keys are sorted lexicographically, which affects the access patterns. For efficient querying, row keys are often designed with application-specific patterns that align with the intended access patterns. For example, in the **`user_profile`**, as shown in *Table 11.1*, the row key is **`user_id`** (e.g., **`user_1234`**), which provides quick access to a specific user's profile. In **`user_posts`**, as shown in *Table 11.3*, a composite row key is created using **`user_id`** and timestamp to support efficient retrieval of recent posts by each user (e.g., **`user_1234_202401010830`**). Similarly, in **`post_interactions`**, as shown in *Table 11.4*. The row key is a combination of **`post_id`** and **`interaction_type`**, with **`user_id`** appended to distinguish interactions from different users. This design allows HBase to efficiently store and retrieve specific interactions (likes, comments, shares) for each post.
- **Column families**: In HBase, column families are defined during table creation, and they represent the primary unit of physical storage. All columns are grouped into column families. As shown in *Table 11.2*, column families **info** and **settings** logically group profile data and user settings. Similarly, the **content** column family stores post-specific information like text and media, while the **metadata** column family holds additional information, enabling selective reads based on the type of data needed. The **info** column family holds interaction-specific details, such as the user ID and timestamp for likes and comments, as well as the text of each comment, when applicable. All columns within a column family are stored together on disk. This structure enables HBase to retrieve only the relevant columns and helps to improve performance for column-oriented queries. You should choose the column families judiciously, as each family is stored separately on disk and requires its own in-memory structures. Creation of too many column families can lead to inefficient memory usage and performance degradation.
- **Columns and column qualifiers**: Unlike relational databases, columns are not predefined and can vary from row to row. *Table 11.4* has variable columns. This table stores different types of interactions (like, comment, share) on posts, which may require different columns based on the interaction type. For example, likes might only require **`user_id`** and **timestamp**. Comments might require additional columns like **`comment_text`**. This variability enables HBase to efficiently store and retrieve only the required columns for each type of interaction, avoiding the need for a fixed schema. This flexibility also empowers HBase to handle semi-structured or evolving data easily. Columns within a column family are identified by column qualifiers, which are also byte arrays and can be assigned dynamically. For example, in the **`user_profiles`** table, the **info** column family includes qualifiers like **`name`**, **`email`**, **`age`**, and **`location`**. In the **`user_posts`** table, the **content** column family has qualifiers like **text** and **`media_url`**. Similarly, the **metadata** column family has qualifiers such as **timestamp** and **location**. Qualifiers give each column family the flexibility to store structured data without enforcing a fixed schema across all rows.
- **Cells and timestamps**: A cell is the smallest unit of data in HBase. It represents a value stored at the intersection of a row key and a column (column family and qualifier). Each cell has an associated timestamp, which allows multiple versions of data to be stored and retrieved based on need.

By default, HBase stores cell versions in descending order, with the latest version returned first. This feature is very useful for applications that require historical data or time-series storage. HBase assigns timestamps automatically when data is written. However, custom timestamps can be set by clients, allowing specific versioning schemes or retention policies.

HBase architecture

The architecture of HBase presents various components and their interactions in the system. It defines how HBase operates within a distributed environment and handles the requests for data processing. It consists of servers that are in a master-slave relationship, as shown in *Figure 11.1*. The HBase cluster has one master node, called **HMaster**, and multiple region servers called **HRegionServer**. Each Region Server contains multiple regions known as **HRegions**. Similar to RDBMS, data in HBase is stored in tables, and these tables are stored in regions. When the size of the table becomes too big, it is partitioned into multiple regions. These regions are assigned to region servers across the cluster. Each region server usually hosts the same number of regions.

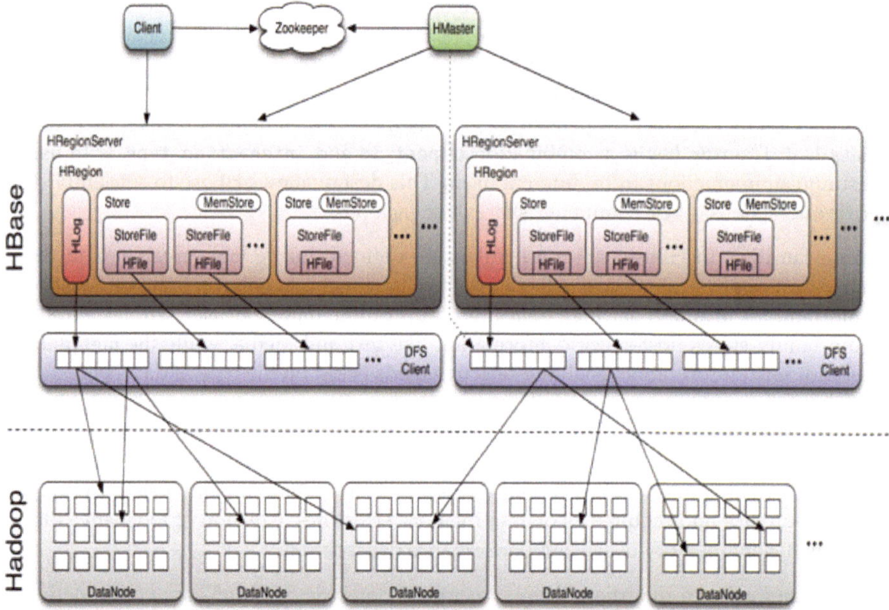

***Figure 11.1**: HBase architecture*

Let us now understand the detailed working of each component:

- **HBase architecture—HMaster**: The HMaster is a primary node that is responsible for managing the entire HBase cluster. As shown in *Figure 11.1*, HMaster handles a collection of region servers that reside on DataNodes. It assigns regions to region servers and keeps track of where data is stored. It is to be noted that the HMaster node is not involved directly in read and write operations. Instead, it manages and coordinates the region servers that handle the actual data operations. It performs load balancing across region servers to ensure even distribution of data. HMaster maintains metadata information, such as schema and configuration of tables and column families, to ensure that region servers access the latest configurations. HMaster monitors all the region servers' instances in the cluster (with the help of ZooKeeper) and, in case of a region server failure, it reassigns regions to other healthy servers to ensure data availability and fault tolerance.

- **HBase architecture—Region servers**: Region servers are the core nodes responsible for handling client read and write requests. Each region server hosts one or more regions, each of which holds data for a specific range of rows in a table. Regions are further divided into *stores* and *store files*. Region server also processes client requests and interacts with HDFS to store and retrieve data. The read and write operations, like Get, Scan, Put, Delete, and other client operations, are processed by the region server only. The various tasks performed by region servers are illustrated in the following figure:

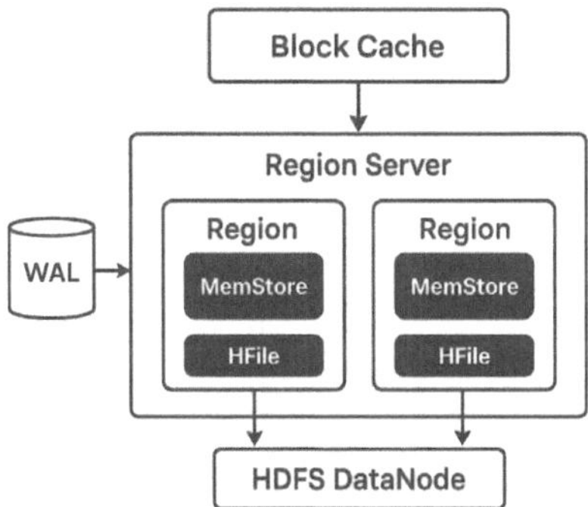

***Figure 11.2**: Components of the region server*

- **Region management**: A region is a contiguous range of rows in a HBase table, storing data between a start key and an end key. HBase tables are divided into a number of regions in such a way that all the columns of a column family are stored in one region. All rows in a region are stored in a sorted order. A region has a default size of 256 MB, which can be configured according to need. As data grows above the configured size, regions are split further into two smaller regions. A group of regions is served to the clients by a region server. A region server can serve approximately 1000 regions to the client. Regions are assigned to region servers by the HMaster. Region servers periodically report their status to the HMaster to provide information about regions load, health, and resource utilization.

  The mapping of regions to the region server is kept in a system table called **.META**. This table is treated like other HBase tables. Each row in the .META table contains metadata, such as the region name, start key, end key, region server information, and the name of the table to which the region belongs. The HMaster relies on the .META table for managing region assignments and monitoring the state of the cluster. Region servers use .META table entries to ensure that regions are correctly assigned and also update metadata when regions are split or moved. When trying to read or write data from HBase, clients query the .META table to locate the region containing the target row key. If the .META table itself is split into multiple regions; clients first use ZooKeeper to locate the region server hosting the .META table and then directly communicate with the appropriate region server to perform read or write operations.

- **Write operations in region servers**: When a client sends a write request (e.g., a Put operation), it is first received by the ZooKeeper to locate the region server that holds the region containing the target row. Once located, the client communicates directly with the appropriate region server. The region server first writes the incoming data to the **write-ahead log (WAL)**. The WAL is an append-only file attached to every region server stored on HDFS. HBase ensures durability via this method. If the region server crashes, the WAL can be replayed to recover any unflushed data. After writing to the WAL, the data is added to the **MemStore**, which is an in-memory storage layer associated with each column family. MemStore holds the data temporarily in memory for fast access before it is persisted to disk as **HFiles**. When the MemStore reaches a configured size threshold (e.g., 64 MB), its contents are flushed to disk and stored as an HFile. HFile is the actual on-disk storage format for HBase data, which is stored on HDFS. HFiles are immutable and contain the final, persistent representation of data after it is flushed from MemStore. Region servers mainly rely on

HDFS for data persistence. The WAL is also stored on HDFS to ensure durability and recovery in case of crashes. Each column family in a region has its own MemStore and corresponding HFiles.

- **Read operations in region servers**: When a client sends a read request (e.g., a Get or Scan operation), ZooKeeper is used to determine the location of the region server responsible for the requested data. The client then directly communicates with the identified region server. The region server first checks the **MemStore** for the requested data. MemStore holds the latest, in-memory data that has not yet been flushed to disk. If the data is not found in MemStore, the region server looks into the **HFiles** stored on **HDFS**. Once the data is located (from either MemStore or HFiles), it is returned to the client. Depending on the data layout and versions, multiple HFiles may need to be read and merged to provide the final result. To optimize the read operation:
    - **Bloom filters** are used to quickly determine whether a specific key exists in an HFile to avoid unnecessary disk reads.

      Frequently accessed data is cached in memory (using the **block cache**) to speed up subsequent reads. Block cache resides at the top of the region server. If the data in the block cache is least recently used, then that data is removed from the block cache.
- **Compactions**: Compactions are an essential maintenance task being performed by region servers to optimize storage and improve read performance. The two types of compactions performed by region servers are as follows:
    - **Minor compaction**: The consolidation of smaller HFiles into a larger HFile without deleting any data is called minor compaction. It helps in reducing the number of HFiles and hence minimizes the overhead during read operations.
    - **Major compaction**: The merging of all HFiles for a region into a single file is termed major compaction. During this process, deleted data (tombstones) and old versions exceeding the configured limit are removed.
- **Fault tolerance and recovery**: If a region server fails, ZooKeeper detects the failure and informs the HMaster. The HMaster reassigns the affected regions to other region servers. The WAL stored in HDFS is replayed to recover any unflushed data.
- **Monitoring and communication**: Region servers send periodic heartbeats to the HMaster to report their status, such as region loads (e.g., number of regions handled, size), Resource utilization (**central processing unit** (**CPU**), memory, disk I/O), etc. The HMaster uses this information for load balancing, reassigning regions as and when required.
- **HBase architecture—ZooKeeper**: ZooKeeper is the backbone of HBase's distributed coordination. It plays an important role in ensuring consistency, fault tolerance, and synchronization. ZooKeeper acts as a centralized registry for the HBase cluster, which maintains information about the state of the HMaster and region servers. The various tasks performed by ZooKeeper in HBase are:
    - **HMaster management**: HBase relies on ZooKeeper for managing the HMaster node. There exists only one active HMaster at a time. If the active HMaster fails, ZooKeeper coordinates the failover to a backup HMaster, as shown in *Figure 11.3*. It maintains a special **ZooKeeper node** (**znode**) to track the currently active HMaster.

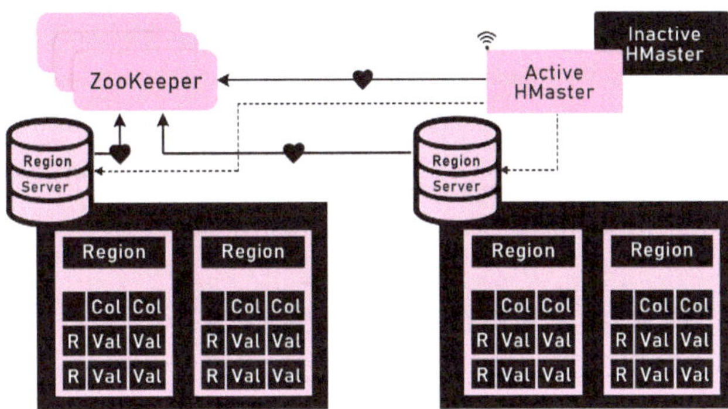

***Figure 11.3** :HMaster management*

- **Region server management**: When region servers start, they register themselves with ZooKeeper. This process creates znodes for each region server, which ZooKeeper uses to track their status. ZooKeeper monitors the health of region servers through heartbeat signals. If a heartbeat is missed, ZooKeeper marks the server as failed. When a region server fails, ZooKeeper notifies the HMaster. The HMaster then reassigns the regions managed by the failed server to other active servers.
- **Metadata management**: ZooKeeper stores metadata about the .META table and the ROOT region (used in earlier versions of HBase; now merged into .META). Clients query ZooKeeper to locate the region server hosting the .META table, which is crucial for mapping row keys to regions.
- **Failure detection and recovery**: ZooKeeper continuously monitors the state of all HBase components. When a failure is detected (e.g., a region server crash or HMaster failure), ZooKeeper triggers recovery actions, such as:
  - Informs the HMaster about the failure.
  - Coordinates with backup HMasters for failover.
- **Distributed locking**: ZooKeeper also ensures that distributed operations like schema changes, table splits, or compactions are synchronized and do not conflict with each other. For example, when a table is being split or regions are reassigned, ZooKeeper prevents other operations from interfering by using distributed locks.
- **ZooKeeper data structure in HBase**: ZooKeeper organizes its data in a hierarchical tree structure of znodes. Key znodes used by HBase include:
  - **/hbase/master**: Tracks the active HMaster.
  - **/hbase/regionserver**: Contains znodes for each active region server.
  - **/hbase/meta-region-server**: Tracks the region server hosting the .META table.
  - **/hbase/recovery**: Used for failover and recovery mechanisms.

HBase vs. RDBMS

HBase and RDBMS are both used for storing and managing data, but they cater to different types of use cases due to their architectural differences. The following table provides a detailed comparison:

Aspect	HBase	RDBMS
Structure	NoSQL database with column-family-based data.	Table-based with rows and columns.
Schema	Schema-less, flexible column families.	The schema is predefined and rigid.
Data storage	Sparse, hierarchical storage in key-value pairs.	Row-oriented structured data.
Primary unit	Row key (unique identifier).	Primary key (unique identifier).

Table 11.5: Comparison of HBase with RDBMS

HBase applications and use cases

Some real-life applications of HBase across industries are as follows:

- **Social media and networking**: *Facebook* and *LinkedIn* use HBase to manage massive datasets, such as user profiles, activity logs, and social graphs.
- **E-commerce and retail**: *Flipkart* or *Amazon* uses HBase to store and query user interaction data for delivering personalized product recommendations. It is also used to track millions of **stock keeping units** (**SKUs**) with details like stock levels and pricing.
- **Finance and banking**: Banks use HBase to store transaction logs, analyze patterns, and identify anomalies in real-time. HBase is also used to maintain extensive credit history and other customer data for loan approvals and credit scoring. It is suitable for processing millions of transactions per second during peak financial trading hours.
- **Telecommunications**: Telecom operators like *Verizon* use HBase to store and analyze billions of call and data records for billing, compliance, and analytics. It is also used for real-time tracking of network performance metrics.
- **Healthcare**: Hospitals use HBase for storing **electronic health records** (**EHR**), which include clinical notes, imaging data, and test results. It is used in Genomic research to analyze and store massive genetic sequencing data.
- **Streaming platforms**: *Netflix* and *Spotify* store metadata for millions of movies, songs, and user preferences, which is used to generate dynamic playlists and deliver optimized video quality.

Start HBase shell in Cloudera

To start the HBase shell in Cloudera, follow these steps:

1. **Ensure HBase is running**: Log into your Cloudera Manager interface and verify that the HBase service is up and running. If it is not, start it from Cloudera Manager.
2. **Access the terminal**: Open a terminal on the Cloudera environment (directly on the Cloudera virtual machine).
3. **Start the HBase shell**: Enter the `hbase shell` command to start the HBase shell. Once the shell starts, you should see a prompt as shown in *Figure 11.4*:

```
[cloudera@quickstart ~]$ hbase shell
2024-11-16 22:22:12,327 INFO  [main] Configuration.deprecation: hadoop.native.li
b is deprecated. Instead, use io.native.lib.available
HBase Shell; enter 'help<RETURN>' for list of supported commands.
Type "exit<RETURN>" to leave the HBase Shell
Version 1.2.0-cdh5.13.0, rUnknown, Wed Oct  4 11:16:18 PDT 2017

hbase(main):001:0>
```

***Figure 11.4**: HBase shell*

Perform basic operations in the shell

Let us learn to perform the basic operations and analysis of data in HBase with the help of a case study on stock data analysis.

Create

It is used to create a new table in HBase. The general syntax is:

```
create '<table_name>', '<column_family_1>', '<column_family_2>',…….
```

<table_name> is the position to specify the name of the table. It should be unique within the HBase namespace. **<column_family>** refers to the user-defined name of the column family to be specified by you. A column family groups related columns. Each column family must be specified during table creation and cannot be added later without re-creating the table. Other additional options you can specify are **'VERSIONS'**, which refer to the number of versions of a column to retain. **'BLOOMFILTER'** to indicate the type of bloom filter to use, and **'TTL'**, which is the **time-to-live** (TTL) for the data in seconds.

In the following example, we have created a table with the name **stocks_prices** with two column families, **"info"** and **"adjusted"**, to store stock-related data as shown in *Figure 11.5*. Column family **'info'** will be used for grouping columns like **open_price**, **high_price**, etc. and **'adjusted'** column family will be used to group columns related to adjusted stock prices (e.g., **adj_close_price**).

Example: **create 'stock_prices', 'info', 'adjusted'**

```
hbase(main):068:0> create 'stock_prices', 'info','adjusted'
0 row(s) in 1.2270 seconds

=> Hbase::Table - stock_prices
```

***Figure 11.5**: create table command for stock_prices*

Put

The put command is used in HBase to add or update data in a specific table. The general syntax is:

```
put '<table_name>', '<row_key>', '<column_family:column_qualifier>', '<value>'
```

<table_name> refers to the name of the HBase table (e.g., **stock_prices**), **<row_key>** is a unique identifier for a row, e.g., a combination of values (e.g., ticker + date) to ensure uniqueness. **<column_family:column_qualifier>** defines where the data is stored. The **column_family** groups data logically, and **column_qualifier** specifies the exact field; **<value>** is the actual data to store in the specified cell. Let us now use the **'put'** command to insert data into the **"stock_prices"** table.

The following commands insert data for the **'info'** column family, which includes fields like **open_price**, **high_price**, **low_price**, **close_price**, and **volume**, and the **'adjusted'** column family, which includes only one field, **adj_close_price**, as shown in *Figure 11.6*.

```
put 'stock_prices', 'A_2007-03-01', 'info:open_price', '31.15'
put 'stock_prices', 'A_2007-03-01', 'info:high_price', '31.66'
put 'stock_prices', 'A_2007-03-01', 'info:low_price', '30.81'
put 'stock_prices', 'A_2007-03-01', 'info:close_price', '31.44'
put 'stock_prices', 'A_2007-03-01', 'info:volume', '2909300.0'
```

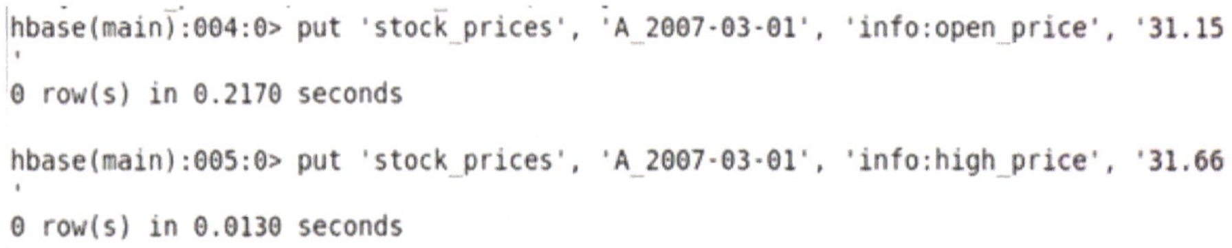

```
hbase(main):004:0> put 'stock_prices', 'A_2007-03-01', 'info:open_price', '31.15
'
0 row(s) in 0.2170 seconds

hbase(main):005:0> put 'stock_prices', 'A_2007-03-01', 'info:high_price', '31.66
'
0 row(s) in 0.0130 seconds
```

***Figure 11.6:** Usage of put command for info column family*

Similarly, we can add multiple records for the **'info'** column family. For the **'adjusted'** column family, insert adjusted closing prices for the same records created above. The same row key indicates the same row for respective column families. *Figure 11.7* shows the insertion of a record for the **'adjusted'** column family using the **'put'** command:

```
put 'stock_prices', 'A_2007-03-01', 'adjusted:adj_close_price', '29.965363317911'
```

```
hbase(main):020:0> put 'stock_prices', 'A_2007-03-01', 'adjusted:adj_close_price', '29.96536
3317911'
0 row(s) in 0.0660 seconds

hbase(main):021:0> put 'stock_prices', 'A_2007-03-02', 'adjusted:adj_close_price', '29.27913
3623608'
0 row(s) in 0.0330 seconds

hbase(main):022:0> put 'stock_prices', 'A_2007-03-03', 'adjusted:adj_close_price', '29.43156
6273693'
0 row(s) in 0.0210 seconds
```

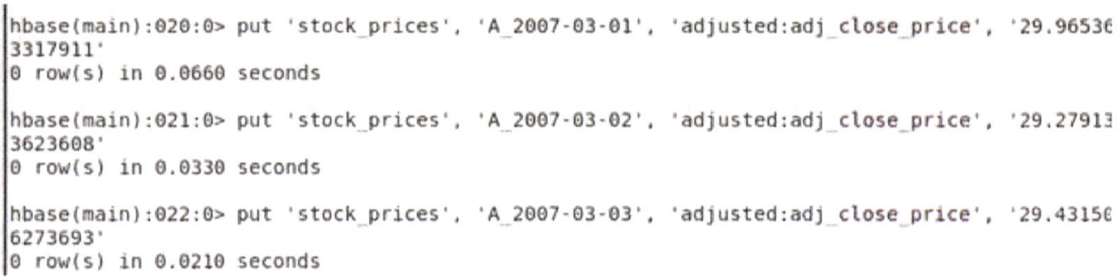

***Figure 11.7:** Usage of put command for adjusted column family*

Logical view of data in HBase: HBase stores data in rows identified by row keys, and data is grouped into column families. Each column family can have multiple columns (column qualifiers). After executing put commands, a logical view of the data stored in the **stock_prices** table is outlined in *Table 11.6*. For all records, each row key will represent a unique stock and date combination (e.g., **A_2007-03-01**, **A_2007-03-02**, etc.), with data spread across the info and adjusted column families. The following table will grow row-by-row, but the schema remains the same:

Row key	Column family (info)	Column qualifier	Value	Column family (adjusted)	Column qualifier	Value
A_2007-03-01	info	Open_price	31.15	adjusted	adj_close_price	29.965363317911
		High_price	31.66			
		Low_price	30.81			
		Close_price	31.44			
		volume	2909300.0			
A_2007-03-02	info	Open_price	31.35	adjusted	adj_close_price	29.279133623608
		High_price	31.53			

Row key	Column family (info)	Column qualifier	Value	Column family (adjusted)	Column qualifier	Value
		Low_price	30.69			
		Close_price	30.72			
		volume	2455500.0			

***Table 11.6**: Logical view of the data stored in the stock_prices table*

Get

This command is used to retrieve a specific record using the row key. It fetches a specific record by its row key. Optionally, you can also retrieve specific columns. The general syntax for get commands is as follows:

Syntax: get '<table_name>', '<row_key>', {COLUMNS => ['<column_family:column_qualifier>']}

Example: **get 'stock_prices', 'A_2007-03-01'**

The following figure illustrates the use of commands to retrieve records:

```
hbase(main):056:0> get 'stock_prices', 'A_2007-03-01'
COLUMN                CELL
 adjusted:adj_close_p timestamp=1733462233154, value=29.965363317911
 rice
 info:close_price     timestamp=1733462137438, value=31.44
 info:high_price      timestamp=1733462121687, value=31.66
 info:low_price       timestamp=1733462129595, value=30.81
 info:volume          timestamp=1733462150106, value=2909300.0
5 row(s) in 0.0160 seconds
```

***Figure 11.8**: Usage of the get command to retrieve records for a key*

The preceding example retrieves all columns for row key **A_2007-03-01** using the **'get'** command.

The following example retrieves only the **high_price** from the info column family for row key **A_2007-03-01**:

Example: **get 'stock_prices', 'A_2007-03-01', {COLUMNS => ['info:high_price']}**

```
hbase(main):058:0> get 'stock_prices', 'A_2007-03-01', {COLUMNS => ['info:high_pric
e']}
COLUMN                  CELL
 info:high_price        timestamp=1733462121687, value=31.66
1 row(s) in 0.0020 seconds
```

***Figure 11.9**: Usage of get command to retrieve data of a column*

Scan

It is used to retrieve all rows from the table. You can also filter columns or rows as per application requirements. It is suitable when you need to retrieve data from multiple rows, such as when performing range queries or filtering data. *Figure 11.10* and *Figure 11.11* show the examples of **'scan'** command to retrieve all rows and filtered rows, respectively:

Syntax: **scan '<table_name>'**

Example: **scan 'stock_prices'**

```
hbase(main):036:0> scan 'stock_prices'
ROW                     COLUMN+CELL
 A_2007-03-01           column=adjusted:adj_close_price, timestamp=1733462233154, val
                        ue=29.965363317911
 A_2007-03-01           column=info:close_price, timestamp=1733462137438, value=31.44
 A_2007-03-01           column=info:high_price, timestamp=1733462121687, value=31.66
 A_2007-03-01           column=info:low_price, timestamp=1733462129595, value=30.81
 A_2007-03-01           column=info:open_price, timestamp=1733462111851, value=31.15
 A_2007-03-01           column=info:volume, timestamp=1733462150106, value=2909300.0
 A_2007-03-02           column=adjusted:adj_close_price, timestamp=1733462267913, val
                        ue=29.279133623608
 A_2007-03-02           column=info:close_price, timestamp=1733462176152, value=30.72
 A_2007-03-02           column=info:high_price, timestamp=1733462168036, value=31.53
 A_2007-03-02           column=info:low_price, timestamp=1733462170517, value=30.69
 A_2007-03-02           column=info:open_price, timestamp=1733462156298, value=31.35
 A_2007-03-02           column=info:volume, timestamp=1733462192491, value=2455500.0
 A_2007-03-03           column=adjusted:adj_close_price, timestamp=1733462273951, val
                        ue=29.431506273693
 A_2007-03-03           column=info:close_price, timestamp=1733462217700, value=30.95
 A_2007-03-03           column=info:high_price, timestamp=1733462204823, value=31.30
 A_2007-03-03           column=info:low_price, timestamp=1733462210587, value=30.50
 A_2007-03-03           column=info:open_price, timestamp=1733462198546, value=30.90
 A_2007-03-04           column=adjusted:adj_close_price, timestamp=1733462279905, val
                        ue=30.154204623432
 A_2007-03-05           column=adjusted:adj_close_price, timestamp=1733462285193, val
                        ue=30.746520154274
 A_2007-03-05           column=info:volume, timestamp=1733462223379, value=4125000.0
5 row(s) in 0.0450 seconds
```

***Figure 11.10**: Usage of scan to retrieve all records*

Example: `scan 'stock_prices', {COLUMNS => ['info:close_price', 'adjusted:adj_close_price']}`:

```
ıbase(main):052:0> scan 'stock_prices', {COLUMNS => ['info:open_price', 'adjusted:a
ıj_close_price']}
ROW                     COLUMN+CELL
 A_2007-03-01           column=adjusted:adj_close_price, timestamp=1733462233154, val
                        ue=29.965363317911
 A_2007-03-02           column=adjusted:adj_close_price, timestamp=1733462267913, val
                        ue=29.279133623608
 A_2007-03-02           column=info:open_price, timestamp=1733462156298, value=31.35
 A_2007-03-03           column=adjusted:adj_close_price, timestamp=1733462273951, val
                        ue=29.431506273693
 A_2007-03-03           column=info:open_price, timestamp=1733462198546, value=30.90
 A_2007-03-04           column=adjusted:adj_close_price, timestamp=1733462279905, val
                        ue=30.154204623432
 A_2007-03-05           column=adjusted:adj_close_price, timestamp=1733462285193, val
                        ue=30.746520154274
5 row(s) in 0.0130 seconds
```

***Figure 11.11**: Usage of scan to retrieve specific columns*

List

This command is used to list all tables in the HBase database. You can use this command to check the tables available in HBase. *Figure 11.12* shows the output of the list, where:

Syntax: `list`

Example: `list`

```
hbase(main):030:0> list
TABLE
education
stock_prices
2 row(s) in 0.0050 seconds
```

***Figure 11.12**: Output of the list command*

Describe table

It provides metadata or table schema for the specified table, including column families, versions, and storage options. It helps to understand the structure of a table. *Figure 11.13* shows the output of **'describe'** command:

Syntax: **describe '<table_name>'**

Example: **describe 'stock_prices'**

Output is as follows:

```
hbase(main):031:0> describe 'stock_prices'
Table stock_prices is ENABLED
stock_prices
COLUMN FAMILIES DESCRIPTION
{NAME => 'adjusted', DATA_BLOCK_ENCODING => 'NONE', BLOOMFILTER => 'ROW', REPLICATI
ON_SCOPE => '0', VERSIONS => '1', COMPRESSION => 'NONE', MIN_VERSIONS => '0', TTL =
> 'FOREVER', KEEP_DELETED_CELLS => 'FALSE', BLOCKSIZE => '65536', IN_MEMORY => 'fal
se', BLOCKCACHE => 'true'}
{NAME => 'info', DATA_BLOCK_ENCODING => 'NONE', BLOOMFILTER => 'ROW', REPLICATION_S
COPE => '0', VERSIONS => '1', COMPRESSION => 'NONE', MIN_VERSIONS => '0', TTL => 'F
OREVER', KEEP_DELETED_CELLS => 'FALSE', BLOCKSIZE => '65536', IN_MEMORY => 'false',
 BLOCKCACHE => 'true'}
2 row(s) in 0.0140 seconds
```

***Figure 11.13**: Output of describe command*

Disable/enable table

These commands are used to disable and enable a table. Disabling a table ensures no operations (e.g., put, get) can be performed temporarily while enabling restoration of access to the table. You can temporarily disable a table before altering its schema and re-enable it afterward. *Figure 11.14* shows the usage of **'disable'** command:

Syntax: **disable '<table_name>'**

Example: **disable 'stock_prices'**

Syntax: **enable '<table_name>'**

Example: **enable 'stock_prices'**

```
hbase(main):065:0> disable 'stock_prices'
0 row(s) in 2.2480 seconds
```

***Figure 11.14**: Usage of disable command*

Similarly, you can use **'disable_all'** or **'enable_all'** command to disable/enable all tables matching a given regex pattern. It can be used to manage multiple tables simultaneously. The following example disables/enables all tables whose names start with stock:

Syntax: **disable_all '<regex>'**

Example: `disable_all 'stock.*'`

Syntax: `enable_all '<regex>'`

Example: `enable_all 'stock.*'`

Drop /drop_all

It is used to delete a table. The table must be disabled before dropping. As shown in *Figure 11.15*, when you try to drop a table, you get an error message indicating that the table must be disabled before dropping. In *Figure 11.16*, the table is first disabled and then dropped. The same is validated by executing the **'list'** commands, which indicate that the **'stock_prices'** table is deleted:

Syntax: `drop '<table_name>'`

Example: `disable 'stock_prices'`

`drop 'stock_prices'`

```
hbase(main):060:0> drop 'stock_prices'

ERROR: Table stock_prices is enabled. Disable it first.

Drop the named table. Table must first be disabled:
  hbase> drop 't1'
  hbase> drop 'ns1:t1'
```

***Figure 11.15**: Usage of drop command showing error message*

```
hbase(main):065:0> disable 'stock_prices'
0 row(s) in 2.2480 seconds

hbase(main):066:0> drop 'stock_prices'
0 row(s) in 1.2570 seconds

hbase(main):067:0> list
TABLE
education
stock
2 row(s) in 0.0030 seconds

=> ["education", "stock"]
```

***Figure 11.16**: Usage of the drop command with successful execution*

Similarly, you can use **drop_all** to drop all tables that match a given regex pattern. However, all matching tables must be disabled first:

Syntax: `'drop_all '<regex>'`

Example: `disable_all 'stock.*' .`

`drop_all 'stock.*'`

Show filters

It shows the list of all available filters for table scans in HBase. *Figure 11.17* shows the output of this command. Filters help in narrowing down the data to be retrieved and hence improve efficiency and relevance:

Syntax: `show_filters`

Example: `show_filters`

```
hbase(main):032:0> show_filters
ColumnPrefixFilter
TimestampsFilter
PageFilter
MultipleColumnPrefixFilter
FamilyFilter
ColumnPaginationFilter
SingleColumnValueFilter
RowFilter
QualifierFilter
ColumnRangeFilter
ValueFilter
PrefixFilter
SingleColumnValueExcludeFilter
ColumnCountGetFilter
InclusiveStopFilter
DependentColumnFilter
FirstKeyOnlyFilter
KeyOnlyFilter
```

***Figure 11.17**: Usage of drop command with successful execution*

Alter schema

It is used to modify the schema of a table, such as adding or updating a column family. *Figure 11.18* shows the output of adding a new column family **'metadata'** to the table:

Syntax: `alter '<table_name>', {NAME => '<column_family>', ...}`

Example: `alter 'stock_prices', {NAME => 'metadata'}`

```
hbase(main):034:0> describe 'stock_prices'
Table stock_prices is ENABLED
stock_prices
COLUMN FAMILIES DESCRIPTION
{NAME => 'adjusted', DATA_BLOCK_ENCODING => 'NONE', BLOOMFILTER => 'ROW', REPLICATI
ON_SCOPE => '0', VERSIONS => '1', COMPRESSION => 'NONE', MIN_VERSIONS => '0', TTL =
> 'FOREVER', KEEP_DELETED_CELLS => 'FALSE', BLOCKSIZE => '65536', IN_MEMORY => 'fal
se', BLOCKCACHE => 'true'}
{NAME => 'info', DATA_BLOCK_ENCODING => 'NONE', BLOOMFILTER => 'ROW', REPLICATION_S
COPE => '0', VERSIONS => '1', COMPRESSION => 'NONE', MIN_VERSIONS => '0', TTL => 'F
OREVER', KEEP_DELETED_CELLS => 'FALSE', BLOCKSIZE => '65536', IN_MEMORY => 'false',
 BLOCKCACHE => 'true'}
{NAME => 'metadata', DATA_BLOCK_ENCODING => 'NONE', BLOOMFILTER => 'ROW', REPLICATI
ON_SCOPE => '0', COMPRESSION => 'NONE', VERSIONS => '1', TTL => 'FOREVER', MIN_VERS
IONS => '0', KEEP_DELETED_CELLS => 'FALSE', BLOCKSIZE => '65536', IN_MEMORY => 'fal
se', BLOCKCACHE => 'true'}
3 row(s) in 0.0130 seconds
```

Figure 11.18: *Usage of alter schema command*

Count

It is used to count the total number of rows in a table. *Figure 11.19* shows the output of **'count'** command for **'stock_prices'** table:

Syntax: `count '<table_name>'`

Example: `count 'stock_prices'`

```
hbase(main):035:0> count 'stock_prices'
5 row(s) in 0.0190 seconds

=> 5
```

Figure 11.19: *Usage of 'count' rows command*

Delete

It is used to delete a specific column from a row. *Figure 11.20* shows the execution of **'delete'** command and the deletion of column is verified by executing the scan command:

Syntax: `delete '<table_name>', '<row_key>', '<column_family:column_qualifier>'`

Example: `delete 'stock_prices', 'A_2007-03-01', 'info:open_price'`

```
hbase(main):037:0> delete 'stock_prices', 'A_2007-03-01', 'info:open_price'
0 row(s) in 0.0170 seconds

hbase(main):038:0> scan 'stock_prices'
ROW                    COLUMN+CELL
 A_2007-03-01          column=adjusted:adj_close_price, timestamp=1733462233154, val
                       ue=29.965363317911
 A_2007-03-01          column=info:close_price, timestamp=1733462137438, value=31.44
 A_2007-03-01          column=info:high_price, timestamp=1733462121687, value=31.66
 A_2007-03-01          column=info:low_price, timestamp=1733462129595, value=30.81
 A_2007-03-01          column=info:volume, timestamp=1733462150106, value=2909300.0
 A_2007-03-02          column=adjusted:adj_close_price, timestamp=1733462267913, val
                       ue=29.279133623608
 A_2007-03-02          column=info:close_price, timestamp=1733462176152, value=30.72
 A_2007-03-02          column=info:high_price, timestamp=1733462168036, value=31.53
 A_2007-03-02          column=info:low_price, timestamp=1733462170517, value=30.69
 A_2007-03-02          column=info:open_price, timestamp=1733462156298, value=31.35
 A_2007-03-02          column=info:volume, timestamp=1733462192491, value=2455500.0
 A_2007-03-03          column=adjusted:adj_close_price, timestamp=1733462273951, val
                       ue=29.431506273693
 A_2007-03-03          column=info:close_price, timestamp=1733462217700, value=30.95
 A_2007-03-03          column=info:high_price, timestamp=1733462204823, value=31.30
 A_2007-03-03          column=info:low_price, timestamp=1733462210587, value=30.50
 A_2007-03-03          column=info:open_price, timestamp=1733462198546, value=30.90
 A_2007-03-04          column=adjusted:adj_close_price, timestamp=1733462279905, val
                       ue=30.154204623432
 A_2007-03-05          column=adjusted:adj_close_price, timestamp=1733462285193, val
                       ue=30.746520154274
 A_2007-03-05          column=info:volume, timestamp=1733462223379, value=4125000.0
5 row(s) in 0.0130 seconds
```

***Figure 11.20:** Usage of delete rows command*

Truncate

This command deletes all rows in a table but retains the schema. *Figure 11.21* shows the execution of this command. Successful execution of the **'describe'** command confirms the existence of a schema for the **'stock_prices'** table in the example, as shown:

Syntax: `truncate '<table_name>'`

Example: `truncate 'stock_prices'`

```
hbase(main):061:0> truncate 'stock_prices'
Truncating 'stock_prices' table (it may take a while):
 - Disabling table...
 - Truncating table...
0 row(s) in 3.3870 seconds

hbase(main):062:0> describe 'stock_prices'
Table stock_prices is ENABLED
stock_prices
COLUMN FAMILIES DESCRIPTION
{NAME => 'adjusted', DATA_BLOCK_ENCODING => 'NONE', BLOOMFILTER => 'ROW', REPLICATI
ON_SCOPE => '0', VERSIONS => '1', COMPRESSION => 'NONE', MIN_VERSIONS => '0', TTL =
> 'FOREVER', KEEP_DELETED_CELLS => 'FALSE', BLOCKSIZE => '65536', IN_MEMORY => 'fal
se', BLOCKCACHE => 'true'}
{NAME => 'info', DATA_BLOCK_ENCODING => 'NONE', BLOOMFILTER => 'ROW', REPLICATION_S
COPE => '0', VERSIONS => '1', COMPRESSION => 'NONE', MIN_VERSIONS => '0', TTL => 'F
OREVER', KEEP_DELETED_CELLS => 'FALSE', BLOCKSIZE => '65536', IN_MEMORY => 'false',
 BLOCKCACHE => 'true'}
{NAME => 'metadata', DATA_BLOCK_ENCODING => 'NONE', BLOOMFILTER => 'ROW', REPLICATI
ON_SCOPE => '0', COMPRESSION => 'NONE', VERSIONS => '1', TTL => 'FOREVER', MIN_VERS
IONS => '0', KEEP_DELETED_CELLS => 'FALSE', BLOCKSIZE => '65536', IN_MEMORY => 'fal
se', BLOCKCACHE => 'true'}
3 row(s) in 0.0270 seconds
```

***Figure 11.21**: Usage of truncate command*

Conclusion

The chapter introduced Apache HBase, which is a distributed NoSQL database tailored for managing vast volumes of structured and semi-structured data with high scalability and real-time performance. Starting with an overview of HBase's evolution and its necessity in handling big data challenges, this chapter explored its physical model, including key components such as the HBase master, region servers, regions, and HBase clients, which collectively ensure seamless data distribution and access. The discussion on data organization and architecture highlighted its column-family oriented design, enabling efficient storage and retrieval of sparse datasets. The data storage model was analyzed in depth, covering critical elements like tables, rows, columns, values, keys, and column families, which collectively define HBase's schema-less yet organized structure. By contrasting HBase with traditional RDBMS, the chapter underscored its unique advantages, particularly for real-time analytics, while acknowledging trade-offs such as limited advanced querying capabilities. Practical use cases on stock market analysis demonstrated HBase's applicability across industries. The chapter also provided a hands-on guide to start the HBase shell in Cloudera and run essential data management commands for creating, managing, and querying tables, offering a comprehensive understanding of its operational capabilities. Overall, HBase stands out as a robust solution for big data applications requiring real-time, scalable, and reliable data management. In the next chapter, we will build a comprehensive understanding NOSQL databases, its types and MongoDB in detail.

Points to remember

The following list outlines the essential pointers:

- HBase is a distributed, scalable, NoSQL database built on Hadoop for managing large datasets with real-time access.
- It addresses limitations of traditional databases in handling sparse, large-scale, and real-time big data applications.
- HBase physical model describes the components ensuring distributed data management.

- HBase master manages metadata and assigns regions to region servers.
- Region refers to a subset of a table's rows, split for efficient distribution and storage.
- HBase region server handles client requests for specific regions and manages data storage.
- HBase client interfaces with HBase for performing data operations.

- In HBase, data is stored in tables, organized into rows and columns within column families.
- HBase architecture is a layered system with master-slave architecture enabling distributed data management.
- HBase data storage model is a schema-less structure supporting dynamic data.
    - **Table**: A logical grouping of rows and column families.
    - **Row**: The fundamental unit identified by a row key.
    - **Column**: Stores data, grouped into families for efficient management.
    - **Value**: The actual data stored within a column.
    - **Keys**: Unique identifiers for rows and column versions.
    - **Column families**: Groups of related columns stored together.
- HBase is a NoSQL database designed for distributed, real-time access to large datasets, offering scalability and schema flexibility, while RDBMS provides structured data management with rigid schemas and support for advanced querying, but struggles with horizontal scalability.
- Data management commands in HBase are used for data analysis.
    - **Create**: Create a new table in HBase.
    - **List**: List all tables in the database.
    - **Describe**: View the schema of a table.
    - **Disable, Disable_all**: Disable a table or multiple tables.
    - **Enable, Enable_all**: Enable a table or multiple tables.
    - **Drop, Drop_all**: Remove a table or multiple tables.
    - **Show_filters**: Display available filters for queries.
    - **Alter**: Modify the schema of a table.
    - **Count**: Count the number of rows in a table.
    - **Put**: Insert or update a value in a table.
    - **Scan**: Retrieve multiple rows from a table.
    - **Get**: Retrieve a specific row or cell.
    - **Delete**: Remove a specific cell or row.
    - **Delete_all**: Remove all rows matching a key.
    - **Truncate**: Empty a table while preserving its schema.

Multiple choice questions

1. **What is Apache HBase primarily designed for?**
    a. Storing images and multimedia files
    b. Real-time access to large-scale, distributed datasets
    c. Performing advanced SQL joins and queries
    d. Managing relational data in a structured format

2. **Which of the following is not a component of HBase's physical model?**
   a. HBase master
   b. Region
   c. Region server
   d. Transaction coordinator
3. **In HBase, what is a column family?**
   a. A set of rows grouped together
   b. A collection of related columns stored together
   c. A logical representation of a database schema
   d. A group of keys stored in a region
4. **What differentiates HBase from traditional RDBMS?**
   a. HBase uses fixed schemas, while RDBMS does not.
   b. HBase is row-oriented, while RDBMS is column-oriented.
   c. HBase is schema-less and highly scalable, while RDBMS has a rigid schema and limited scalability.
   d. HBase supports advanced SQL joins, while RDBMS does not.
5. **What is the primary role of the HBase master?**
   a. Executing client queries
   b. Managing regions and metadata
   c. Handling data replication
   d. Performing backups
6. **Which command is used to retrieve multiple rows from an HBase table?**
   a. Get
   b. Scan
   c. Put
   d. Count
7. **What happens when the truncate command is used in HBase?**
   a. It deletes the table and its schema.
   b. It removes all rows but retains the table schema.
   c. It disables and deletes all regions of a table.
   d. It combines multiple rows into a single row.
8. **In HBase, what is a region server responsible for?**
   a. Coordinating cluster-wide tasks
   b. Handling data read and write requests for assigned regions
   c. Managing distributed transactions
   d. Aggregating data across tables
9. **Which use case is best suited for HBase?**
   a. Processing complex SQL queries on relational data
   b. Real-time analytics on stock market data
   c. Hosting small-scale e-commerce websites
   d. Managing multimedia content storage

10. **How does the Show_filters command assist in HBase?**
    a. It displays the schema of a table.
    b. It lists all the available filters for data queries.
    c. It retrieves specific rows from a table.
    d. It enables filtering rows during table creation.

Answers

1. b.	2. d.	3. b.	4. c.	5. b.
6. b.	7. b.	8. b.	9. b.	10. b.

Questions

1. Define HBase and explain its primary purpose in handling big data.
2. List the major components of HBase's architecture and briefly describe their roles.
3. Differentiate between HBase and RDBMS in terms of schema design and scalability.
4. Explain the significance of column families in HBase and how they optimize data storage.
5. Create a table stocks with column families prices and metadata, insert data for multiple stock symbols (e.g., AAPL, GOOGL) with their prices and associated metadata, and write a query to retrieve all stocks priced above $1000.
6. Demonstrate how to filter rows in a table where the column volume in the stats column family is greater than 1,000,000 and display only the stock symbol and its corresponding volume using the appropriate HBase filter.
7. Write the series of HBase shell commands to:
    - Create a table iot_data with column families sensors and location.
    - Insert data for multiple IoT devices with attributes like temperature, humidity, and location.
    - Query the table to return all devices located in New York with a temperature above 30°C.
8. Assume a table web_logs with the column families metadata and details. The rows include fields such as user_id, timestamp, and action. Write commands to:
    - Count the number of distinct users (user_id) who performed the login action.
    - Retrieve the first 10 rows sorted by the timestamp colu!mn.
9. Evaluate the advantages and limitations of using HBase for real-time analytics compared to other NoSQL databases.
10. Assess the effectiveness of the Truncate and Delete commands for managing table data in HBase, and provide scenarios where each is more appropriate.

Join our Discord space

Join our Discord workspace for latest updates, offers, tech happenings around the world, new releases, and sessions with the authors:

https://discord.bpbonline.com

CHAPTER 12
MongoDB

Data really powers everything that we do.

-Jeff Weiner (LinkedIn CEO)

Introduction

This chapter introduces the concept of **not only SQL** (**NoSQL**) databases and their types. It explains the **consistency, availability, partition tolerance** (**CAP**) theorem, a fundamental trade-off in distributed systems. This chapter next explains MongoDB, the document-oriented NoSQL database, in detail. It covers the data model, **create, read, update, and delete** (**CRUD**) operations, and installation and execution of CRUD operations with the help of examples and case studies. It also covers aggregation operators, which are used to perform complex queries and transformations on data in MongoDB.

Structure

In this chapter, we will cover the following topics:

- Introducing NoSQL databases
- Types of NoSQL databases
- Limitations of key-value stores
- CAP theorem
- Introducing MongoDB
- Installing and running MongoDB
- MongoDB data model
- MongoDB data hierarchy
- Application development in MongoDB

Objectives

By the end of this chapter, readers will gain a comprehensive understanding of NoSQL databases. By exploring the various types of NoSQL databases and the principles of the CAP theorem, they will grasp the foundational concepts that differentiate NoSQL from traditional relational databases. Readers will also learn the NoSQL database MongoDB in detail, and they will be introduced to its features, data modeling techniques, and the practical need for a flexible, scalable database solution. Finally, the readers will gain hands-on skills in performing CRUD operations, understanding aggregation operators, and developing MongoDB applications.

Introducing NoSQL databases

NoSQL databases are non-relational databases designed to handle large volumes of unstructured, semi-structured, or structured data. Unlike traditional relational databases, which use tables, rows, and fixed schemas, NoSQL databases offer flexible schemas and are optimized for scalability, high performance, and distributed systems.

They are particularly suited for modern applications that deal with large-scale, real-time data, such as social media platforms, e-commerce systems, and big data analytics.

The term NoSQL was officially coined in 2009 by *Johan Oskarsson* of *Last.fm* during a meetup to discuss alternatives to relational databases. While it originally stood for *not only SQL,* it came to represent a class of databases that focussed on scalability, performance, and flexibility that moved beyond the rigid schemas and consistency models of **relational database management** (**RDBMS**) moving beyond the rigid schemas and consistency models of RDBMS. This new family of databases was built to handle the big data era, where massive volumes of diverse data were required to be processed with low latency.

The emergence of NoSQL databases was driven by the need to address the limitations of traditional relational databases in handling the scale, speed, and flexibility demands of modern applications. RDBMS, based on *Edgar F. Codd's* relational model introduced in 1970, were designed to store structured data in predefined schemas using SQL as the query language.

They were ideal for enterprise systems requiring consistency and transactional integrity. However, the evolution of the internet in the late 1990s and early 2000s led to the explosion of unstructured and semi-structured data (e.g., logs, user interactions, multimedia). The need for distributed, global-scale applications in the digital era exposed several limitations of traditional **Relational Database Management Systems** (**RDBMS**).

One of the first signs of this shift came from companies like *Google, Amazon,* and *Facebook,* which faced unprecedented challenges. For instance, Google developed *Bigtable* (published in 2006) to manage vast amounts of structured data for applications like Gmail and Google Search. It introduced the concept of column-family storage, which enabled efficient data retrieval for specific use cases. Meanwhile, Amazon tackled high-availability requirements with Dynamo, a key-value store designed to handle large-scale shopping cart systems with eventual consistency. Dynamo's architecture, detailed in a 2007 research paper by *Werner Vogels* and others, became a cornerstone for distributed database designs.

Followed by this, *Avinash Lakshman* (co-author of Dynamo) and *Prashant Malik* from Facebook soon developed *Cassandra* in 2008. Cassandra blended ideas from Dynamo and Bigtable, combining the fault-tolerant, peer-to-peer distribution model of Dynamo with the column-family storage of Bigtable. Around the same time, other innovations began emerging, such as MongoDB (launched in 2009), a document-oriented database designed for schema-less data, and Neo4j (2007), a graph database tailored for relationships and connections.

NoSQL impacted businesses profoundly by enabling them to scale horizontally by adding servers rather than upgrading hardware, adapting to changing data models without schema migrations, and maintaining performance under high traffic. Companies like *Netflix, Twitter,* and *LinkedIn* adopted NoSQL to power critical systems like recommendation engines, caching layers, and real-time analytics. Over time, NoSQL databases have evolved further to integrate with traditional SQL features, resulting in hybrid solutions (e.g., NewSQL databases like CockroachDB) that combine the scalability of NoSQL with the **atomicity, consistency, isolation, durability** (**ACID**) compliance of RDBMS.

The need for NoSQL arose as the digital age demanded new ways to store, process, and access data at an unprecedented scale and speed. From the foundational work at Google, Amazon, and Facebook to the innovations of independent projects like MongoDB and Redis, NoSQL databases have become integral to powering the modern web and enterprise systems. In this chapter, you will learn about MongoDB in detail. Before that, you will learn about different types of NoSQL databases.

Types of NoSQL databases

NoSQL databases are categorized into four main types to address specific requirements: key-value stores (e.g., Redis, Riak) for simplicity and speed; document stores (e.g., MongoDB, CouchDB) for handling semi-structured data like JSON; column-family stores (e.g., Cassandra, HBase) for analytical workloads and large datasets; and graph databases (e.g., Neo4j) for relationship-heavy data like social networks and recommendation engines.

Figure 12.1 shows the various types of NoSQL datatypes:

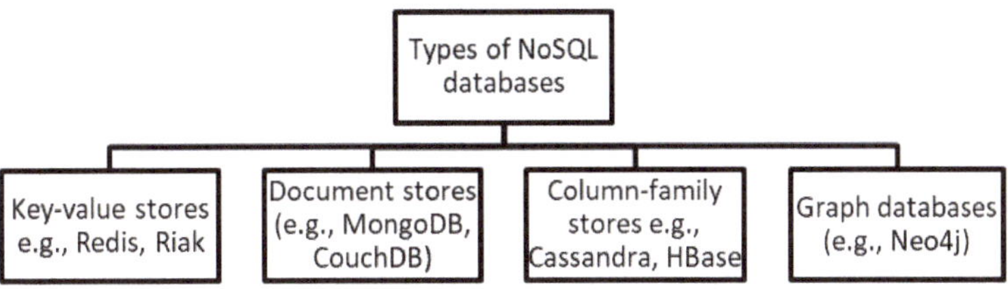

***Figure 12.1**: Types of NoSQL databases*

Key-value stores

These databases are designed to store, retrieve, and manage data using a simple key-value pair structure, as shown in *Table 12.1*. These storage systems are associative arrays of keys and values. In this model, each key is unique and serves as a distinct identifier to store or retrieve data. It is usually a string, but sometimes binary [e.g., hashed IDs or **Universally Unique Identifiers** (**UUIDs**)].

The value holds the data associated with the key. It can be simple (e.g., Strings, integers, or floats) and complex [e.g., **JavaScript Object Notation** (**JSON**) objects, serialized binary data, images, or files]. They are highly optimized for simplicity, speed, and scalability, making them ideal for applications requiring high performance and low latency.

Key	Value
User:101	Aayush Mehta
cart:12345	{"items": [{"id": 1, "qty": 2}, {"id": 2, "qty": 1}]}
image:profile:101	(Binary data for an image)
config/database/url	"db.example.com"

***Table 12.1**: Key-value store*

Key characteristics of key-value stores are as follows:

- **Simplicity**: The data is stored as pairs, where the key is a unique identifier, and the value can be any kind of data (string, number, JSON, binary blob, etc.). The schema-free nature enables you to store and retrieve data without worrying about defining tables or relationships, e.g., if you want to add a new field to a user profile, just update the JSON value without modifying the database schema.
- **High performance**: They are optimized for quick read and write operations, often at in-memory speeds (constant time (*O(1)*) for read/write) due to the direct mapping of keys to memory locations, e.g., Redis stores keys in RAM, making operations like fetching user session data instantaneous.
- **Scalability**: Key-value stores are designed to scale horizontally, making them suitable for distributed systems. You can shard (divide) data across multiple servers easily by distributing keys; for example, a system with billions of keys can distribute them across 10 servers using consistent hashing.
- **Schema-less**: Unlike relational databases, key-value stores do not require a predefined schema, so they provide flexibility to store various types of data. For example, product:12345 can hold a small string or a large JSON object, depending on the business requirements.

These key-value stores are used to fulfil various types of application requirements, for example, e-commerce websites, such as Amazon, which uses Redis or Memcached to cache product details, reducing database hits for frequently accessed products. Facebook stores session tokens with a TTL for authentication and session tracking, Microservices use **etc directory daemon** (**etcd**) to store service configurations or feature flags (e.g. `Key: /config/serviceA/feature1`, `Value: enabled`), Smart home systems (e.g., Nest) use DynamoDB to store telemetry data from **Internet of Things** (**IoT**) devices (`Key: device:12345:timestamp`, `Value: { "temperature": 22.5, "humidity": 60 }`), Online games like Fortnite use Redis sorted sets to store scores (`Key: leaderboard:game1`, `Value: Sorted list of player scores`).

Here are some limitations of key-value stores:

- Data can only be retrieved by its key. Hence, extra efforts (e.g., external indexes or application-layer code) are required to search for values, e.g., to query all users whose age is greater than 30 is impossible natively unless additional data structures are added.
- Key-value stores lack the ability to manage relationships like SQL databases do; for example, a relational database can easily query all orders for a given user, but a key-value store would need a custom implementation to achieve this.
- Since the value is often unstructured, data might be duplicated across keys, leading to inefficiency. For example, storing user preferences in every session object leads to redundant data storage.
- Some key-value stores lack strong consistency or multi-step transaction capabilities, e.g., atomic operations like increment/decrement might be supported, but executing multiple operations as a single transaction is more complex.
- Managing distributed systems comes with challenges like handling network partitions, maintaining consistent hashing for sharded keys, dealing with eventual consistency in some systems, etc.
- Key-value stores are not designed for aggregation or analytics, e.g., summing up all product sales across a store is inefficient compared to SQL-based systems.

Document stores

It (or document-oriented database) is a type of NoSQL database that manages data in a flexible, document-like format, typically JSON, **Binary JavaScript Object Notation** (**BSON**), or **Extensible Markup Language** (**XML**). Unlike relational databases, which store data in structured tables with fixed schemas, document stores are meant for the storage of semi-structured or unstructured data, making them ideal for modern, dynamic applications.

To meet the varied application requirements, numerous document stores are developed. One of the earliest document databases is CouchDB (2005), which uses JSON for data storage and replication. MongoDB (2009) then became the most widely used document database, offering high scalability and flexibility. Amazon DynamoDB, developed in 2012, is a cloud-based NoSQL service optimized for document storage. Firebase Firestore (2017) is a real-time document store for mobile and web applications.

Key features of document stores are as follows:

- They are schema-less with no predefined schema. Each document (typically in JSON, BSON, or XML) can have a different structure, making it easy to store dynamic and evolving data.
- Data can be stored in human-readable formats, e.g., JSON/BSON/XML. These formats are easy for developers to read and debug and are optimized for quick retrieval and processing.
- Documents can have nested objects and arrays, unlike relational databases that require separate tables and joins.
- Document stores scale out by distributing data across multiple servers (horizontal scaling), unlike relational databases, which primarily scale up by upgrading a single server. These stores use sharding (splitting data across multiple nodes) and replication (copying data across nodes for high availability), e.g., a social media platform like Instagram needs to handle millions of posts per second, and MongoDB or Amazon DynamoDB can distribute these posts across multiple servers for faster performance.

- Document stores support automatic replication, ensuring that data is available even if some nodes fail, e.g., in MongoDB, replica sets allow automatic failover if the primary server goes down. Amazon DynamoDB replicates data across multiple AWS regions to prevent downtime.
- Unlike traditional key-value NoSQL stores, document stores support indexing on specific fields for fast query processing.
- Many document databases include built-in full-text search (MongoDB Atlas Search, Couchbase FTS, Elasticsearch integration).
- They are designed for modern applications, so ideal for web, mobile, and real-time analytics.

Today, documents power many modern applications, including e-commerce platforms, social media, content management systems, and real-time applications. For example, an e-commerce platform stores product details in MongoDB. Since products have varying attributes (e.g., a laptop has different specs than a phone), it helps in full-text search for product descriptions and in handling millions of queries efficiently. For example, the document for a laptop in MongoDB is stored as:

```
{
  "product_id": 12345,
  "name": "Gaming Laptop",
  "brand": "Acer",
  "price": 1299.99,
  "specifications": {
    "RAM": "16GB",
    "Processor": "Intel i7",
    "Storage": "512GB SSD"
  },
  "reviews": [
    { "user": "JohnDoe", "rating": 5, "comment": "Great performance!" },
    { "user": "JaneDoe", "rating": 4, "comment": "Good, but expensive." }
  ]
}
```

Similarly, online multiplayer games like *Fortnite*, *Call of Duty*, etc., need to track active player sessions. Couchbase is used to store session data as JSON documents, as it provides low-latency access for real-time gameplay and syncs across multiple regions for a smooth gaming experience. For example, the document may look like the following code:

```
{
  "session_id": "abc123",
  "user": "GamerX",
  "game": "Call of Duty",
  "status": "active",
  "score": 1500,
  "inventory": ["AK-47", "Medkit", "Grenade"]
}
```

Although document stores offer flexibility, scalability, and high performance, they also have some limitations that may make them unsuitable for certain use cases. The key drawbacks of document stores are as follows:

- Unlike relational databases that use **structured query language** (**SQL**), document stores have different query languages depending on the database (e.g., MongoDB uses MQL, Couchbase has N1QL, and DynamoDB uses its API). Therefore, developers familiar with SQL may need to learn different query syntaxes for each document store.
- Document stores do not support join operations like relational databases. Instead, data must be denormalized (duplicated) across documents, which leads to data redundancy, increased storage usage, and complex updates (multiple documents need to be updated instead of a single join query). For example, if customer information changes, multiple documents must be updated instead of one.
- Many document stores prioritize performance and availability over consistency (following the CAP theorem). Some document databases use eventual consistency, which means updates are not immediately reflected across all nodes, making it unsuitable for banking or financial systems. E.g., in a distributed e-commerce application, if a user updates their shipping address, the old address might still appear for some time due to replication lag.
- Document stores are optimized for **online transaction processing** (**OLTP**) but not for **online analytical processing** (**OLAP**). Complex aggregations (e.g., calculating average sales per region) are slower in document stores as compared to relational databases. E.g., a sales report calculating total revenue per month may be slower in a document store than in a columnar database like *Amazon Redshift* or *Google BigQuery*.

Column-family stores

A column-family store (or wide-column database) is a type of NoSQL database that stores data in columns instead of rows. This type of storage provides high performance for write-heavy workloads and real-time analytics. Unlike relational databases, which store data in tables (rows and columns), column-family stores group-related data into column families for faster retrieval.

The concept of column-family stores originates from Google's Bigtable, which was introduced in 2006 to handle massive-scale structured data for Google applications like Search, Maps, and Analytics. This inspired the emergence of open-source alternatives like Apache Cassandra (developed at Facebook in 2008) and Apache HBase (built for Hadoop in 2007), making this database model popular in big data and distributed computing. Today, column-family stores are widely used in real-time analytics, IoT, messaging apps, and recommendation engines due to their high scalability and fault tolerance.

Key features of column-family stores are as follows:

- Unlike relational databases, which require a fixed schema, column-family stores allow dynamic schemas. That is, different rows in the same column family can have different columns. New columns can be added dynamically without altering the entire structure, which makes it ideal for heterogeneous data like logs, sensor readings, and user profiles.
- Column-family stores are designed for horizontal scaling, that is, they can seamlessly distribute data across multiple servers (nodes). Unlike SQL databases, which often require vertical scaling (adding more CPU/RAM to a single server), column-family stores expand horizontally. For example, Facebook Messenger handles billions of messages daily using Apache Cassandra by distributing data across hundreds of servers worldwide. Google Cloud Bigtable powers services like Google Search and Maps, dynamically scaling with demand.
- Column-family stores prioritize fast writes, making them ideal for high-throughput applications, such as IoT sensors generating millions of events per second, log storage for cybersecurity or system monitoring, financial transactions, and stock market feeds. For example, Uber's real-time location tracking uses Apache

Cassandra to instantly store and process ride requests. Twitter's analytics system logs billions of tweets, likes, and retweets per day.

- Column-family stores store data column-wise instead of row-wise, reducing storage costs and improving query performance.
- Column-family stores automatically replicate data across multiple servers, ensuring high availability and fault tolerance. For example, Netflix uses Apache Cassandra to ensure continuous streaming, even if a data center fails. Amazon DynamoDB (which uses a column-family-like model) stores shopping cart data redundantly, ensuring items never disappear due to server failure.

Column-family stores (e.g., Cassandra) and relational databases (e.g., PostgreSQL) fundamentally differ in how they physically organize data on disk. This structural difference impacts performance, scalability, and ideal use cases. Relational databases like PostgreSQL use a row-oriented storage approach, where all columns of a single record are stored together in contiguous disk blocks. For example, a user's complete data (ID, name, age, email) would be stored as one continuous unit. The details are as follows:

- **Relational database**: User's data:

  ```
  [Block 1: 1, "Alia", 30, "alia@example.com"]
  [Block 2: 2, "Babita", 25, "babita@example.com"]
  ```

  This structure excels at retrieving full rows quickly, making it ideal for transactional workloads (OLTP) where operations typically access complete records. However, it becomes inefficient for analytical queries that only need specific columns, as the database must read entire rows to access just a few fields.

  In contrast, column-family stores like Apache Cassandra employ a column-oriented approach, where data is organized by columns rather than rows. Related columns are grouped into *families*, and each column is stored separately. For instance, all user IDs would be stored together, all names together, and so on. This design provides significant advantages for analytical workloads, as queries can read just the required columns without scanning unnecessary data. It also handles sparse data efficiently, as missing columns consume no storage space. Column-family stores are particularly well-suited for write-heavy applications and large-scale data analysis, though they may be less optimal for retrieving complete records spanning multiple column-families.

- **Column-family store**: User's data:

  ```
  [Block 1 (IDs):     1, 2, ...]
  [Block 2 (Names):   "Alia", "Babita", ...]
  [Block 3 (Ages):    30, 25, ...]
  ```

  The choice between these storage models depends on the use case: row-oriented for transactional systems needing full record access, and column-family for analytical systems or applications with massive write volumes. This fundamental difference in data organization directly impacts performance, scalability, and the types of operations each system handles most efficiently.

Here are some limitations of column-family stores:

- Unlike relational databases (SQL), column-family stores do not support traditional joins between tables. To retrieve related data, you must denormalize and store redundant information, thus increasing complexity.
- Since joins are not supported, related data is often stored in the same column family. This increases data redundancy, leading to higher storage costs and update complexity.
- ACID ensures reliable transactions, but most column-family stores prioritize availability and scalability over strict consistency. They typically follow the BASE model: **basically available, soft state, eventually** (**BASE**) consistent.

- Column-family stores do not support SQL-style querying, making complex data retrieval more difficult. Queries require custom APIs, indexing, or MapReduce processing, increasing development effort.

Graph databases

A graph database is a type of NoSQL database designed to store and manage relationships between data using a graph structure. Unlike relational databases (SQL), which use tables and rows, graph databases use nodes (entities) and edges (relationships) to represent and query data efficiently. Graph databases emerged to overcome the limitations of traditional relational databases in handling highly connected data.

The concept of graph-based data modelling originates from graph theory, which was first introduced by *Leonhard Euler* in 1736 with the famous *Seven Bridges of Königsberg* problem. Over time, graph theory became fundamental in computer science, networking, and AI. Modern graph databases evolved in the 2000s, with Neo4j (2007), one of the most widely adopted graph database systems. Today, companies such as *Facebook*, *Google*, *LinkedIn*, and *Amazon* utilize graph databases for social networking, recommendations, and fraud detection.

Key features in graph databases are as follows:

- **Nodes**: Represent entities (e.g., people, products, locations).
- **Edges (Relationships)**: Represent connections between nodes (e.g., `"FRIEND_OF"`, `"PURCHASED"`, `"LOCATED_IN"`).
- **Properties**: These are the attributes describing nodes or edges (e.g., a Person node may have name and age properties).
- **Traversal**: It refers to the process of exploring relationships between nodes, making graph queries extremely fast.

Here are some advantages of graph databases:

- Graph databases are optimized for managing highly connected data, which makes it easy to query relationships between entities. This is often faster and more efficient than using complex joins in traditional relational databases.
- The graph structure (nodes and edges) naturally matches real-world systems like social networks, recommendation engines, or organizational hierarchies. This makes it easier to model and query data in a way that aligns with real-world scenarios.
- Graph databases allow for dynamic schemas, which means you can add or modify nodes, relationships, and properties without needing to restructure entire tables. This flexibility is beneficial for evolving data models.
- Graph databases excel at traversing relationships and finding paths between entities. Tasks like finding the shortest route between two points or identifying connected entities are much faster than SQL-based databases.
- Graph databases scale horizontally (across multiple servers) when dealing with large, interconnected datasets. This makes them suitable for distributed systems where relationships between data points are critical.

Here are some limitations of graph databases:

- Graph databases are not ideal for simple, flat datasets or applications that do not require complex relationships (like basic transactional data).
- Querying connected data is efficient in graph databases. However, sometimes, querying graph-specific queries can be complex and might require specialized knowledge of graph query languages like Cypher in Neo4j.

- Compared to relational databases, the tools and ecosystem around graph databases are less mature, making integrations with other systems or third-party tools a bit challenging.
- Storing large graphs with millions of nodes and relationships can strain memory and performance, particularly when the graph becomes very large and complex.
- While many graph databases are improving, some may not offer complete ACID guarantees for transactions, which can be a limitation for applications requiring strict data consistency.

The following table provides a comparison of the four NoSQL database types based on use cases, data format, and scalability strategy:

Database type	Examples	Use cases	Data format	Scalability strategy
Key-value stores	Redis, Riak	Caching, session management, and real-time apps	Simple key-value pairs	Horizontal scaling (sharding, replication)
Document stores	MongoDB, CouchDB	Content management, user profiles, and catalogs	JSON/ **Binary JSON** (**BSON**) documents (nested structures)	Horizontal scaling (sharding, replica sets)
Column-family stores	Cassandra, HBase	Time-series data, big data analytics	Column families (rows with dynamic columns)	Horizontal scaling (partitioning, distributed clusters)
Graph databases	Neo4j, ArangoDB	Social networks, fraud detection, and recommendation engines	Nodes, edges, and properties (relationships)	Vertical scaling (or limited horizontal via clustering)

***Table 12.2**: Comparison of the NoSQL database*

CAP theorem

The CAP theorem, also known as **Brewer's theorem**, is a fundamental principle in distributed systems that states that a distributed database system can only guarantee two out of the following three properties at any given time:

- **Consistency (C)**: It ensures that every read operation receives the most recent write or an error. In other words, all nodes in the system see the same data simultaneously.
- **Availability (A)**: This means every request receives a response, without guarantee that it contains the most recent write. The system remains operational and accessible even if some nodes are down.
- **Partition tolerance (P)**: The system continues to function even if there is a network partition (a break in communication between nodes). Network partitions are a reality in distributed systems, so partition tolerance is a must-have.

The following figure illustrates the CAP theorem in distributed systems:

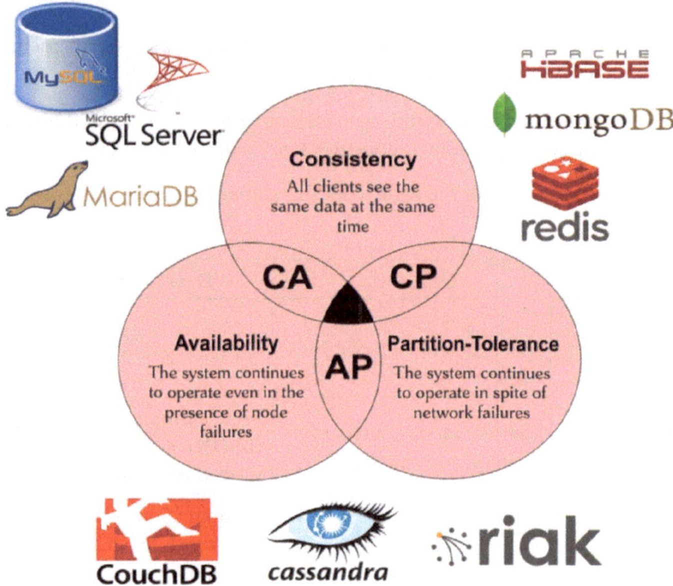

Figure 12.2: CAP theorem in distributed systems

NoSQL databases are designed to handle large-scale, distributed data systems, and they often prioritize scalability and flexibility over strict consistency. The CAP theorem plays a crucial role in understanding how different NoSQL databases are designed and the trade-offs they make.

NoSQL databases are designed to prioritize different aspects based on their use cases:

- **Consistency and partition tolerance (CP systems)**: These systems prioritize consistency and partition tolerance over availability. In the event of a network partition, the system will ensure data consistency but may become unavailable until the partition is resolved. For example, by default, MongoDB is a CP system. It ensures strong consistency but may become unavailable during a network partition. HBase, on the other hand, is a distributed column-store database that prioritizes consistency and partition tolerance. For example, a stock trading platform where consistency is critical (e.g., ensuring stock prices are accurate across all nodes) and temporary unavailability is acceptable during partitions.
- **Availability and partition tolerance (AP systems)**: These systems prioritize availability and partition tolerance over consistency. In the event of a network partition, the system remains available but may return stale or inconsistent data. Cassandra is a distributed, wide-column store that prioritizes availability and partition tolerance. It uses eventual consistency to ensure high availability. CouchDB is a document-oriented database focusing on availability and partition tolerance, allowing for eventual consistency. For example, a social media platform where availability is critical (e.g., users can still post and read content even during network issues), and temporary inconsistencies are acceptable (e.g., a user might see slightly outdated posts).
- **Consistency and availability (CA systems)**: These systems prioritize consistency and availability over partition tolerance. These systems work well in environments where network partitions are rare or non-existent. However, they are unsuitable for distributed systems that must handle network failures. Traditional relational databases (e.g., MySQL, PostgreSQL) are often CA systems, as they prioritize consistency and availability but are not designed to handle network partitions in distributed environments; for example, in a banking system, consistency is critical (e.g., ensuring account balances are always accurate), and downtime is unacceptable.

Techniques to handle CAP trade-offs in NoSQL databases

Here are some techniques to handle CAP trade-offs in NoSQL databases:

- **Eventual consistency**: Many NoSQL databases (for example, Cassandra, DynamoDB) use eventual consistency to balance availability and partition tolerance. This means that updates to the system will propagate to all nodes over time, but there may be a temporary inconsistency.
- **Tunable consistency**: Some NoSQL databases (for example, Cassandra) allow users to tune the level of consistency based on their needs. For example, you can configure the database to prioritize consistency for critical operations and relax it for others.
- **Quorum-based systems**: Systems like Riak and DynamoDB use quorum-based mechanisms to balance consistency and availability. A quorum ensures that a majority of nodes agree on the data state before proceeding with a read or write operation.
- **Strong consistency**: Databases like MongoDB and HBase prioritize strong consistency, ensuring that all nodes see the same data at the same time. However, this may come at the cost of availability during network partitions.

In the real world, platforms like Facebook or Twitter use AP systems (e.g., Cassandra) to ensure high availability and partition tolerance. They can tolerate temporary inconsistencies (e.g., delayed updates to a user's feed) to keep the system running smoothly. E-commerce platforms like Amazon use CP systems (e.g., MongoDB) for critical operations like inventory management, where consistency is crucial.

However, they may use AP systems for less critical features like product recommendations. Financial systems often use CP systems to ensure strong consistency and partition tolerance. For example, a banking system must ensure that account balances are consistent across all nodes, even if it means sacrificing availability during a network partition.

Overall, the CAP theorem highlights the inherent trade-offs in distributed systems, and NoSQL databases are designed to prioritize different aspects based on their use cases. CP systems prioritize consistency and partition tolerance (for example, MongoDB, HBase). AP systems prioritize availability and partition tolerance (for example, Cassandra, CouchDB). CA systems prioritize consistency and availability, but are less common in distributed NoSQL databases. Understanding the CAP Theorem helps in choosing the right NoSQL database for your application, depending on whether you prioritize consistency, availability, or partition tolerance.

Introducing MongoDB

MongoDB is a NoSQL, document-oriented database allowing scalable, flexible, and high-performance data management. It was developed by 10gen (now MongoDB Inc.) in 2007 and officially released in 2009. The database was designed to handle modern applications requiring rapid development, cloud compatibility, and large-scale data processing. Unlike traditional relational databases that store data in tables with fixed schemas, MongoDB stores data in BSON format, which supports dynamic and schema-less data structures, making it ideal for applications where data models evolve over time.

For example, in e-commerce platforms (e.g., Amazon, eBay, Shopify), initially, products may only have basic fields like name, price, and category, and later, new attributes like discounts, customer reviews, and seller ratings are introduced. Different product types may have unique attributes (e.g., clothing size and electronics processor). Support may also be required for new data types like images, videos, or 3D models of products. In such applications, MongoDB provides a flexible document structure, which allows new fields to be added without breaking existing records.

Significance of MongoDB

Modern applications generate vast amounts of unstructured and semi-structured data, which relational databases struggle to handle efficiently. For example, eBay initially used MySQL for its product catalog. The product schema was rigid, requiring changes every time a new product category was introduced. Scaling issues arose as millions of new products were added daily. eBay migrated parts of its catalog system to MongoDB, leading to faster performance and more straightforward schema evolution.

Similarly, Facebook initially used Apache Cassandra for its Messenger chat service. Cassandra worked well for high write throughput, but retrieving chat history across multiple devices was slow. Facebook shifted parts of Messenger to MongoDB to improve message retrieval performance and flexibility.

MongoDB addressed these challenges by providing the following:

- **Big data and scalability**: It supports horizontal scaling with sharding, making it ideal for handling large data volumes.
- **Flexible schema**: Unlike relational databases, MongoDB allows for dynamic schema changes, making it suitable for applications where data structures evolve over time.
- **High performance**: It provides fast read and write operations with indexing, aggregation, and replication.
- **Cloud and distributed systems**: MongoDB is designed for cloud-based and distributed applications with built-in replication and failover mechanisms.
- **Developer-friendly**: Supports multiple programming languages and provides an easy-to-use query language similar to JSON.

Features of MongoDB

MongoDB is a powerful NoSQL database known for its scalability, flexibility, and high performance.

Key features of MongoDB are as follows:

- **Document-oriented storage**: MongoDB stores data in documents (BSON format, similar to JSON). Each document contains key-value pairs to support flexible and dynamic structures. Documents can contain nested structures and varying attributes, making MongoDB ideal for applications with evolving data models. A JSON document in MongoDB is shown in the following code:

```
{
  "_id": "12345",
  "name": "Teana Mehta”,
  "email": "teana.mehta@example.com",
  "age": 19,
  "address": {
    "street": " Sec 128",
    "city": "Noida",
    "zip": "201301"
  }
}
```

- **Schema-less (flexible data model)**: MongoDB does not require a fixed schema, unlike relational databases, where table structures must be defined in advance. Different documents within the same collection can have different structures, which makes it ideal for applications where data fields change frequently, such as e-commerce, IoT, and healthcare systems. For example, refer to the following code:

```
{
  "_id": "001",
  "name": "Tina",
```

```
  "skills": ["Python", "Java"]
}
{
  "_id": "002",
  "name": "Aayush",
  "experience": 5,
  "certifications": ["AWS Certified", "Google Cloud"]
}
```

- **High scalability**: MongoDB scales horizontally using sharding, which distributes data across multiple servers. It uses a shard key (a shard key is a field (e.g., `customer_id`, `region`, or `order_date`) used to partition and distribute data evenly across shards for horizontal scaling) to partition data among shards (clusters of servers), e.g., data can be split based on customer ID, location, or order date. Accordingly, data in the various shards may be: shard 1 as customers from the USA, shard 2 as customers from Europe, and shard 3 as customers from Asia. Companies like eBay, Uber, and Facebook use it to handle large datasets and high-traffic applications efficiently.
- **Replication (high availability and fault tolerance)**: MongoDB uses replica sets for automatic failover and high availability. A replica set consists of the primary node to handle read/write operations and a secondary node that maintains copies of data. If the primary node fails, one of the secondary nodes is automatically promoted to the primary. It ensures zero downtime for critical applications like banking systems and cloud services.
- **Indexing**: MongoDB automatically creates an index on the _id field, but users can create additional indexes for better performance. It improves query performance 10-100x faster compared to scanning the entire database. It supports multiple types of indexes, such as:
  - **Single-field index**: Improves search speed on a specific field.
  - **Compound index**: Indexes multiple fields together.
  - **Text index**: Enables full-text search capabilities.
  - **Geospatial index**: Optimizes queries for location-based data (e.g., finding nearby restaurants).
  - **Example of an index**: `db.users.createIndex({ "email": 1 })`
- **ACID transactions (Since v4.0)**: Traditional NoSQL databases lack ACID transactions. MongoDB supports multi-document ACID transactions, ensuring data consistency like SQL databases. It is essential for financial applications, e-commerce, and order management systems.
- **Security features (authentication, encryption, role-based access)**: MongoDB offers multiple security features that make it suitable for banking, healthcare, and government systems where security is a top priority. Some of the features are as follows:
  - **Authentication**: Uses **Salted Challenge Response Authentication Mechanism** (**SCRAM**), **Lightweight Directory Access Protocol** (**LDAP**), and Kerberos for user authentication.
  - **Role-based access control (RBAC)**: Restricts access based on user roles.
  - **Encryption**: Supports SSL/TLS for data in transit and encryption at rest.
  - **Auditing and logging**: Tracks user activities for security compliance [e.g., **Health Insurance Portability and Accountability Act** (**HIPAA**), **General Data Protection Regulation** (**GDPR**)].

Installing and running MongoDB

Follow these steps to install and run MongoDB on Windows:

1. Download MongoDB Community Edition from: **https://www.mongodb.com/try/download/community**
2. Choose **Windows** | **MSI Package** | click **Download**.
3. Locate the downloaded file (`mongodb-windows-x86_64-<version>.msi`).
4. Double-click the file to start the installation.
5. Follow the installation wizard, as shown in *Figure 12.3:*

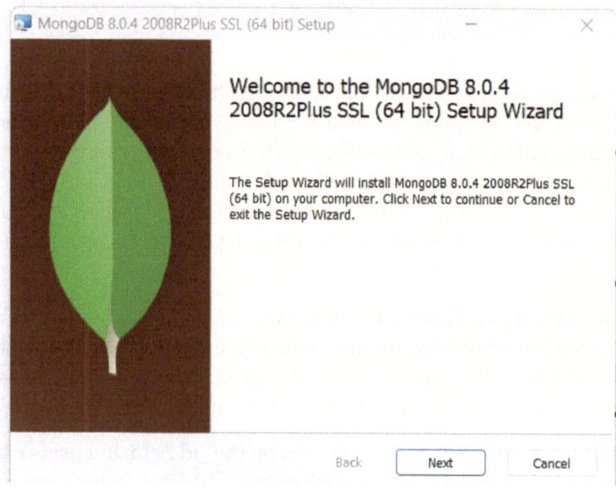

Figure 12.3: *Installation wizard*

6. Accept the license agreement and click **Next**, as shown in *Figure 12.4*:

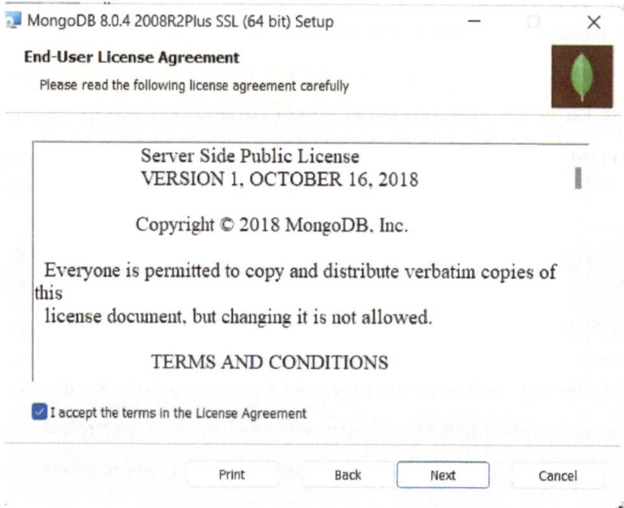

Figure 12.4: *Installation wizard license agreement*

7. Select **Complete** installation for default settings, as shown in *Figure 12.5:*

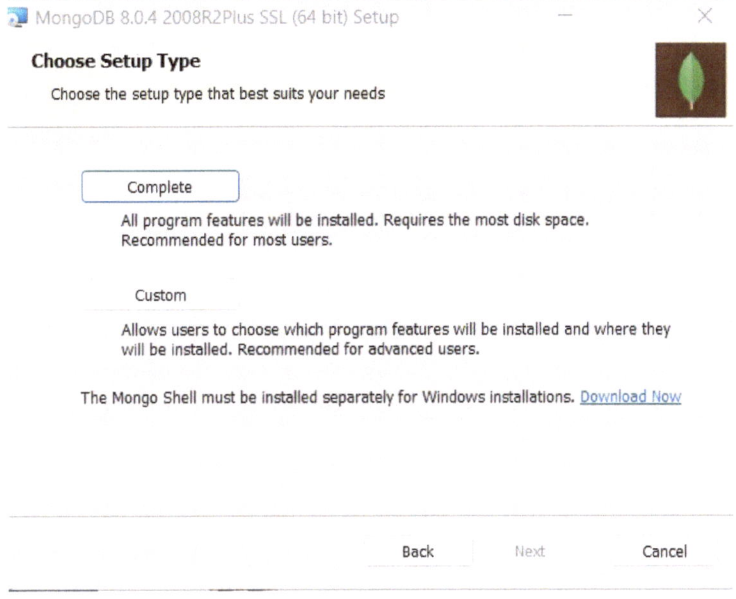

***Figure 12.5:** Installation wizard setup type*

8. Ensure **Run MongoDB as a Windows Service** is checked (recommended), as shown in *Figure 12.6:*

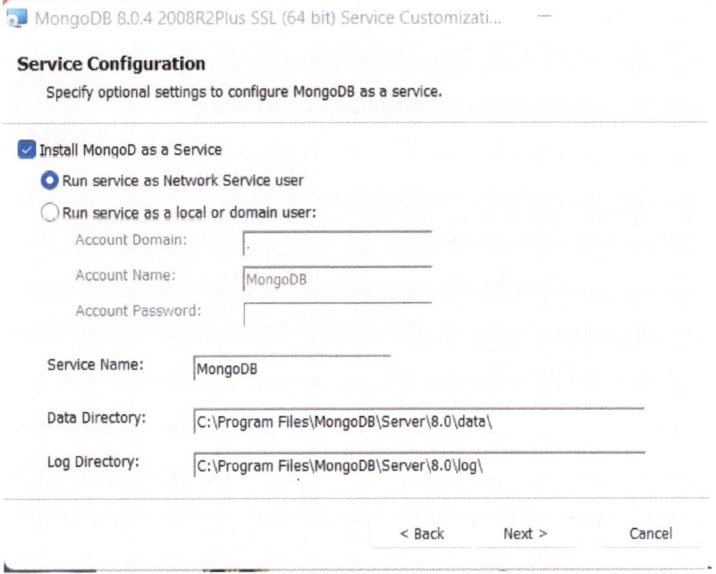

***Figure 12.6:** Choose a directory for installation*

9. Click **Next** and select the option to **Install MongoDB Compass** GUI for MongoDB, and click **Next** to proceed further, as shown in *Figure 12.7:*

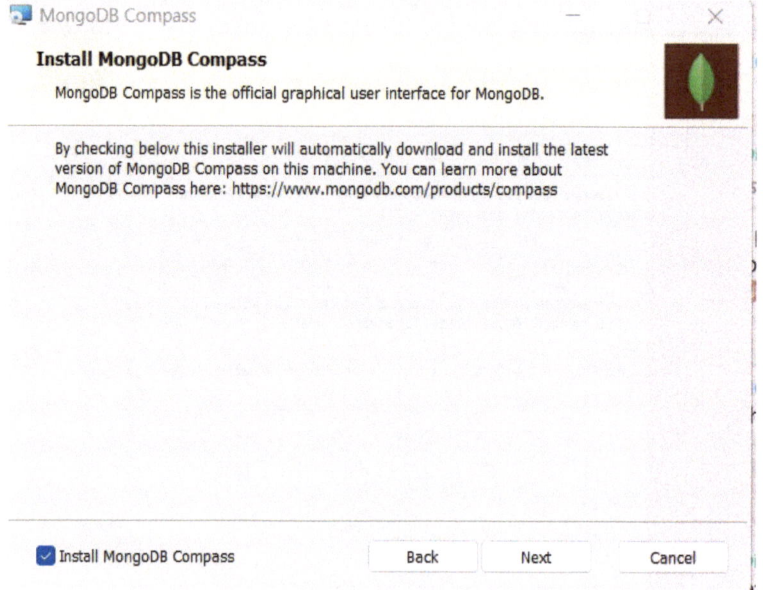

Figure 12.7: *Install MongoDB Compass GUI for MongoDB*

10. Click **Install** to start the installation, as shown in *Figure 12.8:*

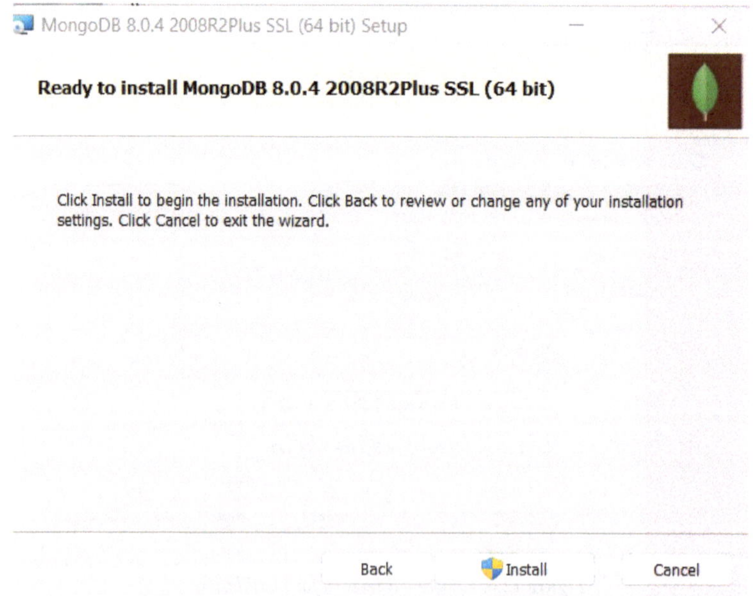

Figure 12.8: *Click Install to begin installation*

11. Next, you will see the installation progress, as shown in *Figure 12.9*:

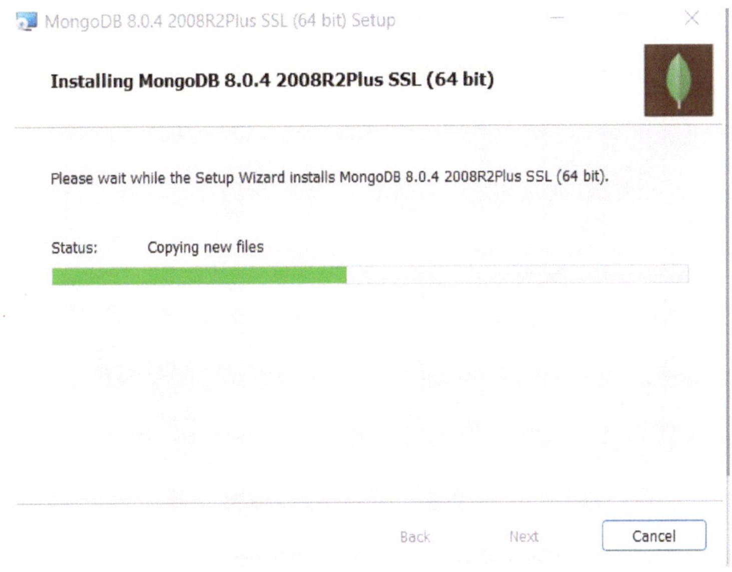

Figure 12.9*: Installation in progress*

12. Finally, once MongoDB is completely installed, you will see the message, as shown in *Figure 12.10*:

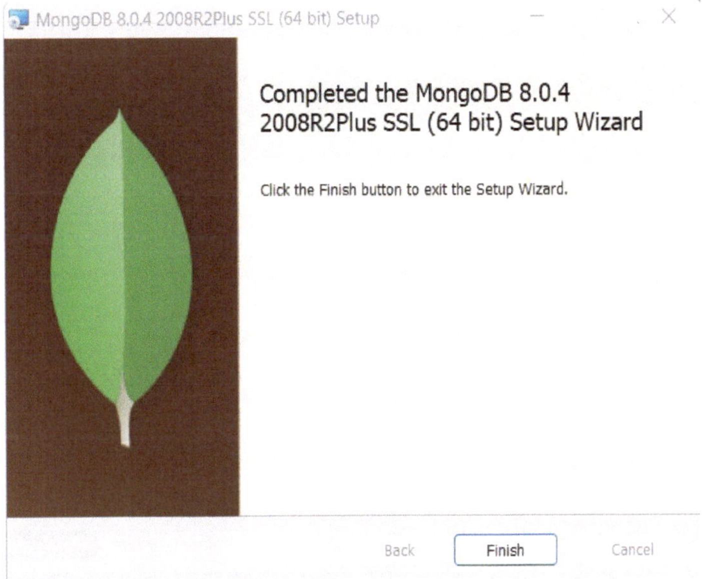

Figure 12.10*: Installation completed*

13. Next, to start working, open the **MongoDBCompass** by clicking on the icon on the desktop, as shown in *Figure 12.11*:

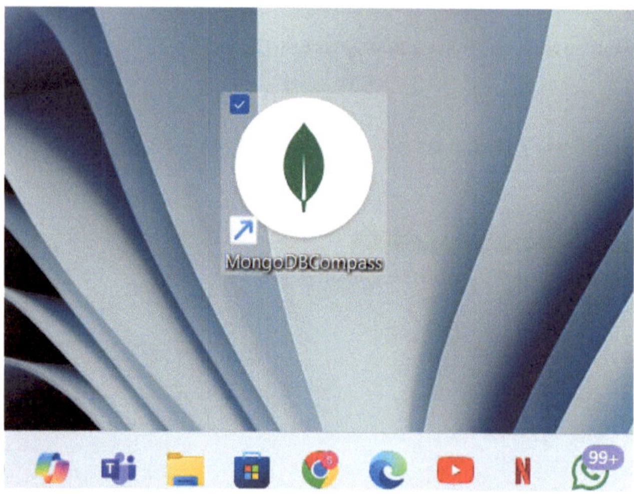

Figure 12.11*: Icon for MongoDB Compass*

14. On clicking the icon, it will open the GUI of **MongoDB Compass**.
15. Next, click on **Add new connection**, which will open a window showing the connection URL to the MongoDB service, as shown in *Figure 12.12*:

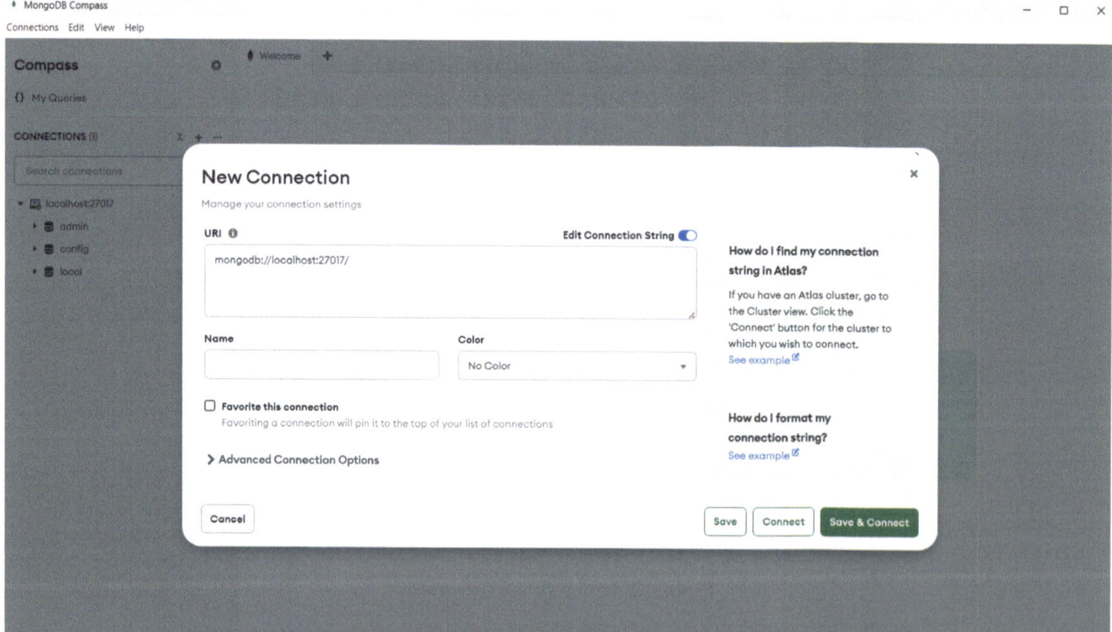

Figure 12.12*: Connection with MongoDB service*

16. This window shows the URI for the MongoDB service. Click on **Connect** to start the service, and you are ready to work.
17. *Figure 12.13* shows the options to **Open MongoDB shell** and **Create database** in the top right corner to begin the work:

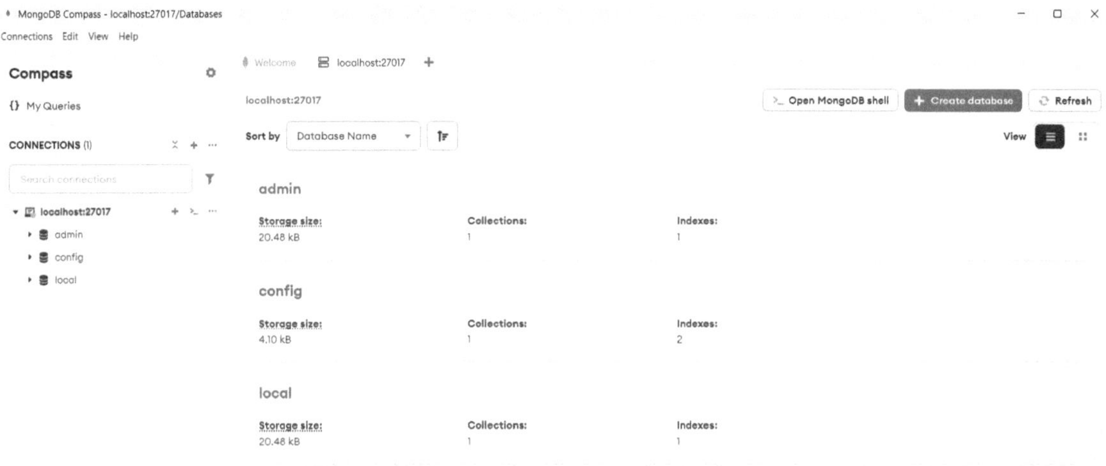

***Figure 12.13**: GUI to work with MongoDB*

To start the MongoDB Shell, follow these steps:

1. Click the MongoDB shell written in the top right corner of *Figure 12.13*.
2. After clicking on the icon MongoDB shell, shell will start as shown in *Figure 12.14:*

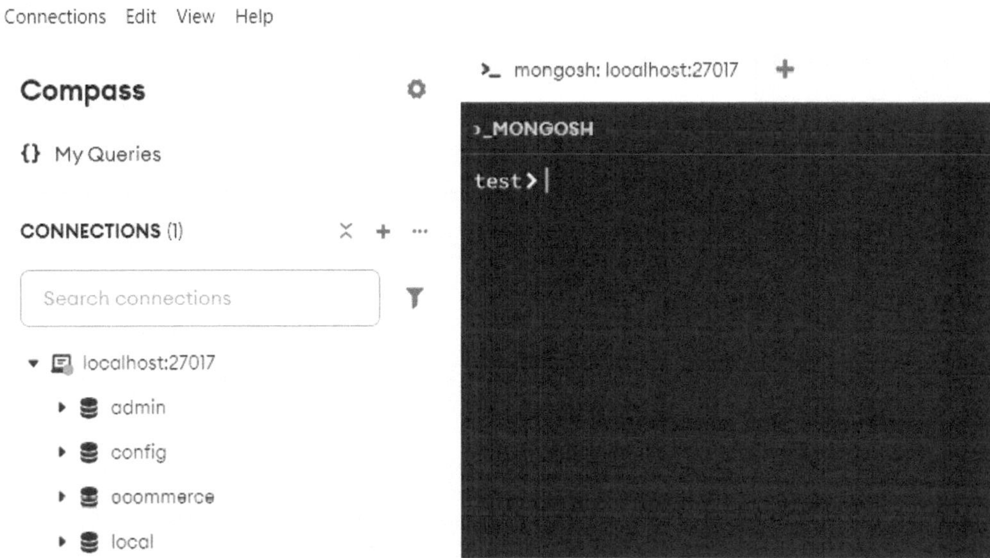

***Figure 12.14**: MongoDB shell*

Refer to the following steps to start MongoDB GUI:

1. To start the MongoDB GUI, click on **Create database**. It will open the new wizard to enter the name of the database and the name of the collection, as shown in *Figure 12.15:*

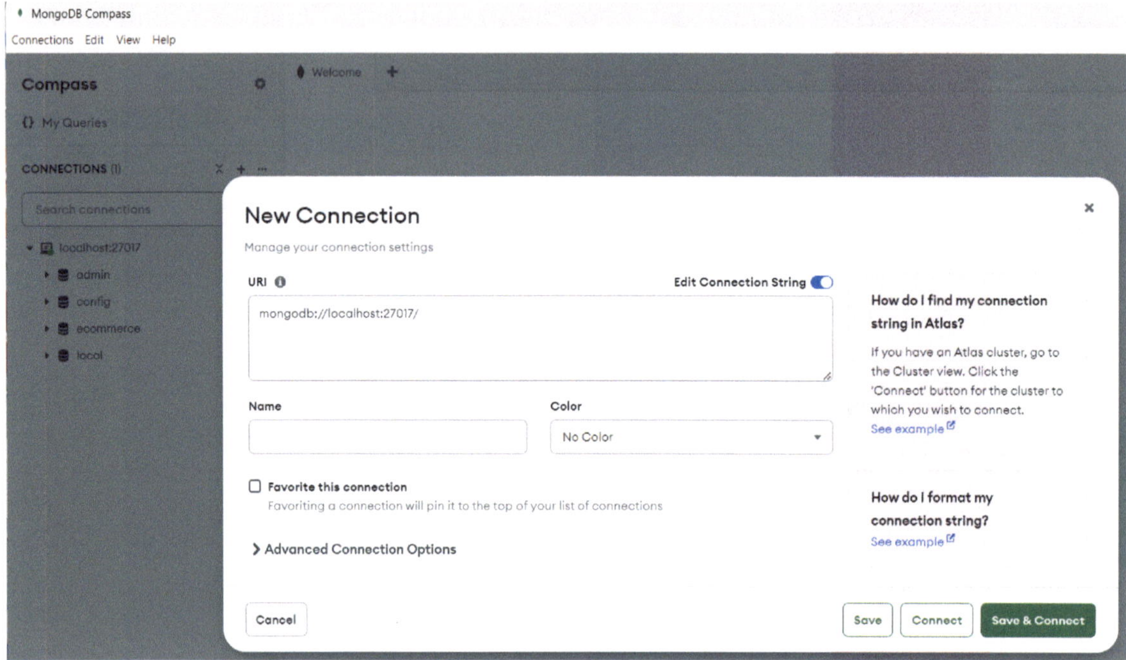

Figure 12.15: Create a database in MongoDB

2. After creating the database, a new window appears. The left panel displays the e-commerce database and provides options for importing and exporting data, updating and deleting data, and more. You can import data from any **comma-separated values (CSV)** or JSON file and begin your analysis, as shown in *Figure 12.16:*

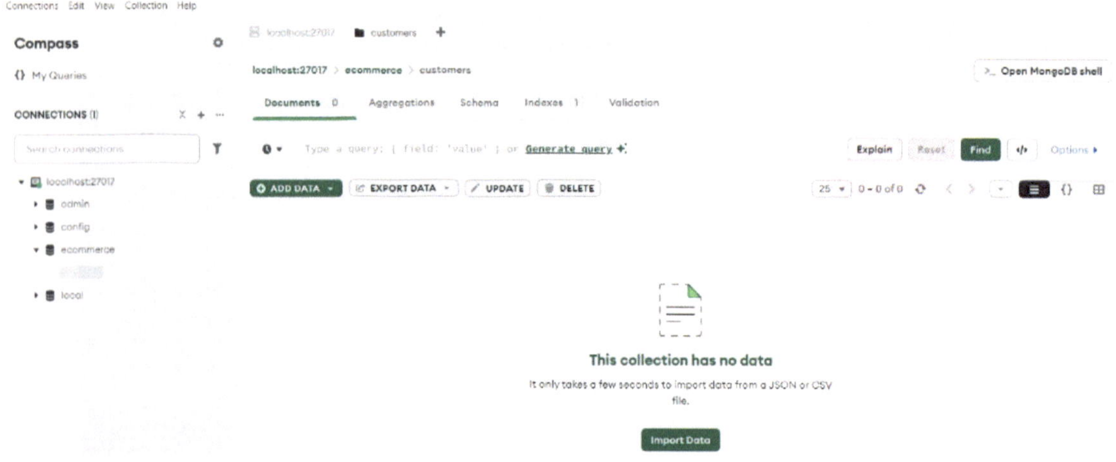

Figure 12.16: GUI for read/write/update operations

MongoDB data model

MongoDB provides two main types of data modelling approaches:

- Embedded data model (Denormalization)
- Referenced data model (Normalization)

The following points provide a clearer understanding of these approaches:

- **Embedded data model**: In this model, related data is stored in the same document as nested sub-documents instead of separate collections, as shown in following code.

  It is suitable for data that is frequently accessed together, applications requiring fast read operations, and for applications where the dataset is not too large, for example, an e-commerce order management system may store order details with embedded customer and product details.

  Refer to the following code:

```
{
  "_id": 1001,
  "customer": {
    "name": "Teana",
    "email": "teana@example.com",
    "city": "Delhi"
  },
  "products": [
    { "name": "iPhone 14", "price": 999 },
    { "name": "Nike Shoes", "price": 120 }
  ],
  "total": 1119,
  "date": "2024-02-06"
}
```

  This model is suitable for faster reads, as joining multiple collections is unnecessary. It provides single-query retrieval as all required data is in one document. It is efficient for write-heavy applications. However, product details are repeated if multiple orders contain the same product. MongoDB enforces a 16 MB document size limit, which can be a constraint when dealing with large datasets.

- **Referenced data model**: This model stores related data in separate collections, and references (foreign keys) are used to link them. It is appropriate when data is shared across multiple documents, and updates are frequent, as changes can be made in a single place without duplication. Additionally, this model is beneficial when documents may exceed the 16 MB size limit imposed by MongoDB.

  For example, refer to the following code for the `Customers` collection (customers) of the referenced data model:

```
{
  "_id": 1,
  "name": "Alice",
  "email": "alice@example.com",
  "city": "New York"
}
```

Products collection (products):

```
{
  "_id": 101,
  "name": "iPhone 14",
  "category": "Electronics",
  "price": 999
}
```

Orders collection (orders):

```
{
  "_id": 1001,
  "customer_id": 1,
  "products": [101, 103],
  "total": 1119,
  "date": "2024-02-06"
}
```

This model avoids data duplication, as product details are stored only once in a separate collection. It also simplifies the updates, as you update once in the product collection; it will be effective for all orders. It is optimized for large datasets. However, reads are slower in this model because they require multiple queries and involve more complex joins to retrieve related data.

MongoDB data hierarchy

MongoDB follows a structured hierarchy of data organization that enables flexible and scalable data storage.

Here is a detailed breakdown of each level in the hierarchy:

- **MongoDB instance**: A MongoDB instance refers to the MongoDB server running on a machine. It manages databases, handles client requests, and performs read/write operations. A single MongoDB instance can manage multiple databases. It can be deployed in standalone mode, replica sets (for high availability), or sharded clusters (for horizontal scaling).

  It can communicate with clients via **MongoDB shell** (**mongosh**) or drivers (Python, Node.js, Java, etc.). In MongoDB Compass, the instance represents the server you connect to, which may be one of the following:

  - A local MongoDB server (localhost:27017 by default).
  - A remote MongoDB server (hosted on a cloud or another machine).
  - A MongoDB Atlas cluster (MongoDB's cloud database service).

- **Database**: A database in MongoDB is a logical container that holds collections (similar to a database in relational databases). Each database stores documents grouped in collections. A MongoDB instance can contain multiple databases, each with its own collection set. MongoDB includes a default database called `admin`, which stores user authentication details.

  Here are some commands to work with databases:

  - **use myDatabase**: This command is used to create or switch to a database. The `use` command switches to the specified database. If the database does not exist, MongoDB will create it automatically once a document is inserted into a collection. Unlike SQL, MongoDB does not create empty databases. It only exists when data is added, e.g., use `shopDB` if you check the database list using `show dbs`, you would not see `shopDB` until you insert a document in it.

- **show dbs**: This command is used to view available databases. It shows only the databases with at least one collection and document. E.g., when you execute this command, the output may look like the following code:

  ```
  > show dbs
  admin     0.000GB
  config    0.000GB
  local     0.000GB
  shopDB    0.002GB
  ```

  The output displays three additional databases, in addition to **shopDB**. The **admin** database stores user authentication and administrative settings. The **local** database stores instance-specific information (e.g., replication), and the **config** database is used in sharded cluster configurations.

- **db.dropDatabase()**: This command is used to delete a database. It deletes the current database that you are using. This command removes all collections and data inside the database. You must ensure that you are using the correct database before executing **db.dropDatabase()**, as once deleted, it cannot be undone.

  Refer to the following code:

  ```
  use shopDB   # Switch to the database
  db.dropDatabase()
  ```

  Example output:

  ```
  { "dropped": "shopDB", "ok": 1 }
  ```

- **Collection**: It is a group of related documents, similar to a table in relational databases, but without a fixed schema. Collections store documents in BSON format. These are schema-less, i.e., documents in a collection can have different structures. Collections are automatically created when inserting the first document.

  Refer to the following code to see the document in the **products** collection:

  ```
  {
     "_id": ObjectId("64a3fbd77d2b3a001e33d45a"),
     "name": "Laptop",
     "brand": "Dell",
     "price": 999.99,
     "stock": 50
  }
  ```

  In this **document**, **_id** refers to the unique **ObjectId** assigned automatically if not provided, **name** is the product name, **brand** is the brand of the product, **price** shows the price of the product, and **stock** refers to the available stock quantity.

  Here are some commands to work with while using collections:

  - **db.createCollection("products")**: This command explicitly creates a new collection named **products**. Although this is not required in most cases because MongoDB automatically creates a collection when you insert a document. The **createCollection** command is useful if you need specific settings like capped collections (size-limited) or validation rules, e.g., you may create a capped collection (max size of 1MB): **db.createCollection("logs", { capped: true, size: 1048576 })**.

  - **show collections**: In MongoDB, the **show collections** command lists all collections within the currently selected database (the one specified using **use <dbname>**). Collections are MongoDB's equivalent of tables in relational databases. For a collection to appear in this list, it must either be explicitly created using `db.createCollection("name")` or contain at least one inserted document (like after running `db.collection.insertOne({...})`). It is important to note that `show dbs` only displays databases that have at least one collection with data, while `show collections` will show all collections in the current database, including empty ones that were manually created. For example, after inserting a document into a new collection (e.g., `db.products.insertOne({ name: "Laptop" })`), running `show collections` will display that collection (e.g., `"products"`). If no collections appear when running this command, it typically means either the database is empty or no data has been inserted yet. Always verify you are working in the correct database using `db.getName()` if you encounter unexpected results.

```
> show collections
products
orders
customers
```

- **db.products.drop()**: This command will delete the entire `products` collection from the database. It will also remove all documents in the collection. This command should be used with caution, as it permanently deletes all data in the collection. Nevertheless, unlike `dropDatabase()`, this only removes a single collection, not the entire database.

- **Document**: A document is a single record stored in a collection. It is the equivalent of a row in relational databases, but it is stored in BSON format for efficiency. Documents have a flexible schema, i.e., documents in the same collection can have different fields. Each document must have a `unique _id` field, which acts as a primary key.

Application development in MongoDB

In this section, you will learn to develop an application using MongoDB with the help of a case study on the online e-commerce platform. Assume ShopEase is an online e-commerce platform where customers can browse and purchase products. The company uses MongoDB to store customer information, order details, and product reviews. We will create a customer collection that stores customer details and an order collection that records purchase transactions. The `Customer` collection and the order collection are given as follows:

```
[
  { "_id": 1, "name": "Rajesh Sharma", "email": "rajesh@gmail.com", "age": 32, "city": "Mumbai",
"state": "Maharashtra" },
  { "_id": 2, "name": "Priya Verma", "email": "priya@gmail.com", "age": 27, "city": "Bangalore",
"state": "Karnataka" },
  { "_id": 3, "name": "Amit Tiwari", "email": "amit@gmail.com", "age": 40, "city": "Delhi",
"state": "Delhi" },
  { "_id": 4, "name": "Sneha Iyer", "email": "sneha@gmail.com", "age": 29, "city": "Chennai",
"state": "Tamil Nadu" },
  { "_id": 5, "name": "Vikram Singh", "email": "vikram@gmail.com", "age": 35, "city": "Jaipur",
"state": "Rajasthan" }
]
```

```
Orders Collection
```

```
  [
  { "_id": 101, "customer_id": 1, "product": "Samsung Smartphone", "amount": 25000, "status":
```

```
"Delivered", "payment_mode": "UPI" },
  { "_id": 102, "customer_id": 2, "product": "Dell Laptop", "amount": 55000, "status": "Shipped", "payment_mode": "Credit Card" },
  { "_id": 103, "customer_id": 3, "product": "Sony Headphones", "amount": 3000, "status": "Delivered", "payment_mode": "Debit Card" },
  { "_id": 104, "customer_id": 4, "product": "Apple iPad", "amount": 45000, "status": "Pending", "payment_mode": "Net Banking" },
  { "_id": 105, "customer_id": 5, "product": "JBL Speaker", "amount": 7000, "status": "Delivered", "payment_mode": "UPI" },
  { "_id": 106, "customer_id": 1, "product": "Canon DSLR", "amount": 60000, "status": "Shipped", "payment_mode": "Credit Card" },
  { "_id": 107, "customer_id": 2, "product": "HP Monitor", "amount": 15000, "status": "Delivered", "payment_mode": "Debit Card" },
  { "_id": 108, "customer_id": 3, "product": "Wireless Keyboard", "amount": 2500, "status": "Pending", "payment_mode": "Net Banking" },
  { "_id": 109, "customer_id": 4, "product": "Gaming Mouse", "amount": 2000, "status": "Shipped", "payment_mode": "UPI" },
  { "_id": 110, "customer_id": 5, "product": "Samsung Charger", "amount": 1500, "status": "Delivered", "payment_mode": "UPI" }
]
```

MongoDB requires a database to store collections. If the database does not exist, MongoDB creates it when you insert data. Let us create a new database for e-commerce using the MongoDB shell as:

```
>show dbs
```

Refer to *Figure 12.17:*

```
test> show dbs
admin        40.00 KiB
config      108.00 KiB
ecommerce   248.00 KiB
local        72.00 KiB
sample        8.00 KiB
test> use ecommerce
switched to db ecommerce
ecommerce>
```

***Figure 12.17**: Create a database using the MongoDB shell*

You can also create a database via the GUI using the following steps:

1. Refer to *Figure 12.18*:

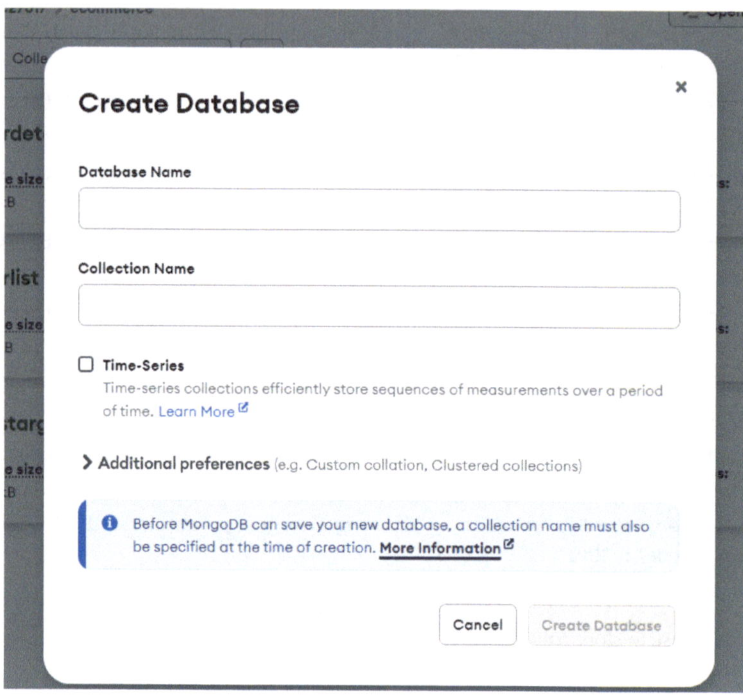

***Figure 12.18:** Create a database using the MongoDB GUI*

2. Another option is to import the data from a `.csv` or JSON file by clicking on the browse data button shown in *Figure 12.19:*

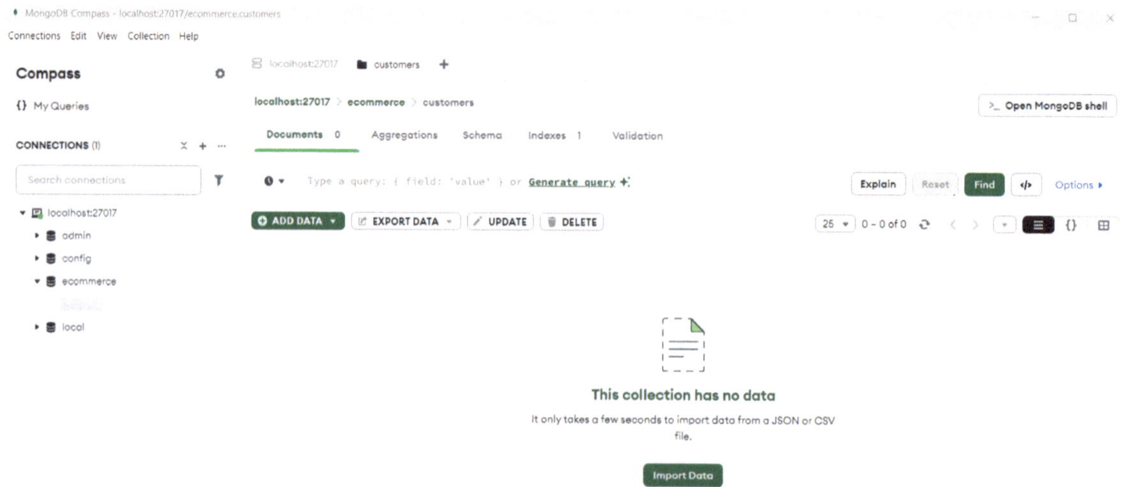

***Figure 12.19:** Import data in MongoDB*

3. Next step is to browse the data file from any location on your device. Here, we import the **orderdetails.csv** file, as shown in *Figure 12.20*:

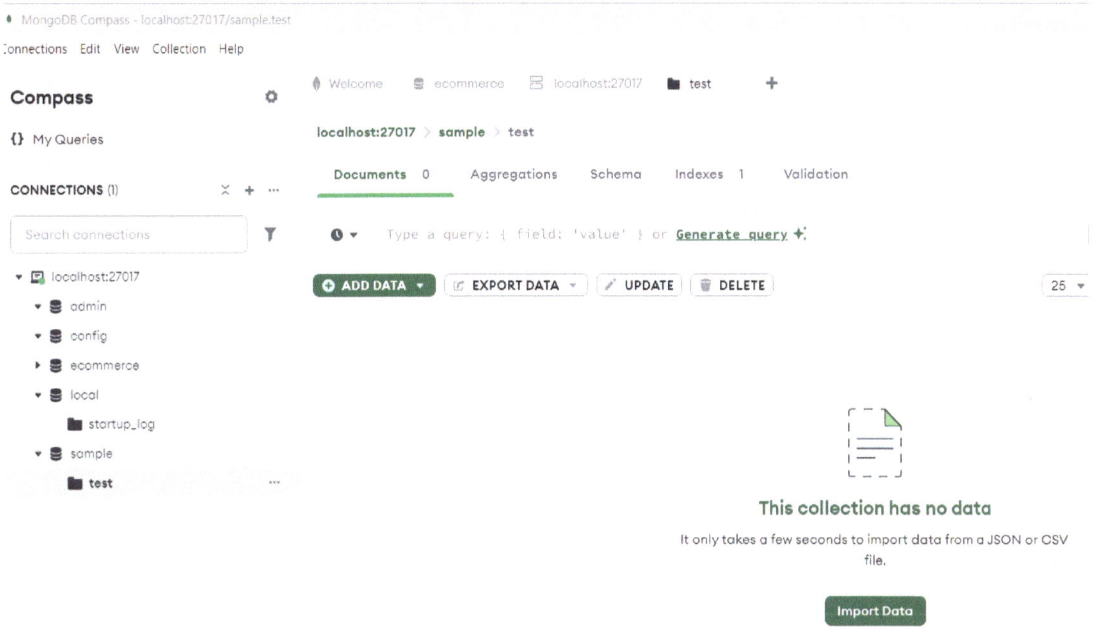

***Figure 12.20**: Import orderdetails.csv file*

4. Finally, on clicking the import, as shown in *Figure 12.19*, the **orderdetails** data gets stored in the MongoDB, as shown in *Figure 12.21:*

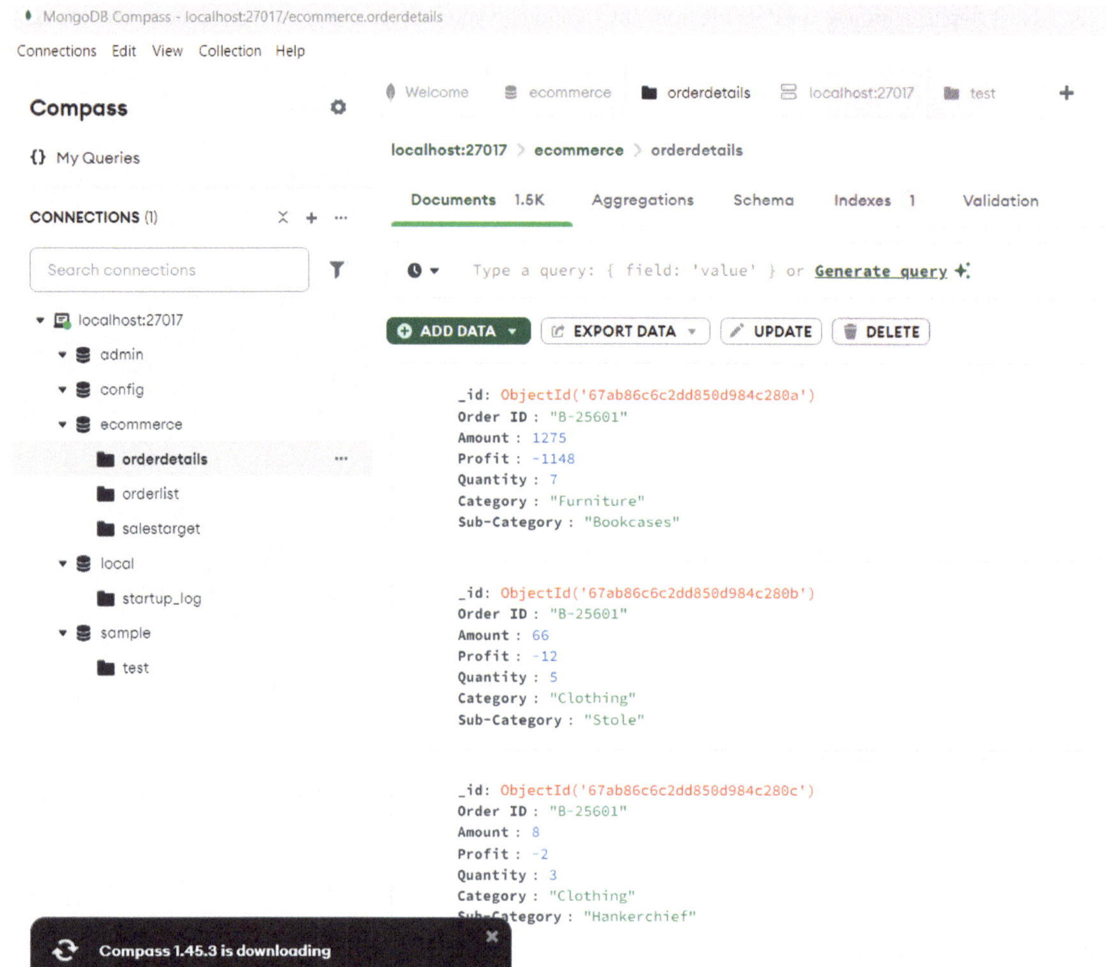

Figure 12.21: Data imported into MongoDB

CRUD operations in MongoDB

Let us apply CRUD operations to our case study:

- **Create/Switch database**: The use command is used to create (or switch to) any database. The following query is used to create/switch to the sales database:

```
>use salesDatabase
```

- **Create collections (optional)**: In MongoDB, the `db.createCollection()` method is used to create a new collection within the current database explicitly. In most cases, MongoDB creates collections automatically when data is inserted. Refer to the following code to explicitly create collections `salestarget`, `orderlist`, and `orderdetails`:

```
db.createCollection("salestarget")
db.createCollection("orderlist")
db.createCollection("orderdetails")
```

- **Insert data**: Now, we insert sample records into the collections. **`db.salestarget.insertOne({...})`** is a MongoDB command to insert a single document into the desired (**`salestarget/orderlist/orderdetails,`** etc.) collection. Internally, MongoDB checks if the collection exists; if not, it creates the collection automatically.

  The following code inserts the document into the **`salestarget`**, **`orderlist`**, and **`orderdetails`** collections. If the **`_id`** already exists, the insertion will fail due to a duplicate key error:

  - Insert into the **`salestarget`** collection:

    ```
    db.salestarget.insertOne({
      "_id": ObjectId("67ab86d2c2dd850d984c2de7"),
      "Month of Order Date": "Apr-18",
      "Category": "Furniture",
      "Target": 10400
    })
    ```

  - Insert into the **`orderlist`** collection:

    ```
    db.orderlist.insertOne({
      "_id": ObjectId("67ab857ac2dd850d984c260c"),
      "Order ID": "B-25601",
      "Order Date": "01-04-2018",
      "CustomerName": "Bharat",
      "State": "Gujarat",
      "City": "Ahmedabad"
    })
    ```

  - Insert into the **`orderdetails`** collection:

    ```
    db.orderdetails.insertOne({
      "_id": ObjectId("67ab86c6c2dd850d984c280a"),
      "Order ID": "B-25601",
      "Amount": 1275,
      "Profit": -1148,
      "Quantity": 7,
      "Category": "Furniture",
      "Sub-Category": "Bookcases"
    })
    ```

- **Read data (find() operation)**: In MongoDB, the **`.find()`** method is used to retrieve documents from different collections. The **`find()`** method, without any filter, returns all documents from the specified collection.

  For example, the following code is used to retrieve all documents from the **`salestarget`**, **`orderlist`**, and **`orderdetails`** collections, respectively:

```
db.salestarget.find()
db.orderlist.find()
db["orderdetails"].find()
```

```
mongosh mongodb://127.0.0.1 ×  +
  2 |

ecommerce> db["orderdetails"].find()
[
  {
    _id: ObjectId('67ab86c6c2dd850d984c280a'),
    'Order ID': 'B-25601',
    Amount: 1275,
    Profit: -1148,
    Quantity: 7,
    Category: 'Furniture',
    'Sub-Category': 'Bookcases'
  },
  {
    _id: ObjectId('67ab86c6c2dd850d984c280b'),
    'Order ID': 'B-25601',
    Amount: 66,
    Profit: -12,
    Quantity: 5,
    Category: 'Clothing',
    'Sub-Category': 'Stole'
  },
  {
    _id: ObjectId('67ab86c6c2dd850d984c280c'),
    'Order ID': 'B-25601',
    Amount: 8,
    Profit: -2,
    Quantity: 3,
    Category: 'Clothing',
    'Sub-Category': 'Hankerchief'
  },
  {
```

Figure 12.22: *Use of the find() method*

The **find()** method can also be used for projections, that is, to retrieve the desired documents based on certain conditions. For example, to find orders from **Gujarat**, use the following query:

```
db.orderlist.find({ "State": "Gujarat" })
```

The output is shown in *Figure 12.23*.

This query retrieves all documents from the **orderlist** where the **State** field is **Gujarat**. MongoDB uses BSON, so string values are case-sensitive.

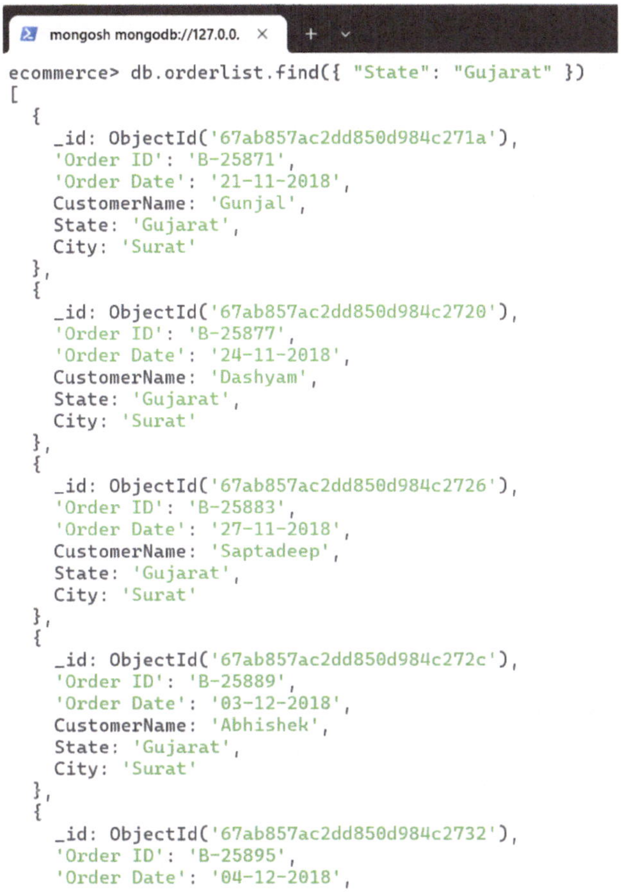

```
mongosh mongodb://127.0.0.

ecommerce> db.orderlist.find({ "State": "Gujarat" })
[
  {
    _id: ObjectId('67ab857ac2dd850d984c271a'),
    'Order ID': 'B-25871',
    'Order Date': '21-11-2018',
    CustomerName: 'Gunjal',
    State: 'Gujarat',
    City: 'Surat'
  },
  {
    _id: ObjectId('67ab857ac2dd850d984c2720'),
    'Order ID': 'B-25877',
    'Order Date': '24-11-2018',
    CustomerName: 'Dashyam',
    State: 'Gujarat',
    City: 'Surat'
  },
  {
    _id: ObjectId('67ab857ac2dd850d984c2726'),
    'Order ID': 'B-25883',
    'Order Date': '27-11-2018',
    CustomerName: 'Saptadeep',
    State: 'Gujarat',
    City: 'Surat'
  },
  {
    _id: ObjectId('67ab857ac2dd850d984c272c'),
    'Order ID': 'B-25889',
    'Order Date': '03-12-2018',
    CustomerName: 'Abhishek',
    State: 'Gujarat',
    City: 'Surat'
  },
  {
    _id: ObjectId('67ab857ac2dd850d984c2732'),
    'Order ID': 'B-25895',
    'Order Date': '04-12-2018',
```

Figure 12.23: find() method to retrieve selected data

In the next query, the **find()** method is used to retrieve all documents from **orderdetails**, where the **Profit** field is less than 0 (**$lt** means less than), also illustrated in *Figure 12.24*:

```
db.orderdetails.find({ "Profit": { $lt: 0 } })
```

```
mongosh mongodb://127.0.0.
ecommerce> db.orderdetails.find({ "Profit": { $lt: 0 }
[
  {
    _id: ObjectId('67ab86c6c2dd850d984c280a'),
    'Order ID': 'B-25601',
    Amount: 1275,
    Profit: -1148,
    Quantity: 7,
    Category: 'Furniture',
    'Sub-Category': 'Bookcases'
  },
  {
    _id: ObjectId('67ab86c6c2dd850d984c280b'),
    'Order ID': 'B-25601',
    Amount: 66,
    Profit: -12,
    Quantity: 5,
    Category: 'Clothing',
    'Sub-Category': 'Stole'
  },
  {
```

Figure 12.24: Find method to filter data

- **Update data (updateOne() and updateMany())**: These methods are used to modify existing documents in a collection. `updateOne()` updates a single document that matches the given filter. If multiple documents match, only the first document found will be updated.

  Syntax: `db.collection.updateOne(filter, update, options)`

  Here, `filter` is used to specify the condition to match documents, **update** defines the update operation using operators like `$set`, `$inc`, `$rename`, etc., and options (optional), e.g., { `upsert: true` } (creates a document if no match is found).

  Example query 1: Update target sales for furniture in April 2018 as:

  ```
  db.salestarget.updateOne(  { "Month of Order Date": "Apr-18", "Category": "Furniture" },{
  $set: { "Target": 11000 } } )
  ```

  The preceding query updates the target from 10,400 to 11,000 only for the first matching document where the `Month of Order Date` is Apr-18, as shown in *Figure 12.25:*

```
}
ecommerce> db.salestarget.updateOne(  { "Month of Order Date": "Jun-18", "Category": "Furnit
ure" },{ $set: { "Target": 15000 } } )
{
  acknowledged: true,
  insertedId: null,
  matchedCount: 1,
  modifiedCount: 1,
  upsertedCount: 0
}
ecommerce> |
```

Figure 12.25: Use of the updateOne() method

Similarly, you can use `updateMany()`. It will update all documents that match the given filter condition. It has similar parameters as `updateOne()`, but applies changes to multiple documents.

Syntax: `db.collection.updateMany(filter, update, options)`

- **Delete data (deleteOne() and deleteMany()**: MongoDB provides two methods to delete documents from a collection. `deleteOne()` to delete a single document that matches the filter and `deleteMany()` to delete all documents that match the filter, as shown in *Figure 12.26*.

  Syntax: `db.collection.deleteOne(filter)`

  Example query 1: Delete a specific order from the `orderlist` as:

```
db.orderlist.deleteOne({ "Order ID": "B-25601" })
```

  The preceding query deletes the first matching order where *Order ID* is *B-25601*.

  Example query 2: Delete all orders from a specific city as:

```
db.orderlist.deleteMany({ "City": "Ahmedabad" })
```

  The preceding query deletes all orders from *Ahmedabad*.

```
ecommerce> db.orderlist.deleteOne({ "Order ID": "B-25603" })
{ acknowledged: true, deletedCount: 1 }
ecommerce> |
```

***Figure 12.26**: Execution of deleteOne() and deleteMany()*

Aggregation in MongoDB for sales analysis

Aggregation in MongoDB is a powerful framework used to process and analyze data by transforming documents through multiple stages. It allows you to perform computations, such as filtering, grouping, sorting, and calculating aggregate values (sum, average, etc.). Aggregation operations help in analyzing sales performance, profit trends, and target achievements. MongoDB provides multiple ways to aggregate data:

- **Map-reduce (mapReduce())**: It is used for complex computations, but is less efficient than an aggregation pipeline.
- **Single-purpose aggregation (count(), distinct(), group())**: Simple aggregation operations.
- **Aggregation pipeline (aggregate())**: The aggregation pipeline processes data through multiple stages, where each stage transforms the documents before passing them to the next stage.

  Syntax:

```
db.collection.aggregate([
  { stage1 },
  { stage2 },
  { stage3 },
  ...
])
```

  Here, `db.collection` refers to the collection on which the aggregation runs, aggregate([]) accepts an array of stages, and each {stage} represents a transformation step.

  Table 12.3 shows the key aggregation stages and their syntax:

Stage	Description	Syntax example
`$match`	Filters documents	`{ $match: { status: "A" } }`
`$group`	Groups documents by expression	`{ $group: { _id: "$department", total: { $sum: "$salary" } } }`
`$sort`	Orders documents	`{ $sort: { age: 1, name: -1 } }`
`$project`	Reshapes documents	`{ $project: { name: 1, department: 1, _id: 0 } }`
`$limit`	Restricts document count	`{ $limit: 5 }`
`$skip`	Skips documents	`{ $skip: 10 }`
`$unwind`	Deconstructs arrays	`{ $unwind: "$tags" }`
`$lookup`	Left outer join	`{ $lookup: { from: "inventory", localField: "item", foreignField: "sku", as: "inventory_docs" } }`
`$count`	Counts documents	`{ $count: "total_employees" }`
`$addFields`	Adds new fields	`{ $addFields: { bonus: { $multiply: ["$salary", 0.1] } } }`

***Table 12.3**: Key aggregation stages and their syntax*

Here are some real-time aggregation examples using our dataset:

- **To find the total sales revenue grouped by category**: The following query helps to analyze which category generates the most revenue:

```
db.orderdetails.aggregate([
  { $group: { _id: "$Category", TotalSales: { $sum: "$Amount" } } }
])
```

  Refer to *Figure 12.27:*

```
ecommerce> db.orderlist.deleteOne({ "Order ID": "B-25603" })
{ acknowledged: true, deletedCount: 1 }
ecommerce> db.orderdetails.aggregate([
...    { $group: { _id: "$Category", TotalSales: { $sum: "$Amount" } } }
... ])
...
[
  { _id: 'Furniture', TotalSales: 127181 },
  { _id: 'Clothing', TotalSales: 139054 },
  { _id: 'Electronics', TotalSales: 165267 }
]
ecommerce> |
```

***Figure 12.27**: Sales revenue grouped by category*

- **Find most profitable categories**: The example query identifies loss-making categories (e.g., furniture is in loss):

```
db.orderdetails.aggregate([
  { $group: { _id: "$Category", TotalProfit: { $sum: "$Profit" } } },
  { $sort: { TotalProfit: -1 } }
])
```

```
ecommerce> db.orderdetails.aggregate([
...     { $group: { _id: "$Category", TotalProfit: { $sum: "$Profit" } } },
...     { $sort: { TotalProfit: -1 } }
... ])
...
[
  { _id: 'Clothing', TotalProfit: 11163 },
  { _id: 'Electronics', TotalProfit: 10494 },
  { _id: 'Furniture', TotalProfit: 2298 }
]
ecommerce> |
```

Figure 12.28: *Profitable categories sorted in descending order*

Conclusion

In this chapter, we explored the fundamental concepts of NoSQL databases and their significance in modern data management. We examined the various types of NoSQL databases and their comparisons to traditional relational databases. The CAP theorem provided insights into the trade-offs between consistency, availability, and partition tolerance in distributed systems. We then learned about MongoDB, its key features, such as schema flexibility, scalability, and high performance. The chapter also covered MongoDB's data model, installation, and how to set up a running instance for development.

Furthermore, we examined CRUD operations and explored the aggregation framework, which enables efficient data processing and analysis. These concepts form the foundation for developing applications using MongoDB, enabling robust data storage and retrieval mechanisms.

In the next chapter, we will delve into Apache Spark, a powerful distributed computing framework used for processing and analyzing big data. We will cover its architecture, key components, and how it enables large-scale data processing with high speed and efficiency.

Points to remember

Here are some key takeaways from this chapter:

- NoSQL databases are non-relational databases designed to handle large-scale, distributed, and unstructured data efficiently.
- NoSQL databases are classified into key-value stores, document stores, column-family stores, and graph databases, each suited for different use cases.
- The CAP theorem states that a distributed database can provide only two out of three guarantees: consistency, availability, and partition tolerance.
- MongoDB is a document-based NoSQL database that provides high performance, scalability, and flexibility for modern applications.
- MongoDB addresses the limitations of relational databases by offering a schema-less design, easy scalability, and support for large-scale applications.
- MongoDB supports flexible document storage, high availability, horizontal scaling, and a powerful aggregation framework.
- MongoDB uses a document-oriented data model where data is stored in JSON-like BSON format, allowing nested and flexible structures.
- MongoDB can be installed on various platforms and run as a service or standalone instance for database operations.

- Involves using MongoDB for data storage, retrieval, and manipulation through its query language and aggregation framework.
- CRUD operations are the basic operations to create, read, update, and delete documents in a MongoDB collection.
- Aggregation operators are used for data transformation, analysis, and complex queries, enabling efficient data processing.

Multiple choice questions

1. **Which of the following is not a type of NoSQL database?**
   a. Document store
   b. Relational store
   c. Key-value store
   d. Column-family store
2. **What does the C in CAP theorem stand for?**
   a. Connectivity
   b. Consistency
   c. Concurrency
   d. Complexity
3. **Which data format does MongoDB primarily use for storing documents?**
   a. JSON
   b. BSON
   c. XML
   d. CSV
4. **Which MongoDB operation is used to retrieve all documents from a collection?**
   a. db.collection.findAll()
   b. collection.fetch()
   c. db.collection.find({})
   d. db.collection.getAll()
5. **What is the purpose of the $group stage in MongoDB aggregation?**
   a. To filter documents
   b. To join collections
   c. To group documents based on a specified field
   d. To delete documents
6. **Which of the following is not a feature of MongoDB?**
   a. Schema-less architecture
   b. Horizontal scaling
   c. ACID Transactions support for all operations
   d. Support for complex queries using aggregation

7. **Which command is used to import data into MongoDB from a JSON file?**
   a. mongoimport
   b. mongodump
   c. mongorestore
   d. mongoexport
8. **In MongoDB, which data type does not exist?**
   a. String
   b. Blob
   c. ObjectId
   d. Array
9. **Which command is used to check all databases in MongoDB?**
   a. Show databases
   b. List dbs
   c. Display databases
   d. db.getAll()
10. **Which of the following is true about MongoDB's indexing?**
    a. Indexing is not supported in MongoDB
    b. Indexes improve query performance by speeding up searches
    c. Indexes slow down read operations
    d. MongoDB automatically creates indexes for all fields

Answers

1. b.	2. b.	3. b.	4. c.	5. c.
6. c.	7. a.	8. b.	9. a.	10. b.

Questions

1. Imagine you are designing a real-time stock trading platform where transactions must be recorded instantly and accurately across multiple servers. Based on the CAP theorem, which two guarantees (consistency, availability, or partition tolerance) would you prioritize, and why?
2. A startup is developing a social media platform that needs to store user profiles, posts, and comments while handling millions of users globally. Would you recommend an SQL or NoSQL database? Justify your choice with at least two reasons.
3. An online marketplace like Amazon or Flipkart needs to store diverse product details, including specifications, reviews, and seller information. How does MongoDB's document-based model provide an advantage over a relational database in this scenario?
4. Describe MongoDB's aggregation framework and how it helps in data analysis.
5. A ride-sharing company like Uber wants to store real-time ride requests, driver locations, and trip details. They need a database that supports fast queries and scales easily as the number of users grows. Would you recommend MongoDB or a relational database for this use case? Justify your choice by discussing scalability, flexibility, and performance.

6. **Case**: Online food delivery app (e.g., Swiggy, Uber Eats, Zomato).

   A food delivery service wants to analyze customer orders, revenue, and restaurant performance. The `orders` collection has the following sample data:

   { "order_id": 101, "customer": "John", "restaurant": "Pizza Hub", "amount": 25, "items": ["Pizza", "Soda"], "date": "2024-02-10", "rating": 4 },

   { "order_id": 102, "customer": "Alice", "restaurant": "Sushi Place", "amount": 40, "items": ["Sushi", "Miso Soup"], "date": "2024-02-11", "rating": 5 },

   { "order_id": 103, "customer": "Bob", "restaurant": "Burger Corner", "amount": 15, "items": ["Burger", "Fries"], "date": "2024-02-12", "rating": 3 },

   { "order_id": 104, "customer": "Alice", "restaurant": "Pizza Hub", "amount": 30, "items": ["Pasta", "Garlic Bread"], "date": "2024-02-13", "rating": 4 },

   { "order_id": 105, "customer": "John", "restaurant": "Sushi Place", "amount": 50, "items": ["Sashimi", "Green Tea"], "date": "2024-02-14", "rating": 5 }

   ]

   Write queries for the following:

   a. Find the total revenue generated by each restaurant.
   b. Find the average order amount across all orders.
   c. Find all orders with a rating of 4 or above.
   d. Find the most popular restaurants based on order count.
   e. Find the top spending customer.

CHAPTER 13
Introduction to Spark for Big Data Processing

The goal is to turn data into information and information into insight.

-Carly Fiorina

Introduction

In today's data-driven world, organizations are constantly seeking faster and more efficient ways to process massive volumes of data. Apache Spark has emerged as a powerful, open-source distributed computing framework designed for processing large-scale data. This chapter provides a comprehensive introduction to Spark, highlighting its key features, such as in-memory computation, scalability, and fault-tolerance, that make it a preferred choice over traditional systems like Hadoop.

We begin by understanding important features of Spark and how it compares with Hadoop in terms of architecture and performance. Next, you will learn about the Spark ecosystem and its interactive environments, such as Spark shell for Scala and PySpark for Python, which make it easier for users to experiment and execute code in real time.

Further, you will learn the core concepts of Spark applications, including SparkSession, jobs, stages, tasks, transformations, and actions, all illustrated through hands-on examples. This is followed by a detailed understanding of lazy evaluation and its implications on performance.

To reinforce learning, the chapter concludes with a practical case study on analyzing **Indian Premier League** (**IPL**) matches data using Apache Spark. This real-world example ties together the theoretical concepts and demonstrates the practical power of Spark in data analytics.

Structure

In this chapter, we will cover the following topics:

- Spark introduction
- Spark vs. Hadoop
- Apache Spark architecture
- Working with Spark-shell in Cloudera and PySpark
- IPL match data analysis using Apache Spark

Objectives

By the end of this chapter, learners will have a comprehensive understanding of Apache Spark, a fast and general-purpose distributed computing framework designed for large-scale data processing. It introduces Spark's key features, such as in-memory computation, fault tolerance, scalability, and modular design, highlighting how these capabilities make Spark suitable for modern data-intensive applications. A comparative overview with Hadoop MapReduce helps learners understand Spark's performance advantages and architectural improvements. The chapter further explores the Spark ecosystem, including components like Spark SQL, Spark Streaming, **machine learning library** (**MLlib**), and GraphX, emphasizing their role in enabling diverse analytical tasks.

Learners are introduced to essential Spark application concepts, including the role of SparkSession, the structure of jobs, stages, and tasks, and the importance of transformations, actions, and lazy evaluation in optimizing Spark workflows. Through hands-on engagement with Spark-shell, learners gain practical skills in writing and executing Spark programs using Scala in interactive environments like Cloudera.

The chapter also covers the creation and manipulation of **resilient distributed datasets** (**RDDs**) from parallelized collections, external storage, and transformations of existing RDDs. Core RDD operations such as map, filter, reduceByKey, and union are applied in practical scenarios. To consolidate learning, the chapter concludes with a real-world case study analyzing the IPL match data, where students perform data filtering, aggregation, and pattern discovery using Apache Spark. This integrated approach ensures that the learners not only understand the theoretical concepts but also gain hands-on experience in applying Spark to real-world big data problems.

Spark introduction

Apache Spark is an open-source, distributed computing system designed for fast and flexible processing of large-scale datasets. It provides an easy-to-use interface for large-scale data processing with inherent data parallelism and fault tolerance to perform operations efficiently on vast datasets. Spark is optimized for both batch and real-time data processing, making it a popular choice in big data analytics.

Unlike traditional frameworks, Spark processes data in-memory, significantly improving performance for iterative and interactive workloads. It supports multiple programming languages, including Scala, Python, Java, and R, and integrates well with various big data tools such as Hadoop, Hive, HBase, and Cassandra.

Features of Spark

In this section, you will understand *why* Spark has become so popular in the world of big data. The key features that make data processing in Apache Spark faster, smarter, and more scalable, and set it apart are:

- **Speed**: The biggest advantage of Apache Spark is its speed. Unlike traditional frameworks like Hadoop MapReduce, which write intermediate data to disk, Spark processes data in-memory, thereby reducing disk I/O and increasing efficiency. This makes it nearly 100 times faster than MapReduce for iterative operations. For example, suppose you are processing log files to identify errors. In Hadoop MapReduce, each operation, filtering, sorting, and counting, writes data to disk, making it slow. In contrast, Spark loads the data into memory and performs all operations before writing the final result to disk, making it significantly faster.

- **Ease of use**: Spark is designed to be user-friendly and supports multiple programming languages, including Python (PySpark), Java, Scala, and R. It provides high-level APIs that simplify complex data processing tasks. It also has an interactive shell for executing commands. For example, if a data analyst wants to perform SQL-like operations on large datasets, they can use Spark SQL to query structured data without writing extensive code.

- **Unified engine**: Spark is not limited to a single type of workload. It can handle batch processing, real-time streaming, machine learning, and graph processing. This flexibility makes it an all-in-one big data framework. For example, a company like *Uber* uses Spark for real-time data streaming (tracking ride requests), batch processing (calculating monthly revenue), and machine learning (predicting surge pricing based on historical demand).

- **Fault tolerance**: Spark is highly fault-tolerant due to its RDDs, which store information about how data transformations were applied. If a node fails, Spark can automatically recompute the lost data using the RDD lineage, ensuring reliability without replicating data. For example, if a Spark job running on a cluster crashes midway, Spark does not restart from scratch. Instead, it only re-executes the lost computations using the RDD's lineage, saving time and resources.

- **Integration with big data ecosystem**: Spark can be seamlessly integrated with existing big data tools and storage systems like **Hadoop Distributed File System** (**HDFS**), Apache Hive, Apache HBase, Apache Cassandra, and Amazon S3. It can also work with Apache Kafka and Flume for real-time streaming. For example, a large e-commerce company using Hadoop for data storage can integrate Spark with HDFS to analyze customer purchase patterns. If they need real-time recommendations, Spark can connect with Kafka to process live user behavior data and suggest products instantly.

Each of these features makes Spark a powerful and versatile big data framework, capable of handling complex analytics efficiently across various industries.

Spark vs. Hadoop

Apache Spark and Hadoop are two popular big data frameworks, but they differ in how they process and handle data. Hadoop uses a disk-based MapReduce model, making it reliable but slower, while Spark relies on in-memory computing, offering much faster performance and more advanced features. *Table 13.1* highlights the key differences between Spark and Hadoop for quick comparison:

Feature	Apache Hadoop (MapReduce)	Apache Spark
Processing model	Disk-based: data written/read from disk after each step.	**In-memory**: Data stored in RAM for faster computation.
Speed	Slower due to heavy disk I/O.	10–100× faster with in-memory operations.
Ease of use	Complex Java-based MapReduce code.	Easy APIs in Python, Java, Scala, R.
Data processing	It has batch processing only.	Batch, real-time streaming, ML, graph processing.
Fault tolerance	Data replication across nodes.	RDD lineage recomputes lost data efficiently.
Scalability	Highly scalable for very large datasets.	Also scalable, but performs best with enough memory.
Use cases	Large-scale ETL, long-running batch jobs.	Machine learning, real-time analytics, iterative tasks.

***Table 13.1**: Hadoop vs. Spark*

Spark ecosystem

Apache Spark follows a master-slave architecture in which all key components work together to execute big data workloads efficiently. The various components of the Spark ecosystem are shown in *Figure 13.1*:

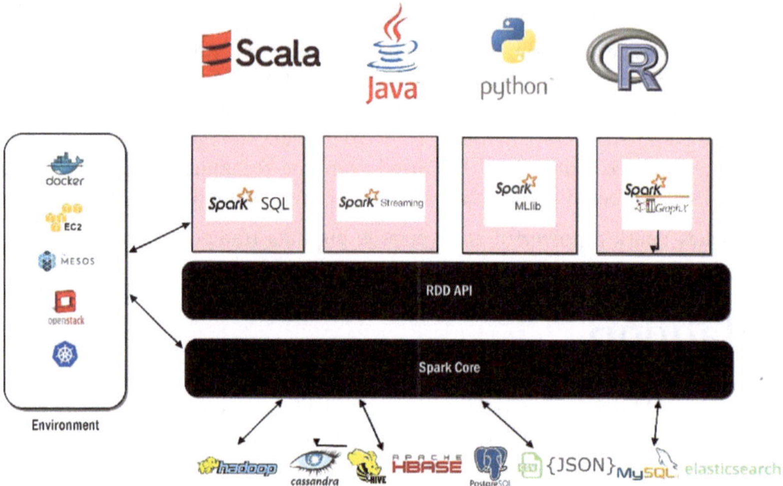

***Figure 13.1**: Spark ecosystem*

They are described as follows:

- **Spark Core**: It is the fundamental execution engine of Apache Spark. It is responsible for memory management, fault recovery, job scheduling, and data interactions with storage systems like HDFS, Amazon S3, and Apache Cassandra. Spark Core provides the foundation for all other Spark components by allowing users to create and manipulate RDDs, which enable efficient parallel data processing. Suppose a company wants to analyze customer transaction data stored in Amazon S3. Spark Core enables them to load the data, filter transactions above Rs 500,000, and compute the total revenue using parallel processing, making the analysis much faster than traditional systems.
- **Spark SQL**: It provides a structured approach to handling data, enabling users to write SQL queries for big data processing. It introduces DataFrames (similar to tables in relational databases) and datasets (strongly typed collections of objects) to optimize query performance. Spark SQL is widely used for ETL operations, interactive queries, and supports integration with existing databases like MySQL and Hive.
- **Spark Streaming**: For real-time data processing, Spark Streaming enables applications to process continuous data streams from sources like Apache Kafka, Flume, or socket connections. Unlike traditional batch processing, Spark Streaming works with micro-batches, providing near real-time processing with high fault tolerance. For example, a banking system can use Spark Streaming to monitor fraudulent transactions in real-time. If an unusual transaction pattern is detected, e.g., multiple high-value transfers from different locations, Spark Streaming can trigger an alert instantly, helping prevent fraud.
- **MLlib**: It is Spark's built-in MLlib that provides classification, regression, clustering, recommendation, and feature transformation algorithms. It is optimized for large-scale data processing, making it easier to develop scalable machine learning models. For example, a streaming platform like *Netflix* can use MLlib to recommend movies based on user behavior. By analyzing past watch history and user ratings, Spark MLlib can build a recommendation system that suggests content similar to what a user has previously watched.
- **GraphX**: It is a Spark distributed graph processing framework to perform graph analytics on large datasets. It is widely used to create the graph structures where data points (nodes) are connected by relationships (edges). For example, social network analysis, fraud detection, and PageRank calculations. Social media platforms like Facebook can use GraphX to identify influencers by analyzing user connections and interactions. By running PageRank algorithms, Spark can determine which users have the highest influence in a network.

Apache Spark architecture

Apache Spark is a powerful distributed computing framework designed to process large datasets quickly and efficiently. It is optimized for in-memory processing and supports various cluster managers to manage its resources effectively. It follows a master-slave architecture, in which a central driver node coordinates multiple executor (slave) nodes to perform parallel computations. The driver, executors, cluster manager, and **directed acyclic graph** (**DAG**) scheduler work together to handle large-scale data workloads efficiently. The detailed flow of data processing in Spark is shown in the following figure:

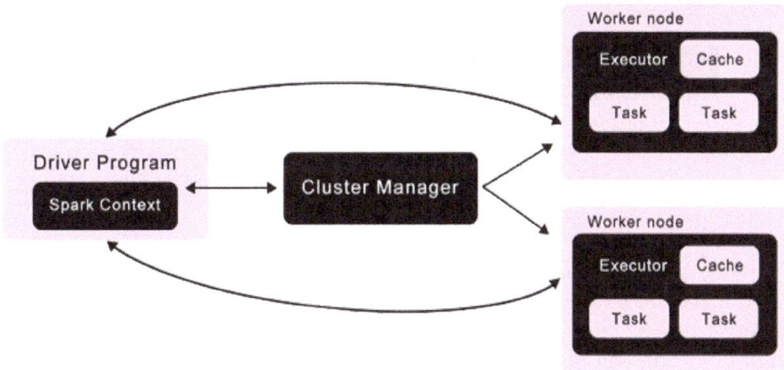

Figure 13.2: *Spark architecture*

The process flow is as follows:

- **Spark driver**: It is the master node that is responsible for managing the entire execution of a Spark application. It converts user-defined code written in Scala, Python, Java, or R into a DAG of tasks. The driver then transforms high-level operations, such as `map()` or `filter()`, into an optimized sequence of execution steps. Next, it schedules these tasks on the available worker nodes and collects the final results. The Spark applications have a SparkSession, which serves as the entry point and is also managed by the driver.
- **Cluster manager**: It is responsible for allocating resources to Spark applications. It decides how many executors to allocate, how much **central processing unit** (**CPU**) and memory each executor should have, and how tasks should be distributed. Spark supports multiple types of cluster managers, where the choice of cluster manager depends on the infrastructure and workload requirements of the application:
    - **Standalone cluster manager**: It is a built-in Spark cluster manager that is useful for small-scale deployments.
    - **Apache Mesos**: It is a general-purpose cluster manager that allows sharing resources among multiple applications.
    - **Hadoop Yet Another Resource Negotiator (YARN)**: It integrates with Hadoop clusters to manage the resources.
    - **Kubernetes**: It is used for containerized deployments, making Spark applications scalable in cloud environments.

The various types of cluster managers in Spark are shown in the following figure:

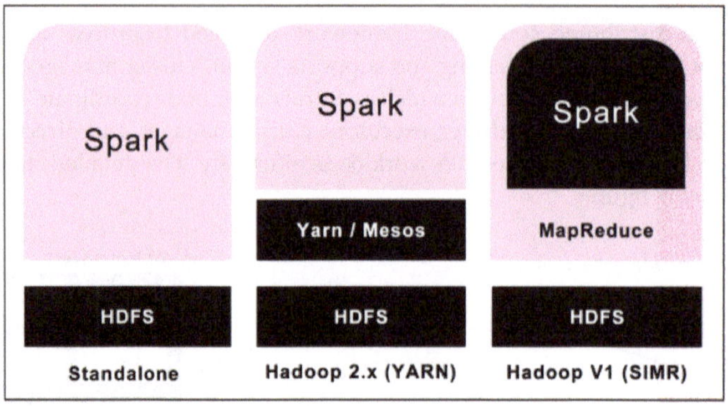

Spark	Spark	Spark
	Yarn / Mesos	MapReduce
HDFS	HDFS	HDFS
Standalone	Hadoop 2.x (YARN)	Hadoop V1 (SIMR)

Figure 13.3: *Types of cluster managers*

- **Executors (Worker Nodes)**: Executors are worker nodes that perform actual computations. When a Spark application starts, the cluster manager launches multiple executors on worker nodes. Each executor processes a portion of the dataset and executes assigned tasks parallelly. Executors also cache intermediate data in memory, which helps in reducing computation time when the same data is needed multiple times. At the end of execution, the results are sent back to the driver node. Since executors are independent, Spark applications remain fault-tolerant such that if an executor fails, Spark can rerun the failed tasks on a different executor without restarting the entire job.
- **Resilient distributed datasets**: It is the fundamental data structure of Spark. It enables fault-tolerant parallel processing of data by distributing it across multiple worker nodes. RDDs are immutable, meaning they cannot be modified once created. Thus, transformation operations generate new RDDs from existing ones. Spark supports two types of operations on RDDs:
    - **Transformations**: They refer to operations that produce new RDDs from existing ones. Spark uses lazy evaluation for transformations, meaning it does not execute them immediately. Instead, it records transformation operations as a logical execution plan in the form of a DAG. This DAG captures the sequence of transformations and their dependencies. When an action (like **`count()`** or **`collect()`**) is called, Spark's DAG scheduler optimizes this plan and sends tasks to the cluster manager for execution, ensuring efficient resource use. Some of the common transformation operations are shown in *Table 13.2*:

Transformation operation	Description
`map()`	Apply the function to each element
`filter()`	Keep elements that match the condition
`flatMap()`	Flatten nested structures
`Distinct`	Remove duplicates
`Union()`	Merge two RDDs
`Intersection()`	Get common elements
`groupByKey()`	Group elements by key
`reduceByKey()`	Aggregate values by key
`sortBy()`	Sort elements

Table 13.2: *List of transformation operations*

In Apache Spark, transformations are classified into narrow and wide transformations based on how they shuffle data across partitions:

  - **Narrow transformations**: A transformation is narrow when each output partition depends on a limited number of input partitions, without requiring a full shuffle across the cluster. These transformations do not require data movement between partitions; that is, data stays within the same partition. Since no network shuffle is involved, they can be executed in a pipeline (one stage), making them more efficient, e.g., `map()`, `filter()`, `flatMap()`, etc.
  - **Wide transformations**: A transformation is wide when the output partition depends on data from multiple input partitions. This requires a shuffle where Spark redistributes data across the cluster, making it computationally expensive, e.g., `groupByKey()`, `reduceByKey()`, `sortBy()`, `join()`, etc.

- **Actions**: These operations trigger the actual computation by forcing Spark to execute the accumulated transformations and return results to the driver program or an external storage system. The various operations, like `collect()`, `count()`, and `reduce()`, etc., which return computed results to the driver or an external storage system, are examples of action operations. The various types of action operations in Spark are shown in *Table 13.3*:

Action operation	Description
`collect()`	Retrieve all elements
`count()`	Count elements
`first()`	Get the first element
`take(n)`	Get the first n elements
`reduce()`	Aggregate all elements
`foreach()`	Apply a function without returning an RDD
`saveAsTextfile()`	Save output to a file

Table 13.3*: List of transformation operations*

RDDs ensure fault tolerance by tracking lineage (the sequence of transformations used to build them), which enables lost partitions to be recomputed in case of node failures. This combination of immutability, distributed processing, lazy evaluation, and fault tolerance makes RDDs a powerful abstraction for large-scale data processing in Spark.

- **DAG scheduler**: The DAG scheduler is responsible for breaking down complex computations into stages and tasks. When an RDD operation is triggered, Spark constructs a DAG representing dependencies between different computations. The DAG scheduler divides the job into multiple stages, each containing multiple tasks. Tasks within a stage can run in parallel, while stages must be executed sequentially based on dependencies. The scheduler then optimizes task execution and ensures that tasks are processed in an efficient sequence, minimizing data shuffling and execution time. This helps Spark achieve efficient distributed computing.

Working with Spark shell in Cloudera and PySpark

Apache Spark supports multiple programming languages, including Scala, Python (PySpark), Java, and R. It provides an interactive shell for Scala and Python to execute Spark commands interactively for testing, development, and debugging.

Running Spark shell (Scala): Apache Spark provides a Spark shell for executing commands in Scala. The steps to launch the Spark shell in Cloudera are as follows:

1. **Ensure Spark is installed**: Download and install Apache Spark from the official website, or install Cloudera by following the steps discussed in *Chapter 4, Introduction to Data Analysis with Cloudera.*
2. Set environment variables (`SPARK_HOME`) and add Spark's bin directory to PATH.
3. Open the terminal and start the Spark shell. Run the following command in your terminal:

   ```
   spark-shell
   ```

   Refer to the following figure:

```
cloudera@quickstart:~
File  Edit  View  Search  Terminal  Help
[cloudera@quickstart ~]$ spark-shell
Setting default log level to "WARN".
To adjust logging level use sc.setLogLevel(newLevel).
SLF4J: Class path contains multiple SLF4J bindings.
SLF4J: Found binding in [jar:file:/usr/lib/zookeeper/lib/slf4j-log4j12-1.7.5.jar
!/org/slf4j/impl/StaticLoggerBinder.class]
SLF4J: Found binding in [jar:file:/usr/lib/flume-ng/lib/slf4j-log4j12-1.7.5.jar!
/org/slf4j/impl/StaticLoggerBinder.class]
SLF4J: Found binding in [jar:file:/usr/lib/parquet/lib/slf4j-log4j12-1.7.5.jar!/
org/slf4j/impl/StaticLoggerBinder.class]
SLF4J: Found binding in [jar:file:/usr/lib/avro/avro-tools-1.7.6-cdh5.13.0.jar!/
org/slf4j/impl/StaticLoggerBinder.class]
SLF4J: See http://www.slf4j.org/codes.html#multiple_bindings for an explanation.
SLF4J: Actual binding is of type [org.slf4j.impl.Log4jLoggerFactory]
Welcome to
      ____              __
     / __/__  ___ _____/ /__
    _\ \/ _ \/ _ `/ __/  '_/
   /___/ .__/\_,_/_/ /_/\_\   version 1.6.0
      /_/

Using Scala version 2.10.5 (Java HotSpot(TM) 64-Bit Server VM, Java 1.7.0_67)
Type in expressions to have them evaluated.
Type :help for more information.
24/11/07 22:15:33 WARN util.NativeCodeLoader: Unable to load native-hadoop libra
ry for your platform... using builtin-java classes where applicable
Spark context available as sc (master = local[*], app id = local-1731046538984).
24/11/07 22:15:44 WARN shortcircuit.DomainSocketFactory: The short-circuit local reads feature cann
ot be used because libhadoop cannot be loaded.
SQL context available as sqlContext.

scala> █
```

Figure 13.4: Execute spark-shell in Cloudera terminal

By default, it will start the Scala terminal to work in Spark. To exit the shell, use the quit command. Once inside the Spark shell, you are ready to execute commands. In the Apache Spark shell, three important contexts are available by default:

- **SparkContext (SC)**: It acts as the entry point for interacting with Spark's core functionalities. It helps you to create RDDs, access cluster resources, and perform parallel computations.
- **SQLContext(sqlContext)**: It provides functionalities for working with structured data using DataFrames and SQL queries. It is mainly useful for handling structured data formats like CSV, JSON, and Parquet.
- **Running PySpark shell (Python)**: For Python users, Apache Spark provides PySpark, an interactive Python API. In the Cloudera terminal, write the following command to start PySpark as done earlier for the Scala shell:

  ```
  pyspark
  ```

  Once inside the PySpark shell, you are ready to execute commands. In the rest of the chapter, we will learn all the commands in Scala.

IPL match data analysis using Apache Spark

The IPL is one of the most popular cricket leagues in the World, which generates vast amounts of data in every season. Authorities may analyse this data to reveal valuable insights, such as team performance, player statistics, win patterns, and match outcomes.

In this section, we will perform IPL match data analysis using Apache Spark. We will download data from *Kaggle*, which is a popular platform for datasets and data science competitions. The dataset includes match details such as team names, scores, venues, player performances, and match results. We will learn to use Spark RDDs to load, process, and analyze this data efficiently in a distributed environment. With Apache Spark, we can process IPL match data at scale, making it ideal for real-time analysis, predictive modeling, and data-driven cricket analytics.

Creating RDD in Spark shell

The various methods to create RDD in Spark are:

- **Using parallelized collections**: A parallelized collection is an in-memory dataset that can be converted into an RDD using `sc.parallelize()`. This method is useful for working with small datasets. Let us assume we have a small dataset containing IPL match results as shown in *Table 13.4*:

Team 1	Team 2	Year	Winner	Score1	Score2
MI	CSK	2023	MI	180	175
RCB	KKR	2023	KKR	190	200
SRH	GT	2023	GT	160	165

***Table 13.4**: Sample IPL dataset*

Scala code to create an RDD for data analysis is as follows:

1. **Create a collection**:

```
val iplData = Seq(  ("MI", "CSK", 2023, "MI", 180, 175),  ("RCB", "KKR", 2023, "KKR", 190, 200), ("SRH", "GT", 2023, "GT", 160, 165))
```

2. **Convert the collection to RDD**:

```
val rdd1 = sc.parallelize(iplData)
```

3. **Display contents of RDD**:

```
rdd1.collect().foreach(println)
```

- **Creating an RDD from external storage (CSV file in HDFS or local)**: If IPL match data is stored in an external file (CSV, JSON, or Parquet format), we can load it into an RDD using `sc.textFile()`. Assume we have an IPL dataset saved as `ipl_matches.csv` in HDFS or the local file system. The Scala code to load data from external storage is as follows:

1. Load CSV file into an RDD (replace with actual HDFS or local path), as shown in *Figure 13.5*:

```
val CKFile = sc.textFile("hdfs:/match/Matches.csv")
```

```
scala> val CKFile = sc.textFile("hdfs:/match/Matches.csv")
```

***Figure 13.5**: Load CSV file into RDD*

2. After loading the data in RDD CKFile, you can display the data stored in RDD in text form (refer to *Figure 13.6*). Here, `collect()` gathers all elements from the RDD across the cluster into the driver, and `foreach(println)` iterates over each element and prints it on the driver node.

```
scala> CKFile.collect.foreach(println)
```

***Figure 13.6**: Display data stored in RDD*

- **Creating an RDD from another RDD**: We can create new RDDs by applying transformations (e.g., **map()**, **filter()**, **flatMap()**, **reduceByKey()**) on an existing RDD. Let us create a new RDD from **rdd1** (from the parallelized collection example) that extracts only the team names and match winners. The Scala code for **rdd2** is as follows:

```
// Extract Team1 and Winner columns
val winnersRDD = rdd1.map(matchData => (matchData._1, matchData._4))
// Display results
winnersRDD.collect().foreach(println)
```

- **map() transformation**: In Apache Spark, the map function is used to apply a transformation to each element in an RDD.

  Let us use it to find the states that participated in the IPL. The following code splits each line of the input data on commas using **_.split(",")**, which converts the line into an array of strings. The expression (1) then selects the second element (index 1) from this array, assuming that this column represents the state.

```
val states = CKFile.map(_.split(",")(1)):
states.collect.foreach(println)
```

  Refer to *Figure 13.7* for the output, which shows the names of states. Here, the code is shown again after execution, but the results are duplicate values. You can apply the following command to print the unique values of states:

```
rdd.map(_.split(",")(1)).distinct().count()
```

```
cloudera@quickstart:~
File Edit View Search Terminal Help
Sharjah
Dubai
Sharjah
Abu Dhabi
Dubai
Dubai
Dubai
Abu Dhabi
Dubai
Dubai
Dubai
Abu Dhabi
Abu Dhabi
Dubai
        CKFile.first()
res5: String = id,city,date,player_of_match,venue,neutral_venue,team1,team2,toss
_winner,toss_decision,winner,result,result_margin,eliminator,method,umpire1,umpi
re2

scala> val states=CKFile.map(_.split(",")(1))
states: org.apache.spark.rdd.RDD[String] = MapPartitionsRDD[4] at map at <consol
e>:29

scala> states.collect.foreach(println)
```

***Figure 13.7**: Number of states that participated in IPL*

- **reduceByKey**: In Apache Spark, **`reduceByKey`** is a transformation used on **`pairRDDs`** (i.e., RDDs of key-value pairs) to aggregate values for each key using a specified reduction function. Let us apply this transformation to identify the state that conducted the maximum number of matches. The following code uses transformation and action operations to identify the state that conducted the maximum number of matches. Let us understand each step in detail.

  Suppose we have an RDD where each element represents a cricket match's state along with a value 1 to indicate one match, for example: **`("Maharashtra", 1)`**, **`("Karnataka", 1)`**, and so on. The operation **`reduceByKey((x, y) => x + y)`** combines the values for each state by summing them, so all the 1s for the same state get added up. This gives us results like **`("Maharashtra", 2)`** for two matches, **`("Karnataka", 3)`** for three matches, and **`("Delhi", 1)`** for one match. Next, **`.map(tup => (tup._2, tup._1))`** reverses each pair so that the match count becomes the key and the state name becomes the value — for example, **`(2, "Maharashtra")`**, **`(3, "Karnataka")`**, **`(1, "Delhi")`**. This reversal is done because Spark's **`sortByKey`** can only sort using the key, so to sort by match count, we make it the key. Then, **`.sortByKey(false)`** sorts these pairs in descending order of match count, resulting in **`(3, "Karnataka")`**, **`(2, "Maharashtra")`**, **`(1, "Delhi")`**. Finally, **`collect().foreach(println)`** prints the results, showing states in order from the highest to lowest number of matches.

  ```
  val statecountm = Scount.reduceByKey((x,y) => x+y).map(tup => (tup._2,tup._1))
  sortByKey(false)
  statecountm.collect().foreach(println)
  ```

  The following figure shows the execution of the given operation and the output:

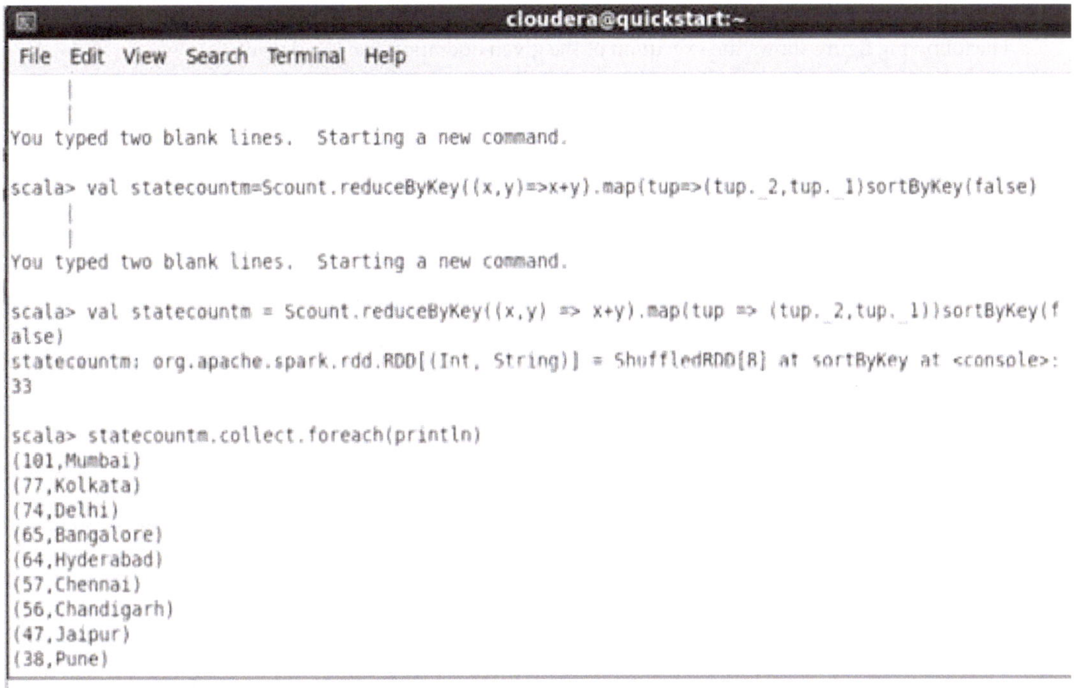

```
cloudera@quickstart:~
File Edit View Search Terminal Help
     |
     |
You typed two blank lines.  Starting a new command.

scala> val statecountm=Scount.reduceByKey((x,y)=>x+y).map(tup=>(tup._2,tup._1)sortByKey(false)
     |
     |
You typed two blank lines.  Starting a new command.

scala> val statecountm = Scount.reduceByKey((x,y) => x+y).map(tup => (tup._2,tup._1))sortByKey(f
alse)
statecountm: org.apache.spark.rdd.RDD[(Int, String)] = ShuffledRDD[8] at sortByKey at <console>:
33

scala> statecountm.collect.foreach(println)
(101,Mumbai)
(77,Kolkata)
(74,Delhi)
(65,Bangalore)
(64,Hyderabad)
(57,Chennai)
(56,Chandigarh)
(47,Jaipur)
(38,Pune)
```

Figure 13.8: States with the maximum number of matches

You may also print only the top 10 states or the top state that hosted the most IPL matches by using the **`take()`** command, as shown in *Figure 13.9*:

```
statecountm.take(10).foreach(println)
```

```
scala> statecountm.take(10).foreach(println)
(101,Mumbai)
(77,Kolkata)
(74,Delhi)
(65,Bangalore)
(64,Hyderabad)
(57,Chennai)
(56,Chandigarh)
(47,Jaipur)
(38,Pune)
(29,Abu Dhabi)

scala> █
```

Figure 13.9: Top 10 states with match count in descending order

- **filter()**: Filter transformation, the name itself describes its use. It is used to select a subset of elements in an RDD that satisfy a given condition; that is, this transformation operation is used to filter out the selective data from a given collection of data. The following code applies a filter operation to get the records of the IPL matches of the year 2017 and stores them in a `filRDD`:

```
val fil = CKfile.filter(line => line.contains("2017"))
fil.collect().foreach(println)
```

Here CKfile is an RDD (created above from a text file with IPL match data), `.filter(line => line.contains("2017"))`, keeps only the lines that contain the string `"2017"`, i.e., matches from the year 2017, and `fil.collect().foreach(println)`, collects the filtered data from all Spark partitions into the driver and prints each line.

The following figure shows the execution of the given operation and the output:

```
scala> val fil = CKFile.filter(line => line.contains("2017"))
fil: org.apache.spark.rdd.RDD[String] = MapPartitionsRDD[11] at filter at <console>:29

scala> fil.collect.foreach(println)
1082591,Hyderabad,2017-04-05,Yuvraj Singh,"Rajiv Gandhi International Stadium, Uppal",0,Sunrisers Hyderabad,Royal C
allengers Bangalore,Royal Challengers Bangalore,field,Sunrisers Hyderabad,runs,35,N,NA,AY Dandekar,NJ Llong
1082592,Pune,2017-04-06,SPD Smith,Maharashtra Cricket Association Stadium,0,Rising Pune Supergiant,Mumbai Indians,F
sing Pune Supergiant,field,Rising Pune Supergiant,wickets,7,N,NA,A Nand Kishore,S Ravi
1082593,Rajkot,2017-04-07,CA Lynn,Saurashtra Cricket Association Stadium,0,Gujarat Lions,Kolkata Knight Riders,Kol
ta Knight Riders,field,Kolkata Knight Riders,wickets,10,N,NA,Nitin Menon,CK Nandan
1082594,Indore,2017-04-08,GJ Maxwell,Holkar Cricket Stadium,0,Kings XI Punjab,Rising Pune Supergiant,Kings XI Punja
,field,Kings XI Punjab,wickets,6,N,NA,AK Chaudhary,C Shamshuddin
1082595,Bengaluru,2017-04-08,KM Jadhav,M.Chinnaswamy Stadium,0,Royal Challengers Bangalore,Delhi Daredevils,Royal C
```

Figure 13.10: Filter operation output

- **flatMap()**: The `flatMap()` transformation is similar to `map()`, but with one key difference: `map()` produces one output per input element, whereas `flatMap()` can produce zero, one, or many outputs per input element. It flattens the results, hence the name `flatMap`. Here we apply `flatMap()` to split out the matches of Hyderabad city and store the data into `filRDD` RDD as follows:

```
val filRDD = fil.flatMap(line => line.split("Hyderabad")).collect()
```

Here, fil is an RDD containing IPL match records. The expression `flatMap(line => line.split("Hyderabad"))`, transformation processes each record by splitting the line wherever the word `"Hyderabad"` occurs. For example, for input line: `"2017,Hyderabad,MI"` is split into an array `["2017,", ",MI"]`. Since the `split()` function returns an array of strings, the use of `flatMap()` ensures that all such arrays generated from different records are flattened into a single RDD of strings rather than an RDD of arrays. Finally, the `collect()` action brings all the elements of the resulting RDD from the executors to the driver program, where they can be printed or further examined. Refer to *Figure 13.11* for execution and output of the preceding code:

```
scala> val filRDD = fil.flatMap(line => line.split("Hyderabad")).collect()
filRDD: Array[String] = Array(1082591,, ",2017-04-05,Yuvraj Singh,"Rajiv Gandhi International Stadium, Uppal",0,Sunr
isers ", ",Royal Challengers Bangalore,Royal Challengers Bangalore,field,Sunrisers ", ,runs,35,N,NA,AY Dandekar,NJ L
long, 1082592,Pune,2017-04-06,SPD Smith,Maharashtra Cricket Association Stadium,0,Rising Pune Supergiant,Mumbai Indi
ans,Rising Pune Supergiant,field,Rising Pune Supergiant,wickets,7,N,NA,A Nand Kishore,S Ravi, 1082593,Rajkot,2017-04
-07,CA Lynn,Saurashtra Cricket Association Stadium,0,Gujarat Lions,Kolkata Knight Riders,Kolkata Knight Riders,fielc
,Kolkata Knight Riders,wickets,10,N,NA,Nitin Menon,CK Nandan, 1082594,Indore,2017-04-08,GJ Maxwell,Holkar Cricket St
adium,0,Kings XI Punjab,Rising Pune Supergiant,Kings XI Punjab,field,Kings XI Punjab,wickets,6,N,NA,A...
scala>
```

Figure 13.11: Output of flatMap()

- **partition()**: Every data we write into an RDD is split into a certain number of partitions. We use this transformation to find the number of partitions the data is actually split into. Let us consider the **'fil'** RDD, as shown in the following code, which stores the data about matches played in the year 2017. Here, **partitions.size** simply tells you how many pieces (partitions) the RDD **fil** has been split into. In Spark, data is divided into these partitions so that different parts can be processed in parallel by different executors. Knowing the number of partitions helps you understand how Spark is breaking up the work. For example, if it prints **4**, it means your data is split into 4 chunks that Spark will process at the same time.

  ```
  val fil = CKfile.filter(line => line.contains("2017"))
  fil.partitions.size
  ```

  Refer to *Figure 13.12* for output. It shows that only one partition is done by Spark in this example:

```
scala> val fil = CKFile.filter(line => line.contains("2017"))
fil: org.apache.spark.rdd.RDD[String] = MapPartitionsRDD[13] at filter at <console>:29

scala> fil.partitions.size
res9: Int = 1

scala>
```

Figure 13.12: Output of the partition() operation

- **mapPartitions()**: It is a transformation in Spark that works on each partition as a whole and not on individual elements, unlike map. It takes an iterator of elements in a partition and returns an iterator of transformed elements. **mapPartitions** is an alternative of **Map()** and **foreach()** together. We use **mapPartitions** here to find the number of rows in each partition. In the following code, the first statement extracts the data of only 2016 IPL matches using the **filter()** transformation as discussed earlier. The next statement is used to count the number of records in each partition. In the code, **idx => ...** is a function that is applied to each partition, where **idx** is an iterator over the elements in that partition, **idx.size** counts the number of elements (rows) in the current partition. **Array(idx.size).iterator** wraps that count into an array and returns it as an iterator, because **mapPartitions** must return an iterator, and finally collect gathers the results from all partitions into the driver program.

  ```
  val fil = CKfile.filter(line => line.contains("2016"))
  fil.mapPartitions(idx => Array(idx.size).iterator).collect
  ```

Refer to *Figure 13.13* for execution and output of the preceding code. The output shows one partition with 60 records:

```
scala> val CKFile = sc.textFile("hdfs:/match/Matches.csv")
CKFile: org.apache.spark.rdd.RDD[String] = hdfs:/match/Matches.csv MapPartitionsRDD[1] at textFile at <console>:27

scala> val fil = CKFile.filter(line => line.contains("2016"))
fil: org.apache.spark.rdd.RDD[String] = MapPartitionsRDD[2] at filter at <console>:29

scala> fil.mapPartitions(idx => Array(idx.size).iterator).collect
res0: Array[Int] = Array(60)

scala> ▌
```

***Figure 13.13**: Output of mapPartitions()*

- **reduceByKey()**: It is a transformation in Apache Spark used to combine values with the same key using a specified function. It groups data by keys and reduces the values using a binary function, like addition, multiplication, or max. Let us use this transformation on our CSV file to find the player with the highest man of the matches.

```
val ManOfTheMatch = CKfile.map(_.split(",")(13))
val MOTMcount = ManOfTheMatch.map(WINcount => (WINcount,1))
val ManOTH = MOTMcount.reduceByKey((x,y) => x+y).map(tup => (tup._2,tup._1))
sortByKey(false)
ManOTH.take(10).foreach(println)
```

In the preceding code the first statement splits each line of the CSV file data stored in `CKfile` using `,` (comma), `split(",")(13)` picks the 14th column, assuming this contains the *Man of the Match* name. `ManOfTheMatch` is now an RDD of player names who won the award in each match. Next, map transformation is used to transform each player name into a (name, 1) pair and prepares the data for counting with `reduceByKey`. Further, `reduceByKey((x, y) => x + y)` adds up the values (1s) for each player to calculate total wins, `map(tup => (tup._2, tup._1))` swaps `(name, count)` | `(count, name)` to sort by count and `sortByKey(false)` sorts by count in descending order (most awards first). Finally, `take(10)` grabs the top 10 (count, player) pairs and `foreach(println)` prints them to the console as shown in *Figure 13.14*:

```
scala> val ManOfTheMatch = CKFile.map(_.split(",")(13))
ManOfTheMatch: org.apache.spark.rdd.RDD[String] = MapPartitionsRDD[4] at map at <console>:29

scala> val MOTMcount = ManOfTheMatch.map(WINcount => (WINcount,1))
MOTMcount: org.apache.spark.rdd.RDD[(String, Int)] = MapPartitionsRDD[5] at map at <console>:31

scala> val ManOTH = MOTMcount.reduceByKey((x,y) => x+y).map(tup => (tup._2,tup._1))sortByKey(false)
ManOTH: org.apache.spark.rdd.RDD[(Int, String)] = ShuffledRDD[8] at sortByKey at <console>:33

scala> ManOTH.take(10).foreach(println)
(610,N)
(23,7)
(23,6)
(22,5)
(15,9)
(13,8)
(10,Y)
(8,4)
(7,NA)
(5,25)

scala> ▌
```

***Figure 13.14**: Highest man of the matches using reduceByKey()*

- **union()**: This transformation is used to club two RDDs together. However, it does not remove duplicates and retains all elements from both RDDs. Here, we are creating two RDDs, namely **fil** and **fil2**. **fil** RDD contains the records of 2017 IPL matches, and **fil2** RDD contains the 2016 IPL match records.

  ```
  val fil = CKFile.filter(line => line.contains("2017"))
  val fil2 = CKFile.filter(line => line.contains("2016"))
  val uninRDD = fil.union(fil2)
  ```

  In the preceding code, after filtering the records of 2016 and 2017 matches, **fil.union(fil2)** is used to combine both 2017 and 2016 match records into a single RDD (here, **unionRDD**) as shown in *Figure 13.15*:

```
scala> val fil = CKFile.filter(line => line.contains("2017"))
fil: org.apache.spark.rdd.RDD[String] = MapPartitionsRDD[9] at filter at <console>:29

scala> val fil2 = CKFile.filter(line => line.contains("2016"))
fil2: org.apache.spark.rdd.RDD[String] = MapPartitionsRDD[10] at filter at <console>:29

scala> val uninRDD = fil.union(fil2)
uninRDD: org.apache.spark.rdd.RDD[String] = UnionRDD[11] at union at <console>:33

scala> uninRDD.collect.foreach(println)
1082591,Hyderabad,2017-04-05,Yuvraj Singh,"Rajiv Gandhi International Stadium, Uppal",0,Sunrisers Hyderabad,Royal Ch
allengers Bangalore,Royal Challengers Bangalore,field,Sunrisers Hyderabad,runs,35,N,NA,AY Dandekar,NJ Llong
1082592,Pune,2017-04-06,SPD Smith,Maharashtra Cricket Association Stadium,0,Rising Pune Supergiant,Mumbai Indians,Ri
sing Pune Supergiant,field,Rising Pune Supergiant,wickets,7,N,NA,A Nand Kishore,S Ravi
1082593,Rajkot,2017-04-07,CA Lynn,Saurashtra Cricket Association Stadium,0,Gujarat Lions,Kolkata Knight Riders,Kolka
ta Knight Riders,field,Kolkata Knight Riders,wickets,10,N,NA,Nitin Menon,CK Nandan
1082594,Indore,2017-04-08,GJ Maxwell,Holkar Cricket Stadium,0,Kings XI Punjab,Rising Pune Supergiant,Kings XI Punjab
,field,Kings XI Punjab,wickets,6,N,NA,AK Chaudhary,C Shamshuddin
1082595,Bengaluru,2017-04-08,KM Jadhav,M.Chinnaswamy Stadium,0,Royal Challengers Bangalore,Delhi Daredevils,Royal Ch
allengers Bangalore,bat,Royal Challengers Bangalore,runs,15,N,NA,S Ravi,VK Sharma
1082596,Hyderabad,2017-04-09,Rashid Khan,"Rajiv Gandhi International Stadium, Uppal",0,Sunrisers Hyderabad,Gujarat L
ions,Sunrisers Hyderabad,field,Sunrisers Hyderabad,wickets,9,N,NA,A Deshmukh,NJ Llong
1082597,Mumbai,2017-04-09,N Rana,Wankhede Stadium,0,Mumbai Indians,Kolkata Knight Riders,Mumbai Indians,field,Mumbai
```

***Figure 13.15**: Execution and output of union()*

Conclusion

This chapter provides learners with both a strong theoretical foundation and practical exposure to Apache Spark, equipping them to efficiently manage large-scale data processing tasks. By exploring Spark's architecture, core features, and ecosystem components, learners gain a deep understanding of how Spark excels as a high-performance, scalable alternative to traditional big data tools such as Hadoop MapReduce. An introduction to Spark application concepts and hands-on practice with RDD operations through Spark-shell enables learners to design and optimize distributed data workflows. The real world case study on IPL match data analysis further reinforces the application of Spark in practical scenarios, ensuring that learners are well-prepared to apply Spark in diverse data analytics projects.

In the next chapter you will learn Scala programming in detail.

Points to remember

Here are some key takeaways from this chapter:

- Apache Spark is an open-source, fast, and general-purpose distributed computing system designed for large-scale data processing with in-memory computation capabilities.
- Spark and Hadoop are both big data frameworks. While Spark offers faster processing through in-memory computation, Hadoop relies on disk-based MapReduce, making Spark more efficient for iterative and real-time tasks.
- The Spark ecosystem includes components like Spark SQL, Spark Streaming, MLlib, and GraphX. These tools enable a wide range of capabilities, including data analytics, machine learning, and graph processing tasks, all within a unified framework.

- A Spark application is a user program that runs on a cluster, and SparkSession serves as the entry point to Spark functionality, allowing users to interact with data and execute queries.
  - Spark Jobs represent the high-level actions triggered by the driver and consist of multiple stages executed across the cluster.
  - Spark Stages are subdivisions of jobs based on data shuffling; each stage contains tasks that can be executed in parallel.
  - Spark Tasks are the smallest units of work in Spark, executed by worker nodes, typically processing a single partition of data.
- In Spark, transformations (e.g., map, filter) specify the operations to be applied on data but are not executed immediately; that is, they are lazily evaluated. Actual execution occurs only when an action (e.g., count, collect) is called, which triggers Spark to process the data using an optimized DAG.
- Spark-shell (Scala) and PySpark (Python) provide interactive command-line environments for running Spark code, ideal for experimentation and learning in platforms like Cloudera.
- **Resilient distributed datasets (RDDs)** are fault-tolerant, immutable collections of objects distributed across nodes, forming the core abstraction in Spark for low-level data manipulation.
- **Creating RDD in Spark shell from**:
  - **Parallelized collections**: RDDs can be created from in-memory Scala or Python collections using parallelize(), enabling fast prototyping.
  - **External storage**: RDDs can also be created by loading data from external sources like HDFS, local files, or databases using textFile() or similar methods.
  - **Another RDD**: RDDs can also be derived from existing RDDs using transformations like map, filter, or flatMap.
- Using IPL match datasets, learners apply Spark operations to perform real-world data analysis tasks such as filtering matches, counting wins, or identifying top players and states, reinforcing Spark's practical utility.

Multiple choice questions

1. **What is Apache Spark primarily designed for?**
   a. Web application development
   b. Real-time data processing and distributed computing
   c. Image processing and rendering
   d. Static data archiving
2. **Which of the following statements best differentiates Apache Spark from Hadoop MapReduce?**
   a. Spark stores all data permanently on disk; Hadoop does not.
   b. Spark uses Map-only jobs while Hadoop uses Reduce-only jobs.
   c. Spark performs in-memory processing, whereas Hadoop MapReduce relies on disk I/O.
   d. Hadoop processes streaming data faster than Spark.
3. **Which of the following is not a component of the Spark ecosystem?**
   a. Spark SQL
   b. Spark Streaming
   c. Spark MLlib
   d. Hadoop Distributed File System (HDFS)

4. **What is the primary entry point for Spark functionality since Spark 2.0?**
   a. SparkConf
   b. SparkContext
   c. SparkSession
   d. SQLContext
5. **Which of the following is the correct order of execution in a Spark application?**
   a. Task | Job | Stage
   b. Job | Task | Stage
   c. Stage | Job | Task
   d. Job | Stage | Task
6. **What does lazy evaluation in Spark mean?**
   a. Spark stops execution if cluster resources are low.
   b. Transformations are only evaluated when an action is called.
   c. Actions are skipped to save memory.
   d. Spark delays scheduling to reduce costs.
7. **In Spark-shell or PySpark, which of the following is a valid way to create an RDD from a Scala collection?**
   a. val rdd = sc.read("file.csv")
   b. val rdd = spark.createRDD(Array(1, 2, 3))
   c. val rdd = sc.parallelize(Array(1, 2, 3))
   d. val rdd = RDD(Array(1, 2, 3))
8. **Which Spark method is used to create an RDD from a file stored on HDFS or local file system?**
   a. spark.load()
   b. sc.readText()
   c. spark.readFile()
   d. sc.textFile()
9. **Which of the following operations creates a new RDD from an existing RDD?**
   a. rdd.saveAsTextFile()
   b. rdd.filter(_ > 50)
   c. rdd.count()
   d. spark.read.rdd()
10. **In analyzing IPL match data, which transformation is best suited for counting the number of times each player won Man of the Match?**
    a. map() followed by reduceByKey()
    b. filter() followed by groupBy()
    c. join() followed by map()
    d. flatMap() followed by union()

Answers

1.	b.	2.	c.	3.	d.	4.	c.	5.	d.
6.	b.	7.	c.	8.	d.	9.	b.	10.	a.

Questions

1. Explain the key advantages of Apache Spark over traditional data processing systems. How does in-memory computation contribute to performance improvements?
2. Compare and contrast Apache Spark and Hadoop MapReduce in terms of architecture, speed, fault tolerance, and use cases.
3. Describe the components of the Spark ecosystem. How do modules like Spark SQL, Spark Streaming, and MLlib enhance Spark's functionality?
4. Explain the life cycle of a Spark application. Describe the roles of SparkSession, jobs, stages, and tasks in the execution of a Spark program.
5. Differentiate between transformations and actions in Apache Spark. Provide at least two examples of each and explain the concept of lazy evaluation with an example.
6. How do you create an RDD using the Spark shell? Explain the three ways to create RDDs in Spark, and describe one practical scenario for each method.
7. Write a Spark (Scala) code snippet to:
   a. Load an IPL match CSV file
   b. Filter matches played in 2016
   c. Count the number of matches per city using map() and reduceByKey()
8. What is the role of DAG in Spark? How does it relate to lazy evaluation and job optimization?
9. Describe a real-world use case where Apache Spark would be the preferred choice over other big data tools. Explain why Spark's architecture fits the problem.
10. Using IPL match data, explain how you would identify the state that hosted the most number of matches. Describe the key transformations and actions used in your approach.

CHAPTER 14
Getting Started with Scala Programming

Data are just summaries of thousands of stories—tell a few of those stories to help make the data meaningful.

— Chip Heath, DigitalDefynd Education

Introduction

This chapter provides a comprehensive introduction to Scala, a powerful, multi-paradigm programming language that seamlessly integrates object-oriented and functional programming concepts. Scala combines Java's robustness with modern syntax, making it ideal for scalable applications, from data processing (e.g., Apache Spark) to web services. The chapter begins with Scala's fundamentals, including basic types and operators. Next, it explores built-in control structures like if-else, for/while loops, and pattern matching for expressive logic flow. Classes and objects are covered to demonstrate Scala's OOP capabilities, followed by functions and closures, highlighting first-class functions and higher-order operations. The discussion on inheritance and traits explains how Scala enables code reuse and composition without multiple inheritance pitfalls. Finally, it provides a practical demonstration of running the Scala shell in Cloudera for interactive data analysis and developing applications using the **Scala build tool** (**sbt**).

Structure

In this chapter, we will cover the following topics:

- Introduction to Scala
- Introduction to Scala basics
- Built-in control structures in Scala
- Classes and objects
- Functions and closures
- Inheritance and traits
- Running Scala Shell in Cloudera
- Application development using Scala

Objectives

By the end of this chapter, the readers will have an in-depth understanding of Scala's core concepts and practical applications. They will understand how Scala uniquely combines object-oriented and functional programming to create more expressive, concise code and will be comfortable working with basic types and operators, leveraging type inference to write cleaner programs. The readers will confidently implement control structures like conditionals, loops, and pattern matching to direct program flow, and will be able to design effective classes and objects while applying functional programming techniques, including first-class functions and closures. The chapter will give the readers a hands-on experience with inheritance and traits, showing you how to build flexible, reusable components, and they will gain practical skills using the Scala REPL in Cloudera environments and learn to develop complete applications with sbt. These fundamentals will prepare you for advanced Scala programming and real-world applications in data processing and distributed systems.

Introduction to Scala

Scala is a high-level, general-purpose programming language that blends the best of object-oriented and functional programming paradigms. The name Scala stands for *scalable language*, due to its ability to grow with the complexity of your applications, from small utility scripts to massive distributed systems.

It was created by *Martin Odersky* in 2004. Scala runs on the **Java Virtual Machine (JVM)** and is fully interoperable with Java, meaning it can use existing Java libraries and frameworks, which makes it a practical choice for modern enterprise applications.

Key features of Scala are as follows:

- **Scala gives you the safety of Java without the clutter**: It catches errors early because it is statically typed, yet it is intelligent enough to figure out types on its own, so you do not have to keep specifying them. The result feels much more natural and lightweight, almost like coding in Python.
- **It blends the best of both worlds**: Object-oriented and functional programming, meaning you can structure your code logically while still writing elegant, reusable, and testable functions.
- **The syntax is clean and expressive**: You can express more with less code, which means you can save time with faster development, have fewer bugs, and easier maintenance.
- **It is the native language of Apache Spark**: If your business uses big data or real-time analytics, Scala gives you a serious performance advantage.
- **It is built for speed and scale**: With native support for concurrent and parallel processing, Scala is ideal for cloud-based systems and distributed applications where speed, responsiveness, and scalability matter.

Real-world applications of Scala are as follows:

- **Big data and Apache Spark**: Scala plays a crucial role in big data processing, particularly through Apache Spark, the leading distributed computing framework. Companies like *Netflix*, *Uber*, and *Databricks* rely on Spark (and thus Scala) to handle massive datasets efficiently. For instance, Netflix uses Spark with Scala to power its real-time recommendation engine, processing terabytes of user data to suggest personalized content. Uber leverages Scala for fraud detection, analyzing millions of transactions to identify suspicious activity. Since Scala is faster than Python for distributed computing and integrates seamlessly with big data tools like Hadoop and Kafka, it has become the go-to language for data engineers and scientists working in large-scale analytics.
- **Financial services and high-frequency trading**: In the *finance and banking sector,* Scala is widely used for risk modeling, algorithmic trading, and real-time data processing. Companies like *Goldman Sachs* and *JPMorgan Chase* employ Scala to build high-performance trading systems that require low latency and high reliability. For example, Goldman Sachs uses Scala to analyze market risks and optimize trading strategies, while JPMorgan applies it to credit risk assessment. *Scala is great at handling many tasks at the same time without slowing down, especially with the help of tools like Akka.* That is why it is often used in financial systems, where things need to happen very quickly, and results must be accurate, like processing trades or detecting fraud in real time.
- **Web development and microservices**: Scala is also a popular choice for backend development, particularly in companies that need *scalable and high-performance APIs. LinkedIn,* for instance, uses Scala to manage its massive user base and real-time notifications. Twitter, which initially relied on Ruby, migrated to Scala to handle its growing traffic and improve system stability. Similarly, *Disney+* uses the Play Framework (a Scala-based web framework) to deliver seamless streaming experiences to millions of users. Since Scala supports asynchronous programming and works well with reactive systems, it is ideal for building microservices that must handle thousands of requests per second.

- **Internet of Things (IoT) and smart manufacturing**: The IoT is another domain where Scala excels. **General electric** (GE) uses Scala in its Predix platform, which collects and analyzes sensor data from industrial machines to predict maintenance needs. By processing real-time data streams, Scala helps GE optimize machine uptime and reduce operational costs. Similarly, *Tesla* employs Scala in autonomous vehicle systems, where rapid data processing is essential for decision-making. Scala's ability to handle asynchronous and event-driven programming makes it a natural fit for IoT applications that require real-time analytics.

Therefore, given its versatility and industry adoption, learning Scala opens doors *to high-paying roles in data engineering, backend development, and financial technology*. Companies value Scala developers for their ability to write efficient, scalable, and maintainable code. Moreover, since Scala is interoperable with Java, developers can leverage existing Java libraries while enjoying a more modern programming experience.

Introduction to Scala basics

Scala is designed to be *concise, expressive, and safe*. At its core, Scala supports two styles of programming:

- **Object-oriented**: Everything is an object, even basic data like numbers. This means you can call methods on numbers and strings, and you define your own classes and objects to structure your program.
- **Functional**: Scala also supports functional programming, where *functions are first-class citizens*, which means you can assign them to variables, pass them as arguments, or return them from other functions. You can also write pure functions that have no side effects (like changing global variables). This leads to more *modular, testable, and predictable code.*

Let us now understand the basic data types, how to declare variables, and how to use operators in Scala.

Basic data types in Scala

These are the basic building blocks. Knowing them helps you store and use data properly. Scala has rich data types similar to Java, but with automatic type inference. *Table 14.1* lists the basic data types in Scala:

Type	Description	Example
Int	32-bit integer	`val x: Int = 10`
Double	64-bit floating-point number	`val y: Double = 3.14`
Boolean	True or false	`val isScalaFun = true`
Char	Single character	`val letter: Char = 'A'`
String	Sequence of characters	`val lang = "Scala"`
Long, Float, Short, Byte	Other numeric types	`val bigNum: Long = 123456789L`

***Table 14.1**: Data types in Scala*

Type inference: You do not always have to specify the type explicitly; Scala figures it out for you. For example:

```
val score = 95          // Automatically inferred as Int
val rating = 4.5        // Inferred as Double
```

Declaring variables

In Scala, there are two ways to declare variables, using the **`var`** and **`val`** keywords. Let us understand each one by one.

val vs. var

In Scala, variables are used to store data values such as numbers, strings, Booleans, or even complex objects. However, Scala brings a very important concept into variable declaration: immutability by default. This is where **`val`** and **`var`** come in:

- **val or immutable variables (Recommended)**: The keyword **val** is used to declare immutable variables, meaning once a value is assigned to a variable, it cannot be changed. This is like declaring a final variable in Java. Using **val** helps make your code more predictable, safer, and easier to debug, especially in large-scale or concurrent applications. For example:

```
val city = "Bangalore"
println(city)
// city = "Delhi"     // ✕ Error: reassignment to val
```

In this example, city is assigned the value **"Bangalore"**. If you try to reassign it to **"Delhi"**, the compiler will throw an error, preventing unintended changes.

- **var or mutable variables**: The keyword **var** is used to declare mutable variables, which means you can change the value of the variable later in your program. While sometimes necessary, using **var** should be done cautiously, as mutable variables can lead to bugs if not handled carefully, especially in concurrent or multi-threaded systems. For example:

```
var age = 25
println(age)          // Output: 25

age = 26              // Value updated
println(age)          // Output: 26
```

Here, the variable **age** is declared using **var**, which allows it to be reassigned later. This is helpful in situations where a variable needs to track state or accumulate values over time.

Operators in Scala

Scala supports several types of operators:

- Arithmetic operators
- Relational (comparison) operators
- Logical operators
- Bitwise operators (advanced use cases)
- Assignment operators

Let us look at each one in detail with examples.

Arithmetic operators

These operators perform basic mathematical operations as shown in *Table 14.2*:

Operator	Meaning	Example	Result
+	Addition	10 + 5	15
-	Subtraction	10 - 5	5
*	Multiplication	4 * 3	12
/	Division	20 / 4	5
%	Modulus (remainder)	10 % 3	1

***Table 14.2**: Arithmetic operators in Scala*

Example in Scala:

```
val a = 10
val b = 3

println(a + b)  // Output: 13
println(a - b)  // Output: 7
println(a * b)  // Output: 30
println(a / b)  // Output: 3
println(a % b)  // Output: 1
```

Relational (comparison) operators

These operators compare two values and return a Boolean result (true or false) as shown in *Table 14.3*:

Operator	Meaning	Example	Result
==	Equal to	5 == 5	true
!=	Not equal to	5 != 4	true
>	Greater than	10 > 5	true
<	Less than	3 < 7	true
>=	Greater or equal	6 >= 6	true
<=	Less or equal	4 <= 2	false

***Table 14.3:** Relational operators*

Example:

```
val x = 5
val y = 10
println(x == y)   // false
println(x != y)   // true
println(x < y)    // true
```

Logical operators

These operators are used to combine multiple Boolean expressions as shown in *Table 14.4:*

<table>
<tr><th>Operator</th><th>Description</th><th>Example</th><th>Result</th></tr>
<tr><td>&&</td><td>Logical AND</td><td>true && false</td><td>false</td></tr>
<tr><td>||</td><td>Logical OR</td><td>true || false</td><td>true</td></tr>
<tr><td>!</td><td>Logical NOT</td><td>!true</td><td>false</td></tr>
</table>

***Table 14.4:** Logical operators*

Example:

```
val isScalaFun = true
val isHard = false
```

```
println(isScalaFun && isHard)  // false
println(isScalaFun || isHard)  // true
println(!isHard)               // true
```

Assignment operators

These operators are used to assign and update values in variables. Mostly used with var since **`val`** is immutable, as shown in *Table 14.5*:

Operator	Description	Example	Equivalent to
=	Assignment	x = 5	Assign value
+=	Add and assign	x += 2	x = x + 2
-=	Subtract and assign	x -= 2	x = x - 2
*=	Multiply and assign	x *= 3	x = x * 3
/=	Divide and assign	x /= 2	x = x / 2

Table 14.5: *Assignment operators*

Example:

```
var score = 50
score += 10      // score is now 60
score -= 5       // score is now 55
```

Bitwise operators

These are used for low-level programming (binary manipulations):

Examples: &, |, ^, ~, <<, >>

Example code:

```
val a = 5       // 0101
val b = 3       // 0011

println(a & b) // 0001 = 1
println(a | b) // 0111 = 7
```

Built-in control structures in Scala

Control structures are the decision-making and flow-control tools in any programming language. In Scala, control structures enable you to:

- Make decisions (if, if-else, match)
- Repeat actions (for, while, do-while)
- Execute expressions conditionally
- Use pattern matching for clean, expressive branching

Scala supports all traditional control structures found in languages like Java and Python, but with more expressive power and conciseness.

Conditional statements

These are used to execute a block of code only when a condition is true, the details are as follows:

For example:

```
val marks = 85

if (marks >= 90)
  println("Grade: A+")
else if (marks >= 75)
  println("Grade: A")
else
  println("Grade: B or below")
```

In Scala, if can also return a value, since it is an expression:

```
val grade = if (marks >= 90) "A+" else "B"
println(grade)
```

Iteration

It is used to iterate through ranges, collections, or conditions as shown in the following examples:

Example: Iterating through a range:

```
for (i <- 1 to 5) {
  println(s"Step $i")
}
```

Example: Iterating through a list:

```
val names = List("Scala", "Java", "Python")

for (name <- names) {
  println(name)
}
```

Example: `for` with `if` filter:

```
for (i <- 1 to 10 if i % 2 == 0)
  println(i)   // prints even numbers
```

While and do-while loops

These are used when the number of iterations is not known in advance. The following are the examples:

Example: `while` loop:

```
var count = 0
while (count < 5) {
  println(s"Count is $count")
  count += 1
}
```

Example: Do-while loop (executes the block at least once, then checks the condition):

```
var num = 0
do {
  println(s"Value: $num")
  num += 1
} while (num < 3)
```

Pattern matching (match)

Scala replaces the traditional switch statement with match, which is more powerful and expressive. For example:

```
val day = 3

val dayType = day match {
  case 1 => "Monday"
  case 2 => "Tuesday"
  case 3 => "Wednesday"
  case _ => "Another day"
}

println(dayType) // Output: Wednesday
```

Match can also match types, conditions, and even deconstruct data structures (very powerful in Scala).

Exception handling

It is used to catch and handle errors gracefully. For example:

```
try {
  val result = 10 / 0
  println(result)
} catch {
  case e: ArithmeticException => println("Cannot divide by zero.")
} finally {
  println("This block always runs.")
}
```

`finally`, is optional and used for cleanup activities like closing files or database connections.

Classes and objects

In Scala, like in many object-oriented languages, a class is a blueprint, and an object is an instance of that blueprint:

- **Class**: Defines properties (also called fields or attributes) and behaviors (methods).
- **Object**: Is a real entity created using a class, containing actual values and logic.

Scala enhances traditional OOP with concise syntax and functional features.

Defining a class in Scala

The following code illustrates a way to define classes in Scala:

```
class Person(val name: String, val age: Int) {
  def greet(): Unit = {
    println(s"Hello, my name is $name and I am $age years old.")
  }
}
```

Here, **class Person(val name: String, val age: Int)**:

- This defines a class named **Person**.
- **It takes two constructor parameters**: name (a String) and age (an Int).
    - The **val** keyword makes these parameters into class fields:
    - They are public and immutable.
    - You can access them from outside the class: **person.name**, **person.age**.

  def greet(): Unit = { ... }:
- This defines a method (also called a function inside a class) called **greet**.
- **()** means the method takes no input parameters.
- **: Unit** indicates the return type of the method is **Unit**. Unit is Scala's equivalent of void in Java or Python's None. It means this method does not return a meaningful value. It is typically used for methods that perform side effects like printing to the screen, writing to a file, sending a message, etc.

  println(s"Hello, my name is $name and I am $age years old."):

  This line prints a greeting to the console.
- **s"...$name..."** is string interpolation in Scala, where variables are directly embedded in strings using **$**.

Creating objects and instances from a class

Let us now create an instance **person1** of the class **Person**. Next, we call the function **greet()** using this instance, as shown in the given code:

```
val person1 = new Person("Riya", 25)
person1.greet()
```

new Person("Riya", 25) creates a new object (instance) of the **Person** class. **"Riya"** is passed as the name, and **25** is passed as the age. These values go into the constructor of the class: **class Person(val name: String, val age: Int)**. Internally, Scala assigns:

```
this.name = "Riya"
this.age = 25
val person1 = ...:
```

This assigns the new **Person** object to a variable named **person1**. The keyword **val** means that the reference **person1** cannot be reassigned; it is immutable. However, the object itself (**person1**) can still perform actions (like calling methods).

```
person1.greet()
```

This calls the **greet()** method on the **person1** object. From the class definition:

```
def greet(): Unit = {
  println(s"Hello, my name is $name and I am $age years old.")
}
```

It prints a message using the values stored in name and age.

Output: **Hello, my name is Riya and I am 25 years old.**

Constructor parameters (val, var, or None): In Scala, you can define constructor parameters with or without **val**/ **var** as shown in example as follows:

```
class Animal(name: String)   // name is private to constructor
class Dog(val breed: String) // breed is accessible and immutable
class Cat(var color: String) // color is accessible and mutable
```

Adding methods and fields

The following code outlines different methods and fields used:

```
class Rectangle(val width: Int, val height: Int) {
  def area(): Int = width * height
  def describe(): Unit = println(s"Width: $width, Height: $height, Area: ${area()}")
}
val r = new Rectangle(10, 5)
r.describe()  // Output: Width: 10, Height: 5, Area: 50
class Rectangle(val width: Int, val height: Int):
```

- This statement defines a class named **Rectangle**.
- It takes two constructor parameters: **width** and **height**, both of type **Int**.
- The keyword **val** before the parameters means:
  - These are public, immutable fields of the class.
  - You can access them as **r.width**, **r.height**.

`def area(): Int = width * height:`

- This is a method called **area**.
- It returns an **Int** (denoted by **: Int**).
- The method multiplies the **width** and **height** to calculate the **area** of the rectangle.
- **width** and **height** refer to the values stored in the object.

`def describe(): Unit = println(...):`

- Another method named **describe**. It returns **Unit** (like **void** in Java), meaning it performs an action but does not return a result.
- Inside the method, it uses **println()** to print:
  - The rectangle's width
  - Height
  - Calculated area using the **area()** method

`val r = new Rectangle(10, 5):`

- This creates an object r of the **`Rectangle`** class.
- The constructor sets:
  - **`width`** = **`10`**
  - **`height`** = **`5`**

`r.describe():`

- Calls the **`describe()`** method on the r object.
- It prints: **`Width: 10, Height: 5, Area: 50`**

Default parameter values and auxiliary constructors

Let us understand with the help of the following example:

```
class Student(val name: String, val grade: String = "A") {
  def info(): Unit = println(s"$name has a grade $grade")
}

val s1 = new Student("Raj")             // Uses default grade
val s2 = new Student("Anita", "B")      // Custom grade

s1.info()  // Output: Raj has a grade A
s2.info()  // Output: Anita has a grade B
```

In the preceding code, **`class Student(val name: String, val grade: String = "A")`**:

- This defines a class **`Student`** with two parameters:
  - **name**: A **`String`**, mandatory
  - **grade**: A **`String`**, optional, with a default value **`"A"`**

Here, grade: **`String = "A"`** implies, if no grade is provided when creating a **`Student`** object, Scala automatically sets **`grade = "A"`**. This is Scala's default argument feature, which helps to avoid writing multiple constructors just to handle optional parameters. For example, in **`val s1 = new Student("Raj")`**, Only the name argument is passed. Since grade is not provided, Scala uses the default value **`"A"`**. Whereas, in **`val s2 = new Student("Anita", "B")`**, both name and grade are provided, the default value is overridden by **`"B"`**.

Auxiliary constructors are additional constructors you define with the keyword def this(...) to offer multiple ways to create an object. However, in modern Scala, you can often avoid auxiliary constructors by using default values, as shown in this example. However, if you needed more control or logic during object creation, you might still define auxiliary constructors.

Companion object

Scala does not have static methods but uses a companion object to define methods and constants related to a class. A companion object is an object with the same name as a class. It sits outside the class, but in the same file. It is used to define methods and values that belong to the class, not to any specific instance, as illustrated in the following code:

```
class Circle(val radius: Double) {
  def area: Double = Circle.pi * radius * radius
}
```

```
object Circle {
  val pi = 3.1415
}
val c = new Circle(5)
println(c.area)  // Output: 78.5375
```

In the preceding code, object `Circle { val pi = 3.1415 }` is the companion object for the `Circle` class. It defines pi as a shared constant available to all instances of `Circle`. Here, `pi` is not tied to any one circle; it is a general constant.

Functions and closures

In Scala, functional programming capability makes Scala powerful for writing concise, modular code as follows:

- Functions are treated as first-class citizens; they can be assigned to variables, passed as arguments, or returned from other functions.
- Closures are functions that capture variables from their surrounding scope, making them powerful for building dynamic behavior.

Basic function syntax is as follows:

```
// Define a function
def add(x: Int, y: Int): Int = {
  x + y
}

// Call it
val result = add(3, 5)  // Returns 8
```

Here, `def` keyword declares a function; explicit return types are optional but recommended

Scala also provides single-expression functions (can omit braces): `def multiply (x: Int, y: Int): Int = x * y`

Lets discuss closures, which represent functions that capture variables from their outer scope. For example, in the following code, the inner function remembers the factor even after the multiplier finishes executing:

```
def multiplier(factor: Int): Int => Int = {
  (x: Int) => x * factor  // `factor` is "closed over"
}

val times3 = multiplier(3)
times3(5)  // Returns 15
```

Anonymous functions in lambdas

An example is as follows:

```
// Syntax: (parameters) => expression
val square = (x: Int) => x * x
square(4)  // Returns 16
```

Here, `val square` is a function value (also called a **function literal**) and `(x: Int) => x * x` is the function definition using the lambda syntax:

```
// Used inline
List(1, 2, 3).map(x => x * 2)  // Returns List(2, 4, 6)
```

Shorthand syntax: _ placeholder can be used for single-use parameters. For example: `List(1, 2, 3).map(_ * 2) // Same as above`

Higher-order functions

Functions that take other functions as arguments or return them. An example is as follows:

```
// Takes a function `f` and applies it to `x`
def applyFunc(x: Int, f: Int => Int): Int = f(x)

val increment = (x: Int) => x + 1
applyFunc(5, increment)  // Returns 6
```

Common HOFs in Scala are as follows:

- **map**: Transforms each element in a collection.
- **filter**: Keeps elements matching a condition.
- **reduce**: Combines elements into a single result.

Example is as follows:

```
List(1, 2, 3)
  .map(_ * 2)       // List(2, 4, 6)
  .filter(_ > 3)   // List(4, 6)
  .reduce(_ + _)    // 10
```

Currying

It means breaking a function into a series of single-argument functions. It enables partial application, that is, pre-filling of some arguments. It is also useful for dependency injection and functional composition. For example:

```
def add(x: Int)(y: Int): Int = x + y

val add5 = add(5)(_)  // Partial application
add5(3)  // Returns 8
```

Inheritance and traits

Scala provides powerful object-oriented features through inheritance and traits to enable code reuse and modular design while avoiding many pitfalls of traditional Java-style inheritance. Inheritance allows one class (child/subclass) to inherit properties and behavior (methods and fields) from another class (parent/superclass). This enables code reuse and supports polymorphism, one interface, many implementations. Inheritance is used for *is-a* relationships (e.g., *Dog is an Animal*), when you need method overriding, or for hierarchical classifications (e.g., UI components). Unlike Java, Scala follows single inheritance for classes—meaning a class can only extend one parent class, but makes up for this limitation through traits, which support multiple inheritance. When a class extends another, it inherits all its non-private members (methods, fields, and nested classes). The child class can:

- Override methods (using the override keyword) to modify behavior.
- Extending functionality by adding new methods.
- Access the parent class using super (e.g., **`super.method()`**).

Let us understand with the help of an example:

Basic syntax: `extends`

```
class Animal {
  def speak(): Unit = println("Animal speaks")
}

class Dog extends Animal {
  override def speak(): Unit = println("Dog barks")
}

val d = new Dog()
d.speak()  // Output: Dog barks
```

In the preceding code, **`class Animal`** defines a base class with a method **`speak()`**, **`class Dog extends Animal`**, inherits from **`Animal`**, and **`override`** is required when a subclass redefines a method from the parent class, and **`d.speak()`** uses the overridden method in **`Dog class`**.

Inheritance with constructor parameters

In the following code, the constructor of **`Person`** is called using extends **`Person(name)`**, which requires a name as a constructor argument, and **`Student`** passes the name to **`Person`** using **`extends Person(name)`**:

```
class Person(val name: String)
class Student(name: String, val school: String) extends Person(name) {
  def info(): Unit = println(s"$name studies at $school")
}

val s = new Student("Riya", "Delhi University")
s.info()  // Output: Riya studies at Delhi University
```

Traits

Traits in Scala are a game-changing feature that combines the best of interfaces and abstract classes from other languages. Unlike traditional interfaces, traits can contain both abstract methods (without implementation) and concrete methods (with default behavior). This makes them incredibly versatile for code reuse and modular design. One of the biggest advantages of traits is multiple inheritance, something classes in Scala cannot do. While a class can only extend one parent class, it can mix in multiple traits using the with keyword. For example, a **`Dog`** class can inherit from **`Animal`** while also mixing in traits like **`Speaker`** and **`TailWagger`**, each adding distinct behaviors without creating a messy inheritance hierarchy.

Traits also solve one of the trickiest problems in object-oriented programming: the diamond problem (where a class inherits from two parents that share a common ancestor). Scala handles this through linearization, a deterministic method resolution strategy that ensures there's no ambiguity in which method gets called. In real-world applications, traits are widely used in:

- Plugin architectures (e.g., adding caching or logging dynamically).
- Functional programming patterns (e.g., type classes).
- Testing (e.g., mock implementations via trait overrides).

You should use traits when:

- **For reusable, cross-cutting concerns**: If your application needs logging, serialization, or authentication across different classes, Traits like Loggable or Secure can be mixed wherever needed.
- **To avoid deep inheritance chains**: Instead of forcing classes into rigid hierarchies, traits let you compose behavior flexibly.
- **For dependency injection**: Traits can define abstract methods that are implemented later, making them perfect for modular design.

Examples are as follows:

```
trait Speaker {
  def speak(): String  // Abstract method
  def greet(): String = "Hello!"  // Concrete method
}

trait TailWagger {
  def wagTail(): String = "Tail wagging!"
}

// Mix multiple traits into a class
class Dog(name: String) extends Animal(name) with Speaker with TailWagger {
  override def speak(): String = "Woof!"
}

val dog = Dog("Buddy")
println(dog.greet())    // "Hello!" (from Speaker)
println(dog.wagTail())  // "Tail wagging!" (from TailWagger)
```

Traits can even modify existing behavior by using super to call the previous implementation in the inheritance chain. This allows for stackable modifications, where each trait adds or tweaks functionality as shown in the following code:

```
trait LoudSpeaker extends Speaker {
  override def speak(): String = super.speak().toUpperCase + "!!!"
}

val loudDog = new Dog("Max") with LoudSpeaker
println(loudDog.speak())  // "WOOF!!!"
```

Running Scala Shell in Cloudera

Cloudera provides a powerful platform for big data processing, and Scala is one of the key programming languages supported for developing distributed applications. The Scala shell **Read-Eval-Print Loop** (**REPL**) is an interactive environment that allows you to quickly test code snippets, explore datasets, and prototype Spark applications without compiling full programs. In Cloudera, you can access the Scala shell either through the standard Scala REPL or via Spark-shell, which includes a built-in Spark context for distributed data processing. This section will guide you through launching the Scala shell in a Cloudera environment, checking the Scala version, and running basic examples to get started. Whether you are working with HDFS, YARN, or Spark, the Scala shell provides a convenient way to interact with Cloudera's ecosystem. The steps are as follows:

1. Launch the Scala shell in Cloudera by using the command Spark shell as shown in *Figure 14.1:*

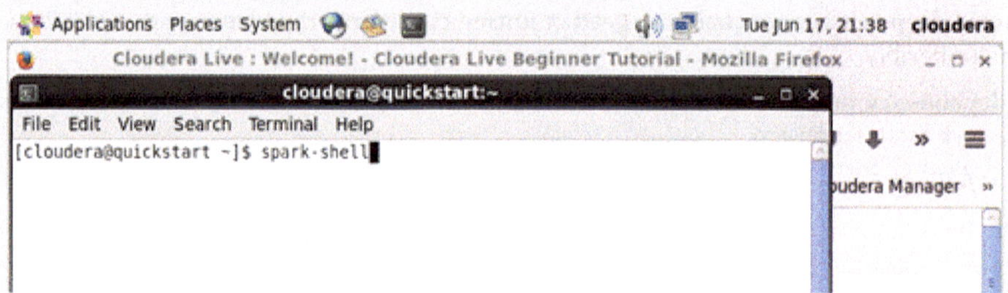

Figure 14.1: *Scala shell command*

2. Next, it loads the Spark environment in a few minutes and prompts the Scala interactive shell as shown in *Figure 14.2:*

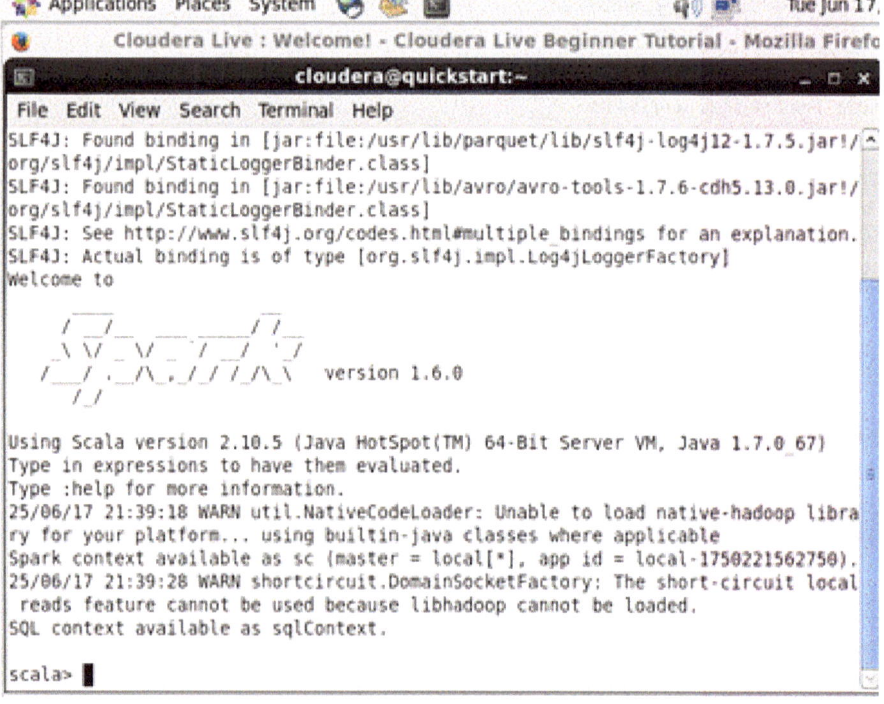

Figure 14.2: *Launch of Scala shell with Spark context*

3. You can work with Scala as well as Spark programming in this shell. *Figure 14.3* is an example of the use of variables and data types in the Scala shell:

```
val name: String = "Cloudera User"
val version = 2.12
println(s"Welcome to $name using Scala $version")
```

```
scala> val name:String="Cloudera User"
name: String = Cloudera User

scala> val version = 1.6
version: Double = 1.6

scala> println(s"Welcome to $name using Scala$version")
Welcome to Cloudera User using Scala1.6

scala>
```

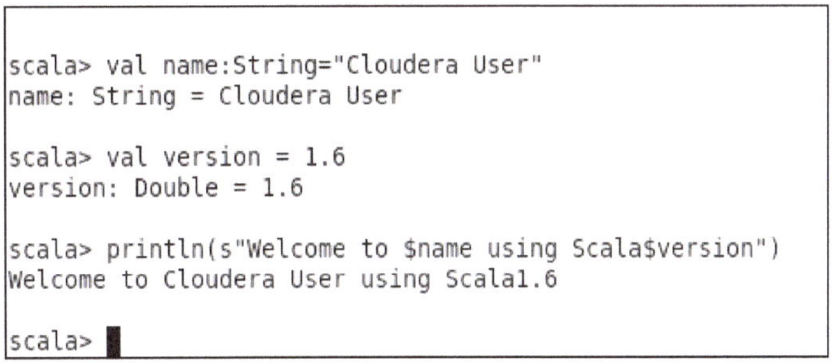

***Figure 14.3**: Scala example variables and data types*

4. The next example shows the **List** operations in Scala (refer to *Figure 14.4*). Similarly, other operations can be performed in the Scala shell, such as:

```
val numbers = List(1, 2, 3, 4, 5)
val doubled = numbers.map(_ * 2)
println(doubled)
```

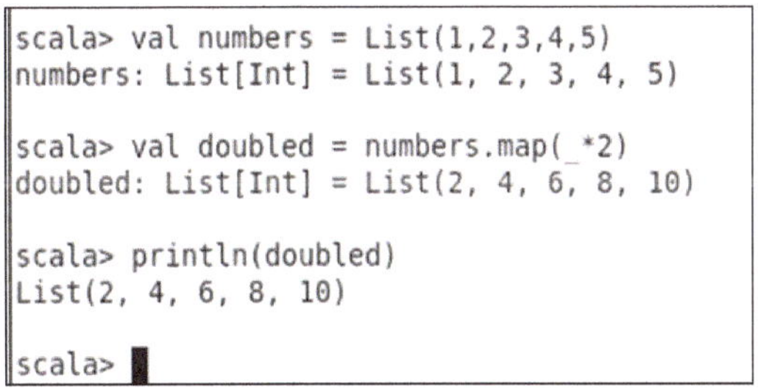

```
scala> val numbers = List(1,2,3,4,5)
numbers: List[Int] = List(1, 2, 3, 4, 5)

scala> val doubled = numbers.map(_*2)
doubled: List[Int] = List(2, 4, 6, 8, 10)

scala> println(doubled)
List(2, 4, 6, 8, 10)

scala>
```

***Figure 14.4**: Example of List operation*

Application development using Scala

sbt is an open-source build tool specifically designed for Scala projects. It was first released in *2008*, and it quickly became the standard build system for Scala due to its tight integration with Scala's ecosystem. Over the years, it has evolved significantly, with *sbt 1.0* launching in *2017*, bringing stability, performance improvements, and better dependency management. Today, sbt remains the most widely used build tool in the Scala community, continuously updated to support modern Scala features and workflows. Its Scala-based DSL allows flexible and customizable build configurations, while plugins like *sbt-assembly* simplify deployment. SBT also excels in parallel task execution, continuous testing *(~testQuick)*, and IDE integration, making it the most powerful and developer-friendly choice for Scala, far more optimized than generic tools like Maven or Gradle.

The following are the steps for downloading and installing sbt:

1. Prerequisites:
   a. Ensure you have Java 8 or later installed (java -version).
   b. SBT works on Windows, macOS, and Linux.

2. Download sbt:
   a. Visit the official sbt website: **https://www.scala-sbt.org/download.html**
   b. Choose the appropriate version for your OS (`.msi` for Windows, `.tgz` for macOS/Linux).
   c. Install sbt on Windows
3. Run the downloaded `.msi` installer:
   a. Follow the setup wizard (default settings are fine).
   b. Verify installation in the command prompt:

```
sbt --version
```

4. Create a project for your desired application:
   a. Open command prompt, first go to the bin in the path where you have installed sbt, like in this case it is installed at `D:\sbt-1.11.2\sbt\bin\` and make a new directory:

```
D:\sbt-1.11.2\sbt\bin\ mkdir todo-app
D:\sbt-1.11.2\sbt\bin\cd todo-app
```

We will now develop a Scala application, i.e., a command-line Todo List manager that allows users to add, list, mark as complete, and delete tasks using a mutable `ListBuffer` for storage. The program starts by displaying a menu with options (1-5), reads user input via `StdIn.readLine()`, and performs actions like adding a task (stored as a `case class Task` with a description and completion status), listing tasks (showing their index, status, and description), marking tasks as complete (by index), or deleting them. The app handles invalid inputs gracefully and loops back to the menu after each operation until the user exits. The state persists in memory (via the mutable tasks buffer) while the app runs. The code for this application is as follows:

Replace the contents of `D:\sbt-1.11.2\sbt\bin\todo-app\src\main\scala\Main.scala` with this code:

```
import scala.collection.mutable.ListBuffer
import scala.io.StdIn.readLine

case class Task(description: String, var completed: Boolean = false)

object TodoApp {
  private val tasks = ListBuffer[Task]()

  def main(args: Array[String]): Unit = {
    println("Welcome to your Todo List!")
    showMenu()
  }

  private def showMenu(): Unit = {
    println("\nChoose an option:")
    println("1. Add task")
    println("2. List tasks")
    println("3. Complete task")
    println("4. Delete task")
    println("5. Exit")
```

```
    readLine() match {
      case "1" => addTask()
      case "2" => listTasks()
      case "3" => completeTask()
      case "4" => deleteTask()
      case "5" => println("Goodbye!")
      case _   =>
        println("Invalid option, try again")
        showMenu()
    }
  }
```

The following is the continuation of the preceding code:

```
  private def addTask(): Unit = {
    println("Enter task description:")
    val desc = readLine()
    tasks += Task(desc)
    println(s"Added: $desc")
    showMenu()
  }

  private def listTasks(): Unit = {
    if (tasks.isEmpty) {
      println("No tasks yet!")
    } else {
      println("\nYour tasks:")
      tasks.zipWithIndex.foreach { case (task, index) =>
        val status = if (task.completed) "[✓]" else "[ ]"
        println(s"${index + 1}. $status ${task.description}")
      }
    }
    showMenu()
  }

  private def completeTask(): Unit = {
    listTasks()
    if (tasks.nonEmpty) {
      println("Enter task number to complete:")
      try {
        val index = readLine().toInt - 1
        if (index >= 0 && index < tasks.size) {
```

```
          tasks(index).completed = true
          println("Task marked as complete!")
        } else {
          println("Invalid task number")
        }
      } catch {
        case _: NumberFormatException => println("Please enter a number")
      }
    }
    showMenu()
  }

  private def deleteTask(): Unit = {
    listTasks()
    if (tasks.nonEmpty) {
      println("Enter task number to delete:")
      try {
        val index = readLine().toInt - 1
        if (index >= 0 && index < tasks.size) {
          val removed = tasks.remove(index)
          println(s"Deleted: ${removed.description}")
        } else {
          println("Invalid task number")
        }
      } catch {
        case _: NumberFormatException => println("Please enter a number")
      }
    }
    showMenu()
  }
}
```

Next, follow the steps as shown in *Figure 14.5*, to run the application:

```
D:\sbt-1.11.2\sbt>cd bin

D:\sbt-1.11.2\sbt\bin>dir
 Volume in drive D is New Volume
 Volume Serial Number is 266B-D016

 Directory of D:\sbt-1.11.2\sbt\bin

06/14/2025  09:09 PM    <DIR>          .
06/14/2025  04:38 PM    <DIR>          ..
06/14/2025  09:09 PM    <DIR>          hello-world
06/14/2025  04:38 PM            29,787 sbt
06/14/2025  04:38 PM         3,847,512 sbt-launch.jar
06/14/2025  04:38 PM            28,655 sbt.bat
06/14/2025  04:38 PM        32,901,160 sbtn-aarch64-pc-linux
06/14/2025  04:38 PM        62,366,088 sbtn-universal-apple-darwin
06/14/2025  04:38 PM        33,851,496 sbtn-x86_64-pc-linux
06/14/2025  04:38 PM        31,756,288 sbtn-x86_64-pc-win32.exe
               7 File(s)    164,780,986 bytes
               3 Dir(s)  52,023,099,392 bytes free

D:\sbt-1.11.2\sbt\bin>sbt new scala/scala3.g8
A template to demonstrate a minimal Scala 3 application

name [Scala 3 Project Template]: todo-app

Template applied in D:\sbt-1.11.2\sbt\bin\.\todo-app

D:\sbt-1.11.2\sbt\bin>
```

Figure 14.5: *Steps to create todo-app project*

Figure 14.6 shows the steps to run the **`todo-app`** application. After executing **`sbt run`**, it will take time to compile and execute and build the project as shown in *Figure 14.7*, demonstrated as follows:

```
Command Prompt - sbt run

Microsoft Windows [Version 10.0.26100.4061]
(c) Microsoft Corporation. All rights reserved.

C:\Users\Hp>d:

D:\>cd sbt*\sbt

D:\sbt-1.11.2\sbt>dir
 Volume in drive D is New Volume
 Volume Serial Number is 266B-D016

 Directory of D:\sbt-1.11.2\sbt

06/14/2025  04:38 PM    <DIR>          .
06/14/2025  04:38 PM    <DIR>          ..
06/15/2025  08:35 AM    <DIR>          bin
06/14/2025  04:38 PM    <DIR>          conf
06/14/2025  04:38 PM            11,436 LICENSE
06/14/2025  04:38 PM             3,021 NOTICE
               2 File(s)         14,457 bytes
               4 Dir(s)  52,023,005,184 bytes free

D:\sbt-1.11.2\sbt>cd bin

D:\sbt-1.11.2\sbt\bin>cd todo-app

D:\sbt-1.11.2\sbt\bin\todo-app>sbt run
[info] welcome to sbt 1.11.2 (Oracle Corporation Java 1.8.0_401)
[info] loading project definition from D:\sbt-1.11.2\sbt\bin\todo-app\project
[info] Updating todo-app-build
```

***Figure 14.6**: Steps to run the todo-app application*

After successful compilation of the todo-app, *Figure 14.7* shows the options to choose the main classes. You enter the choice number, say 1 (over here), to add a task:

```
Command Prompt - sbt run

  100.0% [##########] 1.5 MiB (113.3 KiB / s)
https://repo1.maven.org/maven2/org/scala-lang/scala-library/2.13.16/scala-library-2.13.16.jar
  100.0% [##########] 5.7 MiB (96.1 KiB / s)
https://repo1.maven.org/maven2/org/scala-lang/scaladoc_3/3.7.1/scaladoc_3-3.7.1.jar
  100.0% [##########] 4.7 MiB (79.1 KiB / s)
[info] Fetched artifacts of todo-app_3
[info] compiling 1 Scala source to D:\sbt-1.11.2\sbt\bin\todo-app\target\scala-3.7.1\classes ...

Multiple main classes detected. Select one to run:
 [1] TodoApp
 [2] msg

Enter number: T
Invalid number: 'T'

Multiple main classes detected. Select one to run:
 [1] TodoApp
 [2] msg

Enter number: 1
[info] running TodoApp
Welcome to your Todo List!

Choose an option:
1. Add task
2. List tasks
3. Complete task
4. Delete task
5. Exit
```

***Figure 14.7**: Execution output of todo-app*

After giving choice 1, you are prompted to enter the task as shown in *Figure 14.8*. After adding the task, you may check the list of tasks and so on, as demonstrated as follows:

```
Command Prompt - sbt run

Choose an option:
1. Add task
2. List tasks
3. Complete task
4. Delete task
5. Exit
1
Enter task description:
remind me to read Data Science book
Added: remind me to read Data Science book

Choose an option:
1. Add task
2. List tasks
3. Complete task
4. Delete task
5. Exit
2

Your tasks:
1. [ ] remind me to read Data Science book

Choose an option:
1. Add task
2. List tasks
3. Complete task
4. Delete task
5. Exit
```

Figure 14.8: *Shows the working of todo-app*

Methods to fix the sbt not recognized error

The various ways to fix the error are :

1. Add sbt to Path (permanent fix):
   a. Press *Win + R*, type **`sysdm.cpl`**, go to **Advanced** | **Environment Variables.**
   b. Under **System Variables**, find **Path** and click **Edit**.
   c. Click **New** and add: **`D:\sbt-1.11.2\sbt\bin`**.
   d. Click **OK** and restart your command prompt.
2. Run from the correct directory:
   a. **First, navigate to your project:** `cd D:\sbt-1.11.2\sbt\bin\todo-app`.
   b. **Then run using one of these:** `D:\sbt-1.11.2\sbt\bin\sbt run`.
   c. **Verify project structure**: Your **`todo-app`** folder should contain:

```
todo-app/
 ├─ build.sbt
 ├─ project/
 └─ src/
```

```
└── main/
    └── scala/
        └── Main.scala
```

If files are missing, move to the next step.

a. Create **build.sbt** with:

- name := "todo-app"
- version := "1.0"
- scalaVersion := "2.13.11"

b. Ensure **Main.scala** is in **src/main/scala/**

Conclusion

This chapter has equipped you with essential Scala skills, blending object-oriented and functional programming concepts to write clean, efficient code. You have mastered core features like type inference, pattern matching, and control structures while gaining hands-on experience with classes, traits, and the Scala REPL in Cloudera environments. The practical sbt application development knowledge bridges learning with real-world implementation, preparing you for distributed systems and big data challenges. These fundamentals serve as your toolkit for advanced Scala programming, Spark data processing, and scalable application development.

In the next chapter, you will learn data analysis with Spark SQL and DataFrames in Cloudera.

Points to remember

The following list highlights some key takeaways from this chapter:

- Scala is a high-level language that combines object-oriented and functional programming, running on the JVM and interoperable with Java. It's widely used for scalable, data-intensive applications.
- Scala supports basic data types like int, double, and string, and uses concise syntax for arithmetic and logical operations. Variables are declared using val (immutable) and var (mutable).
- Scala includes standard control structures like if, while, for, and pattern matching, enabling clear and expressive flow control in programs.
- Scala supports class-based design with constructors and methods, and uses companion objects to define static-like members for reusable logic.
- Functions in Scala are first-class citizens and can be anonymous or higher-order. Closures are functions that capture and use variables from their defining scope.
- Scala allows single inheritance through classes and multiple behavior reuse via traits, supporting modular and scalable design with method overriding and mixing.
- The Scala shell in Cloudera provides an interactive REPL environment for testing Scala code, particularly useful for learning and working with Apache Spark.
- Scala is used to build robust applications across domains like data analytics, backend services, and distributed computing, often in conjunction with tools like Spark and Akka.

Exercises

1. **What does Scala infer for val x = List(1, "two", 3.0)?**

   a. List[Any]
   b. List[AnyVal]
   c. List[Serializable]
   d. Compilation error

2. **Which expression is not equivalent to 1 + 2 + 3?**
   a. +(2). +(3)
   b. (1). +(2 +(3))
   c. 1 + (2 + 3)
   d. +. (1, 2, 3)
3. **What does this match expression return?**

```
"hello" match {
  case str if str.length > 3 => "Long"
  case _ => "Short"
}
```

   a. "Long"
   b. "Short"
   c. Compilation error
   d. Runtime exception
4. **Which trait definition causes a compilation error?**
   a. trait A { def x: Int }
   b. trait B { def y = 5 }
   c. trait C { val z: Int = 10 }
   d. trait D { def w: Int = 7 }
5. **What is the output of:**

```
val f: (Int => Int) = _ * 2
f(5)
```

   a. 10
   b. 7
   c. Compilation error
   d. 25
6. **Which is not allowed in Scala?**
   a. class A extends B with C
   b. class A extends B with C with D
   c. class A extends B, C
   d. class A extends B
7. **Which REPL command shows the type of List(1, 2)?**
   a. :type List(1, 2)
   b. :show List(1, 2)
   c. :print List(1, 2)
   d. :kind List(1, 2)
8. **What does for (i <- 1 to 3; j <- 1 to i) yield (i, j) return?**
   a. Vector((1,1), (2,1), (2,2), (3,1), (3,2), (3,3))
   b. List((1,1), (2,2), (3,3))
   c. Seq((1,1), (1,2), (1,3))
   d. Compilation error
9. **What is the output?**

```
def multiplier(x: Int): Int => Int = y => x * y
val triple = multiplier(3)
triple(5)
```

   a. 8
   b. 15
   c. 35
   d. Compilation error

10. **Which command compiles code without running tests?**

    a. sbt test
    b. sbt compile
    c. sbt package
    d. sbt clean

Answers

1. a.	2. d.	3. a.	4. d.	5. a.
6. c.	7. a.	8. a.	9. b.	10. b.

Questions

1. Explain how Scala combines object-oriented and functional programming paradigms. Provide two language features that demonstrate each paradigm.
2. Compare val and var in Scala with examples. When would you prefer one over the other?
3. Describe how pattern matching in Scala differs from Java's switch statement. Write a simple example to illustrate exhaustiveness checking.
4. Given the class Person(name: String, age: Int), write:
    a. A companion object with a factory method apply
    b. A case class version with the same properties.
5. Convert this anonymous function to its explicit form:
    ```
    val square = (x: Int) => x * x
    ```
    Then, explain how it demonstrates *first-class functions*.
6. Identify the issue in this Scala code and fix it:
    ```
    trait Flyable { def fly() }
    class Bird extends Flyable { /* ... */ }
    ```
7. Define a case class 'Person' with fields 'name' (String) and 'age' (Int), then create a List of two Person instances. Filter the list to show only persons with age > 25
8. A colleague claims List(1, "two", 3.0) should infer List[AnyVal]. Explain why this is incorrect and what Scala actually infers.
9. Analyze this code snippet:
    ```
    for {
      i <- 1 to 3
      j <- 1 to 2
    } yield (i, j)
    ```
    What does it return? Rewrite it using map/flatMap.**
10. Design a small Scala application using sbt that:
    a. Creates a class Employee(id: Int, name: String, salary: Double).
    b. Reads a CSV file (employees.csv) with format: id,name,salary.
    c. Filters employees with salary > 50000.
    d. Writes results to "high_earners.txt".
    e. Prints the average salary.

CHAPTER 15
Data Analysis with Spark SQL

Without big data analytics, companies are blind and deaf.

— Geoffrey Moore

Introduction

This chapter presents the concept of Spark SQL, which is a module of Apache Spark that provides a unified interface for structured and semi-structured data processing. The chapter begins with an introduction to fundamental concepts of Spark SQL, its features, and applications. It gives details about Spark SQL interfaces such as SQL queries, DataFrames, Datasets, and SparkSession. The architecture of Spark SQL illustrates the various components, such as the Catalyst optimizer, the Tungsten engine, and the Hive metastore. The multiple ways to import and save data, from different sources and formats, Spark SQL, are demonstrated with the help of practical examples in PySpark. By the end of this chapter, readers will have a comprehensive understanding of Spark SQL and its capabilities. They will be able to use Spark SQL to perform various data processing tasks on structured and semi-structured data.

Structure

In this chapter, we will cover the following topics:

- Introduction to Spark SQL
- Architecture of Spark SQL
- Spark SQL interface
- RDD vs. DataFrame vs. Dataset
- Spark SQL interface with PySpark

Objectives

By the end of this chapter, the readers will have a comprehensive understanding of working with Spark SQL for structured data processing. This chapter introduces the fundamentals of Spark SQL, its architecture, and the Spark SQL Interface, enabling learners to run SQL queries efficiently within the Spark environment. They will explore the evolution and key differences between RDDs, DataFrames, and Datasets, providing clarity on when to use each. Additionally, they will gain hands-on experience in importing and saving data, processing both structured and semi-structured files, and performing essential DataFrame operations such as filtering, aggregating, and transforming data for analytics and real-world applications.

Introduction to Spark SQL

Spark SQL is a module within Apache Spark that provides a structured data processing framework designed to work with both structured and semi-structured data. Its primary purposes are:

- **Unification of APIs**: It bridges the gap between the relational (SQL) and procedural (RDD) worlds in Spark, such that it allows users to mix SQL queries with Spark programs.
- **Performance optimization**: It enables Spark to perform optimizations under the hood that are not possible with traditional RDD operations.
- **Data source integration**: It provides a common way to access a variety of data sources (Hive, JSON, Parquet, JDBC, etc.) using a unified interface.
- **Interactive querying**: It supports interactive SQL queries with low latency, thus making it suitable for both batch processing and interactive analytics. With Spark SQL, users can perform data analysis tasks at scale using familiar SQL expressions, while also leveraging Spark's in-memory computing power for high performance.

Advantages over traditional SQL systems

Spark SQL offers several significant advantages compared to traditional SQL databases and query engines, as follows:

- **Distributed processing capabilities**: One of the key strengths of Spark SQL is its distributed processing capabilities. Unlike traditional SQL databases that primarily scale vertically by upgrading to more powerful hardware, Spark SQL achieves horizontal scalability by distributing workloads across a cluster of machines. This allows it to efficiently process petabytes of data, making it ideal for large-scale analytics tasks. Additionally, Spark SQL offers robust fault tolerance mechanisms. In the event of a node failure, the system can automatically recover lost computations by leveraging lineage information and data replication that ensures reliable and resilient data processing without manual intervention.
- **Integration with the big data ecosystem**: Spark SQL integrates seamlessly with the broader big data ecosystem, thus making it a versatile tool for modern data processing needs. It supports querying data from diverse sources, including HDFS, Hive, Cassandra, relational databases, and more, often within the same query. This flexibility simplifies complex workflows that span multiple data storage systems. A notable advantage of Spark SQL is its ability to perform schema inference. While traditional SQL systems require predefined, rigid schema definitions, Spark SQL can automatically infer schema structures from semi-structured data formats like JSON or Parquet. This capability significantly reduces the overhead of preparing data for analysis, especially in environments where data formats evolve over time.
- **Performance advantages**: Spark SQL is engineered for high-performance analytics. Its in-memory processing architecture allows frequently accessed data to be cached in memory to deliver query speeds that are 10 to 100 times faster than traditional disk-based systems. This is especially valuable for iterative or interactive workloads. The performance is further enhanced by the Catalyst Optimizer, an advanced query optimizer that refines execution plans based on data characteristics and query structure. Catalyst applies both logical and physical optimizations, including predicate pushdown and join strategy selection, ensuring efficient resource utilization. Moreover, Spark SQL employs Whole-Stage Code Generation, a runtime technique that produces compact, low-level code for query execution. This approach minimizes overhead from virtual function calls and significantly boosts execution speed, thus making Spark SQL suitable for complex, large-scale analytical tasks.
- **Flexibility**: Spark SQL provides remarkable flexibility for developers and analysts alike. It supports multiple language APIs, including Java, Scala, R, and SQL, thus enabling teams with varied skill sets to collaborate within the same environment. This multi-language support ensures accessibility for both

programmers and SQL-oriented users. The platform also allows programmatic integration, where SQL queries can be seamlessly combined with complex analytics code, such as machine learning pipelines or graph processing algorithms, all within the same application.

- **Cost efficiency**: Another advantage of Spark SQL is its cost efficiency. Unlike many traditional databases that demand expensive, specialized servers, Spark SQL is designed to run on commodity hardware, reducing infrastructure costs. This makes it a highly economical solution for processing large volumes of data. Additionally, Spark SQL supports dynamic resource allocation, which means it can automatically scale computing resources up or down based on the workload. This elasticity ensures optimal performance during peak demand while minimizing resource consumption during idle periods, leading to significant cost savings for organizations.

Example use cases

Spark SQL is widely adopted across industries for various use cases:

- **ETL pipelines**: Efficiently processes and transforms large datasets from diverse sources into structured formats for downstream analytics.
- **Data warehousing**: Executes complex analytical queries on large, distributed datasets, providing a scalable alternative to traditional data warehouses.
- **Interactive analytics**: Supports Power BI tools and dashboards with fast, SQL-based access to big data, enabling real-time insights.
- **Machine learning feature preparation**: Prepares structured datasets for machine learning algorithms by performing filtering, joins, and aggregations.
- **Real-time analytics**: Processes streaming data with the same API used for batch workloads, enabling consistent, scalable analytics pipelines.

Architecture of Spark SQL

Spark SQL is a fundamental component of the Apache Spark ecosystem. It is designed for structured and semi-structured data processing using SQL queries and programmatic APIs. Its architecture integrates the benefits of distributed computing, in-memory processing, and advanced query optimization to deliver high performance at scale. At a high level, the Spark SQL architecture comprises:

- Unified interfaces for SQL and DataFrame/Dataset APIs.
- Catalyst optimizer for query planning and optimization.
- Tungsten execution engine for efficient query execution.
- Data source API for seamless integration with diverse storage systems.

The Spark SQL architecture, as shown in *Figure 15.1*, follows a layered design that combines SQL query parsing, logical and physical planning, optimization, and distributed execution to process large-scale structured data efficiently. The detailed working of each layer is mentioned in the following sections.

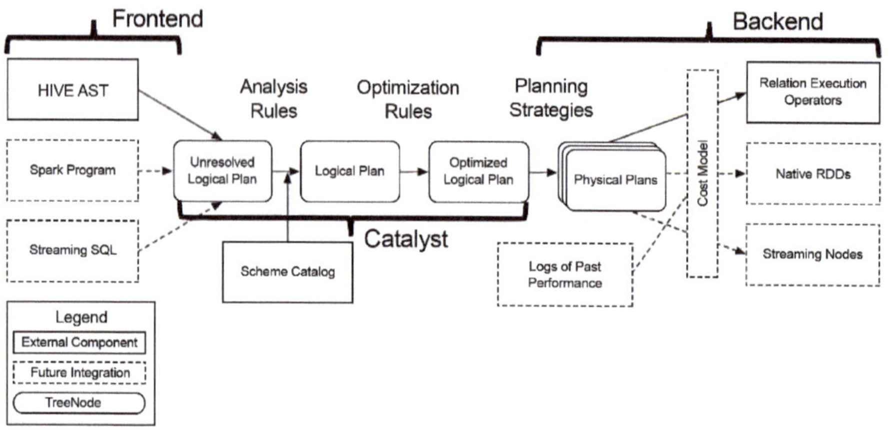

Figure 15.1: Spark SQL architecture

SQL interface and DataFrame/Dataset APIs

Spark SQL provides multiple interfaces for interacting with structured data to provide flexibility for both developers and analysts. Users can execute SQL queries using standard SQL syntax through the `spark.sql()` function that allows users familiar with SQL to work seamlessly with big data. Additionally, Spark introduces the DataFrame API, a high-level abstraction that represents a distributed collection of data organized into named columns. DataFrames provide rich operations like filtering, grouping, and joining, that are accessible across languages, including Scala, Java, and R. For applications requiring compile-time type safety and object-oriented programming, Spark offers the dataset API, available in Scala and Java. Datasets combine the benefits of strong typing with the performance optimizations of Spark's execution engine. Regardless of the interface chosen, all user operations ultimately pass through a common optimization and execution pipeline, ensuring consistency and efficiency.

Typically, the steps involved in the execution of a Spark SQL query are as follows:

1. User interfaces (SQL, DataFrame, Dataset).
2. SQL parser.
3. Unresolved logical plan.
4. Analyzer.
5. Resolved logical plan.
6. Catalyst optimizer.
7. Optimized logical plan.
8. Physical planner.
9. Physical execution plan.
10. Tungsten engine (code gen, memory mgmt).
11. Task distribution across cluster.
12. Results returned to the user.

Thus execution of a query in Spark SQL follows a structured pipeline, where the input SQL or DataFrame operation passes through multiple stages of parsing, analysis, optimization, planning, and execution to ensure efficient and distributed processing of large-scale data as follows:

1. **Query submission**: The user submits a SQL query or a DataFrame operation via supported interfaces.

2. **Logical plan generation**: The SQL parser translates the query into an unresolved logical plan, defining what operations are requested, but without validation.
3. **Analysis**: The analyzer resolves references (tables, columns) and validates the plan, producing a resolved logical plan.
4. **Logical optimization**: Catalyst applies logical transformations to optimize the plan for efficiency.
5. **Physical planning**: The optimized logical plan is converted into one or more candidate physical plans, considering join types, partitioning strategies, etc.
6. **Code generation**: Tungsten's Whole-Stage Code Generation produces optimized bytecode for execution, tailored to the chosen physical plan.
7. **Distributed execution**: Spark breaks the plan into tasks, distributes them across worker nodes, and executes the plan in parallel. In-memory caching, spill-to-disk mechanisms, and fault tolerance ensure reliable and fast execution.

Catalyst optimizer

The catalyst optimizer is the backbone of Spark SQL's query processing, which is designed to improve the performance of user queries intelligently. It performs logical optimizations, which restructure the logical plan to simplify operations. For example, constant folding technique pre-computes constant expressions at compile-time to reduce runtime overhead. Predicate pushdown method applies filtering conditions as close to the data source as possible to minimize unnecessary data transfer. projection planning approach eliminates columns that are not required for the final result, thus conserving computation resources.

In addition to logical improvements, the catalyst optimizer handles physical planning, where it explores multiple candidate physical plans for query execution to evaluate different join strategies and data shuffling techniques. With the introduction of **cost-based optimization** (**CBO**) in Spark 2.x, catalyst can use statistical information like row counts and data sizes to choose the most efficient execution path dynamically. Moreover, the catalyst is designed to be extensible, which allows developers to incorporate custom rules for domain-specific or advanced optimizations, making it highly adaptable to evolving business needs.

Tungsten execution engine

The Tungsten execution engine is Spark's low-level optimization framework focused on maximizing hardware efficiency for large-scale data processing. One of its standout features is Whole-Stage Code Generation, where Spark dynamically generates compact Java bytecode during runtime. This technique reduces the overhead of JVM function calls, which leads to faster **central processing unit** (**CPU**) execution of query operations.

Additionally, Tungsten employs off-heap memory management, managing memory allocations directly rather than relying entirely on the Java Virtual Machine's heap space. This significantly reduces the impact of garbage collection and improves memory utilization, particularly for long-running or large-memory workloads. Cache-aware computations further optimize performance by aligning data access patterns with modern CPU cache designs, minimizing delays caused by cache misses. Tungsten also introduces an efficient binary data format that reduces memory overhead and speeds up both storage and computation.

Data source API

Spark SQL's data source API provides a standardized and unified interface for interacting with various data formats and storage systems. Users can seamlessly read and write structured data stored in formats like Parquet, ORC, JSON, Avro, and CSV, enabling efficient processing of modern, semi-structured datasets. The API also supports external JDBC-compliant relational databases for integration with traditional data sources such as MySQL or PostgreSQL.

For enterprises leveraging existing Hadoop infrastructure, Spark SQL integrates with the Hive Metastore, providing access to legacy Hive tables, along with support for Serializers/Deserializers (SerDes) and custom **user-defined**

functions (**UDFs**). Additionally, the data source API supports custom sources, enabling organizations to build plugins that connect to proprietary or domain-specific storage systems, ensuring flexibility and extensibility within diverse data environments.

Integration with Hive and BI tools

Spark SQL offers deep integration with existing Hive infrastructures and modern **Business Intelligence** (**BI**) tools, making it highly versatile for enterprise data architectures. It provides full Hive compatibility, supporting Hive QL, custom UDFs, and SerDes, allowing organizations to migrate existing Hive workloads to Spark with minimal changes. This compatibility ensures that legacy Hive data can be queried efficiently within Spark's distributed framework, improving performance without disrupting established workflows.

Moreover, Spark SQL includes a Thrift JDBC/ODBC Server, which allows SQL clients and BI tools such as Tableau, Power BI, or custom analytics platforms to connect to Spark using standard protocols. This enables analysts and business users to run interactive queries and generate visual dashboards over massive datasets, using familiar tools, without needing to understand Spark's underlying complexities. As a result, it provides a seamless, scalable, and high-performance environment for both technical and non-technical stakeholders.

Spark SQL interface

Spark SQL provides multiple interfaces to cater to both technical users (developers, engineers) and analysts with varying skill sets. The two primary interfaces are:

- **SQL interface**: The SQL interface in Spark SQL is designed for users who are comfortable with relational databases and SQL syntax. Here, users can run queries using common SQL commands such as `SELECT`, `JOIN`, `GROUP BY`, `ORDER BY`, `HAVING`, and subqueries. As Spark SQL adheres to the ANSI SQL standard, existing SQL workloads can often be reused with minimal modification. This makes Spark SQL ideal for business analysts, BI teams, and data scientists who do not necessarily want to write code. Instead, they interact with data directly using SQL queries. Popular business intelligence platforms, such as Tableau, Power BI, Superset, and Looker, can directly connect to Spark SQL. These tools generate SQL queries under the hood, making it seamless for analysts to visualize and report on data. For enterprises already using relational databases, migrating SQL-based logic into Spark is smooth, since Spark SQL supports a wide range of SQL operations. For example, the following SQL query works inside Spark SQL just like in traditional databases:

```
SELECT department, AVG(salary) AS avg_salary
FROM employees
WHERE age > 30
GROUP BY department
ORDER BY avg_salary DESC;
```

- **DataFrame API**: The DataFrame API is a programmatic interface, designed more for software engineers and developers who want to express data manipulations using code rather than pure SQL. A DataFrame is a distributed collection of rows organized into columns, conceptually similar to a relational table or a DataFrame in Pandas (Python) or R. It supports multiple languages, such as Scala (native Spark language), Java, Python, and R, making it flexible for diverse development teams. Here, instead of writing SQL queries, users can perform operations using method chaining and functional transformations. Developers can write custom code, apply **user-defined functions** (**UDFs**), and perform more complex logic that SQL may not easily support. Since the API is embedded in the programming languages, it integrates neatly within a larger application workflow. For example, the following code produces the same result as the SQL query given in the previous example, but in a programmatic, code-driven style:

```
df = spark.read.csv("employees.csv", header=True, inferSchema=True)
```

```
result = (
    df.filter(df.age > 30)
      .groupBy("department")
      .agg({"salary": "avg"})
      .orderBy("avg(salary)", ascending=False)
)
result.show()
```

So, one of the major strengths of Spark SQL is that SQL queries and DataFrame operations are unified under the same catalyst optimizer and execution engine. This means whether you use SQL or DataFrames, Spark optimizes both queries similarly for efficient distributed execution. In addition, you can freely mix both approaches in a single workflow: execute SQL queries on DataFrames by creating a temporary view and then querying it using standard SQL and convert SQL results into DataFrames for further transformations in code. For example:

```
# Using DataFrame API
df.createOrReplaceTempView("employees")
# Running SQL on the DataFrame
sql_result = spark.sql("""
    SELECT department, AVG(salary) as avg_salary
    FROM employees
    WHERE age > 30
    GROUP BY department
    ORDER BY avg_salary DESC
""")
# Converting SQL output back to DataFrame for further transformations
sql_result.filter(sql_result.avg_salary > 50000).show()
```

In this example, both interfaces are combined, SQL is used for aggregation, and the DataFrame API is used for additional filtering. Both interfaces eventually translate into the same underlying logical and physical execution plans, benefiting from Spark's distributed processing, catalyst optimizer, and Tungsten performance enhancements.

Table 15.1 presents the various characteristics of the SQL interface and the DataFrame API:

Aspect	SQL interface	DataFrame API
Usage style	Pure SQL queries using **`spark.sql()`**.	Object-oriented, chainable method calls.
Language support	Universal SQL; accessed via Scala, etc.	Available in Scala, Java, and R.
User profile	Analysts or users with SQL background.	Developers, data engineers, data scientists.
Examples of operations	**`SELECT`**, **`WHERE`**, **`GROUP BY`**, joins, etc.	**`select()`**, **`filter()`**, **`groupBy()`**, joins, etc.
Integration	Suited for BI tools or adhoc SQL querying.	Ideal for building complex data pipelines.
Schema definition	Inferred from query or data source.	Explicit via code or inferred during read.
Flexibility	SQL syntax-bound.	Highly flexible with functional programming style.

Table 15.1: *SQL interface vs. DataFrame API*

RDD vs. DataFrame vs. dataset

Apache Spark has evolved significantly since its inception, primarily to improve developer productivity, performance, and support for diverse workloads. The evolution of Spark APIs can be summarized in three major stages:

API type	Introduced in	Purpose
RDD	Spark 1.0 (2014)	Low-level distributed data abstraction.
DataFrame	Spark 1.3 (2015)	High-level, SQL-like structured data abstraction.
Dataset	Spark 1.6/2.0 (2016)	Type-safe, object-oriented abstraction with optimized performance.

Table 15.2: *Evolution of Spark APIs*

Each API builds upon the previous one, enhancing ease of use, optimization, and performance while abstracting away complexities like manual data serialization and explicit schema management.

Resilient distributed dataset

RDD is the original, low-level API in Spark that represents an immutable, distributed collection of objects partitioned across the cluster. It offers fine-grained control over distributed processing but requires more effort from the developer. The key characteristics of RDD are:

- It is fault-tolerant and distributed by design.
- It supports transformations (map, filter, flatMap) and actions (count, collect).
- It allows unstructured or semi-structured data (flexible but low-level).
- It requires manual handling of schema and data serialization.
- It supports lazy evaluation for optimization, but minimal query optimization compared to newer APIs.

DataFrame

A DataFrame is a distributed collection of data organized into named columns, like a relational database table. It was introduced to simplify working with structured data and leverage Spark's internal optimizations through Catalyst and Tungsten. The key characteristics of DataFrame are as follows:

- It provides high-level abstraction for structured and semi-structured data.
- It uses Catalyst optimizer for query optimization.
- It supports SQL-like operations (select, filter, groupBy).
- It is schema-aware, enabling more efficient execution.
- It is interoperable with Spark SQL.

Dataset

Dataset API was introduced to combine the benefits of RDDs' strong typing with DataFrame's optimizations. Datasets provide compile-time type safety (in Scala and Java) while using Catalyst and Tungsten under the hood for performance. The key characteristics of DataFrame are as follows:

- It is a type-safe, object-oriented abstraction (Scala/Java only).
- It is schema-aware with Catalyst optimizations.
- It supports both functional and SQL-style operations.
- It is ideal for complex ETL or machine learning pipelines needing type safety.

Table 15.3 presents the comparison of RDD, DataFrame, and Dataset on varied parameters:

Feature	RDD	DataFrame	Dataset
Abstraction level	Low-level	High-level, SQL-like	High-level, type-safe
Schema awareness	None (manual)	Schema-aware	Schema-aware
Optimizations	Minimal (lineage only)	Catalyst and Tungsten	Catalyst and Tungsten
Type safety	Compile-time	Runtime	Compile-time (Scala/Java)
Ease of use	Verbose	Concise, intuitive	Type-safe, slightly verbose
Performance	Lower due to lack of optimizations	High with internal optimizations	High with optimizations and type safety
Language support	All (Scala, Java)	All major languages	Scala and Java only

***Table 15.3**: Performance trade-offs: RDD vs. DataFrame vs. Dataset*

Spark SQL interface with PySpark

Let us now learn to process structured and semi-structured data using the Spark SQL interface, mainly through DataFrames and SQL queries. The SQL interface provides the most familiar experience for those used to querying relational databases. It is accessible through **`spark.sql()`**. This approach offers both programmatic flexibility and powerful optimizations via Catalyst and Tungsten. To demonstrate this, we will use a simple Employee dataset, containing details like employee names, departments, salaries, and ages. This dataset will help us understand how to load data into a DataFrame, register it as a temporary view, and run SQL queries to extract meaningful insights.

A sample employee dataset is as follows:

```
[
  {"name": "Alice", "department": "HR", "salary": 60000, "age": 30},
  {"name": "Bob", "department": "Engineering", "salary": 75000, "age": 28},
  {"name": "Charlie", "department": "Sales", "salary": 50000, "age": 35},
  {"name": "David", "department": "Engineering", "salary": 80000, "age": 40},
  {"name": "Eve", "department": "HR", "salary": 45000, "age": 25},
  {"name": "Frank", "department": "Sales", "salary": 55000, "age": 32},
  {"name": "Grace", "department": "Engineering", "salary": 95000, "age": 45},
  {"name": "Heidi", "department": "Marketing", "salary": 52000, "age": 29}
]
```

Importing and saving data

The following are the steps for importing and saving data:

1. **Import required libraries and create SparkSession**: The **`SparkSession`** is the entry point to Spark SQL functionality:
   ```
   from pyspark.sql import SparkSession
   spark = SparkSession.builder.appName("Spark SQL_Interface").getOrCreate()
   ```
2. **Loading data into DataFrames:** Spark supports reading structured and semi-structured files like JSON, CSV, Parquet, ORC, etc.
   - **Structured data (CSV, Parquet)**: Structured files have a fixed schema (column names and types):

     CSV file:

```
df = spark.read.option("header", True).option("inferSchema", True).csv("employees.
csv")
df.show()
```

Refer to *Figure 15.2* for the execution and output of structured data stored in **`.csv`** file:

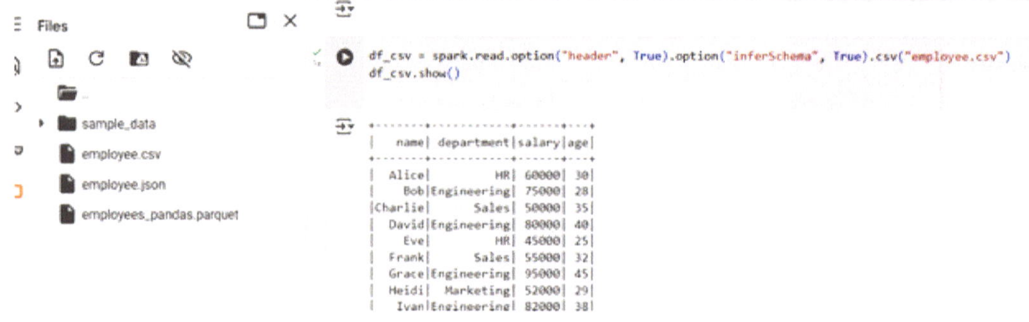

***Figure 15.2**: Structured data processing (.csv file)*

Here, **`header=True`** means the first row contains column names, and **`inferSchema=True`** means it will automatically detect data types. Spark provides automatic schema inference for common formats, enabling SQL-like processing.

- **Reading Parquet (highly optimized, structured)**: Parquet is columnar, compressed, and optimized for big data.

  Parquet file:

  ```
  df_parquet = spark.read.parquet("employees.parquet")
  df_parquet.show()
  ```

  Refer to *Figure 15.3* for the execution and output of structured data stored in a **`.parquet`** file:

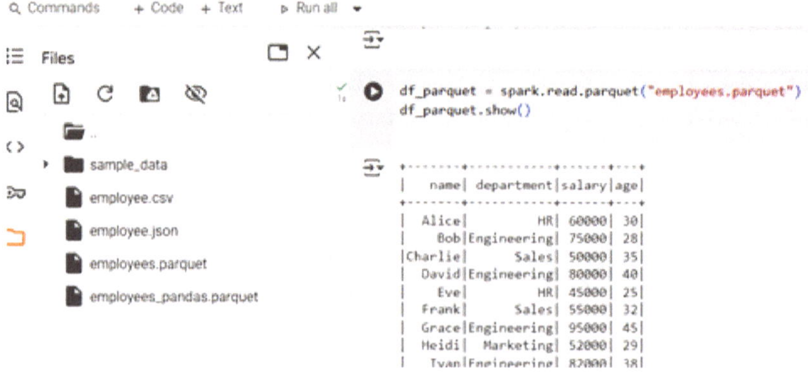

***Figure 15.3**: Structured data processing (.parquet file)*

- **Semi-structured data example (JSON)**: Semi-structured files may contain nested fields or irregular structures:

  ```
  df_json = spark.read.json("employees.json")
  df_json.printSchema()
  df_json.show()
  ```

Refer to *Figure 15.4* for the execution and output of semi-structured data stored in a **`.json`** file:

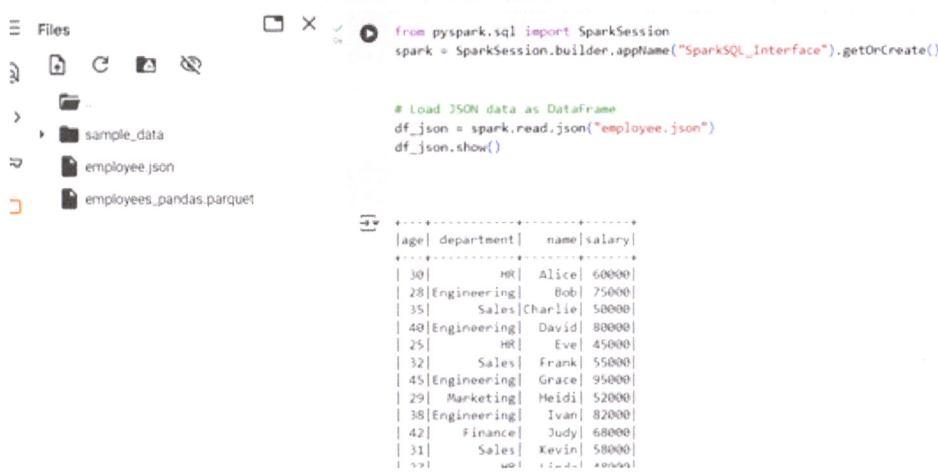

***Figure 15.4**: Semi-structured data processing*

Semi-structured files like JSON can have nested fields and varying schemas, which Spark infers automatically.

3. **Saving data to files**: DataFrames can be saved in multiple formats:

```
# Save as JSON
df_json.write.mode("overwrite").json("output/employees_json")

# Save as CSV
df_csv.write.mode("overwrite").csv("output/employees_csv")

# Save as Parquet
df_parquet.write.mode("overwrite").parquet("output/employees_parquet")
```

Here, mode overwrite means replace existing files, append will add new data, and error will throw an error if the file exists. Refer to *Figure 15.5* for the execution and output of the preceding code. After execution, three new files are created as shown in *Figure 15.5:*

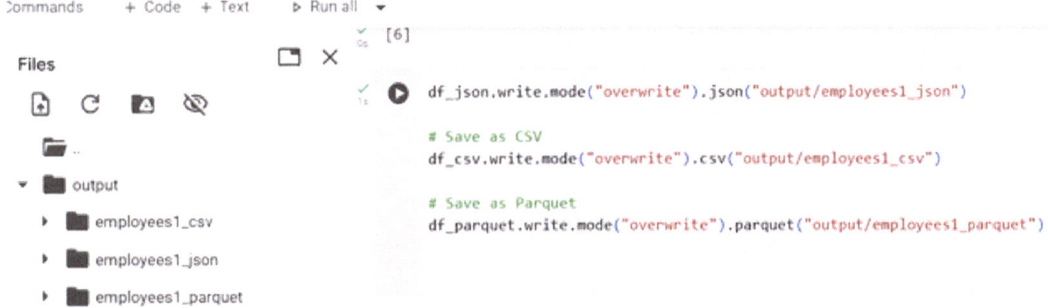

***Figure 15.5**: Saving data in files*

DataFrame operations in PySpark

DataFrames in PySpark are powerful, distributed collections of structured data, similar to tables in relational databases. They allow for rich SQL-like transformations, enabling operations such as filtering, aggregating, joining, and more, all at scale:

1. **Basic operations**:

```
df = spark.read.option("header", True).csv("employees.csv")
```

This loads the employee data from a CSV file into a DataFrame.

a. **Select specific columns**:

```
df.select("name", "salary").show()
```

The preceding code extracts only the name and salary columns, as shown in *Figure 15.6*:

```
df = spark.read.option("header", True).csv("employee.csv")
# Select specific columns
df.select("name", "salary").show()
```

```
+-------+------+
|   name|salary|
+-------+------+
|  Alice| 60000|
|    Bob| 75000|
|Charlie| 50000|
|  David| 80000|
|    Eve| 45000|
|  Frank| 55000|
|  Grace| 95000|
|  Heidi| 52000|
|   Ivan| 82000|
|   Judy| 68000|
```

***Figure 15.6**: Only name and salary columns are extracted*

b. **Filter rows**:

```
df.filter(df.salary > 50000).show()
```

The preceding code shows employees with a salary greater than 50,000, as depicted in *Figure 15.7*:

```
df.filter(df.salary > 50000).show()

+-------+-----------+------+---+
|   name| department|salary|age|
+-------+-----------+------+---+
|  Alice|         HR| 60000| 30|
|    Bob|Engineering| 75000| 28|
|  David|Engineering| 80000| 40|
|  Frank|      Sales| 55000| 32|
|  Grace|Engineering| 95000| 45|
|  Heidi|  Marketing| 52000| 29|
|   Ivan|Engineering| 82000| 38|
|   Judy|    Finance| 68000| 42|
|  Kevin|      Sales| 58000| 31|
|   Mike|Engineering| 88000| 39|
|  Nancy|  Marketing| 54000| 33|
|  Oscar|    Finance| 72000| 36|
|    Pam|         HR| 51000| 29|
|  Quinn|Engineering| 91000| 44|
```

***Figure 15.7**: Filtering rows greater than 50K*

c. **Add a new column:**

```
df = df.withColumn("bonus", df.salary * 0.10)
df.show()
```

The preceding code adds a new column called bonus, which is calculated as 10% of the salary, as depicted in *Figure 15.8*:

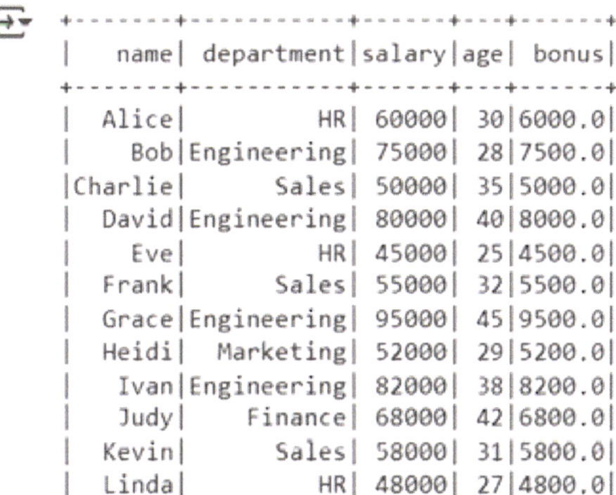

```
df = df.withColumn("bonus", df.salary * 0.10)
df.show()

+-------+-----------+------+---+------+
|   name| department|salary|age| bonus|
+-------+-----------+------+---+------+
|  Alice|         HR| 60000| 30|6000.0|
|    Bob|Engineering| 75000| 28|7500.0|
|Charlie|      Sales| 50000| 35|5000.0|
|  David|Engineering| 80000| 40|8000.0|
|    Eve|         HR| 45000| 25|4500.0|
|  Frank|      Sales| 55000| 32|5500.0|
|  Grace|Engineering| 95000| 45|9500.0|
|  Heidi|  Marketing| 52000| 29|5200.0|
|   Ivan|Engineering| 82000| 38|8200.0|
|   Judy|    Finance| 68000| 42|6800.0|
|  Kevin|      Sales| 58000| 31|5800.0|
|  Linda|         HR| 48000| 27|4800.0|
```

***Figure 15.8**: Added new column Bonus*

2. **Group by and aggregations**: DataFrames make it easy to summarize data with groupings and aggregations:

```
from pyspark.sql.functions import avg, max
df.groupBy("department").agg(
avg("salary").alias("avg_salary"),
max("salary").alias("max_salary")
).show()
```

These operations compute the average and maximum salary for each department, as depicted in *Figure 15.9*:

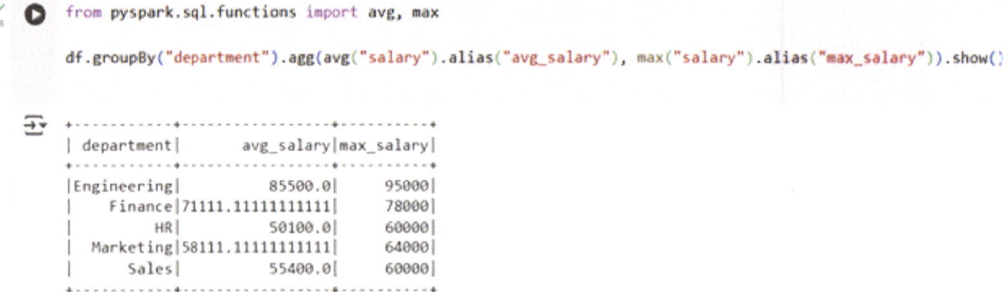

```
from pyspark.sql.functions import avg, max

df.groupBy("department").agg(avg("salary").alias("avg_salary"), max("salary").alias("max_salary")).show()
```

department	avg_salary	max_salary
Engineering	85500.0	95000
Finance	71111.11111111111	78000
HR	50100.0	60000
Marketing	58111.11111111111	64000
Sales	55400.0	60000

***Figure 15.9**: Avg and max salary of each department*

3. **Sorting and ordering:**

```
df.orderBy(df.salary.desc()).show()
```

You can easily sort data based on columns, as depicted in *Figure 15.10*. This displays employees sorted by salary in descending order:

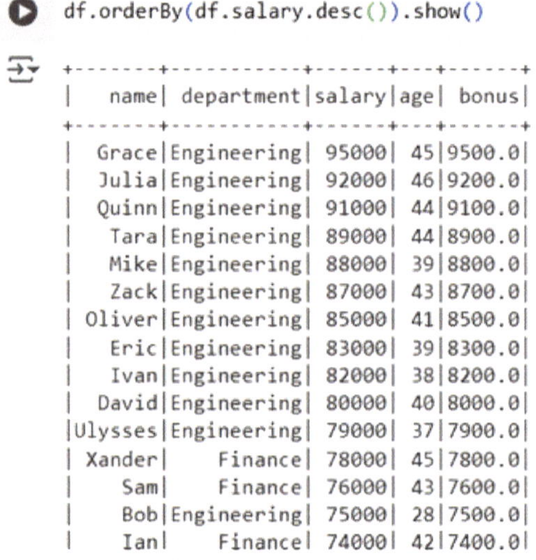

```
df.orderBy(df.salary.desc()).show()
```

name	department	salary	age	bonus
Grace	Engineering	95000	45	9500.0
Julia	Engineering	92000	46	9200.0
Quinn	Engineering	91000	44	9100.0
Tara	Engineering	89000	44	8900.0
Mike	Engineering	88000	39	8800.0
Zack	Engineering	87000	43	8700.0
Oliver	Engineering	85000	41	8500.0
Eric	Engineering	83000	39	8300.0
Ivan	Engineering	82000	38	8200.0
David	Engineering	80000	40	8000.0
Ulysses	Engineering	79000	37	7900.0
Xander	Finance	78000	45	7800.0
Sam	Finance	76000	43	7600.0
Bob	Engineering	75000	28	7500.0
Ian	Finance	74000	42	7400.0

***Figure 15.10**: Employees sorted by salary in descending order*

4. **SQL queries via temporary views:** PySpark allows mixing SQL queries with DataFrame operations for flexibility:

   a. Register DataFrame as a temporary view:

```
df.createOrReplaceTempView("employees")
```

b. Run SQL query:

```
spark.sql("""
    SELECT department, AVG(salary) as avg_salary
    FROM employees
    GROUP BY department
""").show()
```

This performs an SQL-style aggregation to find the average salary by department, as depicted in *Figure 15.11:*

```
df.createOrReplaceTempView("employees")
spark.sql("SELECT department, AVG(salary) as avg_salary FROM employees GROUP BY department").show()
```

```
+-----------+-----------------+
| department|       avg_salary|
+-----------+-----------------+
|      Sales|          55400.0|
|Engineering|          85500.0|
|         HR|          50100.0|
|    Finance|71111.11111111111|
|  Marketing|58111.11111111111|
+-----------+-----------------+
```

Figure 15.11: *SQL-style aggregation*

With PySpark, you can seamlessly blend SQL queries and DataFrame operations, enabling flexible, scalable data processing that is ideal for large datasets and real-time analytics.

Conclusion

In this chapter, we explored the essential components of Spark SQL, gaining insights into its architecture and the practical use of the Spark SQL interface. We understood how Spark SQL bridges the gap between traditional SQL operations and distributed data processing. By comparing RDDs, DataFrames, and Datasets, we highlighted the evolution of Spark APIs and their appropriate use cases. We also covered the complete workflow of importing, saving, and processing structured and semi-structured data, along with performing powerful DataFrame transformations and aggregations. With this knowledge, learners are now equipped to leverage Spark SQL for scalable, high-performance data analytics in real-world scenarios.

In the next chapter, we will build upon this foundation and explore how to implement machine learning pipelines using PySpark, unlocking the full potential of Spark for predictive analytics and intelligent decision-making.

Points to remember

The following are some key takeaways from this chapter:

- Spark SQL is a powerful module of Apache Spark that allows processing of structured data using SQL queries alongside Spark's programming APIs.
- Spark SQL integrates with Spark's core engine, using the Catalyst optimizer and Tungsten execution engine to optimize query performance for both SQL and DataFrame operations.
- The interface lets users run SQL queries directly on DataFrames by creating temporary views, combining

SQL with distributed processing in PySpark.

- RDDs offer low-level data processing, DataFrames provide optimized, tabular data structures, and datasets (in Scala/Java) combine type safety with performance, evolving Spark towards more efficient APIs.
- PySpark allows easy loading and saving of data in formats like CSV, JSON, and Parquet, supporting structured and semi-structured data handling.
- Spark SQL can efficiently process both structured (e.g., CSV, Parquet) and semi-structured (e.g., JSON, XML) data using its unified APIs.
- DataFrames support rich operations like filtering, sorting, aggregations, joins, and SQL-like transformations for scalable, distributed data analytics.

Multiple choice questions

1. **What is the primary benefit of using Spark SQL within PySpark?**
   a. Only for real-time data streaming
   b. Enables SQL queries on structured data within distributed processing
   c. Used exclusively for machine learning models
   d. Replaces DataFrames entirely
2. **Which component of Spark SQL optimizes query execution plans?**
   a. MLlib
   b. Tungsten cache
   c. Catalyst optimizer
   d. Hadoop
3. **In PySpark, how can you run SQL queries on a DataFrame?**
   a. By converting DataFrame to a Pandas DataFrame
   b. By saving it to a database first
   c. By registering it as a temporary view
   d. SQL is not supported in PySpark
4. **Which of the following correctly creates a new column bonus as 10% of salary?**
   a. df = df.addColumn("bonus", df.salary * 0.10)
   b. df = df.withColumn("bonus", df.salary * 0.10)
   c. df = df.newColumn("bonus", df.salary * 10)
   d. df = df.select("bonus", df.salary * 0.10)
5. **What is a key difference between RDD and DataFrame?**
   a. RDDs have automatic optimizations, DataFrames do not
   b. DataFrames offer higher-level, SQL-like operations with optimizations
   c. RDDs support only structured data
   d. DataFrames cannot be used in PySpark
6. **Which command shows employees sorted by salary in descending order?**
   a. df.sort(df.salary.asc()).show()
   b. df.orderBy(df.salary.desc()).show()

c. df.groupBy(df.salary.desc()).show()

d. df.filter(df.salary > 0).show()

7. **When processing semi-structured files like JSON, which Spark component handles it efficiently?**

   a. Spark Core

   b. Spark SQL using DataFrames

   c. Spark Streaming

   d. Hadoop File System

8. **What happens after running this command?**

```
df.createOrReplaceTempView("employees")
```

   a. DataFrame is converted to RDD

   b. You can run SQL queries using employees as a table

   c. It saves the DataFrame permanently

   d. Only filtering operations are allowed

9. **Which is the correct syntax to calculate the average and maximum salary per department?**

   a. df.groupBy("department").agg(avg("salary"), max("salary")).show()

   b. df.groupBy("department").average("salary", "max_salary").show()

   c. df.filter("department").agg("salary").show()

   d. df.select("department").groupBy("salary").show()

10. **DataFrames in PySpark support:**

   a. Only filtering operations

   b. SQL-like operations such as filtering, aggregations, joins, and transformations

   c. Only saving data to files

   d. Only unstructured data processing

Answers

1.	b.	2.	c.	3.	c.	4.	b.	5.	b.
6.	b.	7.	b.	8.	b.	9.	a.	10.	b.

Questions

1. Explain how Spark SQL integrates with the core Spark engine. Why is the Catalyst Optimizer critical for Spark SQL performance? Provide examples of operations where optimization plays a key role.

2. You are working with a dataset containing employee details (name, department, salary, age). Demonstrate how to:

   - Load the data into a DataFrame
   - Select employees with a salary greater than 70,000
   - Add a new column for performance bonus (15% of salary)

   Write the PySpark code for these tasks.

3. Compare and contrast RDDs, DataFrames, and Datasets in Spark. When would you prefer DataFrames over RDDs in a real-world project? Provide a use case to justify your answer.
4. Suppose you are analyzing sales data stored in a JSON file. Explain how Spark SQL can help process semi-structured data efficiently. Write the code to:
    - Load the JSON data
    - Register a temporary SQL view
    - Run a SQL query to calculate total sales by region
5. A manager wants to see the department-wise average and maximum salaries for employees. Using PySpark, explain step-by-step how you would achieve this using both SQL queries and DataFrame transformations.
6. Discuss the advantages of combining SQL queries with DataFrame APIs in PySpark. How does this hybrid approach improve flexibility and performance for large-scale data processing? Provide practical examples.
7. Given the following DataFrame operation:

    ```
    df.groupBy("department").agg(avg("salary").alias("avg_salary"), max("salary").alias("max_
    salary")).show()
    ```

    Explain what this code does. Modify the code also to calculate the minimum salary per department.
8. Your organization is handling large volumes of structured (CSV) and semi-structured (JSON) data. Design an end-to-end PySpark workflow to process both formats and generate department-level summary reports. Include key steps in your explanation.
9. Why is sorting and ordering data essential in distributed data processing? Using an example, explain how to sort employee records by salary in both ascending and descending order using PySpark.
10. Imagine you are tasked with optimizing a Spark SQL job that's running slowly due to complex queries on large datasets. List strategies or Spark features (such as Tungsten or Catalyst Optimizer) you would leverage to improve performance.

Join our Discord space

Join our Discord workspace for latest updates, offers, tech happenings around the world, new releases, and sessions with the authors:

https://discord.bpbonline.com

Chapter 16
Machine Learning Application Using PySpark

Analytics turns curiosity into clarity and decisions into impact.

-Carly Fiorina

Introduction

This chapter explains the concept of **machine learning** (**ML**) and describes different types of ML, such as supervised, unsupervised, and reinforcement learning. It highlights the need to use Spark for ML applications. The next part of the chapter introduces Spark **application programming interface** (**API**) and discusses the two main libraries of Spark for ML, which are spark.mllib and spark.ml. In the rest of the chapter, readers learn to develop classification and clustering applications using Spark ML pipelines. It covers the steps of creating a SparkSession, loading and preparing data, defining a pipeline with stages, fitting and evaluating the model, and making predictions. By the end of this chapter, readers will be able to use spark.ml to perform various machine learning tasks on large-scale data in PySpark.

Structure

In this chapter, we will cover the following topics:

- Introduction to machine learning
- Types of machine learning
- Machine learning with Apache Spark
- Introduction to Spark API for machine learning
- AG News multi-class text classification using PySpark
- Customer segmentation using PySpark clustering

Objectives

By the end of this chapter, readers will have a comprehensive understanding of the fundamentals of ML, including key types such as supervised, unsupervised, and reinforcement learning. They will recognize the need for scalable ML solutions and understand why Apache Spark is well-suited for large-scale ML applications. Learners will also explore Spark's ML libraries, such as spark.mllib and spark.ml, with a focus on building practical ML pipelines. Through hands-on exercises, they will learn to develop classification and clustering applications using PySpark, covering essential steps such as creating a SparkSession, preparing data, defining pipeline stages, training models, evaluating results, and making predictions. By the end of this chapter, learners will be equipped to apply spark.ml for building scalable ML workflows in PySpark.

Introduction to machine learning

ML is a subset of **artificial intelligence** (**AI**) that focuses on developing algorithms that allow computers to learn patterns from data and make predictions or decisions without being explicitly programmed. Unlike traditional rule-based systems, ML systems improve over time by learning from new data.

In today's data-driven world, ML powers a wide range of applications across industries, transforming how businesses operate and improving efficiency, accuracy, and decision-making. The following list outlines several real-world applications where ML is being used:

- **Recommendation systems**: Platforms like *Netflix*, *Amazon*, and *Spotify* use ML to suggest movies, products, or music based on user preferences and past behavior. Similarly, *YouTube* recommends videos tailored to user interests to maximize engagement.
- **Fraud detection and financial security**: Banks and credit card companies such as *Visa* and *Mastercard* rely on ML to detect unusual transactions and prevent fraud in real-time. *PayPal* and other *FinTech* apps use similar techniques to flag suspicious activities and reduce financial scams.
- **Healthcare and medical diagnosis**: *IBM Watson Health* assists doctors in diagnosing complex diseases like cancer by analyzing medical records and imaging data. Wearable devices such as the *Apple Watch* and *Fitbit* leverage ML to monitor health indicators, detect abnormalities, and predict risks.
- **Autonomous vehicles (self-driving cars)**: Companies like *Tesla*, *Waymo*, and *Uber* employ ML for tasks such as object detection, lane tracking, and real-time decision-making to enable safe autonomous driving.
- **Natural language processing (NLP) and chatbots**: Virtual assistants like *ChatGPT*, *Google Assistant*, and *Siri* use ML to interpret and respond to human language effectively. AI-powered chatbots, widely used in customer support platforms like *Zendesk* and *Intercom*, resolve queries instantly.
- **Image and facial recognition**: Technologies like *Apple Face ID* and *Google Photos* use ML to accurately recognize faces for security authentication and photo organization. AI-enhanced surveillance systems monitor public spaces to detect suspicious activities.
- **Predictive maintenance in manufacturing**: Industrial leaders such as *GE* and *Siemens* utilize ML to predict equipment failures in advance, reducing unexpected downtime and maintenance costs.
- **Retail and e-commerce**: ML enables dynamic pricing strategies for platforms like *Uber* and *Amazon*, adjusting prices based on real-time demand. Additionally, intelligent inventory management systems predict stock requirements to avoid shortages or overstocking.
- **Agriculture and precision farming**: Companies like *John Deere* and *IBM AgriTech* use ML to analyze soil health, forecast crop yields, and optimize irrigation practices, boosting efficiency and sustainability in farming.
- **Language translation**: Services like *Google Translate* and *DeepL* leverage neural networks to provide accurate, real-time translations across multiple languages, bridging communication gaps globally.

Types of machine learning

ML algorithms can be broadly classified into two main types, each suited for different kinds of problems and data structures:

- **Supervised learning**: In supervised learning, the model is trained on a labeled dataset, which means each training example includes both input features and the correct output (label). The goal is to learn a function that maps inputs to outputs so that it can make accurate predictions on new, unseen data.

  Supervised learning is widely used for predictive modeling, including tasks like regression (predicting continuous values such as house prices or stock market trends) and classification (predicting categorical outcomes like spam detection or disease diagnosis). Popular algorithms include linear regression, logistic regression, decision trees, random forest, **support vector machines** (**SVM**), and neural networks.

- **Unsupervised learning**: In unsupervised learning, the computer works with data that has no labels. That means we do not tell the machine what the *right answer* is. Instead, the machine tries to explore the data, find hidden patterns, group similar things together, or simplify the information. You can think of it like this - imagine giving a bunch of mixed photos to a computer without telling it what is in them. The computer will try to organize them by finding similarities, maybe grouping all beach photos together, all portraits together, and so on, without any human help.

  The following list outlines different types of unsupervised learning algorithms:

  - **Clustering-grouping similar data together**: Clustering is a popular technique in unsupervised learning where data is divided into groups, known as **clusters**, in such a way that items within the same group are more similar to each other than to those in other groups. This method helps uncover hidden patterns or natural groupings in data without the need for labeled examples.

    A common use of clustering is in customer segmentation, where businesses group customers based on factors like buying behavior or preferences, allowing them to design targeted marketing campaigns or personalized offers. Another example is image compression, where similar pixels are grouped together to reduce the overall file size without significantly affecting image quality. Several algorithms are used for clustering tasks, including k-means clustering, which is fast and widely used for simple groupings; hierarchical clustering, which creates a tree-like structure showing relationships among clusters; and **density-based spatial clustering of applications with noise** (**DBSCAN**), which is effective for finding clusters of various shapes and is capable of handling noise or outliers in the data. Clustering plays a crucial role in fields such as marketing, image processing, biology, and social network analysis.

  - **Dimensionality reduction-simplifying complex data**: Dimensionality reduction is a technique used to simplify large and complex datasets by reducing the number of features or variables while retaining the most important information. In many real-world scenarios, datasets can have hundreds or thousands of columns, making them difficult to analyze, visualize, or process efficiently. Dimensionality reduction helps by eliminating redundant or less significant features, allowing models to work faster and perform better without losing meaningful patterns.

    A common application of this technique is data visualization, where high-dimensional data is transformed into simple **two-dimensional** (**2D**) or 3D charts, making it easier to interpret. It is also widely used to improve model performance by reducing the complexity of the dataset, which leads to faster processing and often better results. Two popular algorithms for dimensionality reduction are **principal component analysis** (**PCA**), which identifies and preserves the most significant patterns while reducing the number of dimensions, and **t-distributed stochastic neighbor embedding** (**t-SNE**), which is particularly effective for visualizing complex, high-dimensional data in two or three dimensions, revealing hidden structures or clusters. Dimensionality reduction is essential in fields like ML, image processing, bioinformatics, and natural language processing, where managing large datasets is common.

  - **Anomaly detection-finding unusual behavior**: Anomaly detection is the process of identifying data points or patterns that deviate significantly from the expected behavior, often referred to as outliers. These unusual instances can indicate critical situations such as fraud, system malfunctions, or security breaches. Detecting such anomalies is like finding a needle in a haystack, especially in large datasets where the abnormal cases are rare but important.

    A common example is fraud detection, where irregular or suspicious transactions are flagged for further investigation. Another key application is fault detection in manufacturing or engineering systems, where identifying equipment malfunctions early can prevent costly breakdowns or accidents. Popular algorithms used for anomaly detection include isolation forest, which efficiently separates outliers from normal data by isolating them in fewer steps, and one-class SVM, which learns the characteristics of *normal* data and identifies anything that does not conform to that pattern. Anomaly detection plays a vital role in finance, cybersecurity, health monitoring, and industrial operations, helping organizations detect problems early and respond proactively.

- **Other emerging types of learning**: As ML continues to advance, several new and hybrid approaches have emerged to tackle real-world challenges more efficiently. These methods combine the strengths of supervised and unsupervised learning or introduce new ways for machines to learn with minimal human involvement.
    - **Semi-supervised learning**: Semi-supervised learning is a technique that combines a small amount of labeled data with a large volume of unlabeled data to train ML models. This approach is particularly useful when labeling data is expensive, time-consuming, or requires expert knowledge. By leveraging the unlabeled data along with the few labeled examples, the model can still learn meaningful patterns and make accurate predictions. A common example is Google Photos, which uses a few labeled images of faces to train its recognition system, while the vast majority of images remain unlabeled, making the process more scalable and efficient.
    - **Self-supervised learning**: Self-supervised learning is a recent advancement where the machine generates its own labels from raw, unlabeled data to teach itself. This approach reduces the need for manual labeling and is commonly used in modern AI systems, especially for language understanding and image processing tasks. In this method, the model creates tasks like predicting missing parts of the data, which allows it to learn underlying patterns. A popular example is **large language models** (**LLMs**) such as GPT-4, which are trained on massive amounts of text by predicting missing words or sentences, enabling them to understand and generate human-like language.
    - **Transfer learning**: Transfer learning is a method where a model trained on one task is adapted to perform a different but related task. Instead of starting the learning process from scratch, the model reuses knowledge gained from the previous task, saving time and computational resources. This approach is especially effective when dealing with small datasets for specialized applications. For example, an image recognition model trained on a general dataset of animals or vehicles can be fine-tuned and applied to medical image analysis, such as detecting diseases in X-rays or **magnetic resonance imaging** (**MRIs**), achieving high performance with minimal additional training.

Machine learning with Apache Spark

Apache Spark is one of the most popular big data platforms for ML, especially when working with large and complex datasets. Traditional ML tools often struggle with huge volumes of data or require time-consuming processing steps. Spark solves this by offering in-memory processing, which means data is processed quickly without constant reading and writing to disk. It also supports distributed computing, allowing ML tasks to run across many machines, handling terabytes or even petabytes of data efficiently.

With Spark, you can build and run scalable ML models directly on large datasets without needing to move the data to separate systems. This is especially valuable in industries like finance, e-commerce, healthcare, and **Internet of Things** (**IoT**), where large amounts of real-time or historical data need to be analyzed for predictions, pattern recognition, or recommendations.

Introduction to Spark API for machine learning

Apache Spark provides powerful APIs for building ML models. These APIs simplify the ML process by integrating data processing, feature engineering, model building, and evaluation within a unified framework. Spark offers two main ML libraries:

- **Spark MLlib (Legacy Library)**: MLlib is Spark's original ML library. It offers basic ML algorithms and utilities such as classification, regression, clustering, collaborative filtering, and dimensionality reduction.

MLlib was designed for **resilient distributed dataset** (**RDD**) based operations, which means it works well for low-level transformations but is less user-friendly compared to newer libraries. Its key features are:

- It provides standard ML algorithms like decision trees, k-means, and **alternating least squares** (**ALS**) for recommendation systems.
- It supports distributed processing for scalable ML.
- It is suitable for quick prototyping with basic ML tasks.

- **Spark ML (DataFrame-based library)**: Spark ML is the newer, high-level API for ML, built on top of Spark's DataFrame abstraction. It provides a more consistent, structured, and easy-to-use interface for building complex ML pipelines. Its key features are:
  - It works with DataFrames, making data processing more intuitive.
  - It provides tools for the full ML workflow, such as data preprocessing, feature extraction, model training, and evaluation.
  - It supports building ML pipelines similar to scikit-learn, enabling easy model tuning and automation.
  - Includes advanced features for hyperparameter tuning, cross-validation, and integration with Spark SQL.

AG News multi-class text classification using PySpark

With the exponential growth of online news platforms, managing, organizing, and retrieving relevant information has become increasingly challenging. Readers are inundated with vast amounts of digital content every day, making automated content categorization a crucial requirement for news providers, search engines, and recommendation systems.

Automatic text classification enables the systematic organization of news articles based on their subject matter, enhancing user experience through personalized content delivery and improving search relevance. One of the most recognized benchmarks for evaluating text classification models in this domain is the AG News Corpus, widely utilized in academic research and NLP competitions. The AG News dataset consists of a large collection of news articles, each labeled with one of four high-level categories, which are as follows:

- World news
- Sports news
- Business news
- Science and technology news

The task involves building a robust multi-class classification model capable of accurately categorizing unseen news articles into these predefined groups. Such a solution not only improves the efficiency of news platforms but also serves as a foundational application for broader NLP tasks, including topic modeling, information filtering, and news recommendation engines.

In this case study, we demonstrate how PySpark's scalable data processing and ML capabilities can be applied to efficiently build and evaluate a text classification pipeline for the AG News dataset, suitable for large-scale, real-world deployments.

Refer to the following steps to build and evaluate a text classification pipeline for the AG News dataset:

1. **Setup and load data**: First step is to initialize Spark and load the dataset from Kaggle (CSV format). You use SparkSession to start a Spark environment and `read.csv()` to import the data, as shown in the following code:

```
from pyspark.sql import SparkSession
from pyspark.sql.functions import concat_ws
from pyspark.ml import Pipeline
from pyspark.ml.feature import RegexTokenizer, StopWordsRemover, HashingTF, IDF,
StringIndexer, VectorAssembler
from pyspark.ml.classification import RandomForestClassifier
from pyspark.ml.evaluation import MulticlassClassificationEvaluator
spark = SparkSession.builder.appName("AGNewsClassification").getOrCreate()
df = spark.read.csv("train.csv", header=False)
df = df.withColumnRenamed("_c0", "class").withColumnRenamed("_c1", "title").
withColumnRenamed("_c2", "description")
df.show()
```

When reading a CSV file with header=False in PySpark, Spark assigns default column names as:**`_c0`**, **`_c1`**, **`_c2`**, ...

Your AG News dataset includes:

- **_c0:** contains the class label (news category: 1, 2, 3, or 4),
- **_c1:** contains the news title,
- **_c2:** contains the news description or body,
- **withColumnRenamed():** It renames these columns to more meaningful names for better readability and clarity. The updated **DataFrame** (**df**) will now have column names as shown in *Figure 16.1*:

```
[1] from pyspark.sql import SparkSession
    from pyspark.sql.functions import concat_ws
    from pyspark.ml import Pipeline
    from pyspark.ml.feature import RegexTokenizer, StopWordsRemover, HashingTF, IDF, StringIndexer, VectorAssembler
    from pyspark.ml.classification import RandomForestClassifier
    from pyspark.ml.evaluation import MulticlassClassificationEvaluator
```

1. Initialize Spark Session

```
[2] spark = SparkSession.builder.appName("AGNewsClassification").getOrCreate()
```

2. Load Dataset (Adjust path to your AG News CSV file)

```
[11] df = spark.read.csv("train.csv", header=True)
     df = df.withColumnRenamed("_c0", "class").withColumnRenamed("_c1", "title").withColumnRenamed("_c2", "description")
```

```
df.show()
```

```
+-----------+--------------------+--------------------+
|Class Index|               Title|         Description|
+-----------+--------------------+--------------------+
|          3|Wall St. Bears Cl...|Reuters - Short-s...|
|          3|Carlyle Looks Tow...|Reuters - Private...|
|          3|Oil and Economy C...|Reuters - Soaring...|
|          3|Iraq Halts Oil Ex...|Reuters - Authori...|
|          3|Oil prices soar t...|AFP - Tearaway wo...|
|          3|Stocks End Up, Bu...|Reuters - Stocks ...|
|          3|Money Funds Fell ...|AP - Assets of th...|
```

Figure 16.1: *Code and output for first step*

2. **Preprocessing**: This code block prepares raw text and labels for ML using PySpark's MLlib:

```
df = df.withColumn("text", concat_ws(" ", "title", "description"))

label_indexer = StringIndexer(inputCol=" Class Index
", outputCol="label")
tokenizer = RegexTokenizer(inputCol="text", outputCol="tokens", pattern="\\W")
remover = StopWordsRemover(inputCol="tokens", outputCol="filtered")
hashing_tf = HashingTF(inputCol="filtered", outputCol="rawFeatures", numFeatures=20000)
idf = IDF(inputCol="rawFeatures", outputCol="features_tfidf")
assembler = VectorAssembler(inputCols=["features_tfidf"], outputCol="features")
```

Figure 16.2 show the execution of preceding code:

```
2. Preprocessing

df = df.withColumn("text", concat_ws(" ", "title", "description"))

label_indexer = StringIndexer(inputCol="Class Index", outputCol="label")
tokenizer = RegexTokenizer(inputCol="text", outputCol="tokens", pattern="\\W")
remover = StopWordsRemover(inputCol="tokens", outputCol="filtered")
hashing_tf = HashingTF(inputCol="filtered", outputCol="rawFeatures", numFeatures=20000)
idf = IDF(inputCol="rawFeatures", outputCol="features_tfidf")
assembler = VectorAssembler(inputCols=["features_tfidf"], outputCol="features")
```

***Figure 16.2**: Preprocessing step*

In the preceding code , following statement combines the **"title"** and **"description"** columns into a single "text" column, Uses space **" "** as the separator. This simplifies downstream text processing by working with a single unified text field:

```
df = df.withColumn("text", concat_ws(" ", "title", "description"))
```

Next statement converts the **"class"** column (1, 2, 3, 4) into a numerical format for ML models.

```
label_indexer = StringIndexer(inputCol="class", outputCol="label")
```

Spark treats even numeric strings as categories for safety. The output column **"label"** will be used as the target for classification. For example:

```
class   label
1       0.0
2       1.0
3       2.0
4       3.0
```

Next statement, splits the **"text"** into individual words **("tokens")**. In this code, **pattern="\\W"** uses non-word characters as separators, so punctuation and spaces split the text:

```
tokenizer = RegexTokenizer(inputCol="text", outputCol="tokens", pattern="\\W")

For example, text        tokens

Wall St. gains U.S. stocks rallied["Wall", "St", "gains", "U", "S", "stocks", "rallied"]
```

Next statement removes common stop words (e.g., `"the"`, `"is"`, `"in"`, `"of"`) that do not contribute to model learning:

```
remover = StopWordsRemover(inputCol="tokens", outputCol="filtered")
```

For example, `tokens` `filtered are ["the", "market", "rallied"] ["market", "rallied"]`

Next statement applies the Hashing Trick to convert words into fixed-length numeric vectors. Here , `"numFeatures"` defines vector size (20,000 features in this case) and counts **term frequency** (TF) of words.

```
hashing_tf = HashingTF(inputCol="filtered", outputCol="rawFeatures", numFeatures=20000)
```

Output example (`rawFeatures is a sparse vector): (20000, [15, 120, 1039], [1.0, 2.0, 1.0]`), where `20000` is the total vector length, The indices (`15, 120, 1039`) correspond to hashed word positions and the values are word counts.

Next we calculate the **Inverse Document Frequency** (IDF) to downweight common words and emphasize rare but informative words. It multiplies TF by IDF to get "features_tfidf" which is a better text representation for ML models. **Term Frequency–Inverse Document Frequency (TF-IDF)** is a technique used in text mining to measure how important a word is in a document relative to a collection of documents. It increases with the word's frequency in a document (TF) but decreases if the word is common across many documents (IDF).

```
idf = IDF(inputCol="rawFeatures", outputCol="features_tfidf")
```

Finally we combine selected feature columns into a single `"features"` vector required by Spark ML models. Here, it is just `"features_tfidf"` but scalable if adding more features later:

```
assembler = VectorAssembler(inputCols=["features_tfidf"], outputCol="features")
```

3. **Define classifier**:

```
classifier = RandomForestClassifier(labelCol="label", featuresCol="features", numTrees=50)
```

The preceding code creates a Random Forest Classifier, a popular ensemble method for classification tasks. Here, `labelCol="label"` specifies the target column, prepared earlier using StringIndexer. `featuresCol="features"` is the input feature vector created after text preprocessing, `numTrees=50` is the number of trees to grow in the forest (more trees generally improve accuracy but increase computation time).

We have chosen Random Forest Classifier as it works well for high-dimensional text data (after TF-IDF). It can handle non-linear patterns and is robust to overfitting compared to single decision trees. It also supports multi-class classification (4 classes for AG News: World, Sports, Business, Sci/Tech).

4. **Build pipeline**:

```
pipeline = Pipeline(stages=[label_indexer, tokenizer, remover, hashing_tf, idf, assembler,
classifier])
```

This code combines all the preprocessing steps and the classifier into a single, reusable pipeline object. It is useful as it automates the entire workflow: text processing | feature extraction | model training. It also ensures consistent transformations during both training and testing phases and makes code modular and readable.

5. **Split data**:

```
train_data, test_data = df.randomSplit([0.8, 0.2], seed=42)
```

The preceding code splits the `df` into training and testing subsets to evaluate model performance on unseen data. Here, [0.8, 0.2] means 80% of the data goes to training, 20% to testing. seed=42 ensures reproducibility;

same random split every time. This step is important as it prevents overfitting by evaluating the model on new data. It mimics real-world scenarios where models predict on unseen inputs.

Refer to *Figure 16.3* for the execution of steps 3 to 5:

3. Define Classifier

```
[15] classifier = RandomForestClassifier(labelCol="label", featuresCol="features", numTrees=50)
```

4. Build Pipeline

```
[16] pipeline = Pipeline(stages=[label_indexer, tokenizer, remover, hashing_tf, idf, assembler, classifier])
```

5. Split Data

```
[17] train_data, test_data = df.randomSplit([0.8, 0.2], seed=42)
```

***Figure 16.3:** execution of Steps 3 to 5*

6. **Train model**:

```
model = pipeline.fit(train_data)
```

In the preceding code, you apply **`.fit()`** to the pipeline using **`train_data`**. The pipeline consists of -label encoding (StringIndexer), text tokenization (RegexTokenizer), stopword removal (StopWordsRemover), feature extraction, TF-IDF, vector assembler, and classifier (random forest). All these steps run in sequence only on the training set. The Random Forest Classifier learns from the features and labels and results in a trained pipeline model that is ready to apply to new/unseen data.

7. **Make predictions**:

```
predictions = model.transform(test_data)
```

In the preceding code, you use **`.transform()`** to apply the trained model to **`test_data`**. The same pipeline steps (tokenizing, stopword removal, TF-IDF, etc.) are applied to test data to maintain consistency. The trained Random Forest model predicts class labels based on test features. A new DataFrame of predictions is generated.

8. **Evaluate model**:

```
evaluator = MulticlassClassificationEvaluator(labelCol="label", predictionCol="prediction", metricName="accuracy")
accuracy = evaluator.evaluate(predictions)
print(f"Test Set Accuracy: {accuracy:.2f}")
```

In the preceding code, first statement creates an Evaluator for multi-class classification. It compares **`"label"`** that is the true label (numeric form from **`StringIndexer`**), **`"prediction"`** that is model's predicted class label. The **`metricName="accuracy"`** specifies that we want overall accuracy, meaning:

Accuracy = (Correct Predictions) ÷ (Total Predictions)

In the next statement, **`.evaluate(predictions)`** applies the evaluator to your results DataFrame that is it internally counts how many rows had label == prediction and divides by total rows to get percentage of correct predictions.

Finally the last statement formats the accuracy to two decimal places and prints results as shown in *Figure 16.4*. Here, **`test Set Accuracy: 0.73`** means 73% of test examples were classified correctly. The model's performance on unseen data is 73%.

Refer to *Figure 16.4* for steps 6 to 8:

6. Train Model

```
[58] model = pipeline.fit(train_data)
```

7. Make Predictions

```
predictions = model.transform(test_data)
```

8. Evaluate Model

```
[60] evaluator = MulticlassClassificationEvaluator(labelCol="label", predictionCol="prediction", metricName="accuracy")
     accuracy = evaluator.evaluate(predictions)
     print(f"Test Set Accuracy: {accuracy:.2f}")

Test Set Accuracy: 0.73
```

***Figure 16.4**: Execution and output for Steps 6 to 8*

9. **Sample predictions**:

```
predictions.select("class", "label", "prediction").show(10)
```

This command displays the first 10 rows of your model's predictions. In the output as shown in *Figure 16.4*, **`"Class Index"`** was originally 1 (actual category label from your dataset), label is 0.0, meaning Spark encoded Class Index = 1 as label 0.0 and prediction is either: 0.0, meaning the model correctly predicted label 0.0 (which corresponds to Class Index = 1), 2.0, meaning the model predicted label 2.0 (incorrect in this case).

10. **Stop Spark session**:

```
spark.stop()
```

This statement is used to stop the current Spark session, as shown in *Figure 16.5:*

9. Sample Predictions

```
predictions.select("Class Index", "label", "prediction").show(10)

+-----------+-----+----------+
|Class Index|label|prediction|
+-----------+-----+----------+
|          1|  0.0|       0.0|
|          1|  0.0|       2.0|
|          1|  0.0|       2.0|
|          1|  0.0|       1.0|
|          1|  0.0|       0.0|
|          1|  0.0|       1.0|
|          1|  0.0|       0.0|
|          1|  0.0|       2.0|
|          1|  0.0|       0.0|
|          1|  0.0|       1.0|
+-----------+-----+----------+
only showing top 10 rows
```

10. Stop Spark Session

```
[63] spark.stop()
```

Figure 16.5: *Execution and output of Step 9 and Step 10*

Customer segmentation using PySpark Clustering

In today's competitive retail landscape, understanding customer purchasing behavior is critical for businesses to drive growth, retention, and profitability. With the rise of e-commerce and digital transactions, companies now have access to detailed datasets that capture every customer interaction.

This case study leverages the popular online retail transaction dataset, which contains historical sales records from a UK-based retailer. The dataset includes:

- Invoice details
- Product descriptions
- Quantities purchased
- Prices
- Customer IDs
- Geographic information

Using this transactional data, we apply unsupervised clustering techniques to segment customers into distinct behavioral groups. By analyzing features such as:

- Total purchase quantity
- Total monetary spend
- Number of purchase events (invoices)

We can identify key customer groups, such as:

- High-value, frequent shoppers
- Occasional or low-spend customers
- Inactive or churn-risk segments

The following is the step-by-step process:

```
from pyspark.sql import SparkSession
from pyspark.sql.functions import col, sum as spark_sum, countDistinct
from pyspark.ml.feature import VectorAssembler
from pyspark.ml.clustering import KMeans
import matplotlib.pyplot as plt
import pandas as pd

# Step 1: Initialize Spark Session
spark = SparkSession.builder.appName("RetailClustering").getOrCreate()

# Step 2: Load Dataset (Update path to your file)
df = spark.read.csv("online_retail_II.csv", header=True, inferSchema=True)
df.show(5)
df.printSchema()
```

First step is to import all libraries as shown here. Next step is to create a session named **"RetailClustering"** to process data using PySpark. It is essential for distributed computing and handling large datasets. Step 2 reads the retail transaction CSV file with headers. Here, **inferSchema=True** automatically detects data types. The next statements display the first 5 rows and print the dataset schema for inspection. Refer to *Figure 16.6* for the execution and output of **Step 1** and **Step 2**:

```
[9] from pyspark.sql import SparkSession
    from pyspark.sql.functions import col, sum as spark_sum, countDistinct
    from pyspark.ml.feature import VectorAssembler
    from pyspark.ml.clustering import KMeans
    import matplotlib.pyplot as plt
    import pandas as pd

    # Step 1: Initialize Spark Session
    spark = SparkSession.builder.appName("RetailClustering").getOrCreate()

    # Step 2: Load Dataset (Update path to your file)
    df = spark.read.csv("online_retail_II.csv", header=True, inferSchema=True)

    df.show(5)
    df.printSchema()
```

```
+-------+---------+--------------------+--------+--------------+-----+-----------+--------------+
|Invoice|StockCode|         Description|Quantity|   InvoiceDate|Price|Customer ID|       Country|
+-------+---------+--------------------+--------+--------------+-----+-----------+--------------+
| 536365|   85123A|WHITE HANGING HEA...|       6|12/1/2010 8:26| 2.55|      17850|United Kingdom|
| 536365|    71053| WHITE METAL LANTERN|       6|12/1/2010 8:26| 3.39|      17850|United Kingdom|
| 536365|   84406B|CREAM CUPID HEART...|       8|12/1/2010 8:26| 2.75|      17850|United Kingdom|
| 536365|   84029G|KNITTED UNION FLA...|       6|12/1/2010 8:26| 3.39|      17850|United Kingdom|
| 536365|   84029E|RED WOOLLY HOTTIE...|       6|12/1/2010 8:26| 3.39|      17850|United Kingdom|
+-------+---------+--------------------+--------+--------------+-----+-----------+--------------+
only showing top 5 rows

root
 |-- Invoice: string (nullable = true)
 |-- StockCode: string (nullable = true)
 |-- Description: string (nullable = true)
 |-- Quantity: integer (nullable = true)
 |-- InvoiceDate: string (nullable = true)
```

***Figure 16.6**: For execution and output of Step 1 and Step 2*

```
# Step 3: Filter valid customer records
df_clean = df.filter(df["Customer ID"].isNotNull())

# Step 4: Aggregate features for clustering
agg_df = df_clean.groupBy("Customer ID").agg(
    spark_sum(col("Quantity")).alias("TotalQuantity"),
    spark_sum(col("Quantity") * col("Price")).alias("TotalSpend"),
    countDistinct("Invoice").alias("InvoiceCount")
)

agg_df.show(5)
```

Step 3 removes records with missing Customer ID so that only complete customer data is used for clustering. In step 4 we group transactions by unique Customer ID. It calculates key features for clustering as:

- **TotalQuantity**: Sum of items purchased per customer
- **TotalSpend**: Total amount spent (Quantity × Price)
- **InvoiceCount**: Number of unique purchase transactions

Refer *Figure 16.7* for the execution and output of **`Step 3`** and **`Step 4`**:

```
[10] # Step 3: Filter valid customer records
     df_clean = df.filter(df["Customer ID"].isNotNull())

     # Step 4: Aggregate features for clustering
     agg_df = df_clean.groupBy("Customer ID").agg(
         spark_sum(col("Quantity")).alias("TotalQuantity"),
         spark_sum(col("Quantity") * col("Price")).alias("TotalSpend"),
         countDistinct("Invoice").alias("InvoiceCount")
     )

     agg_df.show(5)

+-----------+-------------+------------------+------------+
|Customer ID|TotalQuantity|        TotalSpend|InvoiceCount|
+-----------+-------------+------------------+------------+
|      17389|         7430|31300.079999999998|          43|
|      13623|          286|            672.44|           7|
|      14450|          241|            483.25|           3|
|      15727|         3065|           5178.96|           7|
|      13285|         2051|2709.1199999999994|           4|
+-----------+-------------+------------------+------------+
only showing top 5 rows
```

***Figure 16.7**: Execution and output of Step 3 and Step 4*

```
#Step 5: Assemble features
assembler = VectorAssembler(inputCols=["TotalQuantity", "TotalSpend", "InvoiceCount"],
outputCol="features")
data = assembler.transform(agg_df)
data.select("features").show(5, truncate=False)
```

This step combines the selected features into a single features vector.It is required input format for ML models in PySpark.

```
#Step 6: Apply KMeans Clustering
kmeans = KMeans(featuresCol="features", k=4, seed=42)
model = kmeans.fit(data)
predictions = model.transform(data)
```

In this step we initializes k-means clustering with 4 clusters (k=4), use random seed for reproducibility. Next statement fits the model on customer feature data and finally predicts cluster assignments for each customer.

```
#Step 7: Show Cluster Assignments
predictions.select("Customer ID", "TotalQuantity", "TotalSpend", "InvoiceCount", "prediction").
show(10)
```

This code displays the customer features along with assigned cluster labels (prediction) as shown in *Figure 16.8*:

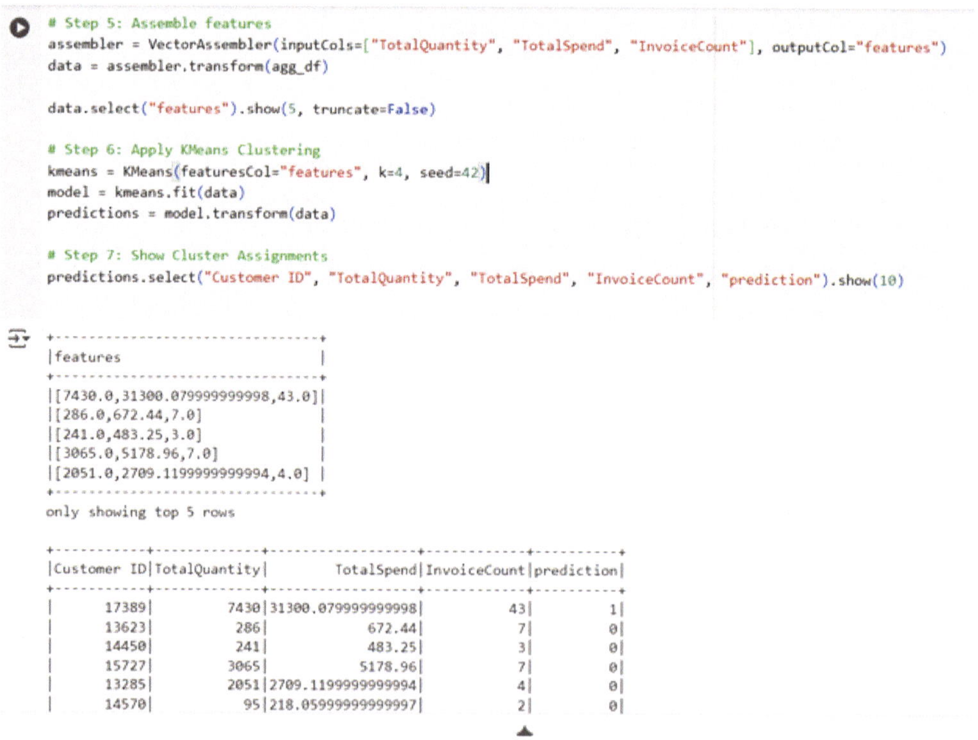

```
# Step 5: Assemble features
assembler = VectorAssembler(inputCols=["TotalQuantity", "TotalSpend", "InvoiceCount"], outputCol="features")
data = assembler.transform(agg_df)

data.select("features").show(5, truncate=False)

# Step 6: Apply KMeans Clustering
kmeans = KMeans(featuresCol="features", k=4, seed=42)
model = kmeans.fit(data)
predictions = model.transform(data)

# Step 7: Show Cluster Assignments
predictions.select("Customer ID", "TotalQuantity", "TotalSpend", "InvoiceCount", "prediction").show(10)
```

```
+-------------------------------+
|features                       |
+-------------------------------+
|[7430.0,31300.079999999998,43.0]|
|[286.0,672.44,7.0]             |
|[241.0,483.25,3.0]             |
|[3065.0,5178.96,7.0]           |
|[2051.0,2709.1199999999994,4.0] |
+-------------------------------+
only showing top 5 rows

+-----------+-------------+------------------+------------+----------+
|Customer ID|TotalQuantity|        TotalSpend|InvoiceCount|prediction|
+-----------+-------------+------------------+------------+----------+
|      17389|         7430|31300.079999999998|          43|         1|
|      13623|          286|            672.44|           7|         0|
|      14450|          241|            483.25|           3|         0|
|      15727|         3065|           5178.96|           7|         0|
|      13285|         2051|2709.1199999999994|           4|         0|
|      14570|           95|218.05999999999997|           2|         0|
```

***Figure 16.8**: Execution and output of Step 5 to Step 7*

```
# Step 8: Analyze Cluster Distribution
predictions.groupBy("prediction").count().show()
```

The preceding code counts how many customers fall into each cluster and thus helps to assess the balance of clusters.

Refer to the following figure for the execution and output of Step 8:

```
# Step 8: Analyze Cluster Distribution
predictions.groupBy("prediction").count().show()

+----------+-----+
|prediction|count|
+----------+-----+
|         1|   29|
|         3|    3|
|         2|    4|
|         0| 4336|
+----------+-----+
```

Figure 16.9: *Execution and output of Step 8*

```
# Step 9: Visualize Clusters
# Convert to Pandas for plotting
df_plot = predictions.select("TotalSpend", "TotalQuantity", "InvoiceCount", "prediction").
toPandas()
plt.figure(figsize=(8,6))
scatter = plt.scatter(df_plot["TotalSpend"], df_plot["TotalQuantity"], c=df_plot["prediction"],
cmap="viridis", alpha=0.6)
plt.colorbar(scatter, label="Cluster")
plt.xlabel("Total Spend")
plt.ylabel("Total Quantity")
plt.title("Customer Clusters: Total Spend vs Total Quantity")
plt.show()

# Optional: Stop Spark Session
spark.stop()
```

In this code, first statement converts selected columns from the Spark DataFrame (predictions) into a Pandas DataFrame. Spark is optimized for distributed computation but not for direct plotting. Pandas is used here because popular plotting libraries like Matplotlib work with Pandas DataFrames. Next statement creates a blank figure of size 8 inches × 6 inches. Then a 2D scatter plot is created in which X-axis represents total spend, Y-axis represents total quantity, color (c) refers to cluster labels to differentiate groups, **`cmap="viridis"`** indicates color scheme (gradient from yellow to green to blue) and **`alpha=0.6`** provides slight transparency for overlapping points. This plot shows how customers group based on how much they spend and purchase. Next statements adds a colorbar to indicate which color corresponds to which cluster label. Next three statements are used to set axis labels and the plot title for clarity. Next statement displays the final scatter plot with clusters visualized. Last statement **"`spark.stop()`"** is used to shut down the Spark session to free system resources.It is a good practice after your PySpark job is completed.

Refer to *Figure 16.10* for the execution of code:

```
# Step 9: Visualize Clusters
# Convert to Pandas for plotting
df_plot = predictions.select("TotalSpend", "TotalQuantity", "InvoiceCount", "prediction").toPandas()

plt.figure(figsize=(8,6))
scatter = plt.scatter(df_plot["TotalSpend"], df_plot["TotalQuantity"], c=df_plot["prediction"], cmap="viridis", alpha=0.6)
plt.colorbar(scatter, label="Cluster")
plt.xlabel("Total Spend")
plt.ylabel("Total Quantity")
plt.title("Customer Clusters: Total Spend vs Total Quantity")
plt.show()

# Optional: Stop Spark Session
spark.stop()
```

Figure 16.10: *Code for Step 10*

Figure 16.11 shows the output of step 9:

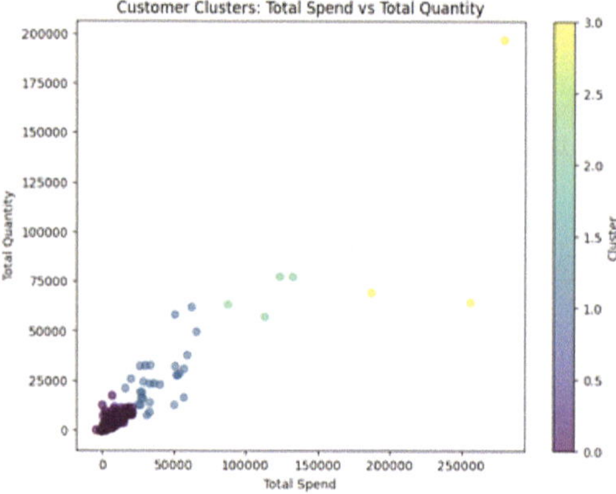

Figure 16.11: *Output for Step 9*

Conclusion

In this chapter, we explored the foundational concepts of ML, its key types, and why Apache Spark has become a preferred engine for large-scale ML applications. We introduced Spark's powerful APIs—Spark.mllib for traditional ML algorithms and Spark.ml for scalable, pipeline-based ML. Through practical case studies, we applied these concepts by building an AG News multi-class text classification model using PySpark, followed by customer segmentation through clustering techniques. Together, these examples demonstrate how Spark empowers organizations to perform complex ML tasks efficiently, making it an essential tool for real-world, data-driven decision-making at scale.

Points to remember

Here are some key takeaways from this chapter:

- ML enables computers to learn patterns from data and make predictions or decisions without being explicitly programmed.
- ML is broadly categorized into supervised, unsupervised, and reinforcement learning, each designed to solve different types of problems.
- Apache Spark offers in-memory, distributed computing, making it ideal for handling large-scale machine learning tasks efficiently.
- Spark provides user-friendly APIs for scalable data processing and machine learning through libraries like Spark.mllib and Spark.ml.

- Spark.mllib is Spark's original machine learning library offering distributed algorithms for classification, regression, and clustering.
- Spark.ml simplifies building scalable ML pipelines by integrating data processing and model building into a unified framework.
- **AG News multi-class text classification using PySpark**: This project demonstrates applying PySpark to build a machine learning model that classifies news articles into multiple categories.
- **Customer segmentation using PySpark Clustering**: Through clustering techniques in PySpark, businesses can segment customers based on purchasing behavior, aiding targeted marketing and personalized strategies.

Multiple choice questions

1. **Which of the following best defines machine learning?**
   a. Writing rules to automate tasks
   b. Enabling systems to learn from data and improve over time
   c. Programming computers to perform only arithmetic operations
   d. Manually feeding outputs to the system
2. **Which type of machine learning uses labeled data for training?**
   a. Supervised Learning
   b. Unsupervised Learning
   c. Reinforcement Learning
   d. Deep Learning
3. **Why is Apache Spark preferred for large-scale ML tasks?**
   a. It uses disk-based processing
   b. It supports in-memory distributed computing
   c. It requires no coding
   d. It only handles small datasets
4. **Which Spark library is designed for building end-to-end ML pipelines?**
   a. Spark Core
   b. Spark Streaming
   c. Spark.mllib
   d. Spark.ml
5. **Which of the following is true about Spark.mllib?**
   a. It is the latest high-level API for ML pipelines
   b. It offers basic distributed ML algorithms
   c. It is used for real-time data streaming only
   d. It processes data only on a single machine
6. **The AG News classification example demonstrates:**
   a. Image segmentation using PySpark
   b. Predicting numerical values using regression
   c. Multi-class text classification using PySpark
   d. Clustering customers based on their behavior
7. **Customer segmentation using PySpark is an example of:**
   a. Supervised Learning
   b. Unsupervised Learning using clustering
   c. Reinforcement Learning
   d. Time series forecasting

8. **In the context of ML with Spark, which statement is correct?**
   a. Spark only supports batch processing, not real-time ML
   b. Spark.ml pipelines help streamline model building and deployment
   c. Spark.mllib is deprecated and no longer usable
   d. Spark cannot handle textual data for ML
9. **Which of the following benefits does Spark provide for ML tasks?**
   a. Scalability across clusters
   b. Real-time and batch processing capability
   c. In-memory computations for speed
   d. All of the above
10. **In PySpark Clustering, customer segmentation helps businesses to:**
   a. Improve only their IT infrastructure
   b. Randomly divide customers without patterns
   c. Understand groups of customers for targeted marketing
   d. Replace all manual decision-making processes

Answers

1. b.	2. a.	3. b.	4. d.	5. b.
6. c.	7. b.	8. b.	9. d.	10. c.

Questions

1. Define ML and explain how it differs from traditional programming approaches.
2. Compare supervised and unsupervised learning with real-world examples for each. How does the choice of learning type impact model development?
3. Why is Apache Spark considered a suitable framework for large-scale ML tasks? Mention at least two technical advantages.
4. Explain how in-memory processing in Spark improves the performance of ML tasks, especially when dealing with iterative algorithms like clustering.
5. Write a simple PySpark code snippet to load a text dataset and create a DataFrame. Mention any two transformations you would apply before building an ML model.
6. A bank wants to detect fraudulent transactions in real-time using PySpark. What ML approach (supervised/unsupervised) would you recommend, and why? Outline your proposed solution architecture.
7. Explain how ML with PySpark can be used to predict the likelihood of a patient being readmitted to a hospital within 30 days. What data features would be critical for this task?
8. A telecom company wants to reduce customer churn using ML with PySpark. Identify the data points that would help predict churn and suggest an appropriate ML approach.
9. Explain the role of Pipelines in Spark.ml. Why are pipelines essential for building scalable and repeatable machine learning workflows?
10. Practical (Code/Design) — Design a basic outline (steps only, code optional) for building a customer segmentation model using PySpark's k-means algorithm. What preprocessing steps would you consider?

Index

A

B

C

D

E

F

G

H

I

J

K

L

M

N

O

P

R

S

T

U

Y